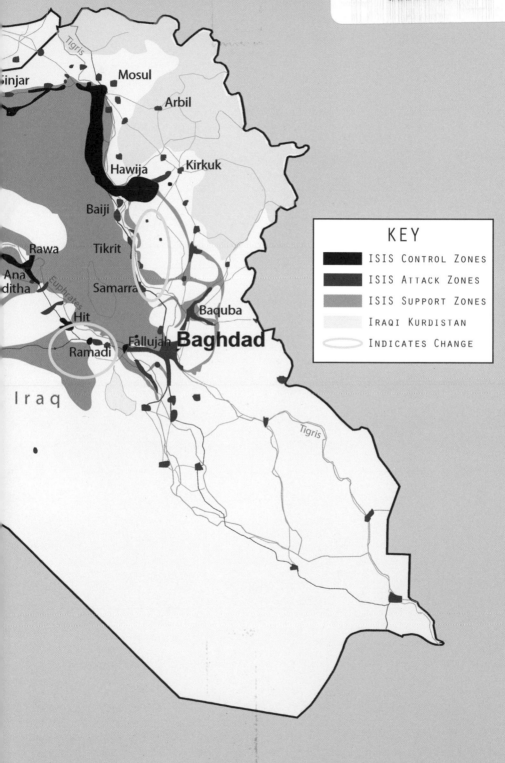

D0559969

KEY

ISIS Control Zones

ISIS Attack Zones

ISIS Support Zones

Iraqi Kurdistan

Indicates Change

Sinjar

Mosul

Arbil

Tigris

Hawija

Kirkuk

Baiji

Rawa

Tikrit

Ana
ditha

Euphrates

Samarra

Hit

Baquba

Ramadi

Fallujah

Baghdad

Iraq

Tigris

"[A] superb piece of journalism, unsparing in its analysis of the folly of the Obama administration."—Nick Cohen, *The Spectator* (UK)

"The first book to fully explain what ISIS is seeking and why they are such a threat to the world. An absolute must-read for anyone who wants to understand the risk we all face from radical Islam." —Douglas E. Schoen, political analyst, author of *The Russia-China Axis: The New Cold War and America's Crisis of Leadership*

"A . . . detailed and nuanced story."—James Traub, *The Wall Street Journal*

"Weiss and Hassan have produced a detailed and readable book. Their informants include American and regional military officials and intelligence operatives, defected Syrian spies and diplomats, and—most fascinating of all—Syrians who work for Isis (these are divided into categories such as politickers, pragmatists, opportunists and fence-sitters). The authors provide useful insights into Isis governance— a combination of divide-and-rule, indoctrination and fear—and are well placed for the task. Hassan, an expert on tribal and jihadist dynamics, is from Syria's east. Weiss reported from liberated al-Bab, outside Aleppo, before Isis took it over."—Robin Yassin-Kassab, *The Guardian*

"Weiss and Hassan have written the most serious book-length study of the Islamic State so far."—*New York Times Book Review* Editors' Choice

"Recounted in painstaking detail . . . the book presents a granular analysis of the IS's organization, ideology, funding and recruitment."—Muhammad Idrees Ahmad, *In These Times*

"Gripping . . . [T]he most comprehensive account to date."—Michael Totten, *Commentary*

ISIS

INSIDE THE
ARMY OF TERROR

REVISED &
UPDATED

MICHAEL WEISS
HASSAN HASSAN

Regan Arts.

NEW YORK

Regan Arts.

65 Bleecker Street
New York, NY 10012

Copyright © 2015, 2016 by Michael Weiss & Hassan Hassan

First edition 2015

Second edition 2016

Library of Congress Control Number: 2016932843

ISBN 978-1-68245-020-8

Cover art © Abaca

Printed in the United States of America

10 9 8 7 6 5 4 3 2 1

CONTENTS

For Amy and Julia, and Ola, Jacob, and Daniel,
who have put up with ISIS
(and us)
more than any family
ever ought to

INTRODUCTION

In late 2011, a sixteen-year-old Bahraini boy named Abdelaziz Kuwan approached his Syrian uncle and asked for an introduction to Riad al-Asaad, a colonel in the Syrian Air Force and one of the first military defectors from the dictatorship of Bashar al-Assad. Abdelaziz wanted to join the armed rebellion in Syria. His parents had forbidden him from doing so, but he was ready to defy their wishes.

In early 2012, he flew to Istanbul and then, as so many other foreign fighters have done, took a thirteen-hour bus ride to the southern Turkish border town of Reyhanli. From there he crossed into the Syrian province of Aleppo, the northern countryside that by then had fallen to the rebels. Abdelaziz fought for moderate factions for several weeks before deeming them too corrupt and ineffectual. Then he moved between various Islamist brigades, including Jabhat al-Nusra, which later revealed itself to be the al-Qaeda franchise in Syria. Despite having earned a reputation as a fearless and devout fighter, Abdelaziz eventually grew disenchanted with his Islamist comrades. He also faced significant pressure from his family to return to Bahrain— pressure to which he caved in at the end of 2012. Upon his arrival, Abdelaziz's mother confiscated his passport.

"I walk in the streets and I feel imprisoned," Abdelaziz said, still pining for his days as a holy warrior. "I feel tied up. It's like someone is always watching me. This world means nothing to me. I want to be free. I want to go back. People are giving their lives. That's the honorable life."

Abdelaziz's family had moved to Bahrain from eastern Syria in the 1980s. His parents provided him with the means to lead a decent life. "His father raised him well," one relative recalled. "He did not make him need anyone and wanted him to be of a high social status." Abdelaziz, the relative said, had been "quiet" and "refined" and had "always behaved like a man."

Abdelaziz stayed in Bahrain for three months before managing to persuade his mother to return his passport. (Why she agreed remains a mystery.) He left for Syria three days later. Once he arrived, Abdelaziz joined the Islamic

State of Iraq and al-Sham (ISIS), which was then rising in prominence as one of the most disciplined and well-organized jihadist groups in Syria. Abdelaziz later confided in us that during his last few months in Bahrain he made the decision to join ISIS, after speaking with "some of the brothers" in Syria via Skype. His prior experience with other Islamist factions ideologically similar to ISIS was an advantage, he said, in joining one that was dominated primarily by foreign fighters. Abdelaziz rose through the ranks of ISIS, first becoming a coordinator among local emirs and other rebel groups, then delivering messages and oral agreements on behalf of his leader. When ISIS seized enormous swaths of territory in both Syria and Iraq in the summer of 2014, Abdelaziz was promoted to the role of security official overseeing three towns near the Syrian-Iraqi border town of Albu Kamal, long a portal between the two countries for men like him.

Abdelaziz discovered in ISIS new things about himself. He learned that he was violent, brutal, and determined. He beheaded enemies. He kept a Yazidi girl in his house as a *sabiyya*, or sex slave. She was his prize for his participation in battles against the Iraqi Kurdish peshmerga forces and other Kurdish militias in Sinjar, Iraq, near the Syrian border. According to ISIS's propaganda magazine, *Dabiq*, one-fifth of the sex slaves taken from Sinjar were distributed to ISIS's central leadership to do with as it so chose; the remainder was divided among the rank and file, like Abdelaziz, as the spoils of war.

Abdelaziz showed us a picture of his sabiyya. She was in her late teens. She "belonged" to him for about a month before being handed off to other ISIS commanders.

One of Abdelaziz's fellow warriors said that during news broadcasts Abdelaziz would cover the television screen to avoid seeing the faces of female presenters. Yet being a rapist never seemed to impinge on what Abdelaziz considered his moral obligations as a pious Muslim. He fervently quoted the Quran and hadith, the oral sayings attributed to the Prophet Muhammad, and spoke pompously about al-Dawla, the "state," which is the term ISIS uses to refer to its project. Asked what he would do if his father were a member of Jabhat al-Nusra, the al-Qaeda group to which Abdelaziz had temporarily belonged, and the two met in battle, he replied promptly: "I would kill him." Abu Obeida, he explained, referring to one of the companions of the Prophet Muhammad, killed his father in battle, and so there was nothing extraordinary about patricide in the name of God: "Anyone who extends his hand to harm al-Dawla will have his hand chopped off." Abdelaziz also called his relatives in the Bahraini army or security forces "apostates," because his adoptive country's military was by then involved in a multinational coalition bombing campaign, led by the United States, against ISIS.

Before he went off to join the jihad in Syria, Abdelaziz was a theological novice who had barely finished a year of Islamic studies at a religious academy in Saudi Arabia. He had dropped out of high school in Bahrain and traveled to Medina to study Sharia, or Islamic jurisprudence. In school, according to one of his family members, he avoided nondevout peers and mingled primarily with hard-line students. Soon he was compulsively using "jihadi speak," referring constantly to the dismal conditions which persist for Sunni Muslims in Africa, the Middle East, and Southeast Asia.

His metamorphosis continued on the Syrian battlefield. He called himself Abu al-Mu'tasim, after the eighth Abbasid caliph, al-Mu'tasim Billah, known for leading an army to avenge the insulting of a woman by Byzantine soldiers. Abdelaziz said he wanted to emulate the caliph in supporting helpless Muslims in Syria and Iraq. Though he had been appointed as a security official, he always looked for opportunities to fight on the front lines. "I cannot sit down," he told one of the authors. "I came here seeking martyrdom, and I have chased it everywhere."

On October 23, 2014, Abdelaziz found what he was looking for. He was shot dead by a Syrian regime sniper in the eastern province of Deir Ezzor.

When ISIS stormed Mosul, the capital city of Iraq's Ninewah province, in mid-June 2014, the world's response was one of confusion as much as of shock. Men very much like Abdelaziz had just conquered an expanse of land in the Middle East roughly the size of Great Britain. That they had done so under the unblinking gaze of orbital satellites and surveillance drones did not mean that world governments were any less surprised by this blitzkrieg than the average citizen.

Even more incredible was *how* ISIS had sacked the city. A thousand of their number had overthrown Mosul, which, according to the Iraqi government, had been guarded by as many as thirty thousand American-trained soldiers and policemen. Those personnel had simply vanished, forfeiting to the black-clad insurgents tens of millions of dollars in American-made Humvees and Abrams tanks. Photographs of jihadists of every ethnicity and skin tone, beaming as they stood in front of newly commandeered state-of-the-art war machinery, circulated across every continent. What kind of terrorists drive armored vehicles and tanks on modern highways? Aren't they meant to be astride mules and donkeys in the Hindu Kush? Is ISIS a fundamentalist guerrilla outfit, or is it more like an army? And how, after nearly a decade of blood and treasure expended in Iraq, did men whose epitaphs had been serially inscribed—and whose deaths just as serially exaggerated—manage to accomplish so much in so little time?

Five months before the fall of Mosul, President Barack Obama had, in an interview with the *New Yorker*'s David Remnick, rather regrettably dismissed ISIS as the "jayvee team" of terrorists. Now that "jayvee team" had razed the berm barriers separating the modern nation-states of Syria and Iraq—barriers that had been in place for nearly a century. They declared that this physical and symbolic act of recombination was the end of a British-French colonial compact that had helped draw the map of the region even before the official end of World War I. There would no longer be any Western fingerprint on that map, according to ISIS. There would now be only the caliphate. If Muslims were strong, intoned Abu Bakr al-Baghdadi, ISIS's newly appointed "caliph," this Islamic empire would eventually reach Spain again and even conquer Rome.

This book is personal. Hassan is a native Syrian from the border town of Albu Kamal, which has long been a gateway for jihadists moving into, and now out of, Iraq. Michael has reported from the Aleppo suburb of al-Bab, once a cradle of Syria's independent and prodemocratic civil society, now a dismal ISIS fief ruled by a malevolent union of Sharia law and Cosa Nostra–style intimidation. Al-Bab is today a place where cigarette smokers are tossed into an outdoor cage for days on end and suspected "traitors" are decapitated in the town square, their heads and corpses left to suppurate on pikes in the hot Levantine sun.

We set out to answer a simple question, one asked repeatedly on cable news shows in the haunting summer and fall of 2014: "Where did ISIS come from?"

The question was understandable, given the images and videos then circulating around the world—most notoriously the horrifying snuff films depicting the executions of several Western hostages, beginning with the American journalist James Foley. But the question was also a strange one, because the United States has been at war with ISIS, in its various incarnations, for the better part of a decade. It has fought ISIS as a group known colloquially to the US military as al-Qaeda in Iraq—a name still in use by force of habit among the many officer-grade veterans of the Iraq War interviewed for this book. It was as if the Vietcong had returned under a different banner and laid siege to a third of Southeast Asia in 1985, only to be goggled at as a heretofore unknown militancy by everyone from CNN to the Reagan administration. If ever there was a familiar foe, ISIS was it.

And yet much about this theocratic, totalitarian enemy remains forgotten or occluded or simply underexamined, lost in a decade-long haze of polemics about the wisdom of invading Iraq or the Islamic-or-not nature of its nastiest terrorists. Debates about ISIS's ideology, war strategy, and internal dynamics persist in every country committed to its defeat. Is it greater or less than the sum of its parts? Is it winning or losing nearly two years into a concerted multinational air campaign, backed by the provision of arms to select allies and proxies? Is the stated US objective articulated by President Obama to "degrade and ultimately destroy" ISIS feasible given the current US policies in Syria and Iraq? Or will this latest iteration of war in the Middle East last for thirty years, as former defense secretary Leon Panetta recently suggested, as ISIS expands the precincts of its power well into Turkey, North Africa, Afghanistan, and Russia—and as it perpetrates or "inspires" atrocities from the Sinai to Paris to San Bernardino?

We begin by examining ISIS as it is now but also as it evolved and adapted over the past decade. The early chapters of this book deal mainly with the complex history of ISIS's prior incarnations, drawing on dozens of original interviews with former US military intelligence and counterterrorism officials and Western diplomats who tracked, fought, and jailed al-Qaeda in Iraq. ISIS is in fact the latest bloody stage in a long-running dispute within the ranks of international jihadism. Namely, how should this holy war be waged, and against whom? Are Shia, Alawites, and other minority sects and ethnicities viable targets for attack, or should they be spared in light of the more urgent need to combat the Americans and their "Zionist-crusader" allies? The fanatical side of this dispute was embodied by Abu Musab al-Zarqawi, the Jordanian founder of al-Qaeda in Iraq, while the relatively "moderate" side was embodied by al-Zarqawi's own patron and nominal superior—Osama bin Laden. The recent split between al-Qaeda and ISIS was inevitable ever since al-Zarqawi and bin Laden first laid eyes on each other in Afghanistan in 1999. Allied, they helped tear Iraq apart, inspired Shia counter-atrocities, and took a bloody toll in American and allied lives. It is this history that ties together the past decade of conflict with the agendas of regimes in Iran and Syria, without which we cannot truly understand ISIS today. Although it is impossible to determine which side of the jihadist argument will ultimately win out, or even if there will be a winner, the fact that al-Qaeda has for the past two years been in a state of fratricidal conflict with its former subsidiary will surely determine how the West continues to fight both.

Having addressed the history of that conflict, we then look at the origins of the Syrian revolution. We demonstrate how the al-Assad regime, which had long facilitated and suborned al-Qaeda terrorism next door, not only attempted to portray itself as the victim of its erstwhile ally, but also perversely created the fertile conditions for such terrorism to take root inside Syria. Bashar al-Assad, like many a dictator who grasps the tenuousness of his rule, has sought for nearly half a decade to eliminate any legitimate or democratic challenge while quietly encouraging the rise of a usurper that no one, least of all Western onlookers, could ever countenance. "Assad, or we burn the country." That was the rallying cry of regime loyalists from the earliest days of the Syrian protest movement in 2011. It was no idle threat. Under the guise of "political reforms," al-Assad released from his prisons the very extremists he had once dispatched into Iraq to murder US and Iraqi forces, and then had them arrested upon their return to Syria. Defectors from his security services have since alleged that they were instructed to arm Islamist guerrillas in the hopes that the latter would attack regime institutions, furnishing the excuse to escalate al-Assad's war. As recounted by numerous eyewitnesses, regime soldiers and mercenaries also purposefully couched their pogroms against protestors in an explicitly sectarian grammar. The aim was to humiliate and demoralize Sunni Muslims, as this would only accelerate a process of radicalization within the insurgency and pull in foreign fighters to the benefit of groups like ISIS. These are merely some of the indirect forms of collaboration between the regime and ISIS. To this day, according to the US Treasury Department and independent analysts, al-Assad continues to subsidize one of ISIS's main sources of income: hydrocarbons. The jihadists now control the majority of Syria's oil wells and refineries, making it what one energy expert has called the "Con Ed" of a Middle Eastern country. They sell al-Assad back his own power, which goes not only to keeping the lights on in the presidential palace in Damascus but also to fueling a barbarous war machine that has mainly targeted Syrian rebels fighting both al-Assad and ISIS.

For the ruling dynasty of Syria, terrorism has never before been viewed as an existential problem, but rather as a nuisance that was easily repurposed into an opportunity. Al-Assad, as we will show, dangled the threat of al-Qaeda before the West, hoping to lure it into a counterterrorism-based entente cordiale with his regime. Why? For two reasons: First, there is no greater insurance policy than for the world's only superpower to consider you indispensable to its national security. Second, there is no better way to project yourself as a regional heavyweight, a power not to be underestimated or antagonized, than to have the ear of the United States. Indeed, in the months leading up to the Syrian revolution, al-Assad was on a sinuous path toward normalizing his relations with a new US administration. Even after that revolution got under way, and well after his henchmen began kidnapping, torturing, and murdering Syrian children, al-Assad could still enjoy hearing himself referred to as a "reformer" by Washington. Indeed, he cunningly exploited this fact in gradually increasing the butcher's bill in Syria, while egging on terrorists to fight back.

In this respect, al-Assad is hardly unique. As Emma Sky, the slight, soft-spoken British adviser to the US military in Iraq, has said: "Corrupt regimes and terrorists keep each other in business. It's a symbiotic relationship." And as we shall see, Saddam Hussein played much the same dangerous game with jihadists committed to his ouster but desperate enough to cut short-term, expedient alliances with him or his followers, such as after the US invasion and occupation of Iraq. Still another skillful manipulator of terrorism has been one of the world's leading state sponsors of it, the Islamic Republic of Iran. As recently as July 2011, Iran stood accused by the US government of allowing the transit of known al-Qaeda recruiters into Syria, no doubt to help supply the very terrorists its client al-Assad had claimed to be fighting all along. And while Iranian proxies have now taken a lead role in fighting ISIS in Iraq, at least where it threatens Iranian interests in the country, they have mainly refrained from going after the terror army in Syria.

That two avowed enemies, ISIS and al-Assad, depend upon and exploit each other's existence in pursuit of a common goal—the wholesale destruction of any and all credible alternatives to themselves—should not be so surprising in the twenty-first century, given the precedents of other absolutist bedfellows in the twentieth. Not least among the tragedies of Syria is that what began as rather transparent agitprop has culminated in US foreign policy.

Al-Assad has now convinced the West to leave him be while it focuses on the degradation and destruction of ISIS. The West is objectively, if not subjectively, aligning itself with his interests, not to mention those of his two main allies, Iran and Russia. Both countries are currently directly intervening in Syria to keep al-Assad's regime alive—not to fight ISIS.

Finally, we look at ISIS as it is today, under al-Baghdadi and his willing executioners, relying on interviews with active or now-deceased ISIS militants, spies, and "sleeper agents"—as well as the victims of the same, including Syrian tribesmen, rebels, and activists. Before the world knew ISIS's name, one brave and defiant schoolteacher in Raqqa said "enough," standing up to the foreign riffraff telling her native Syrians how to dress, where to pray, and, indeed, which houses of worship could even remain standing. We chronicle the *samizdat* resistance that has emerged in Raqqa, led by one furtive but hounded collective of activist-reporters, whose members risk everything to explain to outsiders how the ISIS "capital" looks and feels.

The last eighteen months of international war against ISIS have yielded a surplus of valuable studies in how ISIS proselytizes and recruits, relying on its own vast and well-run propaganda apparatus. This includes a glossy monthly magazine, an entire media division that issues daily videos—in multiple languages and with alarmingly high production value—and more social media accounts relaying and regurgitating the ISIS message than intelligence agencies can keep track of. And these are just the materials designed for *foreign* consumption. Internally, too, ISIS maintains a strict diet for its captive minds, a daily ration of stories of battlefield victories and divine glory, even where the jihadists have suffered total defeat.

How did ISIS learn to brainwash so many, so well? In short, it has had a lot of practice. Among this book's focuses is the role prisons have played for a decade now as organizing hubs and recruitment centers for ISIS. Whether by accident or design, jailhouses in the Middle East have served for years as virtual terror academies, where known extremists can congregate, plot, organize, and hone their leadership skills "inside the wire," as well as, most ominously of all, recruit a brand-new generation of fighters.

"Remaining and expanding" is the motto of the caliphate. While ISIS has lost some territory in Syria and Iraq, it has held firm in the geostrategic heartland of the Sunni Arab tribal regions of both those countries, while also continuing to metastasize worldwide by establishing franchises or having pre-existing jihadist organizations pledge their allegiance to ISIS. It is by no means "contained" according to any working definition of the term. In this revised and expanded edition, we explore how some of these *wilayahs*, or "provinces," got started in Egypt's Sinai peninsula, Yemen, and Libya and weigh which are likely to gain in prominence and lethality in the coming years.

As the caliphate contracts, its terrorism abroad has increased with horrifying consequences. The November 2015 gun-and-bomb massacre in Paris represented a turning point in how the world views ISIS, not least because it was not a singular performance. Three NATO countries were attacked in 2015 in as many months (in Turkey's case, repeatedly) and this does not include other "spectaculars": the immolation of a Russian commercial airliner and a dual suicide attack in Beirut that killed more people than any one act of terror since the end of Lebanon's civil war in 1990. Nearly a year before Paris, a massacre had been narrowly averted in Verviers, Belgium, after a police commando raid on an ISIS safe house resulted in the largest gun battle that country had experienced since World War II. No doubt similar plots are under way as this book goes to press. But just how new is this emphasis by an Iraq-born insurgency on committing mass murder outside of its immediate zone of activity? True, ISIS's spokesman Abu Muhammad al-Adnani issued an injunction in September 2014: "If you can kill a disbelieving American or European—especially the spiteful and filthy French—or an Australian, or a Canadian, or any other disbeliever from the disbelievers waging war, including the citizens of the countries that entered into a coalition against the Islamic State, then rely upon Allah, and kill him in any manner or way however it may be." But, as we shall see, killing "disbelievers" abroad has always been a central tenet of the Zarqawists, one twice-realized in Jordan.

This revised and expanded edition also features a lengthy profile of a former member of one of ISIS's elite spy services, "Abu Khaled." He trained the group's ground infantry and a handful of its foreign operatives, including two French nationals who repatriated months before the grisly Paris attacks in November 2015. Weeks after defecting from ISIS, Abu Khaled sat with one of the authors in Istanbul, where for three straight days he recounted life and death under the black flag. He provided crucial inside information about how ISIS makes and extorts money, manages a surprisingly effective "Islamic welfare state," and withstands a multinational effort to eliminate it. For all that, Abu Khaled conveyed, ISIS remains brittle and unpopular, tolerated by those it rules only for lack of a better alternative, which neither the West nor regional actors have yet been able to proffer.

ISIS is a terrorist organization, but it is not just a terrorist organization. It is a mafia adept at exploiting decades-old transnational gray markets for oil and arms trafficking. It is a conventional army that mobilizes and deploys foot soldiers with a professional acumen that has impressed members of the US military. It is a sophisticated intelligence-gathering apparatus that infiltrates rival organizations and silently recruits within their ranks before taking them over, routing them in combat, or seizing their land. It is also a spectral hold-over of an even earlier foe than al-Qaeda. Most of its top decision makers served either in Saddam Hussein's military or security services. In a sense, then, "secular" Baathism has returned to Iraq under the guise of Islamic fundamentalism—less a contradiction than it may appear.

Most important, ISIS presents itself to an embattled Sunni minority in Iraq, and an even more persecuted and victimized Sunni majority in Syria, as the sect's last line of defense against a host of enemies—the United States and Russia, the Gulf Arab states, or the Alawite dictatorship in Syria, the Shia one in Iran, and the latter's satrapy in Baghdad. Here ISIS relies, as all peddlers of conspiracy theories do, on kernels of truth and awkward geopolitical realities to depict a satanic global enterprise ranged against its followers. Syria's warplanes are now flying the same skies as America's, purportedly bombing the same targets in eastern Syria—while the US government maintains that Assad has no future in Damascus. In Iraq, Iranian-built Shia militias, some of them designated as terrorist entities by the US government (because they have American blood on their hands), now serve as the vanguard of the Iraqi Security Forces' ground campaign to beat back ISIS—and with the advertised supervision and encouragement of Iran's Revolutionary Guards Corps, another US-designated terrorist entity. These militias are also committing acts of ethnic cleansing in Sunni villages along the way, earning the censure of Amnesty International and Human Rights Watch—all while US warplanes provide them with air cover. Whatever Washington's intentions, its perceived alliance of convenience with the murderous regimes of Syria and Iran is keeping Sunnis who loathe or fear ISIS from participating in another grassroots "Awakening" to expel the terrorists from their midst. Those who have tried have been mercilessly slaughtered; others have simply been co-opted and forced to pledge fealty to the slaughterers.

At once oversold and underestimated, brutal and savvy, ISIS has destroyed the boundaries of contemporary nation-states and proclaimed itself the restorer of a lost Islamic empire. An old enemy has become a new one, determined to prolong what has already been a tragically protracted war.

ISIS

1

FOUNDING FATHER
ABU MUSAB AL-ZARQAWI'S JIHAD

"Rush O Muslims to your state. Yes, it is your state. Rush, because Syria is not for the Syrians, and Iraq is not for the Iraqis." Abu Bakr al-Baghdadi—by then anointed Caliph Ibrahim—heralded the birth of the Islamic State on June 28, 2014, the first day of Ramadan, from the pulpit of the Great Mosque of al-Nuri in Mosul. His forces had sacked Mosul, a city in northern Iraq of two and a half million people, just days earlier. The commandeered mosque was named for the twelfth-century ruler Nur al-Din Mahmud Zangi, who reigned over both Aleppo and Mosul and was celebrated as a hero of the Second Crusade. Nur al-Din destroyed Frankish forces in southern Turkey and defeated (and beheaded) the Christian prince Raymond of Poitiers in Antioch. Later, he unified Syria by marrying the daughter of the *atabeg*, or ducal governor, of Damascus. Nur al-Din's vassal, the Kurdish military commander Saladin, a man whom many contemporary jihadists still channel, would become the overlord of Mosul. Before going off to fight the Crusaders, Saladin preached from the very pulpit from which al-Baghdadi now exhorted all Muslims to gather in this ancient land, newly liberated from the hirelings of new Crusaders. And so, the organization that just weeks earlier had been known by its geographical circumscription, the Islamic State of Iraq and al-Sham, was at an end, al-Baghdadi declared, for the simple fact that geography itself was irrelevant. As he saw it, the nations of the Fertile Crescent and indeed of the world no longer existed. Only the Islamic State did. Humanity could now neatly be divided into two camps. The first was "the camp of the Muslims and

1

the *mujahidin*," or holy warriors, bound by no race or country of origin (they were "everywhere," as he put it); the second was "the camp of the Jews, the Crusaders, their allies," a surprisingly baggy coalition consisting of the United States, Saudi Arabia, Jordan, Israel, Russia, Iran, all the nations of Europe, and pretty much everyone else. Standing there, draped in black, his long black beard betraying penumbras of white on either side, al-Baghdadi presented himself as a man of two pasts, one remote, one not so distant. He was the heir to the medieval Abbasid caliphate, the last true glory of Sunni Islam, and he was also the embodied spirit of his heroic predecessor, Abu Musab al-Zarqawi, who had spoken in similarly messianic terms before meeting his fate in 2006 when an F-16 dropped two five-hundred-pound bombs on his head. For his successor to be delivering a sermon to all Muslims from the al-Nuri Mosque was al-Zarqawi's legacy and his revenge. He had, after all, revered this holy place for most of his adult life and he would gladly have died all over again for the chance now given to al-Baghdadi, to preach the fulfillment of a darkling vision eleven years in the making.

THE BOY FROM ZARQA

The scruffy burg of Zarqa lies about twenty-five miles to the northeast of Amman, Jordan. Before its most notorious native son adopted the name of the town for his nom de guerre, it had two main associations, one liturgical and the other humanitarian. Zarqa was the biblical staging ground of Jacob's famous struggle with God; today it is the location of al-Ruseifah, the oldest Palestinian refugee camp in Jordan. Ahmad Fadhil Nazzal al-Khalaylah, as al-Zarqawi was born, hailed not from a nationless people but from the Bani Hassan tribe, a confederation of Bedouins who resided on the East Bank of the Jordan River and were known for their loyalty to the Hashemite King-dom. His father was a *mukhtar*, or village elder, municipally empowered to arbitrate local disputes, although his son was more fond of getting into them. Al-Zarqawi was an unpromising student who wrote Arabic at a semiliterate level, dropped out of school in 1984, the same year his father died, and re-sorted immediately to a life of crime. "He was not so big, but he was bold," one of al-Zarqawi's cousins later recounted to the *New York Times*. He drank and bootlegged alcohol; some contemporaries also claim that he was a pimp. His first stint in prison was for drug possession and sexual assault. His victims in the latter category were not confined to a single gender. "His idea of a sexual conquest," writes Joby Warrick, one of al-Zarqawi's recent biographers, relying on the testimonies of Jordanian security officials and acquaintances of the future jihadist, "was to force himself on younger men as a way to humiliate and assert his own dominance."

Upon his release from prison, al-Zarqawi became known throughout Zarqa as "the green man," owing to the many tattoos he sported on his arms and shoulders—haram, or sinful, markings he would later have cut from his flesh with razors during a second incarceration, this time for terrorism. Worried that her son was descending into an underworld from which he'd never escape, al-Zarqawi's mother, Um Sayel, enrolled him in religious courses at the Al-Husayn Ben Ali Mosque in Amman. The experience was transformative. Faith had the intended effect of supplanting the lawlessness, but not, of course, in the way Um Sayel might have hoped.

Since the 1970s, Jordan had been awash with Islamist ideology in one form or another. The most prevalent was the ideology of the state-indulged Muslim Brotherhood, which, as reward from a grateful King Hussein for its help in ousting the Palestine Liberation Organization from Jordan, was given control of the Ministry of Education. In return, the Brotherhood forswore violent uprising and simply sought to transform the kingdom's politics through the ballot box. For all that, the curricular Islamism that found purchase in the alleyways, mosques, and sitting rooms of Zarqa took Zionism and Israel as its most popular objects of hatred. And when the Hashemite monarchy embarked on creeping accommodation with the Jewish state—culminating in the Oslo Accords, which established formal ties between the two countries—that hatred was directed inward as well. The Brotherhood had competition: a strand of Islamist thinking known as Salafism, which dated back much earlier, to the nineteenth century, and had undergone a complete inside-out transformation of its core philosophy. Originally, the Salafists had sought to marry Islam with Western-style democracy and modernity for use against what was then their bugbear, the corrupt, depraved, and crumbling edifice of the Ottoman Empire. Beginning in the 1920s, however, Salafism was adapted to account for dawning new realities following the close of World War I. Now the enemy was no longer a defunct, notionally Islamic empire but rather the Western-enabled dynastic governments that had risen to take its place, the kingdoms of contemporary Arabia. The Salafist prescription was nothing short of a complete return to Islamic first principles and the seventh-century ways of the Prophet Muhammad. Western-style democracy and modernity were now shunned as irreconcilable with the faith because the pools where these pollutants had gathered were in the very birthplace of a magnificent and now lost civilization, the lands of Egypt, Jordan, Syria, and Iraq, where illegitimate, "apostate" regimes had emerged. The Salafists were revolutionary and uncompromising—Bolsheviks to the Brotherhood's Mensheviks. At the most extreme end of their continuum they practiced jihad, a word that means "struggle" in Arabic and may be defined in a number of ways. But by the late 1970s and 1980s, after the Soviet Union invaded Afghanistan in an act of imperial aggression, jihad meant only one thing: armed resistance.

It was in the Al-Husayn Ben Ali Mosque that al-Zarqawi first imbibed this world-upending doctrine and where he first volunteered to go to Afghanistan to help his fellow Muslims expel the communists. By the time he arrived, the Red Army was already in retreat. And though he would fight—bravely, by most accounts—against the pro-Moscow satellite government left in its wake, al-Zarqawi's more transformative experience would be his immersion in a different kind of civil war, one taking place within the intellectual ranks of Salafi jihadism itself. At issue was the basic question of who the real and immediate enemy of Islam now was in the aftermath of Soviet defeat, and what the acceptable targets were in the prosecution of holy war. These questions preoccupy us still and are being answered, bullet for bullet, suicide bomb for suicide bomb, in every time zone on the planet, between two rival jihadist organizations that once carried the same banner. The first was founded by Osama bin Laden, the second by Abu Musab al-Zarqawi.

THE HAYATABAD MILIEU

Hayatabad is a city on the outskirts of Peshawar, Pakistan, that rests at the base of the Khyber Pass, through which multiple empires have entered, and then exited, Afghanistan. In the late 1980s, the city had become a kind of Casablanca for the Soviet-Afghan war, then winding down. It was a city of perpetual waiting and planning, host to soldiers, spies, peddlers, crooks, warlords, smugglers, refugees, black marketeers, and both veteran and aspiring holy warriors.

It was also the operational headquarters of Osama bin Laden, one of the scions of a billionaire Saudi industrial family, who was busy laying the groundwork and amassing the personnel for his own start-up organization, al-Qaeda. Bin Laden's mentor at the time was also one of Hayatabad's leading Islamist theoreticians, a Palestinian named Abdullah Azzam, who in 1984 had published a book that became a manifesto for the Afghan mujahidin. It argued that Muslims had both an individual and communal obligation to expel conquering or occupying armies from their sacred lands. Certainly galvanized by Israel's military occupation of his birthplace—his famous slogan was "Jihad and the rifle alone; no negotiations, no conferences, no dialogues"—Azzam explicitly made the anti-Soviet campaign the priority for all believing Muslims, not just Afghans. Like al-Baghdadi's exhortations decades later, Azzam's was a global casting call for mujahidin from around the world to join one camp against another. Though not quite advocating a transnational caliphate, Azzam did think that Afghanistan was where a viable Islamic state could be constructed on the ashes of communist hegemony. This war was still a purist one, not yet diluted by competitive and paradoxical ideologies—which the Palestinian cause had lately been, thanks to the secular nationalism of Yasser Arafat and the jet-setting Leninist terrorism of Carlos the Jackal.

So when Azzam relocated to Peshawar, he and bin Laden became den mothers to the arriving "Arab-Afghans," as the foreign mujahidin were colloquially known, who were eager to wage holy war but clueless as to how or where to begin. Together they founded Maktab al-Khadamat, or the Services Bureau, which operated out of a residence bin Laden owned. If Azzam was the Marx, a grand philosopher articulating the concept of a new revolutionary struggle and drawing in the necessary disciples to realize it, then bin Laden was his Engels, the wealthy scion who paid the bills and kept the lights on while the master toiled on texts that would change the world.

About three thousand Arab-Afghans passed through this jihadist orientation center, where they were provided food, money, and housing, as well as being acculturated to a strange and ethnolinguistically heterodox North-West Frontier. Untold millions of dollars passed through the Services Bureau as well, much of it raised by bin Laden and Azzam, and some of it channeled by the Saudi government, with which bin Laden had close ties through his family's construction empire. Some of the world's most infamous international terrorists gained their most valuable commodity—contacts—under the patronage systems set up by bin Laden and Azzam during this period.

Duopolies made up of outsize egos seldom endure, and Azzam and his pupil eventually fell out, owing principally to bin Laden's closeness to another rising celebrity in the jihadist firmament: Ayman al-Zawahiri. Al-Zawahiri was an Egyptian surgeon who had done three months of medical work for the Red Crescent Society in Pakistan in the summer of 1980, and had even taken short jaunts into Afghanistan to observe the war firsthand. By the end of the decade, al-Zawahiri had earned global notoriety for being among the hundreds imprisoned and tortured for his alleged complicity in the assassination of Egyptian president Anwar Sadat in 1981. He had been the emir, or prince, of the Jihad Group, which had sought a coup d'état in Cairo and the establishment of an Islamic theocracy in its place.

After his release, al-Zawahiri returned to Peshawar in 1986 to resume his medical work at a Red Crescent hospital, and to reconstitute his Egyptian organization. His Salafism by that time had grown more extreme; he had been flirting with the concept of *takfirism*—the excommunication of fellow Muslims on the basis of their supposed heresy, and an injunction that almost always carried with it a death sentence. Theologically justified, as all jihadist concepts were, takfirism was also a pragmatic means by which suspect, competitive, or ideologically iffy elements within Sunni Islam could be purged. It was the terrorist's lettre de cachet. Thus, when al-Zawahiri befriended bin Laden, he was put on a direct collision course with Azzam, who was categorically opposed to Muslims killing other Muslims. For Azzam, jihadism's true target was the irreligious and irredeemable West, its denizens and allies, known in the theoretical discourse as the "far enemy." Muslims, he believed, even those who were beneficiaries of backward Arab regimes, were meant to be persuaded, not bombed, into submission. Al-Zawahiri could not disagree more. He had gone to Afghanistan, in fact, with the express purpose of acquiring the training and know-how to destabilize and overthrow the ruling government of his native Egypt, one of those backward Arab regimes, a "near enemy."

And so, like two squabbling courtiers from rival families, al-Zawahiri and Azzam hated each other and competed for bin Laden's attention and good graces. Most of all, they competed for his money.

In late November 1989, Azzam and two of his sons were killed after a roadside bomb blew up their car on the way to a mosque. Theories as to the likely culprits ranged from the KGB to Saudi intelligence to the CIA to bin Laden and/or al-Zawahiri to Mossad. The very next month, one of Azzam's other sons, Huthaifa, went to the Peshawar airport to collect a group of mostly Jordanian Arab-Afghans who were arriving at the tail end of the struggle to fight the Red Army, then about two months shy of a categorical withdrawal from Afghanistan. One of the arrivals was al-Zarqawi.

CLAUSEWITZ FOR TERRORISTS

Rather than return to Amman as the man who had missed the holy war, al-Zarqawi stayed on in the North-West Frontier region until 1993, building up a knowledge base, military résumé, and valuable network of associates among the international retinue that lingered on to determine the fate of a newly liberated Afghanistan. Among those he encountered were the brother of Khalid Sheikh Mohammed, the 9/11 mastermind, and Mohammed Shobana, who published a jihadist magazine called *Al-Bunyan Al-Marsus*, or *The Impenetrable Edifice*. Despite his somewhat impenetrable Arabic, and solely on the basis of his referral by a well-regarded cleric, al-Zarqawi was hired as one of the magazine's cub reporters. He also met his future brother-in-law, Salah al-Hami, a Jordanian-Palestinian journalist affiliated with Abdullah Azzam's own in-house magazine of the Services Bureau. Al-Hami had lost a leg to a land mine in Khost, Afghanistan, and he later claimed that it was during his convalescence in a hospital, after complaining that with his deformity he would never find a wife, that al-Zarqawi offered one of his seven sisters to al-Hami for marriage. She traveled to Peshawar for the wedding, an event that furnished the first and only footage of al-Zarqawi until April 2006, when his al-Qaeda franchise in Iraq released a propaganda video showing its black-clad commander firing a machine gun like Rambo.

According to al-Hami, al-Zarqawi's reportage for *The Impenetrable Edifice* consisted mostly of interviews with veterans of the Soviet-Afghan war, through whom he lived vicariously, tromping through the North-West Frontier, writing no doubt heavily embroidered memoirs of mujahidin who had faced off with Russian Hind attack helicopters and T-62 battle tanks. At night he would try to memorize the Quran. Al-Hami remembers him "crying whenever he said prayers, aloud, even when leading the prayers." Once, on a camping trip with his brother-in-law, al-Zarqawi relayed a rather kitschy epiphany of how he would spend the rest of his life. He said that he had dreamt that a sword had fallen from the sky and upon which the word "jihad" was inscribed.

Al-Hami returned to Jordan after a few months with his new bride, but his brother-in-law stayed on, participating in what was then an incipient civil war between and among manifold belligerents, many of them Islamic warlords. Al-Zarqawi cast his lot with the Pashtun warlord Gulbuddin Hekmatyar, who served intermittently as the prime minister in Kabul; his administration was eventually usurped by the Taliban, whereupon Hekmatyar fled to Iran. He also attended a series of training camps on the Afghanistan-Pakistan border, including the most significant, Sada al-Malahim, or the Echo of Battle. It was al-Qaeda's Fort Dix, graduating the masterminds of the two separate World Trade Center attacks, Ramzi Yousef and Khalid Sheikh Mohammed. As recounted by Loretta Napoleoni in her book *Insurgent Iraq: Al-Zarqawi and the New Generation*, bin Laden's ex-bodyguard, Nasir Ahmad Nasir Abdallah al-Bahari, described camp life at the Echo as three distinct phases of training and indoctrination. The first was "the days of experimentation"—which lasted for fifteen days, to be exact—during which a recruit was subjected to "psychological, as well as moral, exhaustion," evidently to separate the real warriors from the softies. The second was the "military preparation period," which lasted for forty-five days, during which a recruit was taught first how to wield light weapons, then graduated on to shoulder-borne surface-to-air missiles and cartography courses. The third and final phase was "the guerrilla war tactics course," which taught military theory. Clausewitz for terrorists.

Al-Zarqawi is said to have fought well and without fear, at least according to Huthaifa Azzam, the son of the dead cleric, and al-Zarqawi's chauffeur from Peshawar's airport years before; he claims that al-Zarqawi once fended off a dozen Afghan soldiers by himself. What drove him during this transition from two-bit hood to budding commander? Guilt, the younger Azzam maintains. Al-Zarqawi had much to atone for in his wayward youth and felt that a battlefield martyrdom was the surest way to expunge his sins. Whatever the discrepancy here between legend and reality, the Jordanian's days as an avid chronicler of other people's war stories were at an end. He was just beginning to make his own.

HOMECOMING

Al-Zarqawi returned to Jordan in late 1993 and was immediately placed, like every other repatriating Arab-Afghan, under surveillance by the Kingdom's General Intelligence Directorate, or Mukhabarat. It was rightfully reckoned that whatever skills these veterans had learned abroad would be turned against a new enemy at home. The Mukhabarat's fears were borne out within six months.

For al-Zarqawi, return to civilian life was inevitably uneasy and abortive. Jordan was still a largely secular country, saturated with Western popular culture, where alcohol, pornography, and sex could be had relatively easily, as al-Zarqawi well knew firsthand. So, seeking the spiritual sustenance and camaraderie that he had felt in the mountains of the North-West Frontier, he visited Abu Muhammad al-Maqdisi, another Jordanian-Palestinian cleric whom al-Zarqawi had first encountered in Hayatabad. Al-Maqdisi was fast rising up the totem pole of internationally known Salafist theoreticians, and had recently published a blistering anti-Western screed, *Democracy: A Religion*, which drew a stark line between the political economy of the "pagans" and Allah's divine law. Together, in a Levantine shadow play of the bin Laden and Azzam double act, al-Zarqawi and al-Maqdisi proselytized in make-shift salons around Jordan, inveighing against their government's warming relations with Israel and against America's meddling, imperialistic role in the Middle East. Al-Maqdisi was a pedantic scholar, full of invective about the perceived shortcomings of contemporary politics; al-Zarqawi was charismatic but an intellectual lightweight. "He never struck me as intelligent," Mohammed al-Dweik, his future lawyer, recalled years later. It was a view shared by al-Zarqawi's mother, Um Sayel, the person responsible for first introducing him to religion as moral and emotional ballast.

Al-Maqdisi had founded his own Jordanian jihadist cell known as Bayat al-Imam, or the Pledge to the Imam. In spite of the thorough infiltration by the Mukhabarat, he enlisted al-Zarqawi's help in recruiting and plotting attacks. Their first foray into homegrown terrorism smacked more of a Key-stone Kops farce than of a grisly tragedy. Weapons discarded by the retreating Iraqi army at the end of the First Gulf War had furnished a thriving Kuwaiti market for matériel. Al-Maqdisi, who had lived in the Persian Gulf for a time and had the relevant connections, purchased antipersonnel mines, antitank rockets, and hand grenades and had them smuggled into Jordan for future assaults against targets inside the Kingdom. Al-Maqdisi gave al-Zarqawi the contraband to hide, then asked for it back; al-Zarqawi obliged, save for two bombs, which he would later claim were for "use in a suicide operation in the territories occupied by the Zionists." Aware that the Mukhabarat was tracking their movements and had an inventory of their illicit wares, both men tried to flee Jordan. They were caught. In March 1994, al-Maqdisi and al-Zarqawi were arrested—the latter after the Mukhabarat raided his house and found his stockpile of weapons. Discovered in bed, he tried to shoot one officer and then commit suicide. He managed neither. Al-Zarqawi was charged and convicted with illegal weapons possession and belonging to a terrorist organization.

At their trial, the two failed terrorists decided to transform the dock into a bully pulpit, perhaps consciously following in the footsteps of Ayman al-Zawahiri in Egypt, who denounced the court and the government in a famous harangue after being snared in the dragnet following the Sadat assassination. The Jordanian co-conspirators, too, denounced everybody—the court, the state, and the monarchy for violating the laws of God and Islam. According to the judge presiding over the trial, Bayat al-Imam "submitted a letter of accusation in which they claimed that we were acting against the teachings of the Holy Quran." The judge was further instructed to pass on a message to King Hussein, accusing him of sacrilege. Al-Zarqawi was still junior to al-Maqdisi and lacked the cleric's easy way with turning due process into propaganda, but the price he paid was commensurate with that paid by his senior partner. Both men were sentenced in 1994 to fifteen years in prison and transferred to a desert-based maximum-security facility called Swaqa. They would serve four years there before being transferred to an even more notorious prison, an isolated, dank, and vermin-ridden desert fortress built by the British military, known as al-Jabr. It had been shuttered for years but reopened to house a select few of Jordan's most ardent and violent enemies.

"PRISON WAS HIS UNIVERSITY"

Al-Zarqawi's time in Swaqa was not wasted. It made him more focused, brutal, and decisive. As a member of the Bani Hassan, he occupied a station above other inmates, even al-Maqdisi, who was nonetheless ennobled by his comradeship with his nominal pupil. In Jordan, as elsewhere, the gemeinschaft of a jailhouse only emphasized the privileges and perks enjoyed by outlaws beyond their concrete boxes. Al-Zarqawi leveraged his influence with malleable or crooked guards to make his faction, made up of fellow Bayat al-Imam convicts, thrive. He got his underlings out of wearing standard-issue uniforms and exempted from morning roll call in the prison yard. His preferred garb was Afghan, the *shalwar kameez*—a body shirt and pantaloon combination—and a Pashtun hat. His apparent vanity was matched by a steely demeanor and gangland discipline that few would trifle with. "He could order his followers to do things just by moving his eyes," said a prison doctor who tended to him and the small contingent of inmates at al-Jabr after they were transferred there.

By means of coercion or persuasion, al-Zarqawi sought to singularize his interpretation of Islamist ideology, casting himself in the role of supreme jurisprudent. He beat up those he didn't like, such as a contributor to Swaqa's intramural magazine who had turned out articles critical of him. Another inmate, Abu Doma, recalled that al-Zarqawi had caught him reading *Crime and Punishment*, a "book by a heathen." Al-Zarqawi followed up to ensure that Abu Doma abandoned his interest in profane Russian literature, writing him a hectoring letter in which he spelled Dostoyevsky's name "Doseefski." ("The note was full of bad Arabic, like a child wrote it," Doma recounted.) Unable to develop arguments, al-Zarqawi instead developed his body, using his bed frame and olive oil cans filled with rocks for weights. He didn't always get his way with the guards. When he stood up to them, he was sometimes beaten, further impressing those who looked up to him as a leader of men. At one point, he was thrown into solitary confinement for eight and a half months.

Prison was where the role reversal in Bayat al-Imam's leadership finally and definitively occurred. Al-Zarqawi assumed the title of emir in a swapping of honorifics that al-Maqdisi later insisted, possibly to save face, was his suggestion. Despite his fiery tracts against democracy, al-Maqdisi could be a pushover in person, displaying politesse to the "apostate" prison authorities or offering a kind word for the Jordanian parliament when pressed on the matter. Al-Zarqawi, by contrast, gave way neither to man nor to oppositional view, although he apparently displayed an unexpected tenderness in his dealings with his lieutenants, especially where their health or comfort was concerned. As we have seen, al-Zarqawi married off his sister out of pity for the one-legged Salah al-Hami in Afghanistan. Accounts from his incarceration period similarly have him alternating between dead-eyed emir and Florence Nightingale, ministering to his infirm or mutilated jihadists with a loving attentiveness. (This split personality tracks with many of history's monsters.)

That al-Zarqawi eclipsed al-Maqdisi does not mean that he supplanted him outright. The mentor-scholar helped the protégé-commander cultivate ideology as well as brawn. Both composed fatwas, or religious edicts, that were smuggled out of the prison and subsequently uploaded to the Internet for broad dissemination. A few of these even caught the attention of bin Laden, who had followed the trial of the two Jordanians with great interest from Pakistan. According to "Richard," a former top-ranking counterterrorism official at the Pentagon who asked to be quoted in this book under an alias, al-Zarqawi's experience in prison was akin to that of Whitey Bulger. Bulger, the Boston crime boss, was the beneficiary of the same unintended consequence: a penal environment that did not rehabilitate him so much as hone his natural talents for leadership, cunning, and sadism. "We sent him to the Harvard of American penitentiaries," Richard said, referring to Bulger's time in Alcatraz. "He was a wily criminal who had a little IQ and put together some good streams of income. He comes out of the pen with great street cred that helped him form his own gang, which ran Boston for four or five years. Same with al-Zarqawi. Prison was his university."

Much the same would later apply to ISIS's current leader, Abu Bakr al-Baghdadi, as well as to most members of the upper echelons of his organization who, twenty years later, served various stretches as inmates in Camp Bucca, the US-run internment facility in occupied Iraq. Al-Baghdadi, like al-Zarqawi, was looked on by prison authorities as a disciplined and charismatic leader whose followers marched in lockstep with his every instruction. A personality cult that may have been an asset behind bars was a lurking liability outside of them.

Ultimately, owing to changes in Jordan's government, al-Zarqawi served only a fraction of his sentence. When Jordan's King Hussein died he was succeeded by his son Abdullah II, a Western-educated reformist who had intended to live out a professional military career rather than inherit his father's throne. In March 1999, the new king, succumbing to parliamentary pressure, declared a general amnesty for around three thousand prisoners, excepting the worst offenders such as murderers, rapists, and traitors. Many Islamists who hadn't actually (or successfully) committed terrorism against the crown were freed, against the objections of many seasoned spies who knew the recidivism rate of this class of criminal quite well. Halfway through his sentence, al-Zarqawi found himself a free man.

Granted, "free" is a relative term under an Arab autocracy. Al-Zarqawi made one attempt to leave Jordan for Pakistan, posing as a prospective beekeeper; he was snatched at the airport, along with his mother and wife, by the Mukhabarat, which hadn't wanted him let out of prison in the first place. Detained and interrogated about his unlikely newfound interest in honeygathering, he was finally able to depart in the summer of 1999. Of course, he had only ever intended to pick up where he had left off six years prior. Yet fresh problems awaited when he touched down in Pakistan. He was arrested briefly in Peshawar and spent eight days in detention, evidently because his visa had expired. Told that he would only get his passport back if he used it to return to Jordan immediately, al-Zarqawi instead smuggled himself across the border to Afghanistan; he wound up in a jihadist "guest house" in a village west of Kabul, in an area then under the sway of his former warlord confederate, Gulbuddin Hekmatyar. Not long thereafter, a meeting took place that would change the Middle East.

MEETING BIN LADEN

Al-Zarqawi's first audience with Osama bin Laden happened, after many deferrals instigated by the latter, in the city of Kandahar, the de facto capital of what was then the ruling theocratic power in Afghanistan, the Taliban. The encounter went quite badly. Bin Laden suspected the younger jihadist and the cabal of Jordanians he had arrived with of being infiltrated by the very Arab spy service from which they'd just managed to wriggle free. Also, the visible scars of al-Zarqawi's prison-excised tattoos disturbed the puritanical Saudi. More than anything, though, it was al-Zarqawi's arrogance, his "rigid views," that offended bin Laden. Ayman al-Zawahiri, now bin Laden's unchallenged number two, was present at the meeting and agreed that the ex-con was not a prime candidate for enlistment in al-Qaeda. The wariness owed not just to al-Zarqawi's personality, but to what the senior jihadists in Kandahar had by now come to view as an outmoded and de trop path of jihad.

ENEMIES, NEAR AND FAR

In 1996 bin Laden had issued a fatwa. It was titled "Declaration of Jihad Against the Americans Occupying the Land of the Two Holiest Sites," those sites being Mecca and Medina, both in Saudi Arabia, where US and Western garrisons were still kept after the First Gulf War. The declaration was in a sense a dialectical fusion of the rival philosophies espoused by bin Laden's two tutors, Abdullah Azzam (now dead) and al-Zawahiri. As with Afghanistan, al-Qaeda claimed to be fighting another infidel occupier of Muslim land. Only this time, the "occupier," the United States, was there at the invitation and pleasure of a nominally Muslim government, the Saudi monarchy, which had been bin Laden's erstwhile collaborator against a previous Western occupier, the Soviet Union.

In the early 1990s al-Qaeda had targeted American soldiers throughout the Middle East and Africa, from Yemen to Tanzania, putting the organization firmly in the "far enemy" camp of jihad, albeit with the added dispensation for killing any Muslims who collaborated with the democratic superpower.

Therefore, in wanting to bring terrorism back to Jordan, for use against exclusively Muslim targets, al-Zarqawi was still firmly in the "near enemy" camp. In other words, he was exactly where the elder al-Zawahiri had been a decade earlier when he had only wanted to attack the Egyptian government before adapting his views to encompass and prioritize hitting America.

In 1999, the near versus far enemy divergence in jihadism was as much generational as it was ideological. Al-Zarqawi also had a much more promiscuous definition of *kuffar*, the highly derogatory term for "unbelievers," which he took to include all the Shia and any fellow Sunnis who did not abide by a strict Salafist covenant. In yet another sign of a generational schism, where al-Zawahiri had by now given up takfirism, the excommunication of insufficiently pious or doctrinaire Muslims, al-Zarqawi had taken up the practice enthusiastically.

For his part, bin Laden had never drawn a bull's-eye on the Shia minority before, no doubt for filial as much as philosophical reasons. His own mother, after all, was a Syrian Alawite, or a member of the offshoot of the Shia.

From such inauspicious beginnings, then, a marriage of convenience was forged between the two jihadists. Saif al-Adel, al-Qaeda's security chief, seems to have been the principal, if not the only, matchmaker. What did he see in the brash and reckless al-Zarqawi? The same thing all jihadists see when looking to expand their influence and reach: a phalanx of countless others standing right beside him. By 1999, both inside and outside of the walls of Swaqa and al-Jabr prisons, al-Zarqawi had amassed an extensive Rolodex of contacts in the Levant, which al-Adel convinced bin Laden would be of great use to al-Qaeda. One of these contacts was Abu Muhammad al-Adnani, who is today the official "spokesman" for ISIS, although in reality he runs all of his native Syria for the franchise, making him tantamount to one of the caliphate's original framers.

MONOTHEISM AND JIHAD

In 2000 al-Zarqawi was put in charge of a training camp in Herat, Afghanistan's third-largest city, situated near the border with Iran. The camp was built with al-Qaeda money, according to former CIA analyst Nada Bakos, who was later in charge of tracking al-Zarqawi in Iraq. She estimates that bin Laden granted the Jordanian $200,000 in the form of a "loan," a pittance compared to what al-Qaeda was financially capable of disbursing. This may have been a test to see how well al-Zarqawi could get on with so little. "All you needed was a patch of land, a couple of chin-up bars, and guys running around with AK-47s," said Richard, the ex-Pentagon official. "We're not talking about high-end training or even Marine Corps basic training. The physical activity at Herat was to determine who had the stomach for the fight."

Nada Bakos, now retired from the CIA, added that there were many training camps in the Herat area, which "all shared various geography, territory, and resources." One more was meaningless to al-Qaeda. "Al-Zarqawi was not buying into their version of jihad," Bakos said, "and they didn't really give a shit about him. So it was more like: 'Here, go make your jihad in Jordan. That sounds great.' Also, as we now know, bin Laden had a lot more going on at that time."

True to his origins, al-Zarqawi fielded mainly Palestinian and Jordanian recruits for his own independently owned, if al-Qaeda subsidized, franchise, which he named Jund al-Sham, or Soldiers of the Levant. Yet the banner above the entrance to the Herat camp carried a slogan that would eventually become the name of his first terrorist cell in Iraq, where a cognizance of regions or borders was already slipping away. "Tawhid wal-Jihad," the banner read, *tawhid* standing for "monotheism." The word connotes not only a self-evident tenet about an Abrahamic faith but also a dividing line between the true believers and their quarry. "Polytheist" became an epithet used by al-Zarqawi and his minions to defame the Shia, not to mention any number of pre-Islamic confessions, such as Zoroastrianism. It was one of his many capital accusations.

For now, though, the Soldiers of the Levant were being groomed for terrorist operations in Israel, Palestine, Jordan, and other Arab countries, with the ultimate goal being violent regime change and the establishment of Islamic emirates. Some of the camp's graduates did indeed participate in noteworthy "spectaculars." One example is the 2002 shooting at close range of Laurence Foley, an officer for the US Agency for International Development in Amman, whose murder may have been personally ordered by al-Zarqawi. This remains a matter of controversy within intelligence circles. Another is the well-publicized plot to set off chemical bombs in the Jordanian capital in 2004, targeting the prime minister's office, the Mukhabarat headquarters, and the US embassy. The Jordanians claimed that had this attack been successful, it might have killed as many as eighty thousand people. The plot was spearheaded by Azmi al-Jayousi, a Jordanian-Palestinian, who was personally dispatched back into Jordan by al-Zarqawi, equipped with a budget that would eventually swell to $250,000. He used the funds to buy trucks, cars, and twenty tons of chemical agents that were stored in a giant warehouse in the city of Irbid. The man who rented al-Jayousi his warehouse space grew suspicious about his tenant's outsize security measures for so mundane a piece of real estate, and blew the whistle to the Mukhabarat. Were it not for that landlord, who informed on al-Jayousi just as his preparations were being finalized, much of Amman might well have been engulfed in a toxic gas cloud whose epicenter was the headquarters of the General Intelligence Directorate. As al-Jayousi told his interrogator, in a confession that King Abdullah would order broadcast on Jordanian state television, "I promised my loyalty to Abu Musab al-Zarqawi. I agreed to work for him— no questions asked."

While al-Zarqawi accepted responsibility for planning to strike at the General Intelligence Directorate, he denied that his plans had ever involved chemical weapons, claiming that this was a piece of black disinformation cooked up by the Directorate itself. If he had had access to weapons of mass destruction (WMD), al-Zarqawi maintained, he would have used them against Israel. His jihadists in Iraq and later in Syria *would* use chemical "dirty bombs," typically chlorine based, in small-scale but lethal attacks against an assortment of enemies, including the Kurds.

Soldiers of the Levant grew exponentially, deeply impressing Saif al-Adel, the man responsible for bankrolling the operation, who took to visiting al-Zarqawi's training camp monthly to report back to bin Laden on the loan grantee's progress. As a result of his success, or perhaps because bin Laden realized that he was about to need all the manpower he could muster, with the 9/11 attacks imminent, the al-Qaeda leader seems to have reappraised the arrogant Jordanian. Between 2000 and 2001, bin Laden had repeatedly asked al-Zarqawi to return to Kandahar and make bayat—or pledge allegiance— which was the necessary rite of passage for full al-Qaeda enlistment, pending, of course, bin Laden's approval. Al-Zarqawi repeatedly refused. "I never heard him praise anyone apart from the Prophet, this was Abu Mos'ab's character, he never followed anyone, he only ever went out to get what he felt was just to do," a former associate recollected. Whether owing to hubris or (for him) a still very profound difference of opinion with his benefactor, al-Zarqawi retained an arm's-length and opportunistic relationship with al-Qaeda until 2004.

IN NORTHERN IRAQ

One of al-Zarqawi's lieutenants in Herat was a fellow Jordanian named Abu Abdel Rahman al-Shami; al-Zarqawi tasked him with expanding the Soldiers of the Levant network into northern Iraq via Iran. The objective seems to have been to establish a Taliban-style fief in the semiautonomous region of Iraqi Kurdistan, then under protection from Saddam's army and air force by an internationally enforced no-fly zone. Al-Shami got to work, infiltrating the mountainous terrain of Kurdistan, and bivouacking in a five-hundred-square-kilometer area region, where he and his conquering faction, named Jund al-Islam, or the Soldiers of Islam, occupied some two hundred thousand people. These inhabitants were now barred from drinking alcohol, listening to music, or watching satellite television. It was indeed as if Kandahar had come to Kurdistan.

After the September 11 attacks and the start of the US invasion of Afghanistan, al-Shami's Soldiers of Islam merged with other terrorist cells to become Ansar al-Islam, or the Helpers of Islam. The targets of this superconglomerate were two: the Baathist regime in Baghdad and the Patriotic Union of Kurdistan (PUK). The latter was one of two main secular political parties in Iraqi Kurdistan, led by Jalal Talabani, who would become president of a post-Saddam Iraq. The Kurds ran their own intelligence service and paramilitary units, which often clashed with or arrested members of Ansar.

On February 3, 2003, just weeks before the Iraq War began, Secretary of State Colin Powell addressed the United Nations and claimed that Ansar's perch in northern Iraq, which had been identified by Kurdish intelligence, was proof of al-Qaeda's links to Saddam's regime. Al-Zarqawi's network, Powell insisted, was manufacturing ricin and chemical weapons in northern Iraq, while al-Zarqawi, whom the top diplomat incorrectly referred to as Palestinian, had spent months receiving medical treatment in Baghdad, under state supervision. Al-Zarqawi, the rumors ran at the time, had needed a leg amputated and replaced with a prosthetic after sustaining a major injury in an aerial assault in Afghanistan.

Many of the minor and major details of Powell's speech were later debunked after US forces invaded Iraq and recovered scores of Iraqi intelligence files and interrogated plenty of former Iraqi intelligence officers, although there were those who worked in the Bush administration who never bought Powell's argument. "We first knew of Zarqawi in '98 or '99 and we knew what he was about," Richard said. "He was going to be a very brutal guy when he was flushed out of Afghanistan, but we didn't know he was going to head to Iraq. We assumed he was going to go back to Jordan. As for his 'hosting' in Iraq, I don't believe the whole Baghdad hospital story the way the administration sold it—that seems to fall in the 'Dick Cheney imagination' category."

The PUK claimed that Iraqi military intelligence was supplying Ansar with TNT for use in suicide bombings. A senior Iraqi operative in the Kurds' custody also confessed to being sent by Baghdad to make contact with Abu Wael, Ansar's religious leader and the group's liaison to al-Qaeda.

As it happens, the United States had excellent intelligence on Ansar al-Islam's activities, particularly at its base in the Kurdish hamlet of Sargat; the CIA had dispatched an eight-man team there to surveil the group and interrogate any prisoners captured by the pro-American Kurds. The CIA also knew that while Saddam's agents were stationed near Ansar's headquarters, they were there for the same reason: to spy on the jihadist cell, not to second it to do their bidding. Requests by the CIA to destroy the Ansar base were repeatedly rebuffed by the George W. Bush administration, then intent on invading Iraq and fearful of starting a major war too early, and for too small a target.

Al-Zarqawi stayed in Kurdistan for just under a month. By May 2002, he had relocated to Baghdad. There is still debate within the intelligence community as to whether or not al-Qaeda affiliates maintained their presence and ease of movement within Iraq, just prior to the US invasion, with the tacit approval or connivance of Saddam's regime. In his memoir, *At the Center of the Storm*, former CIA director George Tenet writes: "by the spring and summer of 2002, more than a dozen al-Qa'ida-affiliated extremists converged on Baghdad, with apparently no harassment on the part of the Iraqi government. They had found a comfortable and secure environment in which they moved people and supplies to support Zarqawi's operations in northeastern Iraq." Iraq was a police state on the verge of highly probable war with the United States. Might Saddam's Mukhabarat have looked the other way to allow the capital to become a cynosure for mujahidin ready to die fighting a Western occupation? American spies didn't doubt the jihadist infiltration of Iraq; they just argued over what it meant.

According to Richard, the former Pentagon counterterrorism official, al-Zarqawi's presence among the Ansar rank and file was still more a matter of convenience than of any codified hierarchical organization. He had, after all, dispatched al-Shami and other Herat graduates into Kurdistan to found a franchise; that franchise had subsequently merged with other preexisting ones in Kurdistan to form Ansar. The resulting formation had links to al-Qaeda. Exactly the same sort of Rolodex pragmatism that had led to al-Zarqawi's own loose association with bin Laden just three years earlier was now laying the foundation for a new network of Arab and Kurdish jihadists in the mountains of northern Iraq. "Jihadists gain more from friendships and acquaintanceships than they do from being on a list together that says they're part of the same terrorist cell," Richard said. "Look at ISIS today or look at all the groups in Syria, how fungible they are. Ansar al-Islam gave al-Zarqawi refuge in Kurdistan because they knew him and they liked him. Remember, he was always good at cutting deals with various criminal and tribal entities."

Moreover, al-Zarqawi's entry into Sargat, an area outside of Baghdad's control, happened courtesy of a mortal enemy of Saddam: the Islamic Republic of Iran.

When the United States and NATO went to war in Afghanistan, al-Zarqawi's camp in Herat was besieged by the Western-backed Northern Alliance, and al-Zarqawi fled to Kandahar, where he did sustain some injuries from a coalition air strike. But he didn't suffer a mangled or missing leg as reported; he only broke a few ribs, according to Iyad Tobaissi, one of his former trainees. Al-Zarqawi and his convoy of around three hundred militants then departed Afghanistan for Iran, then a willing if wary host of much of the jihadist exodus of an American-made war. Al-Zarqawi allegedly stayed for a week in the city of Zahedan before migrating to Tehran under the auspices of a by-now old and trusted associate, the former Afghan warlord Gulbuddin Hekmatyar. Hekmatyar had by then established a relationship with Iranian intelligence.

IRANIAN PATRONAGE

For a year or so following his flight from Afghanistan, al-Zarqawi was based in Iran and northern Iraq, although he traveled throughout the region. He visited a Palestinian refugee camp in southern Lebanon, where he recruited members to his burgeoning jihadist network, and he moved around the Sunni-majority communities of central and northern Iraq. Shadi Abdalla, bin Laden's former bodyguard, later told German authorities that al-Zarqawi was arrested in Iran for a short time during this period before being released—an allegation that

Jordanian officials claim to have corroborated on a trip to the Islamic Republic in 2003. Al-Zarqawi also went to Syria, where Jordanian spies believe he plotted Foley's assassination, with the connivance of Bashar al-Assad's security services.

Amman's file on the state sponsorship of al-Zarqawi's terrorist activities during the lead-up to the Iraq War stood in marked contrast to what Colin Powell had presented earlier. It was not Baghdad that America should have been looking at, the Jordanians said; it was Tehran.

Counterintuitive though it may seem for a revolutionary Shia Islamist regime to abet Sunni terrorism, Iran understood as well as any regional power that so long as the terrorists' zeal could be directed against a common foe—Saddam or the United States—a nonbinding contract of sorts could be brokered, the main clause of which would read: "We'll help you now, provided you don't attack us." And although he was pathologically hateful of all Shia, al-Zarqawi's priorities had shifted after the violent fall of the Taliban and his own narrow escape from death by way of American warplanes. A new object had taken shape toward which to divert his messianic and annihilationist ambitions, and it was the same as bin Laden's and al-Zawahiri's. "When he came to say goodbye before he left Iran," Saif al-Adel later recalled of al-Zarqawi, "he underlined the importance of taking revenge on the Americans for the crimes they committed during the bombardment of Afghanistan, which he witnessed with his own eyes." To accomplish this task, he'd have to form new short-term alliances. As ever, Washington planned more programmatically than jihadists liked to behave. The Jordanian Mukhabarat, better versed in the subject matter and in a man fast becoming the world's most famous international fugitive, understood far better what al-Zarqawi was up to. A high-level source in Jordanian intelligence told the *Atlantic* magazine in 2006:

> "We know Zarqawi better than he knows himself. And I can assure you that he never had any links to Saddam. Iran is quite a different matter. The Iranians have a policy: they want to control Iraq. And part of this policy has been to support Zarqawi, tactically but not strategically. . . . In the beginning they gave him automatic weapons, uniforms, military equipment, when he was with the army of Ansar al-Islam. Now they essentially just turn a blind eye to his activities, and to those of al-Qaeda generally. The Iranians see Iraq as a fight against the Americans, and overall, they'll get rid of Zarqawi and all of his people once the Americans are out."

There's a triple irony behind this observation.

First, al-Zarqawi's coming reign of terror in Iraq was distinguished by its focus on killing or tormenting the country's Shia-majority population; this, he believed, would create a state of civil war that would force Sunnis into reclaiming their lost power and prestige in Baghdad, which many of them believed the Americans had stolen by toppling Saddam and allowing for a Shia-dominant government to take his place.

Second, Iran later tried to "get rid" of al-Zarqawi's far more formidable disciples in Iraq, transparently and boastfully leading the ground war against ISIS using both its own Revolutionary Guards Corps as well as its proxies, the heavily trained and armed Iraqi Shia militias. Iranian warplanes even reportedly bombed ISIS positions in Iraq.

Third, the Islamic Republic's underwriting of al-Zarqawi's activity in 2001–2002 more adequately meets the accusation leveled by the Bush administration against Saddam's regime—that of maintaining a tactical alliance or condominium with al-Qaeda, a fact that was even owned up to by al-Zarqawi's contemporary, the current ISIS spokesman and plenipotentiary for Syria, Abu Muhammad al-Adnani. In a message directed at Ayman al-Zawahiri in May 2014, months after al-Qaeda formally announced its breakup with its former franchise, al-Adnani wrote to bin Laden's successor that "ISIS has not attacked the Rawafid [Shia] in Iran since its establishment. . . . It has kept its anger all these years and endured accusations of collaboration with its worst enemy, Iran, for refraining from targeting it, leaving the Rawafid there to live in safety, acting upon the orders of al Qaeda to safeguard its interests and supply lines in Iran. Let history record that Iran owes al Qaeda invaluably."

"SOCIALIST INFIDELS" AND NUR AL-DIN

Al-Zarqawi and bin Laden's partnership was struck as a quid pro quo arrangement. It was solidified in the extremities following 9/11 and the war in Afghanistan, and in shared strategic forethought about how best to snare the United States and its Western allies in another Middle Eastern conflict.

As early as October 2002 Ayman al-Zawahiri had anticipated the war, which he said was being perpetrated not to spread democracy, but to eliminate all military opposition to the state of Israel in the Arab and Islamic world. Six months later, bin Laden addressed the people of Iraq with a communiqué aired on Al Jazeera, telling them to prepare for the occupation of an ancient Islamic capital and the installation of a puppet regime that would "pave the way for the establishment of Greater Israel." Mesopotamia would be the epicenter of the unfolding of a Crusader-Jewish conspiracy that would engulf the entire Middle East. In opposition to this, bin Laden advocated urban warfare and "martyrdom operations," or suicide bombings, and he put out a casting call for a mujahidin army on a scale not seen since the days of the Afghan Services Bureau. This appeal carried an intriguing postscript. The "socialist infidels" of Saddam's Baathist regime, bin Laden said, were worthy accomplices in any fight against the Americans. To hurt the "far enemy," jihadists were thus encouraged to collaborate with the remnants of a "near enemy" until the ultimate Islamic victory could be won. The consequences of this sanctioning of an Islamist-Baathist alliance would be lethal and long-lasting.

For al-Zarqawi, war against the Crusader armies in Iraq was also a matter of historical glory and divine prophecy, rooted to the mosque from which Abu Bakr al-Baghdadi would address all Muslims in July 2014. "I think that what he read about Nur al-Din and the launching of his campaign from Mosul in Iraq," recalled Saif al-Adel, "played a large role in influencing al-Zarqawi to move to Iraq following the fall of the Islamic Emirate in Afghanistan."

2

SHEIKH OF THE
SLAUGHTERERS
AL-ZARQAWI AND AL-QAEDA IN IRAQ

Bin Laden's injunction was fully realized in the early months of the occupation of Iraq, when the hybridized nature of the insurgency it was confronting became painfully apparent to the United States military. Saddam Hussein had not anticipated an invasion of Baghdad. But he had very much prepared his regime for a different doomsday scenario: another domestic rebellion from Iraq's Shia majority. At the prompting of the United States, both of these sects had risen up at the end of the First Gulf War, only to be brutally slaughtered (with US acquiescence). Determined not to witness any such revolutionary ferment again, Saddam in the intervening decade constructed an entire underground apparatus for counterrevolution and took precautions to strengthen his conventional military deterrents. He beefed up one of his praetorian divisions, the Fedayeen Saddam, and licensed the creation of a consortium of proxy militias. In *The Endgame: The Inside Story of the Struggle for Iraq, from George W. Bush to Barack Obama*, their magisterial history of the Iraq War, Michael Gordon and General Bernard Trainor note that long before the first American soldier arrived in Iraq, "networks of safe houses and arms caches for paramilitary forces, including materials for making improvised explosives, were also established throughout the country. . . . It was, in effect, a counterinsurgency strategy to fend off what Saddam saw as the most serious threats to his rule."

The man who anatomized this strategy, and who understood that the post-invasion insurgency actually comprised holdover elements from the ancien régime, was Colonel Derek Harvey, a military intelligence officer then working for General Ricardo "Rick" Sanchez's Combined Joint Task Force 7, the American headquarters in Iraq.

Harvey estimated that between sixty-five and ninety-five thousand members of Saddam's other praetorian division, the Special Republican Guard; Iraq's many intelligence directorates (known collectively as the Mukhabarat); the Fedayeen Saddam; and state-subsidized militiamen were all rendered unemployed with the stroke of a pen after L. Paul Bremer, the Bush-appointed head of the Coalition Provisional Authority (CPA), chose to disband the Iraqi military. Many of the sacked officers joined a nascent campaign to expel their expropriators. Added to their ranks were more disaffected Iraqis, the victims of the controversial policy of "de-Baathification" that Bremer announced ten days after his touchdown in Baghdad in May 2003.

Making matters worse, Saddam had licensed a gray market in Iraq designed to evade UN sanctions—in effect, a state-tolerated organized crime network, headed by Izzat Ibrahim al-Douri, his vice president. A member of the Sufi Naqshbandi Order—which claimed direct descent from the first Islamic caliph, Abu Bakr—al-Douri had been born in al-Dawr, near Saddam's own hometown of Tikrit, in the northern Salah ad-Din province of Iraq. As such, he proved an adroit Baathist operator within the country's Sunni heartland. And as vice president, he was also able to stockpile arms of the regime's intelligence services and military with his fellow Sufis. This was a form of ethnic patronage that in 2006, after Saddam's execution, manifested itself in the creation of the Army of the Men of the Naqshbandi Order—one of the most powerful Sunni insurgency groups in Iraq, which would help ISIS take over Mosul in 2014.

Al-Douri was an expert smuggler; he ran a lucrative stolen car ring, importing luxury European models into Iraq via the Jordanian port at Aqaba. It was a vertically integrated racket, Harvey said, because al-Douri also maintained the auto body shops in which these illicit cars were worked on, furnishing both the factories and conveyances for the construction of vehicle-borne improvised explosive devices—or VBIEDs, to use their military acronym—one of the deadliest weapons used against American troops in Iraq.

Saddam employed other counterrevolutionary measures before the war. We tend to remember his regime as "secular," which it was, up to a point. But in the latter years of the long war with Iran, and with added intensity after

the First Gulf War, Saddam sought to fortify his regime against fundamentalist opponents, foreign and domestic, such as the Muslim Brotherhood. Thus
he Islamized his regime. Days before the allied bombing began in 1991, the
phrase "Allahu Akhbar" ("God Is Great") was added to the Iraqi flag, and
after the defeat in Kuwait a host of draconian punishments based on Sharia
law were introduced: thieves would have their hands amputated, while draft
dodgers and deserters from the military would lose their ears. To distinguish
the latter from disfigured veterans of the Iran-Iraq War, Saddamists would
also brand crosses into the amputees' foreheads with hot irons.

Ramping up state religiosity had an ancillary purpose: to distract from or
deflect criticism of an economy battered by international sanctions. The regime
thus introduced a proscription on female employment, hoping to artificially
lower Iraq's lengthening jobless rolls. Most significant was Saddam's inauguration of the Islamic Faith Campaign, which endeavored to marry Baath ideology of regime elites with Islamism. The man he tasked with overseeing this
conversion curriculum was none other than his car-smuggling caporegime,
al-Douri.

Predictably, the Faith Campaign was a Frankenstein patchwork of proselytization and mafia economics. Some of Iraq's new-minted faithful had their
hajj, or annual religious pilgrimage to Mecca, subsidized by the state, while
others were bribed with real estate, cash, and—naturally—expensive cars.
Colonel Joel Rayburn, another US military intelligence officer who served
in Iraq and has written a history of the country, has observed that one of
the unintended consequences of the Faith Campaign was also its most predictable: "Saddam believed he was sending into the Islamic schools committed Baathists who would remain loyal as they established a foothold in the
mosques from which the regime could then monitor or manipulate the Islamist movement. In actuality, the reverse happened. Most of the officers who
were sent to the mosques were not deeply committed to Baathism by that
point, and as they encountered Salafi teachings many became more loyal to
Salafism than to Saddam."

Many graduates of the program, Rayburn notes, found that they had
much to confess and atone for in their pasts and so turned against the very
ideology the Faith Campaign was meant to inculcate, and against the regime
itself. Some of these "Salafist-Baathists" even went on to hold positions in
a new American-fostered Iraqi government while continuing to moonlight
as anti-American terrorists. One such person was Khalaf al-Olayan, who

had been a high-ranking official in Saddam's army before becoming one of the top leaders of Tawafuq, a Sunni Islamist bloc in the post-Saddam Iraqi parliament. Mahmoud al-Mashhadani showed the folly of the Faith Campaign even before the American invasion: he became a full-fledged Salafist and was subsequently imprisoned for attacking the regime responsible for the Faith Campaign. (Al-Mashhadani went on to serve as speaker of the Council of Representatives, Iraq's parliament, in 2006, a year before both he and al-Olayan were implicated in a deadly suicide bombing—against that very state institution.)

The production of extremist Salafists who began attacking the regime was one failure of the Faith Campaign. Another backfire was its claim to be ecumenical; its clear pro-Sunni tilt led to a final breakdown of State-Shia relations, and heightened sectarian tensions in Iraq to a point unheard-of in its modern history. But the Campaign did have some success in the Sunni areas, lowering antagonism with the mainstream Salafi Trend, a longtime opposition movement to the Baath, to such an extent that its members even served in the government. The Faith Campaign also empowered midlevel clerics as social leaders, a role imams had not previously had in the Sunni areas of Iraq, which, in combination with al-Douri's criminal economy, significantly based on tribesmen as it was, reshaped the society in ways that would outlast the regime. Finally, the Campaign also gave the Iraqi security services a deeper, keener apprehension of the country's Sunni Arab cultural and religious identity, and how best to exploit that identity for their own ends—a lesson that would prove especially useful when operatives of those security services joined the anti-American insurgency and, ultimately, the organization we now call ISIS.

In October 2014, at a French cafe on Manhattan's Upper West Side, more than a decade removed from his mapping of the Iraqi insurgency, Derek Harvey recounted for one of the authors how Saddam's bulwark against jihad ended up helping the jihadists. "The Faith Campaign wasn't just about having people in the Baath Party go to religious training one night a week and do their homework and such," Harvey said. "It was about using the intelligence services to reach into the society of Islamic scholars and work with a range of religious leaders such as Harith al-Dari," a prominent Sunni cleric from the Anbar province and the chairman of the Association of Muslim Scholars. "Even Abdullah al-Janabi," Harvey added, referring to the former head of the insurgent Mujahidin Shura Council in Fallujah, "was an Iraqi intelligence agent, although originally he wasn't a Salafist as we portrayed him, but rather a Sufi linked to al-Douri and the Naqshbandi Order. We didn't recognize al-Janabi's true nature. He wasn't a religious extremist at all; he was an Arab nationalist. The thing all these guys had in common was the desire for their tribe, their clan, and themselves. That's a unifying principle. It was the Sunni Arab identity, this search for lost power and prestige, that motivated the Sunni insurgency. Many people miss that when they characterize it. If you talk to the Shiites, they understand it for what it is."

After the US invasion, al-Douri and much of his Baathist network fled to Syria, where they were harbored by Bashar al-Assad's regime. Despite the decades-long enmity between his father, Hafez al-Assad, and Saddam, Bashar al-Assad viewed these fugitives as useful agents for mayhem, for terror-in-reserve, and for disrupting Bush's nation-building experiment next door. For his part, al-Douri had wanted to fuse the Iraqi and Syrian Baath parties into one transnational conglomerate, but al-Assad refused and for a time even tried to catalyze his own alternative Iraqi Baath Party to rival al-Douri's. (Syria, as we will examine later, became one of the leading state sponsors of both Baathist and al-Qaeda terrorism in Iraq.)

What Saddam, al-Assad, al-Zarqawi, and bin Laden all understood, and what the United States had to discover at great cost in blood and treasure, was that the gravest threat posed to a democratic government in Baghdad was not necessarily jihadism or even disenfranchised Baathism. It was Sunni revanchism.

Sunni Arabs constitute at most 20 percent of Iraq's population, whereas Shia Arabs constitute as much as 65 percent. A plurality of Sunni Kurds (17 percent), plus smaller demographics of Christians, Assyrians, Yazidis, and Sunni and Shia Turkomans, account for the remainder. But Saddam had presided over decades of a sectarian patronage system that broadly favored the minority at the expense of a much-impoverished and restive majority. It was for this reason that George H. W. Bush, in prosecuting the First Gulf War, never pursued a policy of total regime change in Iraq—only, fitfully, one of regime decapitation, which failed. (Not that he would have been able to hold together the international coalition he had cobbled together to expel Saddam from Kuwait if he opted for regime change.) The elder Bush had hoped that a Baathist coup, encouraged by the routing of Iraqi forces in Kuwait, would put an end to Saddam once and for all, giving way to a more reformist or at least Western-amenable dictatorship.

The violent implementation of democracy meant the demographic inversion of Iraq's power. It destroyed what many Iraqi Sunnis saw as their birthright. In his book, *Iraq After America: Strongmen, Sectarians, Resistance*, Joel Rayburn recounts what one Sunni in Iraq's northern region told him: "At first no one fought the Americans; not the Baath, not the army officers, and not the tribes. But when the Americans formed the Governing Council [in July 2003] with thirteen Shia and only a few Sunnis, people began to say, 'The Americans mean to give the country to the Shia,' and then they began to fight, and the tribes began to let al Qaeda in." Disenfranchised Saddamists, who had melted back into their native cities and villages along the Euphrates River, were only too happy to accommodate the new arrivals, seeing them as agents for the Americans' expulsion and their own restoration to power. The jihadists had different designs.

AL-ZARQAWI VS. AMERICA

Abu Musab al-Zarqawi's gruesome debut in Iraq took place on August 7, 2003, when operatives from Monotheism and Jihad (his franchise's new name, taken from the banner at the entrance to the Herat training camp) detonated an explosives-laden green van against a barrier wall outside the Jordanian embassy in Baghdad. The blast tore a thirty-foot hole in the wall and killed seventeen people, including entire families. (As ever, al-Zarqawi saw his homeland's government as a primary target.) Twelve days later, al-Zarqawi orchestrated another spectacular attack, this one on the UN headquarters in Baghdad's Canal Hotel. That operation was carried out by a twenty-six-year-old Moroccan man, Abu Osama al-Maghribi, who drove a flatbed truck, similarly outfitted with an enormous bomb, into the wall right beneath the window of Sérgio Vieira de Mello, the UN's charismatic special representative to Iraq. Much of the ceiling crumbled, crushing De Mello in his office; he bled to death. Twenty-one others were also killed and more than two hundred wounded in the explosion. Al-Zarqawi said that he had targeted De Mello specifically for "embellish[ing] the image of America, the crusaders, and the Jews." This "embellishment" evidently included the Brazilian diplomat's role in overseeing Christian East Timor's independence from Muslim Indonesia—a fact that did little to dissuade some of al-Zarqawi's Western apologists' characterization of his terrorism as an expression of "anti-imperialism."

Al-Zarqawi had help. "Originally, the Baathists cooperated in the bombing of the UN and in other suicide bombings in 2003," Harvey said. "The safe houses of the suicide bombers were adjacent to compounds and residences of the Special Security Organization [SSO] officers." The SSO was the most powerful security apparatus in prewar Iraq and was in charge of the Special Republican Guard and Special Forces. According to Harvey, it gave Zarqawi's men the cars that were fashioned into VBIEDs; it also transported the suicide bombers. "The reason we know so much is that one of the suicide bombers didn't die, and we were able to debrief him and backtrack."

By October 2003, bin Laden's call for foreign mujahidin had been heeded, thanks in part to the socialist infidels. The Saddamists had already established "ratlines"—corridors for foreign fighters—to transport them into Iraq from a variety of terrorist cells and organizations around the Middle East and North Africa. "These jihadists had maintained a relationship for at least three years—in some cases longer—with the SSO and a general by the name of Muhammed Khairi al-Barhawi," Harvey said. "He was responsible for their training. The idea was, if you understood who the terrorists were and kept them close to you, you wouldn't have to worry about them striking you."

Al-Barhawi was later appointed police chief in Mosul by Major General David Petraeus, then head of the 101st Airborne Division, stationed in the city. Petraeus insisted that al-Barhawi's transformation from a US-friendly cop to an accomplice of US-slaying terrorists was coerced rather than voluntary. Harvey disagrees, insisting that al-Barhawi simply played the game as it had to be played in Iraq, bartering with whomever was in authority at any given time to ensure the safety and security of his kin. "Barhawi had managed his familial relationships into al-Qaeda when he was police chief, then into Mosul's police force, then into local Awakening councils when they developed," Harvey said, referring to the grassroots Sunni political organizations that later coalesced in revulsion at al-Qaeda's barbarism and for the purpose of forming local partnerships with the US and Iraqi military for al-Qaeda's defeat. "From a tribal perspective, it was the smart thing to do: have that accretion in as many places as possible."

KILLING THE SHIA

Between 2003 and 2005, the Zarqawists were still a minority in Iraq's terrorism. According to a study conducted by the Jamestown Foundation, a Washington-based think tank, a mere 14 percent of what the United States had dubbed "Sunni Arab rejectionists" belonged to al-Zarqawi's network.

This contingent was, however, overrepresented in the media, both because of the prominence Colin Powell gave to al-Zarqawi and because of the fact that al-Zarqawi's terrorism accounted for a full 42 percent of all suicide bombings—the mode of violence with the bloodiest toll—perpetrated in Iraq.

The same month Monotheism and Jihad bombed the Jordanian embassy and the United Nations, it also assassinated Ayatollah Mohammed Baqir al-Hakim, the leader of the Supreme Council for Islamic Revolution in Iraq, with another car bomb. In fact, it was al-Zarqawi's father-in-law, Yassin Jarrad, who led this operation—a suicide mission—which consisted of two car bombs going off in sequence next to the Imam Ali Mosque, one of Shia Islam's holiest shrines, outside the city of Najaf. The explosions killed somewhere around a hundred people and wounded five times that number. Al-Hakim had only minutes earlier finished a sermon denouncing the US occupation as incompetent for failing to protect Iraqis from the depredations of terrorists, citing the previous two major bombings specifically. He was now obliterated. It was the worst assassination of a revered religious figure since the toppling of the Baath, and few were under any illusions as to who was responsible. In the space of just four weeks, al-Zarqawi had successfully damaged or demolished three separate symbols of his own personal loathing—which, not coincidentally, were the three weakest points in a country the US government said was now on "postwar" footing and well on its way to recovery, sovereignty, and democratic stability. One was the Jordanian government, al-Zarqawi's longtime "near enemy," now collaborating with the occupiers of Muslim land—a warning to all other Arab governments not to do likewise. One was the headquarters of an international organization, which was trying to bring aid and relief to a shell-shocked population that was still largely without electricity or basic services. And one was a Shia ayatollah right outside his mosque, whose murder could unleash civil war. Which is exactly what al-Zarqawi wanted.

A letter said to have been written by him, addressed to bin Laden, was intercepted by the Kurds in January 2004. It made plain that al-Zarqawi's conspiratorial obsessions could be repurposed as a Machiavellian plot for tearing Iraq apart and letting his forces inherit the ruins. The Shia, al-Zarqawi wrote, were "the insurmountable obstacle, the lurking snake, the crafty and malicious scorpion, the spying enemy, and the penetrating venom." They were grave-worshippers, idolaters, and polytheists who, as the country's demographic majority, had cut a deal affording them "two-thirds of the booty for having stood in the ranks of the Crusaders against the mujahidin." The only solution for the Shia was, therefore, a final one, and here their own missteps and excesses would be the accelerant for it. Al-Zarqawi sought to exploit what was then an incipient but nevertheless very real problem in Iraq's political evolution: namely, the creeping takeover of state institutions by chauvinistic Shia politicians, many of whom were either spies or agents of influence of Iran's Islamic Revolutionary Guards Corps. One of his named nemeses in the intercepted letter was the Badr Corps. This was the armed wing of the Supreme Council for Islamic Revolution in Iraq, the political party whose leader al-Zarqawi had just blown up and whose name, at least for Sunnis, reified Khomeinist influence in the country. By isolating Badr, which was targeting and abusing the Sunnis, al-Zarqawi managed to translate real sociopolitical grievances into an eschatological showdown: "They have placed cadres in these institutions," he wrote, referring to Badr, "and, in the name of preserving the homeland and the citizen, have begun to settle their scores with the Sunnis."

Al-Zarqawi's prescription was to prompt a civil war between Sunnis and Shia by attacking the latter in their "religious, political, and military depth"; this would "provoke them to show the Sunnis their rabies and bare the teeth of the hidden rancor working in their breasts. If we succeed in dragging them into the arena of sectarian war, it will become possible to awaken the inattentive Sunnis as they feel imminent danger and annihilating death at the hands of these Sabeans."

Even though the Shia outnumbered the Sunnis in Iraq, the broader demography of the Islamic world would be that country's destiny. Sunni mujahidin would heed al-Zarqawi's rallying cry, bear witness to the pogroms and torture chambers of the Badr Corps and other Shia death squads, and, as they once had done in Afghanistan, make Iraq the cynosure of their definitive holy war. It was apocalyptic and insane. It also very nearly worked.

ISIS has couched its current campaign in Syria and Iraq in exactly this kind of sectarian-existential grammar, fondly recalling al-Zarqawi's war strategy in its official propaganda. And it has followed in his footsteps by targeting Shia to prompt their counterreaction (and overreaction), in order to drive Sunnis into ISIS's protective embrace. In June 2014, after sacking Camp Speicher, the former US military base in Tikrit, al-Baghdadi's jihadists boasted, for instance, that they had executed seventeen hundred Shia soldiers that the Iraqi army had surrendered. That figure may have been exaggerated, but not by much: Human Rights Watch later confirmed the existence of mass execution sites of Shia, with a collective death toll of 770. In Mosul, the very same day ISIS took the city, it stormed Badoush Prison and hauled off some fifteen hundred of its inmates. It drove them all out to a nearby desert and separated the Sunnis and Christians from the Shia. Members of the first two categories were taken elsewhere; the Shia were first abused and robbed, then lined up and shot over a ravine after they each called out their number in line.

INVITATION TO A BEHEADING

Al-Zarqawi proved a pioneer in another important respect—he was the first to see the potential of interweaving horrific ultra-violence and mass media. He was especially fond of public or televised beheadings and the attention they received in the West. He personally decapitated the American contractor Nicholas Berg in 2004, then had a video of the execution posted online and circulated around the world. The staging and pageantry of this grotesquerie was also transformational for the future of international terrorism.

As with James Foley, Steven Sotloff, and Peter Kassig, ISIS's latest American victims, Berg was dressed in a Guantanamo or Abu Ghraib–style orange jumpsuit, forced to his knees, and compelled to identify himself. An imprecation was then recited by his captor, before the knife was applied to his throat. One editorial decision was unique to the Berg video: the full carnage of his beheading was featured on-screen, whereas ISIS has preferred (no doubt for added international media exposure) to keep most of the gore off-screen. Berg's body was discovered and his family notified before his snuff film ever got exhibited. ISIS, too, records its murders well in advance of letting the world know its victims are dead. Such was the case with its most famous Arab victim, the Jordanian fighter pilot Mouaz al-Kasasbeh, who was burnt alive in a cage even as ISIS engaged with Amman in a pantomime negotiation of his release.

In its August–September 2004 issue, *Voice of Jihad*, a magazine published by the Saudi branch of al-Qaeda, carried an endorsement of the practice by Abd El-Rahman ibn Salem al-Shamari, who referred specifically to the beheading of an Egyptian by the Zarqawists: "O sheikh of killers Abu Musab al-Zarqawi, continue to follow the straight path with Allah's help, guided by Allah, fight together with the monotheists against the idol-worshippers, together with the warriors of jihad against the collaborators, the hypocrites, and the rebellious ... show him [any soldier from among the Saudi king's legions] no mercy!" Al-Zarqawi's trademark earned him the name "Sheikh of the Slaughterers."

Though al-Zarqawi retained an audiovisual squad of reportedly three people who were fluent in computer editing software and comparatively cruder Internet technology, ISIS has dramatically improved on al-Zarqawi's media savvy, employing its own channel and social media feeds for disseminating information. The spectacle of murder most foul, however, had the same intended effect in the hands of both perpetrators.

Not all jihadists approved of al-Zarqawi's murder of Muslims, though, no matter if they were Shia. His former mentor and collaborator al-Maqdisi was an outspoken critic. Writing to his former protégé from his latest Jordanian prison cell, where he still languished, the cleric chided al-Zarqawi: "The clean hands of mujahidin should be protected from being tarnished with the blood of the protected people." As former CIA analyst Bruce Riedel has observed, these sentiments may not have been genuine. Shortly after the letter was published, Jordan let al-Maqdisi out of jail and placed him under house arrest, prompting allegations by jihadists that his rebuke of al-Zarqawi may have been edited or ghostwritten by the Jordanian General Intelligence Directorate as a form of psychological warfare against the insurgency.

Although al-Zarqawi professed to be profoundly hurt by his former teacher's criticism—he claimed to have wept when he read the letter—al-Maqdisi's counsel did nothing to lessen Monotheism and Jihad's bloodlust for fellow Muslims. Al-Zarqawi told his ex-teacher to take care with issuing such hectoring and restrictive fatwas in the future. Today, al-Maqdisi has lambasted ISIS as "deviant" and criticized its much-publicized atrocities, as well as its alienation of the local Muslim communities and armed groups in Syria.

Al-Maqdisi's denunciation of the heirs of his prodigal student do seem to carry some weight. Because of the cleric's lasting influence as a jihadist theoretician and his inaugural role in al-Zarqawi's career, ISIS has tried to curry favor with al-Maqdisi's followers. As scholar Michael W. S. Ryan has noted, the first issue of ISIS's propaganda magazine, *Dabiq*, features an extensive discussion of Millat Ibrahim, or the Path of Abraham, the ideology of the father of many nations as rendered by the Quran. *Millat Ibrahim* is also the title of a famous tract al-Maqdisi published in 1984, inspiring any number of mujahidin to sojourn to Soviet-occupied Afghanistan.

APPEAL TO THE SUNNIS

Before Blackwater USA attained international notoriety for the lethal shooting of seventeen Iraqis in western Baghdad's Nisour Square in 2007, its mercenaries made headlines three years earlier as corpses horrifically hung upside down from a railroad bridge in Iraq's Anbar province. Then, as now, Fallujah was a byword for hell on earth to scores of American soldiers—and tens of thousands of Iraqi civilians.

Fallujah and Anbar's provincial capital, Ramadi, were meant to have had a sizable US troop presence after the 2003 invasion. Yet the ease with which the military cut through the country and straight into Baghdad altered the military's plans. Instead, the cities that would become the main hot spots for Sunni rejectionism had the lightest American "footprint." The failure of foresight seems staggering in retrospect, given that the Euphrates River Valley consists of what Derek Harvey says was not only the Sunni heartland, but also the national wellspring of Baathism.

Uday and Qusay Hussein, Saddam's sons, fled to Anbar province when their father's high command quit Baghdad in advance of the approaching US army. According to Wael Essam, a Palestinian journalist who was embedded with insurgents in Fallujah, many former Baathists, Mukhabarat officers, and Republican Guardsmen who took up arms to fight coalition forces "all affirmed they were not fighting for Saddam but for Islam and Sunnis." The beheading of Nicholas Berg, US intelligence believed, took place in Jolan, a neighborhood in northwest Fallujah, which the Zarqawists had established as one of their earliest garrisons.

An initial attempt to retake Fallujah in the spring of 2004—named, somewhat infelicitously, Operation Vigilant Resolve—ended in calamity. Integral to the Bush administration's reconstruction project for Iraq was the swift transfer of sovereignty and governance to the Iraqis themselves. This included the extraordinary responsibility of national security for a nation still very much in the throes of war. The Iraqis were hardly ready, willing, or able to assume that role, and so US Marines bore the brunt of the fighting instead. An attempt to stand up to a local Iraqi Fallujah Brigade ended in disaster: the entire outfit disintegrated, and 70 percent of its recruits wound up joining the insurgency instead. The ensuing battle ended with the killing of twenty-seven Americans.

This chapter in the war was instructive in yet another way, apart from showing how unprepared the Iraqis were to defend their own turf. It was closely documented by Abu Anas al-Shami, one of al-Zarqawi's confederates, who kept a wartime "diary" that explained *how* the insurgents had prepped for battle and fought—in a manner eerily reminiscent of how ISIS does now.

First, al-Shami clarified, the boss was never present during the Fallujah fight. Al-Zarqawi was ensconced in nearby Ramadi, overseeing operations remotely, although al-Shami maintained that the emir offered, via a courier, to join his men; they refused, citing concern for al-Zarqawi's safety. The planning for the defense of the city took time. Every jihadist organization has various decision-making departments or bureaus, one of them being a military council. Monotheism and Jihad's had convened about ten days before hostilities kicked off in Fallujah and devised its plan of action. The group had yet to amass any notable victories outside of terrorist spectaculars; it had not been able to sack and retain territory yet. According to al-Shami, days had been used for hiding out, nights for moving men and matériel throughout the city. So the military council determined that Fallujah should be a "safe and impregnable refuge for Muslims and an inviolable and dangerous territory for the Americans which they would enter in fear and leave in shock, pursued and burdened with their dead and wounded."

Fallujah was to be the Zarqawists' briar patch, perilous for outsiders but comfortable for those who knew how to navigate it and vanish into its dark corners. At first, foreign fighters hailing from Saudi Arabia, Egypt, Kuwait, Libya, and Yemen (at this stage, non-Iraqis still made up the majority of Monotheism and Jihad's rank and file) dug tunnels and bunkers underground to avoid incurring the enmity of the local population. Then they learned that this precaution had been unnecessary because, as al-Shami recounted, the jihadists were struck by the "generosity" of Fallujans, who were now joined by Iraqis from other parts of the country, eager to defend their brethren and land from invading American battalions. Nevertheless, al-Shami's war diary goes on to note, the city had yet to formally pick a side in the battle; several local imams, or religious leaders, declined to allow al-Shami and his men to use their mosques to preach jihad directly to the people. More intriguing was how Monotheism and Jihad compromised on one of its core tenets of refusing to acknowledge or negotiate with any US-backed Iraqi institutions. Despite al-Zarqawi's injunction against entering into any dialogue with what was then Iraq's Governing Council, al-Shami says that he did in fact take part in the talks, albeit as an ultrathin slice of the overall delegation from Fallujah.

According to Joel Rayburn, the Iraqi Governing Council had indeed dispatched one of its officials to parley with militants in Fallujah in April 2004. The underlying assumption was that the bulk of the insurgency was still made up of Iraqis and that Iraqis could be cleaved away from the foreign-led jihadists. Nor was this assumption misplaced. As Rayburn put it, "People who in 2005 and 2006 called themselves al-Qaeda would spend 2007 and 2008 hunting down al-Qaeda."

That lesson, which demanded a complete overhaul of the American war strategy in Iraq, would be a hard one for the Pentagon to learn. And in 2004, the main American weapon being deployed against the Zarqawists in Anbar province was Predator drone air strikes, waged by the Joint Special Operations Command (JSOC), headquartered at Balad Air Base north of Baghdad and headed by Major General Stanley McChrystal. JSOC's mission was to go after terrorists in small groups, or even one by one in sorties designed to decapitate the leadership and hollow out the middle cadres of the insurgency. JSOC reckoned that by September 2004, it had killed six out of fourteen "major operators," including al-Zarqawi's newest "spiritual adviser." Regardless, the organizational structure of Monotheism and Jihad remained intact despite this intense aerial bombardment and, if anything, the group only grew in strength, numbers, and popular appeal. What came to be called the First Battle of Fallujah showed how native and foreign forces could blend to bleed a mighty superpower possessed of every kind of conventional military dominance. McChrystal assessed that the threat posed by al-Zarqawi's network was much greater than what US Defense Department analysts had dismissively taken to calling "Former Regime Elements"—an assessment that was greatly bolstered in October 2004 when al-Zarqawi finally did what he had refused to do four years earlier: make *bayat*, or pledge allegiance, to Osama bin Laden.

By then adept at the uses of psychological warfare and agitprop, al-Zarqawi chose to broadcast his pledge of allegiance to the al-Qaeda chief, and did so two weeks after US Secretary of Defense Donald Rumsfeld claimed that he did not believe al-Zarqawi was allied with bin Laden (a reversal of the allegation Colin Powell had advanced a year earlier at the UN).

The Jordanian's bent-knee subordination to his onetime financier resulted in another organizational name change. Monotheism and Jihad now became the more verbose Tanzim Qaedat al-Jihad fi Bilad al-Rafidayn, or Al-Qaeda in the Land of the Two Rivers, which Washington shortened to the simpler al-Qaeda in Iraq (AQI). So where al-Zarqawi had entered the country as a mere affiliate or ally of the world's most sought-after terrorist, he was, a year into the war, fully enlisted as bin Laden's field commander. By one estimate, al-Qaeda already had some two hundred of its own operatives stationed in Iraq, working independently of Monotheism and Jihad. Al-Qaeda also had an "affiliate" in-country in the form of Ansar al-Sunna, yet another autonomous faction, members of which would later turn against al-Qaeda and join the Anbar Awakening. In his open letter pledging allegiance, al-Zarqawi now sounded every inch the loyalist to bin Laden. He praised the "blessed 9/11 attacks" and taunted the United States for thinking its campaign in Iraq would be short-lived and easy. Al-Qaeda, he said, would inherit the country.

A month after making bayat, al-Zarqawi attempted to put his newfound patronage and star power to the test in a second showdown with the Americans—the Second Battle of Fallujah, which began in early November 2004. Dwarfing its predecessor, this operation saw ten American army battalions mobilized, including two Marine regiments, and several hundred Iraqi soldiers, many acting as scouts for viable targets. It was also accompanied by F/A-18 Hornet jets, which dropped two-thousand-pound bombs on points all around the city.

The Marines also discovered what the AQI franchise had achieved by way of community outreach in Fallujah. In addition to a calendar for videorecorded beheadings, soldiers uncovered kidnapping victims who had had their legs removed. In total, three "torture houses" were uncovered in the city, along with an IED-manufacturing facility that gave US forces a clue as to the route taken by foreign fighters pouring into Iraq. Where al-Zarqawi had smuggled himself into Kurdistan from Iranian soil in the east, now the ratlines were tending from the opposite direction. A recovered GPS device showed that its owner had entered the country from the west, via Syria. Intelligence gathered in the aftermath of combat showed what was now obvious to men like Derek Harvey: al-Qaeda and Former Regime Elements were fighting side by side. They even had their own unique ways of communicating. According to historians Michael Gordon and Bernard Trainor, the jihadists used "black-and-green signal flags" to relay information to one another; disbanded Mukhabarat officers wrote their instructions out on Baath Party letterhead.

The Second Battle of Fallujah was catastrophic. Ten thousand homes, or about a fifth of total residences, were destroyed in two weeks of intense urban warfare, matched by punishing air strikes. The aftermath was a pocked moonscape, uninhabitable for many—not that many were left. Fallujah had largely been evacuated, with hundreds of thousands of refugees fleeing before the start of major fighting. Roughly a quarter of all insurgents killed by US troops in 2004—2,175 out of 8,400—died during this single episode in the war, but at a proportionally high price: 70 marines were also killed, and 651 were wounded, in addition to other US casualties.

Like its first installment, the Second Battle of Fallujah was an expensive tactical victory for the United States belying strategic defeat. Whatever was gained in retaken square mileage was rendered negligible because of the enormous propaganda boon it delivered to the insurgents, who treated it as more Dunkirk than Waterloo.

Both the jihadists and the Baathists fled to other cities, towns, and villages in central and northern Iraq. This time, it seems, al-Zarqawi had been present for the fight, if only fleetingly; the marines believed that he repaired to Mosul on the first day of intense combat operations, the better to set up shop in another Sunni-majority city, this one the capital, of Anbar province. Bin Laden, too, watching from thousands of miles away, took the opportunity to transform a territorial setback into a major messianic stride forward. Claiming that he had been personally acquainted with some of the "martyrs" of the battle, bin Laden laid the responsibility for Fallujah's scorched-earth condition squarely at the feet of President Bush. America was waging a "total war against Islam," he declared, while his brave warriors, led by his lieutenant al-Zarqawi, had "written a new page of glory into the history of our community of believers."

What began for the Saudis as a wary collaboration had clearly metamorphosed into an open and celebrated alliance. The al-Qaeda leader's hesitations about his field commander's foolhardiness and sectarian bloodlust were put aside in favor of watching the world's greatest far enemy take a beating. In December 2004 bin Laden answered al-Zarqawi's bayat with warm acceptance, naming him a "noble brother" and calling on the "unification of the jihadi groups under a single standard which recognizes al-Zarqawi as the Emir of al-Qaeda in Iraq."

The title was somewhat misleading, however, because al-Zarqawi had in fact been granted an operational purview that extended well beyond Iraqi territory, into outlying Arab countries as well as Turkey. Arguably, that remit made him a more powerful al-Qaeda leader than bin Laden himself. As the former CIA analyst Bruce Riedel recounts, some jihadist heavyweights even gelled to al-Zarqawi's fanatical anti-Shiism, which was still not endorsed (and would later be criticized) by the al-Qaeda leadership in Pakistan. One Saudi ideologue in particular praised the Jordanian for characterizing the Shia as part of a long, uninterrupted line of perfidious collaborators dating back to the Mongol invasion of the Middle East—an invasion that resulted, infamously, in the obliteration of Baghdad in the thirteenth century. The ideologue invoked Ibn Taymiyyah, the medieval theologian who has become a touchstone for Salafists and ISIS especially: "Beware of the Shiites, fight them, they lie," Ibn Taymiyyah said. The Mongols in the contemporary context were the American occupiers, as well as the "Jews," who were standing right behind them in Iraq. Al-Zarqawi was thus seen as upholding a seven-hundred-year-old tradition of Sunni resistance, the catechism of which consisted of three criteria of *tawhid*, or monotheism. These were: to worship God, to worship *only* God, and to have the right creed in doing so. Ibn Taymiyyah used these categories to declare takfir on the Shia and Sufis of the thirteenth century, establishing that their practices and creeds—including the veneration of imams, which bordered on idolatry, if not polytheism—compromised their worship of the one, true God.

As Riedel observes, al-Zarqawi was not just being celebrated as the rightful heir to Ibn Taymiyyah's line but as the brilliant trap-layer for the new army of Crusaders and infidels marching into the Holy Land. He had intertwined in the popular Sunni imagination the roles of the United States, its European allies, the United Nations, and the Shia-dominant Iraqi government, depicting them as co-conspirators in a plot of antique vintage, the aim of which was the violent disinheritance of 1.3 billion Sunni Muslims. He had, according to his Saudi admirer, "such capabilities that the mind cannot imagine. He prepared for fighting the Americans over a year prior to the American occupation of Iraq. He built the camps and arsenals," and he recruited and enlisted people from all over the region—from Palestine to Yemen.

If al-Zarqawi sounds, in this runaway sermon, like the initiator of the End Times, that is because he was seen as such by his hordes of jihadist admirers. ISIS now relies on the same apocalyptic prophecy about a coming civilizational showdown in the Middle East, in which the Armies of Rome and the Armies of Islam will meet, and the latter will be victorious. In another version of this foretelling, it is the "Persians" whom the Sunni warriors will have to fight. The center of this fated battle? Dabiq, a minuscule town in the Syrian province of Aleppo, whose name now furnishes the title of ISIS's monthly magazine, every issue of which opens with a quote from al-Zarqawi: "The spark has been lit here in Iraq, and its heat will continue to intensify—by Allah's permission— until it burns the crusader armies in Dabiq." It was al-Zarqawi's hosanna to a famous hadith, a saying of the Prophet Muhammad: "The Hour will not be established until the Romans land at Dabiq. Then an army from Medina of the best people on the earth at that time will leave for them. . . . So they will fight them. Then one third of [the fighters] will flee; Allah will never forgive them. One third will be killed; they will be the best martyrs with Allah. And one third will conquer them; they will never be afflicted with sorrow. Then they will conquer Constantinople."

Al-Zarqawi was never going to stop his jihad at the boundaries of Iraq, a "state" he had never believed to exist. "We do not fight for a fistful of dust or the illusory boundaries drawn by Sykes-Picot," he had written, alluding to the British and French imperial carve-up of the Middle East after World War I. Iraq was just the spark; the final conflagration would consume Syria.

3

THE MANAGEMENT
OF SAVAGERY

BIRTH OF THE ISLAMIC STATE OF IRAQ

"Habibi, let me tell you a story."

Mohammed smiled as he began to speak in his small upstairs office in Iraq's Permanent Mission to the United Nations on East Seventy-Sixth Street in New York. It was the spring of 2015, just under a year into an international coalition's effort to degrade and destroy ISIS, and the war was not going very well: in May the jihadists would sack Ramadi, the capital of Anbar province, and Palmyra, the ancient Syrian crossroads of multiple civilizations—Greece, Rome, Persia, Assyria—whose ruins and monuments bore the imprints of them all. *Plus ça change*, seemed to be Mohammed's attitude, and he wanted to explain why the Americans kept making the same mistakes.

Before joining the mission in Manhattan, he had lived in post-Saddam Iraq and had seen up close what life was like under the Americans, al-Qaeda, and a series of corrupt, fearful, or brutish Iraqi governments. A funny, red-haired diplomat, he hails from Mansour, a district in western Baghdad, home to a wealthy Sunni Arab bourgeoisie, many patriarchs of which had been in some way affiliated with Saddam's regime. De-Baathification and the disbandment of the Iraqi military had upended their sense of class entitlement, their dignity, and was allowing never-before-expressed sectarian resentment to congeal. One day, in the mid-2000s, Mohammed said, he was walking down a familiar street in Mansour when he noticed a man in a balaclava trying to

41

affix an object into the side of a house. "Hey, what are you doing?" Mohammed shouted. The masked man nervously turned around and addressed Mohammed by name, suggesting that he was very likely a neighbor. He was—another local from Mansour—but one down on his luck. The neighbor said that he had been unemployed for months, thanks to the US occupation, and could not find a job. "Please, Mohammed. I'm sorry. If I don't do this, I don't eat this month." Sunni insurgents had offered Mohammed's neighbor a cash disbursal if he agreed to lay an improvised explosive device by a well-trafficked boulevard. The reward was payable upon the successful immolation of an American or Iraqi soldier. (The amount differed depending on which one got killed, and how many; Americans, naturally, were worth more.)

"This," Mohammed said in between sips of hot tea, "is why you're losing."

"YES, YES, ZARQAWI"

Eleven years earlier, in the spring of 2004, after the Second Battle of Fallujah, the "spark" of al-Zarqawi's apocalyptic vision was beginning to catch throughout Iraq. This was nowhere more so than where anti-American sentiment was highest, which is to say where US troops were in their densest concentration. One insurgent stronghold was Baghdad's Haifa Street, a two-mile-long thoroughfare that ran parallel to the Tigris River, just north out of the Assassins' Gate, the entrance to the Green Zone and about a fifteen-minute car ride from Mansour. Haifa Street had by now become a totem of Sunni disenfranchisement: residents living in luxury apartments along this Babylonian Champs-Élysées had been the well-paid elites favored by the Saddam regime. But many were unemployed and unemployable in transitional Iraq, thanks to de-Baathification, and so were being drawn into the insurgency in one form or another. They found no promise in the formation of the Iraqi Governing Council or in the prospect of the first free national election, slated for January 2005, which would give them a democratic say in the future of their country. Military officers once bedecked with epaulets (some of them even earned) and favored with multiple homes (some of them even paid for legally) were now being asked to drive taxis. Doctors, lawyers, and engineers who had only ever advanced to university or postgraduate studies because of pro forma Baath Party connections were invited to push kebab carts. It made no difference that Ayad Allawi, a onetime Baathist turned enemy of the party and a secular Shia well-respected by Sunnis, was now the interim prime minister of Iraq. Dignity had become a casualty of war, and for many Sunnis, the sect that for decades had owned Iraq, this would mark the beginning of their personal struggle to win it back—and not through the ballot box. Michael Gordon and Bernard Trainor recount in their definitive history of the Iraq War, *The Endgame*, how one inoperable US Bradley Fighting Vehicle that sat bestride Haifa Street in September 2004 was transformed into a spoil of the Zarqawists. Insurgents slung the black Monotheism and Jihad flag on the vehicle's "25mm gun, and the battalion tasked with controlling the place, from the 1st Cavalry Division, began calling Haifa 'Little Fallujah' and 'Purple Heart Boulevard,' after the medal that would be awarded to 160 of the unit's 800 soldiers by the time they went home in early 2005." Local loyalties in Dora, yet another district of Baghdad infiltrated by insurgents, were even more fully expressed after the Second Battle of Fallujah, Gordon and Trainor write, as the 1st Cavalry battalion glimpsed a new graffiti slogan dotting the neighborhood's infrastructure in the lead-up to the January poll. The slogan read: "No, No, Allawi, Yes, Yes, Zarqawi."

THE (FIRST) FALL OF MOSUL

Mosul, Iraq's second-largest city and the capital of Ninewah province, had seemed a different story. For the first year or so of the occupation, it was a rare spot of good news, having been secured and (relatively) stabilized by David Petraeus's 101st Airborne. But the calm was illusory. As we have seen, al-Zarqawi had made the city his fallback base, personally fleeing there within hours of major combat operations for the Second Battle of Fallujah. With days of that battle's start, Mosul fell to the insurgency.

In truth, Mosul had always been susceptible to Sunni rejectionism, given its demographic cocktail of former regime elements and Salafists. Unemployment in the city hovered at around 75 percent, according to Sadi Ahmed Pire, the Patriotic Union of Kurdistan's security chief in Mosul. As with Mohammed's neighbors in Mansour, locals here were being hired to carry out terrorist operations for as little as fifty dollars a pop. As in prior battles, the Iraqi police and army disappeared altogether in Mosul, their stations either stormed by insurgents facing little resistance or set ablaze. The ease with which the provincial capital collapsed also seemingly vindicated Derek Harvey's prior assessment: namely that the US-appointed police chief, Muhammed Khairi al-Barhawi, had been quietly playing for both sides.

And though al-Barhawi may have been an Iraqi intelligence asset all along, the Zarqawists certainly did not make it easy for other Mosulawis to partner in good faith with the Americans. They were especially brutal to any Iraqi soldier or policeman who refused to abandon his post. In one notorious episode, they even tracked a wounded major to the hospital where he was being treated and beheaded him there. In the end, as with Fallujah, it took another overwhelming commitment of US firepower and manpower—joined by an unusually competent contingent of the Iraqi Special Police Commandos—to regain control of Mosul in the face of a combined Baathist–al-Qaeda onslaught of machine guns and rocket-propelled grenades.

A decade later, history repeated itself, as Mosul once again fell to a hybridized insurgency made up of al-Zarqawi's disciples and the Baathists of ousted Iraqi vice president Izzat al-Douri's Naqshbandi Army. Only this time, there was no US military presence to retake the city. ISIS sacked Mosul in less than a week. The jihadists rule it to this day.

Al-Zarqawi's sinister strategy for fomenting a complete societal breakdown in Iraq hewed closely to a text titled *Idarat al-Tawahhush*, or *The Management of Savagery*. Published online in 2004 as a combined field manual and manifesto for the establishment of the caliphate, it is the jihadist answer to *The Art of War* and *Leviathan*. Its author, Abu Bakr Naji, conceived of a battle plan for weakening enemy states through what he called "power of vexation and exhaustion." Drawing the United States into open as opposed to "proxy" warfare in the Middle East was the whole point, because Naji believed that once American soldiers were killed by mujahidin on the battlefield, the "media halo" surrounding their presumed invincibility would vanish. Muslims would then be "dazzled" at the harm they could inflict on a weak and morally corrupted superpower as well as incensed at the occupation of their holy lands, thus driving them to jihad. He urged that they should then focus on attacking the economic and cultural institutions (such as the hydrocarbon industries) of the "apostate" regimes aligned with the United States. "The public will see how the troops flee," Naji wrote, "heeding nothing. At this point, savagery and chaos begin and these regions will start to suffer from the absence of security. This is in addition to the exhaustion and draining [that results from] attacking the remaining targets and opposing the authorities." He used the time-honored example of Egypt, but he was also implicitly referring to Iraq, where he urged the fast consolidation of jihadist victory in order to "take over the surrounding countries."

There are four "primary objectives" to the power of vexation and exhaustion, according to Naji. The first is to tire out the enemy and those regimes collaborating with it so that they cannot catch their breath. The second is to attract young jihadists to the cause through "qualitative operations," or terror attacks, which need not rise to the level of a 9/11, but could be small and frequent. The third objective is to dislodge regions from the control of the "apostate" regimes entirely: the conquest of land, to be followed by the governance or administration of savagery by the jihadists. The fourth and final goal is the "advancement of groups of vexation through drilling and operational practice so that they will be prepared psychologically and practically for the stage of the management of savagery."

As Naji defines it, this stage is really nothing more than the application of a rudimentary jihadist political economy, the rescue of Muslims from the Hobbesian chaos that was to be brought about by the toppling of the aforementioned regimes. The actual "management" consists of twelve basic needs that must be satisfied:

1. The establishment of internal security such that the local population would be protected from violence other than that meted by the Islamic authority;
2. The provision of food and medicine;
3. The securing of the borders from foreign invaders;
4. The installing of a system of Sharia jurisprudence to govern those ruled;
5. The creation of a pious and "combat-efficient" youth movement;
6. The spread of Islamic jurisprudence as well as "worldly science";
7. The "dissemination of spies" and the creation of an intelligence service;
8. Buying the fealty of the local population through bribery and financial inducements;
9. "Deterring hypocrites," by which Naji meant dissuading any internal resistance to challenges to the ruling Islamic authority;
10. Laying the groundwork for the expansion of this fief and a greater offensive against the enemy, whose money should be plundered and who should be put in a "constant state of apprehension and desire for reconciliation";
11. Building "coalitions" with other groups, including those who have not pledged full allegiance to the Islamic authority (elsewhere in the text, Naji gives a separate disquisition on the role of "affiliates");
12. The advancement of "managerial groups"—bureaucracies, in effect—who would work toward the future establishment of a bona fide Islamic state. This was the end goal of jihad, after all, and the stage of the management

of savagery was to be the "bridge" to such a state, "which has been awaited since the fall of the caliphate." This stage was also the most "critical" through which the global Islamic community would now have to pass, as Naji states in the subtitle to his tract.

One ISIS-affiliated cleric told us that *The Management of Savagery* is today widely circulated among provincial ISIS commanders and some rank-and-file fighters as a way to justify beheadings as not only religiously permissible but recommended by God and his prophet. For ISIS, the manifesto's greatest contribution lies in its differentiation between the meaning of jihad and other religious matters. Naji at one point lectures the reader, arguing that the way jihad is taught "on paper" makes it harder for young mujahidin to understand the true meaning of the concept. "One who previously engaged in jihad knows that it is naught but violence, crudeness, terrorism, frightening [others], and massacring. I am talking about jihad and fighting, not about Islam and one should not confuse them." What he means here is that not all believing Muslims can undertake this sacrosanct responsibility, which brings with it only pain, suffering, and death. "[H]e cannot continue to fight and move from one stage to another unless the beginning stage contains a stage of massacring the enemy and making him homeless. . . ." Such a task is not for the faint of heart. "It is better for those who have the intention to begin a jihadi action and are also soft to sit in their homes. If not, failure will be their lot and they will suffer shock afterwards."

In between offering his own counsel on the proper hows of holy war, Naji was descrying an elite priesthood, to which only the most disciplined and committed might ever belong. All revolutions require a besieged yet romanticized underworld, a sacrificing vanguard, to see them through. Naji was quite deliberately appealing to an army of invisible soldiers sitting in their homes, be they in Manchester, Minneapolis, or Manila. And though the name al-Zarqawi appears nowhere in *The Management of Savagery*, to any Muslim watching the news in 2004, and angered or inspired by events unfolding in Iraq, it was clear that jihad had found its greatest general.

THE SUNNI BOYCOTT

To succeed in his own campaign of vexation and exhaustion, al-Zarqawi needed to both massacre and dispossess the enemy (the Shia and Americans) and keep Sunnis divested of any stake in what he saw as their conspiratorial project: the creation of a democratic Iraqi government. Both the Baathists and al-Qaeda undertook a campaign to enforce a Sunni boycott of the forthcoming January 2005 Iraqi election. It worked. In Anbar province, fewer than 1 percent of all Sunnis cast ballots. The result played wondrously into al-Zarqawi's overall strategy of emboldening Shia triumphalism and further demoralizing Sunnis. Shia parties won the election by an overwhelming margin; Ibrahim al-Jaafari, a candidate from the Dawa Party who had received millions in funding from Iran, became Iraq's first elected prime minister, putting him in charge of a government that would draft the country's post-Saddam constitution, more or less guaranteeing that Sunnis would have even less input than their demographic minority status should have dictated.

The Sunni loss at the ballot box unsurprisingly coincided with a sharp uptick in attacks on "Shia" targets, which included state institutions and the Iraqi Security Forces (ISF). On February 28, 2005, a suicide bomb killed more than 120 people in the Shia-majority city of Hilla, just south of Baghdad, targeting young men tendering job applications with the ISF. In the crucial border town of Tal Afar, which jihadists used as a gateway to import foreign fighters from Syria, al-Qaeda ethnically cleansed mixed communities, "attacking playgrounds and schoolyards and soccer fields," as Colonel Herbert "H. R." McMaster later recalled. In one horrifying instance, they used two mentally disabled girls—ages three and thirteen—as suicide bombers to blow up a police recruitment line.

THE DESERT PROTECTORS

Military progress in Iraq began as improvisation—the innovative thinking of local military actors who apprehended early on that the war for "hearts and minds" would never be won by adhering to a strategy cooked up by planners who had never left the Green Zone in Baghdad or, in some cases, who were mostly confined to the Pentagon. Integral to the insurgency's success was the failure by the Americans to engage with arguably the most important demographic in Sunni Iraq—the tribes. They had suffered enormously from de-Baathification. Saddam had understood the importance of these ancient confederations of families and clans and had thus made them a large part of his state patronage system: the tribes ran smuggling rings, gray-market merchant businesses, all under the auspices of his former vice president, al-Douri.

It was not for a lack of trying that the tribes failed to persuade the coalition of their bellwether status for defeating the insurgency. A sheikh from the influential Albu Nimr tribe had offered to work with the Iraqi Governing Council and the CPA in establishing a much-needed border guard as early as 2003, an offer that was reflected in a memo prepared for the Joint Chiefs of Staff in October of that same year. "Leaders of these tribes—many of whom still occupy key positions of local authority—appear to be increasingly willing to cooperate with the Coalition in order to restore or maintain their influence in post-Saddam Iraq," the memo read. "If they perceive failure, they may take other actions, to include creating alternate governing and security institutions, working with anti-Coalition forces, or engaging in criminal activity to ensure the prosperity and security of their tribes." Nothing came of the memo.

Al-Zarqawi again proved more adept at navigating Iraqi culture than the Coalition Provisional Authority or US military—at least at first. "Zarqawi, or the Iraqis he had working for him, understood who was who in the tribes and he worked them," Derek Harvey said. "That's how he controlled territory in Anbar and the Euphrates River Valley."

But he made a fatal error. Al-Zarqawi overplayed his hand by turning al-Qaeda's protection racket into an asphyxiating mode of jihadist governance. The tribes chafed at the implementation of a seventh-century civil code in areas ruled by fundamentalists, many of whom were foreign-born and behaved exactly as the colonial usurpers they were meant to expel had done. Tribal businesses were disrupted or taken over by those seeking their own monopoly on smuggling, and al-Qaeda protected its confiscated interest with a mafia's thuggish zeal. It justified killing on the basis of market competition.

So when it assassinated a sheikh from the Albu Nimr tribe in 2005, Major Adam Such, who commanded the Army Special Forces Operational Detachment Alpha 555 Company under the 1st Marine Division, seized the opportunity to make al-Qaeda a pariah among its most important constituency. He recruited tribesmen to join an ad hoc militia to monitor the roads near the Anbar city of Hit—another strategically vital town that ISIS would seize in 2014. It was an inspired idea, although it lacked the necessary structural support to become wholly transformative. At the time, there was no permanent US military presence in the area to convince the locals that the expunging of jihadists from Hit would not be a flash in the pan but rather the prelude to a long-term counterinsurgent policing mission. Still, the fact that Iraqis suddenly wanted Americans to stay in their midst indicated that the jihadists had worn out their welcome.

Another city where this proved to be so was Qa'im, which al-Zarqawi had made the capital of his Western Euphrates "emirate" for obvious geostrategic reasons. The Sunni and Bedouin town abuts the Syrian border town of Albu Kamal and is also situated along a main road connecting Iraq to Jordan. It also contains the largest phosphate mines in the Middle East, with an enormous subterranean cave system, which became a guerrilla network for moving men and matériel through undetected.

US marines moved in to take Qa'im in September 2005, followed by subsequent sorties in subordinate al-Qaeda bases in the Western Euphrates. They constructed concrete-fortified outposts to mark an indefinite presence and thereby forestall a jihadist resurgence. Building on Such's experience in Hit, they also reached out to Qa'im's tribes, some of which had already grown so horrified by al-Qaeda's practices that they took up arms against the Zarqawists. In the Albu Mahal tribe's Hamza Battalion, the marines discovered a volunteer army that proved as committed to hammering the insurgents as they were.

Discounting corruption, the main reason why the Iraqi Security Forces often proved inept or simply unwilling to duke it out with al-Qaeda was that many recruits were Shia, who understandably had little interest in fighting in Sunni-majority territory where they were viewed with suspicion or outright contempt. Sunni tribesmen had no such compunction and were fired by self-interest to rid their areas of what may have started out as an applauded anti-American "resistance" but had since devolved into a gang of obscurantist head-loppers. The graduates of the Qa'im program were turned into a battalion called the Desert Protectors, a name more than a little redolent of Lawrentian romanticism but accurate insofar as the battalion safeguarded the December 2005 parliamentary election from terrorist sabotage.

By 2006, security incidents in Qa'im had plummeted. Even in success, though, US forces still failed to discover that the tribes were not motivated by anything so grandiose as patriotism; they only wanted to ensure peace and quiet in their own communities, not in the entire country. A third of the Desert Protectors' members quit after being told that it constituted a national defense force and not just a local Qa'im gendarmerie and so was duly slated for redeployment elsewhere in Iraq.

That said, Iraq's national parliamentary election yielded unforeseen and welcome developments. One of these was the transformation of Dr. Muhammad Mahmoud Latif, a long-sought-after insurgent leader, into a partner of the United States. Appalled by how the Sunni boycott of the January election for a constituent assembly had deprived Sunnis of their say in Iraq's self-determination, Latif realized that al-Zarqawi's plan for delegitimizing the new government was backfiring. He also had political ambitions of his own. In the lead-up to the parliamentary vote, he gathered a collection of Ramadi tribal sheikhs who were eager to declare war on al-Qaeda and, more daringly, work with the Americans to do so, on one condition. Like the Desert Protectors, the Ramadi tribesmen wanted a guarantee that the security portfolio for Anbar's provincial capital would devolve to themselves after al-Qaeda was no more.

Assured of the Americans' good faith in that respect, the Anbar People's Council was born. Its first initiative was to encourage Sunnis to join the Iraqi police, which was about to hold a large recruitment drive at a local glass factory. The council's certification of the effort yielded hundreds of fresh applicants, who in turn became an unavoidable target for al-Zarqawi's jihadists. On the fourth day of the glass factory drive, a suicide bomber exploded a device that killed as many as sixty Iraqis and two Americans. Al-Qaeda then announced all-out war on the Anbari sheikhs who had joined the council, hunting them down individually for weeks after the bombing. Latif fled Iraq to avoid being caught in the terrorists' dragnet. Still too vulnerable to al-Zarqawi's strong-arm tactics, the council folded weeks later.

It took another two years for the US military to make strategic sense of what had transpired in Hit, Qa'im, and Ramadi. Pockets of wholly spontaneous and unforeseen tribal backlashes against the same foreign-led terrorist organization made sense in light of tribal history. For centuries, these clans had survived by cutting pragmatic deals with perceived dominant powers in their midst. They had done it with Saddam, and they had done it with al-Zarqawi, and they were ready to do it with the Americans. And while they still regarded the United States warily, they saw in its army a possible ally against a greater common enemy.

"I had a Marine Corps captain," a former top US military official relayed of this period in the army's anthropological self-education in Iraq. "He was a Sioux. He didn't know shit about Anbar or Iraq. He got out there, and he understood it immediately. The Iraqis could see he knew what was going on, and they loved him for it."

For Derek Harvey, understanding the way Iraq's tribes functioned was the key to all mythologies in understanding Iraq itself. "There were a lot of regime organizations that we didn't figure out very well. The key person might not have been the head guy, but the second or third guy—and this rule of not knowing exactly who's running the show applied to the Saddamists as much as it applies to ISIS today. The tribes had professional and in some cases religious networks that determined informal hierarchies in everything that happened in that country. Our difficulty was in learning who did what." No doubt keeping the enemy in the dark as to its internal hierarchy is very much part of ISIS's strategy today. The way Abu Bakr al-Baghdadi was appointed leader, for instance, has engendered a great deal of speculation about whether or not this was by consensus or reflected native Iraqi—and indeed, Iraqi "Baathist"—usurpation of the house that al-Zarqawi built. That the occlusive terms of Baghdadi's succession (which will be examined in a later chapter) are still being debated by jihadists and intelligence analysts six years later adds a mafia-style grandeur and mystery to an organization that relies on working in the shadows and knowing more about its opponents than they can ever possibly know about it.

If ISIS has made any improvement upon al-Qaeda's ability to answer that question, it has been in relying on Iraqi and Syrian tribes to manage much of the savagery of jihadist rule themselves. This dispensation toward semi-autonomy appears also to have been gleaned from the instructions set down by Abu Bakr Naji a decade earlier. "When we address these tribes that have solidarity we should not appeal to them to abandon their solidarity," Naji wrote. "Rather, we must polarize them and transform them into praiseworthy tribes that have solidarity." Better to use that solidarity by redirecting it toward God, he went on, first by uniting the sheikhs, or tribal leaders, with "money and the like," and then by letting loose association with the true believers work like osmosis on the tribal rank and file. "Of course, solidarity remains, but it has been changed into a praiseworthy solidarity instead of the sinful solidarity which they used to have."

4

AGENTS OF CHAOS

IRAN AND AL-QAEDA

Iraq's Sunnis had just as much of a learning curve to adapt to as did the US military. Having squandered most of their political power through a disastrous boycott of the January 2005 election, they were not about to repeat the blunder again at the one in December 2005. The about-face was statistically staggering. In December, in Ramadi, Sunni voter turnout was around 80 percent, whereas in January it had been a measly 2 percent. The letdown, then, was proportionately disappointing. Shia political blocs again came out on top, albeit with a small margin of victory, which did little to dissuade many Sunnis of the conspiracy theory that al-Zarqawi had cleverly capitalized on and that suddenly appeared wholly realized. They now believed that an Iranian-American alliance was purposefully keeping them from their rightful place as the true masters and custodians of Baghdad.

Sunni participation in the December election also had another disconcerting side effect. As many of the more nationalistic or "moderate" insurgents quit the battlefield in favor of trying their luck at the ballot box, al-Qaeda's role in Iraq's terrorism grew more concentrated. Additionally, less moderate non-al-Qaeda insurgents, such as the 1920 Revolution Brigades, opted to cast their lot with the Zarqawists, who appeared to be the champions of Sunni grievances. And though other insurgencies, such as Jaysh al-Islami, or the Islamic Army, were vying with al-Qaeda for control of territory in Mosul, it was not yet ready to abandon its own avowed rejectionism for national reconciliation. Al-Qaeda's overreach had alienated many, but al-Zarqawi was still able to masterfully exploit demographic anxieties, which long predated the war.

Kanan Makiya, a well-known scholar of Saddam's Iraq, had forecast a dire scenario for a post-Baathist state in his 1993 book, *Cruelty and Silence*: "After Saddam is gone, when people's lives and those of their loved ones look as if they are on the chopping block, Sunni fears of what the Shi'a might do to them in the name of Islam are going to become the major force of Iraqi politics. The more Iraq's Shi'a assert themselves as Shi'a, the greater will be the tendency of Iraq's Sunni minority to fight to the bitter end before allowing anything that so much as smells of an Islamic republic to be established in Iraq. They see in such a state—whether rightly or wrongly is irrelevant—their own annihilation."

As we have seen, al-Zarqawi was counting on it. The stark choice he presented to Sunnis was therefore a simple one: "My barbarism, or theirs." Yet he still had to surmount the greatest obstacle to al-Qaeda's popular appeal—the perception and reality that it was a foreign-run army. Sunnis may have wanted to regain their lost power and prestige in Baghdad, but not so that a cabal of Jordanians, Saudis, Libyans, and Algerians could sit on the throne. The al-Qaeda emir thus needed to "Iraqize" his franchise. In January 2006 al-Zarqawi announced the creation of a new super-assembly called Majlis Shura al-Mujahidin fi al-Iraq, or the Mujahidin Advisory Council of Iraq. Initially this consortium consisted of six different Salafist groups, five of which were Iraqi in composition, leaving al-Qaeda as the sole outlier, albeit with central control over the council's operations. Contributing to what was, in effect, a new marketing or "branding" strategy for jihad was the chauvinistic and authoritarian behavior of the newly elected Iraqi government.

SHIA MILITIAS, SULEIMANI'S PROXIES

Given the world's current preoccupation with ISIS, it is easy to forget that a decade ago, the US military saw as formidable a terrorist threat in the portly, demagogic Shia cleric Muqtada al-Sadr. The son of the revered Muhammad Sadiq al-Sadr, who was killed by Saddam's Mukhabarat in 1999, the younger al-Sadr by rights ought to have been confined to the lower rung of Shia religious leaders. He ruled an impoverished and overcrowded ghetto in northeast Baghdad, formerly known as Saddam City and renamed Sadr City after the invasion. He founded his own paramilitary organization, the Jaysh al-Mahdi, or Mahdi Army, not long after the regime's fall, seeing it as Iraq's counterpart to Hezbollah, the Iranian proxy paramilitary in Lebanon that had long straddled the fault line between US-sanctioned terrorist entity and internationally legitimized political party, occupying posts in the Lebanese cabinet and wielding furtive influence within the country's ostensibly independent intelligence services and armed forces. Hezbollah, or the Party of God, proved the perfect template for carving out a similar terrorist "deep state" in Iraq.

Like all warlords, al-Sadr wanted to rule his fief uncontested. Left largely alone by US forces, he created his own sphere of influence with Iranian assistance. The Sunni conspiracy theory of a Washington-Tehran plot to destroy Iraq can have been met only with anger and bemusement by GIs who experienced firsthand how Iran sought to make life as bloody and difficult for them as possible. The Battle of Najaf in August 2004 was essentially a proxy war between the United States and Iran's elite foreign intelligence and military apparatus, the Revolutionary Guards Corps–Quds Force (IRGC-QF). This was coordinated on the Iraqi side by an Iranian operative named Sheikh Ansari. US intelligence concluded that Ansari was embedded with the Mahdi Army in Najaf and was helping it conduct its combat operations. He was an operative for the Quds Force's Department 1000, which handled Iran's intelligence portfolio in Iraq.

Iran's hegemony in Iraq began well before the regime change. The devastating eight-year war with Iraq had turned the Islamic Republic into a place of refuge for hundreds of thousands of Iraqi Shia who had fled Saddam's depredations. Now, with the Baathist tyrant gone, many of these exiles were able to return home to a country where the Shia were enfranchised by a nascent democracy. They were able, too, to launch both political and paramilitary apparatuses upon an infrastructure that had been quietly and covertly built up for years under Baathist rule.

The Supreme Council for Islamic Revolution in Iraq (SCIRI) was in fact a wholesale creation of Iranian intelligence and Mohammed Baqir al-Hakim, the popular Shia cleric whom al-Zarqawi assassinated in his month-long bombing spree in August 2003. SCIRI's armed wing, al-Zarqawi's hated Badr Corps, operated as Tehran's fifth column in Iraq. "The mullahs ran a very subversive campaign against Saddam long before we got into that country, and we were dealing with those same lines of communications before we got there," said Colonel Jim Hickey, the former commander for the 4th Infantry Division brigade that captured Saddam in December 2003—an operation in which Hickey played a key role.

When the Americans arrived, Tehran's campaign of sabotage and terrorism fell principally to IRGC-QF's commander, Brigadier General Qassem Suleimani, who answered directly to Iran's Supreme Leader, Ayatollah Ali Khamenei.

A former CIA officer not long ago described Suleimani, who has understandably been promoted to major general in the years since, as "the single most powerful operative in the Middle East today and no one's ever heard of him."

When David Petraeus became the top US general in Iraq, he got to know Suleimani quite well, referring to the master spy as "evil" and mulling whether to tell President Bush that "Iran is, in fact, waging war on the United States in Iraq, with all of the US public and governmental responses that could come from that revelation." For Petraeus, Iran had "gone beyond merely striving for influence in Iraq and could be creating proxies to actively fight us, thinking that they [could] keep us distracted while they [tried] to build WMD and set up [the Mahdi Army] to act like Lebanese Hezbollah in Iraq."

In 2007, five American servicemen were killed in an ambush in Karbala carried out by agents of Asa'ib Ahl al-Haq, or the League of the Righteous, a splinter militia of the Mahdi Army set up with al-Sadr and Iran's assistance. Not only had the Quds Force officer stationed at the Iranian consulate in Karbala quit his post shortly before the ambush took place, but one of the leaders of the League of the Righteous, Qais al-Khazali, confessed to Iran's masterminding of the entire operation.

Suleimani's deputy in bleeding America in Iraq was Abu Mahdi al-Muhandis, an Iraqi national who had lived in Iran and had been tied to the 1983 bombing of the US embassy in Kuwait. Al-Muhandis had gone from a Badr Corps member to a full-fledged Quds Force operative before he was elected to Iraq's parliament. He also set up another so-called Special Group— the American euphemism for Sadrist breakaway militias—called Kata'ib Hezbollah, or the Party of God Brigade, which similarly targeted US forces.

Suleimani had spent his career in the 1990s stopping the flow of narcotics into Iran from Afghanistan; he'd spend the subsequent decade in the Iraqi import business. Al-Muhandis was selected to oversee the trafficking of one of the deadliest weapons ever used in the Iraq War: a roadside bomb known as the explosively formed penetrator, or EFP for short. When detonated, the heat from the EFP melts the copper housing of the explosive, turning it into a molten projectile that can cut through steel and battle armor—including tank walls. The US military reckoned that these devices constituted 18 percent of all coalition combat deaths in the last quarter of 2006. They were manufactured in Iran and smuggled across the border by Iranian agents working with the Badr Corps, and then used by all manner of Shia militias, earning them the sobriquet "Persian bombs." In July 2007, two-thirds of US casualties were suffered at the hands of these Shia militias, prompting Petraeus to assess the Mahdi Army as "more of a hindrance to long-term security in Iraq than is AQI," as he wrote to US Defense Secretary Robert Gates. For this reason, many in the military advocated bombing the EFP factories in Iran, regardless of the diplomatic fallout. Regardless of what Petraeus considered telling the president, America was at war with Iran in Iraq.

General McChrystal's JSOC arrested Mohsen Chizari, the head of the Quds Force's Operations and Training staff, along with the Quds Force's station chiefs for Baghdad and Dubai, in late 2006. (Chizari had just come from a meeting at SCIRI headquarters and had been spotted by a US surveillance drone.) Another JSOC raid in Erbil, the capital of the Kurdistan Regional Government, intended to net Brigadier General Mohammad Ali Jafari, a senior Quds Force commander, but instead captured five lower-ranking Iranian officers. Eventually, "countering Iran's influence" in Iraq got to be such a full-time job that JSOC bifurcated its task forces according to quarry. Task Force 16 would hunt down AQI, while Task Force 17 would go after Suleimani's operatives and their proxies in the Special Groups.

In some cases, the United States discovered, its two enemies were secretly collaborating with each other. Suleimani intermittently helped al-Qaeda in Iraq for the simple reason that any agent of chaos and destruction that might hasten the American departure from the country was deemed a net positive for Tehran. In 2011 the US Treasury Department had sanctioned six Iranian-based al-Qaeda operatives, who had helped transport money, messages, and men to and from Pakistan and Afghanistan via Iran. "Iran is the leading state sponsor of terrorism in the world today," Undersecretary for Terrorism and Financial Intelligence David S. Cohen said at the time. "By exposing Iran's secret deal with al-Qa'ida allowing it to funnel funds and operatives through its territory, we are illuminating yet another aspect of Iran's unmatched support for terrorism."

Former US ambassador to Iraq Ryan Crocker told the *New Yorker* in 2013 that a decade earlier US intelligence had confirmed the presence of al-Qaeda in Iran—itself no great revelation, given that al-Zarqawi had made the Islamic Republic his fallback base after fleeing Kandahar the previous year. (According to the London-based Saudi newspaper *Asharq al-Awsat*, Suleimani is reported even to have boasted in 2004 that al-Zarqawi and his first jihadist network in Iraq, Ansar al-Islam, were free to move in and out of Iran at will through multiple border crossings—and that al-Zarqawi had even trained at an Iranian Revolutionary Guards Corps camp in Mehran, Iran.) Crocker, however, claimed that al-Qaeda in Iran was seeking to strike at Western targets in Saudi Arabia in 2003. He enjoyed a somewhat amenable back channel with Iranian officials, given the latter's quiet assistance to the United States in routing the Taliban: a case of enemy-of-my-enemy logic that proved opportunistic and fleeting. When Crocker traveled to Geneva the same year that the United States invaded Iraq and prevailed upon them to halt al-Qaeda's terrorism against America in the Persian Gulf, they refused. On May 12, 2003, three compounds in Riyadh, Saudi Arabia, were blown up in a combination attack involving gunfire and vehicle-borne improvised explosive devices. Dozens were killed, including nine Americans. "They were there, under Iranian protection, planning operations," the ex-diplomat recounted to the *New Yorker*.

Meanwhile, the sectarian deep state of al-Sadr's fantasy and the Sunnis' nightmare was indeed emerging with the collusion of the new Iraq government. After December 2005, SCIRI was placed in charge of Iraq's Ministry of Interior, which commanded sixteen thousand troops. The outgoing interior minister was Falah Naqib, a Sunni who, along with his uncle Adnan Thabit, had cobbled together the first post-Saddam gendarmeries put to use by the Americans in the form of the Special Police Commandos and the Public Order Brigades. Naqib saw nothing but trouble in Iran's fifth column running the national police force of Iraq. "We either stop them or give Iraq to Iran," Naqib reportedly told General George Casey Jr, then the commander of the Multi-National Force—Iraq. "That's it."

Naqib's replacement was Bayan Jabr, an SCIRI functionary whom the Americans viewed as less extremist in orientation than other members of the party. But, by way of trying to limit the damage that he could still do, they arranged for Thabit to stay on as head of the Ministry of Interior's armed forces. This posed no problem for Jabr, whose workaround solution was to not deal with or through Thabit at all and to simply replace the paramilitary forces under his command with loyal Badr Corps and Mahdi Army militiamen. The counterpart brigade in charge of West Baghdad menacingly patrolled the streets, blasting Shia songs on December 15, 2005, just as Sunnis took to the polls to participate in what was for many their first democratic election. A Ministry of Interior uniform conferred authority and impunity on active members of sectarian death squads.

A Badr-influenced Special Police Commando unit, better known as the Wolf Brigade, was one of the worst offenders. The Islamic Organization for Human Rights, an Iraqi nongovernmental organization (NGO), found that the Ministry of Interior was guilty of twenty cases of detainee abuse, six of which resulted in death and most of which were carried out by the Wolf Brigade in Mosul. According to a State Department cable from the US embassy in Baghdad, the NGO "described practices such as use of stun guns, hanging suspects from their wrists with arms behind back, holding detainees in basements with human waste, and beatings."

Other Iraqi government institutions also fell under the sway of Shia sectarians, such as the Health Ministry, the deputy head of which was Hakim al-Zamili, a Mahdi Army agent. Ambulances were used not to transport the sick and injured but to ship weapons. Hospitals, meanwhile, were refashioned into sites for the execution of Sunnis, driving many in Baghdad to travel outside the capital to seek medical treatment.

Iraq's prime minister, Ibrahim al-Jaafari, created his own intelligence agency, the Ministry of State for National Security Affairs, headed by Shirwan al-Waeli, a man who funneled intelligence on US troop movements to the Mahdi Army and gave the Sadrists practical oversight over much of Iraq's travel industry—the commercial airline sector especially. Right under the noses of US civilian and military authorities, then, the Mahdi Army was doing in Baghdad what Hezbollah had done in Beirut: seizing control of the major international airport and its attendant facilities. It ran the customs office, the sky marshal program, even its contracted cleaning company, existing employees of which the Sadrists murdered to create job vacancies for themselves. It imported weapons hidden in the cargo holds of planes from Iran. It also had ready access to the international comings and goings of Sunnis—knowledge that, unsurprisingly, led to many kidnappings and murders.

Nothing better symbolized for Sunnis the new republic of fear being constructed atop the ruins of the former one than Jadriya Bunker. A detention facility situated just south of the Green Zone, the bunker's Special Interrogations Unit was run by Bashir Nasr al-Wandi, nicknamed "Engineer Ahmed." A former senior intelligence operative for the Badr Corps, Engineer Ahmed was, like Hadi al-Amari, seconded to Suleimani's Quds Force. When US soldiers finally opened the door to this dungeon prison, they found 168 blindfolded prisoners, all of whom had been held there for months, in an overcrowded room filled with feces and urine.

Nearly every prisoner was a Sunni, and many bore signs of torture—some were so badly beaten that they had to be taken to the Green Zone for medical treatment. Because it fell under the Ministry of Interior's purview, Bayan Jabr was forced to answer for what had transpired. He claimed never to have visited the prison and dismissed the human rights abuses in a press conference. Only the "most criminal terrorists" were detained, Jabr said, and by way of showing how gently they had been dealt with, he added "no one was beheaded, no one was killed." Testifying to the grim cooperation between Shia-run ministries in al-Jaafari's Iraq, Jabr's predecessor, Falah Naqib, who lived only a few blocks from the Jadriya Bunker, claimed to have seen ambulances coming and going from the building, and speculated that prisoners were being transported in them.

"The Iraq War upset the balance of power in the region in Iran's favor," Emma Sky, the former British adviser to the US military, told one of the authors. "It is common in the Arab world to hear talk of secret deals between Iran and the United States, and laments that the US 'gave Iraq to Iran.'" This geopolitical perception, Sky said, is one of the primary reasons that Sunnis have been attracted to ISIS.

Even more disturbing was the US role in covering up the crimes of these Shia militias. Although the Americans forced al-Jaafari to investigate the torture at Jadriya, the committee published a whitewash that was never released. Reuters obtained a copy of the report a decade later. In mid-December 2015, the news agency disclosed that al-Jaafari's committee blamed "Baathist" police for the crime. The US military conducted its own investigation and found that Jabr, Engineer Ahmed, another Badr official, Brigadier General Ali Sadiq, and an Iraqi jurist, Judge Medhat al-Mahmoud, were the true culprits. Jabr was "indirectly responsible for illegal detentions, abuse, torture, and extra-judicial killings," the US report found, while Judge Medhat "took no steps to correct" the problems, of which he was well aware. Neither faced any legal or political consequences. Today Jabr is Iraq's transport minister; Judge Medhat is the chief justice of Iraq's Supreme Court. The journalist who reported on this exclusive, Ned Parker, was Reuters's Baghdad bureau chief until April 2015, when his life was threatened by Iranian-backed Shia militias. These threats were in reprisal for Parker's candid dispatches from Tikrit, which had then recently been retaken from ISIS by a thirty-thousand-man contingent mostly made up of those militias, with the help of the Iraqi army and Federal Police, not to mention US warplanes providing all of the above air cover. Parker reported on the lynching of alleged ISIS militants and the looting of Sunni homes. A national television channel run by the League of the Righteous broadcast Parker's photograph and called on its viewers to demand his expulsion from Iraq. Other commenters on social media websites called for his death.

RICHER THAN BIN LADEN

Given al-Zarqawi's self-appointed role as defender of all the Sunnis, and his success in making many Iraqis view him as such, it was no great shock to discover that he was fast outstripping his parent organization in revenue generation. In 2006, the US government found that al-Qaeda in Iraq, along with other Sunni insurgent factions, could collect between $70 million and $200 million annually from criminal enterprises. According to Laith Al-khouri, a specialist on Sunni jihadist groups at Flashpoint, a New York–based intelligence firm, al-Zarqawi's gangland past clearly influenced his career as a terrorist warlord. Al-Qaeda "resorted to any number of methods to make money, from stealing US military weapons and trading them with other insurgent groups, to kidnapping and ransoming hostages. They'd raid the houses of top-ranking Iraqi army officers, then interrogate them inside their own homes. They'd tell them: 'Give us the names, addresses, and phone numbers of other high-ranking army officers.' Some of these kidnapping victims were very rich, and their families would pay. When that didn't work, al-Qaeda would simply kill the officers in their houses."

From 2005 to 2010, subsidies from Gulf Arab donors and dubious Middle East "charities" accounted for at most a paltry 5 percent of al-Qaeda in Iraq's overall budget. Oil smuggling from the Bayji Oil Refinery, in Salah ad-Din province, was keeping al-Zarqawi's apparatus in clover. (That refinery was one of the first assets seized by ISIS in 2014; since then, it has changed hands repeatedly.)

A Defense Intelligence Agency assessment conducted in 2006 found that "[e]ven a limited survey of revenue streams available to the insurgency strongly suggests revenues far exceed expenses." Al-Qaeda in Iraq's resources had by then eclipsed those of its Pakistan-based leadership, forcing Osama bin Laden into the embarrassing position of cadging cash from his reluctant subordinate.

In a tape attributed to al-Zarqawi, dated May 2005, the Iraqi emir said that he targeted the Shia only because they were sinister collaborators committed to the extermination of Iraq's Sunnis (surely a case of Freudian projection). They were confiscating Sunni mosques; killing Sunni clerics, doctors, and professionals; and, worst of all, raping Sunni women. Like any paranoid social engineer, al-Zarqawi alternated between the verifiable and the conspiratorial: Shia in positions of government had, after all, run jails and detention centers where widespread abuses were inflicted on Sunni captives.

But was this truly a Shia campaign of extermination against the Sunnis, as al-Zarqawi put it to justify his total war against the former? One person who thought not was his nominal superior. In July 2005 al-Zawahiri sent al-Zarqawi a letter that, though couched in tones of fraternal advice, had an unmistakable message: stop murdering members of Iraq's majority sect. The Egyptian believed that al-Qaeda in Iraq ought to be pursuing a four-phase strategy. First and foremost, expel the American occupier; second, establish an Islamic emirate in the Sunni parts of Iraq; third, use this terrain to plot terrorist attacks against other Arab regimes; fourth, export the war to Israel. Al-Zawahiri counseled al-Zarqawi to avoid the "mistake of the Taliban," which he believed collapsed too quickly because it had played only to its support base in Kandahar and Afghanistan's southern region, at the expense of the rest of the country.

Al-Zawahiri was in effect flirting with a kind of jihadist nationalism, at least as a temporary measure to keep a parasitical organization from alienating its host country. He was the patient planner; al-Zarqawi was the foolhardy warrior who thought he could battle any and all comers at once and who had a nasty habit of believing his own media hype. "You shouldn't be deceived by the praise of some of the zealous young men and their description of you as the shaykh of the slaughterers, etc.," the elder al-Qaeda leader wrote to the Iraq commander. "They do not express the general view of the admirer and the supporter of the resistance in Iraq, and of you in particular by the favor and blessing of God." Anticipating al-Zarqawi's response that the Americans were even more savage with their cluster bombs and detainee torture programs, al-Zawahiri appealed to his own hard-won experience and suffering to urge moderation in his ardent underling. The "author of these lines has tasted the bitterness of American brutality, and that my favorite wife's chest was crushed by a concrete ceiling and she went on calling for aid to lift the stone block off her chest until she breathed her last, may God have mercy on her and accept her among the martyrs." For all that, al-Zawahiri understood that the larger battle was for Muslim "hearts and minds" and that wanton butchery of fellow Muslims or even non-Muslims exhibited on Internet videos was the surest path to defeat. "[W]e can kill the captives by bullet. That would achieve that which is sought after without exposing ourselves to the questions and answering to doubts."

There was one enemy that he did not think it wise to take on, at least not yet: Iran. Fearing that the Islamic Republic's response to any al-Qaeda provocations in Iraq would be formidable (it already had been in response to the US occupation), al-Zawahiri told al-Zarqawi that "we and the Iranians need to refrain from harming each other at this time in which the Americans are targeting us." Al-Zawahiri's July 2005 letter reflected what ISIS spokesman Abu Muhammad al-Adnani would remind the Egyptian of in May 2014: that "Iran owes al-Qaeda invaluably."

The letter was never intended for public dissemination; as far as the rest of the world was supposed to know, al-Qaeda high command looked on their Mesopotamian emir's performance with something less than unmixed enthusiasm. The CIA leaked the critical missive in October 2005 in part to aggravate what was then still a deep fissure running between the Sheikh of the Slaughterers and his masters in Central Asia. A lot of good it did.

On November 5, 2005, suicide bombers detonated military-grade explosive vests at three well-trafficked Amman hotels—the Radisson SAS, the Grand Hyatt, and the Days Inn—within the space of ten minutes of one another. Sixty people were killed in the blasts; in the case of the first strike at the Radisson, the target was a crowded wedding party in the hotel's main ballroom and the explosion brought much of the ceiling down on top of gowned and tuxedoed attendees—including young children. Others were torn to ribbons by the ball bearings in the twenty-two-pound wearable bomb set off by an Iraqi man named Ali Hussein Ali al-Shamari, who got atop a table before pressing the detonator, the better to kill the maximum number of people. The damage might actually have been worse but for the fact that Ali's "wife" Sadija al-Rishawi, a thirty-five-year-old Iraqi girl whose brother had been killed fighting for al-Qaeda by US troops in Fallujah, found that her bomb was not working and fled the Philadelphia Ballroom before Ali went to work. Their wedding was a sham, designed to allow both operatives into Jordan under the guise of seeking fertility treatments. In total, the three hotel hits constituted the worst terror attack in Jordan's history, and even before al-Rishawi's capture at the home of a relative, it was obvious to the country's Mukhabarat who was responsible—the same native son who had tried and failed to turn the Mukhabarat headquarters into an asphyxiating chemical cloud just a year earlier. "They told me I would be killing Americans," al-Rishawi told her interrogator. "All I wanted to do was avenge the deaths of my brothers." As with the abortive chemical plot, al-Zarqawi again became an object of national loathing in Jordan. And again, to mitigate the popular reaction to his sanguinary excesses—excesses whose victims were fellow Sunnis—he lied, claiming that all three hotels had been intensely scouted by the "brothers" for months and that they had been "headquarters for the Israeli and American intelligence."

The summer of 2005 marked the height of al-Zarqawi's rampage against foreign Muslim diplomats in Iraq. Ihab Sherif, an Egyptian who was all but guaranteed to serve as that country's (and the Arab world's) first ambassador to a post-Saddam Iraq, was kidnapped and murdered by al-Qaeda. Pakistan's ambassador and Bahrain's chargé d'affaires were both nearly kidnapped using the same method—gunfire attacks on their convoys—but managed to escape, the latter with mild wounds.

By the end of the year, it was not just Sunni hoi polloi upbraiding the self-appointed defender of the Sunnis. Atiyah Abd al-Rahman, a senior Libyan al-Qaeda lieutenant and confidant of bin Laden who would eventually become the key link between al-Qaeda's leadership in Pakistan and its regional affiliates, wrote him a letter, another lecture larded with praise and encouragement for all al-Zarqawi had accomplished, but obviously containing as much anger as sorrow. Stating that the "[p]olicy must be dominant over militarism," al-Rahman warned al-Zarqawi that he was barreling down the path of other failed jihadists who had proven greater enemies to themselves than to the regimes they sought to extinguish. He cited the example of Algeria's civil war in the mid-1990s, in which al-Rahman had fought. He further counseled al-Zarqawi that all future operations outside of his designated field of the Land of the Two Rivers would require prior approval from "Shaykh Usamah and the Doctor, and their brothers," referring to bin Laden and al-Zawahiri. He should also confer with al-Qaeda's other affiliate in Iraq, Ansar al-Sunna, "no matter how much you have to say about, or reservations about, them, or some of them. An example of this is the issue of announcing a war against the Shi'ite turncoats and killing them. Another is expanding the arena of the war to neighboring countries, and also undertaking some large-scale operations whose impact is great and whose influence is pervasive, and things of that nature."

This offer of fraternal guidance similarly went unheeded. On February 22, 2006, four al-Qaeda in Iraq terrorists, dressed in the uniforms of the Iraqi Ministry of Interior, detonated several explosives inside the al-Askari Mosque in Samarra, one of the holiest shrines in Shia Islam and a mausoleum for two of the sect's twelve revered imams. (The operation was directly led by Haitham al-Badri, a former government official under Saddam.)

The mosque had been built in AD 944 and remodeled in the nineteenth century, although its celebrated gilt dome, which was ruined in the explosions, was only added at the turn of the twentieth century. The day of the bombing, Iraq's vice president, Adel Abdul Mahdi, a Shia, likened it to 9/11. Grand Ayatollah Ali al-Sistani called for peaceful protests, while hinting that if the Iraqi Security Forces could not protect other sacred sites, then Shiite militias might have to. One of Iraq's NGOs found that after the bombing several hundred terrified Shia families had fled Baghdad; US forces announced an emergency mission, Operation Scales of Justice, to mitigate the anticipated wave of retaliatory violence against Sunnis.

The al-Askari Mosque bombing accomplished in the international imagination what al-Zarqawi had intended and what most Iraqis had already been living through for three years—a civil war.

Al-Sistani's plea for restraint was not heeded by the Sadrists and Iranian-run Special Groups, whose weapons of choice for use on Sunni captives included power drills and electrical cords. Bodies were dumped in the Tigris River. The Mahdi Army also set up checkpoints in Ghazaliya, one of several strategically key towns along a major highway from Baghdad to Anbar. Uniformed Iraqi policemen were enlisted to stop cars passing by and check the identity papers of the passengers; if they were Sunni, they would be disappeared in an elaborate show of officialdom that was in fact a Sadrist form of ethnic cleansing.

Sunni insurgents paid the Shia back in their own coin. Al-Qaeda in Iraq and other Islamist insurgent groups, including ones that would eventually turn on it, used every horrific means at their disposal to push the Shia out of Ameriya Fallujah, a Sunni-majority town in western Baghdad that had been choked off and partially starved by the Sadrists. The Iraqi army and police, all answerable to newly installed prime minister Nouri al-Maliki, another Dawa Party member, were seen as accomplices to the rampant killings and abductions, which al-Maliki appeared to be tolerating. This was the issue put forth in a classified memo, subsequently leaked, from Stephen Hadley of the White House National Security Council to President Bush in 2006, after Hadley's visit to Baghdad.

"Reports of nondelivery of services to Sunni areas," the memo read, "intervention by the prime minister's office to stop military action against Shiite targets and to encourage them against Sunni ones, removal of Iraq's most effective commanders on a sectarian basis, and efforts to ensure Shiite majorities in all ministries—when combined with the escalation of [Mahdi Army] kill-ings—all suggest a campaign to consolidate Shiite power in Baghdad."

THE DEATH OF AL-ZARQAWI

Al-Zarqawi's whereabouts had been a mystery to coalition forces since the Second Battle of Fallujah, although, according to Bruce Riedel, he had actu-ally been captured a few times by Iraqis who had no idea of their prisoner's identity. He may once even have escaped from US custody on the sly. To find al-Zarqawi through his underlings, JSOC and the British Special Air Ser-vice (SAS) began rounding up lower-level al-Qaeda members in the spring of 2006. In one raid, during which the group's leader in the town of Abu Ghraib was captured, US commandos found the unedited propaganda video of al-Zarqawi clumsily handling a machine gun. This detainee and another mid-ranking al-Qaeda operative captured separately outlined the jihadist net-work in detail, providing the Americans with the name of al-Zarqawi's latest spiritual adviser, Abd al-Rahman (not to be confused with the Libyan who had written him after the Amman attacks). From there, it was a matter of reverse-engineering al-Rahman's mode of communication with al-Zarqawi, via a series of couriers. US forces discovered that their target had been hiding in plain sight all along: al-Zarqawi's safe house was in Hibhib, a town north-east of Baghdad and just twelve miles away from JSOC's own headquarters at Balad Air Base.

On June 7, 2006, a US drone quietly surveilled al-Rahman making contact with al-Zarqawi. By early evening, an F-16 had dropped a five-hundred-pound laser-guided bomb on the location, followed by a second, satellite-guided mu-nition. Iraqi soldiers found al-Zarqawi first, still alive but mortally wounded. He died as McChrystal's men reached the scene. Jordanian intelligence, which had claimed to know al-Zarqawi better than he knew himself, took partial credit for his discovery.

In death, the Sheikh of the Slaughterers earned the kind of panegyrics from al-Qaeda's core leadership that had eluded him in life. He was a "knight, the lion of jihad," bin Laden announced in a bit of revisionist canonization. All foregoing words of caution to the contrary, he suddenly fully endorsed al-Zarqawi's mass murder of Iraqi Shia as payback for their collaboration with the "Crusaders."

TWO FOR THE PRICE OF ONE

The death of al-Zarqawi hardly meant the demise of his franchise. The Mujahi-din Advisory Council he had installed as a way to domesticate an expat-heavy franchise appointed another nonnative emir: Abu Ayyub al-Masri, an Egyptian national who used the nom de guerre Abu Hamza al-Muhajir.

He knew al-Zawahiri and al-Zarqawi personally. Al-Masri had belonged to al-Jihad in the 1980s. He traveled to Afghanistan the same year as al-Zarqawi, whom he met at an al-Qaeda training camp. When al-Zarqawi headed to Iraq in 2002, al-Masri and more than a dozen senior al-Qaeda operatives went with him. In fact, according to former CIA director George Tenet, US intelligence had followed al-Masri's entry into the country as one of "two Egyptians assessed by a senior al-Qa'ida detainee to be among the Egyptian Islamic Jihad's best operational planners, who arrived by mid-May of 2002. At times we lost track of them, though their associates continued to operate in Baghdad as of October 2002. Their activity in sending recruits to train in al-Zarqawi's camps was compelling enough. There was also concern that these two might be planning operations outside Iraq."

Al-Masri's appointment was at once a continuation and repudiation of al-Zarqawi's legacy. For one thing, he took the Iraqization program further when, in October 2006, he declared that his franchise was part of a mosaic of homegrown Islamic resistance movements, which he named the Islamic State of Iraq (ISI). Its demesne was Ninewah, Anbar, and Salah ad-Din provinces, but also areas where Sunnis did not have numerical strength, such as Babil, Wasit, Diyala, Baghdad, and Kirkuk, an oil-rich and once-cosmopolitan city that had been "Arabized" by Saddam in the 1980s and that the Kurds to this day consider their "Jerusalem." In November, al-Masri gave his allegiance to the organization, formally dissolving al-Qaeda in Iraq, and making himself subordinate, as war minister, to the Islamic State of Iraq's first emir, Abu Omar al-Baghdadi. Al-Baghdadi was a native Iraqi, whom the Mujahidin Shura Council had voted to be its leader; he never appeared in videos or audio files, presumably for security reasons. Some doubted that he existed at all, until his corpse confirmed it. This may have been a deliberate feint, as al-Masri, in fact, ran the new organization, too, but simply made al-Baghdadi the front man for it.

But al-Masri had a different outlook on the purpose of terrorism than did his predecessor. After his succession became public, US forces captured al-Qaeda's emir for southwestern Baghdad, who, in the course of his interrogation, spelled out what divided the two jihadist commanders. Al-Zarqawi, he said, saw himself in messianic terms, as the defender of all Sunnis against the Shia; al-Masri saw himself as a talent scout and exporter of terror, for whom Iraq was but one staging ground in the fight against "Western ideology worldwide." In this respect, al-Masri was closer to al-Zawahiri as a grand strategist. "He came from outside; he was the guy sent by al-Zawahiri and bin Laden to be their man in Iraq," Joel Rayburn, the military intelligence analyst, told one of us. "But he joined up with al-Baghdadi, who was an Iraqi Salafist, so there was this inside-outside partnership. Al-Baghdadi lent the street cred to the operation; al-Masri was the supervisory muhajid standing behind him." Al-Qaeda in Iraq (the name was still in use by the US military, even if al-Masri had dissolved the organization formally) was thus becoming more adept at navigating Iraqi power politics: the person said to be in charge is not necessarily the one in charge.

The al-Masri–al-Baghdadi duo served practical purposes, too. The Egyptian was the point of reference for an uninterrupted supply of foreign fighters, whereas the Iraqi did not want to openly marry himself to al-Qaeda for fear of losing Sunni support among insurgents who believed they were fighting a more nationalistically oriented jihad. Both men wanted to establish an Islamic emirate on the ashes of what the Americans and their Shia helpmeets had built, but the difference was one of emphasis. Most of the Sunni groups that joined ISI protested, as military historian Ahmed Hashim notes, on the grounds that "they were interested in liberating Iraq and not in creating an Islamic state."

ISI focused on hitting what Laith Alkhouri calls "soft targets," like Iraqi military bases and Shia religious leaders. "This was intended as a PR campaign to remaining Salafist factions outside the al-Qaeda fold," said Alkhouri. "The message was: 'We are the only group that is looked upon as legitimate by all jihadi groups around the world. You guys are losing men every day. Why don't you just join us?' Jaysh al-Islami refused to join them, which is true to this day. So al-Masri and al-Baghdadi simply intensified their PR. Ultimately, they resorted to killing jihadists who didn't join ISI in order to take over their operational territory. It was rather like a mafia turf war."

In keeping with its name, the Islamic State of Iraq also transformed the Mujahidin Shura Council's remit by creating and populating various other "ministries," such as ones for agriculture, oil, and health. It was nation-building, or at least giving that impression. Most controversial, al-Masri, while reaffirming his commitment to bin Laden, also made bayat to al-Baghdadi, placing al-Qaeda in Iraq hierarchically under the patronage of a newly formed umbrella. In jihadist terms, this was like taking a mistress and presenting her as your second wife to your first.

Al-Masri was indeed trying to have it both ways: to remain the master of al-Qaeda's franchise in Iraq while also flirting with outright secession from it in order to found his own "state." It was not until ISIS formally broke with al-Zawahiri in early 2014 that the deep and irreparable fissure created by al-Baghdadi's pretensions of statehood, and al-Masri's subordination of his faction to ISI, was at last revealed—by a very angry Ayman al-Zawahiri. In May 2014 he issued a statement in which he quoted an unknown third party who had characterized al-Baghdadi and al-Masri as "repulsive" fools. If al-Qaeda had ever reserved such animadversions for al-Zarqawi, it never publicized them.

BEYOND CAR BOMBS

The rise of ISI also coincided with the rise in the frequency and sophistication of attacks by vehicle-borne improvised explosive devices, or VBIEDs. According to Jessica Lewis McFate, an Iraq analyst at the Institute for the Study of War, one reason why ISIS today projects a much larger military strength than it actually has lies in its expert use of these devices. Not only is the carnage from VBIED bombings extensive, but the weapon is as much about psychologically discombobulating the enemy in advance of a major military push. "We see them at checkpoints mostly," Lewis said. "We're looking more at VBIEDs or suicide VBIEDs as a tool to catalyze an attack or drive tension for one. So, for instance, ISIS will conduct a VBIED bombing somewhere in Baghdad or along the Euphrates River Valley, and then will test to see how the Iraqi Security Forces and Shia militias respond to those attacks."

From 2006 onward, al-Masri had specialized in pursuing these kinds of attacks in and around Baghdad; factories for the outfitting of cars and trucks with ordnance were discovered in the Baghdad "belts"—the towns and villages that surrounded the capital and where, up until the 2007 troop "surge," the United States had maintained a relatively light footprint.

ISI divided Baghdad and the belts into six zones, five centered on the city. Each zone was ruled by its own local emir. Digital intelligence on ISI, obtained in a JSOC raid, found that one such emir, Abu Ghazwan, who lorded over the thirty-thousand-man town of Tarmiya, managed a number of al-Qaeda cells in northern Iraq, including ones that were recruiting women and children for suicide bombing missions. Abu Ghazwan was also intimately acquainted with the schedules of US and Iraqi patrol units, how to avoid them, and how to lay traps for them. The *Wall Street Journal* reported that in mid-February 2007, a "massive truck bomb sheared off the front of the soldiers' base in Tarmiya, sending concrete and glass flying through the air like daggers. The soldiers at the small outpost spent the next four hours fighting for their lives against a force of 70 to 80 insurgents." (More recent, ISIS has targeted Tarmiya with VBIED attacks: in June 2014 it blew up the houses of high-ranking Iraqi Security Forces personnel and a former tribal Awakening leader.)

Abu Ghazwan's overview of how his mini-emirate functioned suggested that ISI was not merely using Tarmiya as a base of terror operations. It was actively building a statelet. "We are running the district, the people's affairs, and the administrative services, and we have committees to run the district headed by my brother Abu Bakr," he said with not a little self-satisfaction. Indeed, al-Qaeda in Iraq's occupation of Tarmiya was reminiscent of the kind of Islamic fief that had characterized Ansar al-Islam's five-hundred-square-kilometer zone in Iraqi Kurdistan, or ISIS's rule in the eastern Syrian province of Raqqa. Abu Ghazwan even had his municipal conveyances for his Tarmiya emirate. He drove around in a white Nissan truck confiscated from the Iraqi police force and repurposed as an ISI car. He also piloted a ferryboat taken from a water treatment plant along the Tigris River.

Abu Ghazwan's personal history also highlighted another alarming trend of ISI warfare—recidivism. He had once been a detainee of the coalition, as had another man by the name of Mazin Abu Abd al-Rahman. Al-Rahman was newly released from Camp Bucca, one of the largest US-run prisons in Iraq based in Basra, Iraq's southern province that borders Kuwait and Iran. The facility had been named for a New York City fire marshal who had perished in the twin towers on 9/11.

As with al-Zarqawi's Swaqa, Camp Bucca gained a deserved reputation for serving as much as a terrorist academy as a detention facility. Islamists reaffirmed their bona fides not only by preaching to the converted, but also by proselytizing to new inmates from the general population of criminals. These prisoners may have gone into the clink as secularists or mildly religious, only to emerge as violent fundamentalists. In Bucca, al-Rahman did not just learn the finer points of Sharia; he also made friends with al-Qaeda bomb makers and thus graduated from US custody as a newly minted expert in the construction of VBIEDs. Another al-Qaeda agent later recalled how al-Rahman's time in the facility also acquainted him with the necessary contacts to start his own jihadist cell in the northern Baghdad belt, once he was released. As Michael Gordon and Bernard Trainor recount: "It took [al-Rahman] and two other men two days to build each car bomb in the Tarmiya farmhouse they used as a workshop . . . using stolen cars driven up from a parking lot where they were stored in Adhamiya and a combination of plastic and homemade explosives. The evening before an attack, the completed car bomb would be driven from Tarmiya back into Baghdad, where it would be stored overnight in a parking lot or garage before the bomber drove it to its final destination and blew it up."

The founder of al-Qaeda's deadliest satellite organization had been found and killed thirteen miles away from JSOC's headquarters at Balad Air Base. A major cottage industry for car bombs was thriving some forty miles north of Camp Victory.

Jordanian intelligence, which had played a major role in hunting its most wanted domestic terrorist, estimated that at the time of al-Zarqawi's death, he had amassed up to three hundred operatives. He had intended to use them for perpetrating attacks outside of Iraq, where they had all been trained before being sent back to their countries of origin as sleepers awaiting activation. While US and European spy agencies placed the figure lower than three hundred, there was evidence to suggest that the Sheikh of the Slaughterers had never been content to confine his slaughter to the Middle East. Germany's Bundesnachrichtendienst, or BND, its foreign intelligence service, at one point arrested eighteen agents of Ansar al-Islam and al-Zarqawi's network who, Berlin alleged, had planned to assassinate Ayad Allawi in 2004 while Iraq's interim prime minister was visiting Germany. Two years earlier, before al-Zarqawi officially joined al-Qaeda, he was linked by French counterterrorism officials to a group of Chechen-trained jihadists operating in Paris. Nevertheless, his European network never achieved a successful terror attack while he was alive. That black accomplishment would fall to the next generation of Zarqawists in ISIS.

5

THE AWAKENING

IRAQIS TURN ON ISI

"The history of the Anbar Awakening is very bitter," a former high-ranking official in the Iraqi government said toward the end of 2014. "The people who fought al-Qaeda were later abandoned by their government. Many of them were also executed by al-Qaeda, and some of them were even arrested by Iraqi forces. Until there is a perceivable change [in] the way business is done by Baghdad, I strongly doubt that people are willing to risk their lives and start something similar against ISIS." His point, which is reflective of the views of many Iraqi Sunnis we have interviewed, is better illuminated by the origins of the Awakening. Like most propitious discoveries, this one happened by accident.

SAHWA

The Desert Protectors program had been a short-lived but useful exercise in American alliance-building with the tribesmen of Ramadi. By 2006, the provincial capital of Anbar had fallen again to al-Qaeda in Iraq's dominance.

The jihadists were so entrenched in the city that they resorted to US Army Corps of Engineers–type innovations for laying undetectable IEDs to deter or kill US and Iraqi columns. They used power saws to cut away large chunks of asphalt in the road and filled the resulting craters with ordnance before reapplying a seemingly untouched blacktop. To the naked eye, it looked like normal road—until the bomb went off, damaging or destroying a Bradley Fighting Vehicle or Abrams tank and killing or maiming its occupants. The holes these inlaid IEDs left in the ground also caused severe infrastructure damage, bursting the city's sewage pipes and flooding the streets with filth.

As elsewhere in Iraq, the provincial government in Ramadi had been keeping two sets of books, one for its official duties on behalf of Baghdad, the other for al-Qaeda, which bribed and cajoled Iraqi Security Forces and municipal officials, using its greatest asset outside of murder: oil-smuggling revenue. Barrels of purloined crude were imported into Ramadi on a regular basis from the Bayji Oil Refinery up north, then exported for resale on Iraq's black market. This had been the tribes' arrangement with the Saddamists for years. But the new bosses proved more difficult to work with. Tribal elders were susceptible to kidnapping or murder. Two sheikhs from the Albu Aetha and Albu Dhiyab tribes had been killed already, and others were being targeted as competition to what had become the jihadists' thriving war economy.

The people of Ramadi turned slowly against terrorism. Nighttime vigilantism gained enough of a following among families of the group's victims (who were joined by vengeful Iraqi policemen and even rival insurgents fed up with takfiris) that soon a bona fide civil resistance movement was born under the banner of Thuwar al-Anbar, or the Revolutionaries of Anbar. It was the beginning of what became known as Sahwa—"Awakening." These native revolutionaries proved so successful in Ramadi that al-Qaeda even attempted to negotiate with them.

What made Ramadi different was that, when the city was retaken by American and Iraqi forces, a post-battle strategy of police recruitment was wisely implemented not in the vulnerable city center—which, as with the glass factory episode two years prior, was an easy target for insurgent attack—but in the adjoining rural tribal districts. Keeping Sahwa confined to the countryside encouraged a growing insurrection to build into an officially sanctioned one, fostered by growing mutual trust between the Americans and the tribes. One of the key tribal allies was the charismatic Abdul Sattar al-Rishawi, whose compound had been raided twice before by US forces after allegations that he was cooperating commercially with the insurgents. Suddenly, out of the very self-interest and pragmatism that had catalyzed the temporary alliance, al-Rishawi was ready to cut a new deal with the enemy of his enemy. "People with ties to the insurgents have us over for tea," a US lieutenant had told the journalist George Packer about a similar experience in Tal Afar in 2005, when H. R. McMaster had overseen that border town's temporary turnaround on much the same principle. Al-Rishawi would prove one of the most significant allies the United States had ever made in Iraq.

Al-Qaeda's attempt to undermine his efforts failed because tribal disaffection had already grown into a significant groundswell. Along with his brother, al-Rishawi formed the Anbar Emergency Council, which claimed to represent seventeen Anbari tribes ready to partner with coalition forces against the franchise. The council quickly expanded and was rebranded the Anbar Awakening. Al-Rishawi oversaw the recruitment of four hundred men to the Iraqi police force in October 2006, and then another five hundred in November. He was also farsighted enough to realize that recruitment did not necessarily translate into immediate security: these cadets all had to be sent off to Jordan for training, creating a vacuum that al-Qaeda was sure to exploit. Al-Rishawi convinced Nouri al-Maliki to authorize the formation of makeshift paramilitary battalions to serve in their stead. And so the Emergency Response Units were born, led not by corrupt or incompetent neophytes but by tribesmen who had served in the former Iraqi army and knew how to fight. Just before New Year 2007, the Units numbered a little more than two thousand men.

To make these ad hoc solutions permanent, the United States also shrewdly set up new police substations throughout the Ramadi region. This created a further psychological bolster for the tribes—a sense that US-imposed and Iraqi-maintained law and order were there to stay—which served as a deterrent for the insurgents. VBIED attacks on the outskirts of the city dropped as a result. Al-Rishawi's general success led him into fits of hyperbole and overconfidence, although both were surely welcome to American cars at the time. "I swear to God, if we have good weapons, if we have good vehicles, if we have good support, I can fight Al Qaeda all the way to Afghanistan," the sheikh told the *New York Times*, and evidently also President Bush, who met him on a visit to Baghdad in 2007. In the end, al-Rishawi was not able to finish seeing al-Qaeda run out of Iraq. He was assassinated by the jihadists just days after his encounter with the president.

The Anbar Awakening was bottom-up rather than top-down, and thus seized upon at the brigade level by other quick-thinking and improvisational commanders who were ready to negotiate with those who only the day before were sharing tea with the insurgents. The December 2005 election had already proved that some Sunni terrorists were reconcilable to Iraq's political system and did not need to be captured or killed.

Lieutenant General Sir Graeme Lamb, General Casey's British deputy, had long held that it was only a matter of a time until al-Qaeda's presence proved too noxious for Sunnis; some of the jihadists' less extremist battlefield partners turned to the coalition for help. The question was determining who could be approached in return and who was too far gone. Al-Qaeda operatives were off-limits, clearly, but what about the organization's more ideologically flexible "affiliates" in the Islamic State of Iraq? Lamb met with an emir from Ansar al-Sunna, a Salafist faction that had recently begun to doubt ISI's methods. The emir told him that while foreign occupiers could and must be fought, Ansar al-Sunna knew that the more exigent evil facing Iraq was al-Masri and al-Baghdadi's head-loppers and rapists. "We have watched you in Anbar for three and a half years," he told Lamb. "We have concluded that you do not threaten our faith or our way of life. Al-Qaeda does."

THE SURGE

Solidifying an incipient popular revolt against al-Qaeda meant adding to the conventional military capability in Iraq. Much has been written and debated about the "surge" of US forces in Iraq, which began in 2007 under a cloud of domestic political controversy in Washington. Overseen by Petraeus, the policy adopted by the president called for the injection of five additional combat brigades—up to thirty thousand more troops—and a completely overhauled war strategy. The new strategy demanded confronting not only al-Qaeda but also the vast network of state-backed Shia militias and Iranian proxies that posed just as much of a security threat to US forces and the Sunni civilians suddenly being asked to help rout jihadism. Not coincidentally, the architect of that strategy was the man in charge of implementing it.

Petraeus and Marine Lieutenant General James Mattis had coauthored a new field manual on counterinsurgency, a 282-page guidebook for beating back a Maoist-style guerrilla resistance by turning the communities it lived among and cooperated with against it—or, to use the oft-cited Maoist metaphor, turning the sea against the fish. A mixture of soldiering and policing, counterinsurgency's magic ratio, as codified by the Petraeus-Mattis manual, was 20:1,000—twenty soldiers for every one thousand civilians. (That math incorporated Iraqi army soldiers and policemen.)

The Sunni tribes did not have to be persuaded that hunting al-Qaeda was in their interest. They were already doing so more bravely and ably than most of the Iraqi army. Petraeus had seen that firsthand. He had been in charge of the training program of the Iraqi Security Forces, a program that had been beset by dysfunction and corruption. Many of the cadets proved incompetent or unwilling to fight. Others stole equipment and ran off to resell it—in some cases, to the very enemy America had hired them to beat. In 2007, the US Government Accountability Office released a report stating that close to 190,000 AK-47s and sidearms had disappeared from registered stocks. That meant weapons purchased by the American taxpayer were very likely floating around Iraq and being used to kill American servicemen.

The first two surge brigades were dispatched to Baghdad, the hornet's nest for al-Qaeda, which wasted no time trying to sabotage the new counter-insurgency strategy. The jihadists were strongest in the belts surrounding the capital, where newly established US outposts were attacked by coordinated VBIED assaults. In a single day in February, five such operations killed around five hundred people. Conditions were particularly nightmarish in areas with mixed Sunni-Shia populations, where Special Groups and insurgents kidnapped, tortured, killed, and ethnically cleansed each other. The US military's solution was a partition: it built enormous and extensive concrete walls to keep one sect away from its rival.

"The key to Baghdad is this terrain, especially the north and south," Jim Hickey, the US Army colonel who helped track and capture Saddam, said. "Sunni tribes and families—they were the support bases [al-Qaeda] used in 2005 and 2007. We ultimately won the battle for Baghdad because we cleared out the supporting belts they spent years building." The clearing would only come once the support bases turned hostile toward their erstwhile guests. These Sunni briar patches, where American troops had once feared the thorns of local resistance, had to begin pricking and bleeding the jihadists.

DIYALA, THEN AND NOW

The failure of the United States to destroy al-Qaeda's purchase on Iraq's capital was actually rooted in some of its deceptive successes. When al-Zarqawi was killed in Hibhib in June 2006, Joint Special Operations Command recovered a cache of intelligence that suggested that the jihadists believed that they were losing their chief stronghold, the so-called Triangle of Death south of Baghdad, to the Americans. Al-Zarqawi had contemplated yet another change of venue for his headquarters just before he was killed. But the coalition's territorial victories were Pyrrhic, because they were tactical, not strategic. Did defeat for al-Qaeda in one place mean defeat nationwide? On that, competing camps within the US defense establishment disagreed. A military intelligence analysis commissioned by George Casey Jr., Petraeus's predecessor, concluded that all the trademarks of Zarqawist violence—suicide bombings, sniper attacks, IED detonations—were noticeably fewer, and the jihadists seemed to be as well. Furthermore, the overwhelming cluster of attacks was confined to only four provinces of Iraq's eighteen, but half the country's population resided in twelve of the remaining ones, which collectively experienced just 6 percent of all attacks. That meant that al-Qaeda was losing badly throughout Iraq, according to Casey.

The rebuttal to Casey's sanguine appraisal was offered by Derek Harvey. Harvey believed that the methodology of the general's study was wrong and that he was mistaking short-term advances for long-term ones. He cited a Defense Intelligence Agency–commissioned plebiscite that had found that Iraqis had minimal confidence in their own government's defense establishment but were still full of admiration for the "armed resistance." That certainly did not bode well, since popular support was its own force multiplier, and one that could keep Iraq's national security in a state of turmoil. Harvey also noted that the way the military was counting terrorist attacks was highly misleading, because it only scored ones that were successful, that is, that resulted in casualties. But what about the failed attacks, the near misses? If a detonated IED turned out to be a dud or if it failed to injure or kill people, did it not still constitute an attack and indicate al-Qaeda's enduring ability to terrorize?

Harvey's more depressing analysis proved correct. Since the jihadists kept relocating their command centers from city to city, Casey's strictly counterterrorism-focused strategy was an agonized game of Whac-A-Mole.

By 2007, al-Qaeda had set up new headquarters in Baqubah, the provincial capital of Diyala province. As they had done the prior year in Ramadi, the jihadists took over not only downtown Baqubah but also the outlying rural areas in the south as well, which ran parallel to the Diyala River and afforded them a verdant canopy to mask their movements and activities. The group's fallback base was in nearby Buhriz, a former Baathist redoubt where it had resorted to publicly executing or kidnapping locals, when not just booting them from their homes. As for Zarqawist "governance," it seized the bread mills outside of the city and rationed food to command the fealty of those it did not dispossess or murder. Buhriz subsequently became the site of one of the most intense battles of the entire Iraq War.

It started in March 2007, when a US Stryker battalion and a paratrooper squadron moved in to take the city, encountering a storm of rocket-propelled grenade (RPG) and sniper fire. The enemy targeted US forces "in small numbers," using "subterfuge," Sergeant 1st Class Benjamin Hanner told the *Washington Post*. "They're controlled, their planning is good, their human intel network and early-warning networks are effective." They were also skillful at using decoys. They laid twenty-seven IEDs in a one-mile expanse of road but ensured that only one out of every three or four bombs was operational. "I have never seen, before or since, organization like that," Shawn McGuire, a staff sergeant, recalled to Michael Gordon and Bernard Trainor. "They were organized. They were well trained. They shot. They could hit things. Instead of just poking around corners and shooting and running, they would bound and maneuver on you. It was almost like watching US soldiers train."

The jihadists also made heavy use of another weapon of choice: house-borne improvised explosive devices—HBIEDs, in the acronym-heavy argot of the US military—which were built into the walls of Buhriz residences and set to explode as soldiers entered. In 2013 ISIS deployed HBIEDs with devastating effect—this time against Iraqi soldiers and policemen in Ninewah, to coerce them into defecting or deserting. Given how easily ISIS sacked Mosul the following year, these attacks clearly weakened an already overwhelmed Iraqi authority.

Long after the battle of Buhriz was over, Diyala saw a return to sectarian warfare, with Shia militias competing against new Sunni Awakening recruits who were committed to opposing the repressive al-Maliki government. The province also represents a crucial battleground for ISIS. Abu Bakr al-Baghdadi belongs to the Bubadri tribe in Diyala. Abu Muhammed al-Adnani, the current ISIS spokesman and contemporary of al-Zarqawi, also said that the jihadist war on Iraq's Shia would be most concentrated there.

LIONS FOR LAMB

The battle for Buhriz also showed the wisdom of Graeme Lamb's attempt to co-opt the less fanatical Sunni insurgents and use them against al-Qaeda. Of all the groups for which this eventually proved feasible, none turned on their former jihadist colleagues with more fervor than the Islamic Army.

In an interview with the *Washington Post* conducted in 2004, not long after the Second Battle of Fallujah, the group's leader, Ismail Jubouri, a Sunni tribesman, insisted that his army was all Iraqi, made up of Sunnis, Shia, and Kurds, and committed only to the expulsion of the occupiers. Maybe, but the

Islamic Army was also the largest group in the Salafist-Baathist insurgency in Iraq, and by April 2007 it had grown so tired of al-Qaeda that it appealed directly to bin Laden to rein in his runaway franchise. When that failed, it appealed to the Americans.

Abu Azzam, an Islamic Army commander, offered to help the US military regain control of the overrun Baghdad belts—especially Abu Ghraib, where Sunnis faced the pincer of al-Qaeda and the Shia militias. Azzam arranged a meeting between US forces and the three thousand volunteers who had signaled their willingness to join an Awakening-style gendarmerie. Among them was a 1920 Revolution Brigades member named Abu Marouf, who had been number seven on the coalition's most-wanted list for Abu Ghraib. Reluctant though they were to collaborate with a top-level terrorist who, not weeks earlier, was hunting and killing their own, the Americans agreed to put Abu Marouf's overtures to the test. After being handed a list of the top-ten al-Qaeda in Iraq operatives in the belt city of Radwaniyah, Abu Marouf returned days later with a cell phone video showing the capture and execution of one of them.

Abu Marouf was backed by the powerful Zobai tribe in the Baghdad region, with which he waged daring raids against the jihadists, further proving his bona fides. In Ameriya, a neighborhood west of Baghdad, an Iraqi volunteer group known as Forsan al-Rafidayn, or Knights of the Two Rivers, called in the coordinates of jihadist targets for American warplanes to bomb.

Eventually, Sahwa went from being a collection of localized civic actions to an institutionalized part of Petraeus's counterinsurgency strategy, with regional Awakening Councils answering directly to the US military and to the Iraqi provincial governments. Initially billed as the Concerned Local Citizens program, it soon became known by the more evocative Sons of Iraq. No doubt leery of seeing a replay of the first Iraqi Security Forces train-and-equip debacle, Petraeus tracked the Awakening volunteers by taking their biometric data and cataloging it on a central database.

While these new political and military forces were key to turning the tide, al-Zarqawi's forces unwittingly helped.

What the al-Qaeda lieutenant Atiyah Abd al-Rahman had once warned al-Zarqawi—that policy must be dominant over militarism—would prove to be the Zarqawists' undoing, after all. The Anbar Awakening was centuries of tribal politics exerting itself against a few years of jihadist domination, bordering on jihadist occupation. Sunnis disliked the Americans, but they hated the black-clad foreigners stealing their land and money, raping their women (and, in some cases, their young girls and boys), and murdering their elders. Like drops of water converging to form streams on a pane of glass, Sahwa happened locally, and in isolation, but soon expanded to become a countrywide movement. This gave Iraq's Sunnis the chance they had missed when they heeded al-Zarqawi's call to boycott elections: the chance for national reconciliation.

"The surge is poorly understood," Ali Khedery, the longest continuously serving American diplomat in Iraq, said. "It was less about a surge of troops and more about a surge of diplomacy with Iraq's national leadership to force it to work together and hammer out political deals. The goal was to buy time for the politicians to reach an accommodation with one another. That's why you saw a reduction in violence by ninety percent from pre-surge highs to the time of provincial election in 2009."

Not coincidentally, that election was largely won in the Sunni provinces by the very tribal figures who had cannibalized al-Qaeda. Al-Rishawi's brother earned a seat on the Anbar Provincial Council. In Diyala and Ninewah provinces, Sunni coalitions likewise came out on top.

AL-QAEDA ON THE ROPES

In a June 2010 Pentagon news briefing, General Raymond T. Odierno claimed that in the same three-month period, US forces had "either picked up or killed 34 out of the top 42 al Qaeda in Iraq leaders. They're clearly now attempting to reorganize themselves. They're struggling a little bit. . . . They've lost connection with [al-Qaeda senior leadership] in Pakistan and Afghanistan."

The franchise was being battered by a combination of JSOC raids, US surge brigades, Sons of Iraq militias, and their own lousy communications. For years, the National Security Agency had been hoovering up telephone chatter between and among jihadists in the field, passing the intercepts along to the CIA and JSOC, which then tracked, arrested, or eliminated them.

"It was Darwinism," said Derek Harvey. "All the guys who were stupid enough to use cell phones in Baghdad kept getting hit, hit, hit, and hit. That was their way of culling the herd, though it had the negative side effect of leaving the smarter and more powerful operatives in place, the ones who were good at internal counterintelligence and buffering access to key leaders. The opaqueness of ISIS today is a reflection of this tradecraft."

Distinct from the surge and the Awakening but equally auspicious was the fact that al-Qaeda's fortunes began to wane in 2007 in the Iraqi imagination. This coincided with the emergence of something resembling a post-Saddam national identity, which transcended sectarianism and fratricidal bloodletting. In 2007, Iraqi-Moroccan singer Shatha Hassoun won *Star Academy*, the Middle East equivalent of *American Idol*, for a heartbreaking rendition of the ballad "Baghdad," which she belted out while wrapped in her nation's flag. Later that year, Iraq took the Asian Cup soccer tournament, beating Saudi Arabia. Al-Qaeda's celebrity, meanwhile, dimmed among its key demographic, young Sunnis. In *Iraq After America*, Joel Rayburn recounts a telling anecdote relayed to him by a police commander in Habbaniyah, a city in Anbar, around that time:

"Stepping from his home on Christmas Eve, 2007, he had been astonished to find the young men of his neighborhood setting off fireworks, with their girlfriends, and drinking alcohol—all distinctly 'Christian' activities that Al Qaeda had banned. The bemused policeman had teased the youths, 'You're celebrating like Christians, but last year you were all Al Qaeda!' The young men had laughed, the police officer later recalled, answering, 'Al Qaeda? That was last year!'"

That the takfiris could be reduced to the level of a passing fad would prove a valuable lesson for the US military's Central Command in Iraq, but a hard one for it to remember when that fad returned with a vengeance five years later.

As al-Qaeda's reputation sagged externally, its internal decision-making was apparently also in crisis. Mullah Nadhim al-Jibouri was originally from the town of Dhuluiya, just north of Baghdad, and had sat on al-Zarqawi's Mujahidin Shura Council. He had then joined the Awakening before moving for a time to Jordan, where a lot of the tribes' Islamic outreach was being conducted remotely. Al-Jibouri appeared on Jordanian national television frequently, denouncing al-Qaeda for its atrocities back home. Then, in the spring of 2011, he returned to Baghdad for reconciliation talks with the al-Maliki government. Al-Jibouri gave an interview to an Iraqi television station. The next day, he was murdered in a drive-by shooting in the western part of the capital.

Several months before his death, he conducted a Skype call with members of the US military. According to one of the officers dialed into the conversation, al-Jibouri confirmed that the creation of the Islamic State of Iraq, the conglomerate announced by al-Masri, was in effect a putsch by al-Qaeda, which sought to dress up its own foreign jihadism in a nationalist costume. But other Sunni insurgents saw through it. The Islamic State of Iraq created a backlash among nationalists who had not been fighting and dying just to see a Zarqawist emirate installed in the Green Zone. Many of these insurgents, furthermore, had only ever accepted the hard-core jihadists on an ad hoc military basis. "[The Islamic State of Iraq] represented al-Qaeda's attempt to hijack the political channel of the Iraqi insurgency," al-Jibouri said.

All totalitarianisms thrive on myths that transcend or erase national boundaries, even ones that begin as expressions of nationalism and then have to retroactively justify their inevitable anschluss of foreign land. Al-Qaeda was no different. For the first years of the war, it had created a powerful dual perception of itself—first, as the vanguard of an Iraqi insurgency committed to seeing the Western occupiers pummeled and expelled, and second, as the guardian of a stolen Sunni patrimony. In its apocalyptic extremism, it erased both perceptions. Petraeus's army had administered the powerful drug of counterinsurgency warfare, which helped Iraq's own antibodies in turn to destroy a deadly foreign pathogen.

But that was with nearly 170,000 American soldiers in Iraq. Today the challenge is far more difficult, because the tribes mistrust Baghdad and, with rare exceptions, they are not inclined to partner with Shia militias against ISIS. "People don't believe in the term 'Awakening' anymore because when the Iraqi government finished using the tribes, it turned against the Sons of Iraq," Dr. Jaber al-Jaberi, a senior political adviser to the former deputy prime minister Rafi al-Issawi, told one of the authors. "It didn't give them rights, it didn't pay their salaries, and it put a lot of them in jail. I don't think the tribes will do another Awakening. What they need is a provincial National Guard, which can be part of the Iraqi Security Forces but from the tribal people, who can work as not army or police but as a militia."

ISIS has taken every precaution against seeing anything of the sort occur again. *Sahwat*, or a practitioner of *sahwa*, is a frequent term of abuse in its propaganda; it boasts of destroying the homes of tribesmen who oppose it and of allowing former Awakening militiamen to "repent" and rejoin ISIS. "Nobody has talked to me about a new Awakening, of forming a national guard," Sheikh Ahmed Abu Risha, al-Rishawi's brother, told the *Guardian* in October 2014. That same month a mass grave filled with 150 bodies was uncovered in a ditch in Ramadi. All the corpses belonged to the Albu Nimr tribe.

6

WITHDRAWAL SYMPTOMS
ISI AND AL-MALIKI WAIT OUT
THE UNITED STATES

The success of Sahwa and the counterinsurgency meant that more jihadists were not only being killed, but also rounded up and jailed in American-run detention facilities in Iraq. The current leader of ISIS and a host of his lieutenants were once prisoners of the United States; they were released either because the United States deemed them negligible security threats or because the al-Maliki government had motives unrelated to the military's security concerns. This failure of foresight, many former US officials have stated, had to do with how these prisoners were identified and categorized once in custody. "Guys we ID'd and reported to be this thing in an organization—we did that because it made it easy to understand them," a former Bush administration official said. "So we'd say, 'Well, he's the emir.' Fuck you, he's the emir. It's the fifth guy standing behind him who counts."

CAMP CALIPHATE

Al-Qaeda in Iraq and its putative umbrella, the Islamic State of Iraq, were not just using US-run prisons as "jihadi universities," according to Major General Doug Stone; they were actively trying to infiltrate those prisons to cultivate new recruits. In 2007, Stone assumed control over the entire detention and interrogation program in Iraq, with an aim to rehabilitate rehabilitation. The internationally publicized and condemned torture of detainees at Abu Ghraib prison left a permanent stain on the occupation and on America's credibility in the war. To make matters worse, detainment facilities had also been used as little more than social networking furloughs for jihadists. Camp Bucca, based in the southern province of Basra, was especially notorious.

According to one US military estimate, Bucca housed 1,350 hardened terrorists amid a general population of 15,000, yet there was little to no oversight as to who was allowed to integrate with whom. Owing to the spike in military operations coinciding with the surge, the detainee number had nearly doubled to 26,000 when Stone took command in 2007.

"Intimidation was weekly, killing was bimonthly," Stone recalled. "It was a pretty nasty place that was out of control when I got there. They used cigarettes and matches to burn down their tents and mattresses, and when we tried to rebuild the tents, they'd just burn them down again. We thought they'd burn the whole goddamn prison down."

Stone introduced a deradicalization program, featuring lectures by moderate Muslim imams who used the Quran and hadith to try to persuade extremists that theirs was a distorted interpretation of Islam. He started to compartmentalize inmates into what were known as Modular Detainee Housing Units, or MDHUs. "Before that, we had guys in thousand-man camp blocs. We used the MDHUs to segregate those who had been intimidated or beaten from those who did the intimidating and beating up."

During his eighteen-month tenure, Stone either led, oversaw, or consulted on more than eight hundred thousand detainee interrogations, observing several "trends" among the AQI population. In a PowerPoint presentation he prepared for Central Command, summarizing his findings, Stone corroborated much of what Mullah Nadhim al-Jibouri had told military officials about this period, namely that foreign fighters were looked on unfavorably as "Iraqis [who were] trying to re-assume leadership roles." Baathists were "attempting to use the ISI banner to regain control of some areas." Jihadists cared more about their hometowns or local areas than they did about global or regional terrorism. Al-Qaeda's use of women and children as suicide bombers had "disgusted" many. Money, not ideology, was the primary motivation for joining the franchise. Finally, its newest emir, Abu Ayyub al-Masri, was "not an influential figure to most." Rather, the "younger, more impressionable detainees" were swayed by the figure of Islamic State of Iraq emir Abu Omar al-Baghdadi (not to be mistaken for his near namesake, the current ISIS leader, Abu Bakr al-Baghdadi).

Early on in his command, Stone noticed a strange phenomenon that pertained exclusively to the jihadist detainees—they would enter Camp Bucca asking to join the al-Qaeda bloc, often with foreknowledge of how the prison worked and how detainees were housed. "Sometimes guys would allow themselves to be caught. Then, in the intake process, they'd ask to be put in a specific compound which housed a lot of the al-Qaeda guys. The jihadists were extremely well organized in Bucca; they arranged where their people slept and where they were moved to based on their Friday night prayers. In fact, one of the large cell areas was nicknamed Camp Caliphate. The more I heard it, the more I began to think, 'Even if they can't get it done, they sure as shit believe they can.'"

Prison culture in Iraq was such that anyone picked up by US forces without any form of identification would give his name and then have his biometric data processed. Iris scans, fingerprints, and DNA samples were collected from all detainees. But often the names given during the intake were fake. "Some of them would have a different name for every interrogation," Stone said. "It was only through biometrics that we were later able to track recidivism rates."

Early on, Stone said, he came across a detainee whose listed surname was Baghdadi. There was nothing inherently eyebrow-raising about that—insurgents often take their city or country of origin (or the city or country they would like people to believe they hail from) as a nom de guerre. But this Baghdadi stood apart from others. Stone said, "His name came up on a list of people that I had. They listed him as a guy who had significant al-Qaeda links. The psychologists rated him as someone who was a really strong wannabe—not in the sociopathic category, but a serious guy who [had] a serious plan. He called himself an imam and viewed himself not as a descendant of Muhammad—we had a few of those at Bucca—but someone with a very strong religious orientation. He was holding Sharia court and conducting Friday services from the platform of being an imam."

This Baghdadi was pensive and hardly a jailhouse troublemaker. "We had hundreds like him in what we termed the 'leadership category,'" Stone said. "We ended up referring to him as an 'irreconcilable,' someone for whom sermons by moderate imams wasn't going to make the slightest difference. So here's the quiet, unassuming guy who had a very strong religious viewpoint, and what does he do? He starts to meet the 'generals.' By that I mean, we had a lot of criminals and guys who were in the Iraqi army who called themselves generals, but they were low-ranking officers in Saddam's army." All the high-level former Iraqi military officials and hard-core Baathists, including Saddam himself, were detained at Camp Cropper, another US-run facility, based in Baghdad International Airport. Cropper was also the processing center for Bucca detainees. "Some of the generals shared Baghdadi's religious perspective and joined the takfiris—big beards and all of that."

Stone said he believes that this man was in fact a decoy sent by the Islamic State of Iraq to pose as the elusive Abu Omar al-Baghdadi to penetrate Bucca and use his time there to mint new holy warriors. "If you were looking to build an army, prison is the perfect place to do it. We gave them health care, dental, fed them, and, most importantly, we kept them from getting killed in combat. Who needs a safe house in Anbar when there's an American jail in Basra?"

A former ISIS member interviewed by the *Guardian* confirmed Stone's appraisal. "We could never have all got together like this in Baghdad, or any-where else," Abu Ahmed told the newspaper. "It would have been impossibly dangerous. Here, we were not only safe, but we were only a few hundred [me-ters] away from the entire al-Qaida leadership."

Abu Ahmed recounted how jihadist detainees scribbled one another's phone numbers and hometowns on the elastic waistbands of their underwear and had a ready-made network upon their release. "When we got out, we called. Everyone who was important to me was written on white elastic. I had their phone numbers, their villages. By 2009 many of us were back doing what we did before we were caught. But this time we were doing it better."

That a decoy al-Baghdadi was recruiting from the ranks of the lower or middle cadres of the former Iraqi army made perfect sense to Richard, the former Pentagon official. "We tend to look at the Iraqi army as a joke, but it was a professional army, a very large army," he said. "What we would consider junior officers—such as captains, majors, warrant officers—we'd be dismissive of those guys in Iraq. In Arab armies, usually those are the guys that are the true professionals. The guys that rise higher than major, the real generals in Saddam's military, have tribal connections, family money. They buy their way in. The mid-grade officers are the ones who matter. Those dudes rocked. How else are they going to make money? Their families are starving, they gotta make money. 'I'll put together a convoy ambush, piece together a couple of rounds into an IED, and these guys will pay me.' Eventually they became pretty successful and they joined up with various insurgent groups, including al-Qaeda."

Around 70 percent of Bucca inmates in 2008 were there for about a year or so. "What this meant in reality," wrote Craig Whiteside, a professor at the Naval War College in Newport, Rhode Island, in an essay for the website War on the Rocks, "is that your average Bucca detainee was incarcerated for a year or two before being released, despite being involved in fairly serious violence against the coalition or Iraqi government. There were even examples of insurgents who were sent to and then released from Bucca multiple times—despite specializing in making roadside bombs."

All of which made it distinctly unpropitious for then–senator and presidential candidate Barack Obama to tell David Petraeus, while on a tour of Iraq in 2008, that if al-Qaeda "has morphed into a kind of mafia then they are not going to be blowing up buildings."

AL-MALIKI'S AMNESTY

Camp Bucca was closed in 2009 in line with the Status of Forces Agreement (SOFA) signed between Washington and Baghdad, which mandated that US-held prisoners either be let go or transferred into Iraqi custody, and that US troops be withdrawn from Iraqi cities by June 30, 2009, handing over all security responsibilities to their Iraqi counterparts. In December 2008, President Bush and Prime Minister al-Maliki signed SOFA in Baghdad at a ceremony more remembered for its violent disruption—an audience member threw his shoes at Bush—than its diplomatic breakthrough.

In reality, by late 2008, US soldiers were already largely confined to the outskirts of Iraq's cities and were acting more as a stopgap on sectarianism than anything else. They protected Sunni and mixed communities from Shia death squads, which operated with state impunity, and they protected the Shia communities from the equally vicious violence of the remaining Sunni insurgency.

SOFA was certainly billed by al-Maliki as a major victory over the United States rather than a mutually agreed compact marking the end of a war. Its implementation date, June 30, 2009, was turned into a national holiday commemorating the "repulsion of foreign occupiers." But it was what the prime minister did with his newfound internment authority that had the direst repercussions for Iraq. "The vast majority of prisoners were just let go, even the crazy Sunni ones," said Joel Rayburn, who has made a close study of SOFA and its consequences for Iraq's security. "Maliki thought that, as of 2008 and 2009, we were just holding innocent people who had been caught up in a sweep. The big problem was, we would capture someone based on intelligence—either signals intelligence or human intelligence—and then not be able to share our methodology with the Iraqis to explain why the captured dude was a bad dude. If it was intelligence where you had to take out all the sources, the Iraqis would say, 'Based on whose say-so?' They'd dismiss it. The entire Iraqi legal system runs on the authority of witness testimony. If you get two witnesses to say something, then it's unshakable."

Plenty of incorrigible al-Qaeda in Iraq jihadists were also let out of jail after the end of US oversight of Iraq's wartime penal system, as the late Anthony Shadid, then a foreign correspondent for the *Washington Post*, reported in March 2009. That month, 106 prisoners were released and headed straight for the Umm al-Qura Mosque in Baghdad—the "Mother of all Battles" mosque Saddam had constructed to commemorate his "victory" in Kuwait, and which had become a citadel of the insurgency. One of the prisoners was Mohammed Ali Mourad, al-Zarqawi's former driver. Despite his likely involvement in two deadly VBIED attacks against a police station, Mourad had been let out of Camp Bucca—even after he was suspected of having founded a new jihadist cell with his fellow detainees. Shadid cited a senior intelligence official at the Iraqi Ministry of Interior who reckoned that 60 percent of freed detainees, be they Sunni or Shia, were getting up to their old habits again, rejoining active insurgencies or Special Groups. "Al-Qaeda is preparing itself for the departure of the Americans," the official said. "And they want to stage a revolution."

Where Baghdad did not rubber-stamp their freedom, the jihadists took matters into their own hands, mounting jailbreaks of their incarcerated associates, often by paying off or intimidating Ministry of Interior personnel to help them.

"It was easy to capture al-Qaeda people," Rayburn said. "We'd get them by the dozen, but they had an entire system for getting their guys back out, either by ensuring that their case was dropped in court or that through bribery they could be released early or, in the last resort, that a physical break of the prison could take place. They even had, at one point in 2008 or 2009, a 'detainee emir'—a guy who was responsible for springing jihadis from the clink—just like they had a 'border emir' who'd coordinate the foreign fighter ratlines into Iraq from Syria. 'Hey, Ahmad's trial is coming up, here's a list of

the key witnesses. Go around, get them to recant or leave, or just kill them.'
Mosul was the worst spot in the country for that. We never got a full handle
on the justice and prison systems up there."

THE AWAKENING PUT TO SLEEP

Al-Maliki may have believed that many US-captured insurgents were innocent, but his definition of the threats to a post-American Iraq derived from his
own political and sectarian biases. Detainees whose only crime was fighting
US forces were not deemed true criminals in need of further incarceration.
Members of the Awakening who had previously fought Iraqi Security Forces
or Shia militias were not subject to the same magnanimous gloss on rehabilitation.

Long-dormant criminal cases against the Sons of Iraq remained open
even after the suspects had been deputized as state-sanctioned militiamen.
No longer useful to al-Maliki, and with ever-diminishing US protection, they
were instead harassed and bullied by the government they had served. Many
were also arrested on spurious "terrorism" grounds. "Sunnis always talk about
the release of prisoners who were convicted illegally or extrajudicially," a former Iraqi government official said. "The dropping of all these terror cases is a
main demand of them now."

Conditions were especially grim in Diyala province, which had been pac-
ified at great expense in the preceding years and yet fell into chaos again after
the surge. In August 2008, the prime minister had dispatched personnel from
the Iraqi Special Operations Forces—one of the few effective counterterrorism units in the Iraqi security apparatus—into the office of the provincial
governor of Diyala to arrest both a local councilman and the president of the
University of Diyala, a Sunni.

By the summer of 2009, the 3rd Stryker Brigade of the US 2nd Infantry
Division had returned to Diyala, where it spent a year observing the crackdown on Sunni political power. It was not enough that al-Qaeda in Iraq was
hunting Sunnis who had repudiated it; anyone affiliated with the Awakening
was targeted for arrest by the state on dubious or nonexistent evidence. Such
prejudicial justice didn't apply to Shia prisoners, many of whom were released
back into society with no questions asked. So, at any rate, claimed the Diyala
governor, who left Iraq in 2012 after a systematic campaign of intimidation

by al-Maliki–appointed officials following the murder of his press secretary. More ominous, the Stryker brigade found, the central government was no longer paying the salaries of Awakening members. After a month or two without pay, they would be liable to quit or even return to the arms of the insurgency that they had previously repudiated.

The problem was no better in Anbar. Shadid interviewed Colonel Saad Abbas Mahmoud, the police chief of al-Karmah, northeast of Fallujah. Mahmoud claimed to have been nearly assassinated twenty-five times, by means crude and creative. "He was delivered a Quran rigged with explosives buried in the pages between its green covers," Shadid reported, "then, less than two weeks later, his dish of dulaymiya, a mix of chicken, lamb, a slab of fat, and rice, was poisoned, sending him to the hospital for ten days. When he got out, two bombs detonated near his house in Fallujah." Mahmoud was in charge of three thousand Sons of Iraq in al-Karmah, who were paid a measly $130 per month—or were supposed to be. They had not received their salaries in three months.

The original plan for the Awakening was to integrate these volunteers into a more official form of government service, such as hiring them to work in state ministries. The Iraqi agency tasked with transitioning them was called the Implementation and Follow-up Committee for National Reconciliation. While it is true that, by 2010, nearly thirty thousand volunteers had moved from being watchmen into certified candidates for state employment, they still had to compete for government jobs, many of which were extremely low-level. Al-Maliki showed little interest in carrying forward a program originally instigated by the United States.

Mullah Nadhim al-Jibouri claimed before he was assassinated that as of mid-2010, a full 40 percent of al-Qaeda was composed of deserters or defectors from the Sons of Iraq. This figure may be exaggerated, but it was certainly plausible given two key events that year that helped deepen the fissures reemerging between the tribes and the central government.

The first was Iraq's national election, which al-Maliki did not win as easily as he had expected to, and technically did not win at all. The second was the US departure from the country, which followed the fraying of Washington's ties to the Sunni tribes, a relationship that had been the most difficult to cultivate and whose deterioration would ultimately spell the return of the Zarqawists under a revitalized and much-expanded organization called ISIS.

THE STRONGMAN'S SECOND TERM

The US assessment of al-Maliki's dictatorial tendencies was such that, even before the polls opened, Odierno feared a defeat for the incumbent might result in a putsch to retain power. Many Sunnis say that is exactly what happened anyway.

Even before the election, Iraq's Accountability and Justice Commission—the sequel bureaucracy to the CPA's de-Baathification Commission—banned more than five hundred candidates from running for parliament because of their links to the Baath Party. Naturally, the majority of these were Sunnis and part of the Iraqiya alliance led by former interim prime minister Ayad Allawi's faction. (Allawi, despite being a Shia, was seen as the mainstream Sunni electorate's best hope for regaining the premiership.) Odierno, with good reason, saw that behind this broad-brush campaign of delegitimization lurked the hand of Iran's Quds Force.

For one thing, the Accountability and Justice Commission was headed by two men of dubious records themselves. The first was Ahmed Chalabi, the Shiite politician who rose to prominence within Iraq's western diaspora. He would become, in effect, the principal whisperer in Washington for regime change in Baghdad, despite having been convicted in absentia for embezzlement and theft by a Jordanian military court in 1992. Since the US invasion, many in the US military had come to view Chalabi as a con artist with blood on his hands, not least because he enjoyed an incredibly close relationship with Qassem Suleimani, the commander of the Quds Force—the organization that, apart from al-Qaeda, had been responsible for the most violence and instability in Iraq. To make matters worse, Chalabi's co-head on the commission was an actual agent of that violence and instability. Faisal al-Lami stood accused by the US military of being involved in a Shia death squad responsible for killing American soldiers. Al-Lami had, in fact, been detained for a year after he was implicated in a 2008 bombing in Sadr City, perpetrated by the League of the Righteous, the same militia that killed five US servicemen in Karbala in 2007.

That two Iraqis seen as factotums of Tehran sat in judgment of the viability of Sunni parliamentary candidates was certainly enough to trigger alarm at the US embassy in Baghdad, then presided over by newly installed ambassador Christopher Hill. Among the candidates the commission disqualified was Salih al-Mutlaq, a Sunni who had *already been* elected to parliament before without raising eyebrows about his supposed Baathist past but whom al-Maliki now accused of conspiring secretly with Izzat al-Douri and Mohammed Younis al-Ahmed, the two Saddamists plotting terrorist attacks in Iraq from their safe haven in Syria. Ultimately, US pressure was all that kept runaway de-Baathification from undermining the election before it occurred.

Despite preelection skulduggery, the vote went smoothly on March 7, 2010, with 60 percent turnout and little reported violence throughout the country. The one person for whom it did not go so smoothly was al-Maliki.

Allawi's Iraqiya bloc won two more seats than did al-Maliki's State of Law Coalition, holding a 91-to-89 margin of victory. Iraqiya even performed remarkably well in the Shiite south, winning some two hundred thousand votes. The new parliament had been increased by fifty seats, from 275 to 325, but the addition of legislators belied the near-categorical housecleaning that the election represented. There were 262 seats that went to first-time candidates, meaning that almost the equivalent of the previous parliament had been sacked. By all accounts, al-Maliki's polling had been way off. He would need to form a government by partnering with any of the other major blocs, which would perforce hinder any further consolidation of power. Defeat unleashed his paranoia in grand fashion.

Despite the election being deemed fair by UN monitors, al-Maliki accused the body of conspiring with Iraq's electoral commission to oust him. It was all a neo-Baathist plot, abetted by the United States, and he demanded a recount.

Al-Maliki used every means at his disposable to push the election toward power for his government. Chalabi and al-Lami's commission prevailed upon Iraq's judiciary to nullify eight victors for their alleged ties to the old regime.

According to Article 76 of Iraq's constitution, the bloc that wins the most seats in an election was entitled to the first opportunity to form a government. To circumvent this reading, al-Maliki instructed Medhat al-Mahmoud, now the chief justice of Iraq's highest court—and one of the jurists identified by a US military investigation as a conspirator in the Jadriya Bunker affair—to answer a question that had already been answered by the constitution's framers. Namely, did the "largest bloc" text in Article 76 refer to the one with the most elected seats or to one that could stitch together the biggest bloc *after* the election? The verdict delivered by Judge Medhat was the one al-Maliki had sought in bringing the case to court. The prime minister who sniffed conspiracy everywhere now stood accused of engineering a slippery and self-serving reinterpretation of Iraq's legal foundation for the purpose of his own conspiracy.

Neglected in this imaginative reinterpretation of a document that was just over five years old was the fact that a prominent framer of the constitution, the Shiite sheikh Humam Hammoudi, had once taken to the nation's airwaves to specify that "largest bloc" referred to election results, not to opportunistic horse-trading after the fact. (The entire reason for voting in blocs, after all, had been to rack up the highest number of seats at the polls.) The verdict was delivered the same day as the electoral commission certified Iraqiya's win.

The following day, Iraq's president, Jalal Talabani, flew to Tehran for negotiations between the State of Law Coalition and the Iraqi National Alliance. Iraqiya was to be stopped at all costs, even if it meant that rival Shia parties had to work together under the supervision and blessing of their foreign state sponsor, Iran. The new government would be decided, at last, through these negotiations and through more judicial maneuvering. Al-Maliki eventually formed a national unity government that also included Kurds and Iraqiya—but with the incumbent returning as prime minister.

Odierno saw how flagrant manipulation and Iranian meddling in a sovereign state's election would be viewed by Iraq's Sunnis. So did Ali Khedery, the former US diplomat who arrived in the Green Zone in 2003, and served as Ryan Crocker's aide during the surge and Awakening period. Khedery maintains today that the US handling of the 2009 election only exacerbated Sunni grievances in Iraq, convincing many that they were being purposefully kept from power. The history of the postelection period did little to dispel this assumption. Ambassador Hill had likened an Iraqiya win to the return of the Afrikaners in South Africa. Vice President Joe Biden, whom President Obama put in charge of the administration's Iraq policy, is recorded as having said, "Maliki hates the goddamn Sunnis," but Biden nevertheless acceded to the return of this sectarian incumbent. "I know one guy, one of the most peaceful, moderate Iraqis you can imagine," Khedery said. "He had been a bottom-level Baathist, one of Saddam's engineers. He says, 'Look, I was never sectarian before. I never liked Iran, we fought a war with them. I love my country, I'm a nationalist. But I've become sectarian now because there's nowhere else for a moderate or a secularist to be. We're losers. I've become as sectarian as the people I used to hate.'"

GOODBYE, AND GOOD LUCK

As much as the consequences of the surge have been debated in US policy circles, so too has the wisdom or lack thereof of a categorical troop withdrawal from Iraq in 2011. Did this enable the easy reconstitution of the Islamic State of Iraq? Could it have been avoided with more fleet-footed or energetic diplomacy by the Obama administration? The administration had intended to renew and extend SOFA, but had come to the negotiating table late in the day and with an air of being even less interested in maintaining a postwar US garrison than was the supposedly hard-bargaining al-Maliki.

There was actually very little debate within the ranks of both the US and Iraqi militaries about the necessity of extending SOFA. Obama's then–chairman of the Joint Chiefs of Staff, Admiral Mike Mullen, had advocated leaving a minimum of sixteen thousand troops. The figure was deemed far too high by the White House's national security team. "I'll bet you my vice presidency Maliki will extend SOFA," Biden had said. But al-Maliki did not, owing to the fact that the minuscule troop number Obama ultimately decided on—3,500 personnel permanently stationed in Iraq, with 1,500 more rotated in at regular intervals for training Iraqi forces and conducting counterterrorism operations—wasn't worth the cost of wrangling with his own deeply divided parliament, which had to ratify any bilateral agreement.

What the debate over military disengagement obscures is that the United States withdrew politically from Iraq even sooner, and arguably with more lasting consequence for the country's future.

Colonel Rick Welch ran the national tribal leader program for the US military during the Awakening and helped transfer the responsibility for continued Sunni and Shia tribal outreach over to the State Department. What he found was a US foreign service ill-equipped to ensure that the Sons of Iraq remained on the right side of the conflict. As Welch recounted, "The joke of the day at the embassy was: 'If you want to know what the embassy is doing, go to the [commissary] on Thursday, and look at how much alcohol was on the shelf and compare that to how much was there by Saturday.'

"It was as if Iraq wasn't still a conflict or war zone. The time when it needed the keenest and sharpest minds that understood the country was in that preelection and immediate postelection period because Maliki pulled a fast one with his supreme court. And the Sons of Iraq, the tribal leaders, would complain about what he was doing. They called it the 'purge.' Yet the State

Department's talking point was, 'We're really sorry to hear that, but Iraq is a sovereign country. We cannot interfere.'

"I remember this moderate tribal leader, with this look of incredulity on his face. 'You cannot interfere?' he asked. 'Yes, we can't interfere.' 'Didn't I just see President Obama authorize the bombing of Libya? Wasn't that a sovereign country? And didn't I hear President Obama interfere in Egypt and say that Mubarak had to go? And didn't I hear the president intervene in Syria and say that Assad has to go? Don't you have sanctions against Iran, another sovereign country? Didn't you invade our country and aren't you still here? It's not that you can't intervene—we've watched you intervene all around us to remove long-standing dictators. What we hear you say is that you won't intervene to stop a rising dictator right here and restore the democracy you brought to us.'"

Undermining Obama's rosy prognosis in 2011—that Iraq was a democratic success—Salih al-Mutlaq, al-Maliki's deputy prime minister, had gone on CNN and said that Iraq was spiraling into "dictatorship." Al-Mutlaq had been one of the early candidates for parliament barred by the Accountability and Justice Commission and branded a terror accomplice by the man he now accused, in turn, of running "a one-party show and one-man show. Yes, al-Maliki is the worst dictator we have ever seen in our history." The United States, al-Mutlaq charged, was blind and stupid to think that it had the kind of leverage over Baghdad that it believed itself to. "The whole set of the government, from the president to the prime minister," he said, "was the decision of Iran."

To counter this criticism from his own cabinet, al-Maliki ordered tanks to surround both al-Mutlaq's home and the homes of Rafi al-Issawi, now the finance minister, and his vice president, Tariq al-Hashimi, a man known for offering his unvarnished opinions to the Americans about how their experiment in democracy-building was faring in Iraq. Al-Hashimi had boycotted the January 2005 election, against the pleas of Robert Ford, then one of the few Arabic-fluent diplomats working for the State Department in Baghdad. He also had correctly explained the societal driver of pro-Zarqawist sentiment among Sunnis, and it was not for any sneaking ideological sympathy. Al-Hashimi lost three siblings, two brothers and one sister, to al-Qaeda's terrorism before becoming vice president. Yet still al-Maliki considered him a terrorist. On December 18, al-Hashimi fled to Iraqi Kurdistan after al-Maliki's security forces held his plane on the tarmac at Baghdad International Airport while he awaited departure. Al-Hashimi was allowed to fly off, but three of his bodyguards were detained for "suspected terrorist activity." (One later died in custody.) The next day, an arrest warrant was issued for al-Hashimi himself. He remained in exile in Iraqi Kurdistan before moving to Turkey. In 2012 he was sentenced to death by hanging in absentia by a judiciary widely perceived as having acted under al-Maliki's personal instructions.

These and other crackdowns on Sunni politicians precipitated Arab Spring–style protests in Sunni areas throughout Iraq—and a counterresponse from al-Maliki, which only aggravated them.

On April 23, 2013, three days after Iraq's provincial elections were held, the Iraqi Security Forces razed one protest site in Hawija, near Kirkuk. They claimed to be searching the site for the killer of an Iraqi soldier, and although stories differ as to what happened next, the aftermath is not in dispute: twenty Sunnis were killed and more than one hundred were injured. The Hawija violence led to Sunni violence throughout Iraq, targeting police stations and army checkpoints. The speaker of Iraq's parliament, Osama al-Nujaifi, called for al-Maliki's resignation in response to the carnage. Clashes spread to Mosul and Baghdad, where Sunni mosques were blown up and Iraqi security officials were yanked from their cars and murdered, and then to Shia cities, where al-Qaeda–style terrorist attacks took place. Sunnis began calling for an armed national revolution, agitating for al-Douri's Naqshbandi Army and Sahwa militias.

BREAKING THE WALLS

Baghdad had shattered the confidence of Iraq's Sunnis who had trusted that the routing of al-Qaeda would lead to greater enfranchisement and fair treatment by a Shia-led government. Now al-Qaeda would spring its cohort out of the clink. In 2012 and 2013, it executed the Breaking the Walls campaign, characterized by eight daring attacks on Iraqi prisons, all designed to spring former operatives and thus to replenish the ranks of the organization.

The growth of the ISIS campaign was separated into four distinct phases, according to Jessica Lewis McFate of the Institute for the Study of War. The first phase saw four prison attacks, including one against the Tasfirat prison in Tikrit in September 2012, an operation that freed one hundred inmates, nearly half of whom were believed to be al-Qaeda operatives slated for state execution. The second phase targeted locations along the Green Line—the demarcation point between Iraq proper and the Kurdistan Regional Government's semiautonomous zone—no doubt designed to capitalize on roiling political and economic tensions between Erbil and Baghdad. The third phase saw the return of VBIED sorties in Baghdad and its belts, targeting Iraqi Security Forces and Shia civilian areas. Here the jihadists sought to exploit another widening gulf in Iraqi society: that between the al-Maliki government and the Sunni protestors who, inspired by the Arab Spring but mainly driven by domestic turmoil, had taken to the streets of Fallujah and elsewhere. The fourth and final phase began in mid-May 2013 and was meant to terrorize the Shia, clearly to precipitate another sectarian civil war and the return of Shia militias. Almost half of the VBIED waves during Breaking the Walls, Lewis McFate found, occurred in this phase, coinciding with the Sunni protests, which culminated in the most successful jailbreak of the entire campaign: the July 2013 freeing of five hundred inmates from Abu Ghraib prison. According to the Obama administration, suicide bombings in Iraq averaged between five and ten per month in the years 2011 and 2012; during the last three months of Breaking the Walls, that number jumped to thirty per month.

By the end of the summer, more than seven hundred Iraqis were being killed each month. The conditions for Sunni rejectionism turning in force to jihadist extremism had returned. At the end of December, in response to an ISIS killing spree, al-Maliki deployed security forces to Ramadi to put an end to the antigovernment protests. They withdrew in the face of tribal resistance. A number of actors were involved in the initial sack of Fallujah on New Year's Day 2014, not just ISIS, among them the Naqshbandi Army, the Army of the Mujahidin, and 1920 Revolution Brigades. But as it had done in Syria the prior year, ISIS set up an Islamic court that same month and harassed and assassinated its erstwhile allies. The complete ISIS takeover of Fallujah was complete by June 2014. By late August, the organization routed the Army of the Mujahidin in the latter's stronghold of al-Karma to the east of Fallujah city, allowing it to declare a new "Fallujah Province." "Maliki pushed the Sunnis so far that they had to rise up," Rick Welch said. "They tried to get reforms, but they couldn't. Tribal honor was on the line and revenge thinking was on the line. Maliki made this crisis."

7

ASSAD'S PROXY
SYRIA AND AL-QAEDA

ISIS's resurgence in Iraq coincided with its takeover of a large swath of territory in Syria, a fact that Bashar al-Assad's regime had tried to exploit to claim victimhood at the hands of international terrorism. The Assad regime's absurd claim was proven false by the uncovering of undeniable forensic evidence that Syria helped keep al-Qaeda in Iraq afloat prior to the US military withdrawal. Abd Sattar al-Rishawi, the Anbar Awakening leader, told the *New York Times* before he was murdered by Zarqawists, "This is all Syria's doing. Syria is doing bad things."

It was. Al-Assad has managed to unite a chorus of varied global accusers—including the US military, the Sons of Iraq, his own former diplomats and security officials, innumerable Syrian rebels, and even the al-Maliki government—in affirming and condemning his sponsorship of the very jihadism he claims is devouring his own country. The proliferation of ISIS in both Iraq and Syria cannot be understood without examining Damascus's long-running collaboration with its forerunner organization.

HAFEZ'S ISLAMISM

We have seen how secular Iraqi Baathism has had a habit, in the last century, of making an accommodation with Islamism in order to preempt its revolutionary potential. The Syrian counterpart was no different.

The Muslim Brotherhood uprising in Syria, which began in 1976 and was brutally suppressed in 1982 by forces loyal to Hafez al-Assad, had tended to obscure the regime's strategic alliance with a host of Sunni Islamist parties and paramilitaries. These alliances were premised on mutually beneficial geopolitical needs: chiefly, confronting the United States and Israel. As scholar Eyal Zisser has noted, by the mid-1990s, Hafez al-Assad was no longer the dread nemesis of those seeking a marriage between mosque and state because "Damascus started to see the Islamists as perhaps the only possible means by which to enhance its regional standing, gain influence in neighboring countries, and bring domestic tranquility to Syria itself."

When the elder al-Assad died in 2000 and his London-trained ophthalmologist son ascended to the presidency, this arrangement intensified. Up until recently, for example, despite a national Syrian law banning the Brotherhood as a party or organization, Damascus had no qualms about hosting Khaled Mashal, the chairman of the politburo of Hamas. Today the regime relies overwhelmingly on the paramilitary assets of Hezbollah and Iran's Revolutionary Guards Corps—both US-designated terrorist entities—to continue its grueling war of attrition against a legion of domestic and foreign-backed insurgents. These of course consist of Islamist and jihadist rebels, some of whom are former prisoners of the regime, if not former accomplices of it in Iraq.

Even before the United States toppled Saddam, al-Assad had embarked on a policy of facilitating foreign fighters' movement into Iraq to destabilize the occupation. An office situated across from the US embassy in Damascus helped would-be insurgents book bus travel to the Syria-Iraq border. In 2007, US Central Command announced that it had captured a "Saddam Fedayeen leader involved in setting up training camps in Syria for Iraqi and foreign fighters," although the individual's name was not released.

That same year, US forces killed Muthanna, a man designated as al-Qaeda's emir for the Syrian-Iraqi border region, in the city of Sinjar. According to Major General Kevin Bergner, the spokesman for coalition forces, Muthanna acted as "a key facilitator of the movement of foreign terrorists" from the one country into the other. As was the case with other high-value targets, Muthanna possessed a cache of useful intelligence, which became known as the Sinjar Records. A study published in 2008 by the Combating Terrorism Center at West Point (CTC) analyzed these records and found that more than half of 376 foreign fighters in Iraq listed their occupation as "suicide bomber," indicating yet again the expendable nature of non-Iraqi jihadists to al-Qaeda in Iraq. It also underscored one reason why sending such cannon fodder to their deaths abroad was not seen as potentially self-defeating for Damascus. The Sinjar Records also confirmed that foreign fighters were entering Iraq from the Syrian province of Deir Ezzor, typically using the Syrian border town of Albu Kamal, which lies adjacent to the Iraqi city of Qa'im—where al-Zarqawi established his headquarters after fleeing Fallujah in 2004 and where a proto-Awakening got started the following year. The flow, the CTC concluded, came in three distinct "waves."

The first began shortly before the invasion, when Saddam exhorted Arabs from around the region to join in the forthcoming insurgency. It fielded a number of Bedouin tribesmen hailing from Deir Ezzor and Hasaka, as well as other jihadists egged on by Sheikh Ahmad Kuftaro, Syria's mufti, who wasted no time in lending state legitimacy to the incendiary sermons wafting out of mosques and madrassas in his country. "In border villages and cities," the CTC study stated, "houses were donated for volunteers to live in while local notables—both religious and tribal figures—organized transportation and accommodations for them in Iraq. According to local sources, hundreds of fighters passed through Albu Kamal and [Hasaka] just before the US invasion, leading to rapid increases in the cost of housing, food, and weapons—all of which greatly benefited the locals. The Syrian authorities monitored the flow, but made no move to stop it."

The second wave arrived with the First Battle of Fallujah, when the al-Assad regime's new show of trying to stop the ratlines was eclipsed by rampant corruption: Syrian Mukhabarat officers were bribed into letting Syrians cross the border anyway.

The third wave of foreign fighters followed the 2005 Cedar Revolution, which brought an end to Syria's military occupation of Lebanon and was prompted by popular revulsion at the assassination of former Lebanese prime minister Rafik Hariri, for which a UN tribunal indicted members of Hezbollah, al-Assad's terrorist ally.

"CALL US"

Al-Assad, of course, has always denied orchestrating or coordinating the jihadist activities in Iraq in any way, and he has even played up his supposed cooperation with Washington in the war on terror. Yet many of his regime's former officials now allege that his state sponsorship of al-Qaeda was hardly a secret and was quite clearly premised on two separate but related motives. The dictator had hoped it would be a severe warning to the Bush administration after Iraq, and as Jason Burke's *The 9/11 Wars* demonstrates, he also wanted to divert Islamists' attention away from his regime by keeping them preoccupied next door.

"For Assad the problem was much bigger than America invading Arab countries for regime change," Bassam Barabandi, a former diplomat at the Syrian embassy in Washington, D.C., said. After the 2011 uprising, Barabandi covertly helped hundreds of dissidents and activists obtain passports for relatives trying to flee a war-ravaged country. "Assad understood that part of Bush's strategy in Iraq was to end minority rule of Sunnis ruling over majority Shiite. He feared that he would be next. From then on, he started to work with mujahidin; he did everything possible to convince the Americans, 'Don't come after me, otherwise I'll send more terrorists next door to kill your soldiers.'"

For about five years, the US reply to this ultimatum was mainly diplomatic, and al-Assad sometimes acceded to Washington's demands, lending the impression that he was dismantling the jihadist networks on his soil. It was all a feint, Barabandi said, part of the strategy to use Syria's facilitation of terrorism as a bargaining chip. The former diplomat described for us how Sabawi Ibrahim al-Hassan al-Tikriti, Saddam's half brother who had been hiding in Syria and was wanted by both the Americans and Iraqis, finally came to be handed over. "The Americans went to Assad in 2005 and asked for his help in catching Sabawi," Barabandi said. "He was on the border of Syria and Iraq, and he was leading the Baathist terrorists. Bashar was of course hosting him. Practically, the Americans and Iraqis were asking for his help: 'We will try to improve our relations with you in return.' Assad agreed. Imad Moustapha [the Syrian ambassador to the United States at the time] was in the meeting in Damascus with the US undersecretary of state, where this was discussed and decided. Imad told us the story. In fact, he told everyone this story. After two days, Assef Shawkat," Barabandi said, referring to al-Assad's own brother-in-law and Syria's top intelligence officer, "contacted Imad to tell him to tell his American friends that Sabawi would be in such-and-such area of Iraq. They informed the Americans exactly where he was, and they captured him."

Tony Badran, an expert on Syria at the Washington-based Foundation for Defense of Democracies, has characterized al-Assad's underwriting of al-Qaeda as a form of attention-seeking. "It's about the regime's conception of its role and position in the region," Badran said. "It believes that its longevity lies in being perceived as an indispensable regional power, and so its foreign policy with respect to the West is: 'You have to talk to us. Just pick up the phone and talk to us; it doesn't matter what's discussed, we just want to hear from you.' For Assad, the ability to boast that the United States is an interlocutor is a matter of power projection. It lets him pretend that he's the linchpin for Arab-Israeli peace or a real force for counterterrorism. He creates the problems he then oh-so-magnanimously offers to solve."

Badran mentioned, as an example, the curious case of an Islamist Kurdish cleric named Sheikh Mahmoud Gul Aghasi, who more commonly went by the name Abu al-Qaqa. Having called for US soldiers to be "slaughtered like cattle" in Iraq, al-Qaqa was allowed to preach openly in Aleppo—following his brief arrest by the regime after 9/11—despite his loud championship of Syria's transformation into a Sharia-compliant Islamic state. As recounted by journalist Nicholas Blanford, who interviewed the cleric in 2003, al-Qaqa organized "festivals denouncing the [United States] and Jews. Many of these festivals were attended by Syrian officials, and some of al-Qaqa's followers grew suspicious of their leader. Those suspicions hardened when it was learned that al-Qaqa had delivered a list of Wahhabis, individuals influenced by the Saudi version of Islamic Salafism, to the state security agency. Was al-Qaqa playing a double game, preaching jihad while handing over jihadists to the authorities?"

Blanford argued that al-Qaqa was tolerated by the regime so long as he stayed in the terrorist export business; forswearing attacks at home was the price for running jihadists. This was why, on the wall of al-Qaqa's mosque in Aleppo, there was a sign displaying "a bomb with a red line drawn through it."

The Syrian Mukhabarat's relationship with this demagogue was hardly al-Assad's best-kept secret. "Abu al-Qaqa was a strange phenomenon," said Muhammad Habash, a former Syrian MP who, in 2008, headed the deradicalization program at the Sednaya prison in Damascus. "He was preaching about jihad in a mosque situation in one of Aleppo's most crowded neighborhoods. In the Sakhour mosque, he not only preached about jihad, but he held military training for young people heading to Iraq. With a sermon like that, an imam would usually spend the rest of his life in prison, along with his family and relatives and those who attended the sermon."

Habash said that he first met al-Qaqa in 2006:

"I was giving a lecture at the Islamic Research Centre and someone stood up to talk. He spoke with such charisma, so I asked to meet him afterward in my office. I told him, 'I would like to know you, you have such a strong presence when you speak.' He was accompanied by two young men who were listening attentively to what he was saying, and he was engaging them in the talk. He seemed to have strong leadership skills. I told him of my plans in Aleppo since it was announced as the new capital of Islamic culture in that year. I had a project for Islamic reform, and I wanted the help of someone like him in Aleppo. We both agreed that there was some room for such activism under this regime. When he left, someone came out and told me he was Abu al-Qaqa, and asked why I talked to him. I did not believe that. He was wearing a suit and tie, and had a tidy beard. His presence gave no indication of his infamous violent side."

Following that initial encounter, Habash met with al-Qaqa regularly. "He spoke to me proudly about his role in preventing the Americans from entering Syria. He was a tool for the regime, and in the end he was shot." A gunman opened fire on al-Qaqa outside the cleric's Imam Mosque in Aleppo in September 2007. Most eyes fell on the regime itself, although Sheikh Samir Abu Khashbeh, an aide to al-Qaqa, claimed that the shooter apprehended after the assassination said he had done it "because he [al-Qaqa] was an agent of the Americans." This was a contingency that seemed remote at the time but was a likely cover story concocted by Syrian intelligence to cover its own tracks.

Yet another famous case was that of Shaker al-Absi, the Palestinian leader of an al-Qaeda–linked militant group called Fatah al-Islam, who had also worked with al-Zarqawi in planning the murder of USAID worker Laurence Foley in 2002. "Shaker al-Absi was the mastermind for the Foley assassination, which was put together in Damascus," said David Schenker, formerly the Pentagon's top policy aide on the Levant and now the director of the Program on Arab Politics at the Washington Institute for Near East Policy. "I am one hundred percent convinced that it was planned in Syria with Assad's involvement, tolerance, permission, and support. In fact, I don't think there's any debate about that anymore. The smoking gun isn't Zarqawi, it's al-Absi, who was in Syria, and then went to Jordan to oversee the assassination."

The Jordanians sentenced both al-Zarqawi and al-Absi to death in absentia and requested the latter's extradition from Damascus. Al-Assad refused and claimed to have put al-Absi in prison. "According to reports in the Arabic press, he was subsequently released and ended up running a terrorist training camp for al-Qaeda operatives going into Iraq from Syrian territory," Schenker said. Regardless of what happened to him in Syria, he was clearly free to leave the country in 2007, because he led Fatah al-Islam's armed uprising against the Lebanese Armed Forces (LAF) in the Nahr al-Bared Palestinian refugee camp. Although the LAF put down the rebellion, al-Absi was never apprehended. Fatah al-Islam later posted to its website that al-Absi had returned to Syria, where he may have been killed by the security services. According to Schenker, he had in fact been "exported" to Lebanon in 2007 and maintained ties to the Syrian Mukhabarat throughout the Nahr al-Bared siege. "How do we know that? There was a Lebanese [pro-Assad] cleric named Fathi Yakan from the Tripoli area who went several times into the camp to serve as an intermediary to contact Absi. A week or so later, he showed up in pictures with Assad in Damascus."

THE ASSASSINATION OF ABU GHADIYAH

Even before the Iraq War, the United States had redoubled its efforts to garner human and signals intelligence, related to a host of national security threats, in the Levant. Al-Assad, after all, was known to possess extensive stockpiles of chemical weapons and was pursuing a nuclear weapons program with the assistance of both North Korea and Iran. In 2002, when tracking the movements of international jihadists became the Pentagon's priority, Secretary of Defense Donald Rumsfeld authorized Joint Special Operations Command (JSOC) to conduct clandestine missions in countries with which the United States was not at war, such as Lebanon and Syria. To do this, JSOC would rely on its own elite team of spy-commandos. They were called Task Force Orange. And because Washington did not have official diplomatic relations with Damascus until 2005, Orange had to conduct itself discreetly. In his book, *Relentless Strike: The Secret History of Joint Special Operations Command*, Sean Naylor writes that in Syria, "the personnel Orange sent in were unarmed and were largely commercial cover operatives, meaning they posed as businessmen and had what a special mission unit veteran called 'established presence' in the region. . . . During the middle of the decade, Orange had fewer than a dozen personnel operating under a commercial cover, about half a dozen of whom were conducting the Syrian operations."

Task Force Orange was deployed into Syria even before the first boots touched down on Iraqi soil in 2003 to perform reconnaissance and surveil

Iraq's border. Its remit soon shifted to trying to uncover evidence that Saddam's own WMD program had been smuggled into Syria prior to the US
invasion, and to mapping the network of foreign jihadists being garrisoned
next door for war against the American occupiers. As Naylor notes, Orange
operatives working closely with the National Security Agency, the US signals
intelligence arm, could use a jihadist's IP address to uncover the whereabouts
of his safe house in Syria. From there they could geolocate and track his daily
routine: which mosque he attended, which people he met, which transport
lines he traveled. In more daring circumstances, Orange operatives would raid
a safe house and make copies of any printed or digital material the jihadist
kept in his possession, or leave their own recording devices to spy on him in
his own home. When the Iraq insurgency kicked off, the intelligence obtained
by these methods would be dressed up as the yield of JSOC raids inside Iraq
and used to try to shame al-Assad into rolling up the foreign fighter networks
he always denied existed in Syria—because they were almost always there
with the complicity and connivance of his Mukhabarat.

Indeed, most of the insurgents Syria had funneled into Iraq were hosted
under the auspices of Assef Shawkat, the aforementioned Syrian intelligence
chief and brother-in-law of the dictator, who was killed in a stunning assassination plot in Damascus in 2012. That plot also wiped out the regime's "crisis
management cell," the ad hoc security committee tasked with quashing the
Syrian revolution. Though it was originally thought to have been the work
of Syrian rebels who infiltrated the cell, new evidence emerged suggesting
that this assassination may have been an inside job, waged by Iranian-backed
hard-liners against Shawkat, who advocated negotiating with the al-Assad
opposition.

Shawkat's history gives no indication of his being a pushover. One of
his jihadist charges was a man known as Badran Turki Hishan al-Mazidih,
or Abu Ghadiyah, an Iraqi from Mosul whom the US Treasury Department
designated as a terrorist in February 2008. Abu Ghadiyah, the Treasury Department alleged, had been appointed AQI's commander of logistics in 2004
by al-Zarqawi and had subsequently taken orders from Abu Ayyub al-Masri
upon the Jordanian's death. "As of the spring of 2007, Abu Ghadiyah facilitated the movement of AQI operatives into Iraq via the Syrian border," the
designation stated, while also listing and sanctioning the rest of Abu Ghadiyah's Syria-based network. According to a State Department cable, subsequently published by WikiLeaks, "Bashar al-Asad was well aware that his

brother-in-law ... had detailed knowledge of the activities of AQI facilitator Abu Ghadiyah."

Abu Ghadiyah was evidently in the family business. His "right-hand man," Ghazy Fezzaa Hishan, also known as Abu Faysal, was his cousin; Hishan resided in Zabadani, a city northeast of Damascus known for being an important concourse for smuggling and transporting weapons from Syria into Lebanon. As of September 2006, both Abu Ghadiyah and Abu Faysal, according to the Treasury, "planned to use rockets to attack multiple Coalition forces outposts and Iraqi police stations, in an attempt to facilitate an AQI takeover in Western Iraq."

Another member of the network was Abu Ghadiyah's brother Akram Turki Hishan al-Mazidih, or Abu Jarrah. He was also based in Zabadani and in charge of weapons smuggling and, as the US government noted, "order[ing] the execution of all persons found to be working with the Iraqi Government or US Forces."

Finally, there was another cousin, Saddah Jalut al-Marsumi, who went by Saddah. He was an al-Qaeda financier and helped his enterprising clan transport suicide bombers from Syria into Iraq.

Abu Ghadiyah's predecessor, the Syrian national Sulayman Khalid Darwish (who was, rather confusingly, also known as Abu Ghadiyah), had been killed by JSOC in Qa'im in 2005. That city's strategic value is that it lies directly across from the Syrian border town of Albu Kamal, and functions a bit like El Paso does for Juarez, as a transnational portal through which men and money can flow relatively freely in either direction.

By 2008, numerous diplomatic attempts by the United States to disrupt Abu Ghadiyah's ratlines had failed. The Iraqi government, using intelligence obtained by the Americans, had pressured al-Assad to pick up al-Qaeda's human resources department head for Syria. He demurred. Petraeus had even sought permission from the Bush administration to parley with al-Assad directly in Damascus, in hopes that another Sabawi-style deal might be arranged. The White House said no. Attempts to cajole al-Assad via the UN Security Council also failed.

Then, in October 2008, the cajoling stopped. Stanley McChrystal's JSOC, overseen by the CIA, was authorized to conduct a covert cross-border raid into Albu Kamal to kill Abu Ghadiyah, which it executed on October 26. This special operation resembled the assassination of Osama bin Laden in Abbottabad, Pakistan, in 2011. An Orange operative had done preliminary work on the ground in the village of Sukkariyah, close to Albu Kamal, following Abu Ghadiyah's movements. "Among his tasks," Naylor writes, "was to position and move equipment that allowed the NSA to precisely locate Abu Ghadiya's cell phone in a particular building. JSOC also had access to a spy in Abu Ghadiya's inner circle who was originally recruited by Syrian intelligence." The mission went off perfectly. Within a minute and a half of Black Hawk helicopters landing at Sukkariyah, Abu Ghadiyah and all of his associates were dead; after an hour of gathering intelligence from the target site, the entire JSOC team was en route back to Al Asad Air Base in Anbar.

Despite the irrefutable habeas corpus nature of the evidence, al-Assad continued to deny any involvement in sending terrorists into Iraq. The United States had even warned al-Assad's top officials that a raid to snare or kill Abu Ghadiyah might be forthcoming. Weeks after the raid, British foreign secretary David Miliband traveled to Damascus and once again tried the talking cure. He asked al-Assad to end his noxious activities and was met only with further professions of ignorance and innocence. Maura Connelly, the chargé d'affaires at the US embassy in Damascus, recounted the meeting in a State Department cable:

"Bashar reportedly complained about the October 26 US military operation at Albu Kamal. Miliband replied that the US had hit known [foreign fighter] facilitator Abu Ghadiya. What Syria needed to do was to cooperate with the US and West. Miliband asked why Syria had not taken action against Abu Ghadiya when the US had provided a lot of information regarding his presence in Syria. 'Even if Abu Ghadiya was there (in Albu Kamal),' the US strike was not the way to deal with the issue, replied [al-Assad]."

Perhaps it was with the foregoing episode in mind that a year later Connelly minuted her overall impression of dealing with a regime whose "officials at every level lie. They persist in a lie even in the face of evidence to the contrary. They are not embarrassed to be caught in a lie."

Although it garnered little media attention at the time, the most damning indictment of the al-Assad–jihadist alliance came in the form of a US federal court civil judgment issued in 2008, which found Damascus liable for the kidnapping and murder of Olin Eugene "Jack" Armstrong and Jack Hensley, two American contractors who were beheaded by agents of al-Qaeda in Iraq.

The families of Armstrong and Hensley had originally filed their complaint against not only the regime but also its military intelligence apparatus—and al-Assad and Shawkat personally. The court, citing the Foreign Sovereign Immunities Act—which places limitations on lawsuits filed in the United States against foreign states—and the fact that al-Assad and Shawkat were never served subpoenas, listed Syria as the sole defendant. The judgment, written by Judge Rosemary Collyer, brought it all up—Shaker al-Absi, Abu al-Qaqa, the first Abu Ghadiyah, and the Foley assassination—and concluded that "Syria provided substantial assistance to Zarqawi and al-Qaeda in Iraq and that this led to the deaths by beheading of Jack Armstrong and Jack Hensley," and that "Syria's provision of material support and resources was inevitably approved and overseen by President Assad and General Shawkat, acting within the scope of their official duties." The regime appealed this decision in May 2011. It lost.

ROLLED UP?

The conventional wisdom in US counterterrorism circles maintained that al-Assad's alliance with al-Qaeda in Iraq more or less ended in 2008, after Abu Ghadiyah was killed, because the regime "rolled up" its jihadist networks in eastern Syria and arrested returning foreign fighters. New evidence complicates this assessment.

In December 2014, Martin Chulov of the *Guardian* newspaper published an in-depth profile of ISIS confirming what the al-Maliki government had long alleged—that al-Assad was complicit in a devastating series of attacks against Iraqi state institutions on August 19, 2009. Sequential VBIED operations targeted the Iraqi Finance and Foreign Ministries and a police convoy in Baghdad. More than one hundred people were killed, including government employees and journalists, and around six hundred more were injured.

Al-Maliki had immediately accused the Baathists of masterminding both plots. In November 2009, his government aired what it claimed were confessions obtained from three Baathist operatives involved in the August explosions.

At first, Baghdad was reluctant to assign any blame directly to the al-Assad regime, insisting only that the plots had been formulated in Syria. But it recalled its ambassador from Damascus after the regime failed to turn over two fugitive Baathists. Al-Assad responded by removing his own envoy from Baghdad. One of the men he refused to turn over was Mohammed Younis al-Ahmed, whom he said he had already expelled from his territory. For a short time, al-Assad had tried to make al-Ahmed a Syrian-controlled leader of an Iraqi Baathist insurgency to rival the more established and self-financed Naqshbandi Army, led by al-Douri, who was also being hosted on Syrian soil.

As 2009 wore on, Baghdad's allegations against its neighbor grew more serious. Iraqi foreign minister Hoshyar Zebari told members of the media in Bahrain, "Intelligence confirms that Saddamist Baathists are working from Syrian soil and enjoy the support of [the Syrian] intelligence services." Major General Hussein Ali Kamal, the director of intelligence at the Iraqi Ministry of Interior, was absolutely convinced that this was so. Well respected by American diplomats and military officials for his professionalism, Kamal, who died of cancer in June 2014, told Chulov that he had obtained hard proof of Syria's hosting and supervision of "two secret meetings" between al-Qaeda agents and Iraqi Baathists in 2009. Both meetings were held in Zabadani, the same town that the US Treasury Department had listed as Abu Ghadiyah's main area of operations. Chulov wrote of Kamal's reconstruction of these meetings: "[H]e laid out his evidence, using maps that plotted the routes they used to enter western Iraq and confessions that linked their journey to specific mid-ranking officers in Syria's military intelligence units."

Apparently Kamal had an asset wear a wire at one of the Zabadani meetings, which he said the Baathists had led. "He is the most sensitive source we have ever had," he told Chulov. "As far as we know, this is the first time there has been a strategic level meeting between all of these groups. It marks a new point in history."

US forces were still stationed in Iraq at that point, but the objective shared by Syrian intelligence, the Baathists, and al-Qaeda was instead to destabilize al-Maliki's government. Kamal relayed to Chulov that a source inside Syria had told him that the plotters had noticed an uptick in Iraqi security around the original targets; they had decided on different ones. The Iraqi general struggled for months, in vain, to determine where the new targets might be—until the August bombings made the truth horribly clear.

ALI MAMLOUK'S GUIDE TO COUNTERTERRORISM

No one has better explained both the motive and nature of Syria's collaboration with Sunni jihadism than Ali Mamlouk, al-Assad's director of general intelligence. In February 2010, Mamlouk surprised US diplomats in Damascus by turning up at a meeting between the State Department's Coordinator for Counterterrorism Daniel Benjamin and Syria's Vice Foreign Minister Faisal al-Miqdad. Mamlouk arrived, as he explained, at the prompting of al-Assad, who claimed to be seeking improved Syrian-US relations under the new American president. Obama had come to office promising a fresh policy of engagement with Damascus. Mamlouk, clearly capitalizing on the opportunity that the regime's destabilization strategy had created, explained that cracking down on terrorism would be contingent on seeing that engagement policy carried through to something approaching a full normalization of bilateral relations. As relayed in a State Department cable about the meeting, Mamlouk and al-Assad sought three dispensations from Washington, all of which confirmed Tony Badran's gloss on the regime's purpose for misbehavior: "(1) Syria must be able to take the lead in any regional actions; (2) politics are an integral part of combating terrorism, and a 'political umbrella' of improved US-Syrian bilateral relations should facilitate cooperation against terrorism; and (3) in order to convince the Syrian people that cooperation with the US was benefiting them, progress must be made on issues related to economic sanctions against Syria including spare parts for airplanes and a plane for President [Assad]."

But then Mamlouk made an interesting admission. He explained that his own peculiar method of dealing with jihadists was "practical and not theoretical. . . . In principle, we don't attack or kill them immediately. Instead, we embed ourselves in them and only at the opportune moment do we move." But what constituted an "opportune moment" for Syria did not necessarily seem like one for the United States, as the preceding decade had demonstrated amply.

Was this acknowledgment of state infiltration of jihadist cells merely edifying, or did it contain an implied threat? The answer to that question lay in Mamlouk's follow-up point to Daniel Benjamin, wherein he reminded the US diplomat that foreign fighters were still slipping into Iraq through Syria. This was about sixteen months after the Abu Ghadiyah assassination and about seven months since the most recent series of VBIED bombings rocked Baghdad. Yet, Mamlouk continued, the regime was cracking down, and "[b]y all means we will continue to do all this, but if we start cooperation with you it will lead to better results and we can better protect our interests."

The Syrian regime has been likened by other US diplomats to a mafia crime family. Mamlouk made the new White House an offer it couldn't refuse.

8

REBIRTH

ABU BAKR AL-BAGHDADI TAKES OVER

ISIS's history, according to its magazine *Dabiq*'s reconstruction, was an eleven-year utopian quest made sweeter by suffering, and which ended in 2014 with the establishment of the caliphate. Abu Omar al-Baghdadi built the "first state in 'modern' times set up exclusively by the mujahidin—the active participants in the jihad—in the heart of the Muslim world just a stone's throw away from" Mecca, Medina, and Jerusalem. And even through Sahwa and the surge, and the elimination of its own leadership, that state had endured, retreating "mostly into the desert regions of al-Anbar, where its soldiers regrouped, planned, and trained." They had gone to ground in the face of near-strategic defeat at the hands of Joint Special Operations Command, who were killing and capturing their leaders at a rate faster than they could appoint successors. The most significant scalps since al-Zarqawi would belong to his dual successors, Abu Ayyub al-Masri and Abu Omar al-Baghdadi.

THE DEATH OF AL-MASRI AND AL-BAGHDADI

In June 2008, Stanley McChrystal had been replaced as commander of JSOC by Vice Admiral William McRaven, a Navy SEAL who later coordinated 2011's Operation Neptune Spear, the raid in Abbottabad, Pakistan, that killed Osama bin Laden. Although by 2010 most JSOC operations were in the AfPak theater—in line with the Obama administration's commitment to drawing down in Iraq and winning the "good war" against core al-Qaeda and the Taliban in Afghanistan—McRaven's team did strike a number of important victories against the Mesopotamian franchise.

The first victory was the killing of Sa'ad Uwayyid 'Ubayd Mu'jil al-Shammari, or Abu Khalaf, Abu Ghadiyah's kinsman, who briefly assumed responsibility for the Syria-based facilitation network after the latter's killing in October 2008. A US official later said that "Khalaf was perhaps the most dangerous [al-Qaeda] facilitator in Iraq" and that his death left a "void in [al-Qaeda] hierarchy."

The second victory came after Iraqi forces arrested Manaf Abd al-Rahim al-Rawi, al-Qaeda's emir in Baghdad, known to his subordinates as "the dictator." Al-Rawi had collaborated with Baathists and Syrian intelligence to perpetrate the devastating series of bombings in Baghdad in 2009, all aimed at the al-Maliki government rather than the US military. The Iraqis initially kept his arrest a secret. It was only after the Americans captured his twin brother that they forced al-Maliki to allow them to interrogate the dictator, who duly gave up information about his network. Al-Rawi named two couriers, whom JSOC tracked in April 2010 to a location in the Tharthar region, along Salah ad-Din's border with Anbar.

The courier's safe house turned out to contain none other than Abu Ayyub al-Masri, hiding in a secret basement accessible only through a door underneath the kitchen sink. His companion was a man some had doubted even existed: Abu Omar al-Baghdadi.

"Their killing was a reflection of [the Islamic State of Iraq's] weakness," Laith Alkhouri, the counterterrorism expert, said. "Masri had been preaching on operational cautiousness to Muslims, how to secure their communications and such to avoid being hit by the Americans. The power he held as the head of al-Qaeda in Iraq was more in the realm of public relations. He'd released a document to supporters that was a step-by-step guideline showing them how they might burnish the image of global jihad. He wanted his recruits to learn how to hack websites and marry scientific advancement with Islamist ideology."

But this focus on the more Don Draper-ish aspects of takfirism happened to coincide with the nadir of ISI's popularity and prowess, owing to some of its commanders' worst tactical decision-making since the war started. Eighty percent of the leadership had been killed along with them. Nor was the "Iraqi face" supposedly created by al-Baghdadi's appointment as emir particularly working anymore. Al-Baghdadi himself had pretensions of something higher than his nominal role as caporegime of the Sunni insurgency, at least judging by the name that he had bestowed upon himself—"Emir of the Believers"—an honorific usually reserved for only the highest positions of Islamic rulership. (Mullah Omar, the fugitive Taliban leader, went by that name.) "The adoption of that title," said Laith Alkhouri, "created a huge question for jihadists unsure of where the Islamic State of Iraq was headed." That question would be answered by Baghdadi's successor, a man that few who knew him would have expected to lead the world's most successful terrorist organization.

THE NEW AL-BAGHDADI

Ibrahim Awwad al-Badari might have been an obscure Islamic scholar, writing arcane commentaries on the Quran and Hadith, had he not become a prisoner of Saddam's regime for his Salafist orientation. The Iraq War and its many discontents instead pushed him into the leadership of the Islamic State of Iraq.

Born in 1971 near the city of Samarra, al-Baghdadi became a scholar of Islamic studies, obtaining a master's degree in the subject in 1999 from the Saddam University of Islamic Studies, in Baghdad's Adhamiya suburb. He is said to have lived in modest quarters attached to a mosque in Tobchi, a western district of Baghdad that was fairly mixed between Sunni and Shiite residents. As is often the case when mass murderers are recollected by those who knew them in their nonage, his friends and acquaintances say he was the quiet, retiring type who in no way resembled the dangerous fanatic of recent imagination. He wore glasses for nearsightedness, an impairment that may have saved his life in that it kept him from being conscripted into Saddam's military during Iraq's eight-year war with Iran; one of his brothers was, in fact, killed in that conflict. Al-Baghdadi famously excelled at soccer, and would be compared to famous Argentine players of the sport throughout his adulthood, as he transitioned from academic to professional jihadist.

Dr. Hisham al-Hashimi, an expert on ISIS who consults with the Iraqi government, met al-Baghdadi in the late 1990s. "He did not have the charisma of a leader," al-Hashimi said. "When I met him, he was extremely shy and did not speak much. He was interested in religious studies, and the focus of his interest was the Quran. He was from a poor rural family, and he was not envious of urban people, as others often are. His ambition was limited to obtaining a government job within the Islamic endowment ministry."

According to one of his neighbors, Abu Ali, who spoke to the *Daily Telegraph*, al-Baghdadi came to Tobchi when he was eighteen years old: "The mosque here had its own imam. When he was away, religious students would take his place. [Al-Baghdadi] would sometimes lead the prayers but not give any sermons." His speciality was Quranic recitation, an art form about which al-Baghdadi had written his master's thesis. He also grew more reactionary as time wore on. Abu Ali recounted al-Baghdadi's response to a wedding in Tobchi at which men and women were dancing with each other and the young zealot shouted at the assembly: "How can men and women be dancing together like this? It's irreligious." So al-Baghdadi stopped the dance.

Wael Essam, a Palestinian journalist with extensive experience reporting from Iraq, talked to many Sunnis who were al-Baghdadi's colleagues during his academic years at the University for Islamic Studies. Al-Baghdadi, they claimed, was either a member or an affiliate of the Muslim Brotherhood when he matriculated. His Salafist inclinations came later, well into his curriculum. "Al-Baghdadi was close to Mohammed Hardan, one of the Brotherhood's leaders," Essam said. "Hardan had left to fight with the mujahidin in Afghanistan and returned in the 1990s and adopted a clear Salafist ideology. Al-Baghdadi joined Hardan's group organizationally and ideologically." For a short time, he also belonged to a separate Sunni militant group known as the Army of the Mujahidin.

When the United States invaded Iraq in March 2003, Abu Ali told the *Telegraph*, al-Baghdadi bore no discernible grievance against the conquering Western army: "He wasn't like the hot-blooded ones. He must have been a quiet planner."

So quiet, indeed, that by late 2003 al-Baghdadi had founded his own Islamist insurgency, Jaysh Ahl al-Sunnah wa al-Jamaah, or the Army of the People of the Sunni Community. His tenure as battlefield commander was short-lived. A year later, he was arrested in a raid on Fallujah—one that had targeted a friend of his—and subsequently enrolled in another sort of university. Al-Baghdadi was remanded to Camp Bucca.

Contrary to numerous claims in the Western press that suggest that al-Baghdadi was released from Bucca in 2009, when it was shuttered, he actually served only a single, nearly yearlong stint in the internment facility, in 2004, as the Pentagon's eventual release of his prison file makes clear. "He was visiting a friend of his in Fallujah named Nessayif Numan Nessayif," al-Hashimi recalled. "With him was another man, Abdul Wahed al-Semayyir. The US Army intelligence arrested all of them. Baghdadi was not the target— it was Nessayif. He was arrested on January 31, 2004, and was released on December 6, 2004. He was never arrested again after that."

Abu Ahmed, the former high-ranking ISIS member who knew al-Baghdadi at Bucca, told the *Guardian* that prison administrators at first took al-Baghdadi to be something of a problem solver. He did not possess the alpha male mystique that al-Zarqawi had at Swaqa and al-Jabr; by all accounts, he was much more congenial an inmate. As such, the Americans let him travel among the different camp blocs at Bucca, as a conflict resolution specialist, breaking up disputes among rival prison gangs; they deferred to his clerical authority and religious erudition. In reality, al-Baghdadi used the indulgence of the Bucca administrators to do what any aspiring jihadist heavyweight would do: recruit foot soldiers. In time, he did begin to don the mantle of a new al-Zarqawi-in-the-making, according to Abu Ahmed. Al-Baghdadi started causing problems in the prison, using "a policy of conquer and divide to get what he wanted, which was status. And it worked."

That rise in status was swift indeed. Al-Baghdadi served just two months shy of a year at the American-run detention facility. He was released at the end of 2004, owing to the US assessment that he posed a low risk to the coalition or Iraqi institutions. This assessment actually coincided with his growing *more* extremist in orientation, according to Essam. By this point, he also had at least one family member in al-Qaeda and so he was able to connect with the foremost jihadist network operating in Iraq. When al-Zarqawi installed the Mujahidin Shura Council to nationalize the insurgency, al-Baghdadi and his small cell joined. He was given the role of clerical consultant to that group's "provinces" in the Iraqi countryside—provinces that at the time existed in name only. Al-Baghdadi's purism and his mercurial alliance-making meant that he was not really interested in working with an ideologically diverse consortium of insurgent groups, even if al-Qaeda was primus inter pares. An al-Qaeda commander from Fallujah told Essam that al-Baghdadi had turned on just about every faction he ever joined. "He left the Muslim Brotherhood and he then declared them apostates and agents of [former US ambassador to Iraq Zalmay] Khalilzad. He also left Jaysh al-Mujahidin and he engaged in hostilities against them, especially in al-Karmah," a town northeast of Fallujah, Essam said. "Al-Baghdadi was always very consistent about his position on fellow Sunni militant groups that were not part of his own organization. He would say: 'Fighting them is more of a priority than fighting the Americans.'"

His insistence on the need for fratricidal warfare—or *fitna*—between and among Sunnis would remain a hallmark of al-Baghdadi's leadership well into

ISIS's expansion to Syria and Iraq. Essam also maintains that, contrary to the popular belief that al-Baghdadi came out of nowhere, he was actually well-known to both Iraqis and Americans. "His uncle was Ismail al-Badri, member of Iraq's Muslim Ulema Association, which is considered an apostate organization by his nephew. Al-Baghdadi's sister-in-law is also married to a leader of the Iraqi Islamic Party, the vehicle of the Brotherhood in Iraq. Before the Americans withdrew, he was arrested multiple times because of his kinship to Abu Bakr."

The year 2007 proved to be the seminal one in the extremist's life. Brookings Institution analyst Will McCants writes that a spokesman for al-Qaeda convinced him to travel to Damascus, where he could complete his doctoral dissertation in peace—the war and his insurgency had interrupted his studies—and also fulfill tasks for the organization. (He defended his dissertation in Baghdad in March 2007, and officially became a PhD.) Al-Baghdadi's "tribal connections in Iraq and his ties with other jihadist groups there must have also come in handy," McCants notes, "because on several occasions he was able to help foreign jihadists cross Syria's border into his native land." Al-Baghdadi was also no doubt himself a beneficiary of Bashar al-Assad's open-border policy, a fact that would later be used against him by al-Qaeda when ISIS formally and publicly broke apart from it in 2014.

According to al-Hashimi, Abu Bakr al-Baghdadi's ascension to emir of the organization known as the Islamic State of Iraq was decided overwhelmingly, by nine out of eleven members of its Shura Council, following the deaths of Abu Ayyub al-Masri and Abu Omar al-Baghdadi. There were three reasons for his selection. First, al-Baghdadi belonged to the Quraysh tribal confederation, considered one of the most venerable in the Middle East, thanks to its proximity to the Prophet Muhammad. (Abu Omar al-Baghdadi was also said to have hailed from this tribe, the wellspring of all Islamic caliphs.) Today ISIS reveres him as a "messenger." "Whoever comes to you while your condition is united behind a single man, and intends to break your solidarity or disrupt your unity, then kill him," *Dabiq* proclaimed, exhorting all Muslims to pledge allegiance to al-Baghdadi. Second, he had been a member of the Islamic State of Iraq's Shura Council, its main consultative body, and was therefore an intimate of Abu Omar. Finally, he was chosen because of his age. He was a generation younger than the other viable candidates for emir and was viewed as someone with more staying power to lead the Islamic State of Iraq out of the doldrums once US forces had quit the country.

While all three reasons no doubt prevailed upon the eleven-man Shura Council, which, like the College of Cardinals, selects the head of the entire institution, there was one man who worked quietly behind the scenes to ensure al-Baghdadi's selection. His name was Samir Abd Muhammad al-Khlifawi, better known as Hajji Bakr, then the Islamic State of Iraq's Chief of Staff and soon head of its Military Council. He was also a colonel in Saddam's elite air defense intelligence unit and the man who, perhaps not coincidentally, was dispatched by al-Baghdadi to construct ISIS's network in northern Syria, having joined al-Zarqawi's Monotheism and Jihad not long after the US invasion of Iraq. Hajji Bakr was a ten-year veteran of the organization and his acquired talents as an Iraqi operative were not wasted in his capacity as a jihadist one, as ISIS documents obtained by *Der Spiegel*'s Christoph Reuter make clear. He built a Stasi-like apparatus for intelligence- and counterintelligence-gathering in Aleppo, with different cells tasked with spying not only on local populations but also one another, in classic Mukhabarat fashion. Powerful, bellwether families in villages and towns were surveilled and marked for bribery, extortion, or assassination. Soviet-style *kompromat*—embarrassing or incriminating details of targets' personal lives—were kept on members of these clans in order to ensure their loyalty to ISIS. Much of the same tradecraft was brought to bear on rival Syrian rebel groups, which were subsequently routed from Aleppo.

The US military arrested Hajji Bakr in 2006 and imprisoned him in Camp Bucca until 2008; thus he was kept out of harm's way during locust years for the franchise. He was killed in January 2014 by anti-ISIS Syrian rebels after they mounted an offensive against the jihadists who had usurped them in northern Syria.

One account of how al-Baghdadi climbed onto the throne was given by an ISIS defector known as Abu-Ahmad. Hajji Bakr, he says, "resorted to a wicked idea. He corresponded with each official [on the eleven-man Shura Council] separately, making them believe that he had consulted the others and they had agreed to the appointment of [al-Baghdadi] as emir."

He was allegedly appointed by a lopsided vote of nine-to-two on the council. But the independent evidence that Hajji Bakr manipulated the succession is nonexistent. What *is* known of his succession is that Osama bin Laden had nothing to do with it. A letter captured in Abbottabad shows the al-Qaeda leader writing to Atiyah Abd al-Rahman, the Libyan chief of staff who lectured al-Zarqawi after the Amman hotel bombings, on July 6, 2010, to say: "It would be good of you to provide us with detailed information about our brother Abu Bakr al-Baghdadi. . . . It would be better for you to ask several sources among our brothers there, whom you trust, about them so that the matter becomes clear to us. I also would like that you ask our brothers in Ansar al-Islam Organization where they stand on the new Emirs."

GHOSTS OF SADDAM

Al-Baghdadi's rise heralded yet another mutation of the Islamic State of Iraq, or rather a retrogression of it to an earlier period in the Sunni insurgency's history. There were visibly many more former Baathists in the higher ranks, owing no doubt to the continued Iraqization of the organization. As General Odierno noted in his June 2010 Pentagon news briefing, al-Qaeda in Iraq's leadership had been all but destroyed in a very short space of time—thirty-four out of the top forty-two operatives were removed from the battlefield in one way or another over the previous three months—and the franchise had lost its ability to coordinate with al-Qaeda's headquarters in Pakistan. The vacuum this created at the top meant that, before al-Zawahiri and bin Laden could appoint a new emir from afar, the Iraqi wing of ISIS was able to decide on one of its own in Abu Bakr.

According to US officials, that was the internal story told by two disgruntled al-Qaeda members several years later. Their perception of the rise of al-Baghdadi, whatever his level of education, was that it represented the takeover of the Salafist-Jihadist movement within the Islamic State of Iraq by people without strong Salafist-Jihadist credentials—the Baathists, such as Hajji Bakr.

There is no argument among analysts or those who knew al-Baghdadi that he is a true-believing takfirist. But, as we have seen, even rock-ribbed terrorists benefit from their own who's who, mainly in the form of filial or tribal connections that enable them to leverage a birthright afforded to them by the very societies or regimes they seek to destroy. Might al-Baghdadi have benefited from his ties to the ousted Saddam regime? Given what is known of his biography and education, the likelihood is strong. Two of al-Baghdadi's uncles were said to have been agents of the Iraqi Mukhabarat and, as has been noted, one of his brothers died fighting in the Iran-Iraq War.

According to Derek Harvey, "[H]e's clearly not Zarqawi. But the breadth and size of the organization and the things it has going on from financial enterprises to administration to the running of eight separate regional commands, to its tactical partnering with Naqshbandi Army, to its tribal outreach—I see a Baathist style to all of this. And I know that one of Baghdadi's mentors at the University of Islamic Studies was close to Izzat al-Douri. Al-Douri continually operated from Raqqa and the northeastern Syria area early on in ISIS's emergence in Syria."

Al-Hashimi pointed out that al-Baghdadi had sought in his youth to pursue a career at Saddam's Ministry of Islamic Endowments. An active US military official well versed in Iraq's history and politics adds to this tenebrous biography:

"I had a talk with a senior former Iraqi official who was a senior official in Saddam's regime and under al-Maliki. I asked him specifically about al-Baghdadi. 'Did you know who he was?' Not specifically, but he knew the background that he came from and the extended network he came from. In Saddam's time, where this guy was from and where his family was from was very much a Saddamist-Baathist stronghold. The people who came from Samarra were very tight with the regime. Al-Baghdadi went to the Islamic University of Baghdad at exactly the time of Saddam's Faith Campaign—in other words, at a time when the Baath Party was controlling admissions. There's no way you'd get into the Islamic University at that time without getting vetted and approved by the party, and there's no way you'd get vetted and approved by the party without having an extended family network of uncles and cousins and so on who are in the regime and endorsing you. So yeah, al-Baghdadi may not have been a Baathist himself, but I guarantee you he had a lot of Baathist family members who put him into the Islamic University."

As we have examined, the anti-American insurgency in Iraq drew its strength from Sunni revanchism. One way to view Baathism historically is as one among many exponents of Sunni political power. It competed in its heyday with pan-Arab nationalism, as expounded by Egyptian president Gamal Abdel Nasser, the Islamism of Sayyed Qutb's Muslim Brotherhood, and the Salafist-Jihadism of Osama bin Laden. Indeed, the Islamic Faith Campaign was meant to preempt Salafism's usurpation of Baathism. Today the secular socialist ideology is in a tenuous state of coexistence and competition with the caliphate-building jihadism of ISIS. Amatzia Baram and Pesach Malovany, two scholars of contemporary Iraq, take this thesis even further and make an intriguing case for viewing al-Baghdadi as the rightful heir to Saddam Hussein. For one thing, they argue, even though he is originally from Samarra, his chosen nom de guerre, al-Baghdadi, situates the Iraqi capital as ISIS's center of gravity—which it was under the Abbasid caliphate, itself an important Islamic touchstone for the dead Iraqi dictator. "Saddam never declared himself to be a caliph," Baram and Malovany write, "but his conceptual connection with the Abbasid caliphate centered in Baghdad was profound. One of the nicknames attached to his name was 'Al-Mansur,' which means 'Victorious by the grace of God,' but that was also the name of the most important Abbasid caliph. . . . Saddam also gave names derived from the Abbasid history to numerous military units he established. . . . So, as far as the central role of Iraq and Baghdad is concerned, Abu-Bakr al-Baghdadi is Saddam's disciple."

"The brutality, the tradecraft, how ISIS is behaving on and off the battlefield—it's really no different from the Saddamists, in my view," said Derek Harvey, who would surely know.

There is also a grim parallel between Saddam and al-Baghdadi's hatred of the Shia. The Baathist slaughtered 150,000 of them during Saddam's thirty-year reign, most notoriously during the suppression of the Shia and Kurdish uprising against his regime in March 1991, at the end of the First Gulf War. When his tanks rolled into Najaf in 1991, they had the slogan "La Shi'a ba'd al-yawm" ("No Shia after today") painted on their sides.

If there is a difference in the ideology of murderous sectarianism, then, it is one of scale. For all his savagery, Saddam did not make it a matter of state policy to seek the wholesale destruction of the Shia, nor could he—they were still tolerated in the upper echelons of the Iraqi military and in the Baath Party, even after the 1991 massacres. Al-Baghdadi has so far demonstrated nothing short of annihilationist intention, following in the dark pathological tradition of al-Zarqawi. To ISIS, the Shia are religiously void, deceitful, and only marked for death.

ALL THE EMIR'S BAATHISTS

Harvey's insight is all the more compelling for the fact that ISIS's high command consists of former or recovering Saddamists, those who occupied elite posts in the Iraqi military or Mukhabarat. As scholar Romain Caillet has found, *every head* of ISIS's Military Council from its establishment in 2011 has been a "Former Regime Element," which hardly seems a coincidence.

Even more than Hajji Bakr, Hisham al-Hashimi says, two men in particular were integral to al-Baghdadi's advancement in the Islamic State of

Iraq. The first is Abu Abdul Rahman al-Bilawi, a former captain in the Iraqi army, who was killed two days before ISIS's takeover of Mosul in June 2014. He was born in al-Khalidiya, in Anbar province, into the Dulaim tribe, the largest tribe in all of Iraq. According to ISIS's spokesman, Abu Muhammad al-Adnani, al-Bilawi was close to al-Zarqawi from soon after the US invasion. Clearly he was among those affected by the Islamization of the Saddam regime. Al-Bilawi was arrested on January 27, 2005, and put in Camp Bucca. According to Iraqi government sources, he was among those whom ISIS freed when they broke open Abu Ghraib in July 2013 during the Breaking the Walls campaign. When Hajji Bakr was killed by Syrian rebels in January 2014, al-Bilawi succeeded him as head of ISIS's Military Council. He was not long for the job himself. His courier was captured by the Iraqi government in late May 2014 and, after two weeks of interrogation, he finally cracked and gave up al-Bilawi's location in Mosul. Within hours, on June 4, 2014, al-Bilawi was dead. Documentation evidently recovered after the raid that killed him showed that al-Bilawi, as head of the Military Council, had been the effective deputy to al-Baghdadi in terms of power, if he was not exactly heir apparent should the emir perish. Al-Bilawi was the man who planned the blitzkrieg into Mosul that ended with the fall of the city on June 10, 2014, giving ISIS control of its second provincial capital across Syria and Iraq. That operation, carried out after he was dead, was actually named "Bilawi Vengeance."

Other information the Iraqis confiscated from al-Bilawi's death disclosed much about ISIS's internal finances and some other important details about its structure, specifically the power of ISIS's Syrian "governor" Abu Ali al-Anbari, the second man al-Hishimi says boosted al-Baghdadi up ISIS's greasy pole.

A native of Mosul and ISIS's man in charge of operations in Syria, al-Anbari had been an intelligence officer in Saddam's army as well as a graduate of the Islamic Faith Campaign. While it is unclear exactly which part of the intelligence apparatus he served in, al-Anbari is known to have attained the rank of major general before 2003. He also distinguished himself by remaining at his post until the final days of the regime, something held against him by pro–al-Qaeda agitators. Somewhere in between, according to the *Wall Street Journal*, he had been affiliated with Ansar al-Islam before the group kicked him out following accusations of financial corruption. Iraqi and Syrian militants believe that al-Anbari was selected as al-Baghdadi's deputy in the Levant because of his political pragmatism; his "knowledge of Shariah Islamic rules isn't considered as extensive as that of other senior leaders," the *Journal* reported.

Al-Anbari is a member of the Shura Council and the Military Council, and seems to have been a member of at least the former from 2010. The ISIS defector "Abu-Ahmad" portrays al-Anbari as having been close to Hajji Bakr. Indeed, he seems to have been the key deputy to the latter in restructuring the Islamic State of Iraq's counterintelligence system. This was a necessary reform after al-Zarqawi, Abu Ayyub al-Masri, and Abu Omar al-Baghdadi were all dead, owing to the proliferation of traitors in the ranks of the organization. The Shura Council was itself a means of preserving the security of the Islamic State of Iraq's leadership, isolating the top from the other levels, but al-Anbari currently heads the more activist part of ISIS's internal security, the Security and Intelligence Council, which, as its name suggest, handles all espionage and clandestine operations for the organization. It also runs the personal security of the "caliph," and internal discipline of ISIS, weeding out any possible double agents or turncoats. Al-Anbari, in other words, is one of the few people alive today who always know the location of Abu Bakr al-Baghdadi.

Hajji Bakr's other key deputy in Syria was Abu Ayman al-Iraqi, another member of ISIS's Military Council, who was formerly a lieutenant colonel in the same elite unit of Saddam's air force intelligence as Hajji Bakr, according to a cache of internal documents recovered by Iraqi forces. Another former US detainee at Camp Bucca, his previous nom de guerre, under Baathist rule, was Abu Muhannad al-Suweidawi. Upon his release in 2010, he moved to the Aleppo-Latakia area of Syria. So entrenched in his native soil was al-Iraqi that he evidently needed assistance migrating next door. "The moment that ISIS expanded into Syria, al-Iraqi went in," analyst Laith Alkhouri said. "There is no way he went on his own to Syria. He couldn't navigate the place by himself. He led ISIS in Aleppo and Latakia, and he must be the group's top guy for security in Deir Ezzor. He's leading much of ISIS's current efforts against other Syrian rebel factions." Al-Iraqi became known among those rebels as perhaps ISIS's most sadistic commander. He stood accused of a "special brand of savagery": shortly after the assassination of a high-profile rebel leader, al-Iraqi "tortured and executed another rival commander's men, leaving their bodies by the roadside. When a local cleric was sent over to mediate, the story goes, Abu Ayman killed him too."

In early 2014, Syrian rebels speculated that al-Iraqi was the third highest-ranking member of ISIS. This was likely correct: he was chosen to head the Military Council following the death of Abu Abdul Rahman al-Bilawi, who ISIS sources say was a childhood friend of al-Iraqi.

One final graduate of both Camp Bucca and the Baath regime bears brief discussion. This is Fadel Ahmed Abdullah al-Hiyali, also known as Abu Muslim al-Turkmani or Hajji Mutazz, an ethnic Turkoman from Tal Afar. A former lieutenant colonel in Iraq's Special Forces, and personally close to Saddam and Izzat al-Douri, he was apparently one of many victims of the 2003 disbandment of the Iraqi army by L. Paul Bremer, the American envoy who ran Iraq after the war. Al-Turkmani linked up with another Sunni insurgent group before joining al-Qaeda in Iraq. After 2010, if not before, Hajji Mutazz was a member of the Islamic State of Iraq's Military Council and Shura Council. His purview was always his native Iraq and by the time he was killed he was the ISIS "governor" of the country, not to mention al-Baghdadi's overall deputy. His death has been serially heralded by both the US and Iraqi governments, although it does seem to have occurred at last in August 2015, when Hajji Mutazz was hit in a coalition air strike.

That ISIS embodies in many respects the ghosts of Saddam is not all that surprising, given the Faith Campaign, the demography of the early anti-American insurgency, and the fact that state-trained military officers and intelligence operatives were smarter than amateur mujahidin who knew nothing of operational security—the kinds of fighters who would call each other on unencrypted cell phones, for instance.

That the epaulets and regalia of the Iraqi army have been replaced by black beards and dishdashas only makes good on what the departed dictator of Iraq had forecast about the demise and resurrection of his regime. "The Baathists originally said that their return to power was going to be based on Islam," Derek Harvey notes. "That's what Saddam's letters and his guidance said."

Yet these Baathist biographies of the ISIS leadership have percolated to the surface, either through investigative reporting or as a form of information warfare, used by al-Qaeda to defame ISIS as an un-Islamic continuance of the "socialist infidels" with whom bin Laden may have temporarily agreed to partner but never wanted to see leading the vanguard jihadist group in the Middle East. Michael Pregent, another former US military intelligence officer who advised the Kurdish peshmerga in Iraq, argues that ISIS's attempt to mask or elide the curricula vitae of its top commanders is part of its war strategy. "They can't use their old affiliation as a recruitment tool to get people to come over and fight. A return to Baathism isn't a great selling point, especially when you claim to be committed to Baathism's defeat in Syria. It's like saying that every Army Ranger or Special Forces soldier suddenly became a Branch Davidian."

FROM TBILISI TO ALEPPO

There is one prominent exception to the aforementioned ex-Saddamist roll call, a rarity in the upper echelons of the terror army for a second reason: he is not a native Iraqi. Known internationally as the "red-bearded jihadist," Abu Omar al-Shishani, or Tarkhan Batirashvili, as he was born, is an ethnic Chechen in his late twenties from the Pankisi Gorge region of Georgia. He actually served in the US-trained Georgian army as a military intelligence officer. He fought in the 2008 Russo-Georgian war but was later diagnosed with tuberculosis, according to his father, Teimuraz, and so was dismissed from the army. Today his main function for ISIS seems to be as its celebrated Patton of holy war. Allegedly, al-Shishani is also the head of ISIS's elite Jaysh al-Khilafa, or Army of the Caliphate, which acts as a special forces division for organization and whose responsibilities include defending the city of Raqqa and dispatching operatives abroad.

The Batirashvili men were all Christian, but Tcimuraz's sons became radical Muslims. Al-Shishani even hung up the phone when told that his father had not converted to Islam.

He was arrested for arms possession and served time in a Georgian prison, where his evolution into a hard-core Salafist may have taken place. Released in 2010 as part of Georgia's general amnesty for prisoners, al-Shishani traveled sometime thereafter to Turkey, and then crossed into Syria. "Now he says he left because of his faith, but I know he did it because we were poor," Teimuraz told the BBC.

In the summer of 2012, Katibat al-Muhajireen, the Brigade of Foreign Fighters, was formed in the Aleppo-Latakia area and was mostly staffed by Libyans while being led by Chechens, with al-Shishani as emir. In March 2013 it combined with two other Salafi-jihadist groups, renaming the resulting conglomeration Jaysh al-Muhajireen wa-Ansar, or the Army of Emigrants and Partisans, which took as its headquarters Hraytan, a town northwest of Aleppo City. (One of the factions that took part in the merger, Jaysh Muhammad, or Muhammad's Army, later operated independently.)

Chechens, as a rule, are viewed by other ISIS jihadists as the most formidable warriors, owing to decades of experience fighting a grueling insurgency against the Russian army. "Shishani is the most visible commander, even while ISIS's command-and-control is still being directed by Baghdadi and former Baathists," according to Chris Harmer, an analyst at the Institute for the Study of War. "The Chechens stand apart from the other foreign jihadists. If I'm in the ISIS Military Council, I'm not going to take a guy who has experience fighting the Russians and turn him into a suicide bomber. I'm going to make him a platoon commander."

Like a lot of factions in Syria, the Army of Emigrants suffered from internal division and split entirely in November 2013, when al-Shishani tried to have his fighters, who had previously pledged allegiance to him, switch their fealty to al-Baghdadi. Many refused because they had already declared an allegiance to the Caucasus Emirate, an al-Qaeda–linked insurgency in Russia. So al-Shishani quit his own militia, taking a contingent of loyalists with him, one of whom would go on to greater infamy: the London-born Mohammed Emwazi, dubbed "Jihadi John" by the international press after he personally beheaded James Foley in ISIS's first Western-orientated snuff video, exhibited in 2014. (Emwazi was killed in a US drone strike in late 2015 in Raqqa, the "capital" of ISIS's caliphate.)

Al-Shishani's preternatural talents as a military strategist were heralded and taken as received wisdom among observers of the Syrian conflict after the Army of Emigrants and Partisans played a decisive role in sacking the Menagh air base in Aleppo. (The installation had been besieged for months by rebels of all sorts, including ISIS.) Some of them even made impressive incursions inside the base only to then be beaten back by Syrian soldiers. Menagh finally fell after al-Shishani dispatched two foreign suicide bombers—one was reportedly a Saudi—who detonated a VBIED in an armored car they drove right up to the base's command center. Largely a morale boost to the anti-Assad cause, the Menagh operation was generously credited by other rebels as a major ISIS victory over the regime because even before the Army of the Mujahidin formally split apart in November, al-Shishani was acting as ISIS's northern commander.

Lately, his heroic portrayal has come in for revisionist scrutiny by al-Shishani's former comrades, who fought alongside him and insist that his legend is tabloid embroidery. As Radio Free Europe/Radio Liberty reported in November 2014, another Chechen jihadist named Khalid Shishani believes that his namesake is actually a lousy field commander. "Umar Shishani is a person who is absolutely useless in military terms," Khalid wrote in a statement posted to Russian jihadist forums. "He lacks knowledge of military tactics—and that's putting it nicely. Take note that it's only the infidel (i.e., the Western) mass media that has written about Umar Shishani's military genius.

They have greatly inflated his identity and presented him as a genius military specialist, which is the complete opposite of the real picture. This person only knows how to send mujahidin as cannon fodder, and that's it."

Even if we attribute this to sour grapes or an intramural falling-out, it must be said that al-Shishani's reputation has been better served by the *Daily Mail* than by the Salafist-Jihadist cognoscenti. Alkhouri said that he's the butt of innumerable jokes in online jihadist forums because his knowledge of Islam is "shit" and his spoken Arabic is even worse. Regardless, there is no disputing the lead role al-Shishani played in ISIS's consolidation of northern Aleppo in early 2014, as leaked internal ISIS documents make clear.

Serially reported since then as having been killed in combat—typically at the hands of Kurdish militias—he has now even earned the special attention of Ramzan Kadyrov, Vladimir Putin's handpicked warlord-president of Chechnya. In November 2014, Kadyrov announced one of the many alleged deaths of al-Shishani, the "enemy of Islam," on his favorite social media platform, Instagram, before deleting the announcement. This prompted speculation that the Chechen may actually have been killed in Syria and that Kadyrov's obituary was a way of confirming the news. To date, there is no evidence that al-Shishani is dead.

In his 2014 Ramadan sermon, al-Baghdadi referred to Russia right behind the United States as a national leader of the "jews, the crusaders, their allies, and with them the rest of the nations and religions of kufr," by way of emphasizing that now, after the founding of the caliphate, the world could be neatly divided into two "camps": the true Muslims and holy warriors who are with ISIS, and everyone else.

This renewed declaration of war, in other words, came a year before Putin began directly intervening in Syria to prop up al-Assad, an aerial bombing campaign that has overwhelmingly avoided ISIS in favor of other (anti-ISIS) rebel groups, particularly those backed and indirectly armed by the CIA. Syria's multisided proxy war is in many respects a reply to the Soviet-Afghan war, which set Abu Musab al-Zarqawi on his path to jihad. The difference this time is that Washington and Moscow are "de-conflicting" separate air wars in what both maintain are dogged fights against al-Zarqawi's heirs.

9

REVOLUTION BETRAYED
JIHAD COMES TO SYRIA

On January 31, 2011, Bashar al-Assad gave an interview to the *Wall Street Journal*. Reflecting on the revolutions that had swept Tunisia, Egypt, and Libya, he was in a boastful mood about the slim chances of a similar upheaval coming to his own country. "Syria is stable," he proclaimed. "Why? Because you have to be very closely linked to the beliefs of the people. This is the core issue." Al-Assad was right: it was indeed the core issue.

Just three days before his interview took place, soldiers from his regime had dispersed a candlelight vigil organized in solidarity with the Egyptian protestors and which took place in Bab Touma, a Christian quarter in Damascus's Old City. Then, on February 17, a spontaneous protest erupted in the souk in the capital's al-Hariqa neighborhood after a police officer insulted the son of a local merchant. Although the protest was carefully directed against the behavior of the police officer, the slogan transcended a single crime: "The Syrian people will not be humiliated."

That demonstration came to an end after Syria's interior minister arrived on the scene to address the angry crowd and apologize. Yet it was too late. More demonstrations erupted and spread against the atrocities being committed by Muammar Gaddafi in Libya and, implicitly, by the dynastic dictator at home who had just described his reign as unimpeachable.

A reform movement became a full-fledged revolution after a hinge incident in the city of Deraa. Fifteen schoolboys, some as young as ten years old, were arrested by the regime's security forces, under the supervision of al-Assad's cousin, General Atef Najib, for scrawling prodemocracy graffiti on their school's walls. Some of the slogans were adopted from TV broadcasts about other countries, but one especially creative phrase, which rhymes in Arabic, ran, "It's your turn, Doctor" ("Doctor" here refers to al-Assad's ophthalmology degree). A popular account of what followed claims that when the families of the detainees told Najib that these were their only children, he replied: "Send us your wives, and we will make you new children."

Similar protests soon broke out in Damascus, Homs, Baniyas, and then across all of Syria. The response was widespread state violence. Many peaceful demonstrators and activists were shot by soldiers, riot police, Mukhabarat, and pro–al-Assad militiamen. Others were arrested and hauled off to any number of security prisons. As documented by Human Rights Watch, the secret police used a broad array of torture methods against their captives, including pipe beatings, whippings, electrocutions, acid burns, fingernail extractions, bastinadoes, and mock executions. Detainees of all ages and both genders were also raped.

One woman held at the Palestine Branch of Military Intelligence in Damascus, one of the most feared Mukhabarat prisons in Syria, told the BBC what happened to a fellow female prisoner. "He inserted a rat in her vagina. She was screaming. Afterwards we saw blood on the floor. He told her: 'Is this good enough for you?' They were mocking her. It was obvious she was in agony. We could see her. After that she no longer moved."

General Najib's threat had not been idle, as rape was systematically used by the al-Assad regime from the early days of the uprising. According to Farha Barazi, a Virginia-based human rights campaigner, many rapes resulted in unwanted pregnancies, with Syrian gynecologists seeing victims as young as eleven. In April 2012, Barazi recounted the story of "Salma," a young girl from Baba Amr, Homs, whose house was raided by the *shabiha*, mercenary gangs loyal to al-Assad. "She told them, 'Please, please—don't you have sisters? Don't you have mothers? Just leave me, please not in front of my dad.'" The shabiha tied Salma's father to a chair in his own house and forced him to watch as three or four men raped his daughter. "They made him keep his eyes open and watch," Barazi said. "We have documented eleven cases so far of women needing abortions because they were raped. We had to move them all from either Baba Amr or Idlib to Aleppo, where it was safer to perform this procedure. They are all safe now, but when I called some of them, they were in hysterics. All have suffered severe psychological trauma because of what they've gone through."

Since Barazi's interview almost three years ago, those documented cases have skyrocketed. Close to 300,000 people have been killed in Syria, and another 150,000 are still detained in regime prisons, according to "Caesar," a code-named Syrian military police photographer who defected; he was able to smuggle out of the country some fifty thousand photographs depicting horrific detainee atrocities. "Before the uprising," Caesar told French journalist Garance Le Caisne, "the regime tortured prisoners to get information; now they were torturing to kill. I saw marks left by burning candles, and once the round mark of a stove—the sort you use to heat tea—that had burned someone's face and hair. Some people had deep cuts, some had their eyes gouged out, their teeth broken, you could see traces of lashes with those cables you use to start cars. There were wounds full of pus, as if they'd been left untreated for a long time and had got infected. Sometimes the bodies were covered with blood that looked fresh. It was clear they had died very recently." Stephen Rapp, the State Department's ambassador at large for war crimes, has said that Caesar's disclosures constitute "solid evidence of the kind of machinery of cruel death that we haven't seen frankly since the Nazis."

"ASSAD, OR WE BURN THE COUNTRY"

In his epic poem "Child of Europe," which deals in a series of ironic couplets with the intellectual and moral depravities of totalitarianism, Czeslaw Milosz offered this apostrophe to the offspring of the twentieth century: "Learn to predict a fire with unerring precision / Then burn the house down to fulfill the prediction." Al-Assad resorted to much the same logic when faced with months of protests calling for his ouster.

From the outset, he had portrayed his opponents, even those who were only calling for modest economic reforms, as al-Qaeda terrorists or as hirelings of the United States, Saudi Arabia, Qatar, and Israel—surely one of the most elaborate coalitions of the willing in modern history. The goal of this silly-seeming but consistent propaganda and disinformation campaign was simple. As we have seen, al-Assad was always desperate to win the attention and cooperation of the West, even while suborning terrorism against it. Faced with revolution, and blaming the West for the very crimes that he himself had long committed, he sought to ensure his political longevity through self-fulfilling prophecy. His regime undertook several measures to bring violent Islamism home to Syria. It was no coincidence that one of the favored slogans of his loyalists was "Assad, or we burn the country."

Qusai Zakarya is a Palestinian refugee who lived in the Damascus suburb of Moadamiyeh. He survived both the regime's August 2013 chemical weapon attack and a months-long starvation campaign imposed on his town before he was able to leave Syria under complicated circumstances. "From the beginning, if you were Sunni, and especially if you were Palestinian, you were treated as something less than human by Bashar's forces," Zakarya said. " 'There is no god but Bashar,' the shabiha would say as they kicked protestors or pulled the hair from their head or beards. This was very deliberate. It was also genius."

What Zakarya meant was that the verbal, psychological, and corporal abuse unleashed on Sunnis was designed to radicalize them and push them to acts of extremism. "Assad used a lot of the Alawite forces to repress the opposition in key areas," said Shiraz Maher, an expert on radicalization (and a former Islamist himself) at King's College London. "It was physical torture mixed with a campaign to mock the core aspects of Sunni belief. That's what caught the attention and anger all around the world, above and beyond what drew the average guy in the Midwest to pay attention to what was happening in Syria. Assad set the Sunni Muslim world on fire. This is why the foreign fighter trend started from the Gulf and North Africa." Lighting this fuse proved remarkably easy after decades of dictatorial misrule.

Sectarianism in Syria, as in Iraq, long predated civil war. It was as much the by-product of a minority sect lording it over a restive majority as it was of an antique dispute among Muslims about the lineage of the Prophet in the seventh century. In this case, it was the minority Alawites, a mostly cultural offshoot of the Shia, who constitute between 8 percent and 15 percent of the population in Syria, ruling over the Sunnis, who constitute close to 75 percent. As in Saddam's Iraq, the majority sect was also well represented in all levels of government; for instance, al-Assad's wife, Asma al-Assad, is a Sunni, as have been several high-ranking regime security and military officials. And though it was always the case that minorities were represented in the early protest movement, demography in Syria proved revolutionary destiny: Sunnis were viewed as, and most often were, the ones standing up to the regime in number. The expectation of this contingency had created a republic of fear and paranoia in Syria.

In 2010, Nibras Kazimi published an incredibly prescient study, *Syria Through Jihadist Eyes: A Perfect Enemy*, which featured a number of telling vignettes, all drawn from his many interviews with native Syrians of various religious, ethnic, and socioeconomic backgrounds. Kazimi met a "Damascus-born plastic surgeon," for instance, whose father was a high-ranking Alawite officer in the Syrian Arab Army and had been a personal friend of Hafez al-Assad. The surgeon was exhibited in a photograph with Hasan Nasrallah, the leader of Lebanese Hezbollah. As one of the beneficiaries of Assadism, this man ought to have been, writes Kazimi, "the portrait of an assimilated upper middle-class [Alawite], confident of his standing in Syrian society. But he isn't. When he drives his late-model Volvo, he keeps a submachine gun handy on the passenger's seat. He said, 'Do you know the Sunnis have a saying, *mal'oon baba Hassan* ("Cursed is Baba Hassan")? Do you know who Baba Hassan is? He's Ali bin Abi Taleb, the father of Hassan and the first of the twelve Shia Imams. They hate us. That is who they are. . . . If given the chance, they will massacre us.'" Out of such societal dysfunction, a counterrevolutionary strategy was born.

"The sectarianism was carefully manufactured by Assad from the get-go as a tool of his suppression," Maher said. " 'This is not a peaceful uprising, it's a sectarian one, the Sunnis are rising up and will kill all the minorities.' This was the original line, and it tried to do two things. First, peel off the rest of Syria from the Sunnis who were rebelling so that Alawite or Christian dissidents wouldn't join the uprising, even though some of them did. Second, provoke concern in the international community about what was taking place—namely, that minorities were all going to be slaughtered by terrorists."

The shabiha were the main protagonists in furthering this agenda. Named "ghosts" after the Mercedes Shahab cars in which they used to smuggle everything from cigarettes and drugs to food and weapons into Syria's gray-market economy in the years before the revolution, these muscle-bound thugs, most of whom were Alawites, were enlisted by Damascus to commit some of the worst crimes against humanity. According to one who was detained by rebels in 2012, each shabih was paid $460 per month, plus another $150 bonus for every person he killed or captured. "We love Assad because the government gave us all the power—if I wanted to take something, kill a person, or rape a girl I could," he bragged. In the Houla region of Homs, in May 2012, the shabiha embedded with Syrian army regulars and went house to house in the town of Taldou, following its sustained artillery bombardment, slitting the throats of more than one hundred people. Most of them were women and children. (The shabiha were readily identifiable, locals later testified, by their white sneakers; Syrian soldiers wore black boots.) Al-Assad blamed al-Qaeda for the massacre. An investigation by the United Nations, however, found "reasonable basis to believe that the perpetrators . . . were aligned to the Government."

In an early awareness of what would later become al-Assad's main war strategy, State Department spokeswoman Victoria Nuland accused Iran of being an accomplice to the massacre. "The Iranians have clearly supplied support and training and advice to the Syrian army, but this shabiha thug force mirrors the same force that the Iranians use," Nuland said. She added that the Basij, a volunteer paramilitary originally built by Iran's Revolutionary Guards to help fight in the Iran-Iraq War, "and the shabiha are the same type of thing and clearly reflect the tactics and the techniques that the Iranians use for their own suppression of civil rights." Nuland noted that on the very same weekend that the Houla massacre had been carried out, the Quds Force Deputy Commander Esmail Ghani claimed credit for playing a "physical and non-physical" role in Syria's war.

SULEIMANI'S WAR

That role would only increase in the following year. Evidence emerged that the Quds Force and Lebanese Hezbollah were also training a more professionalized Basij guerrilla army, the so-called National Defense Force, and doing so in both Syria and Iran. With as many as one hundred thousand recruits, these irregulars have lately become one of the regime's main bulwarks in light of the successive failures of the Syrian army to beat back the rebels and reclaim territory on its own. Again, the legacy of Assadism bears on the current civil war. Many of the army's rank-and-file soldiers were Sunnis who have defected or deserted, or have been confined to barracks because their commanding (Alawite) officers fear that they might do so. Other infantrymen have been killed by rebels in three years of attritional war.

"The Syrian army couldn't handle this three-year crisis because any army would be fatigued," Revolutionary Guards Corps operative Sayyed Hassan Entezari said by way of accounting for the genesis and necessity of the National Defense Force. "Iran came and said why don't you form popular support for yourself and ask your people for help. . . . Our boys went to one of the biggest Alawite regions. They told the head of one of the major tribes to call upon his youth to take up arms and help the regime." Each brigade of the National Defense Force is supervised by a Revolutionary Guards Corps officer who acts the part of an embedded commissar ensuring ideological discipline.

Reuters conducted interviews with several cadets of this program in April 2013. All were from Homs and most were Alawites, although some hailed from other minority sects. One interviewee, Samer, was one of the rare Christians who had undergone training in Iran. He told the news agency: "The Iranians kept telling us that this war is not against Sunnis but for the sake of Syria. But the Alawites on the course kept saying they want to kill the Sunnis and rape their women in revenge."

The camp at which Samer must have trained is called Amir Al-Momenin, or Commander of the Faithful, located about fifteen miles outside of Tehran; it is where the Quds Force's ballistic missiles are housed. According to an Iranian military officer who spoke to the *Wall Street Journal* in September 2013, the trainee's "are told that the war in Syria is akin to [an] epic battle for Shiite Islam, and if they die they will be martyrs of the highest rank."

Unsurprisingly, the National Defense Force has already been implicated in anti-Sunni pogroms, one having taken place in the town of al-Bayda and a few neighborhoods in the city of Baniyas, in the coastal province of Tartous. In May 2013, eyewitnesses interviewed by Human Rights Watch testified that "government and pro-government forces entered homes, separated men from women and young children, rounded up the men of each neighborhood in one spot, and executed them by shooting them at close range. . . . In many cases, the pro-government forces burnt the bodies of those they had just shot."

Although al-Bayda and Baniyas are home to a minority Christian population, all the Christian witnesses who spoke to the NGO said that pro-regime forces "only killed Sunnis and burned Sunni homes." The regime, meanwhile, claimed that it had killed "terrorists." The leader of one pro-Assad, and predominantly Alawite, militia called Muqawama Suriya, or Syrian Resistance, spoke openly of the need for ethnic cleansing in these 2013 massacres.

The regime has also burned people alive.

In January 2015, as the world awoke to the horror of seeing a Jordanian airman set alight in a cage by ISIS, the United Kingdom–based Syrian Network for Human Rights and the Geneva-based Euro-Mid Observer for Human Rights, publishing evidence that the National Defense Force, backed by pro-Assad foreign militias and armed loyalists, "have burned at least 81 people to death, including 46 civilians; 18 children, 7 women, and 35 of the armed opposition fighters" between March 2011 and February 2015. In many cases, the Iran-backed paramilitaries set houses on fire with the victims still inside—images, needless to add, that Tehran did not find it necessary or self-serving to upload to its state news channels for immediate "viral" effect.

Iran's involvement in Syria has strongly mirrored its involvement in

US-occupied Iraq, with one stark and ironic exception: now it appears to be the occupying military force, desperately trying to hold together a shambolic and undisciplined native army. Suleimani's militias have taken on more and more military responsibility as al-Assad's conventional forces have deteriorated, died, or fled. This has resulted in high-profile Iranian fatalities, most famously that of senior Quds Force Commander Hassan Shater, who was killed on a road that connected Damascus to Beirut. Notably, Tehran has relied not only on operatives from its foreign intelligence arm of the Revolutionary Guards Corps to "assist and train" al-Assad's conventional army, but also on ones from the Guards Corps' Ground Forces. These are men with extensive experience in suppressing ethnically driven insurgencies, such as among Azerbaijanis in Iran's West Azerbaijan province. Several members of the Ground Forces, including a brigade commander, were among forty-eight Iranians captured by Syrian rebels and subsequently released in January 2013 as part of a prisoner swap.

A report published by the Institute for the Study of War found that in one interesting respect, Iran's counterinsurgency tactics in Syria may consciously be replicating America's in Iraq. In Homs, the city known as the "birthplace of the revolution," to which the Syrian army laid merciless siege in 2012, once the rebels were expelled, the regime constructed a ten-foot-high concrete wall reminiscent of the one US forces had constructed around Sadr City in 2008. "Iranian observers working with proxies in Sadr City at that time would have seen the effectiveness of the campaign firsthand and could have advised the Assad regime to adopt a similar approach," the report concluded.

"Syria is occupied by the Iranian regime," former Syrian prime minister Riyad Hijab declared after his defection in August 2012. "The person who runs the country is not Bashar al-Assad but Qassem Soleimani, the head of Iranian regime's Quds Force."

As early as May 2011, Suleimani and his deputy, Mohsen Chizari—the same operative who had been detained by Joint Special Operations Command in 2006 after attending a meeting at the headquarters of the Supreme Council for Islamic Revolution in Iraq—were sanctioned by the US government for their "complicity . . . in the human rights abuses and repression of the Syrian people." Suleimani was designated specifically as the "conduit for Iranian material support" to Syria's General Intelligence Directorate. Such support, as later came to light, included the trafficking of arms, munitions, and Quds Force personnel in civilian and military airliners across Iraq's airspace to Damascus, prompting several demarches from Washington to Baghdad, all met with denials by the al-Maliki government that any such sky corridor existed. (In 2012, when the Iraqis stopped denying it, they claimed that it was "humanitarian aid" and that the United States had failed to provide any evidence of weapons being transferred.) According to US intelligence, Suleimani's helpmeet in smuggling men and arms to Syria via Iraq is Hadi al-Amiri, the head of the Badr Corps, which al-Zarqawi made a lightning rod for al-Qaeda in Iraq's Sunni recruitment efforts in 2004. By 2013, al-Amiri was Iraq's transportation minister. Today his Badr Corps controls Iraq's Interior Ministry, giving it a broad purview over that country's state security, including and especially in the ground campaign against ISIS.

This may account for why the "spillover" of one country's war into another country was not confined merely to the movement of Sunni jihadists. In January 2014, the Meir Amit Intelligence and Terrorism Information Center in Israel calculated that there were actually more foreign Shia fighters helping Assad than there were foreign Sunni fighters trying to overthrow him.

Jaafar Athab, a member of the League of the Righteous, the group responsible for killing five American servicemen in Karbala in 2007, was killed in Syria in 2012, whereupon his body was brought back to Baghdad and given a funeral in Tahrir Square under the supervision of the Iraqi Security Forces. Iraq's Hezbollah Brigades have also lost Shia militiamen in Syria. So has Muqtada al-Sadr's Mahdi Army, which formed a Shia-Alawite Special Group made up of Iraqi, Syrian, and even Afghan and African Shia called the Abu al-Fadhal al-Abbas Brigade. Phillip Smyth, an expert on the Special Groups, documented in August 2013 how the Badr Corps' own Facebook page had announced a 1,500-man-strong presence in Syria and public funerals for its members slain in Iraq. Most of these fighters couched their participation in al-Assad's war in strictly defensive language; they were going off, they said, to "protect holy shrines." Though it is true that many Shia-Alawite militants were deployed to religious sites, notably the Sayyida Zeinab mosque in the Damascus suburbs, this custodianship of sacred architecture became a sectarian euphemism or code for what was, in effect, Shia Islamist holy war—or counterinsurgency à la Suleimani.

Iran has even sent thousands of Afghani refugees to fight on al-Assad's behalf, offering them residency rights and as much as five hundred dollars per month. Others are allegedly ex-Taliban fighters who became Iranian mercenaries to fight "against those who are being assisted by Americans in Syria."

No Iranian-run subsidiary has been more integral to Assad's survival thus far than Lebanese Hezbollah, which was almost single-handedly responsible for expelling Syrian rebels from the town of al-Qusayr, which lies along a vital Syrian-Lebanese supply corridor. "Hezbollah is leading operations in Qusayr," one Party of God paramilitary confessed to the Beirut-based news portal NOW Lebanon. "The Syrian army is only playing a secondary role, deploying after an area is completely 'cleaned' and secured."

Of course, what he meant by "clean[ing]" areas is more accurately described as ethnic cleansing. "There have been obvious examples of denominational cleansing in different areas in Homs," a Syrian activist named Abu Rami told the *Guardian* in July 2013. "It is . . . part of a major Iranian Shia plan, which is obvious through the involvement of Hezbollah and Iranian militias. And it's also part of Assad's personal Alawite state project."

The project alluded to was the supposed creation of an Alawite rump state on the Syrian coast. For a time, when it was still suffering territorial losses, the regime subtly put out indications that this would be its fallback plan if Damascus fell, a way to telegraph to the West that it would remain the guardian of a vulnerable Alawite minority in the face of what it originally and consistently portrayed as the rebel cause: a Sunni supremacist plan for extermination.

BASHAR'S SECOND INTERVIEW

In marked contrast to his serene *Wall Street Journal* interview in 2011, al-Assad's first post-uprising interview with a Western newspaper was a forecast of Armageddon. "Syria is the hub now in this region," he told the Sunday *Telegraph*. "It is the fault line, and if you play with the ground you will cause an earthquake. . . . Do you want to see another Afghanistan, or tens of Afghanistans? Any problem in Syria will burn the whole region." The fire metaphor again. Absent, of course, from this apocalyptic forecast was any mention of who the original arsonists were. But that was of little consequence, because it worked.

Not only did NATO and Washington rule out active military intervention in Syria in the form of a no-fly zone or the establishment of "safe areas" in parts of the country, but also they were equally wary and dismissive of al-Assad's enemies, in a manner that can only have pleased al-Assad. When Hillary Clinton left government, she chastised President Obama for not collaborating with nationalist or secular rebels sooner—a supposed policy failure to which she attributed the rise of ISIS. But in February 2012, when she was still secretary of state, she told CBS News: "We know al Qaeda—Zawahiri is supporting the opposition in Syria. Are we supporting al Qaeda in Syria? Hamas is now supporting the opposition. Are we supporting Hamas in Syria?" Not knowing who or what the opposition was would remain the White House's public posture for years thereafter, until it solved this mystery and professed itself unimpressed with its discovery. "This idea that we could provide some light arms or even more sophisticated arms to what was essentially an opposition made up of former doctors, farmers, pharmacists, and so forth, and that they were going to be able to battle not only a well-armed state but also a well-armed state backed by Russia, backed by Iran, a battle-hardened Hezbollah, that was never in the cards," President Obama told the *New York Times* as late as August 2014, even after the CIA began arming and training a small number of rebels.

The president's assessment suffered from two problems. First, his characterization of the rebels was inaccurate. The Violations Documentation Center, a Syrian opposition source but one trusted for its empiricism, conducted a survey of rebel deaths in the war and found that doctors accounted for a statistically negligible 1 percent, while teachers and farmers accounted for even less than that. Soldiers constituted the majority of fatalities, at 62 percent. As Ambassador Frederic Hof, Obama's former special adviser on Syria at the State Department, has reminded the president, Syria has a conscript army, meaning that most adult males have some prior military experience. Based on our reporting from Antakya, Turkey, we can attest that a single refugee camp houses thousands of low- and mid-level defectors from the Syrian military.

The expectation that Syria's rebels could not defeat a battered and depleted Syrian army, even backed by Iranian proxies and Russian matériel, seemed odd given that the policy Obama ultimately adopted was to have them trained to defeat ISIS, the heirs to an insurgency that had battered the most powerful army on earth in Iraq for nearly a decade. Given that these rebels' raison d'être was fighting the regime, not ISIS, America's proxy counterinsurgents—a Sunni Navy SEALs—were bound to cause resentment and disaffection. "The Americans are using the lies to get information [about jihadists]," one rebel told *Newsweek* in February 2013. "If you ask any rebel in Syria right now, he will say America is our enemy." This was hyperbole, but it became less so after al-Assad's sarin gas attack on rebels and civilians in Damascus in August 2013. When the United States failed to respond militarily, according to Obama's own "red line," many had had their fill of empty or broken promises. Not long after Obama inked a deal with Vladimir Putin to decommission Syria's chemical weapons program, scores of Western-backed rebels either quit the field, mutinied, or invited ISIS to raid their Syrian warehouses filled with US-sent aid and supplies.

THE JIHADISTS' AMNESTY

While rebel disillusionment with the United States and its true prerogatives in Syria took time to come about, al-Assad wasted little time in guaranteeing that extremists dominated the insurgency. On March 26, less than two weeks into the uprising, and again on May 31, 2011, he issued a general amnesty as part of his package of "reforms." These were mostly symbolic gestures aimed at placating the protest movement. In reality, the amnesties were more of a booby trap than a salve. Although meant to free all of Syria's "political prisoners," they were applied selectively. In the first amnesty, 246 of the 260 people freed were from the infamous Sednaya prison that houses the violent Islamists. Plenty of protestors and activists were kept in jail, while an untold number of Salafist-jihadists were let out. Of these, many had not long ago been on ratlines to Iraq, only to return to Syria and be collared and locked up by the very Mukhabarat that had sent them to Iraq in the first place.

Muhammad Habash, the former Syrian parliamentarian, has said that the regime can only have known that at least some of the Islamists it was releasing would take up arms against the state. Three men did: Zahran Alloush, Hassan Abboud, and Ahmad Issa al-Sheikh, the current or former Salafist leaders of the best-organized rebel brigades in Syria. There is a famous photograph of them standing in a row, all smiles, not long after being decreed free men by al-Assad. Future ISIS members were also granted amnesty, including Awwad al-Mahklaf, who is now a local emir in Raqqa, and Abu al-Athir al-Absi, who served time in Sednaya prison in 2007 for membership in al-Qaeda.

In August 2012, after his brother Firas was killed near the Turkish border, al-Absi took charge of the Mujahidin Shura Council, a group that Firas had started. As of mid-July 2014, according to the US State Department, al-Absi became ISIS's provincial leader for Homs, in the Aleppo region.

Habash, as mentioned earlier, had been in charge of the deradicalization program at Sednaya in 2008 after proposing himself for the role to Syria's National Security Bureau. "Salafism could have been controlled or reformed," he said. "The regime drove Salafists and Sufis to violence. Ideology was part of the reason, but let me tell you: if Gandhi spent three months in Syria, he would be a jihadi extremist."

A twelve-year veteran of Syria's own Military Intelligence Directorate told the Abu Dhabi–based newspaper the *National* that al-Assad's general amnesties in 2011 was designed to sow terrorism in Syria for propaganda value. "The regime did not just open the door to the prisons and let these extremists out, it facilitated them in their work, in their creation of armed brigades," the intelligence officer, an Alawite who defected from his unit in northern Syria in the summer of 2011, told the *National*. "This is not something I heard rumours about, I actually heard the orders, I have seen it happening. These orders came down from [Military Intelligence] headquarters [in] Damascus." The regime also made an abundance of weapons available to these extremists in Idlib and Deraa, the officer added.

A revealing anecdote was relayed to the authors by Fawaz Tello, a long-time Syrian dissident who was arrested by the regime on September 11, 2001, when, understandably, the world's attention was diverted elsewhere. He had been an activist associated with the Damascus Declaration, a pro-reform political movement that enjoyed a brief flowering in the initial days of the dauphin's "reformist" presidency, only to be summarily crushed thereafter. Tello was sent to Adra prison, northeast of Damascus, where he made the acquaintance of Nadeem Baloosh. "He was a young man from Latakia," Tello said. "He had been in Turkey, and when he returned to Syria, Turkish intelligence informed the Mukhabarat and they arrested him. He spent more than a year in Adra." Baloosh was in a cell neighboring Tello's, and during that time, the two had discussions at night, "shouting" through the doors. "I found that there was nothing compatible with this man. He had very extremist views. But he was also talking to other Islamists in the other cells and he was spreading his ideology. He hadn't been a member of al-Qaeda, nor had he attended any military training camps. He was just a Salafist, but nonviolent. A lot of people put into prison were like this. During their time in the jail, it was as if they were attending jihadist college—including Baloosh."

After Tello was released from Adra, Baloosh was transferred to Sednaya, where, in 2008, he became one of six ringleaders of a famous prison riot, the events and aftermath of which have been rendered somewhat opaquely. It is known that at least twenty-five people were killed and ninety more were injured. "Directly after he and the others took over the prison, they executed a handful of inmates," Tello recounted, "claiming they were regime informants. Baloosh was personally responsible for executing one of these inmates. His victim wasn't an informant, he just didn't agree with Baloosh's ideology."

When the regime finally regained control of Sednaya, it executed the six ringleaders of the riot—except Nadeem Baloosh. "He received no death sentence and he was released in 2010, well in advance of completing his original sentence, which was supposed to have lasted until 2015. He returned to Latakia and opened up a shop."

In the early days of the Syrian uprising, Baloosh joined the peaceful demonstrations in Latakia, the coastal province whence the al-Assad family claims its ancestry. He was kicked out by other activists because of his viciously sectarian slogans against the Alawites—these, in the Alawite heartland of Syria. "They didn't accept him. Less than a year later, maybe nine months, some rebels took up arms against the regime in Latakia. They ran to the mountains and founded battalions. Baloosh was one of them. Nobody was following him, but he went to the mountains and established his own battalion. His battalion then joined Jabhat al-Nusra," Tello said, referring to the al-Qaeda franchise in Syria.

Although Baloosh was released from Sednaya before the protest movement began, his story generally tracks with what foreign and Syrian officials have said in the past few years about the makeup of the country's now-numerous terrorist cells. For instance, in January 2014, Major General Fayez Dwairi, a former Jordanian military intelligence officer who helped run the kingdom's Syria crisis portfolio, told the *National*, "Many of the people who established Jabhat al-Nusra were captured by the regime in 2008 and were in prison. When the revolution started they were released on the advice of Syrian intelligence officers, who told Assad 'they will do a good job for us. There are many disadvantages to letting them out, but there are more advantages because we will convince the world that we are facing Islamic terrorism.'"

Nawaz Fares was the former Syrian ambassador to Iraq, a country that, as we examined in chapter 7, al-Assad was intent on destabilizing with terrorism up until late 2009. Fares defected in July 2012 and told the press that Damascus was still playing with jihadist fire well into the revolution. Fares was in a position to know firsthand how this collaboration had worked. Before moving to the Syrian embassy in Baghdad, and after the toppling of Saddam, he had served as a regime security chief as well as a provincial governor near the Syrian-Iraqi border. He recalled to the *Sunday Telegraph* how he "was given verbal commandments that any civil servant that wanted to go [to Iraq] would have his trip facilitated, and that his absence would not be noted." He also said that he knew several regime "liaison officers" who were coordinating with al-Qaeda operatives up until the moment of his defection—the summer of 2012. More intriguing, Fares claimed, is the fact that all the large-scale terrorist attacks that had occurred in Syria, beginning in late 2011, were "perpetrated by al-Qaeda through cooperation with the security forces." These included an especially devastating one that had targeted a military intelligence building in a Damascus suburb in May 2012.

Are such allegations invented or politically motivated? Perhaps, although in the case of the Alawite intelligence officer, it bears mentioning that he told the *National* that he still preferred al-Assad's rule to the victory of a radicalized opposition. Whatever the truth, these allegations are founded on the plausible premise of proven past collusion between Damascus and al-Qaeda, which extended almost to 2010. So if the regime categorically terminated its relationship with jihadists in the yearlong space between the bombings in Baghdad and the outbreak of unrest in Deraa, then it is one of the most dramatic recipients of blowback in modern history.

THE ZARQAWISTS COME TO SYRIA

A few months before the last American GI left Iraq, Abu Bakr al-Baghdadi dispatched a handful of operatives into Syria. According to journalist Rania Abouzeid, who has embedded with jihadists in Syria, eight men crossed into the country's northeastern province of Hasaka in August 2011, during Ramadan. Among those making the journey was Abu Mohammed al-Jolani, a Syrian from Damascus who had fought with ISI and was about to redirect his attention against the regime that had likely once facilitated his traffic in the opposite direction.

Although it has been rumored that al-Jolani, who is in his early thirties, had also been released from Sednaya under the general amnesty, there is no hard evidence to substantiate that claim. Major General Dwairi told the *National* that al-Jolani was in regime custody at one point, but he did not specify the time or the prison. Al-Jolani's first point of contact in Hasaka, Abouzeid reported, was a former Sednaya inmate who hosted the ISI cohort, consisting as it did of "several Syrians, a Saudi, and a Jordanian," during their first night in Syria. (What has been established with certainty is that al-Jolani had been a detainee at Camp Bucca, where he was misidentified by US forces as an Iraqi Kurd from Mosul.)

Al-Jolani's cell allegedly waged a series of car bombings in Damascus, targeting the security services and the army in late 2011. It did not claim credit for them until January 23, 2012, when Jabhat al-Nusra, or the Support Front for the People of Greater Syria, declared its formation as a group.

Al-Jolani also took care to hide his organizational ties to the Islamic State of Iraq, so much so that even members of his own cell were not quite sure what al-Nusra was getting up to or how it had carried out its daring attacks. Christoph Reuter, the same correspondent for the German weekly *Der Spiegel* who obtained the documents used by Hajji Bakr to build ISIS's network in northern Syria, said: "The first real al-Nusra groups emerged in July 2012 in Aleppo. When we talked to one of them, asking them, 'Oh, so, you are al-Nusra?' they said, 'Yes, yes yes!' 'So how did you blow up the security building in Damascus?' 'No clue,' they conceded after a while. 'We took the name, because it is a great name, and we get money from the Gulf with it.'"

Al-Jolani, in other words, spent close to six months building—or reconstituting—a clandestine jihadist network in Syria before he debuted it as a strictly homegrown affair. This was incredibly savvy, as it turned out, because not only did al-Nusra prove to be one of the most formidable anti-Assad insurgencies in the civil war, but also its relative "moderation" in its engagement with local communities earned it the respect and approval even of non-Islamists. Al-Nusra, for instance, did not declare war on Syria's minorities, as ISIS later did. In some cases it even protected churches to show Christians that it was very much part of the social and religious mosaic of Syria, not a foreign takfiri group. In this, analysts say, al-Jolani conformed to al-Zawahiri's plan of action following bin Laden's assassination in May 2011. "Zawahiri was strictly against targeting other religious groups or sects such as Shia, Yazidis, Hindus, Christians, and Buddhists unless they targeted Sunnis first," Laith Alkhouri said. "This owed to the enormous negative backlash against al-Qaeda in Iraq from the time of Zarqawi and Masri and Baghdadi. Zawahiri also urged jihadi groups to reach out to the Muslim public, people who he claimed had been absent from true Islamic teaching in Syria, Lebanon, and North Africa. The goal was to unify people around the concept of tawhid, or monotheism."

Takfirism as a binding social contract for al-Qaeda had failed in Iraq, thanks to US and tribal efforts. Al-Nusra was thus the vehicle by which al-Zawahiri hoped to refurbish in Syria the damaged reputation his franchise had incurred next door. Al-Jolani later explained to Al Jazeera the origins of al-Nusra as the belated realization of a long-held ambition of al-Qaeda, to help free the Syrian people from a tyrannical regime:

"Nobody can ignore the significance of the Levant," he said. "It is the land of conflict, ancient and modern. . . . When the [Syrian] uprising started, one of the leaders of [the] Islamic State in Iraq asked us what to do. We said let's begin working there. . . . The regime was grossly oppressive and people were far away from the idea of picking up arms against it or even accepting the path we are taking and unable to beat the consequences of any confrontation with this regime. So this uprising removed many of the setbacks and paved the way for us to enter this blessed land. . . . We asked for [permission to found al-Nusra], but this idea was in the mind of the al-Qaeda leadership for a while."

As commander of al-Nusra, al-Jolani personally oversaw his group's operations all over the country, in some cases posing as a decoy representative dispatched by the real al-Jolani to test the mettle of his rank and file. (As in Camp Bucca, al-Qaeda in Iraq resorted to counterintelligence feints not only to fool its enemies but also to trick its own recruits.)

Al-Zawahiri issued two communiqués in early 2012, implicitly certifying al-Jolani's endeavor without ever acknowledging it. In the second communiqué, released on February 11, the Egyptian "appeal[ed] to every Muslim and every noble, free man in Turkey, Iraq, Jordan, and Lebanon to come to support his brothers in Syria with all that he possesses with himself, his wealth, his opinion, and information." Al-Zawahiri excoriated the al-Assad regime for keeping "the splendor of the Ummah's youth in its prisons, torturing and killing them. It has protected the Israeli borders [for] about forty years, participated with America in the war against Islam in the name of terrorism, shed the blood of Muslims in horrible massacres in Hama, Homs, Jisr al-Shughur and Daraa, for consecutive decades, and includes a group of thieving robbers, who are looting the wealth and resources of Syria using iron and fire."

Not about to let another good war go to waste, al-Zawahiri was once against channeling the Services Bureau era, and his dead boss, in issuing a global casting call for mujahidin.

10

DIVORCE

At the end of December 2014, ISIS released the sixth issue of *Dabiq*. The cover promised a "testimony from within" al-Qaeda's home base of operations, the Waziristan region of southern Pakistan. Written by a man named Abu Jarir al-Shamali, a former associate of Abu Musab al-Zarqawi, the article was a more-in-sorrow-than-in-anger look at the degeneration of a once-noble jihadist enterprise. Al-Shamali said that he had traveled to Waziristan after being released from an Iranian jail in 2010. He expected to find a proud Islamic emirate: "I had thought the mujahidin were the decision makers there and that the Sharia laws were implemented by them there. But alas and sadly, the dominant law was the tribal laws." Children were attending the "secularist government" schools; paved roads indicated that Islamabad was still very much in control of the territory; and women intermingled with men, "making the movement of the mujahid brothers difficult in the case of sudden military action." In short, al-Qaeda's emirate was a busted flush. Moreover, al-Shamali explained, the treachery of the mujahidin in Pakistan, principally Ayman al-Zawahiri and "his cronies who left from the arena of Waziristan carrying secret and private messages," had created a rift within ISI, leading to a civil war within a civil war in Syria. Suddenly, Jabhat al-Nusra was fighting ISIS.

AL-NUSRA AT WAR IN SYRIA

By August 2012, US intelligence estimated that al-Qaeda had roughly two hundred operatives in Syria, a minority of the overall rebel formations battling the regime. But, as the Associated Press reported, their "units [were] spreading from city to city, with veterans of the Iraq insurgency employing their expertise in bomb-building to carry out more than two dozen attacks so far." And al-Zawahiri's exhortation had paid off because, as Daniel Benjamin, the State Department's top counterterrorism official said, "There is a larger group of foreign fighters . . . who are either in or headed to Syria." That said, he claimed that Western-backed rebel groups "assured us that they are being vigilant and want nothing to do with al-Qaeda or with violent extremists."

That vigilance would be severely tested as Free Syrian Army (FSA) brigades and battalions continued to complain about their lack of resources relative to the jihadists. At that point, the United States was sending "nonlethal aid" to the opposition in the form of walkie-talkies, night-vision goggles, and Meals, Ready to Eat (MREs). FSA fighters had to rely on whatever weapons the military defectors in their midst had taken with them from the Syrian army, commandeered stocks from raided regime installations, and black-market purchases where the prices of even "light" arms such as Kalashnikovs, rocket-propelled grenade launchers, and ammunition had been inflated by high demand. The rebels were also growing increasingly dependent on weapons purchased for them by Saudi Arabia and Qatar, two Gulf states with antagonistic agendas and a willingness to work with Islamist fighters deemed unsavory by the West.

A little-explored facet of the Syrian Civil War was how the highly competitive bidding war for arms, by fighters inclined toward nationalism or secularism, accelerated their radicalization—or at least their show of having been radicalized. In a survey of the opposition carried out by the International Republican Institute (IRI) and Pechter Polls of Princeton in June 2012, rebels made their intentions for a post-Assad Syria clear. The survey showed that 40 percent wanted a transitional government in Damascus, leading to elections; 36 percent said they wanted a constitutional assembly, as in post-revolutionary Tunisia, leading to elections. But that would slowly change, or at least appear to. In Antakya—which by the summer of 2011 had become a refugee hub, triage center, and a remote barracks for the rebels—we met with one mainstream FSA fighter who was recuperating from an injury caused by shrapnel. He drank alcohol and smoked marijuana and professed to want to see a democratic state emerge in the wake of Assadism. But his battlefield photo showed a long-bearded Islamic militant resembling the late Chechen separatist warlord Shamil Basayev.

This rebel's brigade, he said, was financed by the Muslim Brotherhood, and so he felt it necessary to play up his religiosity to ensure funding for his men. Another rebel commander complained that he had had to sell everything, from his family mining businesses in Hama to his wife's jewelry, to keep his small start-up battalion of a few hundred afloat; meanwhile, jihadist leaders were turning up in safe houses throughout Syria with bags full of cash, ready to disburse it to their comrades for guns, bullets, and bombs. The eight-year-old arms and jihadist trafficking nexus in eastern Syria and western Iraq was moving in the reverse direction.

On December 11, 2012, the US Treasury Department sanctioned al-Nusra as the Syrian arm of al-Qaeda, which it accused of seeking "to exploit the instability inside Syria for its own purposes, using tactics and espousing an ideology drawn from [al-Qaeda in Iraq] that the Syrian people broadly reject."

The designation failed to marginalize the jihadist cell. Instead, it rallied the opposition behind al-Nusra, not necessarily out of ideological sympathy but out of wartime exigency. Dr. Radwan Ziadeh, a Washington-based Syrian dissident who had belonged to the Syrian National Council, the first political vehicle for the opposition, called the decision misguided precisely because it seemed to certify the al-Assad regime's portrayal of the conflict—as a war against terror. Dissidents within Syria saw it in much the same way.

Having asked for the better part of a year for US military intervention in the form of a no-fly zone or arms for the FSA, activists chafed at America's blacklisting of one of the groups taking the fight most assiduously to their enemy. In December 2012, Syrians held one of their Friday demonstrations throughout the country. This one was called "We are all Jabhat al-Nusra."

THE ISLAMIC STATE OF IRAQ OWNS AL-NUSRA

As it happens, the first al-Qaeda agent to confirm the Treasury Department's intelligence was none other than Abu Bakr al-Baghdadi. This confirmation came in the form of an audio message publicized on April 8, 2013, more than a year after al-Nusra had established itself as one of the vanguard fighting forces. It was also a month after an array of rebel factions, led by Ahrar al-Sham and al-Nusra, took its first provincial capital away from Syrian soldiers in the eastern city of Raqqa; Raqqa was nicknamed the "hotel of the revolution" because its population had tripled from internally displaced persons.

The fall of the city nearly coincided with the anniversary of another hinge moment in the history of the modern Middle East. It had been almost ten years to the day since US forces invaded Iraq in Operation Iraqi Freedom. There was a grim symmetry between the two events. US marines had famously helped local Iraqis tear down a large statue of Saddam in Baghdad's Paradise Square; one soldier even briefly (and controversially) covered the fallen monument with the Stars and Stripes. Suddenly Islamists had just toppled a bronze statue of Hafez al-Assad and hoisted the Muslim *shahada*—the black flag with Arabic script reading, "There is no god but God, and Muhammad is His messenger"—up a flagpole in another Baathist-ruled Arab metropolis. Within days, graffiti appeared on buildings in Raqqa, attributed to al-Nusra, warning that the punishment for theft was the loss of a hand. Pamphlets were distributed with images instructing women in the modesty in dress that would now be expected of them. And while many residents had cheered on the expulsion of the regime, not all welcomed their new masters or the divisive iconography they brought with them.

In the *New Yorker*, Rania Abouzeid reconstructed an intense debate between Raqqans of all generations and an al-Nusra operative. The operative had been handing out leaflets explaining the necessity of replacing the Free Syrian flag—the pre-Baathist tricolor adopted by the opposition in the early months of the protest movement—with an Islamic one. Abu Noor, a man in his twenties, feared the shahada was an open invitation for the wrong kind of US intervention in Syria. "We will become a target for American drone attacks because of the flag—it's huge," he said. "They'll think we're extremist Muslims!" Abu Moayad, an older man who had helped smuggle ammunition to the rebels from Iraq, told al-Nusra that the flag denatured the first principles of the revolution: "We are not an Islamic emirate; we are part of Syria. This is a religious banner, not a country's flag."

The Islamic State of Iraq's seizure of Raqqa had happened by stealth, seemingly overnight, much as had its insertion of al-Nusra into all of Syria. "When the situation in Syria reached that level in terms of bloodshed and violation of honor," al-Baghdadi declared on April 8, 2013, "and when the people of Syria asked for help and everyone abandoned them, we could not but come to their help so we appointed al-Jolani, who is one of our soldiers, along with a group of our sons, and we sent them from Iraq to Syria to meet our cells in Syria. We set plans for them and devised policies for them and we supported them with half of our treasury every month. We also provided them with men with long experience, foreigners and locals. . . . We did not announce it for security reasons and for people to know the truth about [ISI] away from media distortion, falsehood, and twisting."

Al-Baghdadi did not confine his message to confirming what was already widely assumed. He went further, announcing that al-Nusra and the Islamic State of Iraq were uniting into one cross-regional jihadist enterprise to be known as the Islamic State of Iraq and al-Sham (ISIS), which has alternatively been translated as the Islamic State of Iraq and the Levant (ISIL).

No thanks, came al-Jolani's reply, two days later.

Although respectful of his Iraq-based superior, whom he referred to as "honorable sheikh," al-Jolani said that he did not approve of the merger, or indeed even know about it beforehand. He thanked ISI for sharing its straitened operating budget with the Syrian franchise and confirmed al-Baghdadi's deputizing him to lead al-Nusra. Al-Jolani left absolutely no doubt as to where his true loyalty lay—with Ayman al-Zawahiri, the "Sheikh of Jihad," to whom he publicly renewed his and al-Nusra's bayat.

What followed was a brief media intermission by al-Nusra and an attendant escalation in chatter by ISIS. Al-Nusra's official media network, al-Manara al-Bayda, or the White Lighthouse, stopped producing material, as did ISIS's media arm, al-Furqan, until al-Zawahiri issued his decision. But that didn't stop affiliates and fellow travelers of either franchise from producing their own agitprop. With al-Nusra, a "Wilayat Deraa" military council issued content independently in May and June 2013 signposting its loyalty to al-Jolani in southern Syria, whereas in the north and east, Aleppo and Raqqa, al-Nusra suffered defections to ISIS. In one instance, an al-Nusra affiliate that jumped to ISIS jumped right back after al-Zawahiri commented on the dispute in late May and early June 2013 when, like an exhausted father trying to break up a fight between two unruly sons, the al-Qaeda leader intervened publicly.

In a communiqué published by Al Jazeera, he did his best to sound even-handed in his judgment. Al-Baghdadi, he stated, was "wrong when he announced the Islamic State in Iraq and the Levant without asking permission or receiving advice from us and even without notifying us." But al-Jolani, too, was "wrong by announcing his rejection to the Islamic State in Iraq and the Levant, and by showing his links to al-Qaeda without having our permission or advice, even without notifying us." Al-Zawahiri thereby "dissolved" ISIS and ordered both ISI and al-Nusra back to their geographically delimited corners, one having control over Iraq, the other over Syria.

No doubt aware that this pronouncement would not keep his two sub-ordinates from restarting their argument, al-Zawahiri also hedged his bets. He appointed Abu Khalid al-Suri, al-Qaeda's "delegate" in Syria, to act as an on-the-ground arbiter of any further squabbles that might arise from his decree. Also, in the event that al-Nusra attacked the Islamic State of Iraq, or vice versa, al-Zawahiri empowered al-Suri to "set up a Sharia justice court for giving a ruling on the case."

Al-Suri, who was killed in a suicide bombing in Aleppo in February 2014 (possibly at the hands of ISIS), was a veteran al-Qaeda agent, not to mention another beneficiary of al-Assad's general amnesty in 2011. He had helped found Harakat Ahrar al-Sham al-Islamiyya (the Islamic Movement of the Free Men of the Levant), one of the most powerful rebel groups in Syria today. Before his death, al-Suri was the linchpin of the long-standing operational alliance between al-Nusra and Ahrar al-Sham.

AL-ZAWAHIRI, DEFENDER OF SYKES-PICOT

Al-Zawahiri's suspicion that the crisis between his two field commanders would outlast his paternal intervention proved correct. Al-Baghdadi refused to abide by his edict and justified his defiance by claiming that al-Zawahiri, by insisting on a distinction between the lands of Syria and Iraq, was deferring to artificial state borders drawn up by Western imperial powers at the close of World War I, specifically the Sykes-Picot Agreement. That was no mild charge to level at the Sheikh of Jihad.

The brainchild of Sir Mark Sykes, the secretive twentieth-century compact between London and Paris had divided the remnants of the Ottoman Em-pire. "I should like to draw a line from the 'e' in Acre to the last 'k' in Kirkuk," Sykes told the British cabinet in December 1915. In reality, the Sykes-Picot Agreement was never implemented as it was originally envisioned: Mosul, for instance, was meant to fall to France's sphere of influence but in the end became part of the British mandate in Iraq. But despite being drawn along Ottoman boundaries more than one hundred years old, the pact has become a compelling complaint for successive generations of Baathists, communists, pan-Arab nationalists, and Islamists. The agreement was, and still is, a byword for conniving and duplicitous Western designs on the Middle East—so much so, in fact, that when ISIS stormed Mosul in June 2014 and bulldozed the berms dividing Iraq from Syria, it billed the act as a physical and symbolic repudiation of Sykes-Picot. Implicitly, too, it was a rejection of al-Zawahiri's prescription for holy war. Al-Baghdadi's break with the Egyptian elder was therefore more than that of a lieutenant mutinying against a general. The ISIS emir was calling his boss a has-been and a sellout.

The al-Nusra–ISIS rupture led directly to yet another transformation in the ranks of regional, not to say global, jihadism. The majority of foreign fighters in al-Nusra's ranks went over to ISIS, leaving the rump organization under al-Jolani heavily Syrian in constitution.

Inside Iraq, the dynamics and nature of ISIS changed as well. Al-Baghdadi had earnestly taken up the PR gambit inaugurated by al-Zarqawi, and then expanded by al-Masri and the first al-Baghdadi, and further Iraqized ISI, outfitting its upper echelons with former Saddamists. By incorporating al-Nusra's lower and middle cadres, al-Baghdadi thus found himself once again commanding a more internationalized terror army, one that spanned the Levant and Mesopotamia. By renouncing al-Qaeda, al-Baghdadi actually returned ISIS to a version of its earliest incarnation in Iraq.

SYRIA'S SAHWA

Souad Nawfal remembered when the anti-Assad protests gained traction in Raqqa. It was March 15, 2012, shortly after the death of Ali Babinsky, the first resident of the eastern province of Syria to be killed by regime forces. He was seventeen years old. "We buried him and then when we had a funeral and protest on his behalf, they fired on us and killed sixteen of our people."

She also remembered when she began protesting ISIS. "I started demonstrating because they took Father Paolo," she said, referring to the Italian Jesuit priest who for decades ran a parish north of Damascus and who supported the Syrian revolution from its inception. After joining protests in Raqqa in late July, he was kidnapped by ISIS and has not been heard from since. "Paolo was my guest," Nawfal, a short, forty-year-old, hijab-wearing former schoolteacher said during an interview in November 2013. "He used to come to break the fast at Ramadan in my house. He was coming to speak out against ISIS. He wanted to stop the killings and secrecy, all the stuff the regime does. He went in to speak to ISIS, but he never came out."

Nawfal became a hero to Syrian moderate activists, as well as a minor Internet celebrity for a four-minute video she made in which she lambasted ISIS for their draconian rule and religious obscurantism. The video is titled "The

Woman in Pants," in reference to her refusal to adhere to ISIS's dress code for women. Nawfal said that she has spent the last two months protesting the new ideologues in her province, whom she sees not only as tarnishing Islam, but also as the mirror image of the very totalitarians she and her fellow activists wanted to be rid of in the first place. "They treat people horribly. They're exactly like Assad's regime. They scare people into submission."

Much like the Mukhabarat during the early days of the protest movement, ISIS has also banned civilians from taking photographs or making any recordings of provocative behavior in Raqqa. "ISIS would beat people in the street with leather. If anyone was going around taking 'illegal' pictures of this with a camera, they'd be taken into custody. In the month and a half I was protesting in front of the headquarters, no one would take my picture because they were scared."

The jihadi movement has succeeded, Nawfal believes, by preying upon the poverty, illiteracy, and wartime exigencies of this province to curry favor with the population. An especially effective tactic has been the brainwashing of Raqqa's children. "People that are poor and uneducated and not paying attention to what their kids are doing, their ten-year-olds will go out and then ISIS will promise the family food and money. They elevate these kids and call them 'sheikhs' and give them weapons and power, turn them into child soldiers. But these are ten-year-old boys who have never studied theology, and now they're sheikhs! I am worried that this is really ruining the idea of what Muslims are and what Islam is."

Nawfal became a daily fixture in front of ISIS's local headquarters, where she was cursed at, spit on, manhandled, and even run over. "I was standing out in front of this place, and there was an ISIS man with a long white beard who wanted to park his car there. But it's a huge area. He told me I had to move. I told him no. So he started swearing at me, berating me, but I still wouldn't move. So he hit me with the car twice. It wasn't that hard, but more for him to make a point."

She went on: "Every day they'd point a Kalashnikov at my head and threaten to shoot me. I'd tell them, 'Do it. If you kill me first, then the second bullet has to go to Bashar's head.' That'd irritate them."

Where her chutzpah may discombobulate the takfiris, the fact that she is both a small, middle-aged woman and more or less a solo act in defying them likely accounts for her survival and precarious freedom thus far. Nevertheless, she insists that she has narrowly escaped ISIS's distinct brand of social justice more than once, the last time after standing up for the rights of Raqqa's Christian community.

In late September 2013 ISIS attacked and burned two churches in the province, removing the crosses from their spires and replacing them with their black flag of global jihad. On September 25, it did this to the Sayidat al-Bishara Catholic Church, after which around two dozen people turned up at the site to protest. "I told them, 'What are you doing here? Go to the headquarters,'" Nawfal said. She led a march, and some of the protestors began following her, but by the time she reached the headquarters, she found that she was all by herself. Everyone had dropped out of the retinue out of fear. A day later, another church was stormed; Nawfal again went to demonstrate after she heard that people had been arrested. This time she carried a sign that read "Forgive me." The message was intended for her family, because she was certain that that day she would either be killed or abducted. "First they tried to scare me away. They let off a bomb near me. I was there for ten minutes, and a sixteen-year-old member of ISIS came to me and called me an infidel and turned to the other ISIS men and said, 'Why are you letting her live?' He was about to kill me, but apparently he got orders for no one to talk to me.

"Five minutes later, a car came with guns and weapons. Somebody jumped out and started grabbing at my arm, hitting me on the shoulder. Another person was spitting at me, swearing at me. I thought I was finished at this point. I started to call the Syrian people around me. I shouted, 'Are you happy, Syrians? Look what they're doing to me. Look at your women, how they're getting raped, how they're getting attacked, and you're just sitting there, watching.'"

Nawfal said that she will only go outside to protest so long as no one on the street recognizes her. The minute an ISIS militant sees her, she leaves. She never stays in one place now, instead moving from house to house, a fugitive in her own city. She does not believe that the current situation will change in the near future. "If people have fear, Raqqa will not have freedom from ISIS. As long as ISIS continues to use the tactics of the regime, it's not going to become free."

Nawfal has since fled to Turkey.

There are thousands more like Nawfal who have resisted ISIS locally in Raqqa and elsewhere. Abu Jarir al-Shamali's criticism of al-Qaeda's Waziristan operation—that the entire territory was more in thrall to Pashtun tribes than to the mujahidin—was of a piece with ISIS's obsession with sahwats, be they in Iraq or in Syria. Paradoxically, in trying to forestall an Awakening, it ended up precipitating one.

On July 11, 2013, Kamal Hamami, a commander of the FSA's Supreme Military Council, was shot dead by ISIS gunmen at a checkpoint in Latakia. Although tensions following that incident ran high—"We are going to wipe the floor with them," one FSA commander told Reuters—the matter was swiftly hushed up, and Hamami's murder was referred to a Sharia court for "investigation." Similarly, when ISIS "accidentally" beheaded Mohammed Fares, a commander from Ahrar al-Sham, believing him to have been an Iraqi Shia militiaman (he allegedly muttered Shia mantras in his sleep), ISIS asked for "understanding and forgiveness." Neither ISIS nor any mainstream or Islamist rebel group wanted to start a civil war within a civil war. And though many FSA rebels saw ISIS's draconian rule as a long-term danger for Syria, they also understood that Sahwa-come-too-soon would only benefit one man: Bashar al-Assad, who would then either sit back and watch the opposition devour itself, or contribute to this self-cannibalization by helping ISIS attack the FSA.

Nevertheless, ISIS seemed intent on provoking a backlash. It kidnapped revered opposition activists. It terrorized civilians under its sway. It established monopolistic checkpoints that functioned more like choke points for rival factions. And it attacked Syrian rebels. On August 1, 2013, for instance, ISIS sent a car bomb to the base of Ahfad al-Rasoul, or Grandsons of the Prophet, in Raqqa, killing thirty. Then it expelled the brigade from the city.

In late December 2013, the city of Maarat al-Numan, in Syria's Idlib province, staged a protest in favor of rebel unity against the al-Assad regime—and for the release of an FSA officer, Lieutenant Colonel Ahmad Saoud, who had been kidnapped days earlier by ISIS at a checkpoint. Saoud, a defector from the Syrian army, had been traveling with a retinue to the Taftanaz air base in Idlib in order to parley with ISIS and negotiate the release of military equipment— including antiaircraft missiles—that the latter had stolen from Forsan al-Haqq, or the Knights of Justice, an FSA brigade. Saoud also represented the Idlib Military Council, a regional assembly representing all the rebel groups in the province, which had publicly demanded that ISIS free all its kidnapped civilians and pursue any civil or criminal complaints that it had with rebels in the relevant Sharia courts. Saoud's own kidnapping, then, came in the midst of his trying to avoid further confrontation with ISIS. Maarat al-Numan's rally on his behalf had the intended effect. Within hours of the protest action, ISIS released Saoud, making him the first FSA officer to leave its custody alive.

On December 29, ISIS raided several dissident news organizations in Kafranbel, a city in the northwestern Idlib province, which had somehow managed, through two years of regime bombardment and the proliferation of jihadism, to retain the democratic principles of the original Syrian uprising. Among the buildings targeted was the Kafranbel Media Center, run by the forty-one-year-old Raed Fares, an artist whose pro-revolutionary artwork and slogans—all written in colloquial English and very often wittily allusive to Western popular culture—had helped make an Arab revolution intelligible to non-Arab audiences the world over. In one celebrated poster, the famous "king of the world" scene from the movie *Titanic* is reproduced, with Vladimir Putin cast as Leonardo DiCaprio and Bashar al-Assad as Kate Winslet. Lately, Fares had taken to comparing ISIS's depravity to the regime's, making them twin enemies of the Syrian people.

Hours earlier, before the ISIS raid, Fares's Media Center broadcast a radio program featuring Syrian women discussing their recent divorces. This was all too much for the takfiris, who abducted six of Fares's employees (they were released two hours later) and stole or smashed the center's computers and broadcasting equipment.

"The reason Kafranbel became important is because it's been persistently and consistently supporting the revolution in all of its aspects—whether it's the nonviolent revolution or the armed revolution or the humanitarian and civil society work," Fares told one of the authors. "The regime, when we would say something in opposition to them, they'd shell us. ISIS, when we made a drawing against them—the first in June of this year—they wanted to attack us, so they came and raided the Media Center. At the end of the day, they're both the same. They're both tyrants." (Not long after this interview, which took place as Fares was touring the United States, months following the assault on his center, ISIS tried to assassinate him in Idlib. He was shot several times but recovered from his injuries.)

On New Year's Day 2014, ISIS finally overplayed its hand in Syria, killing Hussein al-Suleiman, or Abu Rayyan, a respected physician and commander in Ahrar al-Sham. Like Saoud, Abu Rayyan was abducted while heading to a negotiation meeting with ISIS. He was locked up for twenty days and horribly tortured before being shot. Images of his mutilated corpse were then circulated on social media, outraging even those Ahrar al-Sham supporters who had hitherto urged patience and reconciliation with ISIS. The brigade accused it of exceeding even the barbarity of al-Assad's Mukhabarat and warned that "if ISIS continues with its methodical avoiding of refraining from ... resorting to an independent judicial body, and its stalling and ignoring in settling its injustices against others, the revolution and the jihad will head for the quagmire of internal fighting, in which the Syrian revolution will be the first loser."

A day later, on January 2, ISIS hit another FSA location, this time in Atareb, Aleppo, driving even Islamist fighters into an alliance with the FSA. The Islamic Front, a conglomerate of Islamist and Salafist rebel groups, which not a month earlier had commandeered an FSA warehouse full of weapons and supplies in the Idlib village of Atmeh, declared solidarity with a fellow victim of jihadist fanatics. "We hereby address the Islamic State of the requirement to immediately withdraw from the city of al-Atareb," the Islamic Front stated in a press release, "and to end the killing of the fighters based on false excuses and return all unfairly confiscated properties of weapons and bases to their rightful owners. They must also accept the rule of God by agreeing to the judgments of the independent religious courts to resolve the conflicts that arise between them and the other factions. We remind ISIS that those who originally liberated al-Atareb and the suburbs of Aleppo in general are those whom you are now fighting."

By that point, Lieutenant Colonel Ahmad Saoud had joined with a new rebel formation known as the Syrian Revolutionaries Front, which claimed to have aggregated as many as twenty separate factions belonging to the Idlib Military Council. This new mainstream front, Saoud relayed to one of the authors, was founded with one purpose: "to fight ISIS."

The last group to join the budding Sahwa movement in northern Syria was the Army of the Mujahidin, an alliance of eight rebel brigades, all based in Aleppo. "We, the Army of the Mujahidin," it declared, "pledge to defend ourselves and our honor, wealth, and lands, and to fight [ISIS], which has violated the rule of God, until it announces its dissolution." ISIS was given a stark choice: either it could defect to the mainstream rebellion or it could surrender its arms and leave Syria.

So what had begun as localized skirmishes transformed into a massive armed uprising against ISIS led by three super-militias of diverse ideological orientation: the Islamic Front, the Syrian Revolutionaries Front, and the Army of the Mujahidin. Together they swept ISIS from its territorial perches throughout much of northern Syria. The ad hoc counterinsurgency coincided with an upsurge in popular anti ISIS protests in Idlib and Aleppo, which ISIS tried to suppress by shooting the protestors.

As the FSA had feared, the al-Assad regime was not about to stay neutral in this internecine fight, and it intervened objectively on the side of ISIS. As the ground fighting continued, the Syrian Air Force took to bombing areas from which ISIS had just been expelled, hitting either FSA or Islamic Front targets (when it was not hitting civilians), and prompting further allegations among activists that ISIS was little more than a catspaw of the regime.

By January 4, following an FSA-issued twenty-four-hour deadline for ISIS to surrender and abandon Syria, two hundred jihadists had been arrested. ISIS had executed civilians and rebels and resorted to car bombings and the shelling of rebel-held territories. In a desperate communiqué apparently suing for peace, ISIS issued three demands. All road blockades in cities and villages were to be lifted; no ISIS fighter should be detained, insulted, or harmed; and all ISIS detainees and foreign fighters from any other groups should be released immediately. If these demands were not met, ISIS would issue a general order to withdraw from all the frontline positions against the regime—the clear implication being that it would return territory to al-Assad.

On January 5, the Islamic Front announced that it had been given no choice but to turn on its former ally; it had been "push[ed]" to battle, and while its charter was initially welcoming of foreign fighters offering assistance in the struggle against al-Assad, it would "not accept any group that claims to be a state." Atareb was retaken by the rebels, and the black flag of ISIS replaced with the Free Syrian tricolor. An activist for the Shaam News Network in Raqqa claimed that rebels had "liberat[ed] more than 80 percent of the Idlib countryside and 65 percent of Aleppo and its countryside." Another declared that "the presence of the State of Baghdadi is finished," in what would prove to be too optimistic a prediction.

By the end of the first week of January, al-Nusra was leading the charge against ISIS in its regional headquarters in Raqqa city, joined by Ahrar al-Sham. Some fifty Syrian hostages held by ISIS were released from Raqqa's answer to the DMV—which had been turned into a makeshift prison—as was one of many foreign journalists held captive by the group, the Turkish photographer Bunyamin Aygun, who had been kidnapped the previous month. Two churches that had been burned or confiscated by ISIS were also "liberated" by al-Nusra, which declared its intent to restore them for Christian use.

A shaky truce brokered between ISIS and al-Nusra/Ahrar al-Sham appeared to lower the temperature a bit in the Aleppo suburbs, as did ISIS's withdrawal from strategic areas close to the Turkish border, including Atmeh and al-Dana.

Al-Jolani blamed ISIS for the week of fitna that shook northern Syria but urged the formation of independent legal councils for resolving disputes to accompany the cease-fire. He also said that "detainees will be exchanged between all parties . . . and roads will be opened for everyone."

Throughout the course of Syria's brief Sahwa—an Awakening that suddenly featured al-Qaeda's official franchise on the side of the sahwats—ISIS had raised a defiant slogan: *baqiyya wa tatamaddad* ("remaining and expanding"). It amounted to a promise to defeat this popular turn against it and to reach the Arabian Peninsula. The internecine war had already spilled over into other parts of Syria, with ISIS bombing Ahrar al-Sham's base in Mayadeen, Deir Ezzor, near the Iraqi border. It declared war on the rebels, and threatened suicide attacks and car bombings against Syrians.

In the ten days of Syria's Sahwa, cracks appeared within the various groups duking it out with ISIS. Some were ideologically opposed to going to war against a fellow Muslim army; others rightly understood that doing so would only play right into the hands of al-Assad and his proxies, who could simply sit back and let their revolutionary foes devour themselves. Also, the ease with which fighters migrated from one banner to another, depending on who was seen as the dominant or more disciplined faction, could well erase the gains made against ISIS by creating waves of mass defections to the terror army. So Abu Omar al-Shishani, then ISIS's commander in Aleppo, signed the ceasefire agreement with Abu Khalid al-Suri, al-Zawahiri's delegate in Syria, who was acting on behalf of both Ahrar al-Sham and al-Nusra. For the moment, total fratricidal war among the jihadists had been avoided.

THE AL-NUSRA–ISIS SPLIT

But the damage wrought on the al-Nusra–ISIS relationship was irreparable. On February 2, 2014, global al-Qaeda formally ended its association with ISIS, issuing a public statement: "ISIS is not a branch of the Qaidat al-Jihad [al-Qaida's official name] group, we have no organizational relationship with it, and the group is not responsible for its actions."

One of the jihadists who smuggled himself across the Iraqi-Syrian border with al-Jolani during Ramadan in 2011 was Abu Maria al-Qahtani. His real name is Maysara al-Juburi. He is active on Twitter as a leading exponent for the al-Nusra worldview, particularly its ongoing family feud with ISIS, from which al-Qahtani defected after having served as a top commander. "The rumor is that he used to be a traffic cop before he became al-Nusra's military operative in Deir Ezzor," Laith Alkhouri said. "He accused ISIS of destroying jihad in Iraq and Syria; he called the members 'deviants.'"

The fault lines of this divorce had run throughout the marriage. They were already discernible in that awkward first encounter between bin Laden and al-Zarqawi in Kandahar in 1999, and in AQI's tempestuous eleven-year history. And though al-Nusra and ISIS have cooperated tactically since the split, allegedly even mulling some form of reconciliation (particularly in the face of coalition air strikes against both organizations in Syria), there is little chance that a broad rapprochement will occur. *Dabiq* makes plain that ISIS views al-Qaeda as a spent force in jihad, and views itself as the inheritor of bin Laden's legacy. The differences are too deep and many by now, according to Alkhouri. "ISIS takes the super-rightist ultraconservative route. It is legitimate to kill even those who you cannot otherwise repel their aggression. Jolani is one of those guys. Baghdadi is even rumored to have vowed to kill him. ISIS apostatizes Muslims who didn't know they committed some offense. So if you insulted the divine using a slang expression, they'll behead you even if you didn't know you insulted the divine."

Another major discrepancy is the chicken-or-egg one about Islamic state-building. For ISIS, theocratic legitimacy follows the seizure and administration of terrain. First you "liberate" the people, then you found a government. For al-Qaeda, it's the other way around: Sharia laws come into practice before the holy war overthrows the *taghut* (tyrannical) regime.

ISIS further claims that al-Zarqawi had a five-phase process for establishing the caliphate, and that he had accomplished three of these phases by the time al-Baghdadi arrived on the scene: the emigration of foreign fighters to the land of jihad (*hijrah*), their enlistment in the ranks of a militancy (*jama'ah*), and their undermining of the idolators and the *taghut* (pretty much everyone but the Zarqawists and their allies). The remaining two phases were consolidation of power (*tamkin*), followed finally by the establishment of the caliphate (*khalifah*).

JIHADI RECRIMINATIONS

One of the more curious epiphenomena of this breakup is that of Jolanist loyalists accusing Baghdadis of working for the other side. Many al-Nusra supporters have pointed to how the Syrian Air Force had largely refrained for the better part of a year (2013–2014) from bombing rather conspicuous ISIS installations in Raqqa. Al-Nusra was right.

A study conducted by the Carter Center found that, prior to ISIS's military advances across Syria and Iraq in July and August 2014, the regime had "largely abstained from engaging [ISIS] unless directly threatened. . . . Prior to this [ISIS] offensive, the Syrian government had directed over 90 percent of all air raids against opposition positions."

By Damascus's own admission, it spent the better part of 2013 and 2014 mostly leaving ISIS alone in order to focus its aerial campaign against FSA and other rebel groups—for the simple reason that letting black-clad terrorists run around a provincial capital, crucifying and beheading people, made for great propaganda. One adviser to the regime told the *New York Times* that ignoring ISIS targets helped with the "tarring [of] all insurgents" as extremists.

We have also seen how the regime chooses to deal with terrorism by infiltration. An early defector from ISIS told CNN's Arwa Damon in February 2014 that he witnessed would-be suicide bombers being told by their battlefield emirs that they were going off to attack regime installations. In reality, they were sent on suicide missions against other rebels. "There were a lot of regime locations we could have taken without sustaining losses of our fighters," the defector, Abu Ammara, said, "and we would receive orders to retreat."

Some of this may owe to ISIS's financial dependence on selling Syria's oil back to the regime. As a Western intelligence source told the *Daily Telegraph* in January 2014, just a month before al-Qaeda formally severed its ties with ISIS, "The regime is paying al-Nusra to protect oil and gas pipelines under al-Nusra's control in the north and east of the country, and is also allowing the transport of oil to regime-held areas. We are also now starting to see evidence of oil and gas facilities under ISIS control."

"Whatever Bashar al-Assad and Abu Bakr al-Baghdadi may think of one another personally," Frederic Hof, the former State Department adviser on Syria, wrote, "their top tactical priority in Syria is identical: destroy the Syrian nationalist opposition to the Assad regime."

Alkhouri said that this charge of ISIS's collusion or conspiracy with the regime is widespread in al-Qaeda circles. "I came across a document—the person who released it said it came from air force intelligence—which said that Syrian intelligence has about 250 informants in the ranks of ISIS. I was not shocked in the least. I like to do reverse-engineering. How can I prove this by eliminating the noise? This is what you see: for many months, ISIS was very much capable of attacking regime soldiers but chose not to, preferring instead to transfer literally hundreds of its fighters to other areas in Syria that had been liberated by the FSA, Nusra, and other Islamist brigades. Why is ISIS doing this? Nusra says it's for the expansion of its power: 'Let other fighters repel or expel the regime, we'll move in and rule the land after all the heavy lifting is done.'"

On Twitter, a popular account known as @WikiBaghdady has been reporting what it says is inside intelligence on ISIS—and about the backstory of its emir. No one knows who runs the account, but the likelihood is high that it is either an al-Qaeda operative or affiliate, or, perhaps, a defector from ISIS looking to embarrass his erstwhile confederates by airing their dirty laundry. The portrait made of al-Baghdadi on this account is that of a midlevel member of the Islamic State of Iraq from 2006 to 2010 who rose through the ranks after having used his house as a drop site for secret communications between fighters and their commanders. "His job was apparently that of a go-between," said Alkhouri. "If this is true, then he was definitely privy to secret communications—dates of operations, claims of responsibilities, the top structure of the Islamic State of Iraq's Shura Council, who was powerful and who was not. And that means he was also privy to how Syria's military intelligence was running ratlines into Iraq. This is how Nusra wants to scandalize him. 'Baghdadi called Zawahiri a quisling, an upholder of Sykes-Picot? Yeah, well, look who's talking.'"

11

CONVERTS AND
"FIVE-STAR JIHADISTS"
THE MANAGEMENT OF HYPE

The transformation of foreign fighters into contemporary Saladins is a central plank of jihadist recruitment, going back to al-Zarqawi's days. After all, even the Jordanian had come off as Gomer Pyle with an assault rifle until his tech department edited him into every inch the emir. "Look at who these foreign fighters are, first of all," Richard, the former Pentagon counterterrorism official, said. "In most cases, they're adventurers who don't have a pot to piss in back home, whether that's Belgium, Manchester, Algeria, Yemen, or, okay, Georgia," Richard said, referring to ISIS's photogenic commander, Abu Omar al-Shishani, who originates in the Pankisi Gorge, just south of Chechnya. "They got hopped up through social media or proselytizing outside the mosque and went off to fight jihad. These are the same guys militaries around the world have been counting on forever to be privates or infantrymen. They're knucklehead nineteen-year-olds looking to do something in their life because they don't have shit to do back in Belgium."

Western sensationalism has perversely contributed to the lure or glamour of ISIS as much as it has to its lurid appeal to the young and disaffected. Stories about pretty, middle-class teenage Austrian girls going off to fight with and marry warrior-heroes—and copycats who are stopped en route before they can reach Syria—continue to supply headlines. People are fascinated by the psychopathic spectacle of ISIS, and especially by those they see as "like them" but who are so drawn to it that they abandon seemingly comfortable lives in the West to pursue jihadism.

Scott Atran, an anthropologist at France's National Center for Scientific Research, argues that ISIS is really no different from the revolutionary-romantic movements that have reveled in bloodshed throughout history. "You can't inspire people to kill people and harm others without moral virtue," he said. "It's very much like the French Revolution. When Robespierre introduced the terror as a tool of democracy—they were quite ostentatious about it." Bringing the fever-dream caused by world-historical movements closer to our own time, Atran reminded us of a 1940 essay by George Orwell in which he asked a similar question of a book advocating what he summarized as a "horrible brainless empire in which, essentially, nothing ever happens except the training of young men for war and the endless breeding of fresh cannon-fodder." How, he wondered, could such a "monstrous vision" be put across when liberal democracy was meant to have ended such barbarism? And why was a nation flinging itself at the feet of a man who offered "struggle, danger, and death" where other forms of government were offering a "good time"? Orwell was reviewing *Mein Kampf*.

It was with an appreciation of these macabre precedents that we set out to profile the various sorts of people drawn to the caliphate.

THE INTELLECTUALS

In October 2014, ISIS's security squad arrested Mothanna Abdulsattar, an articulate nineteen-year-old media activist working for the Free Syrian Army, around two months after it assumed control of his region in eastern Syria. He was taken for an interrogation at a nearby jihadist base amid threats to his life, the fate of which, he found out, could be determined by his professional affiliation. Working for the Syrian opposition or Saudi media arms meant death. "If you are working for Orient or Al Arabiya, we'll chop your head off," Abdulsattar was told. Working for Qatar's Al Jazeera, according to the conversation between Abdulsattar and the ISIS members, was evidently less of a problem. Abdulsattar told one of the authors that he was relieved when a smiling, respectful older jihadist stepped in to save him from an ISIS commissar's line of questioning.

"Abu Hamza was quiet and respectful," Abdulsattar remembered, referring to Abu Hamza al-Shami, a senior cleric in ISIS, from the township of

Minbij in eastern Aleppo. "Even his face makes you comfortable. He began by talking about the FSA, and why ISIS was fighting it. He said because they accept ungodly laws and receive funding from America, and God said: 'Whoever aligns with them, he's one of them.' He then talked about al-Dawla. He asked me, 'Why aren't you pledging allegiance? The Prophet said that those who die without having bayat to someone—their death will be a *jahiliyyah* [un-Islamic] death.' Honestly, when I heard that, I was shocked to my core. For the first time, I realized, the hadith is true."

But Abdulsattar still was not ready to pledge allegiance to Abu Bakr al-Baghdadi. So Abu Hamza smiled and asked him to take his time. A week or so later, Abdulsattar decided to commit.

He spoke with gusto about his journey into ISIS, downplaying the eight hours he had spent in its custody as more of a rite of passage than a life-or-death grilling. Abdulsatter said that he was ultimately swayed by ISIS's "intellectualism and the way it spreads religion and fights injustice."

A great number of ISIS members who were interviewed for this book echoed similar sentiments—and hyperbolic appraisals—of the terror army, which has mastered techniques to break down the psyches of those it wishes to recruit, and then build them back up again in its own image. Abdulsattar's reference to "intellectualism" may seem bizarre or even grotesque to a Western observer, but it refers to ISIS's carefully elaborated ideological narrative, a potent blend of Islamic hermeneutics, history, and politics.

"When you listen to the clerics of the al-Dawla," Abdulsattar said, "you are shocked that most of our Islamic societies have deviated from the true religion. They follow a religion that was invented two decades ago, or less. Most of our societies that claim to be Muslim, their religion is full of impurities; ninety percent of it is *bida'a* [religious innovation]. Take *shirk*, for example: we associate in our worship things other than God, and we don't even realize it. Omens, for example. When we adjust our posture in front of other people inside a mosque, that is *riya'* [ostentation]." ISIS offered Abdulsattar something he could not find under Assadism or the Free Syrian Army. It offered him "purified" Islam.

"When you meet a cleric or a foreigner with ISIS, and he sits with you for two hours, believe me you will be convinced," he continued. "I don't know, they have a strange way of persuading people. When they control an area, they enforce religion by force, you have to pray whether you like it or not. We were all oblivious to the most important obligation in Islam—jihad. They shed light on jihad. Every time you watch a video by them, you are going to have a strange feeling that pushes you toward jihad."

Even those victimized or persecuted by ISIS attest to the way the group has of turning opponents into loyalists.

Abu Bilal al-Layli had been in charge of funding the FSA in his hometown, Albu Layl, in Deir Ezzor. When ISIS arrived, he left for Turkey. The jihadists burned down his house and put him on its wanted list. He sees them as a band of illiterate thugs who hold a twisted understanding of religion, but he nonetheless admires their ability to persuade the young and the old, particularly those with little religious background. "ISIS used money and talk of justice and war against thieves to lure people. For some, it worked. In our areas, you see people longing for Islam and wanting someone to fight . . . *haramiya* [thieves]. They bought into the 'Islamic State' idea, thinking that the jihadists were honest. Those who joined Daesh," he said, referring to the derogatory and strident-sounding Arabic acronym for ISIS, "hardly memorized a few Quranic verses. They had no religious base. They were simply lured by the power of persuasion."

THE NOVICE

Hamza Mahmoud was a fifteen-year-old boy from a well-to-do family in Qamishli, in northern Syria. Hamza's parents learned that he had joined ISIS after he started to disappear from their home for long stretches in the summer of 2014. After many failed attempts to prevent him from returning to the group, one of his brothers said, Hamza's father deliberately broke one of Hamza's legs. Once it healed, he left his family home again and severed direct communication with his parents. According to his brother, Omar, Hamza refused to speak to his family lest his mother's cries or his father's admonitions influence his decision to remain with ISIS. He would communicate only with his brothers, who were outside of the country.

During a Skype conversation organized for the authors, Omar unsuccessfully tried to persuade Hamza to quit ISIS and return home. "Hamza, this is not right, you're still young, this is a misguided group," Omar told him. "Nothing in Islam calls for slaughter and violence." Hamza responded, in mechanical but classical Arabic, by citing hadith and verses to validate acts carried out by his new masters. Also, he insisted, the common portrayal of ISIS was biased and wrong. "Don't believe everything you hear in media," Hamza said. "The brothers are true Muslims. They are doing nothing but the right thing. If you see what I see and hear what I hear, you will know."

Omar then told Hamza that Syria has people from various sects and religions who have lived side by side for centuries. Hamza was particularly shocked when his brother added that among his friends who were living in the same residence were Alawites and Yazidis. "You have Yazidis next to you?" Hamza answered. "Kill them and get closer to God."

THE KURDS

Kurdish participation in ISIS seems counterintuitive given that the organization's upper cadres are replete with former Saddamists—members of the Baathist regime responsible for a genocidal campaign against the Kurds. ISIS has targeted Kurdish villages and towns, such as Kobane, on the Syrian-Turkish border, and besieged Erbil, the capital of Iraq's Kurdistan Regional Government, before having its advance halted by US air strikes in August 2014. Kurdish militias in Syria and Iraq, including the Iraqi peshmerga and the People's Defense Units, or YPG, are considered secularists and Marxists, respectively, and are therefore marked for death. And whereas other Sunni insurgencies with strong Baathist composition—particularly al-Douri's Naqshbandi Army—have tried and mostly failed to recruit Kurds, ISIS has had remarkable success in the very site of Saddam's genocide, the Iraqi city of Halabja.

ISIS's spokesman, Abu Muhammad al-Adnani, has justified the campaign against the largest stateless people of the Middle East in the following terms: "Our war with Kurds is a religious war. It is not a nationalistic war—we seek the refuge of Allah. We do not fight Kurds because they are Kurds. Rather, we fight the disbelievers amongst them, the allies of the crusaders and Jews in their war against the Muslims. . . . The Muslim Kurds in the ranks of the Islamic State are many. They are the toughest of fighters against the disbelievers amongst their people." Emphasizing the point, and also driving the wedge among Kurds deeper, in October 2014, one of ISIS's "Muslim Kurds," Abu Khattab al-Kurdi, was reportedly leading the jihadists' battle against the YPG in Kobane. He was joined by other Kurds from Hasaka, Aleppo, and northern Raqqa.

Hussain Jummo, the political editor at the Dubai-based *Al Bayan* newspaper, and a prominent analyst of Kurdish politics, offers the most plausible explanation for why Kurds have joined ISIS. After Saddam's Halabja massacre, many families in the town were left impoverished, while others built new homes and carried on with their lives as before. Charities that were started and meant to tend to the victims of the chemical attacks were mainly Salafist in orientation, organized and funded by Gulf state sponsors, including Kuwait's Society of the Revival of Islamic Heritage, which has been accused by the United States of bankrolling al-Qaeda. So after decades of proselytization in the Kurdish regions of the Middle East, Halabja became the epicenter of Kurdish Islamism.

In Syria the Kurdish turn to ISIS has been less common, although not unheard-of. Syrian Kurds are predominantly secular or Sufi from the Khaznawi order, named after the family that inaugurated it. We spoke with two Kurds from Aleppo and Hasaka, however, who said they were driven to ISIS because of the organization's pan-Sunni, rather than pan-Arab, philosophy. A Kurdish ISIS member from Hasaka related to the authors a conversation he had had with an ISIS recruiter shortly before he joined. The recruiter told him that al-Nusra, which had by then split from ISIS, was essentially an "Arab" organization, rather than an Islamic one. ISIS was blind to ethnicity, he said, and attended only to true faith—a theme that recurs frequently in its propaganda.

In much the same way, ISIS has also attracted large numbers from the Turkoman minority, which has suffered a large share of discrimination and repression under despotic Arab regimes. Turkoman ISIS members have been key to the rise of the organization in Mosul and the areas outlying it. Al-Baghdadi's deputy, Abu Muslim al-Turkmani, who was killed in August 2015, was Turkoman.

THE PRISONERS

A particular breed of jihadist dominates ISIS's middle and upper echelons, subscribing to a narrow set of doctrinal tenets at odds with the more expansive and welcoming ideology previously described. Abu al-Athir al-Absi, the former Sednaya prisoner who was released under al-Assad's general amnesty, is the perfect case study in this category.

Al-Absi formed a group, Usud al-Sunna, or the Sunni Lions, in Aleppo's countryside soon after his release. He then became instrumental in rallying support for ISIS after its 2013 split from Nusra. Al-Absi took a hard line against other Islamist and jihadist groups many months before ISIS was formed—a position that many say was an extension of the ideological conflict among jihadists at Sednaya prison (although it may also be linked to the fact that al-Absi holds many of the groups responsible for the death of his brother Firas).

According to journalist Wael Essam, who met al-Absi after the Syrian uprising started, the jihadist has considered many of his fellow former inmates at Sednaya to be kuffar, including those who now lead rival Islamist brigades and battalions in Syria. Why? Because they refused to pronounce as non-believers the taghut (tyrannical) Muslim rulers in the Middle East and the majority of Muslims in the region. Also, al-Absi explained, these Islamists acceded to the surrender of Sednaya to the Syrian authorities after the bloody 2008 riot.

Al-Absi and his cohort were outliers among Salafists at Sednaya. Few of the inmates shared their ultraist ideology or joined them in defying the regime even after it had amassed soldiers from the 4th Armored Division outside their ward.

The tensions between ISIS and other jihadist and Islamist groups in the Syrian Civil War can be viewed as the resumption of an argument that took place behind bars in the preceding years. According to Abu Adnan, a security official in ISIS, most of the rebel Islamist brigades and battalions were formed as insurgent reunions within the various prison wards. "They did not just come together," he said. "These men all knew each other, and the factions that were formed later already had the personnel and ideological infrastructure in place. The personality conflicts and political differences continued."

When Abu Bakr al-Baghdadi visited Syria in March 2013, al-Absi was the first al-Nusra commander he met and the latter had secretly defected to ISIS before it was even formed. Al-Absi helped al-Baghdadi secure the allegiance of various al-Nusra fighters and other jihadists and militants then part of rival insurgencies in Syria. Later, he was one of al-Baghdadi's staunchest defenders and one of the loudest proponents of the declaration of an Islamic caliphate.

THE FENCE-SITTERS

Another category of ISIS recruits consists of those who already held Islamist or jihadist views but had limited themselves only to orbiting takfiri ideology. The final gravitational pull, as it were, differed depending on circumstance.

Some recruits joined for the simple reason that ISIS overran their territories and became the only Islamist faction available to join. Others were impressed with ISIS's military prowess in campaigns against rival rebel factions. Still others fell out with their original insurgencies and found ISIS more organized, disciplined, and able-bodied.

For what might be called "extra-mile extremists," the conversion experience is hardly as sweeping or comprehensive as it was for men like Abdulsattar. They have tended to trickle into ISIS from the rank and file of the Islamic Front and Islamist-leaning groups in Iraq and Syria as a result of either leadership disputes or the abortive Syrian Sahwa that erupted in late December 2013.

The trend of defections to ISIS was most conspicuous in September 2013. It was during that month that a dozen Islamist factions, including al-Nusra, issued a joint statement disavowing the Western-backed Syrian National Coalition, the political arm of the opposition, and calling for unity under "an Islamic framework." In October, seven Islamist groups then formed the Islamic Front and issued a statement rejecting democracy in favor of an Islamic *shura*-based system.

Over that period, ISIS made significant gains at the ideological level. Many Islamists struggled to reconcile warring against a fellow Salafist group—a position shared by many ordinary Syrians, who believed that any diversion from the main conflict against the al-Assad regime and its Iranian proxies amounted to treason. Younger members of the Islamic Front in particular held to religiously ultra-conservative beliefs and subscribed more ardently to the jihadist discourse of establishing an Islamic state. Some Islamic Front commanders, in fact, provided protection to ISIS convoys or simply refused to turn their guns on them. The dual loyalty only benefited ISIS.

Liwa Dawud, once the most powerful subfaction within the Islamic Front brigade known as Suqour al-Sham, or Falcons of the Levant, saw around one thousand of its own jump ship to ISIS in July 2014. Increasingly, fighters from the Islamic Front and al-Nusra have migrated to ISIS as the franchise has expanded farther into both Syria and Iraq.

ISIS benefits from the absence of a "Syrian" jihadist discourse to keep pace with the intensifying violence in a war-ravaged nation, which, by August 2014, had seen close to two hundred thousand killed. Established Syrian Islamists, especially the Muslim Brotherhood, have steered away from adopting such a discourse and have instead presented themselves as part of the mainstream prodemocracy movement, even though they have financially and politically backed rebel Islamist factions. Even al-Nusra, to some extent, positioned itself as a "nationalist" outcropping without international ambitions. This hypocrisy meant that ISIS more or less had a monopoly on the global Salafist-Jihadist narrative and its intoxicating vision of world conquest.

THE POLITICKERS

As it happens, the closer ISIS came to realizing its territorial ambitions, the less religion played a part in driving people to join the organization. Those who say they are adherents of ISIS as a strictly political project make up a weighty percentage of its lower cadres and support base.

For people in this category, ISIS is the only option for Sunni Muslims who have been dealt a dismal hand in the past decade—first losing control of Iraq and now suffering nationwide atrocities, which many equate to genocide, in Syria. They view the struggle in the Middle East as one between Sunnis and an Iranian-led coalition, and they justify ultra-violence as a necessary tool to counterbalance or deter Shia hegemony. This category often includes the highly educated.

One example is Saleh al-Awad, a secular lawyer from Jarablous, Hasaka, who was a staunch critic of ISIS before deciding that it was the only bulwark against Kurdish expansionism in his region. Saleh took part in the peaceful protest movement against al-Assad and was an advocate of democratic reform in Syria. "We're tired, every day [ISIS cuts] off four or five heads in our town," he said before his conversion experience took place. A few months following that exchange—around the time that ISIS began to besiege Kobane—Saleh said he joined the head-loppers.

A large number of Arabs in Hasaka share views similar to his own. One influential resident of the province said that "thousands" would join ISIS tomorrow if it invaded the city and provincial capital of Hasaka because of fears of what might happen to them under Kurdish domination.

A comparable dynamic exists in mixed communities near Baghdad, such as Baqubah, and in Homs and Hama, where sectarian tensions shape people's political orientations. A dozen ISIS-affiliated Arabs who conform to this political category might even be described as secular or agnostic (many said that they do not pray or attend mosque) and expressed deep objections to us about the atrocities being committed by ISIS. Nevertheless, they see it as the only armed group capable of striking against the "anti-Sunni" regimes and militias in Syria, Iraq, and beyond. By way of justification, Salim told one of us that violence has always been part of Islamic history and always precedes the establishment of strong Islamic empires, including the Ummayads, Abbasids, and the second Ummayad kingdom in what is now Spain.

This sense of dejection, or injustice, felt by many Sunnis who now identify as a persecuted and embattled community is known in Arabic as *madhloumiya*. It is a concept historically associated with the Shia, to whose religious discourse suffering is integral. Equally paradoxical is that even where Sunnis are in the majority, they have taken to behaving as an insecure minority. The Shia in these areas, by contrast, appear more decisive, confident, and well organized, no doubt thanks to Iranian patronage and the militia-ization of their communities by Qassem Suleimani's Quds Force. Shia militants, as we have seen, are crossing national boundaries as much as their Sunni counterparts to participate in a holy war.

Sunnis feel that they are under assault—from al-Assad, Khamenei, and, up until recently, al-Maliki—and lacking any committed or credible political stewards. Their religious and political powerhouses, meanwhile, are perceived as complicit, politically emasculated, discredited, or silent: the Gulf Arab states, which either have Sunni majorities or Sunni-led governments, have been reduced to begging the United States for intervention.

ISIS has exploited this sense of sectarian grievance and vulnerability with devious aplomb. As al-Zarqawi could point to the Badr Corps in 2004, al-Baghdadi can now point to anti-Sunni atrocities being committed by the National Defense Force, the League of the Righteous, Lebanese Hezbollah, Iraq's Hezbollah Brigades, or, indeed, the Badr Corps in Syria and/or Iraq, and offer them up as proof that Sunnis have no hope but the caliphate.

THE PRAGMATISTS

In areas fully controlled by ISIS, people support the group because it is effective in terms of governance and delivery of basic services, such as sanitation and food delivery. ISIS has established a semblance of order in these "governed" territories, and people view the alternatives—al-Assad, the Iraqi government, or other militias—as far worse. For those weary of years of civil war, the ability to live without crime and lawlessness trumps whatever draconian rules ISIS has put into place. Members of this category sometimes keep their distance from ISIS, to avoid trouble; others seek out areas where ISIS is said not to be committing atrocities.

Abu Jasim, a cleric who joined ISIS after it overran his home in eastern Syria in the summer of 2014, said that he would deliberately avoid details of what ISIS did or did not do. "I see them leaving people alone if nobody messes with them," Abu Jasim said. "All I do is to teach people their religion, and I hope to get rewarded by God for what I do."

THE OPPORTUNISTS

There are also those who were drawn to ISIS largely because of personal ambition. The opportunists tend to serve in the group's rank and file as well as its low-level command structures. They join to undermine a rival group, to move up the chain of a dominant military and political force, or simply to preempt ISIS's brutal justice because of some past offense or crime they might have committed against the group.

Saddam al-Jamal, for example, was one of the most powerful FSA commanders in eastern Syria. After his prior rebel outfit, the Allahu Akbar Brigade, lost out to al-Nusra, which killed two of his brothers, al-Jamal pledged allegiance to ISIS. It apparently did not matter that he had a reputation as a drug dealer.

Aamer al-Rafdan joined ISIS after it broke from al-Nusra, owing mainly to a dispute he had with the latter over oil revenues—also, a continuing rivalry between his tribe and the one that had been dominated by al-Nusra in Deir Ezzor. Al-Rafdan was later accused by al-Jolani's organization of stealing $5 million worth of cotton.

THE FOREIGN FIGHTERS

Outside Iraq and Syria, of course, the motivations for joining ISIS differ drastically and are almost always fed by serious misapprehensions of what is taking place in either country.

The radicalization expert Shiraz Maher of King's College London has explained how digital apps or social media platforms such as Twitter, Facebook, and, in the ex-Soviet context, VKontakte (Russia's answer to Facebook) have revolutionized jihadist agitprop. Much of the online chatter among Western-born ISIS recruits sounds more like a satire of the group than an earnest commitment to it: "Does the Islamic State sell hair gel and Nutella in Raqqa?" "Should I bring an iPad to let Mom and Dad know that I arrived safely in caliphate?" "I was told there'd be Grand Theft Auto V."

In an article for the *New Statesman*, Maher observed that "[d]uring the Iraq War, sympathisers of al-Qaeda needed access to password-protected forums, where they could learn about events on the ground. These forums were not easy to find and access was harder to gain. Crucially, most of the conversations were in Arabic, a language alien to most British Muslims." Now every British Muslim who goes off to fight in Syria or Iraq becomes a virtual wrangler or recruitment officer for more of his own kind. One example was Mehdi Hassan, a twenty-year-old from Portsmouth who went off to join ISIS and died fighting in the battle of Kobane in November 2014. Hassan had actually enlisted along with several friends from Portsmouth, all of whom were drawn to the dazzling images of ISIS's martial triumphs and its whitewashed depiction of life under takfiri rule. They were known as the "Pompey lads," and, as Maher wrote, "Of the men he travelled with, only one is still fighting: three are dead and another is in prison in the UK."

In December 2013, Maher's International Centre for the Study of Radicalisation calculated that the number of foreign fighters enjoined with the Syrian opposition was "up to 11,000 . . . from 74 nations." Most of them signed up with ISIS or other jihadist groups, with few going to join mainstream FSA factions. Western Europe, the study found, accounted for 18 percent of the total, with France leading among nations as the number-one donor country for jihadists, followed closely by Britain. That number only grew, particularly in light of the US coalition war against ISIS. By September 2014, the CIA calculated that there were fifteen thousand foreign fighters in Syria, two thousand of whom were Westerners. These figures had doubled by September 2015. The predominant emigration trend has always been from the Middle East and North Africa, with Saudi Arabia, Libya, and Tunisia being the major feeder countries of foreign Sunni militants.

Missionary jihadists who were driven by civilian suffering, according to Maher, constituted a plurality of the Britons who joined ISIS. They saw jihad as an obligation to defend women and children as the war dragged on in Syria, Maher said.

Inside Syria, a similar trend of fighters drifting to extremist groups existed since mid-2012, when reports of civilians being slaughtered by pro-Assad militias became international news.

The impact of those massacres on the psyche of antiregime Syrians was also immense. Those conscious of their own radicalization typically point to the Houla and al-Bayda and similar massacres as the reason for their turn to Islamist and jihadist rebel factions closer to the end of 2012. Native Syrians, however, tended to enlist with homegrown extremist factions rather than the more foreigner-friendly ISIS. Even still, ISIS benefited from the Assadist massacres in another respect: for one, the gruesome manner in which they were carried out helped create some level of tolerance for beheadings, which were accepted by many Syrians as retribution against the regime and its Iranian-built militias.

The worst regime massacres typically occurred in areas where Alawite, Sunni, and Ismaili (another Shia offshoot) villages and hamlets adjoined one another, the better to encourage sectarian reprisal bloodlettings. They also followed a pattern of assault: a village would be shelled overnight by the Syrian Arab Army, and the next morning, militiamen from nearby would storm it. Armed with knives and light weapons, they would go on killing sprees, slaughtering men, women, and children. The killing was portrayed as systematic and driven by sectarian vigilantism. Videos of torture also showed shabiha or popular committees (the precursors to the National Defense Force) anathematizing Sunni symbols and forcing victims to affirm al-Assad's divinity and make other sacrilegious statements.

Maher notes a second category of foreign fighters: martyrdom-seekers, who want nothing more than to carry out a suicide operation and thus be lionized in the annals of jihadism. For many foreign fighters from the Gulf states, the glorification of suicide bombers has been a constant on jihadist chat forums and websites since al-Qaeda in Iraq got started. Saudi nationals often point to the fact that many Saudis carry out these self-immolations, to argue that ISIS leaders discriminate against their compatriots by sending them to their deaths, whereas Iraqis hoard all the leadership positions in the organization for themselves.

The final factor leading foreign fighters to ISIS, according to Maher, is pure adventurism. Adrenaline junkies tend to be nonpracticing Muslims and are often drug users or addicts, or involved in criminality and gang violence back home—much as al-Zarqawi himself was in Jordan before discovering the mosque. Going off to fight in Syria represents just another rush.

12

FROM TWITTER TO *DABIQ*
RECRUITING THE NEW MUJAHIDIN

Many interviewees from other Arab countries admitted that they had not been following developments in Iraq and Syria closely before they started supporting ISIS. That changed after the fall of Mosul. One Egyptian Islamist, for instance, explained that he was not sure which factions in Syria or Iraq were good or bad, but that after ISIS stormed through Ninewah, he began conducting "research" and found that the establishment of the caliphate was "consistent with" stories foretold by Prophet Muhammad. The anthropologist Scott Atran relayed a similar anecdote. "I remember talking with an imam in Spain who said, 'We always rejected violence, but Abu Bakr al-Baghdadi put us on the map. The caliphate doesn't have to be violent. It can be just like the European Union!'"

Detachment from the mundane realities of ISIS has made many Arabs susceptible to its self-aggrandizing portrayal as a God-anointed Sunni resistance movement inspired by early Islamic history and fundamentals. In order to control this carefully cultivated image, ISIS has transformed al-Zarqawi's grainy rough cuts into professionally produced blockbusters of propaganda and disinformation. So prized is its media operation that those in charge of its various departments are given the title of emir, making them equal in rank to ISIS commanders on the battlefield. Jihadist journalism is also a profitable line. According to the *Washington Post*, which queried captured media operatives from ISIS, "hundreds of videographers, producers and editors" responsible for scripting, filming, cutting, and disseminating ISIS films, or laying out the monthly issue of *Dabiq*, "form a privileged, professional class with status, salaries and living arrangements that are the envy of ordinary fighters."

A subject that recurs in our conversations with ISIS recruits is how the organization has learned from the mistakes of its forebears by not allowing detractors in the foreign press to shape popular perceptions about it. "Don't hear about us, hear from us" is a phrase that has come up repeatedly in our interviews. The West, it is implied, traffics in lies and conspiracies whereas the caliphate is the only speaker of truth to power.

Slightly overstating the power of social media in the terror army's ascendance was Iraq's former national security adviser Mowaffak al-Rubaie, who told Al Jazeera that it was more or less Twitter and Facebook that caused thirty thousand Iraqi Security Forces soldiers to drop their weapons, lose their uniforms, and leave Mosul free for the jihadists' taking.

Overstating that case though he may have been, al-Rubaie did have a point. Two weeks before the fall of the city, ISIS had released one of its most popular videos to date, titled "Saleel al-Sawarim," or "Clanging of the Swords." A characteristic example of "jihadist pornography," it demonstrated ISIS's peerless ability to produce hour-long cable news–worthy recruitment films, celebrating the very sort of blood-soaked content that Western politicians and diplomats have hoped would dampen people's attraction to the group.

A preacher brandishing a machete proclaims the Islamic State and warns the kuffar and Jews of Jerusalem that the jihadists are coming for them. He then leads the tearing up of passports.

In one scene, we see so-called Rafidah Hunters—anti-Shia assassins—drive by other cars, blasting their guns at what they say are Shia soldiers headed off to join their "Safavid" Iraqi army units. Inside the perforated vehicles are the bloodied corpses of young boys in civilian clothing; any who stir are fired upon. In another scene, ISIS soldiers shoot a man running away from them. He is injured but still alive and tells them, "I'm a driver." The film then juxtaposes the image of him lying on the ground with his official Iraqi army photograph. He is killed.

At a mosque in Anbar we find ISIS taking what appear to be applications from unarmed civilians. The narrator explains that if one were formerly a member of the Anbar Awakening Councils, or a Sunni politician aligned with the Iraqi government, he would be entitled to "repent and stop waging war against the mujahidin." If he does, he will be granted "clemency" and all his past crimes against ISIS will be forgotten—but this must happen before ISIS gets "a hold of you." Likewise, any Sunni soldiers, policemen, or agents of the Mukhabarat are encouraged to quit and turn in their weapons. "You carried your weapons and stood with those *rafida*, fighting your sons," one masked ISIS fighter tells an assembly gathered inside the mosque. "We are your sons, we are your brothers. We can protect your religion and your honor."

"Clanging of the Swords" also exhibits ISIS's supposed omnipresence and its cloak-and-dagger tradecraft in reaching its enemies.

Its agents dress in Iraqi Security Forces uniforms and raid the home of an Awakening commander. They are the "Sahwat Hunters." When the commander is seized, he says that he must call the army to verify these men's identities because he is afraid that they are really members of ISIS.

In the very next scene, two young boys, the sons of a Sahwa commander, are digging a giant pit in the dirt. They explain that their father convinced them to work with the Iraqi government. Then it is their father's turn to dig. When he falters, the mujahidin taunt him: "You didn't get tired when you set out to become a commander in the Sahwa and were working at the checkpoints." He addresses the camera, advising everyone in the Awakening to repent. "I am now digging my own grave," he says.

A counterterrorism official from Samarra is interrogated in his living room. Then he is led into his bedroom as an ISIS fighter, also dressed as an Iraqi soldier, pulls his security uniforms out of his wardrobe. The man is blindfolded with a scarf. Then he is beheaded.

Not quite reaching the cinematic brilliance of Sergei Eisenstein or Leni Riefenstahl, "Clanging of the Swords" chillingly and compellingly conveys its message to its target audience. The video debuted just as rebel groups in eastern Syria and Aleppo—sahwats of a more recent vintage—were battling ISIS. None of these factions had anything to present to their militants or to outsiders in order to suggest a comparable prowess or unity of purpose. In Iraq, if one were a Shia in an ISIS-infiltrated area, one was doubtless terrified. If one were a Sunni, why would he bother turning up for work as a soldier, policeman, or elected councilman, if a simple pledge of allegiance meant keeping his head for the foreseeable future? ISIS claimed to be unstoppable and indomitable. Many believed it was.

TWEETING THE CALIPHATE

"Clanging of the Swords" was posted on YouTube several times (although it was taken down just as often), and on file-sharing sites such as archive.org and justpaste.it. It was heavily promoted by ISIS members and "fanboys" (groupies or unaffiliated enthusiasts) on Twitter and Facebook. This not only maximized its viewership through crowdsourcing; it also helped drown out antagonists and critics. "Everybody should know that we are not who they think we are," an ISIS media activist in Aleppo said in what has become a common refrain. "We have engineers, we have doctors, we have excellent media activists. We are not *tanzim* [an organization], we are a state."

Such triumphalism to one side, ISIS's propaganda suffers from the same inborn deficiency of all cultish or messianic messaging: false expectations that inevitably lead to anticlimax and disillusionment. As Shiraz Maher put it, describing the general condition of war under less fanatical circumstances, "A lot of foreign jihadists get to Syria and after a few days or weeks start to complain about the downtime and boredom. The videos overdramatize the experience for them."

We found that one of the less scrutinized social media tools used by ISIS is Zello, an application for smartphones and computers that allows users to establish channels to share encrypted audio messages. Often used by prodemocracy activists in the Middle East to hide from an authoritarian government's scrutiny, Zello has lately been repurposed by ISIS as a simple how-to guide for pledging allegiance to al-Baghdadi, thanks to a prominent pro-ISIS user, Ansar al-Dawla al-Islamiya. The application essentially turns mobile phones into walkie-talkies, through which anyone curious about ISIS or seeking to join up can listen to sermons by affiliated clerics, simulcast as Christian revivals might be.

Incredibly user-friendly, Zello is quite popular among ISIS's younger audiences. According to Ahmed Ahmed, a Syrian journalist from Sahl al-Ghab, Hama, two young boys from his village joined ISIS after listening to sermons through Zello. Mohammed, a fourteen-year-old who worked in southern Turkey, disappeared at the Bab al-Hawa border crossing in October 2014. Answering a call for help from Mohammed's father, Ahmed composed a Facebook post asking his friends and followers for any information about the boy. An hour later, Ahmed told one of us, Mohammed called his parents from the Iraqi border and said, "I am with the brothers."

Mohammed's father was shocked to hear the news and later told Ahmed that his son would regularly listen to ISIS sermons through Zello. "His father warned him about them and told him that they were liars. But the boy would respond that he just wanted to hear what they were saying. The majority of young people join ISIS after they listen to their preaching."

ISIS also has offline means for brainwashing youth. In May 2014, it abducted around 153 schoolchildren between the ages of thirteen and fourteen in Minbij as they traveled back to their hometown of Kobane, after having sat for exams in Aleppo. ISIS put the children in a Sharia training camp and kept them hostage for months, releasing them the following September. According to two journalists from Hama close to the families of a few of those abducted, some of the children voluntarily chose to stay on and become members of ISIS even after being offered the opportunity to return to their families.

A relative of one such recruit spoke of how his cousin refused to return to his mother despite contrary advice from a local ISIS emir. The mother had told the emir that the boy, Ahmed Hemak, was her only son and that her husband was dead, which, according to Islamic teachings, ought to have compelled the boy to remain with his mother. But the child had become an obstinate convert and had no wish to abandon the movement.

END TIMES

In much of its public discourse, ISIS relies on Islamic eschatology for legitimacy and mobilization. A hadith attributed to the Prophet Muhammad about an end-of-days battle between Muslims and Christians in Dabiq, a town in rural Aleppo, is a frequent reference point—so pervasive that ISIS's propaganda magazine is named for it. In the videos, this hadith is recited by al-Zarqawi as an ISIS jihadist marches, in slow motion, holding up a black flag: "The spark has been lit here in Iraq and its heat will continue to intensify, by Allah's permission, until it burns the crusader army in Dabiq." As we noted in Chapter 2, this motto also opens every issue of *Dabiq*.

Much like its Baathist forerunners, ISIS has managed to turn outsider or enemy opinion of it into part of its world-historical struggle. For instance, the announcement in August 2014 of an international coalition to fight ISIS in Syria was hailed as a sign that the Islamic prophecy was nigh, especially as it followed the declaration of a caliphate, another event foretold by the Prophet. According to a famous hadith, Muhammad explained to his followers that after him, a caliphate modeled on prophethood would be established, and that it would in turn be followed by a repressive kingdom and tyrannical rule. Finally, another caliphate modeled on prophethood would be established. Both Islamist and jihadist organizations often used this hadith to mean that a caliphate will replace the tyrannical regimes of the Arab world.

ISIS employs Islamic symbolism to animate its fighters and to draw sympathy from Muslims outside of its orbit. Al-Baghdadi claimed to be a descendant of Hussain, the grandson of the Prophet, which is a precondition set by many Islamic scholars for claiming legitimacy to rule Muslims. ISIS's use of lineage tales is particularly important in its arguments with fellow jihadists, for whom these genealogies are profoundly evocative and can mobilize Muslim youth around an imminent project. Frustration with the more gradualist approaches to building an Islamic state endorsed by, for instance, the Muslim Brotherhood sometimes leads Islamists to look at ISIS as an alternative. The fact that it has already announced the caliphate means that the hardest work has been done; Muslims can join and fight for its survival and expansion, even without traveling to Iraq and Syria.

Then there is the very land upon which the supposed caliphate has been founded. Al-Sham refers to both Damascus and Greater Syria (an ancient territory that encompasses most of the contemporary northern Levant, including the Turkish city of Antakya) and was described by the Prophet Muhammad as "blessed" and "the land of resurrection." Iraq and Syria were the cradles of the first Muslim empires, the birthplaces of many of God's prophets, and the burial sites of many of the Prophet's companions. They are also for the staging grounds of End Times events foretold by Muhammad. These symbols are used as ammunition for ISIS to promote its ideology and gain legitimacy among conservative Muslims. They are more effectively used on audiences divorced from the day-to-day reality of ISIS control.

SLAUGHTERING RAQQA

Total control and captive minds require deterrence, an object lesson on what happens to those who dare to speak up. Here ISIS has modified its atrocity media form to serve as a domestic means of psychological warfare. In July 2015, another ISIS video appeared showing two men in the now-characteristic orange jumpsuits. They are Bashir Abduladhim al-Saado and Faisal Hussain al-Habib and they are twenty and twenty-one years old, respectively. Both are made to confess to spying on the jihadists' activities in occupied Raqqa. A masked man flips through a stack of papers, purportedly copies of documents ferreted out by al-Saado and al-Habib. The two victims claim that a neighbor, Hamoud al-Mousa, asked them to make the copies. Al-Mousa evidently provided them with a camera watch and pair of glasses capable of snapping photographs.

"I took photos in [the] Rumaila, Tal Abyad, al-Wadi, streets, main and local streets, panorama, ISIS members—anybody who comes in front of it, any street that has a base for ISIS," al-Saado says, referring to towns in Syria that were formerly or are currently held by ISIS. "[Al-Mousa] also asked me to go to Deir Ezzor to take photos of oil fields and how they extract oil and fill the vehicles." He adds that al-Mousa paid four hundred dollars for pictures of ISIS activities, which he would encrypt and then dispatch another activist to smuggle into Turkey, where they could be safely uploaded to the Internet and spread around the globe. Al-Saado says that he was captured by ISIS in his home, in Raqqa, while al-Habib claims that ISIS security officials found him as he was encrypting his latest material.

Al-Saado and al-Habib are then tied to wooden posts and shot through the head with pistols at point-blank range by two ISIS gunmen. The camera lingers on their corpses and even captures the sound of blood dripping from their head wounds, onto their jumpsuits. The video ends, ominously, with a third man who says, "My name is Mohammed al-Mousa." It is a "teaser" for a forthcoming murder. The man speaking is Hamoud al-Mousa's father, whom ISIS captured three months earlier. Mohammed would be killed, too, in a later video.

Al-Saado and al-Habib worked for a clandestine media activist collective known as Raqqa is Being Slaughtered Silently, or RBSS, which, since April 2014, had risked everything to provide the world a glimpse inside the first provincial capital in the Middle East to fall to the army of terror. Like samizdat writers and printers under Stalinism, they wanted only to record history as it actually happened, not as it was being dictated from above. "They Are the Enemy, Beware of Them" was the name ISIS chose to give to the atrocity video of al-Saado and al-Habib's killing. By 2015, RBSS's work was so relied upon by international journalists, who with rare exception refused to travel into Raqqa to see for themselves, that the entire organization won the Committee to Protect Journalists' International Press Freedom Award.

"A media activist documents the violations committed by the group as much as he can with whatever equipment or tools he has," said Omar Abu Layla, who runs Deir Ezzor 24, an anti-ISIS media organization. "Despite ISIS's monitoring—by checking cell phones at checkpoints, sudden raids into

Internet cafes, arbitrary arrests—media activists working to document violations have become much savvier about security, which helps them to stay safe."

Since the jihadists' loss of crucial towns and villages along the northern Syrian-Turkish borderland, the dragnet on local dissidents has increased. Dozens of young men accused of producing or distributing "illegal" material of life under ISIS rule were arrested. The more land ISIS lost, the more its Murder Inc. pornography proliferated.

Originally seventeen in number, the membership of RBSS dwindled to twelve after one of the group's founding members, Motaz, was captured by ISIS and executed in a public square by being thrown off a high building. Abu Ward al-Raqqawi, one of the pseudonymously named, English-speaking founders of the collective, said weeks before al-Saado and al-Mousa's murders, "I can't imagine it. [ISIS did] this in a crowded area and they asked the people to come to see what would happen. The people who are watching the execution are children—so that the children will be terrorists in the future. They will be killers. ISIS is trying to brainwash the children." Abu Ward also said that the jihadists drove around Raqqa in cars "trying to catch anyone who did anything wrong, such as smoking in the street. Sometimes they make checkpoints in areas to check the civilians' cell phones, to see if anyone has recorded any videos or photos. If he has music on his phone, he's arrested. If he has any picture of the city, ISIS will execute him. That's what happened with our friend."

Nor would ISIS confine itself to killing RBSS members within Syria. On October 30, 2015, days after its operatives perpetrated the worst terror attack in modern Turkish history, in the capital of Ankara, ISIS dispatched a gunman to shoot dead two more RBSS members, Fares Hammadi and Ibrahim Abd al-Qader, in the southern Turkish city of Sanliurfa, or Urfa as it is known in Arabic.

"In the morning, somebody, we don't know who, exactly, but he was from ISIS—entered their apartment and shot them in the head," Abu Ibrahim al-Raqqawi, another pseudonymous Raqqa-based founder of RBSS, said via Skype, his voice at turns tremulous and hoarse. "Then he beheaded them. There was a third friend who was coming to the apartment. He found their bodies. He was shocked." Nothing was confiscated from Ibrahim and Fares's apartment. Their computers and equipment were untouched. "He just killed them and left," Abu Ibrahim said.

"They were very brave people. The bravest people I ever met. They were filming in the very sensitive places, filming ISIS in battle, covering the barrel bombs. Every time there was an air strike in the city, they were the first guys to go and film."

ISIS not only claimed responsibility for the assassinations; its supporters celebrated the crime on social media. An ISIS media account on Twitter published a screenshot from a cell phone showing Ibrahim and Fares posing together in an old photograph, one they'd posted themselves when it was taken. The mocking caption of the tweet read: "A selfie before being slaughtered silently." Two days after Christmas 2015, ISIS murdered RBSS's film director Naji Jerf, a father of two, and revered in Syrian opposition circles for his resistance to both al-Assad and the takfiris. Jerf, like Hammadi and al-Qader, was shot with a silenced pistol in his house, in Gaziantep, Turkey.

Despite ISIS's manhunt for RBSS members, Abu Ibrahim remained committed to exposing the truth of life in Raqqa.

"We are a lot," he said. "We will not stop. It's our city. We will defeat them."

UNPLUGGING RAQQA

ISIS's demand for absolute obeisance took on new form in the summer of 2015 when it tried to pull the plug on the only means for those under its dominion to absorb non-caliphal information: the Internet. In July, ISIS "banned" Wi-Fi in Raqqa in a diktat that didn't require the cutting of coaxial cable lines but rather the elimination of what Abu Ibrahim called the "Space Internet." By this he meant the Broadband Global Area Network, a network accessed by expensive mobile devices that are roughly the size of books and enable users to log on via satellite after paying for data packages from their local Internet cafes.

Raqqa's preferred BGAN is a Hughes model, which, Abu Ibrahim said, sells for about two thousand dollars each. Despite the cost, there are—or were—an abundance of cafes in Raqqa where you could log on; some five thousand by Abu Ibrahim's count. Except the cafes are unlike any you'd see in Western cities.

"You won't find computers in ninety-five percent of them," he said. "It's more like a small shop where not even two or three people can sit down. You go to there, bring your own cell or laptop. You tell them, 'I want an account with you.' The Internet cafe owner will give you a password and account username. He'll give you megabytes. Every hundred megabytes costs three dollars.

The device can take fifty gigabytes. It costs one thousand dollars, maybe twelve hundred dollars every six months to top up the data package for each device. It's very hard to have an Internet at all."

For one thing, BGAN owners have had to travel to Turkey to recharge their data allotments, a routine that even before the Wi-Fi ban was dangerous. Then the BGAN has to be linked up to a Wi-Fi extender in each cafe, which broadcasts the network signal well beyond the shop's confines so that users can get access from their home or within walking distance. "ISIS has always tried to monitor the people's online activity," Abu Ibrahim said. "It was always very risky. Internet cafe owners have been spies for ISIS." The few cafes that will remain open are ones that force users to stay and conduct their online business out in the open. ISIS routinely raids such establishments, forcing users to put their hands and cell phones on the table. If any image or video offering an unauthorized glimpse into the caliphate is found on the phones, ISIS will arrest the owner. "They'll accuse him of being a spy for the coalition or the regime and they'll kill him immediately," Abu Ibrahim said, adding that RBSS has its own BGAN devices, which is how he's still able to talk to journalists via Skype (though each time we switch off with him could be the last we ever hear from him).

Not content with mere spot-checking, ISIS has also taken to driving around Raqqa in surveillance cars that monitor Wi-Fi signals. Anyone caught broadcasting a signal gets the same treatment as an illicit cafe patron. "Most of the people are very angry," Abu Ibrahim said. "Many have left the city because residents want to talk to their families outside. They call each other on WhatsApp or Viber."

Alex Gladstein, chief strategy officer for the Human Rights Foundation, said Internet workarounds for activists living under repressive regimes are still hard to come by. "The closest thing that I've held in my hand is something called a BRCK, a low-cost rugged option that a company out of Kenya created," he said. "You can buy it for a couple hundred dollars."

But that's not cheap, either, particularly in a starvation economy where families are forced to pay as much as thirty dollars a month for electricity from ISIS, in addition to *zakat* (Islamic alms payable to the state) and all the surcharges on everyday goods and services, by which the jihadists enrich themselves. To make matters worse, more twentieth-century methods of trying to foment insurrectionary sentiments against ISIS are backfiring. The US-led coalition so far has dropped three versions of propaganda leaflets designed to draw the population of Raqqa away from their black-clad masters. But the leaflets have only elicited unintentional amusement or irritation.

"The first one said, 'Most of the people of Raqqa are ISIS and be careful of joining ISIS because we will kill you,'" Abu Ibrahim said. "This made people very angry because few here are sympathetic to ISIS, and why does the coalition assume otherwise? The second leaflet was really, really funny. It was written in very bad Arabic, [such that] you couldn't understand any word. I can't even tell you what it was trying to say."

The third one was designed to show ISIS's recent battlefield losses to a combined force of Kurds and Arabs. Four fighters are exhibited, three from the Kurdish People's Defense Units (including a woman fighter) and one from the Free Syrian Army. They're walking along a sunlit street strewn with the corpses of slain terrorists. "But the ISIS flag is hanging upside down. The people of Raqqa don't like the [Kurdish militias] and don't want them coming here. And this flag is for Islam and all Muslims, not just for ISIS. So the people didn't like seeing it upside down."

Not that ISIS sees the irony in a poorly waged counterreformation campaign. It sends street sweepers to clear the roads when these coalition leaflets land. "If they find one of these leaflets with you," Abu Ibrahim said, "it will be big problem for you."

GLOSSY JIHAD

Dabiq's content, which we have cited throughout, explains ISIS's core mission and its behavior through an eschatological prism. The introduction of sex slavery, for example, was defended by the editors as one of the signs of "the Hour," meaning Judgment Day. According to a hadith, the apocalypse will come when a "slave gives birth to her master."

Abolition of slavery, then, would make the realization of this prophecy impossible. So *Dabiq* concludes: "After this, it becomes clear where [ISIS spokesman] al-Adnani gets his inspiration from when saying, 'and so we promise you [O crusaders] by Allah's permission that this campaign will be your final campaign. It will be broken and defeated, just as all your previous campaigns were broken and defeated, except that this time we will raid you thereafter, and you will never raid us. We will conquer your Rome, break your crosses, and enslave your women, by the permission of Allah, the Exalted. This is His promise to us."

Many of the practices that ISIS has revived are intended as heralds of Islamic prophecy, including the blowing up of shrines and the tossing of homosexuals from rooftops. One of ISIS's governors, Hussam Naji Allami, who was captured by Iraqi Security Forces in 2014, issued a fatwa ordering the demolition of shrines in Mosul on the premise that a hadith had called for it. In an interview with the Iraqi newspaper *Al-Sabah*, Allami said that he had issued the fatwa in response to criticism, namely from al-Qaeda, about the illegitimacy of ISIS, which was said not to be the foretold "caliphate modeled on the Prophet's methodology."

Whatever the perversion or barbarity, ISIS has a ready-made justification. The popular appeal of its dark vision cannot be underestimated. Recently, the US State Department created a Twitter account called "Think Again Turn Away." It tweets photographs of ISIS atrocities and casualties and links to news stories describing them. It also engages with pro-ISIS accounts, in effect trolling them. Thus, to @OperationJihad, who tweeted (quoting a jihadist anthem), "We have nothing to achieve in this world, except martyrdom, [i]n the mountains we will be buried and snow will be our shroud," the State Department shot back, "Much more honorable to give a Syrian child a pair of boots than drive him from his home into snow w/your quest for death."

@OperationJihad did not bother with a reply.

Three days earlier, as the world was recovering from the terrorist slaughter of *Charlie Hebdo* journalists in Paris, ISIS or some contingent of its supporters appeared to have hacked the Twitter and YouTube accounts of US Central Command, posting military documents and jihadist threats, including a menacing Tweet that read: "AMERICAN SOLDIERS, WE ARE COMING, WATCH YOUR BACK." Though the White House downplayed the incident as an act of "cybervandalism," one of the documents the "CyberCaliphate" hackers released was less than innocuous: a spreadsheet titled "Retired Army General Officer Roster," which carried the names, retirement dates, and email addresses of US army generals.

As ISIS's "foreign operations" have increased, *Dabiq* has also been used to crow after the fact. The magazine now has its own obituary section celebrating the "martyrs" who have struck in France, Egypt, and elsewhere in 2015, ISIS's most successful year in overseas terrorism. In the first week of January, a little more than a month after the formation of the anti-ISIS coalition, Amedy Coulibaly, another French national who had earlier pledged allegiance to al-Baghdadi, shot sixteen people in France in the space of two days, five of them dead, including an unarmed policewoman in Montrouge and every Jewish shopper who had the bad luck of being at the Hypercasher kosher supermarket at Porte de Vincennes, Paris. Prior to this attack, Coulibaly had managed to dispatch his wife, Umm Basir al-Muhajirah, to Syria. And not long after Coulibaly and his victims had met their end, Umm Basir told *Dabiq*: "His eyes shined every time he would watch the videos of the Islamic State. He would say, 'Don't show me this,' because when he would watch the videos, it would make him want to perform *hijrah* [emigration] immediately and that would have conflicted with his intent to carry out the operations in France." Well before the six coordinated suicide bomb and gun attacks in Paris, ringleader Abdelhamid Abbaoud made his own cameo appearance in *Dabiq*—in the same issue, in fact, in which Coulibaly's wife was interviewed— to brag about how easy it was for him to move about in the land of unbelievers. Photographed with two other Belgian nationals who had joined ISIS while in Syria, Abbaoud told the magazine that he had serially managed to slip a European security dragnet, even after his photograph had been widely shared in the press. "I was even stopped by an officer who contemplated me so as to compare me to the picture," Abbaoud said, "but he let me go, as he did not see the resemblance! This was nothing but a gift from Allah."

Scott Atran is one of many analysts who believe that the US government has not adequately grasped ISIS's appeal to those most susceptible to it. "We keep hearing that the antidote is preaching moderate Islam. I tell people on the National Security Council, 'Don't you have kids? Does anything moderate appeal to them?'"

13

SHAKEDOWN OF
THE SHEIKHS
ISIS CO-OPTS THE TRIBES

"Terrain is fate in ground combat operations," said Jim Hickey, the US Army colonel who helped to capture Saddam in 2003. "Iraq is a tribal society, and families in the tribes are tied to specific pieces of ground. That's going to shape this fight dramatically. It shaped the fight when the British were there in the First and Second World Wars. It shaped the fight when we were there."

Much the same can be said of the Jazira, the plains region spanning from northwestern Iraq to northeastern Syria, which has in the last two years served as ISIS's strategic heartland. So important are these confederations of clans to ISIS's terrain strategy that the organization even has a tribal outreach department known as Diwan al-Asha'ir. This heartland region, after all, is where Abu Ghadiyah maintained his safe house; it was here that countless other ratline runners and "border emirs" kept their forward operating bases for al-Qaeda in Iraq.

The Baathist regimes in Syria and Iraq viewed and dealt with tribes differently. Prewar Iraqi state television channels prominently featured tribal traditions and folklore; Saddam mingled with both Sunni and Shia sheikhs, and dispensed various incentives—such as smuggling and gray-market privileges—for their continued fealty. It was this established patronage system that al-Qaeda in Iraq self-defeatingly tried to disrupt in the mid-2000s, precipitating the Awakening.

In Syria, by contrast, the regimes of both Hafez and Bashar al-Assad were generally ambivalent about the tribes and strategically inept in co-opting them. True, they opportunistically exploited the tribes to create social rifts on demand. The regime Arabized Kurdish-dominated areas in northern Syria, the better to contain restive Kurdish nationalists. The al-Assads never considered the ancient filial confederations in Syria's desert hinterlands as significant as Saddam had those in Iraq.

Since its advent in the 1960s, the Syrian branch of the Baath Party saw in tribalism a twofold threat. First, it regarded tribal bonds between clans in eastern Syria and northwestern Iraq as a potential advantage for its rival Iraqi branch. Second, the Baath Party, particularly in the early years of its ascent to power, regarded "retrograde" tribalism as antithetical to the party's "progressive" ideology.

Damascus's clumsy engagement with the tribes came back to haunt it at the outset of the Syrian uprising. Many of the early demonstrations in Deraa, for example, were driven by these antique connections and made use of pronounced tribal rhetoric. Protestors called for *fazaat houran*, the collective help of the people of the Houran valley, where Deraa is located. When the Syrian security forces used violence to suppress the demonstrations, Deraawis called on their "cousins" in the Gulf to come to their assistance.

Tribal networks played an even more significant role after the rebellion became militarized in early 2012. Coordinators of the rebellion helped arm rebel groups in various parts of the country by appealing to their kin abroad, especially in Saudi Arabia, Kuwait, and Bahrain. Members of the Ugaidat tribe in Homs, for example, reached out to their fellow Ugaidat members from eastern Syria who were living in the Gulf and had readier access to cash or fund-raising mechanisms. Some pan-Syrian rebel coalitions were also formed in part because of tribal links. The Grandsons of the Prophet Brigade was led by Maher al-Nuaimi from Homs and Saddam al-Jamal from Deir Ezzor; both belonged to the same tribe. "People from al-Wa'ar al Qadeem and al-Dar al Kabeera in Homs, and others from the countrysides of Hama and Damascus connected with us," an FSA financier said. "We knew each other through tribal connections." These Syrian networks often operated like a well-organized but far-flung diaspora might, with the paradoxical exception that everyone still resided in the same country. Unfortunately, what was initially an asset for the revolution soon became one for its jihadist iteration.

Al-Qaeda and ISIS's purchase in Syria's tribal regions owes largely to the relationship between population density and geography in those areas. Tribes have their highest concentrations in Deir Ezzor, Hasaka, Raqqa, and Deraa, which is to say the easternmost and southernmost regions of Syria. They constitute a full 90 percent of the population in each of those four provinces. They also number around two million in Aleppo's rural districts. Overall, tribes account for 30 percent of Syria's overall population, and yet they inhabit about 60 percent of its territory. Thus they are bound to the countryside, where insurgents have found it easiest to navigate and bivouac. As in Iraq, this is where Zarqawists tend to coalesce and regroup whenever they have been ejected from urban areas or are plotting a massive offensive against rival groups. It is, in a very real sense, their briar patch.

AL-RAFDAN'S REVENGE

In Syria, the tribes also found themselves pawns in what became the cleavage of the franchise built by al-Zarqawi. One of the first al-Nusra cells in Syria emerged, in fact, in a small town in Deir Ezzor known as al-Ghariba, where nearly every resident belonged to the same family. The province's proximity to a years-long Sunni insurgency explains why. Because Deir Ezzor connects Syria to Iraq, many of al-Ghariba's inhabitants found it easy to cross the border in 2003 and 2004 and to imbibe Zarqawist propaganda.

The al-Assad regime uncovered the al-Nusra cell in al-Ghariba in January 2012, killing dozens of its members and almost completely eliminating it. Al-Nusra then relocated to a nearby town, al-Shuhail, which had long been a hub for arms smuggling between Iraq and Syria. As is common in the region, the town was named for the tribe that inhabits it, and most of the resident families had deep-rooted connections to Salafism. Members of the Hajr family, for instance, joined the Fighting Vanguard, a group that fought the regime in Hama as part of the Muslim Brotherhood's uprising in the 1970s and 1980s. After the US invasion of Iraq, many Hajr kin joined the Sunni insurgency. After the Syrian uprising, when al-Nusra moved in, dozens of Hajr men joined up. By the summer of 2012, al-Shuhail was so thoroughly run by al-Nusra that it earned the nickname "Shuhailistan."

The identity of the occupier, as is often the case, became inextricable from that of the occupied. "If you spoke about Jabhat al-Nusra in a negative way, you were effectively insulting the Shuhail," said Amir al-Dandal, a member of another prominent tribe in Deir Ezzor, and an organizer for the Free Syrian Army. Even the internecine war that eventually erupted between al-Nusra and ISIS took on a tribal inflection. In April 2013, al-Nusra fought alongside Jaysh Muta, another rebel group in Shuhail, against members of the al-Bu Assaf clan, part of the Albu Saraya tribe, which is the third largest in Deir Ezzor. Members of the al-Bu Assaf later backed ISIS in the dispute, and ISIS won.

Similarly, when Aamer al-Rafdan, a senior al-Nusra member, defected to ISIS after the rift, he did so less out of ideological preference than out of patrilineal allegiance. Al-Rafdan was from al-Bekayyir, a tribe based in Jedid Ugaidat, a town in the eastern countryside of Deir Ezzor, near the Iraqi border. Al-Bekayyir had for decades been at odds with the rival Shuhail tribe. Al-Rafdan's ship-jump was pivotal. It allowed ISIS to seize control of Syria's Conoco gas plant in Mayadeen, Deir Ezzor, delivering up a valuable resource prize to al-Baghdadi's forces and exacerbating what had been a long-running territorial dispute between the al-Bekayyir and the Shuhail tribes. It had nothing whatsoever to do with competing ideologies or with jihadist hermeneutics about how and when to found a caliphate. "The fighting had everything to do with the tribes, not with jihadi politics, and it was resolved on a tribal basis," said al-Dandal. "The tension was finally ended because the al-Bekayyir and the Shuhail both realized that any conflict would lead to greater problems in the future. The issue was resolved absent ISIS or al-Nusra's intervention." The truce was short-lived. The Shuhail expelled al-Rafdan and ISIS from Jedid Ugaidat. Then, in July 2014, ISIS conquered the Shuhail altogether, a victory with wide reverberations across Deir Ezzor. A series of towns and villages succumbed swiftly to the jihadist blitz. Fayyadh al-Tayih, a former al-Nusra member who joined ISIS in December 2013, said: "From the beginning, we believed that al-Shuhail was the real problem. If we were to take them, everyone else would surrender." He was correct. Triumphant, al-Rafdan exacted revenge, imposing harsh conditions on the Shuhail, exiling some members for a period of three months. (This itself was an old form of tribal jurisprudence.) The fall of the Shuhail tribe and the town named for it marked a decisive end to al-Nusra's purchase in eastern Syria, granting ISIS more or less total control over the province of Deir Ezzor. This turn of events was stunning. ISIS presence in the area had hitherto been minimal, and confined to Jedid Ugaidat.

Even in that town, ISIS had so alienated the local population that it had been temporarily expelled.

ISIS'S DIVIDE-AND-RULE STRATEGY

In *The Management of Savagery*, Abu Bakr Najji elucidated the importance of manipulating tribal politics and offered his own anthropological gloss on the matter. He observed that it was not necessarily a bad thing for jihadists that confederations of families tended to stick together. In fact, this reality was easily harnessed to the jihadists' benefit by a gradual process of bribery, brainwashing, and co-optation. "When we address these tribes that have solidarity we should not appeal to them to abandon their solidarity," he wrote. "Rather, we must polarize them and transform them into praiseworthy tribes that have solidarity. . . . It is possible to begin doing so by uniting the leaders . . . among them with money and the like. Then, after a period of time in which their followers have mixed with our followers and their hearts have been suffused with the picture of faith, we will find that their followers do not accept anything which contradicts the sharia. Of course, solidarity remains, but it has been changed into a praiseworthy solidarity instead of the sinful solidarity which they used to have."

Given the popularity of this manifesto among ISIS zealots, it was hardly a shock that the organization would be the first one in history to successfully pit members of the same tribe against one another. Such divide-and-rule tactics were on grim display in August 2014, when members of the Shaitat tribe in Deir Ezzor participated in the killing of hundreds of their fellow tribesmen at ISIS's behest. The same kind of coerced fratricide occurred in the Iraqi town of Hit, where members of the Albu Nimr took part in the execution of dozens of their own in October 2014. Making the ruled complicit in the crimes of the ruler, and individuals more loyal to the state than to their own flesh and blood, is a hallmark of totalitarianism.

As per Najji, the exchange of money for loyalty has played a major role in tearing families apart. In April 2013, after the rupture with al-Nusra, ISIS secretly sought to co-opt young tribal leaders by offering to share oil and smuggling revenues with them. It also promised them positions of authority currently held by their elders. Younger tribesmen were generally more credible and popular, owing to their participation in the anti-Assad rebellion; their elders had mainly sided with the regime or stayed neutral.

One figure from the Syrian border town of Albu Kamal explained how ISIS had exploited this generational schism to snare members of a prominent family, months before the jihadists had even established a presence there. "They are giving him a portion of an oil well in the area," the figure said, referring to a younger relative who had joined the jihadists. "They know that if they are to be eradicated in our area, who would be able to rally up people around him? Most of the other tribes in our area have no leadership; we have leadership and influence. They give him money, they protect him and consult with him on everything. The other option is, they would assassinate him."

Bribing the youth is how ISIS took otherwise impervious towns in Deir Ezzor in the summer of 2014. The seizure of Mo Hassan, for instance, came as a shock to most local rebels, as the town was known to be hostile to the takfiris. This town's population is famously secular and has produced many professional soldiers and officers in the Syrian Arab Army. Ideology played no role whatsoever in its mass defection to ISIS. The group had simply bought its way in before fighting its way through—which it did using the enormous stocks of American- and Saudi-made weapons that it had seized from the Iraqi Security Forces in Mosul in June 2014.

ISIS AS PROBLEM SOLVER

Much as Abu Bakr al-Baghdadi was seen by the Americans as a kind of Dr. Phil for bickering jihadist factions in Camp Bucca, so too has the movement he leads attained a reputation for problem-solving and arbitration in Syrian tribal areas. It mediated a historic reconciliation in November 2014 between two warring tribes in Albu Kamal, putting an end to what had been a War of the Roses–style thirty-year argument between al-Hassoun and al-Rehabiyeen.

As part of its administration of ruled territory, ISIS has appointed an emir in charge of tribal affairs, a Saudi national known as Dhaigham Abu Abdullah, based in Qa'im, the town just opposite Albu Kamal on the Iraqi side of the border. He receives envoys to discuss local grievances or complaints. In many cases, the residents of newly captured areas in eastern Syria cross the now-erased national boundary to meet with Abu Abdullah as they would a federal court judge. "People are racing to win the trust of the state," said an ISIS member from Deir Ezzor, who accompanied a convoy of arbitration-seekers to Anbar province. ISIS, he added, "is a new authority in our area and people rush to present themselves as leaders to push for their personal interests, and tribalism is above everything for these people. Our leaders know this. We're not stupid."

In areas where killings have been carried out by fellow tribesmen or a tribe from a neighboring town, ISIS uses foreign jihadists or leaders from other regions to keep the peace. Here the importation of nonnatives appears to be well considered. Saddam al-Jamal, who was responsible for the execution of seventy locals in his hometown of Albu Kamal, was not given a leadership role when ISIS returned to the area. Instead, he was tasked with the management of a refugee camp near Iraq. Al-Rafdan, the vengeance taker from Shuhail, was reassigned to Raqqa.

Hybridized tribal outreach—part Saddam and part Najji—has become an integral part of ISIS's governing strategy. The overarching objective is forestalling another Awakening, which, as it did a decade ago, poses the greatest internal threat to jihadist supremacy in the Euphrates River Valley. Where it has not frightened or tempted tribesmen into submission with propaganda about "repentance"—"forgiveness" of unbelieving or "apostate" tribal leaders being another theme of *The Management of Savagery*—it has inserted itself as a buffer between feuding clans. Not for nothing did al-Baghdadi, in announcing the formation of ISIS in April 2013, explicitly refer to two categories of people: Muslims and the tribes of Syria.

As Frederic Wehrey of the Carnegie Endowment for International Peace wrote, ISIS "has proven to be a more adaptable and entrenched opponent today than its predecessor was in the mid-2000s, deploying a potent mix of extreme violence and soft power to both coerce and co-opt the tribes. Underpinning all of this are truisms that often elude tribal enthusiasts: tribal authority is fickle, hyper-localized, often artificially constructed, and therefore hard to fully harness."

ISIS's tribal exploitation does have limitations, the greatest being that it is still regarded as a temporary governing force, an ally of convenience or brute necessity. The tribes accept ISIS's presence on a short-term basis because they do not want their homelands turned into combat zones. Smaller tribes joining ISIS are typically driven to do so by power politics rather than genuine sympathy for the caliphate. Generally speaking, the tribes do not endorse ISIS ideologically or join it en masse; they do not believe that its reign will last forever.

The volte-face in Iraqi Sunni areas was a product of the policies of Nouri al-Maliki and of the military campaign in Anbar in early 2014. The anti-government protests in that province following the US withdrawal saw the rise of mainstream Sunni religious and tribal figures, politically in the protests camps and militarily in the Anbar desert—even though ISI was present in the background. Instead of taking these figures' concerns seriously, al-Maliki portrayed his military campaign in Anbar in unequivocally sectarian terms. In a speech he delivered on Christmas 2013, he characterized it as an ancient war between the partisans of the Prophet's grandson Hussain and the son of the first Ummayad ruler, Yazid, in the seventh century.

This disastrous miscalculation arguably cost al-Maliki his premiership. It certainly helped open the door for ISIS's return in Anbar. In the final months before Abu Omar al-Baghdadi was killed, the Islamic State of Iraq produced its "Strategic Plan for Reinforcing the Political Position of the Islamic State of Iraq," an internal report that in many ways resembled *The Management of Savagery*. Acknowledging that America's enlistment of the tribes had been "a clever, bold idea," the report recommended emulation: Replace the Americans in providing security and a sustainable income, and the local Awakening Councils would surely switch sides, preferring to answer to fellow Muslims. The jihadists could always eliminate any Awakening leaders who refused, and had already begun doing so: between 2009 and late 2014, ISIS assassinated more than thirteen hundred Awakening militiamen. But just as in Syria, where ISIS found al-Assad cooperative in removing all non-ISIS alternatives to the government, in Iraq al-Maliki, by commission and neglect, removed the Awakening leaders most dangerous to ISIS, fostering an environment of sectarianism and opening a security vacuum that ISIS filled. "Once things settle down, the tribes will realize how the [al-Assad and al-Maliki] regimes marginalized them and get back to their senses," the ISIS mediation official told one of the authors. "They are our people, but they need to know that they cannot get it their way. They have to understand we are the only ones who can help them and protect them."

14

AL-DAWLA
THE ISLAMIC "STATE" SLEEPER CELLS

We met Abu Adnan in a five-star hotel in Sanliurfa, also known as Urfa, in southern Turkey, near the Syrian border. He was in his late thirties and had been referred by a contact as someone with inside knowledge of ISIS. He introduced himself as a doctor who worked in makeshift hospitals in ISIS-controlled territories. Initially he seemed curious to know what we thought of the "state," for which he provided medical services, and our appraisal of attitudes toward it in the Middle East and internationally. He listened attentively, as did a younger companion who sat next to him.

Then Abu Adnan came clean. He revealed that he was not merely a doctor but also an *amni*, a security official for ISIS. He declined to answer specific questions about his job, and was vague in answering other ones, but he proudly explained that there are dozens of men like him working with ISIS outside of Syria, many in neighboring countries. "A believer does not get stung from the same hole twice," Abu Adnan said, referring to a saying attributed to the Prophet Muhammad, which is more or less the Islamic equivalent of "Fool me once . . ."

"We cannot afford to wait for others to spy on us," he said. "Information is the foundation and the pillar for everything. We need to know if there are activities outside the borders that might affect us in the future. We need to have a presence outside our territories. We need to do all that without compromising the state, so it is important to have reliable, efficient, and trusted people doing that."

Amniyat, or security units, are one of the vital organs of ISIS intelligence and counterintelligence, developed by the former Iraqi Mukhabarat officers in its ranks. The entire spy sector of ISIS is headed by Abu Ali al-Anbari, the former operative in Saddam's regime. In ISIS territories these units are responsible both for arresting wanted individuals and for probing security-related cases. Within a local ISIS structure, the Amniyat have to operate apart from other sectors, such as the clerical authority, the military, and *khidmat al-muslimeen* ("Muslim Services").

Abu Moawiya al-Sharii, who serves ISIS as a *sharii*, or cleric, confirmed that walls of separation exist between and within local ISIS affiliates. "Each one has a speciality," Abu Moawiya said. "I don't know what the military commanders do or know, and they don't know what an amni knows."

Such separation of powers bolsters ISIS's pretense of statehood, reminiscent as it is of the walled-off bureaucracies and departments of any legitimate government. It also guards against infiltration and espionage—a particular obsession among ISIS's upper cadres and no doubt also a holdover from their Baathist origins. Even though ISIS tends to be more flexible in its recruitment and membership requirements than al-Nusra, it has established an elaborate and layered internal security apparatus to insulate its core leadership from provincial officers, and vice versa. "Our enemies are clever and determined," Abu Adnan said. "What we can do is to make sure the body of the state is strong, so that it can heal no matter how far they weaken it. So even if they destroy us in one area, you can be sure we're still there. We don't have to be exposed and visible."

At the hotel in Sanliurfa, Abu Adnan gave no outward sign of belonging to a takfiri organization known for its bearded and black-clad militants. He was clean-shaven and dressed in modern attire, more Mohamed Atta than Abu Bakr al-Baghdadi. Yet in the course of our interview he thumbed through his mobile phone photos to show himself mingling and posing with ISIS leaders in Raqqa, northern Hasaka, and Aleppo. He said that security officers, depending on the seniority of their positions, must learn a range of skills; they must master basic military training, political orientation, communications, and clandestine activity. Abu Adnan claimed to have a network of smugglers on the Syrian-Turkish border who would help potential fighters enter Syria to join ISIS. They operated in plain sight of the Turkish authorities and, like Abu Adnan, would not be conspicuous in any Western city.

"ISIS moves with incredible speed," Chris Harmer, an analyst at the

Institute for the Study of War, said, trying to explain how ISIS mobilizes its forces and, indeed, springs up in places where it previously had no discernible presence. "They have embedded, nested sleeper cells that start picking people off. We saw this in Mosul in June. Clearly, they had a list of people they were going to kill in the first seventy-two hours in the seizure of the city."

Mayser Hussain, a paramedic from Sahl al-Ghab, Hama, explained how ISIS has outfoxed the Free Syrian Army there. "We have a group of five hundred and eighty fighters from Sahl al-Ghab and Mount Shahshabu; many of them have secretly pledged allegiance to ISIS, as a sleeper cell. They're ready to fight. They haven't made it public because the FSA group in the region, Suqour al-Ghab Brigades, is dominant. Suqour al-Ghab has around four thousand fighters, so they can't fight it."

Hussain said that the group that pledged allegiance to ISIS used to be known as al-Farouq; now it is called Jabhat Sham. "I used to work with them when they were al-Farouq. Lately they offered me to join them as a paramedic. They told me that because I've been defending them in public and online, because I grew a beard and trimmed my mustache . . . 'We are ready, and we are preparing ourselves to take the whole region.'"

ISIS, Hussain said, has experience recruiting from FSA cadres and offers incentives for mainstream rebels to defect to its ranks. Per a current policy, anyone who has fought with the FSA, Ahrar al-Sham, or al-Nusra against ISIS and leaves to join al-Baghdadi's army is more likely to be promoted within its ranks. Abu Bilal, the FSA financier whose house was burned down by ISIS, recounted the story of Obeida al-Hindawi, a former FSA fighter, who had worked for ISIS in secret for three to six months before declaring his affiliation. During that time, al-Hindawi received funding through local channels, all linked to external FSA donors. He was in regular communication with a Tunisian emir in al-Muhassan, a town in Deir Ezzor whence his mother's family hails and where, as we examined in the previous chapter, ISIS has had good luck recruiting tribesmen.

"During his secret allegiance," Abu Bilal informed us, "Obeida objected to our plan to join the fight against ISIS and he said that we should distance ourselves from it. He single-handedly recruited FSA members and convinced his former colleagues to join. Two of his brothers who led the brigade in the town were killed. He then became the commander of the brigade. Suddenly, he stopped fighting and said he no longer had any money or that his cars stopped working. It was all a ruse; he'd been with ISIS for a while at that point."

The one group that knew al-Hindawi's true affiliation was al-Nusra, which Abu Bilal said possessed better intelligence than anyone else in the area. "Nusra stormed Obeida's house in April or May. Everyone was asking why. Nusra said he was an ISIS member who paid money to people to join. He fled and went to Raqqa. He announced his allegiance when he returned from Raqqa to al-Muhassan, as ISIS took Busaira, a town in Deir Ezzor, in June, and two days before they advanced into Nusra's stronghold in the town of Shuhail. He raised the ISIS flag and built a checkpoint and activated all the sleeper cells." Al-Hindawi was later involved in the execution of Shaitat tribesmen in nearby villages.

Zakaria Zakaria, a journalist from Hasaka, said that ISIS's infiltration of al-Nusra was equally impressive. When a number of al-Nusra jihadists in Hasaka wanted to defect to ISIS in early 2012, ISIS told them to stay put for the time being. "When ISIS made it public later on, already half of the members were with them, and the rest either fled to Turkey or joined."

OVERTAKING THE FSA

A mere twenty-six miles north of Aleppo, al-Bab had fallen to the FSA the previous summer. It served as a fallback base for battalions laying siege to Aleppo, sections of which were progressively being peeled away from the regime.

One of the authors met Barry Abdul Lattif while reporting from al-Bab and the Bab al-Hadid quarter of Aleppo in late July 2012, in the midst of Ramadan. Lattif, an early pro-revolution media activist, had earned a reputation among foreign correspondents for being a charismatic but sometimes unnerving adrenaline junkie. He loved to chase the regime's Sukhoi fighter jets and attack helicopters as much as he loved to take queasy Western journalists into the most forbidding war zones in Syria. A day before our visit, he had sustained a small shrapnel injury, the result of sniper bullets ricocheting off the ground in Salaheddine, which was then the fiercely contested Stalingrad of Aleppo, a city laid waste by aerial bombardment and round-the-clock shelling.

The al-Bab of Ramadan 2012 had offered one of the most encouraging signs of the anti-Assad revolution. The FSA presence guarding the town was mostly financed by local merchants, not foreign donors, and perhaps because it was salaried by the community it protected, it exhibited none of the taints of corruption or venality that would come to characterize the larger rebel camp.

Fighters stationed in the downtown barracks of the al-Khatib Brigade (one of the many units named for Hamza al-Khatib, a thirteen-year-old boy who was killed by al-Assad's forces in 2011) would flash the peace sign or insist on posing for photographs.

It was al-Bab's civil society that seemed so pregnant with promise. The Assad regime had all but destroyed al-Bab's hospital and so, in order to tend to the wounded, local volunteers and professional doctors set up a makeshift field hospital in the basement of a mosque. They kept meticulous records of those they treated, including civilians and FSA fighters as well as al-Assad's soldiers and even some shabiha. By nightfall, the streets of a pastoral Levantine hamlet were transformed into jubilant scenes of protest and municipal action. Because all government services were stopped after al-Bab fell to the opposition, the people of the town had to take care of themselves. So FSA fighters put down their Kalashnikovs and picked up brooms and garbage bags, joined by white-gloved volunteers on motorbikes.

"Where are the terrorists here?" Lattif had asked that summer, mocking the regime's propaganda that all of its enemies belonged to al-Qaeda.

The terrorists arrived a year later.

Now living in Turkey and working for RMTeam, a Syrian research and humanitarian aid organization, Lattif recounted how ISIS had moved into al-Bab and ultimately seized control of the entire town. "After they announced their 'state' and after they defected from al-Qaeda, they started to arrest activists around the liberated areas. For the first time, I saw it—it was August 2013, they came to al-Bab and they captured some bad FSA battalions."

What made the battalions "bad"? "They were thieves," Lattif said. "They kidnapped some civilians and asked for money to set them free. So Daesh arrested the battalions. In the early days, the civilians liked Daesh; they didn't know that it had its own project and its own plans for al-Bab."

The regime had never stopped bombarding al-Bab. According to Lattif, it had hit a school next to the hospital, which by then had been partially restored to working order. Twelve medics were killed in that attack. Believing that the presence of takfiris would only invite further punishment on the town, the people began protesting against ISIS. "It lasted for three or four days. After that, some FSA brigades negotiated with Daesh for Daesh to leave the city. So they withdrew to the farmland around al-Bab. But they stayed there, just above the city, hovering, very close. And every day they captured new people, more FSA fighters from the bad battalions. They didn't yet capture any activists, they just issued threats against them—for me, especially. Almost everybody in the city asked me every day on Facebook if I was still free. They warned me that I was in danger, that Daesh was coming for me."

It was after ISIS seized near-total control of Raqqa, Lattif said, that it returned to al-Bab in force, laying siege to the city. It clashed with the FSA battalions as well as with Ahrar al-Sham and al-Nusra fighters. "There were not too many men from those two groups in al-Bab at this point," Lattif said. The FSA was still the predominant insurgency, with around 1,500 fighters in al-Bab (many of them imported from neighboring areas, such as Minbij and Aleppo), followed distantly by Ahrar al-Sham, and then al-Nusra.

To force al-Bab to surrender, ISIS resorted to a favored tactic of the regime: starvation. It stole the wheat from silos just outside the city; the FSA was enlisted to stop the plunder lest the residents, already suffering, run out of bread. ISIS raided the main al-Bab headquarters for Liwa al-Tawhid, Lattif said, the largest brigade in Aleppo, killing around twenty-one men. Then the "regime bombarded the city with helicopters. It targeted only civilians in the center of the city. So Daesh took advantage of that attack and came inside. It saw the opportunity created by the regime."

Al-Assad, Lattif insisted, was very crafty. "He wanted to give the impression to the civilians that Daesh and the regime are one. His goal was to start a civil war with the FSA."

By January 2014—the month that Syria's minor sahwa began—ISIS had brought snipers to strategic locations throughout al-Bab. They began picking off civilians and rebels. "They shot everyone," Lattif said. "I was in the al-Bab media office when Daesh took about a quarter of the city, in the southern district. Suddenly, everything went silent. There was no sound at all. All the fighting had stopped.

"We closed our office and went back to our homes. At about eleven at night, I went to take a look around the city to see what was happening. I saw Liwa al-Tawhid leave. There were no armed fighters left in al-Bab. I don't know where they went."

Ahrar al-Sham, he said, maintained a presence around the city but not inside it. "I stayed with them until morning. It was Friday night. I saw many Ahrar al-Sham fighters with cars with machine guns enter the city at around four a.m. Then, about an hour and a half later, three trucks, all filled with ammunition and rockets and all belonging to Ahrar al-Sham, drove out of al-Bab. There was an emir of Ahrar al-Sham who came over to us and asked the fighters I was with to leave our checkpoint because we were the last checkpoint in the city. Everyone had left for Aleppo, he told us."

ISIS took sole control of al-Bab that morning.

The safe house where one of the authors had stayed belonged to a rebel fighter named Abu Ali, a personal friend of Lattif. "He left his wife and children with my family. ISIS took control of his house. Abu Ali's family stayed for four, maybe five months. Now they're with him in Aleppo." Lattif's family is still in al-Bab.

WHEN ISIS RULES

At first, Lattif said, ISIS treated civilians "gently," even assuming some of the civil administrative duties that had been handled by volunteers and the FSA. They fixed damaged roads, planted flowers in the street, cultivated gardens, and cleaned the local schools. But not long thereafter, Lattif said, ISIS instituted Sharia law, forcing women to wear what he called "the Daesh clothes"—the niqab or full head-and-face covering. "They banned hairdressing. Beard shaving is also forbidden. No woman can leave her house without a male escort now. There's no smoking, no *shisha* [flavored tobacco smoked in hookahs], no playing cards. They've made everything bad for civilians now. They force the people to go to the mosque for prayers, to close their businesses. No one can walk in the street during prayers. They kidnapped almost everybody working in the relief centers. About a month ago [November 2014], they closed the school. If you want to study now, you have to go to the Daesh school in the mosque."

Torture is common, too. ISIS has taken to arresting members of the FSA, whom they accuse of being agents of foreign intelligence services. Sentences for various ISIS-designated crimes are carried out publicly in al-Bab's town square. These range, depending on the offense, from dismemberment to beheading. "They cut off heads and hands in the square. Do you remember the hookah place?" Lattif was referring to a popular cafe in central al-Bab where, in 2012, he had outlined his vision of a free and democratic Syria. "The beheadings are taking place now in front of there. They shut down the hookah place, of course."

In the first months after ISIS seized control of al-Bab, the regime refrained from bombing the city. Then, in November 2014, the Syrian Air Force started up again, dropping barrel bombs—"flying IEDs," which have proved some of the deadliest ordnance used by the regime in the war—that killed sixty-two civilians in one air strike. According to Lattif, the air force dropped a barrel bomb in the main street of al-Bab, nowhere near any ISIS location.

This followed ISIS's eastern offensive against a series of regime military installations, such as the Tabqa air base in Deir Ezzor, the Division 17 base in Raqqa, and the Regiment 121 base in Hasaka—a noticeable uptick in the group's antiregime sorties that followed directly after its blitz into central and northern Iraq. "The regime wants al-Bab to stay under the control of Daesh," Lattif said. "Assad has soldiers about fifteen kilometers west of al-Bab, but they never try to take the city back. Now, every time the regime sends its forces against the north areas of Aleppo, ISIS also attacks some places in the north. Both [the] regime and ISIS are attacking the FSA at the same time, but separately. The regime sees many benefits of ISIS's control of al-Bab and Raqqa—without them, allied forces won't strike Syria. The regime lost its authority in the beginning of the revolution. To get it back, it needs terrorists in Syria. Now there are many voices in the West saying that al-Assad is the only force against terrorists in the Middle East. Now the main players in Syria are the terrorists, Daesh, Jabhat al-Nusra, and the regime."

ISIS VS. ASSAD

Lattif's story conforms not only to what the Syrian opposition has been saying for years—that al-Assad and ISIS are, at the very least, tacit allies in a common war against the FSA and Islamist rebels—but also to what regime loyalists have begun to say as well. To sack Tabqa, Division 17, and Regiment 121, ISIS relied on weapons looted from fallen Iraqi Security Forces bases in Ninewah and Anbar. As we have seen, prior to June 2014, when Mosul fell to ISIS, al-Assad's forces had largely refrained from fighting the takfiris in Syria while insisting in their propaganda that those were the only forces they had ever fought. After the fall of Mosul, however, the regime sensed a renewed opportunity to partner with the West as an agent of counterterrorism. So Syrian warplanes began bombing dozens of ISIS targets in Raqqa, or so they made a show of doing. "They did not bomb the [ISIS] headquarters until June, and even then only after it had been evacuated," Masrour Barzani, the Iraqi Kurdish intelligence head, told the *Guardian* in late August 2014. "We are all paying the price now."

After the takeover of Division 17, ISIS executed upwards of fifty Syrian soldiers, beheading some and then photographing the lopped-off heads in Raqqa. This is according to Rami Abdel Rahman of the London-based Syrian Observatory for Human Rights, who told Agence France-Presse: "There is a clear shift in the ISIS strategy. It has moved from consolidating its total control in areas under its grip. It is now spreading. For ISIS, fighting the regime is not about bringing down Assad. It is about expanding its control."

This was all too much for many Assad loyalists. By the summer of 2014, after seeing how little resistance ISIS faced in its eastern offensive, many pro-regime activists began denouncing their own side. In a video posted online, they accused the regime of nothing short of treason at Tabqa air base, justifying their criticism by citing a statement once made by Hafez al-Assad: "I don't want anyone to be silent about a mistake." The video shows Syrian officers speaking confidently about their fight against ISIS, but the narrator explains that they were duped into believing that helicopters full of fifty tons of ammunition and supplies were on the way. In the event, the only helicopters that arrived carried no cargo to Tabqa but plenty of it away: namely, the head of the air base, Adel Issa, along with three of his generals. This was eighteen hours before the base was stormed by ISIS militants. The video also accuses Syria's information minister, Omran al-Zoubi, of covering up this treachery and then lying about its grisly aftermath. Assad's own cousin, Douraid al-Assad, is quoted as saying: "I call for the expulsion of the defense minister, the chief of staff, the air force chief, the information minister, and everyone involved in the fall of the Tabqa military base and its consequences." Finally, the video ends with statements such as "Our bullets—nine of them are directed to the traitors and one to the enemy."

Elia Samaan, a Syrian official with the Ministry of Reconciliation, had openly inquired into the absence of the Syrian Air Force in the war against ISIS in June 2014, after al-Baghdadi's men tore back into Syria from Iraq with renewed vigor and much stolen matériel. Though he discounted the allegation that the regime had in any way colluded or cooperated with ISIS, Samaan admitted to the *New York Times*'s Anne Barnard that fighting the terrorist group was not a "first priority" for Damascus. Instead, al-Assad had been all too "happy to see ISIS killing" the FSA and Islamic Front instead of his own troops. When the Syrian Air Force finally escalated its air campaign against ISIS, it ended up killing, as per Lattif's account, more innocents than militants. Khaled, an ISIS fighter, told Barnard, "Most of the air strikes have targeted civilians and not ISIS headquarters. Thank God."

ISIS VS. "BAD" REBELS

Where ISIS may have thrived in part from the Assad regime's malign neglect, it also benefited from savvy politicking against what Lattif called the "bad FSA battalions."

Ayman al-Zawahiri had counseled al-Zarqawi, in the early years of AQI, not only about the folly of slaughtering Iraq's Shia but also about the need for effective Islamic governance in the areas ruled by al-Qaeda in Iraq. "[I]t's imperative that, in addition to force, there be an appeasement of Muslims and a sharing with them in governance," al-Zawahiri wrote to his field commander in 2005. What he had advocated was something akin to the steady application of jihadist soft power. While clearly shirking al-Zawahiri's injunction about Shia, ISIS has more or less heeded his advice on creating popular incentives for Islamic governance. Minbij is a case in point.

A city of approximately two hundred thousand, situated strategically between Aleppo, Raqqa, and the Turkish border, Minbij was abandoned by Syrian regime forces in November 2012, after which residents set up a municipal administration for self-rule. Soon the city became an important but temporary symbol for the Syrian revolution, proof that a post-Assad state need not be a Hobbesian nightmare at all. That idyll lasted for about a year.

Accusations that nationalistic or secular rebel groups were behaving like brigands or gangsters were rife throughout Syria, often making more hard-line Islamist factions, including al-Nusra, seem models of discipline and fairness by comparison. Fortified with nearly all of al-Nusra's former foreign fighter contingent, ISIS established a base in the city in April 2013, operating side by side with several other armed factions, and continued to serve as a small but feared gendarmerie of about fifty men.

ISIS used its base to reach out quietly to the local population, inviting people to its *madhafa*, or meeting place, to socialize and also to learn about al-Baghdadi's broad Islamic project for the region. ISIS mediated disputes and responded to complaints from locals, acting as de facto mukhtars in a city devoid of any state authority. ISIS's presence in Minbij grew steadily and without ostentation; rented houses were used as secret weapon and ammunition stockpiles, making the true extent of the jihadist presence publicly incalculable. Also, its policy of arbitration grew less transparent and more severe. ISIS arrested FSA fighters without resorting to the Sharia commissions established by the rebels. It intimidated secular activists and controlled whatever resources it could lay its hands on to try to buy off the rest of the population through the dispensation of social services. It kept its fighters away from the front lines and instead struck tactical deals with FSA and other Islamist groups: in exchange for suicide bombers, who could be used to detonate VBIEDs at regime checkpoints or to blow up military installations with surplus matériel, the rebels who were fighting al-Assad's forces would share their war booty with ISIS. By September 2013 ISIS's heavy-handedness and its play for monopoly control of the city's services boiled over into outright confrontation with rival groups.

It declared war against Kurds in Minbij, vowing to "cleanse" the region of the Kurdistan Workers' Party, whose Syrian branch, the Democratic Union Party of Kurdistan, was the most powerful armed faction among Syria's Kurdish minority.

In October, rebel forces in Minbij seized the flour mills from ISIS and told the jihadists to refrain from bypassing military and Sharia councils in the city in the settlement of public disputes. When the rebels in Aleppo and Idlib declared war against ISIS in January 2014, local forces in Minbij overran the ISIS base and killed or captured all of its fighters.

According to several residents from Minbij who spoke to the authors, locals sympathized with ISIS and lamented its expulsion. "People did not see anything but good things from ISIS, even though they did not like its religious ideas," said resident Shadi al-Hassan. "They also know that those who fought it were the worst people in the area." ISIS's retreat from Idlib and northern Aleppo helped it return to Minbij with a vengeance. It took control of the city after sending reinforcements from Raqqa and northeastern Aleppo. Soon it established a full-fledged system of governance, impressing city denizens and displaced refugees alike. Hard as it may be to believe, given the lurid nature of ISIS's atrocities, Syrians actually flocked in large numbers to join the jihadist group or to work with it at the local level. ISIS members had different roles: some were dedicated to fighting, while others acted as security, administered medical services, operated bakeries, ran Sharia courts, and so on. For the local community, the difference was quickly felt. ISIS provided safety and security. Its methods of justice were swift. Nobody was exempt from punishment, including its own fighters, when they deviated from the strict moral code it had laid down. Consequently, kidnappings, robberies, and acts of extortion all but ceased.

Ayman al-Mit'ib, a Minbij resident who since November 2013 had been internally displaced in Minbij, said, "There is no absolute support for its acts but no absolute opposition to its acts, either. The reason why people support the Islamic State is its honesty and practices compared to the corruption of most of the FSA groups. Some FSA groups joined it, too."

The story of how ISIS grew in Minbij rings true in other areas under its control, particularly where FSA factions failed to rein in corruption or human rights abuses. A defector from the Syrian army, for instance, told the *Guardian* in November 2013 about how ISIS operated like a virus in Syria, taking over other battalions and the territories they controlled. "What they do is attack the weaker units on the pretext that their commander is a bandit or a looter—they only fight one force at a time," he said, adding that once ISIS was ensconced in a city, it spread outward, seizing towns and villages surrounding that urban hub.

Indeed, one of the first rebel leaders to be publicly executed by ISIS was Hassan Jazra of the Ghuraba al-Sham Front, a choice calculated to meet little local resistance given the group's reputation for robbery and even connections to the regime. Jazra had been a watermelon merchant before the revolution, then a peaceful protestor against al-Assad, and finally a rebel who stole to finance his military activity. In one obituary for Jazra, journalist Orwa Moqdad wrote, "Aleppo knew Hassan Jazra as a thief. Yet he did not leave his post at the front for a year and a half in the face of regular army attacks. He was a son of the protest movement who was driven by deteriorating circumstances to become a military leader . . . that became increasingly typical over the course of the war." ISIS executed him, along with six of his fighters, in November 2013. The execution was used by ISIS to prove a point, that those who sought personal gain from the war, or who strayed from a pure revolutionary path, were as culpable as the regime. Although in death Jazra's reputation depended on whom you asked, for ISIS his execution was a necessary form of justice. Its popularity went up accordingly. After that, it began to assert itself even more forcefully in rebel-held areas.

Strong governance has been a winning strategy for ISIS, driving many to join its ranks, to work with it, or at least not to oppose its existence. Since this is key to its existence and viability, it is important to understand how the group set out winning hearts and minds in spite of its pathological brutality.

When the Syrian rebels began to control areas across the country, lawlessness was somewhat tolerated by the local communities as a necessary price before the removal of the regime. Also, as came to be seen later, some FSA-affiliated groups engaged in theft and robbery and claimed that Assad forces were behind them. As time went on, however, lawlessness became more pronounced and provoked serious complaints from locals. Some FSA factions opted to leave the front lines and busy themselves with moneymaking activities in their areas. Factionalism, profit-making, and incompetence started to alienate people.

Toward the end of 2012, independent Islamist factions gained a foothold as they proved more effective, in terms of governance and fighting, than the militias of the FSA. As the Islamists expanded their rule, they established Sharia committees, regulated resources, and ran government facilities. In some areas, al-Nusra worked with Islamists to strengthen the enforcement mechanism of the Sharia courts. But, for several reasons, this model did not prove sustainable.

Since most Islamist insurgents received financial backing from a variety of donors—donors who demanded a say in how funds were to be spent—division was inevitable. Ideological differences also contributed to difficulty establishing strong courts and security forces. Islamists were attuned to local communities, and could enforce Sharia law only through mediation and public consent, especially when the matter involved another armed group or a powerful family. Even al-Nusra, which was far more powerful and disciplined than other forces up until the rise of ISIS, had to retract some of its decisions to avoid clashes with local families. Al-Nusra, as well as other Islamists, typically shied away from enforcing their rules, to avoid alienating the population.

ISIS's model was high-risk. The group was consistent and determined about enforcing its rules, often at the cost of turning more powerful local forces against it. Even at times when it seemed clear that ISIS had little future in Syria—around February 2014, for instance—it insisted on its methods. It would not tolerate any rivalry or recognize any Sharia commissions other than its own. It demanded uniformity at any cost. "If you're an FSA commander and you have a civilian relative, [FSA and other rebels] would accept mediation," said Hassan al-Salloum, a former rebel commander from Idlib residing in Antakya, Turkey, referring to a time when ISIS was still a marginal player in Syria. "But with ISIS, if I complain about an FSA member, they would go and bring him to interrogate him. They would not accept mediation. People started to go to complain to them. People made them intervene. A person comes to them and asks for help. FSA would not do it. ISIS gets you what you want, and then you start talking about it. If I hit one of my soldiers, he goes to ISIS. They give him weapons, salary, pocket money."

Once ISIS controls an area, it establishes a semblance of order and shows zero tolerance for any rivalry or public display of weaponry. It immediately disarms the locals, primarily of their heavy weapons. For Syrians who lived under the control of FSA militias, the change was welcome. "You can drive from Aleppo to Raqqa to Deir Ezzor and into Iraq, and nobody will bother you," a resident of Deir Ezzor said. "Before, you'd have to be stopped at ad hoc checkpoints and you [would] have to bribe this and tolerate that."

Lawlessness has been even more irksome for those who work in transportation or trade or who live in areas that have oil fields. Whole armed groups were formed to control oil fields, impose road taxes, escort oil traders, perpetrate smuggling, or accumulate wealth in any way possible. Constant gunfire, random killing, kidnapping, and extortion were common in most places. It was often the case that when a person with heavily armed relatives killed another person, the family of the victim despaired of justice, unless they had allies in a militia that could ask for justice through a Sharia commission. The situation virtually reversed upon ISIS's arrival. People seemed pleasantly surprised at first, sometimes to the extent that they would overplay their sense of relief. "We never felt this safe for twenty years," said one old resident of Deir Ezzor. "We no longer hear shooting. We no longer hear so-and-so killed so-and-so. We can travel with no problems." Later, the same people expressed satisfaction with the current situation but were less keen to praise ISIS's rule.

One of the most common claims in ISIS's favor in its territories is that it does, so to speak, get the job done. Unlike the FSA and Islamist groups, ISIS will send a patrol to fetch someone if another person files a complaint about him. Even if the complaint in question dates back to the years before the uprising, said one resident who was involved in such a case, ISIS will settle the situation, provided that the complainant has the appropriate documents. Rifaat al-Hassan, from Albu Kamal, told the story of an uncle who lost hundreds of thousands of Syrian pounds years before the uprising, in a fraud scheme by a local businessman. When ISIS controlled Albu Kamal, the fraud was arrested and forced by ISIS to return all funds taken unlawfully.

More important, laws apply to ISIS members and commanders, too; ISIS has executed scores of members and commanders for profiteering or abusing power. In November 2014, ISIS executed one of its leaders in Deir Ezzor after accusing him of embezzlement and robbery. According to the group, the commander had robbed residents after claiming that they were apostates. Similar stories are often told by members of communities under ISIS control. Imad al-Rawi, from al-Qa'im, pledged allegiance to ISIS in August 2014. He spoke of ten ISIS members who were executed because they sold tobacco that they had seized from smugglers. "When they raid shops that sell tobacco, they don't burn the tobacco," al-Rawi said. "When they raid a house, they also steal from it. The state executed them when it discovered them. None of those members smoked, they just sold the tobacco."

"The regime made mistakes and repeated them," said Ghassan al-Juma, from Hasaka. "The FSA, too, made mistakes, and nobody could stop them. But when ISIS makes mistakes, it does not repeat them. You go and complain. If nobody responds to your complaint, you go to the perpetrator's leader, and you always get what you want if you are right."

In Iraq, ISIS also sought to avoid the mistakes and pitfalls of the years before the Awakening. After the takeover of Mosul, ISIS members avoided making their presence heavily known in the streets. Residents of Mosul said that in the first weeks after the Iraqi Security Forces left the city, most of the fighters roaming the streets were from the neighborhoods.

In Mosul and elsewhere, ISIS allowed local forces to govern their own affairs, especially in areas where it felt relatively secure or, conversely, where it lacked manpower. ISIS's reduced visibility helped to establish confidence in the new order, especially in the Iraqi cities. In Syrian areas, before ISIS established control, it had less leeway to do so given the dominance of hostile rebel groups. It relied instead on sleeper cells and loyalists from within those communities to establish a foothold incrementally. The group's reputation for brutality became a form of crowd control.

"People were terrified of ISIS because its reputation preceded it," said al-Rawi from al-Qa'im. "At first, people avoided them, but once they started meeting people in mosques and engaging them, people became too comfortable with them. They liked their dedication and slowly started working with them even if they were still not with them. [ISIS] interfered when they had to. Local people were more present."

That is still particularly the case in areas where ISIS is in need of manpower. After the takeover of Mosul, ISIS came up with a new system of membership for existing local forces that it does not fully trust. It termed them *munasir*, or "supporter"—to be distinguished from *ansar*, a term jihadists use to refer to local members of a group as opposed to *muhajirin*, or foreign fighters.

A munasir must pledge allegiance to ISIS without having direct access to the organization. These second-tier members receive salaries and mostly work to fill low-level municipal and police roles in their areas, tasks ISIS often refers to as *khidmat al-muslimeen.* This strategy helps ISIS to be less visible and thus more capable of dodging responsibility; it also increases rivalry over governance within the local community. ISIS can call on such forces to serve as reinforcement for its troops on the front lines, such as in Kobane, according to residents in Raqqa. Despite the leeway it gives local forces, ISIS still maintains an overarching military, religious, and political control.

EVERYWHERE AND NOWHERE

Just as it tends to be minimally visible as a military force, ISIS also refrains from micromanaging towns, to whatever extent possible. Local forces and their relatives often run day-to-day administrative affairs. Typically, when ISIS takes over a new town, the first facility it establishes is a so-called Hudud Square, to carry out Sharia punishments such as crucifixions, beheadings, lashings, and hand amputations. It then establishes a Sharia court, police force, and security operation station. The work of Sharia police, known as al-Hisbah, is not restricted to the implementation of the religious code, but also includes regulation of the marketplace. These police forces are more active in urban centers. ISIS divides regions into *wilayat*, or provinces, of which there are roughly sixteen in Iraq and Syria, and smaller *qawati*, or townships. One military commander, one or more security commanders, and a general emir are appointed for each township. They all answer to a *wali*, or governor.

Top leaders do not live in the provinces over which they rule. For example, the governors of Minbij, al-Bab, and the parts of Deir Ezzor ISIS designated as Wilayat al-Khair—stretching from the city of Deir Ezzor to the borders of Albu Kamal—tend to live in Raqqa or in Shaddadi, in Hasaka. The governor of Wilayat al-Furat (Albu Kamal and Qa'im) lives in Iraq and rarely travels to Syria. The same applies to the governors of Iraqi provinces.

Raqqa and Mosul serve as ISIS's de facto capitals, and envoys from its territories often meet in palaces occupied by the group. Members of ISIS are instructed to display very few of their weapons in public; as in Minbij, they hide arms in confiscated homes. Checkpoints are also manned by a small number of fighters, in some cases by those who have recently joined ISIS and are still undergoing basic training.

When ISIS security units carry out an operation, foreign and local fighters from the target town and nearby ones gather as reinforcements. This exaggerated show of force during security operations is a hallmark of ISIS's deterrent strategy. This everywhere-but-nowhere strategy deters local forces from rebelling against ISIS, because it allows flexibility, albeit limited, for locals to run their own affairs. It also enlists ISIS as the sole jurisprudent. It is very common for residents to voice their anger at one another rather than at ISIS as an organization, with some going so far as to claim that foreign fighters are more disciplined and better behaved than natural-born residents.

ISIS allows fighters from other groups to keep their arms after it overruns an area, so long as these fighters continue to fight exclusively on the front lines. Anyone who receives weapons, ammunition, or food from ISIS must report to an ISIS emir and serve a specified number of hours per week. One cannot take a leave of absence from the battlefield without relinquishing his weapons. Members of other groups have to follow a similar routine if they wish to govern in their own respective areas. In Fallujah and newly captured regions of Syria, ISIS offers a stark choice: pledge allegiance or leave. "At first, ISIS sets harsh conditions to pressure them," an FSA fighter from Deir Ezzor said of the jihadists' administration of the province in the summer of 2013. "It tells them that if you don't turn up at the [Deir Ezzor] airport regularly, you have to hand over your arms."

Enforced disarmament—ISIS's answer to gun control—also helped the jihadists gain popularity. During FSA rule, buying and carrying weapons became necessary protection for moving from place to place in the face of rampant lawlessness and theft. As one resident from Hasaka put it, "Everybody carried weapons, from children on up. If you didn't have a gun, you'd walk into the market and be scared. If you got into a small fight, you were doomed." ISIS thus caters to popular fears about the absence of law and order by offering itself as the only alternative to societal collapse. Like any government, it seeks to retain a monopoly on violence.

TAKFIRINOMICS

FSA and Islamist groups that controlled oil fields in eastern Syria dedicated some of their revenue to running schools and supplying electricity, telecommunications, water, food, and other services. Some villages and towns saw a decline in such services because ISIS distributed oil revenue to other towns under its control in Syria and Iraq, establishing its own pan-territorial patronage system. As a result, in oil-rich areas, warlordism—a side effect of strictly localized rebel governance—dropped steadily. ISIS has wedded its authoritarian governance to a remarkably successful war economy.

ISIS also forced municipal personnel to work, unlike previous groups that had allowed Syrian state employees to continue to receive their salaries (mostly from the regime) while they sat at home and did nothing, no doubt with no great loss of kickbacks. "The streets are cleaner now; seventy percent of the employees were not working, even though they received salaries," said a former media activist with the FSA from Deir Ezzor. "They canceled the customary day off on Saturday; they're supposed to make Thursday the day off instead."

Regulations and price controls are other areas in which ISIS's governance proved successful. It banned fishermen from using dynamite and electricity to catch fish. It also prohibited residents in the Jazira from using the chaos of war to stake new land claims; this was especially true in the Syrian desert, where opportunistic residents had attempted to build new homes or establish new businesses, much to the chagrin of their neighbors. ISIS also limited the profit margins on oil by-products, ice, flour, and other essential commodities. Before ISIS controlled eastern Syria, an oil well produced around thirty thousand barrels per day, and each barrel sold for two thousand Syrian pounds—eleven dollars at the current exchange rate. Local families that worked in refineries would make two hundred liras (a little more than one dollar) on each barrel that they refined primitively. After ISIS took over, a barrel of oil became cheaper because it fixed the price of a liter of oil at fifty pounds (thirty cents).

ISIS also prohibited families from setting up refineries close to private residences, under the threat of confiscation—a policy that led some families to quit the oil business altogether. Collectively, price control and regulations balanced the decline in resources and services. Subsidies from Gulf countries, where many of those who live in ISIS-controlled areas work, helped some families to afford electricity-generating engines and oil by-products. "Those in the Gulf who used to send once a month now send twice a month because they understand the situation," said the former FSA media activist. "Also, there is no big difference in value. In 2010 a kilo of chicken was 190 pounds [$1] and is now 470 [$2.60]."

Oil was a major revenue generator for ISIS prior to the spring of 2015, when the coalition, acting with newly obtained intelligence, was better able to map ISIS's hydrocarbon industry and understand how the jihadists had been able to keep their wells functioning in the face of punishing airstrikes. According to the trade magazine *Iraq Oil Report*, ISIS "has nearly shut down its oil operations in Iraq and has hampered its more lucrative business in Syria," owing to Operation Tidal Wave II, the coalition's code name for a renewed assault on the jihadists' petroleum sector, which began in October 2015. Internal ISIS documents captured in a US Special Forces raid months earlier on the Deir Ezzor compound of Abu Sayyaf, the group's deputy oil emir, established that ISIS managed to produce "as much as $40 million per month from the sale of crude oil." ISIS functioned very much like a state oil company by outsourcing its production and transportation business. It dispatched operatives to scout and hire regional engineers and specialists who could then demand ultracompetitive salaries to keep the caliphate in black gold. ISIS's oil trade at its peak is now estimated to have been a staggering 70,000 barrels per day. It should shock no one that one of its largest buyers was Bashar al-Assad.

In November 2015, the US Treasury Department, following the European Union's lead, designated George Haswani as al-Assad's middleman for buying back Syria's oil from the jihadists. Haswani also used his own company, HESCO Engineering and Construction Company, to service ISIS-run oil fields. A Greek Catholic industrialist, he has elsewhere been described as having "strong ties" to the Syrian dictator and to agents of the Mukhabarat. HESCO has also done a brisk business in Moscow. It subcontracted with the Russian engineering company Stroytransgaz, with which it was in the midst of constructing a gas processing plant in Palmyra before ISIS sacked the ancient city in May 2015. (Stroytransgaz was formerly a subsidiary of Russia's state-owned gas behemoth Gazprom. It is now privately owned by oligarch Gennady Timchenko, a longtime friend of Vladimir Putin; because of his status as a member of the Kremlin inner circle, Timchenko was sanctioned by the United States after Russia's invasion and annexation of Crimea in 2014.) According to a Syrian opposition website, Haswani once lived and studied in Russia, where he met not only his first wife but also, evidently, men who would go on to prominent roles in Russia's state intelligence services. Tony Badran, the Syria expert at the Foundation for the Defense of Democracies, has suggested that the oilman's liaising between al-Assad and ISIS has not gone unnoticed in Moscow and has been tolerated, whatever the Kremlin's avowed commitment to destroying ISIS.

Furthermore, as Matthew Reed, the vice president of Foreign Reports Inc., a Washington, D.C.–based consultancy, has written, ISIS also sells natural gas to Damascus. "These deals are durable because ISIS can't use it or sell it to anyone else: it must be captured at the source and moved by pipeline. The only users connected to the gas fields are power plants, refineries, and industries, which are concentrated in Assad's strongholds." The regime supposedly committed to vanquishing terrorists keeps electricity running in ISIS-run territories, in a literal power-sharing arrangement. At all events, there can be no plausible deniability as to how Syria's natural gas sector is kept alive. "At natural gas fields like those around Palmyra, which produce lighter liquid hydrocarbons in addition to gas, ISIS takes whatever it can turn into fuel," Reed writes. "The gas goes west to Assad."

Oil smuggling to neighboring countries such as Turkey and Jordan, and to other areas in Syria and Iraq, still produces significant revenue for the jihadists. The sharp decline in oil production affected civilians more than it did ISIS, which could still generate wealth from other sources. Importantly, though, it hampered ISIS's ability to provide for the local communities, especially much-coveted materials such as gas cylinders. "I estimate that the impact of air strikes was five percent," said one anti-ISIS media activist, who still lives in Deir Ezzor, prior to Operation Tidal Wave II. "They affected oil primarily. Food is plenty, and most of it comes from Turkey or Iraq. Borders are open; if you don't like prices here, you go to Anbar. I see the situation as normal."

ISIS's oil trade has impressed and shocked many observers, although Derek Harvey is not one of them. "I know for a fact that the Saddamists who were smuggling the oil in the nineties, to evade UN sanctions, are now doing so for ISIS," the former US military intelligence officer said. It may be true, as the latest analysis has concluded, that ISIS was at one point selling oil for $10 to $20 per barrel, but, Harvey said, the price points may be misleading. "These middlemen are selling it, and there's a kickback coming back in to ISIS's senior leaders. . . . It's going back into the kitty of financiers at the top of the pyramid. The ISIS fighters in Deir Ezzor would not be aware of that."

Locals in eastern Syria had learned to survive on remittances from the Gulf and local economies even before the uprising. High oil prices led many to rely less on agricultural products since the energy had to be spent pumping water from the Euphrates or Tigris rivers to their farmlands many miles away. After the war started, cheaper oil revived Syrian agribusiness, and smuggling and livestock trade markets began booming again. When ISIS seized control of the Jazira, people were already buying their own oil for irrigation and electricity and did not need to rely on subsidized services.

The BND, Germany's foreign intelligence agency, has cautioned against "overblown" speculation about ISIS's high oil revenue because there is a tendency to discount the massive overhead and spending inside its territories. Yet, as per Harvey, ISIS pockets most of this revenue, as it sometimes taxes residents for services supplied by the regime, such as electricity and telecommunication. Unlike Islamist groups that operated regime-established facilities for the local communities gratis, ISIS has developed a surcharge economy to replenish its own coffers.

ISIS makes millions from zakat (different forms of Islamic alms payable to the state). Zakat is extracted from annual savings or capital assets (2.5 percent), gold (on values exceeding $4,500), livestock (two heads out of 100 heads owned by a farmer), dates, crops (10 percent if irrigated by rain or a nearby stream or river, and 5 percent if irrigation costs money), and profits (2.5 percent).

ISIS also imposes annual taxes on non-Muslims living in its territories, especially Christians (4.25 grams of gold for the rich and half that for moderate-income individuals). It makes money by theft dressed up as civil penalties: it confiscates the properties of displaced or wanted individuals, and as punishment for fighting against ISIS. This includes, of course, enormous stocks of weapons and ammunition as part of its community disarmament policies. In October 2015, analyst Aymenn Jawad al-Tamimi obtained documents produced by ISIS's Finance Ministry in Deir Ezzor. Oil and gas proceeds accounted for 27.7 percent of ISIS moneymaking, but "confiscations," such as from contraband cigarette or alcohol smuggling or the seizure of homes and assets from declared enemies, accounted for 44.7 percent, while taxation accounted for 23.7 percent. Nearly 70 percent of ISIS's income for an entire province came from the population it "governs."

Ghanima, or war spoils—in ISIS's definition, this encompasses robbery and theft—remains one of the group's largest and most valuable sources of income. ISIS seized hundreds of millions of dollars' worth of American and foreign military equipment after it forced the Iraqi army to flee in June 2014, and it has also seized large stockpiles of weapons, as well as equipment, facilities, and cash from al-Assad's regime and rebel groups.

Artifacts, the stolen patrimony of Syria and Iraq, are also a booming business, although it's one ISIS has inherited rather than pioneered. (Both Saddam's and al-Assad's regimes have partaken of it; other Syrian rebel groups and Kurdish insurgents continue to do so, too.) But one man we interviewed in

Turkey said that trade in antiquities grew during ISIS's reign. One of his cousins, he said, smuggled into Turkey golden statues and coins found in Mari's ancient ruins, about seven miles away from Albu Kamal. Other items, such as statues, lamps, and pottery, have reportedly turned up for sale in London, suggesting that a mere fraction of the total international trade in looted works of art has been empirically verified. The now-deceased ISIS operative Abu Sayyaf was in charge of the "Antiquities Division in the al-Sham Wilayahs." According to declassified State Department documents, Abu Sayyaf had several pieces in his possession when he was killed by American special forces in May 2015. And the trade was strictly regulated, with excavators being "licensed" to dig artifacts out of the ground. Anyone caught smuggling antiquities without ISIS's permission was remanded for punishment. As with everything else, the licensees were taxed—20 percent, according to Syrian archaeologist Amr al-Azm. By mid-2014, ISIS had sufficiently institutionalized a decades-old black-market pillage and grave-robbing business that, as al-Azm told the *Guardian*, it started "to hire their own archaeologists, digging teams and machinery—and that's when we saw a peak of looting activity." Black-market buyers have connected with ISIS sellers on eBay, Skype, and social media platforms with ease.

The world looked on in horror as ISIS thugs took sledgehammers to thousand-year-old monuments and statues—dating back to the Assyrian and Akkadian empires—in the central museum in Mosul in February 2015, demonstrating what happens to antiquities ISIS does not sell. A month later, they bulldozed the Assyrian city of Nimrud to Mosul's south and a month after that it was the turn of Hatra, a city built by the Seleucid Empire two thousand years ago and founded by a former infantry general of Alexander the Great. In April 2015, ISIS released a video showing the demolition of Hatra's ruins, a UNESCO World Heritage Site, with sledgehammers, bulldozers, and assault rifles. "Some of the infidel organizations say the destruction of these alleged artifacts is a war crime," one of the militants on screen says. "We will destroy your artifacts and idols anywhere and Islamic State will rule your lands." For those who had never been there, Hatra became a popular cultural touchstone after featuring in the memorable opening scenes of *The Exorcist*. Now the cultural patrimony of the cradle of civilization would fall to another form of demoniacal possession.

15

LOYALTY AND DISLOYALTY
ISIS IDEOLOGY IN THEORY AND PRACTICE

Hamid Ghannam's first day at training camp was intense. Very early on the morning of August 13, 2014, he picked up his packed clothes and walked quickly to the main street in his Syrian village to meet three of his cousins. As with Abdelaziz, the Bahraini fighter whose story we recounted in the introduction, and as with many young men who dream of the caliphate, Ghannam went on to join ISIS without informing his parents.

The cousins drove in a white minibus to an ISIS-run camp at the Omar oil field in the desert of Mayadeen, Deir Ezzor. Their recruiter was a distant relative who had enlisted around eight others from his village since he was put in charge of its security. He accompanied his cousins to their new lodgings, where they would spend the next few weeks.

"Make us proud," the recruiter told the cousins as he drove away. Another jihadist welcomed the three fresh recruits and asked them to prepare themselves for Sharia lessons. "It is not easy, you have to be patient," Ghannam said. "They test you first. They speak with you for a while. They check your knowledge of religion. They discuss everything. They talk to you about the Nusayri regime," he continued, referring to the pejorative term used by ISIS to describe Alawites, and therefore al-Assad's loyalists, "and then about the Free Syrian Army and all the misguided groups. It is exhausting at first."

ISIS ideology has been generally viewed by outsiders as being identical to al-Qaeda's or the Saudi version of Salafism—an adherence to fundamental Islamic tenets. The debate often stops here. Crucially, though, outsiders' ability to grasp the ideology is further muddled by reliance on books and documents without examining how these texts are interpreted and absorbed within the organization.

Understanding ISIS's ideological appeal is not only the key to understanding why tens of thousands of men and women, many of them not even pious or practicing Muslims, set out to enlist in a death cult, and why so many stay committed long past the point of diminishing returns. It's also the key to defeating the army of terror. General John Allen, the retired marine who was formerly in charge of leading the international coalition against ISIS, told the London-based Saudi newspaper *Asharq Alawsat* in October 2015, "the long-term direction of ISIS that we will have to deal with beyond the choking off of its revenues, which diminishes its capacity, its operational flexibility and discretion, is its brand and idea."

ISIS ideology hangs over the battlefield, affecting even separate and putatively antagonistic rebel factions. Field commanders in Syria also say that it's been a key impediment to mobilizing forces against ISIS, as many fighters refuse to fight fellow Muslims, especially if the effort is backed by non-Muslim powers. A commander of Usud al-Sharqiyyah, or the Eastern Lions, an armed group from Deir Ezzor that has fought ISIS bitterly, spoke of a "culture of takfir" pervasive within rebel groups' rank and file undermining any attempt at a grassroots counterinsurgency. Not for nothing have the Islamist militias most effective at resisting ISIS—notably Jaysh al-Islam, or the Islamic Army, near Damascus—provided their men with a religious curriculum to immunize them from

ISIS'S FORT BRAGG

Sharia training varies from one member to another, depending on ISIS's assessment of one's value or loyalty. New recruits have to be indoctrinated first, a process that can take from two weeks to forty-five days to a year. Inside the camps, students receive a mix of military, political, and Sharia orientation, usually given by around five instructors. During training, cadets can be dispatched to checkpoints, but not to the front lines, in order to observe martial discipline. After graduation they remain under supervision and can be expelled or punished in cases of noncompliance—including being lashed if they express reservations about obeying orders or the group's acts. It's not uncommon for many new members who struggle with the brutality of the

ISIS's Sharia justice to be sent back to receive more training to "strengthen" their faith.

"You first get the basics about religion," said Abu Moussa, an ISIS-affiliated religious cleric, originally from Aleppo, who is operating in eastern Syria. "They cleanse you from religious innovations and Baathist ideas. Issuing fatwas is restricted to clerics and nobody can kill without a fatwa unless in the battlefield. You also study Arabic and learn how to speak in standard Arabic if you don't know."

Clerics in charge of religious training, known as *sharii*, or Sharia specialists, are mostly academically qualified or have long experience within the organization. ISIS likes to rely on young clerics who have recently joined up to compensate for the shortage of imams. There are approximately twenty mosques in each town under ISIS control, and all have to be fully staffed to cater to their flocks. Religious services, such as Friday prayers, are strictly enforced. It's also more convenient to hire younger, more impressionable prelates who are easier to brainwash. Imams with limited theological experience are thus selected to speak from pulpits across eastern Syria and northwestern Iraq, where mosques were hitherto run by Sufis from the Naqshbandi Order or its Khaznawi branch.

Abu Moussa denied that ISIS excommunicates Muslims. "We don't do that," he said. "Yes, we have no tolerance for anybody who opposes our message. Why do we fight the Free Syrian Army? We spread our message by proselytization and sword." Abu Moussa cited fourteenth-century Islamic theologian Ibn Taymiyyah, who said "the foundation of this religion is a book that guides and a sword that brings victory." "We guide and the sword brings victory. If someone opposes the message of the Prophet, he faces nothing but the sword. As the Prophet spread the message across the earth, we are doing the same."

Another ISIS member echoed this reasoning, telling one of the authors: "The Prophet said: 'I have been given victory by means of terror.' As for slaughter, beheading and crucifixion, this is in the Quran and Sunna," he said, referring to oral sayings attributed to Prophet Muhammad. "In the videos we produce, you see the sentence 'deal with them in a way that strikes fear in those behind them,' and that verse speaks for itself."

ISIS generally steers clear of exposing new members to teachings that are not derived from Sharia texts. Fresh recruits are given religious books almost exclusively, while established figures or military commanders are permitted to study manuals such as Abu Bakr Naji's *The Management of Savagery*. The restriction of religious indoctrination to purely theological texts is in line with ISIS's avowal that it is an extension of authentic Islam rather than one among competing schools of Islamic interpretation.

ISIS is so wedded to purity of vision that it actually presents the "mainstream" Islam practiced by Muslims today as one that was "invented" over the past few decades. To dismantle this invention, ISIS looks to Islamic Sharia and history to find the most arcane teachings and then magnifies them as though they were the norm, selling itself as the new exegetical standard-bearer. Recruits are thus treated to a fabricated Islam only a few years old, while believing they're channeling centuries of tradition. Take, for instance, the caliphate's punishment for homosexuality: throwing people off rooftops. Those cheering this form of murder from the ground are made to believe that this is nothing but a perfectly condign punishment for deviant sexuality, when, in fact, hurling people from great heights to certain death is unheard of, even in countries such as Saudi Arabia where brute Sharia jurisprudence is practiced openly.

Unlike previous modes of execution—stoning and crucifixion, both of which have generated innumerable Islamic commentaries, in favor and against—many people in the Middle East weren't even aware that throwing people from rooftops was a Sharia penalty in the first place, which was precisely the point. The obscurity of the practice is what makes it valuable to ISIS; while most cast about in the dark to find an appropriate hermeneutics to justify or condemn the practice, ISIS has its answers ready-made. It has fabricated a twenty-first century ethos as a seventh-century Guide for the Perplexed. And only the elect can understand it. Indeed, many ISIS members interviewed for this book were eager to emphasize that they were stirred by such recondite teachings—it made them feel like part of a priesthood, a secret society—and were drawn to the way ISIS presents Islam with absolute clarity.

Nor does it do much good to argue with ISIS about how its practices are un-Islamic. A common story told within the organization recounts the Prophet Muhammad's commander in chief, Khaled bin al-Walid, who killed hundreds of captives after the seventh-century battle of Ullais in Iraq. Bin al-Walid's behavior seemingly ran contrary to the faith, but he had pledged to God that he would make a "river of blood" from the Persian army in the event that God granted him victory. Keeping a promise to the Almighty took precedence over the Islamic proscription against murdering captives. Bin al-Walid struggled even so in fulfilling his pledge when he couldn't exsanguinate enough victims to make his river. He innovatively solved this problem by having a dam opened onto enough bleeding corpses to at least give the on rushing water a reddish hue. ISIS repurposes this story to justify the murder of captives because surely the military commander deemed by the Prophet himself as the "Unleashed Sword of God," and hailed for his martial prowess by the first Muslim caliph, Abu Bakr, cannot be a heretic.

THE SALAFIST "AWAKENING"

ISIS also thrives by homing in on the stories or texts that mainstream Islamic clerics have preferred to ignore, either because they deemed these too marginal or because they're too difficult or embarrassing to square with modern morality. ISIS feels no such queasiness or reluctance to tackle these sacred lessons, and its willing executioners graduate from boot camp feeling that they have stumbled on the unexpurgated message of Islam. More than that, they believe, mainstream Muslims have conspired to hide this message from the faithful. Ghannam and his cousins left the Omar training camp knowing not just how to fire a Kalashnikov but how to argue a point of theology against those they consider to be blinded by a kind of Islamic false consciousness.

Other extreme wings of the religion are challenged by ISIS. Wahhabism, the school of Salafism founded by Mohammed bin Abdulwahab in the eighteenth century and officially enforced in Saudi Arabia today, is glibly used by pundits to account for the entirety of the organization's ideological underpinnings. While Wahhabist influence on ISIS cannot be denied, it's hardly the whole story. For instance, both ISIS and the Taliban exhibited strikingly similar behavior in their implementation of Sharia. Both come from countries that share the same school of Islamic jurisprudence, the Hanafi school. Wahhabists, however, adhere to the Hanbali school. Yet one cannot argue that ISIS is simply the Taliban relocated to Syria and Iraq. Also, why does a reputedly secular country like Tunisia, which historically fended off Wahhabist currents wafting into North Africa from the Gulf, export more jihadists into ISIS ranks per capita than Saudi Arabia? Wahhabism also forbids many of the practices that ISIS embraces, such as suicide bombing, the destruction of mosques, targeting Shia civilians, and rebellion against established rulers.

It pays to look at ISIS ideology as a hodgepodge of regional influences. Syrian, Egyptian, and Palestinian Islamism imprinted on traditional Salafism during the period commonly known as the Islamic Awakening, a period that saw the influx of multinational Arabs into the Gulf states, especially Saudi Arabia and Kuwait. It produced most of today's jihadist ideologues and theoreticians, including the current generation of al-Qaeda leaders. As we've seen, the war of ideas taking place between the Muslim Brotherhood, the organization founded by Egyptian schoolteacher Hassan al-Banna in the 1920s, and more reactionary Salafist competitors was formative in producing figures like Abdullah Azzam and Ayman al-Zawahiri, bin Laden's first and second spiritual mentors, and Abu Muhammad al-Maqdisi, al-Zarqawi's formative mentor and partner in Jordanian crime. Bin Laden was part of the Muslim Brotherhood in Saudi Arabia and Abu Bakr al-Baghdadi was at least close to Iraq's Muslim Brotherhood, as were many of today's jihadists in the ranks of Jabhat al-Nusra and Ahrar al-Sham in Syria.

The Brotherhood's focus on transforming Arab politics gradually, through preexisting institutions (be they democratic or not), clashed dialectically with the Salafists' rejection of the ruling order, *tout court*. In Saudi Arabia and Egypt, an awkward fusion was taking place between these two Islamist currents. The result was that Brotherhood-style politics was made still more conservative, while Salafism was made more political. Salafists took up political takfirism under the banner of restoring the caliphate. Jihad and rebellion became their campaign strategy.

The Muslim Brotherhood's philosopher-in-chief Sayyed Qutb drew on some of the Salafists' tear-it-up-and-start-again radicalism. He argued that Muslim-majority societies were living in a state of *jahiliyya*, or pre-Islamic obliviousness. All secular ideologies, including capitalism, communism, and pan-Arab nationalism, had failed. The only system that could and would succeed was Islam—not just in Muslim-majority countries but everywhere. Qutb espoused *ustadhiyyat al-alam*, or supremacy over the world.

In order for these transformative goals to be achieved, a vanguard of Muslim youth would have to reject their societies and lead the change through complete disassociation, or *mufasala*, and the taking of Islam as their only societal reference point, a concept known as *hakimiyya*. Qutb's brother, Muhammed, sometimes known as the "father of Islamic Awakening" in Saudi Arabia, made a vital contribution to the ideological fusion between Salafism and Islamist ideas by adding hakimiyya to Ibn Taymiyyah's three criteria for *tawhid*: belief in God, belief only in God, and following the right creed. Islamic supremacy has thus become a determinant of one's belief in monotheism.

Salafist-jihadists mostly agree with Qutb's diagnosis, although for them he was still too much of a squish and too little concerned with revolutionizing Islamic jurisprudence for everyday life. Qutb gave these jihadists the contours of their ideology, a way of reading of the world through the prism of Islamic supremacism, even if they disagreed with him on how to get to utopia.

The chain-link progression of Islamist revolutionary thinking, from the Brotherhood to the caliphate, was best captured by the Yemeni journalist Abdulelah Haider Shaye. "The Islamic State," he said, "was drafted by Sayyid Qutb, taught by Abdullah Azzam, globalized by Osama bin Laden, transferred to reality by Abu Musab al-Zarqawi, and implemented by the al-Baghdadis: Abu Omar and Abu Bakr."

The Qutbist concepts of hakimiyya, jahiliyya, and mufasala shape the way ISIS deals with diverse religious and ethnic communities it rules. Local populations need to be "reconverted" to Islam. Accusing a Muslim of apostasy doesn't have to adhere to traditional clerical guidelines because takfir is a root-and-branch business for changing the world and, as per Qutb, Muslims have fundamentally deviated from the true meaning of their faith. Nothing nothing short of a total, coercive revolution can save them.

"If you think people will accept the Islamic project [voluntarily], you're wrong," one ISIS member said. "They have to be forced at first. The other groups think that they can convince people and win them over but they're wrong. You have a ready project, you should place it on society like a tooth crown and make sure to maintain it."

THE CLERGY OF TAKFIR

In its territories, ISIS relies on the jihadist literature of ideologues who agree with its stance. Four of those clerics, namely Nasir bin Hamad al-Fahad, Sulaiman bin Nasir al-Alwan, Ali bin Khidr al-Khudair, and Hamoud bin Uqla al-Shuaibi, were part of a network that heavily influenced al-Qaeda in Saudi Arabia in the early 2000s, as well as the transnational jihadi movement. Remarkably, the four clerics were active members of the Islamic Awakening, which blended conservative traditions with revolutionary ideas. They wrote extensively on the apostasy of Saudi Arabia for helping the United States in its regional interventions, especially during the First Gulf War. The entry of

Western troops into Saudi Arabia as a base to expel Saddam Hussein from Kuwait was widely used by extremist clerics to apostatize Riyadh. Al-Shuaibi has also written an important and influential book for ISIS on the impermissibility of seeking the help of infidels, titled "The Chosen Word in the Rules Regarding Seeking Help from Infidels." Al-Fahad has also reportedly pledged allegiance to ISIS.

Also, the fact that the four clerics were theologically trained—rare within jihadi ideologues, which tend to lack official religious training—and were at the same time in stark disagreement with the clerical establishment in Saudi Arabia makes them a huge asset for ISIS.

Al-Khudair and Khaled Muhammed al-Rashed, two Saudi clerics, are heavily referenced by ISIS. Al-Khudair has an unequivocal position on modern legislative systems and any Muslim who becomes involved in them in one way or another. Anyone who voluntarily joins a parliament, he deems an infidel; anyone who swears loyalty to a constitution, even if compelled to do so, is an apostate; and anyone who opposes a constitution through democratic means, is a sinner. Al-Khudair's writings are essentially a one-stop shop for ISIS: he stipulates that non-Islamic systems and followers are illegitimate and that ordinary people's adherence to them is inexcusable.

All four clerics further underwrite ISIS's exterminationist project with respect to the Shia, preaching that members of this sect simply have no excuse in maintaining their faith. Al-Rashed, for example, held a series of sermons dedicated to attacking Shia under the title "The Sharp-Edged Sword on the Evil Shiites," featuring explicit language, such as "freezing the blood in their veins" and "cancer sweeps them away." Al-Fahad wrote a treatise titled "The Permissibility of Excessiveness Against the Rafida," which is also replete with abusive and denigrating language directed at Shia.

Another key influencer of ISIS's ideology is Abu Muhammad al-Maqdisi, al-Zarqawi's father figure in jihad, even though he has vehemently opposed the organization since the start of its expansion in Syria and criticized their war against fellow jihadists. Al-Maqdisi's contribution to ISIS's overall ideology is profound. "I am their sheikh who taught them the concept of tawhid," he recently boasted, whatever his disagreement with these epigones' methods. ISIS does not publicly promote his books due to the sensitivity of relying on a man who has repudiated the organization. But, paradoxically, it uses his ideas to debunk the arguments of ISIS detractors. His books are also in heavy circulation in ISIS-controlled areas, according to many jihadists in Syria.

One volume in particular is instrumental. This is *Millat Ibrahim*, or *The Path of Abraham*, the book cited in the first volume of *Dabiq*, which is also used by other Salafist factions in Syria, such as al-Nusra and Ahrar al-Sham, even though it has been highly criticized by their members as the root of all evil: the origin of ISIS-style takfiri currents within these non-ISIS Islamist groups. Ahmed Abazaid, a Syrian expert closely studying Islamists and jihadists in Syria, described al-Maqdisi's writings as "the basis of the takfiri cancer and the cause of the ease with which the blood of people and mujahidin is shed."

The Path of Abraham applies the concept of *wala* and *baraa*—loyalty to Islam and disloyalty to anything un-Islamic—as the religion's foundational creed and uses it to label other Muslims as apostates, even if they're family members. Based on al-Maqdisi's rendering, the criterion for determining a true or false Muslim has so narrowed that jihadists in Syria use *ikhwat al-manhaj*, or brothers in methodology, to designate those revolving in the orbit of ISIS, al-Nusra and Ahrar al-Sham. Tantamount to a jihadist Popular Front, this assemblage of ideologically similar but politically disparate factions is meant to keep everyone else out—any Sunnis who do not adhere to these ideas, and all Shia and members of other Islamic sects.

This sectarian bias is also on full display in the figure of, Turki al-Binali, the single most influential cleric to ISIS. In 2007, he was expelled from Dubai, where he was studying, and he was later banned from Kuwait, Egypt, Qatar, and his home country, Bahrain, because of his takfirism and his pathological hatred of Shia. Al-Binali has been a prolific critic of this sect and what he calls its "warped ideology." In July 2015, after ISIS carried out a series of suicide bombings against Shia mosques in Kuwait and Saudi Arabia, he threatened similar attacks against Shia targets in Bahrain. But his usefulness to ISIS derives from his more establishment jihadist pedigree. Before he traveled to Syria to join the organization in 2013, he had gained credibility as a mufti through close association with fourteen known clerics in the Middle East. In 2009, al-Maqdisi authorized al-Binali to teach and issue fatwas, which he did on prominent jihadi forums for years under the nom de guerre Abu Hummam al-Athari. ISIS members highlight this part of his career to counter attempts by clerics, such as al-Maqdisi, to downplay al-Binali's religious authority.

As one ISIS cleric put it, al-Binali's bona fides before the organization was founded is a testament not only to its credibility but to its many al-Qaeda detractors' hypocrisy, since the latter had previously approved of him. He also undercuts a common criticism leveled at ISIS, that it has no clerical support base older than itself. Although theologically a relative lightweight, al-Binali's pre-ISIS career helps the organization situate him in a long line of jihadist jurists.

For those reasons al-Binali has been at the forefront of building credibility for ISIS as well for al-Baghdadi's personality cult. As a former al-Qaeda associate, he is seen as better positioned to address the issue of reversing the allegiance some had pledged to al-Qaeda or the Taliban. Al-Binali also authored a booklet on the new caliph and his historical and theological pretensions for being such, "Extend the Hands to Pledge Allegiance to al-Baghdadi." He was reportedly dispatched to the Libyan city of Sirte in March 2013 and in 2014 to proselytize, chiefly through a series of lectures in the Rabat Mosque on his favorite subject: the evil of the Shia.

What all this shows us is that ISIS is an even more extremist outcropping of extremism. As part of its long-term enterprise, it has constructed a Frankenstein theology unto itself, complete with a bespoke penal code, using Islamic concepts that lifelong scholars and clerics have no means of engaging with, and borrowing promiscuously from a decades-old philosophical tradition. When new recruits leave ISIS training camps charged and sometimes even willing to kill their own relatives, they're galvanized not by religion alone. They are animated by an exclusivist, puritanical, and elitist political ideology not long in the making.

16

BACK TO IRAQ

ISIS COMES HOME

The birth of any "state" is a nasty and brutal affair but no parturition has been quite so nightmarish as that of the caliphate. In mid-2014, as ISIS expanded its territory in a lightning push across thousands of square miles of Syria and Iraq, it took millions of people hostage either as willing or coerced subjects of its new theocracy, put an untold number to the sword, and revived a long-dormant practice of religiously codified slavery for a vulnerable ethnic minority. The jihadists massacred hundreds of Shia Iraqi soldiers at Camp Speicher. They burned a fellow Sunni Arab alive in a cage. They kidnapped and sold at auction thousands of Yazidi girls—many of premenstrual age—for the purpose of raping them around the clock. Fresh humanitarian outrages would scandalize the world into military action against the army of terror, which seemed to up its quotient for evil with each passing news cycle. Surely the modern world had never seen anything like this.

A cultural amnesia set in among those who presumed history had begun with the fall of Mosul, or that the last eleven years had never happened. And the syndrome was worst in the one place it could least afford to be: US policy-making circles. Forgotten was the Zarqawists' long, bloody history of divide-and-conquer, which had once made front-page headlines and shocked even al-Qaeda stalwarts. The United States under President Obama could not wait to be done with Iraq, and behaved in the first year of war as if the hard-won lessons of the occupation had never been learned. Unfortunately, ISIS behaved as if it had learned those lessons all too well and happily spent the early months of Operation Inherent Resolve sussing out the inherent contradictions and weaknesses of the strategy to destroy it. Two thousand fourteen would mark a return to takfiri first principles. ISIS started by eliminating "polytheists" and "apostates" in its midst, or taking them as captives for the pleasure of its holy warriors. It waged a campaign of mass slaughter against Iraq's Shia, the better to both radicalize them onto their own sectarian war footing and push them into an inevitable reliance on Iranian-run militias. This of course would terrify a nervous Sunni minority into the arms of Abu Bakr al-Baghdadi. It exploited internal divisions within another important demographic—Iraqi Kurds—through mass expulsion and genocide, and staged an unconscionable and demoralizing attack on its original "near enemy," Jordan.

These atrocities were clearly committed to advance the underlying political ambition of Sunni restoration. Having seized so much terrain—roughly the size of Great Britain—ISIS was never closer to realizing al-Zarqawi's darkling vision of re-creating a Sunni Islamic dynasty across the Levant and Mesopotamia. And what ISIS lacked in an order of battle, it more than made up for in espionage capabilities and sociological cunning. Adhering to the Bonapartist principle of never interrupting an enemy when he is making a mistake, ISIS let its many enemies make many mistakes. The result was a needless loss in blood and treasure. And even in places where ISIS was tactically defeated, "liberation" was often viewed by those who had just suffered under the jihadist yoke as merely the arrival of another kind of oppression.

THE DESTRUCTION OF THE YAZIDIS

In August 2014, ISIS trapped tens of thousands of Yazidis on top of a mountain and laid waste to their historic community below. This humanitarian catastrophe, coupled with the horrific prospect of ISIS's sacking Erbil, the capital of the Kurdistan Regional Government and home to an important US consulate in the Middle East, forced President Obama to finally go to war with the group he had recently described as the junior varsity of terror outfits. It was no small climb-down for an antiwar commander in chief who had a year earlier also seen his "red line" violated with spectacular bravado by the al-Assad regime, which gassed Syria's ethnic majority in Damascus; now Obama would be committing to military action in order to rescue an ethnic minority in Iraq and enforce a threshold of a different color: the so-called Green Line, which for twelve years before the fall of his regime kept Saddam's jets and helicopters out of Iraqi Kurdistan by way of a US-implemented no-fly zone.

Although not yet part of the coalition that would prosecute Operation Inherent Resolve, the US Air Force was tasked with conducting two separate operations. The first was a series of limited air strikes against ISIS in and around the region of Sinjar, a border community in northwestern Iraq, to halt their advance toward Erbil and protect the US consulate in the city. The second was airdrops of thousands of gallons of potable water and even more meals to the forty thousand Yazidis stranded on Mount Sinjar, a craggy hunk of rock thought to be where Noah's Ark eventually washed up. Those who tried to escape the desolation by coming down off the rock were murdered by ISIS, and dozens of those who remained, mainly the elderly and at least forty children, had already died of dehydration. The stranded dead were buried the only way possible, in shallow graves, "their bodies covered with stones," as the *Washington Post*'s Loveday Morris wrote. Nothing could grow on Mount Sinjar; only death awaited those who tried to escape the desolation by coming down off the rock. "There is no water, there is no vegetation, they are completely cut off and surrounded by" ISIS, Marzio Babille, the Iraq representative for the United Nations Children's Fund (UNICEF), told Morris. "It's a disaster, a total disaster." The full extent of that disaster, which met the legal definition of genocide, would take another year to uncover.

Why was ISIS targeting the Yazidis? One of Iraq's smallest religious minorities, they represent a mere 1.5 percent of the country's total population and have exactly one member of Iraqi parliament, Vian Dakhil, who would earn international fame for her speech in that chamber demanding the world intervene to save her people from extermination. Considered by Kurds to be their ethnic kin, the Yazidis have maintained a sense of singular identity, owing to the uniqueness of their faith, which borrows liberally from Islam, Christianity, and Zoroastrianism. Their godhead is Melek Taus, the peacock angel. ISIS considers him to be Lucifer, which makes the Yazidis "devil-worshippers." And there is only one thing to do with devil-worshippers: kill them or take them as chattel.

To veterans of the Iraq War, there was a sense of déjà vu to the siege of Sinjar that warned of much of the carnage to come. Throughout the mid-2000s, the town had acted as a "waypoint for foreign fighters coming from Syria across the Jazira toward Mosul and the Tigris valley," Joel Rayburn, the former military intelligence officer, said, adding that it was also the epicenter of the single deadliest terror attack of the entire war. In August 2007, just south of Sinjar, four large truck bombs were detonated by al-Qaeda in Iraq jihadists, collapsing Yazidi apartment blocks, killing around eight hundred and injuring another 1,500. A former CIA operative stationed in Iraq at the time remembered the atrocity as wholly gratuitous. "There was nothing out there of any strategic or military value," he told us. "They just did it as a 'Fuck you.'"

By 2014, Sinjar was to be an important conduit between ISIS's two main provincial capitals, Raqqa and Mosul. Now, absent US troops, the only bulwark the Yazidis had to avoid an encore performance was the Kurdish peshmerga, the powerful paramilitary under the control of the Kurdistan Regional Government (KRG), headed by President Massoud Barzani in Erbil. Long considered one of the few success stories out of Iraq—a cosmopolitan, largely secular, pro-American enclave—the KRG has territorial and geopolitical ambitions of its own. When ISIS invaded northern Iraq in June 2014, for instance, the KRG ordered its peshmerga to take full military control of Kirkuk, an oil-rich city that lies south of the Green Line in the eponymous province, justifying the seizure as defensive in nature. Baghdad, Erbil said with some justification, had been wholly unprepared for the jihadist onslaught and so the Kurds would now have to fortify vulnerable likely targets. In reality, the seizure of Kirkuk was opportunistic and shrewd; Iraqi Kurds have no intention of ever relinquishing their "Jerusalem," which Saddam's Baath regime notoriously "Arabized" in the 1980s. As a hydrocarbon juggernaut, the city also represents a huge commercial prize for the KRG, which has serious, cyclical budget disputes with the central government in Baghdad. The taking of Kirkuk was a unified action. The loss of Sinjar was not.

There are two peshmergas, each commanded by one of the two main political parties in the KRG. There is the peshmerga answerable to Barzani's Kurdistan Democratic Party (KDP), and there is the peshmerga answerable to the Patriotic Union of Kurdistan (PUK), which is headed by Iraq's first democratic president, Jalal Talabani. The KDP's peshmerga was responsible for safeguarding Sinjar when ISIS rolled in. But, owing to localized political tribalism, only the most KDP-loyal corps of Yazidi residents of the town were armed by Barzani's paramilitary. The rest had to fend for themselves, either by using weapons they had confiscated from retreating Iraqi soldiers—weapons for which resupplies would not be forthcoming—or by using whatever arms they had in their personal possession, such as hunting rifles. There were also reports that the peshmerga had disarmed the Yazidi communal defense militias and, in some cases, prevented villagers from leaving Sinjar. What isn't in dispute is how ignominiously the peshmerga commanders behaved while ISIS was at the gates of the town. They deserted. And while the KDP politburo promised to send in reinforcements, none ever arrived.

ISIS doesn't just conquer a place physically; it seeks to expropriate the cultural memory of those who survive its grim reign. Robbing a community of its capacity for truth and reconciliation once the jihadists have been booted out of a village or town or provincial capital is a staple of ISIS's psychological warfare. Rifts are not just widened among antagonistic tribes, sects, or ethnicities; they are *created* within them—particularly where the bonds of kinship are tenuous or imaginary. Abu Bakr Naji's instruction of co-opting tribal solidarity to advance the management of savagery has been taken up and amplified by ISIS's atrocity-making. And so the pillage of the Yazidis' ancestral home didn't just elicit horror and revulsion against the pillagers; it led to a wave of anger and recrimination against the negligent defenders.

A former KRG official conceded to the authors that the fall of the town was not exactly his government's finest hour. "It's a big shame and those peshmerga commanders should have fought and died," he said. "But they were facing ISIS, who had captured the Iraqi army's heavy weaponry from Mosul and they were really no match for the jihadists." Baghdad, it's true, has long been at odds with Erbil over oil revenue sharing and territorial control and has not adequately armed its Kurdish confederates since Iraq's independence from Saddam. But Barzani's camp has now resorted to rewriting recent history in order to evade responsibility for how the Yazidis came to near extinction. The peshmerga commanders who fled were never prosecuted for desertion; instead, the KRG now blames its main rivals the Kurdish Workers' Party, or PKK (its Kurdish acronym), and the PKK's Syrian branch, the Democratic Union Party, or PYD, both of which sent militias into Sinjar to fight ISIS and both of which, Barzani has alleged, made tactical mistakes that prevented the town's timelier recapture. Many Yazidis, on the contrary, see the PKK and PYD guerrillas as their true saviors.

The price for ISIS's exploitation of internal Iraqi politicking would be paid, as ever, by innocent men, women, and children. ISIS kidnapped 5,000 Yazidis during the siege, 3,000 of whom are still being held. The fall of Sinjar created a massive refugee crisis when 36,000 Yazidis fled into Iraqi Kurdistan. By December 2014, almost half of all internally displaced Iraqis, including Christians, Turkomans, and other minorities, would pour into one of the four

KRG provinces—around 890,000 people—overwhelming Barzani's regional government, which had already been steadily absorbing Kurdish refugees from Syria.

In August 2014, ISIS justified attacks on peshmerga positions in the towns of Gwer and Makhmour, both in Mosul province, as a reaction against burgeoning rapprochement between Erbil and Baghdad. "The [Kurdish] co-alition with the Safavid Shia and the cross worshippers to attack the Sunni Muslims to stop them from their 'project' to create an Islamic state resulted in all the Mujahideen standing up and fighting back," it said in a statement.

According to Wladimir van Wilgenburg, an Erbil-based journalist and expert on the Kurds, the influx of refugees was *designed* to undermine the KRG; the waves of internally displaced persons (IDPs) were ISIS weapons in its war against Iraqi Kurds. "Sunni Arabs had already fled the crackdown of the al-Maliki government, and then the fall of Mosul," van Wilgenburg said. "So when ISIS attacked the Kurdistan region in August, all the streets were full of IDPs. Ainkawa, the Christian neighborhood of Erbil, was full of Christian IDPs from everywhere, fleeing the ISIS advances."

A jihadist syndicate whose war-planning and intelligence-gathering echelons are staffed by former Iraqi spies and military officials well knew how to exploit latent tensions within the Kurdish-Yazidi community and exacerbate not-so-latent ones between the KRG and Iraq's central government. Genocide and mass displacement would constitute major chapters in Saddam Hussein's handbook for social engineering. But what happened to the feminine contingent of ISIS's Yazidis captives would leave human rights organizations and investigative journalists in utter disbelief.

THE MANAGEMENT OF RAPE

A fifteen-year-old girl known only as "F" told the *New York Times*' Rukmini Callimachi that after her family's car overheated, leaving them stranded by the side of a road in Sinjar, ISIS caught them. "There, they separated me from my mom. The young, unmarried girls were forced to get into buses," F said. Her bus, crammed with so many young girls that they had to sit on one another's laps, was driven to the Galaxy Wedding Hall in Mosul, one of several venues in both Syria and Iraq where ISIS first kept its quarry in purdah, then sold them at modern slave auctions. These are highly bureaucratic and time-consuming processes. F was held along with 1,300 Yazidi girls. Three ISIS fighters turned up, Callimachi writes, "holding a register. They told the girls to stand. Each one was instructed to state her first, middle and last name, her age, her hometown, whether she was married, and if she had children. For two months, F was held inside the Galaxy Hall. Then one day, they came and began removing young women. Those who refused were dragged out by their hair."

Another girl, sixteen-year-old Randa, was abducted by ISIS from her village south of Mount Sinjar. She told Amnesty International that she was driven to Mosul and kept at a *maqarr*, or headquarters, along with 150 girls and five women.

> "A man called Salwan took me from there to an abandoned house. He also took my cousin, who is 13 years old; we resisted and they beat us. He took me as his wife by force. I told him I did not want to and tried to resist but he beat me. My nose was bleeding, I could not do anything to stop him. I ran away as soon as I could. Luckily they did not do anything to my cousin, did not force her to marry, and she escaped with me. I went to a doctor here, who said that I was not pregnant and didn't have any disease, but I can't forget what happened to me. It is so painful what they did to me and to my family. Da'esh . . . has ruined our lives. My mum gave birth while being held by Da'esh in Tal 'Afar; now she is being held in Mosul with my little sister and the baby. My 10-year-old brother was separated from my mum and is being held in Tal 'Afar with my aunt. What will happen to them? I don't know if I will ever see them again."

Many fellow travelers or supporters of ISIS, including "local businessmen," as another Amnesty witness said, were also eager buyers of Yazidi females at the various slave markets that were held in Iraq and Syria. Of all the natural resources ISIS has plundered, human beings remain the most valuable.

Curiously, jihadist disinformation about rape spread internally as well as externally. ISIS's extensive online fan base had few objections to the UN's conclusion that their holy warriors had murdered five thousand Yazidi men and boys as they took Sinjar, but quite a few rejected out of hand the allegation that ISIS had women and girls for pleasure, considering this just another Western lie to blacken the black flag. So in order to justify the revival of a bygone Islamic practice, ISIS's apparatchik clerisy did what it does best: came up with a theological basis for atrocity.

On October 12, the fourth edition of *Dabiq* was published, containing an essay titled "The Revival of Slavery Before the Hour." The record was corrected and consecrated. "Prior to the taking of Sinjar, Shari'ah students in the Islamic State were tasked to research the Yazidis to determine if they should be treated as an originally mushrik [polytheist] group or one that originated as Muslims and then apostatized," the article read. "[I]t was determined that this group is one that existed since the pre-Islamic *jahiliyyah* [state of ignorance], but became 'Islamized' by the surrounding Muslim population, language, and culture, although they never accepted Islam nor claimed to have adopted it." The Yazidis were unfit for *jizya*, the tax levied on non-Muslims, and so they could be taken as slaves, in accordance with Sharia. More generally, ISIS decreed, this was a dispensation applicable to all "original kuffar," or those "disbelievers" by birth and without any faith from which to apostatize. Original kuffar here consisted of all Shia as well as any Jews and Christians who refused to subordinate themselves to dhimmitude, or second-class citizenship under Islamic rule. In practice, the only demographic of slaves ISIS has yet taken is the Yazidis.

The recurring phrase in the Quran, "Those your right hand possesses," which exegetes maintain refers to slaves, kept at various points by the Prophet and his Companions, is the armature upon which ISIS constructed its catechism of rape. Here, again, it caught mainstream Muslim clerics off guard because this practice had long ago been abandoned in light of the modern world's abolition of human bondage. But ISIS repudiates modernity outright, and so could renew slavery with gusto, remarking on how it has even brought enlightenment to the benighted. "Many of the *mushrik* women and children have willingly accepted Islam," the same *Dabiq* article stated, "and now race to practice it with evident sincerity after their exit from the darkness of" polytheism. Thus was rape turned into an edifying experience for the victim. A twelve-year-old girl interviewed by Callimachi recounted that her tormentor kept justifying his violation on the basis of this creed: "I kept telling him it hurts—please stop. He told me that according to Islam he is allowed to rape an unbeliever. He said that by raping me, he is drawing closer to God." The jihadist here seems to be convincing himself, rather than his victim, of his own savage rectitude.

In a separate pamphlet ISIS issued to its rank-and-file, the terror army gave a highly specific and horrifying set of instructions—rendered in the form of answers to twenty-seven "questions"—for the keeping and raping of slaves of all ages. Here are three:

"If she is a virgin, he [her master] can have intercourse with her immediately after taking possession of her. However, if she isn't, her uterus must be purified [first]."

"It is forbidden to have intercourse with a female captive if [the master] does not own her exclusively. One who owns [a captive] in partnership [with others] may not have sexual intercourse with her until the other [owners] sell or give him [their share]."

"It is permissible to have intercourse with the female slave who hasn't reached puberty if she is fit for intercourse; however if she is not fit for intercourse, then it is enough to enjoy her without intercourse."

AL-BAGHDADI'S "PRIZE"

Temporal temptations and personal preferences evidently furnish their own exceptions to ISIS's theology of rape. Much like the Austrian anti-Semite Karl Lueger's famous judgment, when asked how it was that he kept quite so many Jewish friends—"I decide who is a Jew," he replied—ISIS has bent and broken its own definitions of "People of the Book" and "original kuffar" as needed. This is how Kayla Mueller, the twenty-six-year-old American aid worker abducted by ISIS in Syria in 2013, was repeatedly raped by Abu Bakr al-Baghdadi.

Mueller was a Christian from Prescott, Arizona, motivated to do charitable work throughout the Middle East and India. And yet, according to two former Yazidi captives, Dalal and Susan, ages fifteen and thirteen, respectively, who say they were kept with Mueller at a house in the Syrian town of al-Shadadiya, she was told that she could either become the caliph's fourth "wife" or be beheaded. Not much of a choice there, and no doubt a nuptial dispensation was made by al-Baghdadi to classify his unwilling concubine as something other than a slave. But that's what Mueller undoubtedly was.

She acted as a kindly big sister to the underage girls, and offered them solace when they, too, were taken as prizes by senior ISIS commanders. A seventeen-year-old named Amshe, who was made a "wife" to al-Baghdadi's deputy, Hajji Mutazz, told the BBC's Paul Wood that Mueller was coveted most of all among the Shura Council members for "her pale skin and because she was an American."

Umm Sayyaf, the wife of ISIS's Tunisian energy and antiquities emir, Abu

Sayyaf, was the grim den mother of the organization's sex trafficking network. Mueller's serial torture at the hands of the most wanted terrorist on the planet was a motivating factor in the White House's decision to dispatch US Special Forces to raid Abu Sayyaf's compound in Deir Ezzor in May 2015. He was killed, but Umm Sayyaf was captured and rendered into Kurdish custody, where she is said to be cooperating with Western intelligence. While the only prior US Special Forces raid into Syria, in July 2014, had held out the hope of rescuing journalists James Foley and Steven Sotloff, there was no prospect of this raid rescuing Mueller. She had been announced killed by ISIS the February before, something confirmed by her family four days later when ISIS provided them with a photograph of her corpse, authenticated by US intelligence. The circumstances of her death are to this day not entirely clear. Amshe alleges that Hajji Mutazz boasted to her that ISIS murdered Mueller in retaliation for the actions of the American's "stupid government," an account deemed plausible by US officials.

The tragedy of Mueller's death was compounded by ISIS publicly repurposing it into a convenient propaganda foil against the one country it had done more to weaken and destabilize outside of Iraq and Syria: the Hashemite Kingdom of Jordan. Jordan was the original "near enemy" against which Abu Musab al-Zarqawi had declared holy war years before meeting Osama bin Laden in Kandahar or smuggling himself and the graduates of his al-Qaeda–financed Herat training camp into the foothills of Iraqi Kurdistan. ISIS made Mueller a prop in its ongoing jihad against the Kingdom.

BURNED ALIVE

On January 3, 2015, twenty-six-year-old Mouaz al-Kasasbeh was marched into a metal cage in an undisclosed desert location and set on fire. His body cooked until it was charred to brittle crisp, and then ISIS bulldozers leveled the cage and his unrecognizable remains. His murder was not confirmed in real time. It took a month and came by way of ISIS's most sadistic snuff video to date, a full twenty-two minutes and thirty-four seconds—the length of a prime-time television show. Only the last third of "Healing the Believers' Chests" was actually devoted to the horror-film immolation of the Arab pilot; that clip, in its truncated form, was either shared or written about around the world. But the first two-thirds of the video constituted ISIS's indictment of al-Kasasbeh and his nation, and its eye-for-an-eye justification for the mode of his murder.

Sat at a table with a black eye, dressed in the orange jumpsuit of the world's most luckless prisoners, he was made to give up operational details of Jordan's air war in Syria, along with that of other Arab members of the coalition. The models and makes of fighter jets were rattled off on-screen, in an elaborate and high-tech presentation—the kind you'd find in a Michael Bay–directed action sequence. Al-Kasasbeh's confession was also juxtaposed with footage of buildings being reduced to plumes of smoke, and the charred corpses of infants and small children and adults being pulled from the rubble—the aftermath, according to ISIS, of coalition bombing runs in Syria, where the pilot's plane had crashed owing to a technical malfunction and he'd had to parachute right into jihadist-controlled territory. Al-Kasasbeh then walks before a column of ISIS fighters in beige balaclavas and digital desert camouflage, all holding assault rifles. Multiple camera angles show other militants positioned everywhere in half-destroyed buildings, amid broken concrete and rebar. Next he's shown in the cage, only now his jumpsuit is wet, doused with gasoline.... The video doesn't end with the bulldozing of the cage. It ends with a roll call of names and photographs of other known Jordanian pilots flying missions in Syria, along with their home addresses in Jordan. The message is clear: they're next.

As a piece of agitprop, the video was many things: ominous, infuriating, disgusting—and effective. True, ISIS provoked an enormous backlash in Jordan against its war crime; al-Kasasbeh had belonged to the prominent Bararsheh tribe, and his highly respected family was outspoken in its grief, eliciting sympathy and solidarity, but also in its criticism of the government for not securing Mouaz's release. There was probably no way Amman could have done so because the takfiris were intentionally turning recent history on its head—using the Jordanian Mukhabarat's preferred form of information warfare against the monarchy their founding father despised.

Not only did ISIS continue to negotiate with Jordan over al-Kasasbeh's fate (as well as the fates of two Japanese hostages) well after it had already killed him; they parleyed directly with none other than Abu Muhammad al-Maqdisi, then still a prisoner in Jordan, who was being used or manipulated by Jordan's security service, the General Intelligence Directorate, as a convincing go-between. First in the hostage-takers' list of demands was the release of their "sister" Sajida al-Rishawi, the only surviving members of the 2005

Amman hotel bombings, planned and then implausibly denied by al-Zarqawi when the Mukhabarat showed how his henchmen had killed Sunni wedding-goers and innocent Muslims. That Jordan was talking at all to ISIS was potentially devastating to the coalition's cohesion.

The United States has consistently declined to legitimate ISIS's pretensions of "statehood" and categorically refused to negotiate with it over the fate of its own captive citizens, threatening, in the cases of both Foley and Sotloff, to prosecute the family members of those hostages should they try to barter with the organization. ISIS media had mocked the seeming double standards of America's "we don't negotiate with terrorists" posture, noting that the Obama administration had just traded five Taliban detainees held at Guantanamo Bay for Bowe Bergdahl, a US Army soldier accused of deserting his post in Afghanistan and being captured by the Taliban-linked Haqqani network, which held him for five years. (The US government classifies the Taliban, unlike ISIS, as an armed insurgency rather than a foreign terrorist organization—a bit of Orwellian double-speak that plenty of pundits, not to mention jihadists, would seize upon during the Bergdahl exchange.) Well, now here was a prominent Sunni Arab ally negotiating with the terrorists *and* using one of the terrorists' most influential theoreticians to do it.

Had al-Kasasbeh been returned to Amman in one piece, the whole sub rosa interaction no doubt would have been excused and al-Maqdisi, who had famously upbraided his former protégé for his sanguinary excesses, may well have been applauded in Jordan and even in the West for acting as a constructive intermediary. Instead, King Abdullah and al-Zarqawi's spiritual mentor were both badly humiliated by the deceitful takfiris. ISIS released the video showing it had killed al-Kasasbeh on February 3, 2015. (Al-Maqdisi realized he had been played by his interlocutors when they sent him a computer file with a password calling him a "pimp.") Three days later, ISIS publicly blamed Jordan for inadvertently killing Kayla Mueller, releasing a photograph of what it said was the building in al-Raqqa where Mueller was being held and which Jordanian bombers had just hit. No evidence to corroborate this claim was provided and it almost certainly wasn't true.

But the reaction from Jordan was swift and furious. "So they behead innocent #US #UK & Japan hostages & BURN a brave #Jordan pilot ALIVE & now a hostage is killed by an airstrike? Sure! Sick!" tweeted Jordanian foreign minister Nasser Judeh, who somewhat lent credence to the ISIS allegation by saying that using human shields to blame counterterrorists for collateral damage was an "old and sick trick."

It was also comeuppance for what Jordan's security service did to al-Zarqawi a decade earlier, when he was forced to call his government a liar when it exhibited (admittedly far more persuasive) evidence of how his operatives in 2004 nearly deployed chemical weapons in central Amman, and in 2005 blew up three hotels in the same city.

In the days after the al-Kasasbeh snuff video, there was serious talk of Jordan possibly sending ground forces into Syria to go after ISIS. Much of the chatter was sensationalist hyperbole, complete with claims that King Abdullah himself was now flying bombing missions in Raqqa. But Hashemite hawkishness would prove to be short-lived. No doubt fearing what ISIS was capable of doing on Jordanian soil (such as going after the remaining fighter pilots, as promised) and that it might continue to use Jordan's involvement in the coalition's air campaign as proof that a Sunni Arab nation was bombing Sunni women and children, Amman quietly deescalated. By August 2015, it had stopped bombing ISIS altogether.

THE AYATOLLAH'S REVENGE

If ISIS could strain President Obama's coalition by executing a single Arab fighter pilot, then what could it achieve through mechanized mayhem on its original battlefield of Iraq? Days before its first recorded murder meant for global consumption, the YouTubed beheading of American journalist James Foley on August 19, 2014, Iraq's authoritarian prime minister, Nouri al-Maliki, bowed to US and Iranian pressure and gave up his bid to remain in power, ostensibly addressing the political impasse that supposedly gave rise to ISIS. His successor was a fellow member of the Dawa Party, the sixty-two-year-old Haider al-Abadi, who had spent years of exile in London. Many Iraqi Sunnis we talked to at the time praised al-Abadi as an improvement on al-Maliki, but none thought he could or would make a substantive difference in the way Iraq was governed. This, they all said, owed to the endemic sectarian dimensions of the nation's politics and Tehran's overweening influence on Baghdad.

It didn't bode well for the new premier's tenure that in one of his first press conferences he advocated a strategic partnership between the United States and Iran in combating ISIS—a partnership that many Sunnis believed started in 2003. "The American approach is to leave Iraq to the Iraqis," Sami al-Askari, a former Iraqi MP and senior adviser to al-Maliki, told Reuters. "The Iranians don't say leave Iraq to the Iraqis. They say leave Iraq to us." One of the world's leading state sponsors of terrorism would now present itself as the last line of defense against terrorism.

Shia militias beholden to Iran were first mobilized by al-Maliki during his offensive in Anbar in late December 2013, which reignited the Iraqi civil war and saw ISIS flying its banner over Fallujah within days. As the Iraq front spiraled, Shia militiamen whom Iran had sent to Syria to bolster the al-Assad regime were returning to Iraq, and in April 2014 a major recruitment drive was begun by Iran's Iraqi cutouts, with volunteers assembled not only under old banners like the Hezbollah Brigades but new front groups—helping to hide Iran's hand and give the appearance of a popular reaction against ISIS. The collapse of the Iraqi security forces during the ISIS takeover of Mosul in June 2014, and the Iraqi government's response to it, would give Iran further opportunities to entrench its power in Iraq.

Three days after the fall of Mosul, a fatwa was issued by Iraq's most senior Shia cleric, Grand Ayatollah Ali al-Sistani, calling on those who are "capable of carrying arms and fighting the terrorists in defense of their country" to do so. Al-Sistani specified that he wanted volunteers to "join the security forces to achieve this sacred goal." The reaction was instantaneous. According to one Iraqi official, thirty thousand men had signed up before the end of the day. Al-Sistani's fatwa was the first of its kind since the 1914 declaration of jihad against the invading British forces in Mesopotamia, and the cleric had to know that managing the fallout would be difficult. But it was an act of desperation. In the summer of 2014, many Iraqis, not to mention a handful of US intelligence officials, feared the jihadists would march on Baghdad and possibly ransack the fortified Green Zone, home to America's largest and most expensive embassy in the world.

Unfortunately for al-Sistani, who had spent years trying to blunt Iran's influence in Iraq, Iran quickly co-opted the mass mobilization of Shia Iraqi volunteers triggered by his fatwa, diverting them into militia formations that bypassed the formal command structures in Baghdad. Quds Force commander Qassem Suleimani was able to oversee the creation of a multipronged sectarian army. According to Phillip Smyth, there are "at least 200 Shia militias operating in Iraq. A large cross section of those groups are controlled by Iran—they follow the Islamic Republic's radical ideology, are anti-American, and push rabidly sectarian agendas." Collectively they form the umbrella brand of al-Hashd al-Shaabi, or the Population Mobilization Units, which operate under multiple chains of command, the most important of which comprises a "Hashd Shaabi committee" nominally beholden to the prime minister's office but in reality under the thumb of Tehran. Indeed, the most powerful militias within the Popular Mobilization Units—the Badr Corps, the Hezbollah Brigades, and the League of the Righteous—are the very same Special Groups not only responsible for killing US soldiers and countless Sunni civilians in Iraq, but now equally committed to propping up the murderous regime in Damascus and warring against the Sunni rebels fighting ISIS. The Iranian-controlled Shia militias have also stolen American gear. The Hezbollah Brigades have been seen driving around in Abrams tanks, Humvees, armored personnel carriers, and MRAPs (Mine-Resistant Ambush-Protected vehicles), and toting M4 and M16 rifles—all the unintended largesse of US taxpayers, who have sent $1 billion in military equipment to Baghdad but have no oversight as to which actors, foreign or domestic, ultimately receive it or what they then do with it. ISIS wasn't the only terrorist organization with American blood on its hands using purloined American matériel to threaten the lives of Americans.

In March 2015, General Martin Dempsey, then still chairman of the Joint Chiefs of Staff, took a helicopter tour of Baghdad and noticed a "plethora of flags, only one of which happens to be the Iraqi flag." The rest, he told reporters, to evident dismay, belonged to Shia militias. He might have also added that posters of Ayatollah Ruhollah Khomeini and Ayatollah Ali Khamenei are now omnipresent in the Iraqi capital. Dempscy was formerly the commander of the 1st Armored Division in Baghdad, and he knows just as much about Iraq's militias as he does about ISIS. Nevertheless, and perhaps owing to administration pressure, he remarked on the "positive" role Iran might yet play in the country. Alas, this view was not shared by many of his former colleagues, who have witnessed the inevitable return to the bad old days of ethnic cleansing and disappeared families. David Petraeus, now out of government owing to an extramarital affair and a violation of his classified intelligence clearance as director of the CIA, and Masrour Barzani, the long-serving Iraqi Kurdish intelligence chief, would both acknowledge that Shia militias pose more of a long-term threat to the stability of the country than does ISIS. Once a deep state has been built, it's almost impossible to unbuild it. Just ask Lebanon.

Al-Zarqawi couldn't have scripted Iraq's militia craze better himself. This was the necessary precondition for the sectarian total war he envisaged in

2004, when he identified the Badr Corps as al-Qaeda in Iraq's nemesis. In attacking the Shia, al-Zarqawi had written, "striking at the heart of [their] religious, political, and military structures we will trigger their rage against the Sunnis . . . [forcing them] to bare their fangs and reveal the sly rancor that drives them from deep within. If we manage to draw them onto the terrain of partisan war, it will be possible to tear the Sunnis away from their heedlessness, for they will feel the weight of the imminence of danger and the devastating threat of death wielded by these Sabeans."

In 2004, the US military was the only thing standing in the way of realizing this apocalyptic fever-dream, and only just. Though al-Zarqawi wouldn't live to see it, his plans were now coalescing across two separate countries in the Middle East at a time when, owing little to his own strategizing, the region's geopolitics would align almost perfectly with his blueprint. Four years into the Syria catastrophe, many Sunni Arabs had come to believe that al-Zarqawi had been right all along. If anything, he hadn't gone far enough in his analysis. He believed that George W. Bush blundered into Iraq and, in deposing Saddam Hussein, had "accidentally" handed the country on a platter to Iran. But, by the time Mosul fell to ISIS, Sunnis would come to speculate that maybe it wasn't an accident, after all. Why else were US warplanes and drones bombing *Sunni* extremists but leaving their Alawite and Shia counterparts alone? Forces loyal to al-Assad, after all, had burned civilians alive, ethnically cleansed whole villages, disappeared tens of thousands of protestors and activists into dungeons, displaced millions internally and externally, and systematically murdered hundreds of thousands using every weapon of the modern state arsenal, save biological and nuclear. Bush had fought both al-Qaeda and the Quds Force in Iraq. Now President Obama was not only acquiescing to the latter's military campaign but actually helping it gain more territory. Obama spent the first two years of his second term seeking a "legacy" accomplishment, a nuclear deal with Iran, at the expense of the wholesale destruction of Sunnis in Syria. Now he was describing Iran's possible emergence as a "very successful regional power" as "good" for the Middle East and "good for the United States." By the autumn of 2015, the American executive was also allowing Russia to establish its own no-fly zone in western and central Syria, not for the purpose of bombing ISIS, as Vladimir Putin falsely claimed, but to prop up al-Assad and eliminate any credible Sunni rebel challenge to the regime.

Al-Zarqawi had outlined the broad contours of the answer to all this the year he pledged allegiance to bin Laden. For him, it was simple: the United

States had cast its lot with the Shia, who had taken over the Iraqi state in order to eliminate the only defenders of the true Islam. As he seemingly so presciently said: "They began by killing many mujahidin brothers, and they then set about liquidating scientists, thinkers, doctors, engineers, and others. God only knows what will happen, but for my part I believe that the worst will not be behind us so long as the American army is standing firmly in its rear positions and the secret Shiite army and its military brigades continue to fight at its side."

MILITIA RULE

Despite al-Abadi's calls for national unity, the sectarian bloodletting has continued. According to Human Rights Watch, Iraqi Security Forces and Shia militias executed 255 prisoners in six villages and towns between June 9, 2014—a day before the fall of Mosul—and July 11. Eight of the victims were boys younger than eighteen. On August 22, 2014, Iraqi military personnel and League of the Righteous militants dressed in plainclothes raided the Musab bin Omair Mosque in Diyala—where ISIS has anticipated its fiercest battles and where anti-Sunni violence spiked in the early months of 2015. Dozens were massacred. On March 10, 2015, the UN Office of the High Commissioner for Human Rights released a comprehensive study of human rights violations committed by both ISIS and pro-Iraqi forces. "Throughout the summer of 2014," the report noted, the Popular Mobilization Units, "other volunteers and [Shia] militia moved from their southern heartlands towards [ISIS]-controlled areas in central and northern Iraq. While their military campaign against the group gained ground, the militias seem to operate with total impunity, *leaving a trail of death and destruction in their wake*" (emphasis added). More worrying, a six-month investigation by ABC News found that US-trained Iraqi Security Force personnel were also guilty of anti-Sunni pogroms, with officers from Iraq's Special Forces shown in one video accusing an unarmed teenaged boy of being a shooter (a charge the boy denies) before opening fire on him.

If the evidence ABC compiled is correct, then the continued US arming of Iraq clearly violates the Leahy Law, which prevents the State and Defense Departments from providing military aid to a foreign country that commits gross violations of human rights. Whenever allegations of extrajudicial killings or torture emerge, the Iraqi government promises to "investigate" them, though the nation's judiciary and police are often accomplices in the very crimes they're meant to uncover.

Nor was the US government unaware of what a harvest it might reap when the coalition got under way. In 2011, Obama told Nouri al-Maliki, then on a state visit to Washington, D.C.: "Some people will think that our withdrawal will bring more influence by Iran. I am confident in your independent leadership and we accept that Iraq needs a normal relationship with Iran. But as partners we must say our main problem with Iran is their nuclear ambition. We said we would not use Iraq as a platform to attack Iran, but in Iraq there are groups supported by Iran who target our people. This is a major concern. Iran has not responded to our approaches. We would prefer to resolve the issue of the militias by diplomatic means."

Ironically, diplomatic means would largely enable the militias.

Hadi al-Amiri is a salient example of a militia leader empowered by the US policy of disengagement. Al-Amiri is the leader of the Badr Corps, Iran's oldest Iraqi proxy that is the seedbed for many of the others, and the primary foil against which al-Zarqawi rallied Sunnis fearful of Shia domination. Al-Amiri was in Washington with al-Maliki when Obama said his piece, and would boast in late January 2015 that Stuart Jones, the US ambassador to Iraq, was now offering the Popular Mobilization Units, which al-Amiri formally commanded, American air support. To this day, the US envoy to the anti-ISIS coalition, Brett McGurk, tweets congratulations to the militias after their conspicuous battlefield advances. And even where these are not in evidence, militia penetration of Iraqi state security structures has scarcely diminished since the bad old days of the mid-2000s. The current interior minister, for instance, is Mohammed al-Ghabban, a senior official in the Badr Corps, an appointment that once again has granted a power drill–wielding death squad purview over Iraq's Federal Police. According to Human Rights Watch's Iraq researcher Erin Evers, the Badr Corps has lately been accused of "kidnapping and summarily executing people [and] expelling Sunnis from their homes, then looting and burning them, in some cases razing entire villages." The United States, she added, "is basically paving the way for these guys to take over the country even more than they already have."

Nearly every Iraqi ground offensive against ISIS in the first year of Inherent Resolve bore Suleimani's fingerprints. Often, the Quds Force commander would be photographed in well-crafted war propaganda images circulated on social media to underscore his role as the Eisenhower of the war and, of course, embarrass the Americans who denied he was any such thing. In late October 2014, when ISIS was driven from Jurf al-Sakher, a town about thirty miles southwest of Baghdad along the Euphrates River Valley, agents of the Quds Force and Lebanese Hezbollah were embedded with some seven thousand Iraqi Security Forces soldiers and militiamen, providing training and distributing arms. The entire operation was planned by Suleimani and led by the Badr Corps.

Now enabled by US warplanes, the League of the Righteous and the Hezbollah Brigades, a US-designated terrorist organization, played a lead combat role in ending ISIS's months-long siege of Amerli, a Shia Turkoman town of about 15,000, in August 2014. Suleimani was photographed smiling in Amerli shortly after it was retaken, and he had every reason to be. The commander of the Hezbollah Brigades is still Abu Mahdi al-Muhandis, the Iranian spy who is widely believed to have planned the bombings of both the US and French embassies in Kuwait in the 1980s. (There's even a photograph of al-Muhandis holding up a Kuwaiti newspaper blaming him for this act of international terrorism.)

If Amerli was "liberated," it certainly didn't seem that way to the Sunni villagers there. Their homes were looted or destroyed by militiamen operating on the specious assumption that all local inhabitants once ruled by ISIS must necessarily be ISIS sympathizers or "collaborators." Human Rights Watch charged that the aim of this spate of retaliatory violence had risen to the level of ethnic cleansing. "Building destruction in at least 47 predominantly Sunni villages was methodical and driven by revenge and intended to alter the demographic composition of Iraq's traditionally diverse provinces of Salah al-Din and Kirkuk," it declared. The Hezbollah Brigades's fighters have also been seen, on uploaded YouTube videos, playing "bongos" with severed human heads. (ISIS wasn't the only insurgency eager to exhibit its atrocities for recruitment and morale purposes.) In one video, a celebrated Shia militiaman, the burly, bearded, and shaven-headed Abu Azrael—the name means "Angel of Death"—is shown cutting slices of charred human flesh from an upside-down corpse as though it were shawarma. Whether or not these were sick trophies of slain jihadists matters not to international humanitarian law or to Sunnis' perception of what awaits them once they've gained their freedom from ISIS.

Civil wars driven by ethnic or confessional chauvinism create new internal laws as they grind on. Sunnis were by no means the only demographic subjected to collective punishment by the Popular Mobilization Units. A twenty-one-year-old Shia Turkoman from the Yengija village was "burned with cigarettes and tied to a ceiling fan" by militants of Saraya Tala'a al-Khorasani, another proxy of Suleimani. "They kept saying, 'You are ISIS,' and I kept denying it," he said. "They were beating me randomly on my face, head, shoulders using water pipes and the butts of their weapons. . . . They went to have lunch and then came back and beat us for an hour and a half. Later that night they asked me if I was Shia or Sunni. I told them I was Shia Turkoman and they ordered me to prove it by praying the Shia way. . . . They kept me for nine days."

Michael Pregent, a former US military intelligence officer who advised the peshmerga, traveled, in 2014, to Baghdad, where he witnessed how the Quds Force was feeding its own tendentious intelligence up the chain of command and right into the US Air Force's targeting queue. "Are we meant to be bombing ISIS or to be paving the way for Iran's consolidation of power in Iraq?" Pregent asked. As he explained it, the Quds Force would give targets to Iraqi military commanders, many of whom were in fact operatives of the Badr Corps, who would pass them along to the Iraqi Defense Ministry liaisons in the Joint Operations Center, the coalition war room in Baghdad. Here US advisers would receive the targets and send them along to the Pentagon ready for use in upcoming US air strikes.

Pregent was astounded by this arm's-length coordination with Iran. Keeping the Quds Force's self-interested intelligence from being filtered through Baghdad was one of the biggest security challenges US officials faced during the occupation of Iraq. But then, unlike now, the Pentagon was just as committed to countering Iran's influence as it was al-Qaeda's. "Today, the Quds Force is America's eyes and ears in Iraq," Pregent said. "With the *consent* of the US government."

Another difference is one of transnational scope. Countering Iran's influence had once been geographically delimited to Iraq. Now it extends to Syria. According to *Politico*, US war planners are worried that any decision to engage or isolate the al-Assad regime in Syria will encourage the Quds Force or its proxies to attack the three-thousand-plus US military trainers currently stationed in Iraq as many of them have threatened to do regardless.

It is admittedly difficult to tell where America's genuine fear of Iranian retaliation grades into a rationalization for outsourcing the anti-ISIS ground campaign to Iranian operatives. The net outcome is the same: Washington behaves as if it needs Tehran's express permission to prosecute its own war against ISIS. Sunnis consequently feel (at best) marginalized and (at worst) susceptible to ISIS's us-versus-them dichotomy.

"Many of the people in Mosul will stand with ISIS if Shia militias invade," said General Najim al-Jabouri, the former mayor and police chief of Tal Afar, a town that now belongs to ISIS but where the first stirrings of the Sunni Awakening were experienced a decade ago. "Eighty percent of the population does not like ISIS, but if the militias are involved—eighty percent will stand very strong with them. I told the Americans before the image now is not like it was in 2003. Now the Sunni people want American forces. They will throw the flowers on them now, because the battle now is not between them and the United States and ISIS, it's between the Sunnis and Iran."

DESTROYING TIKRIT TO SAVE IT

The campaign to retake Tikrit, Saddam Hussein's hometown, in the province of Salah ad-Din, was originally billed as "revenge" for the ISIS massacre at Camp Speicher the previous June, where ISIS claimed to have murdered 1,700 Shia soldiers. The operation was launched without any consultation with al-Abadi, who found out about it after the fact and meekly asked Suleimani to add a token contingent of Iraqi Security Forces to allow him to claim the entire operation was under prime ministerial command. As it turned out, that was the least of Baghdad's problems.

Determining the order of battle in Iraq is more a matter of alchemy than computation, given the predilection of all sides in the war to exaggerate their numbers. Nonetheless, most analysts agree that when the Tikrit operation got under way, the Popular Mobilization Units far outnumbered, likely even doubled, the ranks of the Iraqi Security Forces. The Iraqi Security Forces had about 48,000 troops remaining after their scuttle from Mosul, according to Iraqi and American officials, while low-end estimates for the Popular Mobilization Units were 100,000. This imbalance continues to the present day.

Still, the resort to the militias could be justified by exigency. The whole battle was meant to be over by the end of the month. US officials variously estimated that either 23,000 or 30,000 "pro-government" forces were marshaled for the job, of which only a slender minority consisted of actual Iraqi soldiers. The majority by a margin of at least two-to-one was the Popular Mobilization Units. But against this force of tens of thousands of paramilitary and army soldiers, a mere 400 to 1,000 ISIS fighters held their ground for weeks, forcing Baghdad into a pathetic stalemate.

How did so few get the better of so many?

ISIS resorted to the kind of trap-laying its predecessor organization mastered against a far more professional and better-equipped US military. With hundreds of square miles of terrain at its disposal, it has amassed an underground military-industrial complex, with untold bomb manufacturing factories where it builds its vehicle- or house-borne IEDs. Iraq's main traffic arteries have been turned into concrete minefields. And the sophistication of ISIS's deadliest weapon has increased with time. *Everything* lying about on the ground, such as Shia prayer beads, could be a bomb in disguise. According to a report by BuzzFeed, since August 2014 Kurdish peshmerga fighters alone "defused or detonated more than 6,000 IEDs along their 650-mile front with ISIS."

The toll these IEDs have taken on Iraqi forces is underreported and undoubtedly being covered up by Baghdad. Cemetery workers in Najaf, one of Shia Islam's holiest cities, told the *Washington Post* that as many as sixty corpses were arriving per day. Derek Harvey, fresh from a trip to Iraq, noted in mid-March 2015 that an Iraqi Shia source confided in him that the number of militia war dead from the Tikrit offensive at that point may have been as high as 6,000. (If true, that would mean that ISIS at the height of battle was capable of a staggering 6:1 kill ratio.)

The militias' triumphalism proved badly misplaced. "They just didn't have the sufficient desire and determination to take the fight forward given the casualties they've been sustaining," said Jeffrey White, a former Defense Intelligence Agency analyst now at the Washington Institute for Near East Policy.

In the end, Baghdad was compelled to put in an eleventh-hour request for an F-16 bailout, well after the militias had dismissed the need for American airpower to loosen up the terrain in advance of their march. Which didn't stop the Popular Mobilization Units from claiming credit for ISIS's expulsion in early April 2015, at an all-too-predictable cost in human rights and American credibility.

Reuters's correspondents in the city (whose names had to be withheld for fear for their safety) saw the militias drag a corpse through the streets in a Toyota pickup truck. One suspected ISIS fighter, an Egyptian national, was lynched in front of numerous international journalists by two uniformed Iraqi police officers, as Iraqi intelligence agents and at least one other policeman tried in vain to stop them. The policeman appealed to them for the sake of Iraq's image: "There are dozens of media here. This is not the suitable time. Why do you want to embarrass us?" But locals and the militias egged them on to exact revenge for the Egyptian's alleged knife murder of a fellow federal police officer. "The killer started to saw through the neck, but it was slow-going. He lifted the blade again and slammed it into the Egyptian's neck another four times. Then he sawed back and forth," the Reuters article stated.

Sunni homes in Tikrit were also set alight, as militiamen and government agents looted them, piling their vehicles high with stolen "refrigerators, air conditioners, computer printers, and furniture." The news agency's Baghdad bureau chief, Ned Parker, the only byline in this story, subsequently had his life threatened by the militias on social media, and the League of the Righteous's Iraqi television station. Parker, a veteran journalist, left Iraq not long afterward.

An unnamed US official told Al Jazeera that members of the League of the Righteous had been responsible for burning down homes in Albu Ajil, a village near Tikrit, in retaliation for massacres carried out by ISIS and members of the village's eponymous tribe, who took part in the Camp Speicher atrocity. The League of the Righteous had also recently been implicated in the abduction and murder of Sheik Qassem Sweidan al-Janabi, one of the Sunni tribal leaders who worked alongside US forces during the Awakening.

The Pope doubting the existence of God is one way to satisfy Bertrand Russell's concept of "evidence against interest." Another way is to hear former clerical ward heeler turned warlord Muqtada al-Sadr not only condemn al-Janabi's killing—in language more severe than anything contrived by the US State Department—but also issue a blanket denunciation of the Popular Mobilization Units. "Did not I tell you that Iraq will suffer from the brazen militias?" the father of the most notorious Shia militia said. "Did I tell you that the army must handle the reins?" Al-Sadr then demanded that justice be meted out to the decapitators within his own sect and even temporarily suspended the participation of his own al-Salam, or "Peace," Brigades (the rebranded Mahdi Army in 2015) in the final push for Tikrit.

General al-Jabouri, the former mayor and police chief of Tal Afar, relayed to the authors the shocking fact that Khaled al-Obaidi, Iraq's defense minister, was barred from entering the city that his own military was purportedly in the midst of besieging, because the Popular Mobilization Units wouldn't allow him. "He had to stay in Samarra," he told us.

Equally remarkable was how the Pentagon pretended that these militias had all vanished from the field upon the start of US aerial sorties—their withdrawal being an ostensible precondition set forth by Washington before the sorties could begin. General Lloyd Austin, the commander of US Central Command, briefed the Senate on March 19, 2015, about what were then ongoing operations. "Currently, there are no [Shia] militia and as reported by the Iraqis today, no [Popular Mobilization Units] in that area as well," he said. This was simply not the case, as the *Guardian*'s correspondent Martin Chulov, who returned from Tikrit shortly after Austin's briefing, confirmed to the authors. Chulov personally spotted both al-Amiri and his sidekick al-Muhandis in the center of the city on March 26. In fact, the United States even made overtures to some of the militias they found more palatable, such as Kataib Jund al-Imam, or the Brigade of the Soldiers of the Imam, which played a lead role in the recapture of the city, but whose ideological affinity with Iranian Khomeinists is hardly Iraq's best-kept secret.

Human Rights Watch further determined, based on satellite footage and local testimony, that in the weeks following ISIS's expulsion from Tikrit, hundreds of homes were demolished in the city's northern al-Qadisiyya neighborhood. "Officials and residents in Tikrit also alleged that the militias were involved in widespread looting and extrajudicial killings." There were some Sunni volunteers embedded with the Popular Mobilization Units, and they engaged in much the same retaliatory violence. "We burned and destroyed al-Dur, because they [the residents] are ISIS and Baathists," one Sunni member of the Tikriti Popular Mobilization Units told Human Rights Watch, referring to a town just outside the city.

According to analyst Aymenn Jawad al-Tamimi, Sunni participation in the militias was limited, and largely determined by intertribal politics. "Some tribesmen participated in the Tikrit operation," al-Tamimi told us, "but they were a minor component and they have traditionally been pro-government. Some of them even revel in the beheading of ISIS fighters."

The good news is that no large-scale revenge massacres have been recorded and between 70 and 90 percent of Tikrit's inhabitants have returned. A year on, there are almost miraculously positive foreign dispatches from the city, but the militias still primarily control it, and, according to al-Tamimi, "kidnappings have been a routine problem. In addition, scores of individuals have been kidnapped from the al-Dur district in the wider area and remain unaccounted for." When one zooms out to assess all of Salah ad-Din province, the picture is bleaker. One hundred twenty thousand displaced Sunnis are still not allowed to return home to Shia areas.

ISIS TAKES RAMADI

The Second Battle of Fallujah in November 2004 showed how the Zarqawists used the guerrilla tactic of bait-and-switch to devastating effect. They put up minimal to moderate fight for one place, drawing the enemy's disproportionate attention there, while planning and executing opportunistic pinprick attacks, if not all-out assaults, on another. Yet Baghdad's military decision-making has seldom taken this predictable behavior into account. Or, rather, the balkanization of its security apparatus means that it simply can't focus on several hot zones at the same time.

Well before the Iraqi government had finished mopping up the city center in Tikrit, it foolishly launched a separate offensive, on April 14, 2015, against al-Karmah, an ISIS-held city close to Fallujah in Anbar province, over which Abu Bakr al-Baghdadi had been given authority in 2006, his first job for ISIS. The jihadists responded the very next day by launching their own offensive around the provincial capital of Ramadi. They took three villages within the first twenty-four hours—Sjariyah, Albu-Ghanim, and Soufiya—on the eastern edge of the city and fought with Iraqi Security Forces within a mile of government buildings.

ISIS had been trying to take Ramadi since January 2014, drawing on popular discontent with al-Maliki's heavy-handed policies: his administration had sacked a protest camp in the city on December 30, 2013, reigniting the Sunni insurgency and giving ISIS an opening. By January 3, 2014, ISIS had its flag flying over Fallujah, although it wouldn't have categorical dominance until after it sacked Mosul six months later.

Ramadi took almost another year of distracting warfare to succumb. In April 2015, al-Baghdadi mobilized jihadists from Syria to fortify combat zones in Anbar and Salah ad-Din, as internal ISIS documents found by al-Tamimi demonstrate. "In this context, it's clear he was referring primarily to Ramadi in Anbar and Baiji in Salah ad-Din," the analyst told us. "Baiji was used by ISIS as a diversion to pin down government forces and Shia militias, which is partly why the Ramadi effort was poorly managed culminating in its downfall."

The final ISIS push began in the Albu Alwan neighborhood in the eastern district of the city at about 9 a.m. on May 14. Well-armed jihadist fighters sailed in skiffs down the Euphrates, taking government authorities in Ramadi by surprise. When Colonel Hamid Shandoukh, the local police commander, began shooting back at the waterborne militants, having called up the local security forces of police and tribal militias, he found he was also facing fire from behind. "We thought the areas behind us were secured," Shandoukh said. But ISIS had activated its Ramadi sleeper cells. Some of the infiltrators had entered Albu Alwan from the northern area of Albu Farraj and were able to cross the Euphrates on foot because parts of the river had actually dried up. VBIEDs were the battering rams that smashed through Ramadi's defenses. In total, thirty of them went off during the final three-day siege; ten were reportedly as powerful as the bomb that tore apart the Alfred P. Murrah Federal Building in Oklahoma City in 1995. ISIS's equivalents "took out entire city blocks," according to a senior State Department official. The suicide car bombers were able to get close to the government buildings by masquerading as Iraqi Security Forces personnel in stolen uniforms and driving official-looking Humvees. The Golden Division, the elite, US-trained Special Forces group commanded by Major General Fadhil Jalil al-Barwari, pulled back to the "Stadium" neighborhood of southern Ramadi on May 15 in what he termed a "tactical" withdrawal. His men would not reenter the fight.

Longtime Iraq watcher Joel Wing has made a close study of the fall of Ramadi. He noted that on the same day that the Golden Division pulled back, the black flag was raised over a whole section of the provincial government complex. "Baghdad responded by sending three regiments to relieve the city," Wing wrote, "but they never arrived, going to the surrounding cities like Habaniya and Khalidya without ever entering Ramadi. On May 17 [ISIS] launched its final assault upon the Anbar Operations Command with three suicide car bombs, and forced the [Iraqi Security Forces] and several thousand refugees to flee west. During the taking of the city [ISIS] members were said to be roaming the streets looking for government workers and sahwa members to execute. In the first two days [ISIS] executed 500 police, sahwa and civilians. On May 16 they killed another 20, and then 33 more the following day. This victory was the culmination of months of fighting by [ISIS], which slowly made its way from the southern part of Ramadi to the middle. Several times this year [ISIS] had made an attempt on the government center, but had been pushed back. This time they were finally able to break through, and took the city as a result."

Iraqi forces' chain of command was thrown into total disarray. Sunni tribal fighters resorted to trying to buy ammunition off the black market. The coalition was slow to respond to the jihadist invasion, launching just four air strikes on May 15 and 16, and only seven more over the twenty-four-hour period between May 16 and 17. An attempt by the Federal Police to send in reinforcements failed when their thirty-vehicle convoy came under attack from the al-Dawlah al-Kabir Mosque in the city center. More policemen retreated to a street in southern Ramadi, hoping to find the Golden Division there. Instead they discovered that Iraq's foremost counterterrorists had already quit the battle. They were further (mis)informed that the United States could not launch air strikes because a sandstorm had closed in around the area, depriving pilots of visibility. What was left of Iraqi Security Forces' morale broke. Ramadi belonged to ISIS.

US defense secretary Ashton Carter would later tell CNN's Barbara Starr, "What apparently happened was that the Iraqi forces just showed no will to fight. They were not outnumbered. In fact, they vastly outnumbered the opposing force, and yet they failed to fight, they withdrew from the site, and that says to me, and I think to most of us, that we have an issue with the will of the Iraqis to fight [ISIS] and defend themselves." But this was not quite the whole story.

In fairness, Iraqi Security Forces in Ramadi had not been resupplied for a month, many of their vehicles were in disrepair, and many soldiers had not received salaries for as long as six months. They were being asked to defend, pro bono, a government that, as far as they were concerned, had already left them to confront well-armed and well-paid insurgents.

Characteristically, the killings started even before Ramadi had entirely fallen. On May 16, a Sunni tribesman told McClatchy: "They're executing people in the streets, I have seen at least 20 myself and there are no government forces left in the main sections of the city. We have been abandoned to [Daesh]." Two days later, ISIS went door-to-door killing scores of any remaining Iraqi policemen and government-affiliated militiamen left in Ramadi, dumping their bodies in the Euphrates. One of the communities to suffer worst was the Albu Alwan tribe, at least thirty of whom were "arrested" by ISIS. At the end of the three-day offensive, 500 civilians were dead and 25,000 were displaced, according to the United Nations.

AL-ABADI VS. THE MILITIAS

The third provincial capital to come under the control of the caliphate within the space of a year gave the jihadists another garrison that was well within striking distance of Baghdad, where suicide and car bombings had already begun to surge. Ramadi's sacking also damaged al-Abadi's reputation as an improvement on his thuggish and venal predecessor and threatened to reverse the perceived progress made at Tikrit the previous month. Little did it matter that that city had been recaptured as a direct result of US airpower; Iranian and militia propaganda had sold it as the exclusive accomplishment of all Shia Islamists, having been billed as the symbolic restitution for the Iran-Iraq War (given the city's notoriety as the birthplace of Saddam). Now it really was time to crow. Suleimani's proxies presented the humiliating defeat at Ramadi as confirmation that the Popular Mobilization Units were Iraq's first and only lines of defense and ought to have been included in the fight all along—a contingency al-Abadi had ruled out, in deference to the Americans, who were now (quietly) growing queasy about how the militias "cleared" ISIS-held terrain. Iranian-choreographed agitprop went even further: the United States, it claimed, was *helping* ISIS by dropping weapons and aid to the terror group. Only Iran could save Iraq from the takfiris.

Al-Amiri vowed to send his men into Anbar, whether the prime minister authorized the decision or not. He then planned to direct the Popular Mobilization Units to retake Fallujah, completely undercutting the pretense that the supposedly sovereign leader of Iraq was in charge of the nation's most powerful security organs.

The Ramadi counteroffensive got off to a very unpromising start when, on May 26, the Popular Mobilization spokesmen announced that the name for their operation would be "Labeyk Ya Hussein," a slogan roughly translated as "At your service, Hussein," in tribute to one of the Shia's central religious figures. The connotations were redolent of sectarian holy war, not a national counterterrorism effort. A day later, after a demarche from US officials and the objection of Iraqi leaders—including, impressively, al-Sadr—the motto was changed to the more catholic "Labeyk Ya Iraq." But the public relations reboot still didn't address underlying Sunni anxieties.

Osama al-Nujaifi, one of Iraq's vice presidents and the former parliamentary speaker, noted that political missteps were conspiring with militia excesses to permanently damage any prospect of Sunni reconciliation with

Baghdad. On May 27, during a parliamentary session, the Sunni governor of Diyala province was sacked and replaced with a Shia. "This is a real threat and a very negative message to Iraqis," Nujaifi told us. "This is considered a break to the rules and it contradicts what has been agreed. The majority in Diyala are Sunnis." Diyala was also, as we've seen, where ISIS anticipated the mother of all sectarian battles.

THE RECAPTURE OF RAMADI

On July 13, 2015, the al-Abadi government formally launched the offensive to retake the capital of Anbar province from four directions. At the same time, the Popular Mobilization Units launched their separate operation against Fallujah and al-Karma. Once again, ISIS capitalized on the split manpower ranged against it and held its ground against both ground forces. Even where the jihadists could be forced from a suburb or village, the Iraqi Security Forces and the militias were stretched too thin to hold on to it. Adding to this atomized battlefield was a crisis of confidence within Iraq's political establishment, a crisis that reached its apex on July 31 after protests broke out throughout the country due to the lack of basic services and endemic government corruption. The militias, especially the League of the Righteous, tried to hijack these demonstrations and redirect them against the prime minister. Only the timely intervention of Ayatollah al-Sistani and al-Abadi's announced reforms, on August 7, neutralized what may well have been an Iranian-enabled coup against Baghdad. Yet the "reform" era lasted a mere eleven weeks, ending when a vote in Iraqi parliament revoked any mandate for al-Abadi to conduct the kind of administrative housecleaning he had promised, which included the elimination of superfluous cabinet positions, many added by al-Maliki as a means of co-opting opponents during his time in office. (The former premier himself now occupied a post, one of Iraq's several vice presidencies, that had been on the prospective chopping block.)

Al-Abadi maintained an important albeit quiet ally throughout his abortive tub-thumping phase. The United States was heavily involved in planning the Ramadi operation. Iraq's counterterrorism forces, federal police, and army soldiers, it was determined, would be the sole ground contingent, backed by US airpower. The *New York Times* reported in early July that around 6,000 troops in total would fight, "according to an Iraqi war plan that has been significantly shaped by American advisers sent to Al Taqqadum, a base east of Ramadi. An

Iraqi follow-on force of up to 5,000 tribal fighters along with Iraqi provincial police officers would be assigned to hold the city and nearby areas in Anbar Province if they were retaken from the Islamic State." Most important, the *Times* noted, the Popular Mobilization Units would have *no* frontline combat role; rather, they would be relegated to "blocking positions south and west of the city, hoping to prevent Islamic State fighters from escaping."

By July 2015, the US advisers had trained 8,300 Iraqi soldiers at five sites in Iraq. Additionally, another 2,000 Iraqi soldiers were working through the US training camps at that time—which meant there was space for 2,000 more. About five hundred Sunni tribesmen entered training at al-Taqqadum in late June, and the United States was directly coordinating between the tribes and the Iraqi Security Forces, specifically the Iraqi 8th Division and the Anbar Operations Center. The Americans were also training three hundred provincial policemen as a potential "hold" force for the city to ensure that hard-won victory against ISIS wasn't immediately squandered by a lack of manpower.

Under US pressure, about 1,500 members of the Popular Mobilization Units left their bases where US trainers were stationed in Anbar. By October, essentially all of the Shia militias had been moved out of the Ramadi theater, either to Fallujah or Baiji, in Salah ad-Din. The only listed volunteer corps were a handful of Sunni tribal fighters, and as these were technically not a part of any Iraqi state institution, their deputation required a creative workaround to enable them to receive government salaries for their service. Counter-intuitively, the tribesmen were bundled into the Popular Mobilization Units, at the behest of Washington. (A more lasting measure, the creation of an Iraqi National Guard that mandates 5,000 Sunni soldiers for every one million Iraqis, was approved by parliament in 2015, but hasn't yet materialized as law.)

In the end, around 630 US air strikes between July and December broke the ISIS siege on Ramadi. "This was attrition warfare," a defense adviser to the coalition told the *Daily Beast*, adding that the Iraqi Security Forces did little actual ground fighting as ISIS fighters melted away. "They were mostly coordinating and providing security for the counter terrorism unit and maintaining a perimeter, which can be quite taxing. It was mostly about pinpointing ISIS positions to call in airstrikes, clearing booby traps so you could open up mobility corridors."

Several Iraqi newspapers would allege that US Special Forces and helicopters were also involved in the decisive push into the city that occurred in the second week of December. The Pentagon has steadfastly disclaimed such rumors, although a dozen Kurdish fighters told the *Guardian* that US Special Forces had indeed been fighting alongside them for six months, naming specific battles in and around Kirkuk and giving up operational details (such as the number of mortars the Americans fired). It also bears mentioning that the first—and so far only—US fatality of the war was Master Sergeant Joshua L. Wheeler, a member of Delta Force and an adviser to the peshmerga. He was killed after coming to the aid of a Kurdish rescue party seeking to liberate dozens of ISIS hostages in Kirkuk province. (There are two US Special Forces units embedded with the Kurdish Counter Terrorism Force and recent video footage aired on Kurdish television showing at least three commandos on the front line with peshmerga actively repulsing an ISIS attack in Kirkuk province. No doubt the true extent of an American combat role will not be known until much later.)

The bulk of the heavy lifting in Ramadi was done by Iraq's own Special Forces, the Golden Division in particular. In a harrowing documentary shown from the war zone in December 2015, the news outlet *Vice* embedded with these commandos—who back in May had beat a "tactical" retreat in the face of advancing ISIS columns—as they swept bomb-rigged houses and sat and talked about the future of Ramadi. The Golden Division is one of the few multi-confessional and multiethnic units in the entire Iraqi military, with Sunnis, Shia, and Christians working alongside one another with no apparent antagonism or chauvinism. In fact, one commando interviewed by *Vice*, "Ahmed," who is himself a Shia, claimed to have been kidnapped, tortured, nearly shot to death—not by ISIS but by an unnamed Shia militia.

As in Tikrit, the number of jihadists hanging on to Ramadi was staggeringly small: 600 to 1,000, with the total ISIS buildup never exceeding more than 2,000 for the entire six-month period in which the city was occupied. US officials say that most of these militants were either killed by air strikes or quit the scene. On December 22, the Iraqi Security Forces broke into the city center from two different directions and, five days later, hoisted the Iraqi flag over the government compound and declared victory.

The Ramadi operation had been strictly planned by the United States to bolster the prime minister, and it did. But the challenges from Iranian satraps didn't stop. On December 16, at a fulcrum point in the Ramadi battle, al-Abadi was caught off guard when the Popular Mobilization Units unilaterally recommenced an offensive that had been dormant for two months, against Fallujah, which was conceived and planned expressly to undermine his leadership. The gambit failed owing to how poorly the militias' own offensive proceeded. A senior US military official said in late 2015, "the Shia militias are too beaten and tired to fight ISIS in the long term. Only the Kurds have the morale and capacity to fight."

The cheerleading of total victory coming out of al-Abadi's office also failed to match reality on the ground. Baghdad claimed to have "completely cleared" Ramadi weeks before this was true. By the end of 2015, ISIS still held 20 to 25 percent of the provincial capital, notably in districts to the east. On January 3, 2016, ISIS even captured the Iraqi army base in al-Tarah by breaking in with suicide bombers, before being driven out.

More worrying, the Iraqi government's effort to construct a police force to hold the liberated areas in Ramadi is, as of this writing, inchoate. The US defense adviser who gave a less romanticized assessment of the operation to the *Daily Beast* was not overstating matters when he said that the "hard part of Ramadi is still to come. This is the easy stuff. How are you going to hold it if you have not addressed the political, economic and humanitarian issues? How are you going to hold it if you don't have the military structure that is reliable? You can't hold Ramadi, and Tikrit, and the area around the Tigris River valley and take Mosul."

The most convenient return invitation for ISIS would indeed be for the continued Hezbollah-ization of Iraq's security establishment, which entails not just the proliferation of runaway rogue proxies of Iran but also the infiltration of them into state institutions. If men in army uniforms whose real loyalty is to an Iranian Special Group round up, arrest, torture, or try to expel Sunni tribesmen, the liberation of Ramadi will have been for naught. And should this dire contingency be avoided, there is the reconstruction of the ruined provincial capital to bear in mind. Between 60 and 80 percent of the city now lies in rubble after six months of air strikes and artillery shelling—and ISIS's bomb-rigged departure. Everything was blown up or left to explode. The *New York Times'* Michael Gordon toured Ramadi with General Ali Jameel, an Iraqi counterterrorism officer, after the battle. "In one neighborhood," Gordon wrote, General Ali "stood before a panorama of wreckage so vast that it was unclear where the original buildings had stood. He paused when asked how residents would return to their homes. 'Homes?' he said. 'There are no homes.'"

The head of the Anbar Provincial Council, Gordon noted, reckons that the rebuilding of Ramadi will cost $12 billion. The United States and its partners have committed less than one-half of 1 percent of that amount in reconstruction money.

Even more worrisome is the parlous condition of Iraq's budget for financing the rest of the war. Both the central government and the KRG are on the verge of bankruptcy because of rock-bottom oil prices. "Neither government can pay for all the ghost soldiers and ghost civil servants they have hired while courting political support," Joel Rayburn said. "So they are digging themselves a deep hole, and it can't go on. At some point they will have to cut employees and troops, and that's when their political support will erode." And materialism coupled with the now-unavoidable reality of an Iranian-built deep state threaten to fundamentally alter Iraq's political landscape.

Provincial elections are scheduled for early 2017. There are two loose Shia coalitions that will battle for control of Baghdad and the southern provinces. On one side are al-Abadi, al-Sadr, and Ammar Hakim, the nephew of Ayatollah Mohammed Baqir al-Hakim, the Shia cleric whom al-Zarqawi assassinated in 2003. This bloc has Sistani's support. On the other side are al-Maliki (still very much a player in Iraqi politics), al-Amiri, the League of the Righteous, and the Hezbollah Brigades. This bloc is backed by Iran. "The former have more popular support, probably," Rayburn said. "But the latter have money and political influence."

The main theater of Inherent Resolve is therefore heavily reliant on the assumption that a barrel of Brent crude doesn't dip below $60 and that Tammany-style politics, which purchases support through the provision of civil and military sinecures, can be maintained indefinitely. Qubad Talabani, the deputy prime minister of Iraqi Kurdistan, put it bluntly. An economic "tsunami," he told reporters in January 2016, could wash away all the victories against ISIS on the battlefield.

Finally, what David Petraeus, Masrour Barzani, and many analysts have forecasted about a future post-ISIS Iraq remains the private worry of US officials, who put an optimistic face on a progressively worsening situation. The cure might not be worse than the disease, but it might still kill the patient.

"There's a panic among military commanders over the growth and strength of Shia militias," an American intelligence officer in Baghdad told us in late January 2016. "This is so much so the case that they can barely muster the words 'Shia militias' as a bad thing. It's the coming wave from these groups that is our next major shit storm. Sadly, the White House refuses to acknowledge this for fear of looking like they don't know what they're doing. Or that they've made a mistake."

17

AT WAR IN SYRIA
REMAINING, IF NOT EXPANDING

By 2014, ISIS's successes had lured Washington into an alliance of inconvenience with Iranian-backed militias in Iraq in a seeming confirmation of al-Zarqawi's conspiracy theory that the world's only superpower was leading a global war of extermination and dispossession of the Sunnis. Nothing could better undercut the potential for a second Awakening than the perceived corroboration of this appraisal, which US policy was accidentally facilitating.

In Syria, the army of terror was just as deviously committed to exploiting sectarian fault lines, although its chances for success were far less certain owing to demography. Here Sunni Arabs constituted the majority of the population—about 60 percent—and once they had had enough, ISIS would be subsumed and cannibalized by the masses, assuming, that is, the masses had a credible alternative on offer. This could never be the al-Assad regime or his Quds Force–overseen consortium of Shia and Alawite militias, which *were* waging a brutal sectarian war against the Sunnis. A brief moment of sahwa did occur across seven provinces in the early weeks of 2014, forcing ISIS wholly from two provinces, to which they still have not returned. Yet it was never capitalized on by the so-called Friends of Syria nations. The main beneficiary of this uprising therefore became al-Qaeda, the former patron turned fratricidal enemy of the Zarqawists.

Throughout the first eighteen months of Operation Inherent Resolve, Syria's Sunni Arabs, particularly those in the ISIS briar patches of the Jazira, would find themselves treated more as an American afterthought than as the sine qua non for defeating Sunni jihadism. By 2015, US Central Command had found its one true proxy army in the minority Kurds, specifically, the People's Defense Units. These were militias run by the Democratic Union Party (PYD), which was the undeniable (and undenied) Syrian affiliate of the Kurdish Workers' Party (PKK). And the PKK is blacklisted by both the United States and Turkey, against which it had waged an on-again, off-again forty-year insurgency. A leitmotif in the Obama administration's anti-ISIS strategy was thus coming into focus across the Levant and Mesopotamia. In the name of counterterrorism, one deeply authoritarian and cultist terrorist franchise would be empowered to defeat another. The ironies and unintended consequences of this approach, not to say the more Lewis Carroll–ish aspects of its logic, were not lost on ISIS. The jihadists' merciless assault on Syria's Kurds was conducted, as always, on Islamic fundamentalist tenets. It wasn't a war against the Kurds per se—many Kurds had, after all, joined ISIS and were believing Muslims. It was rather a war against a godless communist guerrilla movement and enemy of Islam. As ever, behind the messianic zeal lay a well-crafted geopolitical motive.

Since 2011, Syria's Kurds had been less interested in overthrowing the al-Assad regime than in using the revolution as a pathway for their own creeping independence. The PYD had adopted a "wait-and-see" policy, though in some cases, such as after the sarin gas attack on Ghouta in 2013, it came out on the side of the regime. PYD cochairman Salih Muslim Muhammad denied that al-Assad was capable of such a war crime. For his part, al-Assad had sought to enervate Turkey, which had become an all-too-willing barracks and command center for rebels devoted to his overthrow, by withdrawing his military and security personnel from Syrian Kurdish areas. He knew full well that the PYD, the largest and best-organized Kurdish party, would take over and that Ankara would take notice. As such, many Sunni Arabs were wary of the Kurds, seeing them as separatist spoilers rather than comrades-in-arms against the Baathist dictatorship. Any US-abetted military endeavor led by the Kurds against ISIS would therefore transform into a different kind of state-building project in Syria—a Kurdish one, specifically to realize the dreamt-of Rojava, or "West Kurdistan," which would stretch from eastern regions of Aleppo all the way to the end of Hasaka province, encompassing most of the 565-mile expanse of the Syrian-Turkish border. And such an outcome would automatically split NATO because Ankara would never acquiesce to the rise of an autonomous Kurdish fief on its southern doorstep, led by a sister organization of its foremost national security threat, any more than Israel would concede a Palestinian state to Hamas. If the United States armed or partnered with the PYD while Turkey contained it, then the coalition would be turned inside out and ISIS would gain. If the United States abandoned the Kurds, in deference to Turkish considerations, then ISIS would sweep the remainder of northern Syria, winning valuable new border crossings and supply lines for replenishing men and matériel in the caliphate. As an added bonus, any outward American alliance with the PYD would further alienate Sunni Arabs in the tribal heartland of the Jazira, who, as much as they disliked or hated ISIS, would view the People's Defense Units the way their Iraqi confederates had viewed the Popular Mobilization Units—as conquerors rather than liberators.

THE SIEGE OF KOBANE

Within the space of a week in October 2014, Kobane, the Syrian-Kurdish city on Turkey's southern lip that had been besieged for a month by ISIS, went from being "not strategically vital" to "symbolically important." Such was the *Wall Street Journal*'s paraphrase of official US government thinking on the subject. The air mission to keep the jihadist army from sacking Kobane represented Inherent Resolve's first foray into Syria, with the number of coalition sorties there far outstripping that of any other target in either Syria or Iraq during the remainder of 2014.

Earlier in October, both US Central Command and the Turkish government announced that Kobane's fall was imminent. "As horrific as it is to watch in real time what's happening in Kobane," US Secretary of State John Kerry said on October 8, "you have to step back and understand the strategic objective." Kobane didn't meet the criteria, at least not for another twelve days. "We cannot take our eyes off the prize here," Kerry announced on October 20. "It would be irresponsible of us, as well as morally very difficult, to turn your back on a community fighting [ISIS], as hard as it is, at this particular moment."

The ISIS assault on Kobane, which is known as Ayn al-Arab in Arabic, began in mid-September when the jihadists managed to get the better of the People's Defense Units, or YPG. These battle-savvy Kurdish militias had been the ablest forces ranged against ISIS in northern Syria. The rebel groups operating under the FSA brand who went to war with ISIS were drawn from an agriculturalist demographic—albeit one subjected to universal conscription—motivated to take up arms in defense of themselves and their families against the al-Assad regime, giving them the character of neighborhood watch militias. Subordinate to the PKK and led by hundreds and now thousands of its fighters, the People's Defense Units had decades of experience of guerrilla warfare to draw on. They were savvier at politics than the FSA—as proven by their very existence, which allowed the US deniability in arming a designated terrorist organization. There was also no ambiguity or indecision about their commitment to battle ISIS; the YPG had been doing so far longer than any Syrian rebel faction. Indeed, many FSA brigades and battalions had formerly partnered with ISIS in missions against the People's Defense Units out of a shared hostility to Kurdish nationalism (or out of a shared sense of Arab chauvinism, which amounted to the same thing). It was these Kurdish militias that had sent crucial reinforcements into Sinjar in August 2014 to assist the Iraqi Kurds when peshmerga fighters ran out of ammunition.

The State Department's legal fiction of a distinction between the PYD and PKK might not have been very convincing, but there was no other way to save Kobane, as Lloyd Austin informed President Obama. So within days, Soviet-era weapons, such as AK-47s, procured by the United States from Albania for resupplying the peshmerga were instead en route from Erbil to Kuwait, where they were stowed aboard C-130 cargo planes and flown to Kobane. There they were dropped to waiting People's Defense Units, although one errant package filled with grenades and mortar rounds apparently fell into ISIS's hands and was immediately shown on jihadist media.

On September 21, ISIS's spokesman Abu Muhammad al-Adnani issued a statement attempting to dispel the notion that ISIS was warring against the Kurds as an ethnic group, no doubt aware of the many Kurds who had joined ISIS, but rather as disbelievers—the YPG being a secular force with ideological origins in Marxism-Leninism—who collaborated with the West and the Jews. ISIS was careful to make the public face of its campaign in Kobane a Kurd, from Halabja no less, Abu Khattab al-Kurdi, though how much control al-Kurdi actually had over the ISIS offensive is open to doubt. The statement was significant for another reason: al-Adnani delivered what amounted to an international call for foreign terrorist attacks and thus a return to the earlier period in al-Qaeda in Iraq's dual-pronged strategy of taking terrain locally while carrying out bombings globally. Rather than emigrating to the land of the caliphate, mujahidin were now exhorted to stay put in their native lands and kill the kuffar there, by any means necessary. "Strike their police, security, and intelligence members, as well as their treacherous agents," al-Adnani said.

"If you can kill a disbelieving American or European—especially the spiteful and filthy French—or an Australian, or a Canadian, or any other disbeliever from the disbelievers waging war, including the citizens of the countries that entered into a coalition against the Islamic State, then rely upon Allah, and kill him in any manner or way however it may be. Do not ask for anyone's advice and do not seek anyone's verdict. Kill the disbeliever whether he is civilian or military, for they have the same ruling." And use whatever tool you had at your disposal, be it a rock to smash an infidel's head in, a knife to stab him, a car to run him over, a high place to toss him off. At the very least, it was incumbent upon believing Muslims to spit in his face. "If your self refuses to do so, while your brothers are being bombarded and killed," al-Adnani warned, "and while their blood and wealth everywhere is deemed lawful by their enemies, then review your religion."

America's swift, unambiguous military support for the Kurds did not go unnoticed by advocates of the mainly Sunni Arab Free Syrian Army. Jad Bantha, an Oxford-educated activist from Damascus, tweeted a series of observations and complaints on October 20: "Obama sent 1 tonne of medical supplies & loads of military supplies to PYD kurds only, neglecting thousands of Syrians who have fought ISIS. . . . Obama & his admin lied to us so many times, I would rather trust ISIS than Obama & his jokers! The US admin again prove they are our enemies."

Bantha's disillusionment attended the exposure of yet another ISIS massacre of Sunni Arabs in Syria. For three days in early August, according to the *Washington Post*, the jihadists had "shelled, beheaded, crucified and shot hundreds of members of the Shaitat tribe after they dared to rise up" against them in Abu Hamam, a village in Deir Ezzor. "By the time the killing stopped, 700 people were dead, activists and survivors say, making this the bloodiest single atrocity committed by the Islamic State in Syria since it declared its existence 18 months ago." Men and boys older than fifteen were summarily killed once ISIS took Abu Hamam. Abu Salem, a tribesman who survived this massacre, spoke to a newspaper from the Turkish town of Reyhanli: "We saw what the Americans did to help the Yazidis and the Kurds," he said. "But they have done nothing to help the Sunnis against the Islamic State."

ISIS was eventually expelled from Kobane on January 27, 2015, after a 112-day siege. By February 2, the People's Defense Units had established a five-mile cordon around the city, driving ISIS back more than two miles overnight. By this point, the jihadist front line had all but deteriorated. As in Tikrit, US airpower proved the deciding factor. The coalition waged more than seven hundred air strikes—75 percent of all its sorties in Syria—in defense of the city. According to one estimate of the casualties from the Battle of Kobane, sixteen hundred people were killed, a thousand of them ISIS fighters and the majority of the rest Kurdish militiamen. At least seventy Free Syrian Army rebels also died resisting the jihadists, although, as Jad Bantha correctly noted, they were not direct recipients of US matériel. Abu Saif, the field commander of the Raqqa Revolutionaries Brigade, told one of the authors in early October 2014 that he and his men had fought against the People's Defense Units until ISIS booted the brigade out of its home base of Raqqa. "There was a sort of cease-fire or truce between the [Free Syrian Army] and the YPG," Abu Saif said, which resulted in the former coming to the latter's assistance in Kobane. Initially, the Raqqa Revolutionaries Brigade commanded about 1,250 rebels, he added, but that figure dwindled to a mere 300 because of wartime exigencies—a lack of money, food, and ammunition to keep so many men at the front. Nor were any resupplies forthcoming from those C-130 cargo planes. "We asked for assistance, but no one gave us anything," Abu Saif said at the time. "There were no anti-tank weapons. When Daesh breached the defenses and made their way into the city, the fighting became street-to-street. We decided we had to withdraw at least half of our forces to save their lives." Both the Kurds and Sunni Arabs defending Kobane, he added, resorted to their own scorched-earth insurgency tactics to keep ISIS from seizing still more square miles: they planted their own car bombs and rigged houses and buildings with explosives to deter the jihadists.

ISIS's physical siege of the city coincided with a heightened campaign of information warfare, intended to both dissuade greater military escalation on the part of the West and to debunk Western claims that the enemy was being steadily defeated. Another beheading video was released, this time of British aid worker Alan Henning, on October 3, during some of the most intense fighting in and around the city. Henning's execution, ISIS declared, was an act of retribution following British Parliament's decision on September 26 to allow air strikes in Iraq—moral equivalence that did not quite account for why a previous British hostage, David Haines, was murdered a fortnight before that legislative decision was taken. Then, on October 27, the organization released a video titled "Inside Ayn al-Islam" (their name for Kobane), which opened with an impressive piece of ISIS-operated drone footage showing the cityscape relatively quiet. The film was narrated by yet another British hostage,

John Cantlie, who was now—no doubt under duress—used as a full-time Western apologist for his hostage takers. Cantlie was shown walking around Kobane with ease, with only sporadic and distant gunfire in the background. The message was simple: The international media were lying. ISIS was in full control of most of the city.

For a time, the "hear from us, not about us" strategy translated into material gain. Rashid Taku, a former commander of Jaysh al-Sham, or the Army of Greater Syria, an Islamist rebel group established in early 2014 to be independent of both al-Qaeda and ISIS, defected to the latter on October 17. A Saudi Sharia official from Abu Umar al-Shishani's Army of Emigrants and Partisans, Abu Azzam al-Najdi, announced his defection to ISIS four days later. The flow of foreign fighters was also increasing, as the takfiris portrayed Kobane as their own "symbolic" watershed moment in a war against infidels, crusaders, and apostates. It was estimated that, by late October 2014, more than one thousand foreigners per month were pouring into Syria to enlist in the army of terror.

In many ways, this was to be the apex of ISIS's good fortune in the war. Air strikes, combined with dogged resistance by the People's Defense Units, Free Syrian Army, and arriving convoys of Kurdish Peshmerga from Iraq, combined to reverse the momentum of the siege by January 2015. Human waves of jihadists simply poured into the city, as cannon fodder, and were easily targeted and bombed by coalition warplanes. By February, Kobane was lost to ISIS, but the city lay in ruins. Three hundred thousand Kurdish refugees had crossed the border into Turkey, which had done little for half a year to help the Kurdish resistance. Ankara feared the rise of a PKK-aligned political power—and the establishment of contiguous Kurdish cantons, if not a Kurdish "statelet"—at its southern doorstep more than it did the caliphate.

Turkish president Recep Tayyip Erdogan had been clear about his government's position back in October: "There has been talk about forming a front against [ISIS] by giving the PYD arms," he told reporters, just before President Obama called him to say that the United States was going to ally with the People's Defense Units. "But the PYD, for us, is equal to the PKK; it is a terrorist organization." And while Turkey did eventually allow convoys of peshmerga from Iraqi Kurdistan to bypass its territory to enter Kobane, it refused to countenance any direct military assistance or matériel for the People's Defense Units. Also not helping its international public relations profile during this period was the fact that journalists were able to snap photographs of the Turkish gendarmerie spraying water cannons at incoming refugees from Kobane, while armed ISIS jihadists on the *Turkish* side of the border stood smiling in the refugees' midst. Turkish warplanes also bombed PKK sites in October 2014, at the height of the Kobane siege, definitively ending what had been a fitfully progressive round of peace negotiations between Ankara and its longest-running domestic insurgency. Whatever the geopolitics or understandable Turkish national security considerations, global opinion was decided: when it came to the war in Syria, NATO's second-largest member state would rather hamper the Kurds than defeat ISIS, a point sometimes highlighted by US officials including Vice President Joe Biden.

Unfortunately, ISIS wasn't quite done with Kobane after it was pushed out. In the last week of June 2015, it committed one of the worst massacres of civilians since the establishment of its "state" when around thirty of its jihadists smuggled themselves back into the city, then just beginning to absorb returning families and slowly recover from its near eradication. These operatives set off car bombs and waged lethal gunfire attacks. By the end of the month, when ISIS was pushed out of the city, 220 civilians, including women, children, and the elderly, had been killed.

ISIS's return to Kobane, although abortive, was hugely demoralizing due to what it represented—the Kurds' inability to stop opportunistic attacks even in areas where the militants had lost control. ISIS could be defeated, but would it ever be definitively gone? Contained within the carnage for carnage's sake was an insidious military motive: divide and conquer. ISIS sought to exacerbate lingering sectarian tensions between the Arabs and Kurds who, by the early summer of 2015, had been burning through hundreds of square miles of territory in northeast Syria like an avenging flame, delivering defeat after defeat to the takfiris. As Abu Saif, the military commander of the Raqqa Revolutionaries Brigade, explained to one of the authors, the jihadists penetrated Kobane by posing as some of the city's heterogeneous defenders.

It was around five o'clock in the morning on June 25 when they struck, dressed in the uniforms of the Free Syrian Army and People's Defense Units. "They first fired shots in the air, and people were happy because they thought these were friendly forces," Abu Saif said. "But when they came out to greet them, the militants opened fire. When I went up to the rooftop [of my building], I saw that they were dressed in YPG fatigues. Then, they started killing people."

They embedded deep within the city center, taking control of the Mishta

Nur Hospital and fifty civilian hostages along with a secondary school and other buildings. The one military target the militants had in mind, it seems, was the home of Abu Issa al-Raqqawi, the top commander of the Raqqa Revolutionaries Brigade. They raided his house, critically injuring Abu Issa's wife and two of his children, according to Abu Saif. Even the *Washington Post* reported that the infiltrators were all Kurdish, many from Iraq; they had snuck back into the city in the first place posing as repatriating refugees. Clearly, then, the Arab minority in Kobane were meant to think that their majority Kurdish allies had turned on them in a bid at elimination.

As a tactic of psychological warfare, this ruse succeeded well, given how resentful the Free Syrian Army fighters aligned with the People's Defense Units were at the asymmetry of the coalition's war. While they fought and died for the same turf, the United States refused to arm or share intelligence with them. They were expendable helpmeets, invisible soldiers. Abu Saif described how his rebels had to call in US air strikes against ISIS by proxy, via their Kurdish partners. "We gave the Kurds coordinates, and the Kurds passed them along to the Americans. There was a vehicle operated by them that was in the rear of our convoy, and we would scout ISIS positions, tell the Kurds the coordinates and they'd send them onto the coalition." Angrily, Abu Saif added, Central Command wouldn't liaise directly with his brigade or other Arab contingent, granting the Kurds a favored status that allowed them to recruit allies out of desperation rather than genuine camaraderie. These included Christian Assyrian forces from Aleppo, Raqqa, and Hasaka, who were eager for even indirect international assistance. ISIS was well aware of this imbalance in the coalition's designation of proxies because it had been reported extensively. So it sought to exacerbate latent (or not-so-latent) sensitivities by posing as fifth columnists.

The attack on Kobane, furthermore, came right after a series of impressive Arab-Kurdish joint victories, however lopsided in favor of the Kurds these may have been. A mere forty-eight hours was all it took, in mid-June, for the crucial border town of Tal Abyad to be retaken from ISIS, formerly its most prized gateway into Turkey for the smuggling of wares, weapons, and foreign fighters. For some reason, ISIS had beat a tactical retreat rather than put up a serious fight. Abu Saif said that he intercepted communications between the jihadists in Tal Abyad and their superiors in ISIS's high command, in Raqqa. "We heard their commanders calling for reinforcements, which never materialized. When we moved on Tal Abyad, some of their fighters withdrew, some stayed and fought. But that was a small number." One hundred ISIS fighters were killed, while an untold number escaped north into Akcakale, southern Turkey. Some of the latter were then taken into custody by Turkish soldiers, while others, according to US officials, shaved off their beards and melted into the exodus of thousands of civilian refugees marching north.

The fall of Tal Abyad was attended by two more successive victories for the People's Defense Units. First, they took Brigade 93, a Syrian regime installation that had been under ISIS control, with just as little pushback as in Tal Abyad. Hours later, they seized the town of Ain Issa, just thirty miles north of Raqqa City, and the closest any anti-ISIS ground force has come to the jihadist "capital" in three years. Misdirection worked again for ISIS. By attacking Kobane, they were able to briefly retake some of Tal Abyad and Ain Issa.

But the damage to morale would be long-lasting. Reports soon emerged that the People's Defense Units were guilty of ethnic cleansing and the burning of Arab homes in these areas—allegations that Turkey, seeking to justify its wariness of Syria's Kurds, was all too happy to promote and emphasize. The Kurds swiftly returned the gesture by accusing Turkey and its Free Syrian Army proxies of being behind ISIS terrorism. "Without support of a regional country, ISIS could not [have infiltrated Kobane]," Democratic Union Party member Sheruan Hassan told the *Daily Beast*, noting that the ISIS attackers had entered the city from Turkish soil—with the connivance of Ankara. Salih Muslim, the cochairman of the party, suggested that Syrian rebels inside Kobane "might" have cooperated with ISIS in the operation.

"You can say that the [Free Syrian Army] and [People's Defense Units] are both fighting ISIS," said Chris Harmer, of the Institute for the Study of War. "You cannot say that they have the same interests. Because ISIS is geographically in the center of the fight, they sense these gaps in the opposition very easily and exploit them."

By late June 2015, ISIS was retrenching to its Sunni Arab tribal heartland of Raqqa, laying land mines around the provincial capital city and constructing blast walls. Rami Abdulrahman, the director of the Syrian Observatory for Human Rights, told CNN that ISIS had already moved about one hundred military vehicles filled with fighters, weapons, and ammunition into the city from the east of Raqqa.

Were the jihadists hunkering down for a long, bloody fight on their own terrain? A US attempt to reinvigorate a heterogeneous counterinsurgency in the fall of 2015 was blessed with a new operational name, the Syrian

Democratic Forces. Christians, Turkomans, Arab tribesmen, and palatable Free Syrian Army units are, in theory, united with the People's Defense Units in a common struggle, although no one denied the disproportionate number of, and influence wielded by, the Kurds in this ground coalition. In October, US planes dropped fifty tons of ammunition on the Syrian Democratic Forces. None of the constituent factions apart from the People's Defense Units had the logistical capability to make use of the cargo, according to Tim Lister, a journalist who has reported on Operation Inherent Resolve from both the Syrian and Iraqi front lines, and embedded with the Kurdish-led militias. In an essay published in December 2015 in *CTC Sentinel*, the in-house journal of the Combating Terrorism Center at West Point, Lister noted that the "non-Kurdish constituents can, at best, field fighters in the low thousands, and in many instances their training is non-existent. They are more akin to defensive neighborhood militia." The odds that such a congeries will march on ISIS's center of gravity in eastern Syria behind screaming US F-18s are long indeed. People's Defense Units commanders "do not envisage taking a leading role closer to Deir Ezzour," he wrote. "They regard it as an Arab city where Kurdish fighters would not be welcome and where losses would likely be high."

"There's no possibility that American airpower can be employed in Raqqa the way it was in Kobane," Chris Harmer, the analyst at the Institute for the Study of War, said. "For all practical purposes, Kobane was depopulated before the battle started. There's no way we're going to incur mass casualties in Raqqa in order to get a few ISIS fighters."

And the materialized effort to do just that failed precipitously. In October 2015, around two thousand Sunni tribes had assembled under the umbrella of Jabhat Thuwar al-Raqqa, into Jaysh al-Ashair, or the Tribes' Army. Based in Tal Abyad, the Tribes' Army was going to be the Sunni Arab wing of the People's Defense Units, and so an important demographic cover for any further advances into predominantly Arab ISIS-held territory in northern and eastern Syria. "The Kurds are our brothers, with the shared objective of liberating Al-Raqqa province from the oppression of IS," one commander declared in the uploaded video heralding the formation of the Tribes' Army. But fraternal solidarity quickly descended into accusations of extrajudicial murder and the forced displacement of Arabs from villages and towns by the Kurds— accusations that Amnesty International corroborated.

The Tribes' Army had instructed the People's Defense Units to stay clear of these areas; instead, the Kurdish forces blockaded them in Tal Abyad. On December 29, the group Raqqa Is Being Slaughtered Silently reported on the claims of internecine conflict on its Facebook page: "The YPG and its allies are imposing a strangling siege on Jabhat Thuwar a-Raqqa and the Tribes' Army for the 15th consecutive day—they're preventing them from entering Tel Abyad with their wounded, and depriving [those inside] of foodstuffs and all essential supplies." Meanwhile, the website Syria Direct quoted a Kurdish journalist denying these allegations and countering that the Tribes' Army "was spread over too-wide an area" to even be blockaded, especially as there were no Kurdish forces stationed there. Never one to miss an opportunity to capitalize on division in its enemies' ranks, ISIS waged a VBIED and gun attack on Ain Issa on January 2, 2016, overwhelming the Raqqa Revolutionaries Brigade entirely. The People's Defense Units lost nine fighters in defense of the town that had been won back six months earlier. Days later, the Tribes' Army was disbanded completely.

THE FALL OF PALMYRA

If victory at "symbolic" Kobane came at a dramatically high price, at least it could be counted an unambiguous coalition success. But ISIS was hardly on the ropes in Syria. Within days of Ramadi's collapse in May 2015, ISIS scored another dramatic and unforeseen victory, sweeping through the desert table-land of eastern Syria and sacking Palmyra, a city that holds a dual significance as being home to both some of the world's most celebrated classical archaeological wonders and one of the al-Assad regime's most feared detention and torture facilities, the Tadmor prison. Both, as it happened, would meet the same end—immolation, one earning the world's censure, the other giving even avowed ISIS enemies cause for guilty celebration.

The loss of the oasis city, once a vital trade route linking East and West, was a clear and present danger to still more world heritage, consisting as it does of the standing remnants of two-thousand-year-old temples, tombs, and colonnades, built by Greeks, Romans, Persians, and Assyrians. "The fighting is putting at risk one of the most significant sites in the Middle East," Irina Bokova, the director general of UNESCO, said in a statement, while Syria's chief of antiquities, Maamoun Abdulkarim, told Agence France-Presse that many of the statues and artifacts in Palmyra's museum had already been relocated but that immovable monuments were now helpless.

The prospective evaporation of history would follow the actual evaporation of any regime resistance to the jihadist invasion. So desperate were al-Assad's troops that they resorted to freeing the city's prisoners to coerce them into fortifying Palmyra in a last-ditch and pathetically unsuccessful attempt to hang on, as a local resident told one of the authors. Khaled Omran, a member of Palmyra's pro-rebel Coordinating Committee, said that the regime tried to reinforce its collapsing front lines with detainees from Tadmor prison. Most, however, ran away from ISIS's advancing convoys rather than stay and fight for their jailers. "I saw about ten busloads of prisoners being driven to the front," Omran said in a Skype interview shortly after the siege on the city. "Maybe one thousand men." They added to the regime's "thousands" of soldiers and forcibly conscripted tribal militias who were used, in Omran's words, as "cannon fodder." Al-Assad's military was stationed throughout the city and its outlying districts, which are home to several security installations, including an important air base that Iran's Revolutionary Guards Corps has used in the past to deliver resupplies to its overstretched and attrited ally, and the Syrian Air Force has used to wage sorties on mostly civilian and non-ISIS targets. "Regime forces called in reinforcements, mainly to the military security branch and the citadel, but relied heavily on their air force," Omran said. "The number of ISIS fighters was quite small—they were in the hundreds. They weren't very heavily equipped, save for antiaircraft guns mounted on trucks in six positions around the city." These rudimentary air defenses were enough to deter the fighter planes and attack helicopters. "I didn't see them down any jets, but the guns were enough to deter most of the aerial assaults."

The Syrian Observatory for Human Rights claimed that the regime withdrew or evacuated its forces on Wednesday, though Omran insisted that many of these also deserted because of fear of inevitable ISIS atrocities, such as beheadings, photographs of which were circulated on social media as the militants moved in. "Regime troops were fleeing left and right," he said. "Most of the senior Alawite officers in the army fled earlier and left their men— Sunnis—to their own devices." Assad's forces also evidently pulled away from the phosphate mines next to the main M3 highway system, theoretically giving ISIS a straight shot to Homs and Damascus.

Omran's account read like an uncanny replay of the regime's ignominious regime defeat in August 2014 at Tabqa air base: a feckless, halfhearted defense of an important strategic foothold. Mohammed Ghanem, the director of government relations at the Washington, D.C.–based Syrian American Council, an anti-Assad organization, told us that he could not understand how an imminent ISIS advance wasn't interdicted by either regime or coalition aircraft. "We are mystified as to how ISIS columns with hundreds of fighters were able to traverse the Syrian desert and reach Palmyra without suffering a single air raid," Ghanem said at the time. "The areas between ISIS-controlled cities and Palmyra are sparsely populated, and any significant military convoy should have been extremely easy to spot. Yet neither Assad nor the coalition conducted raids against ISIS."

Regime forces tried to destroy whatever infrastructure they could as they retreated. The departing Syrian army destroyed the electrical transformers, Omran said, bathing the ancient city in darkness. As of May 2015, batteries were being used to power computers, but Internet access was spotty. Another source of concern was Damascus's propaganda after the withdrawal. Syrian state television made false claims that the regime evacuated all of Palmyra's civilians before its military withdrew. "We're worried that this was to lay the groundwork for an imminent bombing raid that will make no distinction between Daesh and us," he said. "Some people have resigned to their fate. Most of the key services have been shut down. The bakery has run out of flour. The regime shut the lights. People are fearful. They're not sure what tomorrow holds." Not long after giving this interview, Omran fled to Turkey.

Despite international fears over the destruction of monuments in Palmyra, ISIS made its first order of business the demolition, on May 30, 2015, of Tadmor prison, an infamous detention center not only for Islamists—including those who had tried to assassinate Hafez al-Assad—but secular dissidents, too, as well as many Lebanese activists and politicians who have long opposed the regime. The latter had been kidnapped rather than arrested in the 1970s and 1980s when Syria occupied Lebanon, and remanded to the desert jail. A different kind of "amnesty" would be issued as the custodians of this facility opened the cell doors to let everyone out to face down the advancing jihadist columns.

ISIS released a statement on May 27 titled "The Ancient City of Tadmor" (Tadmor being the Arabic name for Palmyra), which also had ten photographs showing the area in perfect condition. In fact, ISIS seemed to have wanted the world to genuinely believe that it had no malign intentions on razing thousands of years of archaeological splendors. In a ninety-second video clip, released on the ISIS "auxiliary" Amaq news agency, the ruins of Palmyra were shown unscathed. Abu Leith, the ISIS commander for the city, spoke to a local Syrian opposition radio station and declared: "Concerning the historical city, we will preserve it and it will not undergo damages [God willing], but what we will do is to pulverize statues that the miscreants used to pray for. As for the historical monuments, we will not touch it with our bulldozers as some tend to believe." The statues here referred to any "pagan" or "idolatrous" art, the presumption being that any colonnades absent graven images of pre-Islamic deities would be spared. Abu Leith also claimed Tadmor prison was virtually empty, but among the prisoners who were there, he said ominously, were "non-Syrian Christians that will convert to Islam."

On June 23, ISIS blew up the tomb of Mohammed bin Ali, a descendant of Muhammad's cousin and considered by the Shia to have been a saint. At the same time, it also laid and detonated mines around the five-hundred-year-old Shrine of Abu Behaeddine, a Sufi religious scholar, completely annihilating the structure. As for other objects of "miscreant" worship, here ISIS also made good on Abu Leith's vow. On August 24 it blew up the Temples of Baalshamin and Bel, both dating back about two thousand years, and exhibited a video in which children shot twenty-five regime soldiers in the back of the head in the center of the city's Roman theater.

Khalid al-Asaad, an archaeologist then in his eighties, who when he retired in 2003 had been head of antiquities for the ancient city for more than forty years, helped evacuate not only the people but also the relics in Palmyra's famed museum. It is unclear whether he was arrested by ISIS when they first took over the city, as some reports say, but al-Asaad was confirmed as being in the jihadists' custody as of July. They spent a month interrogating him about the locations of these ancient treasures—information, it seems, al-Asaad refused to give up. So in August, masked ISIS executioners dragged him into a public square and beheaded the octogenarian with a sword. They then strung al-Asaad's body up on a set of traffic lights with a sign attached to it declaring him an "apostate." His various offenses to the caliphate were also listed: "the director of idolatry," who had represented Syria at "infidel conferences," visited Iran, and maintained contact with a brother in the regime's security services.

Shortly after ISIS had Palmyra under complete control, it commandeered numerous gas facilities in the surrounding deserts, which were responsible for producing most of Syria's electricity. In total, the group took over 45 percent of Syria's electricity-producing infrastructure, intensifying the trend whereby the nation's energy sector became, in effect, a partnership between ISIS and al-Assad. Requiring know-how that they lacked, the jihadists simply left the regime's technicians in place and, for additional money or in-kind payments, agreed to continue to supply Damascus with power.

By October 2015, with ISIS in control of three hydroelectric facilities, Syria's largest gas plant, and at least four other power plants, the regime was, by one estimate, buying approximately 40 percent of ISIS's oil output. Some of the few areas where ISIS and the regime fought, paradoxically, were around these same power plants. As one Syrian energy executive explained: "This is 1920s Chicago mafia-style negotiation. You kill and fight to influence the deal, but the deal doesn't end."

ISIS IN DAMASCUS

The sacking of Palmyra also gave the army of terror a valuable point of ingress for another, albeit smaller, foothold in central Syria: the town of al-Qaryatain. Located in Homs province, and roughly equidistant from Palmyra as it is from Damascus, al-Qaryatain is, or was, residence to an estimated forty thousand inhabitants, many of them internally displaced from other parts of Syria. An unknown number of these had already fled by the time the jihadists arrived in early August 2015. Another 230 inhabitants, including thirty Assyrian Christians, were not so lucky. They were taken as hostages, while hundreds of other Assyrian families sought refuge in the neighboring town of Sadad.

Where Ramadi gave ISIS a launchpad for waging attacks on Baghdad, al-Qaryatain served a similar function for Syria's capital. Its fall also represented something of a hinge moment for an organization that had hitherto failed to establish a significant perch in southern Syria, owing largely to the preemptive action taken by other rebel groups in the area as well as al-Nusra.

ISIS espionage and infiltration hasn't worked as well in southern Syria as it has in the north, for a variety of reasons. Primarily, rival armed groups are more smartly integrated into the local populations of Deraa and eastern Quneitra (the westernmost part of that province having fallen under Israeli occupation following the 1967 Six-Day War) and enjoy a far better reputation than that of their counterparts in Idlib and Aleppo. Secondarily, opposite Syria's southern border are two countries, Israel and Jordan, that, unlike Turkey, consider Islamists an immediate threat to their national security. Israel has long acted as an ambulance corps and triage center for Syria's southern rebels and has reportedly even dispensed light arms (Kalashnikovs and rocket-propelled grenades) to certain factions in exchange for battlefield intelligence.

As one would expect, there has been a great deal of conspiracy-mongering about this relationship, much of it emanating from Damascus, but the reality is straightforward. The Israelis see the Free Syrian Army as a low-cost buffer against both al-Assad's forces, Iran's Revolutionary Guards, Hezbollah (which are now supervising those forces' activities and embedding with Shia and Alawite proxies in southern Syria), and Sunni jihadists. The Israelis also seek to protect the indigenous and influential Druze community in the Golan Heights. In the case of Jordan, the patronage is more coordinated and complicated, having arrived by way of a joint spook task force: US, European, and regional intelligence services, working alongside the Jordanian Mukhabarat at the so-called Military Operations Command, a Syria-dedicated war room located in Amman.

The yield of this multilateral proxy-wrangling is known as the Southern Front, a collection of fifty-four nationalist rebel militias totaling some thirty-five thousand fighters, whose operational purview is in its very name (they fight in Deraa and southern Damascus). Their soldiers are made to subscribe to the norms and rules of modern warfare governing international humanitarian law, in exchange for which they receive bullets. But the Military Operations Command is no Afghan Services Bureau, and the stream of matériel is more of a trickle than a deluge. And its continued existence rests upon a rather unusual principle for proxy warfare: not winning. Issam El Rayyes, a spokesperson for the group, told one of the authors in August, just as ISIS had sacked al-Qaryatain, that for the most part, help has been modest but steady. "We don't get any weapons, just ammunition. And the condition for continuing to get anything is that we not try to advance on Damascus." The reason for this is twofold: Washington's reluctance to see the al-Assad regime fall for fear that ISIS would be the main beneficiary of the ensuing chaos and Jordan's national security interest to see Syrian insurgents keep jihadists well away from its border and not dilute their garrisons by fanning out across the country. For all that, the Southern Front had remarkable success against the regime in the spring of 2015, but a much-heralded plan to sack Deraa City, the capital of the province, alongside Islamist groups, including al-Nusra, came to dust in June. The Southern Front then began parroting Washington's line about a negotiated "political solution" for Syria, albeit without al-Assad taking any part in the transition of the country's governance. "As much as we are strong on the ground, we are [also] able to achieve positive results on the debating table," Brigadier General Fayez Mjareesh told pro-opposition outlet

All4Syria in September 2015. As of January 2016, the Southern Front was apparently being ordered by the Military Operations Command to redirect its focus away from al-Assad and against al-Nusra, its former ally in the abortive Deraa siege, as Washington has begun to realize that ISIS isn't the only jihadist enterprise that requires degradation and destruction in Syria.

Adding to the difficulty of this policy pivot is the fact that ISIS has been largely kept out of central Damascus by insurgent groups the United States wants nothing to do with: namely, Jaysh al-Islam, or the Islamic Army, and al-Nusra, both of which have systematically attacked anyone suspected of creeping takfiri sympathies. Al-Baghdadi's split from al-Zawahiri's brand in 2014 put paid, albeit temporarily, to ISIS's plan for territorial expansion and ideological supremacy in the Syrian capital.

In 2013, the organization had been able to found a military training camp named for al-Zarqawi in Ghouta, site of the regime's sarin gas attack that year, as well as a second camp for child soldiers. But after Syria's brief sahwa, ISIS withdrew from the outlying districts of Damascus to better fortify its headquarters in Raqqa and its dug-in positions in Deir Ezzor. Its return to the capital region happened in 2014, and in characteristic fashion: its sleeper agents infiltrated and absorbed rebel groups, which ultimately pledged allegiance to al-Baghdadi. As analysts Aaron Zelin and Oula Rifai have noted, ISIS's "most important accomplishment during this period" was its takeover in April 2015 of al-Yarmouk Refugee Camp, home to some eighteen thousand Palestinian refugees. A reported one thousand ISIS militants routed two umbrella groups: the first led by the regime and backed by certain Palestinian proxies, the other led by the Islamic Army and backed by Free Syrian Army groups. Al-Nusra, which maintained a presence in the camp, stayed "neutral," although objectively it became an ally of ISIS. Together both jihadist outfits would at one point control 80 percent of al-Yarmouk. ISIS subsequently released video presenting itself as the upholder of the Palestinian cause, more honest and trustworthy than the corrupt Hamas and its subsidiaries. To better ensure that the refugees all saw it that way, ISIS did what it does best. As one camp resident told CNN, any rival militias within the camp's confines were "slaughtered . . . in the streets."

It was no coincidence that al-Yarmouk, which had been under a devastating regime siege for two years prior to the ISIS incursion, was a high-value target of the jihadists, who were "angling to isolate Damascus," as Zelin and Rifai note. Integral to this campaign was the interdiction of strategic road systems used both by the regime to resupply its forces in central Syria and by rebels to attack regime bases for the booty—something ISIS would have preferred to do. It followed its capture of al-Qaryatain with an (unsuccessful) attempt at a far more significant spoil, the T4 air base, a major regime weapons depot, where it proceeded to launch a series of suicide attacks. The closer ISIS inches toward al-Assad's seat of power, the more the regime seems willing to put up a fight and tear up the tenuous detente it had previously maintained with the jihadists. The regime has acquitted itself pathetically as an agent of counterterrorism whenever ISIS has contested a more remote military installation, a fact even remarked upon, as we've already noted, by Assad's loyalist Alawite constituency. Al-Qaryatain hit too close to home. Shortly after ISIS took it, Syrian helicopters began dropping barrel bombs on the town, this deadliest airborne munition having typically been reserved for Free Syrian Army or Islamist rebel groups or, as human rights monitors have found, Syrian civilians.

THE TRAIN-AND-EQUIP DEBACLE

Speaking at West Point in May 2014, President Obama announced what would constitute the main plank of his ground strategy for containing ISIS in Syria. As opposed to an earlier, somewhat successful covert program of arming Syria's rebels through the CIA, now the Pentagon would take charge of creating the New Syrian Forces, a small army of counterterrorism proxies who would be tasked with fighting ISIS, and only ISIS. Known colloquially in the defense establishment as "train-and-equip," the program came with a $500 million price tag and set out to produce as many as five thousand ISIS-slayers each year for the next three years. The training was to take place in Turkey and Jordan, under the auspices of the US military. From its initial conception to its final epitaph, in October 2015, train-and-equip was an unmitigated disaster, one that cost American taxpayers $384 million.

The first graduating class of New Syrian Forces, consisting of fifty-four men, was dispatched into northern Syria from Turkey in mid-July 2015. Two weeks later, in apparent retaliation for a US air strike on one of its outposts, al-Nusra kidnapped ten of the fighters, putting a pause on the whole program. Weeks later, General Lloyd Austin, the head of US Central Command, sheepishly informed Congress that only "four or five" of the remainder were still left in the fight. In a well-reported postmortem on the Pentagon's folly,

McClatchy's Roy Gutman noted that the entire philosophy of repurposing anti-Assad militants into anti-ISIS ones was backward. Gutman quotes Ibrahim, the commander of the first NSF class, who says he repeatedly thought about quitting the program because his American sponsors seemed wholly removed from the raison d'être of the very pool of applicants they were recruiting. "Every day I had a meeting with [the American trainers]. I told them the whole idea is wrong. I said: 'We are Syrians. Our problem is with the regime. Help us to get rid of the regime.' The response was: 'You should not shoot a bullet against the regime.'"

In fact, New Syrian Forces recruits were asked to sign a pledge forswearing any intent to use their newfound martial skills or any US-provided gear to go after any al-Assad regime targets. They were only authorized to fight ISIS. But what would happen if, say, they came under fire from Syrian army forces or Hezbollah or an Iranian-built militia? Would the United States protect its own assets in that event?

Our own extensive reporting on train-and-equip throughout 2015, drawing on interviews with US military personnel and rebels acquainted with the program, has convinced us that the answer was a resounding "no." Yet this only partly accounts for why the whole thing collapsed in ignominy.

On September 22, 2015, the *Daily Beast* reported that Major Anais Ibrahim Obaid, more commonly known as Abu Zayd, was rumored to have defected from Division 30, one of the Free Syrian Army rebel units from which the Pentagon fielded New Syrian Forces applicants, to al-Nusra. This fresh folly was said to have occurred within hours of the deployment of the second graduating class of New Syrian Forces, again into northern Syria via Turkey. In fairness, there was little substantive proof to the scuttlebutt; al-Nusra, which had vigorously promoted the story, tweeted a photograph purportedly showing US matériel in its possession (in fact, the picture had been taken at Division 30's own base). Moreover, the Defense Department was adamant that all of its proxies and their hardware were accounted for, issuing a categorical press statement on September 23 that there was "no indication that any NSF fighters have defected to Al Nusra Front" and "all Coalition-issued weapons and equipment are under the positive control of NSF fighters." Abu Zayd, the Pentagon added, hadn't received training for the New Syrian Forces program.

So had al-Nusra concocted the whole thing to embarrass the United States?

Not quite. The Pentagon had been half-right. Abu Zayd didn't defect to al-Nusra; he just handed over millions of dollars in US equipment, including four-by-four pickup trucks with mounted machine guns, flak jackets, and M16 rifles to the terror network in exchange for safe passage through a part of Aleppo where, as he himself announced on Facebook, he planned to found a new rebel outfit neither beholden to nor backed by the Americans. This fact was established when one of the authors uncovered a video showing Abu Zayd surrounded by New Syrian Forces graduates. The video was apparently shot in Atareb, the Aleppo suburb where Abu Zayd had vanished a few days earlier, and it was unmistakably the New Syrian Forces fighters surrounded by US supplies, with Abu Zayd being deferred to as the clear man of authority.

But how did he come to command a group of New Syrian Forces rebels if he himself had never been part of the program? According to a US military officer who worked on train-and-equip, this was, bizarrely, standard operating procedure. Because the Pentagon was fielding counterterrorists from already established and active Free Syrian Army groups, who had developed loyalty to their brigade or battalion commanders. The military vetted but did not train those commanders, allowing them to continue to lead their men into battle— men who were trained by the United States and outfitted with US weaponry. "We don't train the senior leaders, just the tactical-level fighters," the military source told one of the authors. "But the leaders are vetted and coordinated with, so this isn't really a distinction with a difference. The commanders are definitely 'our guys' without being actual graduates of the training pipeline."

Within twenty-four hours of the Abu Zayd video being published by the *Daily Beast*, US Central Command issued a mea culpa. "In this particular instance," spokesman Air Force Colonel Patrick Ryder said, "the [vetted] commander leading the [US-trained] graduates self-reported to coalition forces that under threat from al-Nusra, they surrendered six trucks and some ammunition to a suspected al-Nusra Front intermediary to secure safe passage. We will look at what we can do to prevent such a situation in the future, but given the complexity of the battlefield it is not possible to eliminate all risk. We are using all means at our disposal to look into what exactly happened and determine the appropriate response."

Train-and-equip was shelved not long thereafter. According to McClatchy's Roy Gutman, quoting a separate Pentagon spokesman, Major Roger Cabiness, 180 Syrians in total graduated from the program. Of that number, 145 were still active, but only 95 were currently fighting in Syria. No one knows what happened to the other thirty-five graduates.

THE RUSSIAN INTERVENTION

In February 2015, Aleksandr Bortnikov, the director of Russia's Federal Security Service (FSB), traveled to Washington to attend a two-day conference
at the White House on "Countering Violent Extremism." Although the European Union and Canada had placed sanctions on Bortnikov for his role
in Russia's illegal invasion and annexation of Crimea the previous year, the
US government had conspicuously left him off its own sanctions regime, en-
abling the Kremlin to put what was, in effect, the head of its FBI at the head
of a delegation to a meeting about international terrorism. In his presentation, Bortnikov claimed that there were up to 1,700 Russian citizens fighting
with ISIS in Iraq, but many more from other former Soviet states. He urged
stronger efforts to prevent their departure from Russia but also their return
to Russia, and chastised the United States for its support of moderate Syrian
rebels. An irony of Bortnikov's comments was that as he was lambasting his
host government's role in exacerbating Syria's civil war, his own FSB was quietly acting as a consultant to ISIS's personnel department. Based on extensive
fieldwork in one village in the North Caucasus, Elena Milashina, a reporter
for *Novaya Gazeta*, one of the few independent newspapers left in Vladimir
Putin's Russia, found that the "Russian special services have controlled" the
flow of jihadists *into* Syria, where they have lately joined up not only with ISIS
but with other radical Islamist factions.

It may sound paradoxical—helping the sworn enemy of your client—but
the logic is actually straightforward: better the terrorists go abroad and fight
in Syria than blow things up in Russia. Penetrating and co-opting terrorism
also has a long, well-attested history in the annals of Russian intelligence back
to the nineteenth century, and has recurred at some key moments in recent
history, from the still-unsolved apartment bombings that killed hundreds in
Moscow in 1999 to the arrest and six-month detention of Ayman al-Zawahiri
in Dagestan three years earlier, a high-value prisoner who the FSB claimed it
didn't realize was the al-Qaeda number two.

Milashina made her case study the village of Novosasitili in Dagestan's Khasavyurt district. Since 2011, she reported, nearly one percent of the
total population of Novosasitili has gone to Syria—twenty-two out of 2,500
residents. Of that figure, five were killed and five have returned home. But
they didn't leave Russia, a difficult country to enter and exit, without outside
help. The FSB established a "green corridor" to allow them to migrate first to

Turkey, and then to Syria. (Russians, including those living in the North Caucasus, can catch any of the daily nonstop flights to Istanbul and visit Turkey without a visa.)

"I know someone who has been at war for 15 years," Akhyad Abdullaev, head of the village, told Milashina. "He fought in Chechnya, Afghanistan, Iraq, and now in Syria. He surely cannot live peacefully. If such people go off to war, it's no loss. In our village there is a person, a negotiator. He, together with the FSB, brought several leaders out of the underground and sent them off abroad on jihad. The underground resistance has been weakened, we're well off. They want to fight—let them fight, just not here."

Milashina next interviewed the "negotiator" Abdullaev mentioned. He told her of his role as an intermediary between the FSB and local militants in arranging the latter's departure to the Levant. In 2012, for instance, he helped arrange for a man known as the "emir of the northern sector"—a "very dangerous man," believed by the FSB to have been behind several terrorist bombings—to go to Turkey if he agreed to quit jihadism in Dagestan. The FSB gave the emir a passport and acted as his travel agent. The condition was that he'd deal exclusively with the FSB and not inform any of his confederates of his true sponsor. The emir has since been killed in Syria, but the "negotiator" insists that he'd subsequently brought another five militants to the FSB who benefited from the same quid pro quo arrangement. "This was in 2012," he told Milashina. "Just before the Syrian path opened up. More precisely, [the FSB] opened it."

So far the tactic of encouraging hijrah, or jihadist emigration, has appeared to help the Russian government pacify its decades-long insurgency in the North Caucasus. By all accounts, the result has been great for counterterrorism officials, who are now able to claim direct credit for seeing terrorist violence in the region halved since the Syria crisis kicked off. Tanya Lokshina, the Russia program director and a senior researcher at Human Rights Watch, told us that while she can neither confirm nor deny the allegations put forward in *Novaya Gazeta*, "[i]t is also evident that [Russian] law enforcement and security agencies are proud of the fact that the number of casualties in armed clashes between insurgent forces and security has declined very significantly by some fifty percent. Officials attribute it to the success of the government in fighting the insurgency; in reality, it seems the drop derives from the fact that all the aggressive, competent fighters are no longer fighting in Dagestan but are in Syria as part of ISIS."

Oleg Kalugin, a former KGB general who once headed Moscow's counterintelligence First Chief Directorate, said that not only is the *Novaya Gazeta* story plausible, it's likely. "I'm pretty sure that what has been reported did in fact happen," he told us, noting that Russian intelligence has a long, ignominious history of "pushing forward the more extremist elements and use their facilities to do the most damage to a local population." A former CIA operative who has liaised with the FSB in Central Asia agrees that sending violent religious zealots to foreign countries is an old tool of clandestine tradecraft. "It's perfectly conceivable that the FSB would take their most violent types and say, 'Yeah, you want your caliphate? Go set it up in Raqqa.' The Saudis did this in the eighties with the Afghans. It's sort of tried and true. We could do the same thing. Of course, we're not."

This was the strategy, after all, during the early '90s, when jihadist-warlords such as Shamil Basayev were co-opted by Russia's military intelligence in order to vitiate the secular or democratic Chechen movement. Basayev was a useful tool for the Kremlin—at least until the FSB (probably) assassinated him in 2006—because he wasn't really interested in secession from the Russian Federation; he wanted to establish an "emirate" in the Caucasus. His carnage accomplished two things at once: it cast a pall on the legitimate separatist struggle and offered a wag-the-dog national security justification for a scorched-earth Russian counterinsurgency, which did nothing short of leveling Grozny, the capital of Chechnya.

Added to the direct underwriting of ISIS recruitment, the Russian government has a tendency to coerce jihadists into joining up with an Islamic militancy through campaigns of harassment and intimidation. Suspects in the North Caucasus are put on Salafist watch lists, interrogated, photographed, and fingerprinted repeatedly. Some have to submit DNA samples. "All the ones I spoke to," Lokshina said, "say that once you're on the watch list, you no longer have a normal life. It's as if law enforcement and the security officials are trying to push them out into the forest." One man in his forties who didn't support violence, she remembered, was stopped in Dagestan and taken into custody by an official who asked him, "Hey, how come you're not in the woods yet? Your cousin is already with the insurgents, all these people you know are with them and yet how come you're not?"

If there is indeed a cynical FSB plot to push jihadists into ISIS, then Lokshina thinks it's occurring at the local rather than national level, as a way for field agents in the North Caucasus to impress their higher-ups back in Moscow with improved security quotas. "This is something members of the police force told me off the record: if you have ten people registered this month, then there is pressure for you to register twelve next month. It's all about numbers." Andrei Soldatov, a journalist specializing in the Russian security services, agrees. "To me, it looks like a desperate attempt in Dagestan where the FSB tried everything to support radical Islamists to try and pacify the situation," Soldatov said. "It doesn't look like a well-thought-out campaign to steer trouble away from the North Caucasus into Syria."

Regardless, trouble has been conveniently steered away from Russia—terrorist incidents have decreased fifty percent since the Syria crisis began—and into the Middle East, leaving many analysts to wonder at the ability of even well-known clerics under twenty-four-hour surveillance to slip the watchful eye of one of the successor organs of the KGB. Joanna Paraszczuk, a journalist with Radio Free Europe/Radio Liberty, covers the Russian contingent of ISIS fighters, whom she estimates to be in the "hundreds," not thousands, based on documentary evidence she has examined including videos and social media usage. "Many are youngish boys who get recruited in Russia or Dagestan and then go to Istanbul. Then they get taken to ISIS territory, usually Raqqa. Are they on watch lists? How'd they get passports to leave the country? Here's the weird thing: Some of the radical preachers from Dagestan are turning up in the 'caliphate,' too." One of these, Paraszczuk told us, is Nadir Abu Khalid, who was under house arrest in Dagestan but has suddenly "popped up" in Iraq with another insurgent called Abu Jihad, a close friend of Abu Umar al-Shishani, the ethnic Chechen field commander for ISIS in Aleppo. "What we have right now is a growing number of Dagestani preachers who are forming the core group of recruiters in Iraq."

In June 2015, some members of the Caucasus Emirate, the leading jihadist insurgency in Russia, pledged allegiance to ISIS, giving al-Baghdadi's army a nominal "province" in a major Eurasian country. Characteristically, ISIS has worried the cracks running throughout Russia's decades-old insurgency and, according to Geidar Dzhemal, chairman of the Islamic Committee of Russia, "We're talking about initiative groups that have taken a peculiar kind of 'franchise' with ISIS. Such people, who call themselves supporters of ISIS, can appear in Alaska or Florida. But their actions should not be ascribed to Raqqa or al-Baghdadi. . . . They say they are supporters of ISIS, because that's popular now. And then they take action. But to connect their actions with ISIS is entirely incorrect."

Nevertheless, the emergence of a pro-ISIS fief on Russian soil ought to be terrifying to Moscow. Except that it isn't. "Russia is very happy about this because it means that it can now blame the local insurgency on ISIS—'an international group created by the West'—rather than on local problems in the Caucasus," Paraszczuk said.

That the Kremlin sees in ISIS an opportunity for spreading disinformation was borne out in July 2015, when Chechnya's warlord "president," Ramzan Kadyrov, took to Instagram to claim that the organization was, in fact, an invention of "Western intelligence agencies. . . . Everyone knows that Abu Bakr al-Baghdadi is also fed by the USA CIA, and was recruited by Gen. David Petraeus during al-Baghdadi's time as a POW in Camp Bucca in Iraq." Kadyrov is in many ways the Russian government's id, and while many in the Kremlin hate him, Putin does not, having bestowed medal upon medal on his plenipotentiary in Grozny. Such conspiracy-mongering, needless to add, plays right into the hand of Suleimani's Quds Force and its array of Shia militias in Iraq, which already believe that ISIS is a sinister American plot to destabilize the Middle East, and prefer dealing with Moscow over Washington. The Popular Mobilization Units have threatened repeatedly to turn their guns on US military trainers of the Iraqi Security Forces, while Putin has been hailed in pro-Iranian media as a heroic leader and more reliable ally in the war against ISIS.

Also, the rumored enmity between Kadyrov and the Russian intelligence establishment is overblown, according to Soldatov, who insists that the FSB relies on the Chechen president for actionable intelligence as to the whereabouts and goings-on of Caucasian jihadists—including those who've run off to Syria. "All my contacts inside the FSB and Interior Ministry tell me that it's extremely difficult to penetrate militant groups. In the mid-2000s, they set up big detention centers in Chechnya to process as many Chechens as possible, to recruit them in prison and release them as informants. We had only a few real examples of successful penetration." The eventual killing of Basayev, Soldatov noted, was done by agents recruited by the FSB, which has spent the better part of ten years cultivating Russian Muslims abroad. "They had a diaspora of Circassians," he said, referring to a Russian ethnic group from the North Caucasus, "they used to try to make contact with Zarqawi. Well, the first thing they needed to start with was a list of those who trained and studied Islam abroad. But the FSB didn't have such a list. So this raised the profile of Kadyrov; he was able to use his connections inside Chechnya and among the diaspora to become indispensable to Moscow."

For other analysts, it beggars belief that the central Russian government is unaware of this dirty nexus between the regional officialdom and the state's most radical opponents. "The Russian government has several aims and they're mixed together and it's very difficult to say which one applies in any particular case," Paul Goble, an expert on Russia's ethnic minorities and a former adviser to both the US State Department and the CIA, told us. "First, the Russians are not idiots. They've thoroughly penetrated militant groups in the North Caucasus. These aren't 'controlled' by Moscow, but they're wholly penetrated. The easiest way to garner intelligence is to get these militants to go to Syria posing as freedom fighters. Second, Moscow is running out of money to buy off the North Caucasus and needs a new way to oppress the opposition there. Well, the best way to oppress it is to exile it. Better that they should be fighting the US-led coalition in Syria and Iraq than fighting Russian government in Dagestan or Ingushetia. It's like Victor Serge's *Comrade Tulayev*," Goble said, referring to the 1948 novel based on the assassination of a Stalinist official, Sergei Kirov, and the consequent dragnet of paranoiac purges that swept the Soviet Union. "Moscow comes up with a broad prescription and you get all sorts of people coming up with ways to implement it."

On June 21, 2015, Caucasian Knot, a regional news site covering human rights and terrorist attacks, claimed that a video had appeared on YouTube showing militants from four regional divisions, including Chechnya, Ingushetia, Kabardino-Balkaria, and Karachai (the areas had made up the Caucasus Emirate), pledging allegiance to al-Baghdadi. Caucasian Knot questioned the authenticity of the allegiance and regional experts have suggested that, as with al-Shishani's Army of Emigrants and Partisans, there is a cleavage taking place within the ranks of the Caucasus Emirate, with some fighters wanting to join ISIS, while others seek to remain independent of the organization.

Whatever the case, ISIS took direct responsibility for two attacks in Dagestan, the first on September 2, 2015, in Magaramkent, and the second in Derbent, where a border guard was killed. Local residents never confirmed an attack in Magaramkent and regional experts have hotly disputed whether or not ISIS, as such, is even capable of one attack in the North Caucasus. Akhmet Yarlykapov of the Russian Academy of Sciences' Institute of Ethnology and Anthropology told Caucasian Knot: "Today in the North Caucasus, the most capable of battle are the members of ISIS. Meanwhile, the Caucasus Emirate is so weakened that it no longer exists as a unified whole."

A little less than a month later, Putin went to war in Syria. The Russian president had told Charlie Rose in an interview that aired September 27, 2015, as the UN General Assembly in New York opened, that "sixty percent of the territory in Syria [is] controlled by either ISIS or by others . . . such as al-Nusra and other terrorist organizations," recognized as such by "the United States, by other states and by the United Nations." Except that Russian bombers, which began their raids three days later, would expend the majority of their payloads bombing not ISIS or al-Nusra or US-designated terrorist entities but rather US-*backed* units of the Free Syrian Army, and scores of Syrian civilians.

In the first forty-eight hours of its war, the Russian Air Force targeted al-Lataminah in northern Hama three times, hitting the Free Syrian Army's Tajammu al-Aaza, or the Coalition for Dignity, a rebel group backed by the CIA and a rare recipient of US-provided TOW antitank missiles. "The attack [on September 30] targeted the main headquarters of Tajammu al-Aaza," Major Jamil al-Saleh, once a defector from the Syrian Arab Army and now the commander of the rebel brigade, told us just after the bombing raid had ceased. "There were two air strikes yesterday, then two more last night, and two this morning. So far, we have fourteen wounded fighters but no fatalities." Al-Saleh added that four Russian aircraft flew in formation and conducted five circular sweeps over northern Hama before striking. "We thought these were drones at first, because drones have been hovering over the area for a week now," he said. "There was actually one drone ahead of the jets, which we knew were Russian because they were white and flying at higher altitudes than the regime's planes."

"We have been fighting for four years in north Hama," he said, "and there is nothing called Daesh or ISIS in this area. The closest ISIS position from us is one hundred kilometers."

These rebel claims were seemingly corroborated by the US military. "We don't believe that [Russia] struck [ISIS] targets. So that is a problem," Colonel Steve Warren, the Pentagon spokesman for the coalition, said on October 1.

Nor did the trend dissipate. A week later, on October 7, 2015, Russian jets rocketed an ammunition storehouse, destroying artillery, armored personnel carriers, and even tanks belonging to Liwa Suqour al-Jabal, or the Mountain Eagles, a CIA-armed rebel brigade. A video uploaded to YouTube shows the burning wreckage of the Russian air strike, in Mansoura, in the western suburbs of Aleppo, as the local commander of the Mountain Eagles, known as Abu Mohammed, taunted a newly blatant enemy in the five-year-old conflict: "Thank God, we are all fine. We don't fear Russia or anyone helping the Russians. Bashar, we will remain resistant fighting you even without any ammunition or bullets. We will fight you with knives. We don't need ammunition, Allahu Akbar." The cameraman then adds that the Russians weren't the only ones hitting the brigade yesterday. "The Russian airplanes are targeting Suqour al-Jabal's weapon depots in Aleppo and ISIS attacked the bases with explosives at the same time."

The Mountain Eagles are led by Hasan Hagali, a former captain in the Syrian Arab Army. He explained to us via Skype that one of his bases in Mansoura, the brigade's main weapons depot, was hit in two consecutive Russian air raids. "At the same exact time—5:30 p.m.—ISIS sent a car bomb against us in Deir Jemal, against our base. This is about one hundred thirty kilometers away from Mansoura." An earlier ISIS attack against a Mountain Eagles frontline position, Hagali added, occurred in Ehres, also in western Aleppo, at around three o'clock. But ISIS locations in the province, no doubt equally visible from the air, were left unscathed by the same bombers.

In the first week of Putin's war in Syria, less than ten percent of all Russian missiles (and shipborne cruise missiles) were said to have struck ISIS or al-Qaeda–affiliated targets, according to the US State Department. In actual fact, as American intelligence officials would go on to tell various news outlets, Moscow's air war was objectively *helping* ISIS by vitiating its nemesis—the Free Syrian Army. The proof of this proposition came quickly, when ISIS sacked six villages in the Aleppo countryside held by the rebels, who had kept them out of jihadists' reach for more than a year but could no longer do so under round-the-clock Russian bombardment. Putin's adventurism, then, wasn't counterterrorist in nature at all—it was designed and implemented to fortify a teetering client regime, help it regain lost territory, and above all eliminate any credible threat to its legitimacy or longevity, a threat ISIS did not pose but other opponents of al-Assad did.

It was also meant to telegraph the return of Russian hard power and hegemony in the Middle East. The Kremlin had poured $52 billion of its state budget into the military in 2015, and, ever since helping to secure a (never fully satisfied) chemical disarmament program for Syria, Putin had promoted himself as the go-to interlocutor for solving diplomatic crises after a turbulent and bloody Arab Spring. Here, at last, was a trustworthy and reliable ally to have against the fickle and foolhardy United States, which scuttled decades-old partners—such as then-Egyptian president Hosni Mubarak—for a phantom concept called "democracy." What, Putin would ask in the lead-up to his intervention, has US foreign policy brought the region but chaos and terror, from Iraq to Libya? The Obama administration's touted "pivot" to Asia—and implicitly away from the turbulent Middle East—also offered an enticing opportunity for another great power to swoop in as guarantor of stability, making Moscow if not the primus inter pares than a necessary cosigner on all internationally brokered business in the neighborhood. Going to war in Syria had already given Putin a new forward operating base and airfield in Latakia, adding to Russia's longtime warm-water port (really more of a naval service facility) at Tartous. As many as four thousand Russian military and support personnel were also stationed in-country, including some of the elite marines and airborne troops who had seized Crimea in 2014.

As a dramatic demonstration of its renascent role in the region, Russia fired long-distance cruise missiles from naval vessels in the Caspian Sea that sailed across Iranian, Iraqi, and Syrian airspace, hitting indeterminate targets in eastern Raqqa (where ISIS is present) but also in western Aleppo and Idlib (where ISIS is not). Footage of these strikes, accompanied by swishy computer-generated simulations of their flight paths, were disseminated almost in real time throughout Russia's state-controlled propaganda organs, including the English-language Russia Today. The missile strikes at unknown targets were meant to project "strength and power," according to Lilia Shevtsova, a nonresident fellow and Russia expert at the Brookings Institution. "The Kremlin's adventure has both psychological and systemic dimensions," she said. "On the one hand, this is an act of blackmail against the West—Putin's way of trying to force the Americans to accept the Kremlin's rules of the game. On the other hand, it's a desperate attempt to reproduce the military patriotic legitimacy of the Russian government. But erasing terrorists? Come on!"

Jeffrey White, a military specialist at the Washington Institute for Near East Policy, said that while he did not doubt that the Russians would eventually set their sights on ISIS, for the time being it behooved Moscow to indirectly allow ISIS to devour US-armed rebels to make this dichotomy a fait accompli. The Russians, White added, have strategic form here. "We had the classic case of the destruction of the Polish Army in 1944. As the Soviets approached Warsaw, they stopped and let the Germans crush the Polish rebellion. The Red Army did nothing to help the Poles. But then they chased Germans out of Poland. It's possible that a similar plan is unfolding in Syria."

By the end of October, its first month at war in Syria, Russia's air force had struck at non-ISIS targets 80 percent of the time, according to an independent

Reuters investigation. As events wore on, Russian helicopter gunships and artillery would train their sights on ISIS targets whenever the jihadists threatened al-Assad installations, such in the north of Damascus or at Kuweires air base in Aleppo province, the site of a year-long ISIS siege that was broken only by Russian airpower and extra injections of Iranian and Iranian-backed manpower, devised and led by Qassem Suleimani. (It was the Quds Force commander, in fact, who prevailed upon the Kremlin in secret trips to Moscow—all of which violated a UN-imposed travel ban on Suleimani—to go to war on behalf of al-Assad.) That said, any engagement with ISIS is far outweighed by a continued focus on the mainstream armed opposition in areas where the jihadists have no presence, or any extremely minimal one, such as Idlib, Deraa, Hama, and Homs. The sortie trend lines that emerged in October continue to the present day, according to Hugo Spaulding of the Institute for the Study of War, with the proportions having changed only "marginally." In some cases, as Spaulding points out, Moscow has *invented* nonexistent jihadist groups, such as the wondrously named "Sham Taliban," said to populate Syria's coastal region, to justify its merciless campaign against the rebels. As of January 2016, well after both the Russian airliner bombing in Sinai and the attacks in Paris, when the Kremlin's bloodlust for ISIS was said to have been at record highs, a US official would tell Reuters that Russia was hitting ISIS targets only 30 percent of the time. In the same issue of *Dabiq* in which the jihadists explained how they took down the Metrojet Flight 9268 with a smuggled-aboard improvised explosive device, they mocked Moscow for going after everyone but them. "The drunken brown bear—Russia—savagely but clumsily strikes here and there in a manner that has even confused American analysts, think tanks, intelligence, and policy-makers," *Dabiq* read. "And while it is at war with its Western rivals in the Ukraine, it has decided to enter into yet another conflict with the West, by targeting the Sahwah allies of America in Sham."

One of the closest observers of Russia's intervention in Syria is the website Bellingcat. Made up of citizen journalists who use open-source information to analyze the forensics of modern warfare, the site has been lauded by NGOs, governments, and human rights monitors for its objectivity and methodological rigor. Its founder, Eliot Higgins, was one of the first analysts to locate and identify Croatian-supplied weapons in the hands of Syrian rebels in 2013. He maintains that the Russian government is flat-out lying about the purpose and scale of its campaign in the Levant. "By examining Russian Ministry of

Defense airstrike videos posted on their own YouTube channel it was possible to establish the majority of videos were described using false information," Higgins explained. "In all cases the videos were described with the incorrect location, or claiming strikes on ISIS in areas where there was known to be no ISIS presence, or both. In at least one case two videos showed the same location being bombed, but was described as showing two entirely different locations." Eventually, the Defense Ministry realized its disinformation was being swiftly debunked, so it altered its approach. Videos began to be uploaded with less precise locations. "For example, instead of videos being described as being near a town they were now described as being in a province of Syria. Instead of ISIS being described as the targets videos now describe militants or terrorists as the targets. It was still clear that the majority of videos were not in ISIS controlled territory, even based on the ministry's own maps of what was controlled by ISIS in Syria." A mere 7.5 percent of documented Russian air strikes hit areas known to be controlled by ISIS, Bellingcat has found.

The Russian government was accidentally providing evidence of its own war crimes. Videos purportedly showing ISIS oil facilities being bombed were, upon closer inspection, of grain silos or water treatment plants. Hospitals and marketplaces are also frequent targets. This is especially the case in Aleppo City, where ISIS has no discernible footprint.

SECOND CITY, PRIMARY TARGET

"When I'm sitting here and we hear a plane, which is a lot now, I know from the sound. If the plane is above us—you can tell if it's above you, because that's when it's the loudest—and if it's a Russian plane, then it doesn't attack where we are. It attacks two or three kilometers away."

Rami Jarrah was describing for us how he distinguishes which government is now bombing civilians in Syria's Aleppo City. It's a question that used to answer itself—but no more, given the presence of Syrian, Russian, and coalition aircraft in the skies. Syrian jets, he says, once flew so low that you could actually see the pilots in the cockpits; Russian fixed-wing aircraft fly at much higher altitudes such that they look like crosses or plus signs in the clouds. They fire from far away, the better to evade the bullets of the Dushka (the name means "sweetie" in Russian), a Soviet-era antiaircraft machine gun, which is typically all anti-Assad rebels have to deter helicopters and attack jets, sometimes successfully.

Jarrah lives in the war-ravaged provincial capital of Syria's industrial province, documenting the gruesomeness of multisided civil war for his open-source newsgathering service, ANA Press. Born in Cyprus and educated in London, he first became famous in 2011 as an English-speaking eyewitness on Western TV channels to what was then still a peaceful protest movement against a Baathist dictatorship. He used to call himself Alexander Page, a pseudonym he doesn't need anymore because what good is a pseudonym against one of Putin's jets?

In the last five years, he has moved in and out of Syria. He returned to what had once been the country's largest city and took an apartment there, very close to the front line between the pro-Assad forces and anti-Assad rebels. "Two hundred meters from where I am right now are regime soldiers." For that reason, he added, Aleppo's children are now being educated in apartments on the front lines, because their open-air schools have been bombed by Russia. In these makeshift academies, the primary fear is "elephant bombs," the regime's "locally made" ground-to-ground missiles (so called because they sound like an elephant's trunk-blow when they're launched), which can hit sixty or seventy times a day.

Jarrah returned to Aleppo two months ago because he wanted to see for himself what the Russian intervention was really like. Were his fellow countrymen lying about the scale of devastation now being unleashed, with civilian death tolls starting to exceed those of the regime? Moscow maintains that it is going after ISIS and other "terrorists"—not fruit carts, bakeries, and hospitals. The Russian Defense Ministry has yet to claim responsibility for any civilian casualties and often denies striking in civilian-heavy locations that evidence suggests they have in fact struck. But the claims of Russian collateral damage, Jarrah told us, are "absolutely true. Russia is killing civilians and waging an information war. I want every single person on this planet to know that, whether they [the Russians] admit it or not."

Other observers of the conflict agree. According to the Syrian Network for Human Rights, 570 civilians were killed in Russian air strikes between September 30, 2015, the first day those air strikes began, and December 1. Human Rights Watch has documented Russia's use of cluster bombs, violating United Nations Security Council Resolution 2139, which Moscow helped to pass, calling for an end to "indiscriminate employment of weapons in populated areas." And in a twenty-eight-page report released in December 2015, Amnesty International claimed to have examined six separate Russian air strikes—and confirmed the deaths of 132 noncombatants. "Some Russian air strikes appear to have directly attacked civilians or civilian objects by striking residential areas with no evident military target and even medical facilities, resulting in deaths and injuries to civilians," according to Philip Luther, director of Amnesty's Middle East and North Africa Programme. In response, Russia's Defense Ministry demanded to know the identities of the NGO's on-the-ground sources, or else, it threatened, the ministry will attempt to out them itself.

On December 15, Russian warplanes bombed Mash'had market in an area called Saif al-Dawla, a central marketplace in Aleppo. "Ten meters to the right and the missile would have landed inside the market, killing two hundred or three hundred people," Jarrah said. "The attacks are not that precise." At first, he was puzzled why the Russians would risk killing so many people. Then he remembered the kill logic of the Assad regime in the early days of the revolution.

"Shoot one person in a protest," Jarrah told us, "and he runs away. Then the next day, more come. Then you have to shoot five people to make the same point. The Russians want to kill a lot of people at once so they don't have to kill even more later. The marketplace, it's like the veins of the city. If you open the veins, you bleed the city."

Within a month, Russian air strikes in Aleppo province had directly displaced 35,000 people, and indirectly displaced more than 100,000 by providing air cover for regime offensives in other provinces. But so far, there has been no conspicuous hemorrhage of civilians from Aleppo City because the inhabitants don't want to leave, according to Jarrah. This isn't because they're patriots or defiant in the face of a brutal onslaught but because most of them are already internally displaced, refugees from other cities and towns and villages of Syria who have come to occupy abandoned apartments and set up stalls using the resources that had never before been available to them. Jarrah reckons that, apart from Aleppo's historic Old City, where longtime residents still remain, in the "modern" districts only about 20 percent of the current population is native. "The rest are Syria's poorest. If they leave, they'll have nowhere else to go."

18

"WE WILL CONQUER YOUR ROME"

A YEAR OF ISIS TERRORISM

On January 6, 2015, a woman in a niqab walked into a tourism police station in Sultan Ahmet Square, a heavily trafficked district of Istanbul home to the celebrated Blue Mosque and Hagia Sophia museum. Speaking English with a "thick accent," the woman told the on-duty officers she had lost her wallet, a ruse maintained just long enough for her to detonate a bomb she'd been carrying. The resulting blast mortally wounded one police officer and injured another. The attacker, Diana Ramazov, who had two hand grenades in her possession, was dead by her own hand.

An eighteen-year-old woman who held Russian citizenship, Ramazov was two months pregnant at the time and a recent émigré to Turkey. She entered the country, as was later learned, in May 2014 and shortly thereafter married a man named Abu Aluevitsj Edelbijev, a Norwegian citizen of Chechen origin, whom she had met in an online forum. There is no state record of Edelbijev's entry into Turkey, which means he probably entered the country illegally. After a three-month "honeymoon period" in Istanbul, the couple relocated to Syria and joined ISIS. Whether their marriage took place in Istanbul or the caliphate is not exactly clear, but the speed of Ramazov's transformation shocked those who knew her. She went from being a normal Russian teenager who wore miniskirts to being a conservative Muslim in a headscarf, friends and relatives would later remember. Edelbijev was already known to Norwegian Police Security Services, which opened a public criminal investigation into his activities in October 2014, having issued an Interpol Red Notice for his arrest in secret in July 2014. The investigation and international warrant were rendered moot by his death in December 2014. Edelbijev was killed fighting for ISIS in Syria. Whether he prompted Ramazov to become a "black widow," as female Russian suicide bombers are known, or she took the decision herself is unclear.

2015 would be the year that ISIS metamorphosed from a "terrorist organization that runs a state . . . [to] a state that sponsors terrorism," in the words of Richard Barrett, a former British diplomat and intelligence officer. He was writing a month after the choreographed nine-man massacres carried out on November 12 in the streets of Paris, a transformative event in the popular imagination. Far from the "jayvee team" of President Obama's description, and now no longer a guerrilla insurgency dedicated to superimposing its "state" across the Levant and Mesopotamia, ISIS had made good on one of its promises, to bring the war on terror back home to the West. On January 7, 2015, a day after Ramazov blew herself up in Istanbul, Amedy Coulibaly shot and wounded a jogger in Fontenay-aux-Roses area southwest of Paris, and planted a car bomb, which failed to explode, in the Parisian suburb of Villejuif. On January 8, Coulibaly would lethally shoot a policewoman in Montrouge, before butchering five patrons of the Hypercacher kosher market in the same city on January 9. ISIS would claim Coulibaly as one of their own cultivated martyrs after it was revealed that his widow, Umm Basir al-Muhajirah, was already back in Syria to write her dead husband's legend in the pages of *Dabiq* as an example for all would-be mujahidin living in the Lands of Disbelievers to emulate.

Months earlier, before the first US air strikes began in Syria, in support of the People's Defense Units at the siege of Kobane, ISIS spokesman Abu Mohammed al-Adnani had issued a kind of draft notice for an invisible army of mujahidin, instructing them to strike at the disbelievers without leaving their hometowns and risking the fraught journey into caliphate country. "If you are not able to find an IED or a bullet, then single out the disbelieving American, Frenchman, or any of their allies," he'd said in a communiqué released on September 21, 2014. "Smash his head with a rock, or slaughter him with a knife, or run him over with your car, or throw him down from a high place, or choke him, or poison him."

Al-Adnani would bring Diyala to the kuffar, in do-it-yourself fashion. Sure, ISIS high command would still plan and facilitate complex and multifaceted operations, but it no longer needed trained-up operatives to inflict the maximum amount of pain on its enemies. Anyone with Internet access could imbibe ISIS propaganda in his native tongue, then shoot up his place of work, or a naval recruitment center, or a cop parked at a stoplight, without even being known by name to the organization on whose behalf he murdered. ISIS was mobilizing an invisible army of jihadists to wage total war against everyone, the better to ultimately conquer the world in advance of ending it.

As ever, there was temporal cunning to this apocalyptic endgame. As al-Adnani surely knew, egging on Muslims to kill citizens of liberal democracies—particularly those in Europe, where a Syria-loosed refugee crisis was now shaping domestic politics on the basis of Muslim immigration—would grant ISIS a protest vote in all forthcoming European elections, possibly destabilizing the very governments that were waging war against ISIS thousands of miles away. The terror organization's us-or-them worldview dovetailed perfectly, for instance, with the bigoted, demagogic platforms espoused by onetime outlier, now increasingly mainstream, political currents wafting throughout the continent. There was neofascist Le Front National, which called for an end to all Muslim immigration in France; Jobbik, which now has trouble deciding whether its foremost civilizational menace is the Jews or the Muslims; UKIP, which resorts to more dog-whistle politics but nonetheless wants Britain's borders sealed and London to withdraw from a European Union; Pegida, which leaves no mystery as to its ambitions in Germany because its very name stands for Patriotic Europeans Against the Islamization of the Occident. If any or all of these groups rose in membership or at the polls on the back of ISIS-concocted or "inspired" attacks, Sunnis would be persuaded that their only salvation rested with the armies of Abu Bakr al-Baghdadi.

ISIS'S ANTI-KURD STRATEGY

Ramazov's suicide bombing in January 2015 may have been the first in a series of ISIS terror attacks in Turkey throughout that year, but it was an aberration in terms of its designated target. Turkey would suffer four subsequent bombings in 2015, all linked to the sprawling terror syndicate located just opposite its southern border, which ISIS used as a sieve. All four would all target in some way Turkey's Kurdish community, prompting allegations by opponents of the ruling Justice and Development Party (AKP) that the government had actually staged these attacks as false flags, or at the very least turned a blind eye to their execution. AKP, after all, had been funneling arms and matériel to any number of Islamist rebel groups fighting the al-Assad regime in Syria, whose overthrow had become a signal foreign policy goal of President Recep Tayyip Erdogan. Moreover, the government was now embroiled in collapsing peace negotiations with a forty-year-old domestic guerrilla insurgency, the Kurdish Workers Party (PKK), whose cross-border affiliate was running by far the most successful anti-ISIS ground campaign in northern Syria and, in the process, carving out a de facto statelet for itself, much to Ankara's consternation.

ISIS's leadership was aware of the well-publicized dynamics and antagonisms of Turkish politics, and also savvy to Kurdish ambitions to found an independent state in northern Syria. It also had every strategic reason to batter and bloody affiliates of the PKK, on either side of the border, following the loss of Kobane. Untold numbers of ISIS sleeper agents were living and mixing not just in the borderland communities of Gaziantep and Antakya, where they would sometimes assassinate Syrian exiles opposed to ISIS rule in Raqqa, but also in international cities such as Ankara and Istanbul, to which Diana Ramazov had even hired a taxi to drive her the 1,250-mile distance from the Syrian border. As even the Obama administration had more than hinted in public statements, the Erdogan government viewed the PKK and PYD, now virtually unassailable American assets in Operation Inherent Resolve, as greater menaces than it did ISIS, causing a rift between the two NATO member states. ISIS wanted revenge for its series of humiliating defeats across hundreds of square miles of northern Syria and knew that the easiest way to destabilize Turkish politics was to murder Kurds deemed by ISIS to be godless Marxists. "Our war with Kurds is a religious war," al-Adnani had decreed in his September 21 message. "It is not a nationalistic war—we seek the refuge of Allah. We do not fight Kurds because they are Kurds. Rather we fight the disbelievers amongst them, the allies of the crusaders and Jews in their war against the Muslims." Such "disbelievers," as al-Adnani understood, would also turn their resentment inward, toward their own state, prompting a heavy-handed Turkish reaction.

On May 18, 2015, twin bombs ripped through two local headquarters of the People's Democratic Party (HDP), the leading left-wing Kurdish party affiliated with the PKK, in the cities of Adana and Mersin, both in southern Turkey. No one was killed, but six people were injured, and police later identified the bomber as Savas Yildiz, a thirty-two-year-old Turk who had joined a jihadist group in Syria in early 2014. Because of Yildiz's prior association with Marxist militants, Turkish prime minister Ahmet Davutoglu initially hinted that the attack had been a radical leftist plot, although Yildiz would later be named as one of four ISIS bombers-at-large in Turkey. He's now thought to have gone back to Syria.

On June 5, the jihadists struck again, this time at an HDP rally held just two days before a Turkish general election in which the party was expected to perform quite well. Two bombs went off minutes before HDP's charismatic cochairman, Selahattin Demirtas, seen within his constituency as something of a counterweight to Erdogan, was due to take the stage. Detonated within five minutes of each other, they killed two people instantly and injured more than a hundred, two of whom would later die at a nearby hospital. The rally was canceled, but many of HDP's youthful supporters remained at the site, protesting against the AKP government. Almost everybody instinctively fingered ISIS for the atrocity, but they leveled almost as much blame at the incumbent, who, they thought, was secretly in league with the terrorists. The crowd threw stones at Turkish police, who then turned water cannons on the stone throwers. While the bombs had initially been thought to be connected to nearby transformers—indeed, the immediate reaction of the authorities had been to blame the explosions on an electrical malfunction—it was soon established that the devices had consisted of two gas canisters packed with marbles and hidden in trash cans.

The follow-up attack came, again, a month after the last. On July 20, outside the Amara Culture Centre in the town of Suruc, in Urfa province, a suicide bomber detonated in a crowd gathered by two other Kurdish parties: the Marxist-Leninist Socialist Party of the Oppressed and the less radical Socialist Youth Associations Federation, which was formally headed by Figen Yuksekdag, the cochair of HDP with Demirtas. The federation had been known for sending pro-communist Turks into Syria to fight alongside the People's Defense Units. The activists, mostly university students, had been giving a press statement on their intention to travel into Syria to help with the reconstruction of Kobane, then just six months ISIS-free, when a twenty-year-old Turkish Kurd, Seyh Abdurrahman Alagoz, walked into their midst and blew himself up, massacring thirty-two people. Alagoz had joined ISIS in Syria around the time that Kobane was being recaptured, according to his family. His older brother followed him soon afterward. As al-Adnani had put it, "Muslim Kurds" were ISIS's "people and brothers wherever they may be. We spill our blood to save their blood. The Muslim Kurds in the ranks of the Islamic State are many. They are the toughest of fighters against the disbelievers amongst their people."

Making matters worse was how Erdogan's scorn was directed at the same constituency al-Adnani had just declared war against. Months before going into a hotly contested Turkish general election, on June 7, the president had rhetorically denigrated the Kurds and HDP in particular, because Demirtas's stated goal was to overcome the 10 percent legislative threshold and thereby block Erdogan's own overriding ambition to legally amend Turkey's constitution and transform the country from a parliamentary democracy into a presidential one (granting himself, naturally, more executive powers). An incendiary anti-Kurdish atmosphere had thus been created by both Turkey's head of state and the state of terror next door. All any one of the three main parties to this conflict had to do was light a match.

The Kurdish answer to the Amara bombing came the very next day, on July 21, when PKK militants shot and killed two Turkish police officers in a "revenge operation," accusing them—and the government as a whole—of "collaborating with Daesh." The policemen had been called to a car accident in Diyarbakir, a city in southeastern Turkey that doubles as the de facto Kurdish capital, when they were ambushed by gunmen. Two days later the PKK operatives shot a third policeman in the head in Diyarbakir, killing him, and injured another. Turkey next began escalating attacks on both ISIS and the PKK simultaneously. On July 23, its army exchanged fire with ISIS at the Syrian-Turkish border, resulting in the death of one Turkish soldier. (Unsubstantiated reports in the Turkish press also suggested at the time that another soldier may have been captured.) In the early morning of July 24, under a hard-argued agreement finalized between Erdogan and President Obama just hours before, Turkey's air force launched its first air strikes inside Syria, killing nine ISIS fighters and "completely destroy[ing]" three ISIS positions, according to Davutoglu.

The air strikes in Syria were accompanied by an arrest wave in Turkey, purportedly to round up the many ISIS networks and cells active throughout the country. If not quite a feint, then the massive dragnet had an ulterior motive because jihadists weren't the only, or even primary, targets. More than five thousand police officers in Istanbul raided 140 locations, the majority of them belonging to the PKK and a radical leftist group called the Revolutionary

People's Liberation Party/Front, both registered terrorist organizations by Turkey, the European Union, and the United States. Then a third round of air strikes on July 25 hit at PKK targets in northern Iraq, prompting diplomatic protests from Ankara's close commercial and political ally, the Kurdistan Regional Government, in Erbil.

The perceived focus on a secular insurgency over the world's most hated and feared Islamic fundamentalist one was taken as confirmation by Kurds that Ankara had indeed played some sinister role in the Suruc attack to give itself a casus belli for reactivating the war it preferred to fight—the one against the PKK. That the government had banned the publication of photographs and videos from the Amara Cultural Centre attack, and even temporarily blocked Twitter in the wake of the attack, only aided this perspective.

"For many Kurds in Turkey, the Justice and Development Party has become synonymous with ISIS," Aaron Stein, a senior resident fellow with the Rafik Hariri Center for the Middle East at the Washington, D.C.–based Atlantic Council, told us. "The belief that they support ISIS is widely felt, with both HDP cochairs, Demirtas and Yuksekdag, routinely accusing the government of working with the group to attack the PYD in northern Syria. ISIS, whether consciously or not, has helped to spark the PKK insurgency in southeast Turkey, a conflict that has claimed hundreds of lives, destroyed large areas in Turkey's Kurdish majority cities, and displaced over a hundred thousand people."

So ISIS might have left well enough alone, sat back, and watched as Turkish society devoured itself and a Muslim-majority US ally went to war with America's favored anti-ISIS proxy in Syria. But the jihadists were just getting warmed up.

On October 10, 2015, just after 10 a.m., two suicide bombers detonated, within seconds of each other, at a rally outside Ankara Central railway station, and within sight of the headquarters of the National Intelligence Organization, or MIT, the security organ in charge of Turkey's Syria file, including its clandestine arms network to rebel groups. One hundred and two people were massacred instantly and more than three hundred more badly injured. It was the worst terrorist attack in Turkey's modern history. The target could not have been better chosen.

The Labor, Peace, and Democracy rally, as it was called, was organized by four powerful Turkish trades unions and HDP, which acted as majordomo of the demonstration. The entire event was planned in opposition to the ongoing war against the PKK outside the country; it was also a call for Ankara to recognize and make an accommodation with the party. After the devastation, many Kurds again turned the bulk of their resentment and scorn against the government. Demirtas condemned the "barbaric attack" in the same breath as he reprehended "a state mentality which acts like a serial killer," apparently drawing a not-too-subtle correlation between the actions of ISIS and those of his own government.

The two suicide bombers in Ankara were identified as Omer Deniz Dundar and Yunus Emre Alagoz, the brother of Seyh, who perpetrated the Suruc massacre in July. The Alagoz brothers had run the Islam Tea House in Adiyaman City, an obvious ISIS front business in an area that the Turkish press had been reporting on for two years as a cynosure of radicalism and terrorist recruitment. Dundar had frequented the teahouse, as had Orhan Gonder, who allegedly rigged the charges in the explosives used in the pro-Kurdish rally back in June. Dundar was on a MIT list of twenty-one suspected suicide bombers; his own parents had beseeched the police to arrest him back in 2013 when he joined an Islamist faction. Instead, Dundar went to Syria, only returning after his father persuaded him to in 2014. "I went to the police countless times to try and get my son back from Syria," the father said. "I told the police, please take him and imprison him. They took his statement and then they let him go." It was when Dundar's parents succeeded in closing the Islam Tea House in late 2014 that Dundar and the Alagoz brothers returned to Syria. Their radicalization, evidently, quickened with the loss of Kobane.

Within a week, Turkey had arrested four people connected to the Ankara bombings. By December 18, 2015, it had officially concluded its largest investigation to date into ISIS activities on its soil, producing a 315-page indictment in which sixty-seven suspects were blacklisted. Of the three major ISIS operatives in Turkey named in reports of the indictment, two had already been apprehended: Halis Bayancuk, also known as Abu Hanzala, a young preacher based in Istanbul who was at least the "spiritual leader" of ISIS in Turkey, and Asaad Khelifalkhadr, or Abu Suhayf, a key provider of logistics, particularly false identity documents, and supplies to ISIS's foreign fighters as they arrive in Turkey before stealing across the border. (Khelifalkhadr was actually held on charges related to his fake-passport production rather than terrorism.) One man still at large, Ilyas Aydin, is considered the leader of the entire ISIS network in Turkey.

"If you follow Turkish ISIS social media long enough," Ilhan Tanir, a Washington, D.C.–based journalist with the Turkish newspaper *Cumhuriyet Daily*, told us, "you begin to realize that these hundreds, maybe thousands, of accounts—which appear to be managed by young radical Muslim Turks or Kurds—understand the nation's politics really well. ISIS members consistently and sharply criticize Turkish political leaders and security forces for being soft on the Kurds and the PKK, while they react angrily against the arrest of ISIS members. Their effort to re-spark a war between Erdogan and the PKK, which both sides seemed eager to do anyway since the summer of 2014, is not a far-fetched conclusion at all."

EUROPE'S 9/11

Many eyes in Europe were fixed on the television at 9:20 p.m. on Friday, November 13, 2015, just twenty minutes into a much-awaited soccer match between France and Germany, when the first loud noise, like a tractor-trailer backfiring, was heard outside the Stade de France, in Paris's Saint-Denis district. The game played on for another seventy minutes or so, through two more not-so-distant booms, and finished with much of the crowd still inside. By this point, there was a crescendoing murmur moving throughout the stands as news quickly spread that the three sounds, which were audible for the viewers of the game at home, had been explosions. The first suicide bombing had gone off early; then, within the space of about half an hour, two more ISIS operatives had self-immolated at the entrance to the stadium or several hundred yards away on a side road.

Seeking to murder as many of the eighty thousand spectators—and, if at all possible, French president François Hollande and German foreign minister Frank-Walter Steinmeier, who were in attendance—the attacks largely failed because none of the operatives could gain access to the Stade de France. So they detonated outside the venue. Apart from the three terrorists themselves, just one passerby was killed. And if this had been the single locus, and the biggest brunt of ISIS's carnage on French soil, we might not now be writing about it. But in between the first and last explosion, five separate *attentats*, some of them carried out by the same assailants, were being perpetrated all throughout the French capital. A timeline of events would later be compiled by the nation's public prosecutor, demonstrating the speed and scale with which the terrorists had unleashed hell in a world city.

At 9:25 p.m., on the terraces of the Le Carillon café-bar and the Petit Cambodge, a Cambodian restaurant, in the tenth arrondissement, gunmen shot to death fifteen people and badly wounded ten.

At 9:32 p.m., another shooting, this one front of the A La Bonne Bière bar in the eleventh arrondissement. Five dead, eight injured.

At 9:36, another restaurant terrace—that of La Belle Équipe—in rue de Charonne, in the same neighborhood, was covered under a hail of bullets. No one was killed, but nine were injured.

At 9:40, a suicide bomber blew himself up inside Le Comptoir Voltaire, a restaurant in the same district. One person was seriously hurt.

At the same time, a car was pulling up in front of the Bataclan concert hall, not far from Le Comptoir Voltaire, where an American rock band, Eagles of Death Metal, were playing to a full house. Three gunmen got out of their black Volkswagen Polo rental car, which had been idle not far from the Bataclan for a while, waiting for the right moment to proceed forward. Taking out Kalashnikovs, they first shot three people dead in front of the concert hall. Survivors of this initial assault actually fled *into* the Bataclan for safety, not realizing that that's exactly where the assailants were headed.

The French daily *Le Monde* later gave a precise account of what transpired next. Two shooters went to the pit orchestra and started mowing down concertgoers. The third man was waiting outside an emergency exit; when it was opened and people started pouring out, he opened fire on them, too:

> "The audience, which is now trapped in the area of the pit orchestra, is lying down on the floor pretending to be dead. 'I will shoot the first one who is moving, you will see' one of the attackers says after methodically shooting into the crowd. 'I told you not to move!'
>
> "Some of the hostage takers play with the hostages: 'Come on, the ones who want to leave, just go!' one of them says. Of course, all those who stood up got shot.
>
> "One survivor explains: 'The terrorists started again and other hostages stood up. Again, they shot at them. They were having fun. It made them laugh.'"

The shooters knew well who was playing that night, and must have also done a reconnaissance run on the Bataclan, whose security protocol did not include metal detectors. The shooters asked their victims where the "yanks" had gone, meaning the Eagles of Death Metal. "It's an American group, you are bombing together with the Americans, so we are now targeting you and the Americans," they said, according to witnesses. "Now you will see what the bombing in Iraq feels like. We are doing what you have been doing in Syria, listen to the people scream. It's what people in Syria are living through. You are killing our wives, our brothers, our children, we are doing the same, we are here to get you, we are not in Syria but we are acting here. You do this to us, we do this to you!"

Some in the audience managed to hide or escape the bloodbath. Eighty-nine weren't so lucky. They were killed in the single deadliest event of the evening. One witness, who hid in a tiny room in the theater, told reporters that when he finally emerged under police escort, he was told not to scan the aftermath, which he of course did. "There was blood everywhere. Even people alive were covered with blood," Denis Plaud said. "There was especially on the ground floor a lot of dead bodies and blood, and some people had been alive and had to stay for several hours among dead corpses and they went out covered with blood." Another witness, radio journalist Julien Pearce, told CNN that the assailants, all dressed in black but without any masks on, "were just standing at the back of the concert room and shooting at us. Like if we were birds." Many were shot execution-style by "very calm, very determined" shooters.

Just after 10 p.m., police, having raided the Bataclan, shot one of the terrorists, Samy Amimour. He fell to the floor, then lifted his head up slightly before activating his suicide belt. His head and one of his legs were blown onstage, and bits of his flesh into the hair of a concertgoer. His accomplices, Ismail Mostefai and Foued Mohamed Aggad, found this hilarious. "It made them laugh," the concertgoer told *Le Monde*. "I told myself that they were really retarded."

The reason it took so long for the Bataclan to be cleared, even after Amimour, Mostefai, and Aggad were dead, was that the French SWAT teams from the Brigade de Recherché et Intervention, or BRI, had to check each survivor in the theater to make sure they weren't rigged with explosives. They also uncovered the hiding places of those lucky enough, but still terrified, to have passed more than three hours in a miniature war zone and hung on to their lives. And Mostefai and Aggad had taken human shields and hidden behind a door. A hostage crisis ensued for more than an hour. One of the two gunmen gave their demand: "I want that you remove your armies. I want a paper and a signed paper that proves it, it is now [11:32]. If in five minutes I do not

have anything, at [11:37] I will kill a hostage and throw him out the window."
The French negotiators managed to distract Mostefai and Aggad long enough
shortly thereafter to allow the SWAT teams to storm the corridor where they
and their human shields were. None of the hostages were killed, but Aggad
was shot twice and detonated his belt, killing him and Mostefai.

All eight attentats combined to constitute France's worst terror attack, ever, and left 130 civilians dead. What we would later learn of the ten
operatives—one of whom evidently chickened out at the last minute—was
as infuriating as it was informative. Almost all fit what has by now become a
stereotypical European terrorist profile. Signs of radicalization observed, but
not necessarily reported by friends, family, and colleagues, over the course
of years. Alarming paeans to existing terrorist groups posted to social media
networks. As with Abu Aluevitsj Edelbijev, the Norwegian-Chechen jihadist
who was husband to Diana Ramazov, most of the suspects had been on various state watch lists before, or had rap sheets. On November 20, the French
Interior Ministry announced that in the wake of the Paris atrocities, it had
searched 793 premises, taken 90 people in for questioning, put 164 under
house arrest, and confiscated 174 weapons, including assault rifles.

A major terror attack in France was all but inevitable. That country has
been the largest feeder, among European nations, of foreign fighters into Syria
and Iraq, with more than two thousand citizens having emigrated to link up
with some jihadist movement or another—not necessarily ISIS. Two hundred
and fifty French nationals are thought to have gone over and come back to
France. Most of the Paris attackers were French nationals, although many had
lived in the Molenbeek district of Brussels, long a hotbed of Islamist proselytization and recruitment. All but the one who didn't go through with his
mission (and is still at large somewhere in the world) had recently returned
from fighting with ISIS in Syria, and most had repatriated within the three
months prior to the attack.

Bilal Hadfi, for instance, the twenty-year-old "baby-faced jihadi," and one
of the Stade de France suicide bombers, was a French national who lived in
Neder-over-Heembeek, Belgium, not far from Molenbeek, and had been, as
his Facebook page attested, obsessed with soccer. Then something changed in
2014. His online behavior began to betray extremist leanings. A trainee elec-
trician, Hadfi was apparently radicalized by a Belgian imam. He had been in
touch, through Facebook, with a well-known ISIS jihadist named Abu Isleym
al-Belgiki, also Belgian, who was a member of the organization's elite special

forces unit, the al-Battar Battalion, which had consisted primarily of Libyan fighters until ISIS disbanded it for suspected disloyalty. One of Hadfi's teachers recalled him speaking admiringly of the conquest of territory in Nigeria by Boko Haram, a jihadist group that has now joined ISIS. "To the brothers who reside in the lands of the infidels," Hadfi said on a Facebook-posted video that's since been taken offline, "those dogs are our citizens everywhere. Hit the pigs in their communities so they no longer feel safe even in their dreams." The faculty at Instituut Anneessens-Funck in Brussels, where he studied until he dropped out in February 2015, noticed his transformation. The school would notify the Brussels education board two months later that Hadfi was in Syria. According to two Belgian newspapers, the country's police oversight body, known as "Committee P," is trying to find out why the authorities were not notified of Hadfi's flight to Jihadistan.

Hadfi took a *kunya*, or jihadist nom de guerre—two, in fact. He was now Abu Mujahid al-Belgiki (also spelled al-Baljiki) and, alternatively, Bilal al-Muhajir. When he returned to Belgium, his registered apartment was bugged by Belgian intelligence, but he never turned up there. Brussels lost track of him.

One of his fellow bombers, one M. al-Mahmod, had traveled into Europe with the third Stade de France bomber, who used a fake Syrian passport with the name "Ahmad al-Mohammad." The holder of the fake passport had entered Europe initially via the Greek island of Leros on October 3, then registered with Serbia's border guard at Macedonia on October 7, checked into a refugee center in Croatia the following day, before moving on to Austria, where his trail, too, went cold. How he arrived in France remains a mystery.

All three Bataclan gunmen had similar résumés. Twenty-nine-year-old Omar Ismail Mostefai, a native of Courcouronnes, a suburb of Paris, was the first suspect to be identified after his fingertip was found at the scene of the crime following his self-immolation. The son of Algerian immigrants, he was arrested eight times but never went to jail; his crimes were petty in nature, the least of which seems to have been driving without a license. "He wasn't a troublemaker," a childhood friend told the *Guardian*. "He was someone who stood up for himself; you wouldn't provoke him because you knew that he'd stand up for himself if you did. But he wasn't someone who went looking for problems. He was calm; he wasn't someone who you'd notice, who stood out." In 2010, Mostefai's turn to radicalism earned the attention of French police and inclusion on its *la fiche S* or "S Files"—a database of more than ten thousand people suspected, in one way or another, of being a threat to state security—although he had no known ties with a jihadist organization. He had trained with ISIS in Syria, having entered the country sometime in late 2013. According to Britain's *Daily Telegraph*, "A senior Turkish official said the country had also identified Omar Ismail Mostefai as a possible 'terror suspect' in October 2014 and notified the French in December 2014 and then June 2015." The Turks received no reply.

Twenty-eight-year-old Samy Amimour, the first Bataclan terrorist to be killed, had been a bus driver, also driven to espouse Islamic extremism through sermons and literature found on the Internet. He'd been arrested for terrorism-related offenses in October 2012 and placed under supervision after an attempt to travel to Yemen with Charaffe al-Mouadan, an ISIS fighter who would be killed in Iraq on December 24, 2015, and Abdelhamid Abaaoud, the tactical commander of the Paris operation. Yet somehow Amimour managed to successfully leave France and make it to Syria the following year. His presence in ISIS country was known to his parents. His father, Mohamed, even traveled to Raqqa a few months later to try to convince his son, who had by now sustained injury on the battlefield as Abu Haji ("father of war"), to return home. Amimour refused the money Mohamed offered him; he stayed with ISIS and took a wife, Kahina. Much like Coulibaly's jihadist bride, Umm Basir, she'd make the proud widow. Emails uncovered by French investigators three days after the attacks showed Kahina claiming credit for Amimour's martyrdom. "I encouraged my husband to leave in order to terrorize the people of France who have so much blood on their hands. . . . I'm so proud of my husband and to boast about his virtue, ah la la, I am so happy," they read.

Twenty-three-year-old Foued Mohamed Aggad, from Strasbourg, one of two men deemed "retarded" for their sick sense of humor, was the last Bataclan attacker to be identified—by his own mother. She received a text message from ISIS on November 13 informing her that her son had become a "martyr," and she turned over Aggad's DNA to the French authorities.

RINGLEADER OR MASTERMIND?

The unquestioned man in charge that night was also a gunman at three of the target locations. Abdelhamid Abaaoud, a twenty-eight-year-old Belgian of Moroccan descent, was killed in a shoot-out with French security forces the next day, November 18, 2015, at an apartment in Saint-Denis, not far from the Stade de France. After Paris went on lockdown following the attacks, Abaaoud, who had taken part in three of the separate gun massacres against the "soft" targets of Friday night bar- and restaurant-goers, holed up under a bridge for four days with Chakib Akrouh, another shooter. They both stole into an apartment used by Abaaoud's cousin, Hasna Aitboulahcen, which was under police surveillance. Five thousand rounds of ammunition were used in the raid to arrest them. In the end, Abaaoud and his two accomplices were dead; Abaaoud's body was so torn to ribbons that it took a full day for forensic investigators to properly identify him. The raid happened just as the three terrorists were preparing to carry out a sequel performance, launching suicide bombings against police and retail targets in the business district of La Défense, either that very day or the next. Abaaoud had even asked Aitboulahcen to buy two five-thousand-euro suits so that he and Akrouh could blend into the crowd at La Défense.

If not exactly a foreordained end for a third-generation immigrant from Molenbeek who had enrolled, at the age of twelve, in the elite Catholic College of Saint-Pierre in Brussels's tony district of Uccle, Abaaoud's trajectory from bourgeois first-generation European to jihadist did follow an all-too-familiar script. He had dropped out of the school because of poor academic performance and, like al-Zarqawi, became a minor hood. And, like the founder of his terror organization, he stole, he beat people up, he broke and entered, he resisted arrest; he did time. Belgian journalist Guy Van Vlierden has written the fullest biography of Abaaoud to date. According to him, in 2010, after Abaaoud and his friend Salah Abdeslam—the only Paris attacker still at large, who doesn't appear to have gone through with his part in the multipronged operation—broke into a garage in a town southeast of Brussels. They evaded capture from the police and Abaaoud "jumped in a river, where he was found suffering from hypothermia. 'Probably they were all a little bit drunk,' his long-time lawyer Alexandre Chateau said about that incident." Following another assault charge in 2012, Abaaoud went back to prison, where his metamorphosis from petty thug to Islamist took place. Van Vlierden notes that it was upon his release that Abaaoud grew his beard long in the Salafist fashion, severed old friendships (though not, presumably, with Abdeslam), and linked up with infamous jihadist figures in Belgium, including a veteran of the Soviet-Afghan war.

Abaaoud made an attempt to enter Syria in March 2013, but wound up back in Belgium shortly thereafter. He tried again in January 2014, this time snatching his thirteen-year-old brother, Younes, from the boy's school in Brussels, at least according to the Abaaoud family, before traveling to the Cologne Bonn Airport, in Germany, where they intended to fly to Istanbul. They very nearly didn't make it onto the plane. German police would later state that they had questioned Abaaoud at the airport on January 20 because his name had been flagged in Belgium. They let him go.

Once inside Syria, Abaaoud joined up with Abu Umar al-Shishani's Brigade of Foreign Fighters, where he gained a reputation for sadism. A cell phone video of him dragging Free Syrian Army corpses behind a pickup truck was confiscated by anti-ISIS rebels and uploaded online before Abaaoud migrated into the caliphate's answer to janissaries: the Libyan-heavy al-Battar Brigade. He evidently faked his own death, persuading al-Battar to include his name in a tweeted list of killed jihadists, in order to dupe Europe's security services, all of which by now had Abaaoud in their sights. He was, as the mother of a slain Belgian ISIS jihadist told the *New York Times*, "in the database of every single European country, but he returned to Europe like he was going on a vacation to Club Med." In fact, Abaaoud found the ease with which he passed in and out of European soil, outmaneuvering Western intelligence services, highly amusing. Before earning international notoriety as the Mohamed Atta of Parisian terror, he made his own cameo appearance in *Dabiq*—in the same issue in which Coulibaly's widow was interviewed—to brag about how easy it was for him to move about in the land of the kuffar. Photographed with two other Belgian nationals who had joined ISIS while in Syria, Abaaoud told the magazine, "I was even stopped by an officer who contemplated me so as to compare me to the picture, but he let me go, as he did not see the resemblance! This was nothing but a gift from Allah." The *Dabiq* issue appeared in February 2015.

Abaaoud had been in Europe just a month earlier. On January 15, 2015, Belgian police raided a safe house in the town of Verviers, killing two Belgian ISIS operatives and arresting a third man. Abaaoud wasn't present at the location but Belgian counterterrorism officials say he was overseeing a forthcoming plot against Belgian targets, via cell phone, from Greece. The raid in Verviers was dramatic, the largest firefight to occur in the country since World War II. Inside the house, police found an arsenal: Kalashnikovs and the precursor of triacetone triperoxide, or TATP, the same chemical agent found in the suicide vests of the Paris bombers. Also uncovered were bundles of cash, fake passports, and GoPro cameras, indicating that the planned operation, said to have included the beheading of a Belgian police officer, was to have been filmed in real time for dissemination by ISIS media later. (Coulibaly also used a GoPro to video-record his attacks.) The efforts of spy agencies from multiple countries, including the United States, in trying to find Abaaoud based on his cell phone calls—all of which came from an area close to Athens, according to Van Vlierden—failed, and he returned to Syria.

Among the other plots in which Abaaoud has been implicated were two that made international headlines. The first was the May 2014 gun attack on the Jewish Museum of Belgium, which killed four people and was carried out by French national Mehdi Nemmouche, whom Abaaoud may have "guid[ed]." French journalist Nicolas Hénin, who was held captive by ISIS in Syria but released, had said that Nemmouche was one of his captors and a true psychopath. "It's such a pleasure to cut off a baby's head," Hénin overheard Nemmouche say back in Syria. The other plot was the abortive August 2015 massacre aboard a high-speed train headed from Paris to Amsterdam. Twenty-five-year-old Moroccan Ayoub el-Khazzani emerged from a bathroom with a Kalashnikov, a pistol, 270 rounds of ammunition, and a bottle of gasoline. He was stopped by several of the train's passengers, including three Americans—among them a member of the US Air Force and a National Guardsman just back from Afghanistan—before he could kill anyone. According to a French intelligence official, "From late summer [2015] we knew something big was being planned," and that "Abaaoud was involved in it but we didn't know what, or where, or when." Marc Trévidic, France's chief counterterrorism judge until September 2015, has said that Abaaoud "kept security services busy and distracted with these mini-plots while preparing the real attack."

But his Zelig-like ability to turn up everywhere a European counterterrorism investigation was under way didn't necessarily bespeak seniority as an ISIS foreign operative. Western intelligence sources have told CNN's Paul Cruickshank that a Tunisian ISIS member, "one of the most senior figures in ISIS's external operations unit," is "believed to have been one of the brains" behind the Paris attacks. That jihadist is now thought to be working with a Frenchman around Raqqa. Moreover, if there is a European citizen who was the mastermind of the entire operation, it was likely Fabien Clain, "one of the suspected brains" of the Paris attacks, a longtime jihadist previously convicted in France in 2005 for sending foreign fighters into Iraq. Clain joined ISIS in 2014; he was the one to claim credit for the Paris attacks on behalf of the organization via audiotape released a day after the attacks. French authorities matched his voice to that of the tape's speaker, who said that all of the targets were chosen with care. According to Cruickshank, Clain and Abaaoud were "working in tandem to recruit operatives for a string of attacks against France this past year."

Clain also referred to an additional attentat that never took place, in the eighteenth arrondissement, which likely was to have been perpetrated by Salah Abdeslam, Abaaoud's childhood friend, who acted as a driver on the night of the attacks but then disappeared. (His brother Brahim was the suicide bomber who detonated at Le Comptoir Voltaire in the eleventh arrondissement.) Abdeslam was reported to have been caught on CCTV in the "Jacques Quarter," the bustling homosexual district of Brussels, several times in late October 2015. Belgian officials have said that he was possibly there to target-spot or steal identification documents. But one bartender in the areas says that, on the contrary, the jihadist was a loyal customer and very much au fait with the quarter's gay scene. "We had him down as a rent boy," the bartender told Britain's *Sunday Times*. "He was always hanging out with that kind of crowd." Others say he was also an alcoholic and drug taker. There is no evidence that Abdeslam ever went to Syria to team up with ISIS there, unlike all nine of his co-conspirators. If these allegations about his nightlife are true, or even if they aren't, they're reason enough for the most wanted man in Europe to stay well away.

Abaaoud's role as ringleader rather than mastermind was somewhat confirmed by French terrorism expert Jean-Charles Brisard, who reported that an eyewitness spotted Abaaoud near the Bataclan, "huddling in the doorway of a residential building where he remained for about one hour. The witness described him as very agitated and shouting into the phone with an earpiece. The witness left and came back to the car several times and each time Abaaoud was still there yelling into his phone." After the theater siege was lifted, Abaaoud, the witness said, was still lingering in the doorway.

NINE "LIONS OF KHALIFA"

On January 24, 2016, ISIS released a seventeen-minute video meant to leave no doubt that the events of November 12, or at least the broad contours of them, were preconceived in Raqqa, under the auspices of ISIS high command. They are now meant to inspire Muslims to follow in the footsteps of the nine operatives, because the title of the video is named for al-Adnani's phrase, "Kill Them Wherever You Find Them." Shot and edited with characteristic production value, the film opens with news footage of the attacks and a kind of roll call of many of the attackers, as they were seen in Syria, dressed in camouflage, cutting people's heads off. A *nasheed*, or rhythmic Islamic chant, plays in the background. It's in French, not Arabic. A statement celebrating the "lions of the Khalifa who were mobilized from their dens to bring an entire country—France—to her knees" is brandished underneath a mosaic of all nine attackers. The image is familiar because it's so recent: it was published as a kind of teaser movie poster—*The Expendables* of ISIS—in the thirteenth issue of *Dabiq* five days before. The only Paris operative absent in both the poster and video is Salah Abdeslam.

Abdelhamid Abaaoud speaks, slowly, and in French, over a montage sequence of a French aircraft carrier in the Persian Gulf, along with fighter jets—all stamped with moving gunsights by ISIS's CGI masters—and more scenes from the night of the massacres:

> "I have a message to these disbelievers who are fighting the Muslims, and to all the nations taking part in the coalition. You are the ones who came to us. You are the ones who dared to come. You fly in the sky of Allah (the Glorified and Exalted). . . . You have declared a war that you have lost before even starting it! By Allah, we will make you taste terror, and you will taste it in your very stronghold. . . . By Allah, we will come to you. Rather, we are already in your lands. We will slaughter you inside your homes. All this is a result of your policy— your policy of war—or should I say, the policy of your rulers. Indeed, you voted for these rulers, and this is the result."

Scenes of President François Hollande and other French politicians speaking—gunsights superimposed upon their faces, too—are exhibited amid the street views of Paris and stock footage of missiles being loaded onto French warplanes.

Next, Bataclan shooter Samy Amimour, here presented by his nom de guerre Abu Qital al-Faransi, is shown in a desert region, dressed in the digital camouflage often worn by ISIS infantry. He claims that he was dispatched by Abu Bakr al-Baghdadi to "cleanse the earth of disbelievers, whoever they may be and wherever they may be." As the camera pans down, we see a man dressed in an orange jumpsuit kneeling at Amimour's feet, identified as *murtad*—apostate. "And by Allah, we will fight you . . . in the heart of Paris at the corner of the Eiffel Tower," Amimour declares. He then addresses those "remaining in France who claim to be Muslims" and asks what they're doing there. "We are being killed every day and you are sitting idly, living among [the disbelievers] . . . while it is within your ability to display some honor and spit in their faces—if you can't find a weapon—or smash their heads with a rock, or run them over with your car and terrorize them." The allusion to Abu Mohammed al-Adnani is so obvious as to obviate attribution.

The next speaker is Foued Mohamed Aggad, now Abu Fu'ad al-Faransi, who issues much the same imprecations against disbelievers. Only now Amimour's captive is kneeling at Aggad's feet. Clearly less confident in front of the lens (it looks as if he's reading, haltingly, off a cue card), Aggad finishes his sermon and then proceeds to behead the captive with his knife. Amimour takes the severed, gory head to the camera and grins. "Soon," he says, "in Champs-Élysées."

The remaining four Paris attackers are introduced, and another beheading is shown. "Kill Them Wherever You Find Them" ends with footage of British prime minister David Cameron expressing his solidarity with France. Another gunsight is superimposed on his face. "Whoever stands in the ranks of kuffar will be a target for our swords and will fall in humiliation."

ISIS IN AMERICA

Even before Paris, thirty-six people in the United States were under federal surveillance for their suspected links to ISIS, the *New York Times* reported in mid-November. According to FBI director James Comey, there were nine hundred open inquiries related to the organization; in February 2015, he had told the National Association of Attorneys General, the bureau was looking into cases of radicalization in all fifty states. For much of the year, any acts of ISIS-inspired violence were more aspirational than accomplished, either disrupted by vigilant law enforcement agencies while still in the planning stages— the FBI in particular was quite good at undercover sting operations, chatting up would-be jihadists as co-thinkers—or, in the case of two shooters at Garland, Texas, aborted while in the process of being carried out. Teenagers, losers, and the mentally ill were fecund constituencies for online ISIS recruiters— assuming, that is, the latter actually *were* online ISIS recruiters and not the feds. Some US criminal complaints make for amusing reading, given the exuberance and concomitant lack of skill or IQ on the part of many wannabe mujahidin.

In the summer of 2015, nineteen-year-old Jaelyn Delshaun Young and twenty-two-year-old Muhammad Oda Dakhlalla, both from Starkville, Mississippi, chatted online with a series of undercover FBI agents, one of whom posed as an ISIS facilitator for making hijrah to Syria. The two southerners planned to be married in June, Young said, to give themselves a plausible "honeymoon" cover story for traveling from Mississippi to the Mediterranean— Greece, rather than Turkey, to further lower suspicions about their true itinerary. Dakhlalla said he wanted to work in ISIS media to "correct the falsehoods heard here. IS has a thick cloud of falsehood and very little truth about Dawlah makes it through and if it does then usually the links are deleted (like on youtube and stuff)." He also apparently didn't know much about ISIS governance. "In sha Allah I will go through training and Shariah first? I am not familiar with Shariah but from what Aaminah [Young] and I researched, Dawlah follows Shariah correctly, right Akhi [sister]?" FBI Employee 1 told him that it was just so. Young later vented about the American press reporting on ISIS's sex slave trafficking. "These likes [*sic*] are so toxic, I am getting very angry at them for believing such stupidity," she wrote. In August, the young couple had their visas to Turkey and passports in hand. Young told the uncover agent that she tried to allay Dakhlalla's fears of being arrested once they landed in Istanbul because "I don't think they would put so much effort to arrest us in Turkey when they could just give Intel to US to arrest us before leaving." She was right. They were both picked up by the FBI on August 8 at the Golden Triangle Regional Airport in Columbus, Mississippi.

The Irish Republican Army said after it tried and failed to assassinate Margaret Thatcher that governments have to be lucky all the time; terrorists have only to be lucky once. There was a palpable sense in the United States after Paris that ISIS would get lucky eventually. How it would happen was unclear. Perhaps another synchronized series of attacks by well-trained returnees from the caliphate. Perhaps a low-grade, do-it-yourself operation, the handiwork of an unmonitored "lone wolf" who simply liked what ISIS was selling on the Internet and sought to enlist in its ranks virtually, and after many kuffar were dead.

A pattern had become discernible. Robin Simcox, an expert on homegrown radicalization, made a study of all known ISIS plots in the West between July 2014 and August 2015. There were thirteen attacks spanning ten countries and carried out by fourteen different nationalities, he found. "In the majority of plots (a total of 24 cases, or 75%), there was no proof of contact

with IS fighters or leaders; but the group's ideology or propaganda was integral to each schemes' inspiration," Simcox wrote. "IS fighters encouraged, on
five occasions (16% of the total number of schemes), individuals with whom
they were in contact in the West to carry out attacks in their home countries,
though without providing operational guidance."

Only two cases—six percent—involved people with "known connections"
to the organization. Published before Paris, Simcox's report found that only
one plot—the Verviers one, overseen by Abdelhamid Abaaoud—had any direction from senior commanders in Raqqa.

Seeking to defend his record on prosecuting the war on terror, President
Obama had spent the anxious weeks in the aftermath of Paris, which still
dominated international news headlines, downplaying the threat that ISIS
posed to the United States or to Americans at large. On November 22, while
in Malaysia, had had vowed once again to destroy the organization and said,
somewhat infelicitously, that ISIS "cannot strike a mortal blow" against the
United States (practically speaking, and rhetorical grandiosity aside, not even
al-Baghdadi thinks he can do that). Then, on November 25, the day before
Thanksgiving, Obama once again tried to reassure a nervous electorate. He
and his national security team, with which he had just met back in Washington, "know of no specific and credible intelligence indicating a plot on the
homeland and that is based on the latest information I just received in the Situation Room. I want the American people to know, entering the holidays, that
the combined resources of our military, our intelligence, and our homeland
security agencies are on the case. They're vigilant, relentless, and effective."

SAN BERNARDINO

For a Christmas party, it was meant to be fairly humdrum. "Ready to be
bored?" Patrick Baccari asked his colleague Syed Farook as he sat down at
Farook's table. "I'm ready," Farook responded and smiled. This was their inside
joke with each other.

The San Bernardino County Department of Public Health was holding
its biannual all-staff meeting and training session on December 2, 2015, in the
conference hall of the Inland Regional Center headquarters, but the attendant luncheon was given over to seasonal festivities. Ninety-one people were
invited, but only around eighty turned up. Fourteen would die in the single
worst terrorist attack on American soil since 9/11.

Farook, 28, had arrived at the meeting at 9:05 a.m., and left less than an hour into the presentation, leaving his papers on the table and his jacket on the back of his seat. At 10:37, got into his black SUV and drove home to pick up his wife, Tashfeen Malik, at their rented apartment in Redlands, six miles away. They left their six-month-old baby daughter with Farook's mother and by 10:58, were back at Inland Regional Center, where they proceeded to shoot Farook's coworkers. According to the *Washington Post*, "65 to 75 rounds [were] fired over the course of about a minute, coming from a Smith & Wesson and two AR-15s. . . . Dozens of people were shot, at least one as many as five times." The whole massacre happened in under four minutes. By 11:14, Tashfeen had used her cell phone to post a message to Facebook: "We pledge allegiance to Khalifa bu bkr al baghdadi al quraishi."

Farook and Malik were on the road for four hours before police spotted them just outside their apartment in Redlands. They actually drove back to the scene of their crime and were stopped two miles away, on San Bernardino Avenue, where twenty-three police officers unloaded 380 bullets into the SUV, while taking seventy-six in return fire from the couple. Farook and Malik were dead.

Their victims might well have been more but for the fact that the Bonnie and Clyde of Islamic terrorism were bad bomb makers. They constructed an improvised explosive device—"composed of three galvanized steel pipe bombs . . . attached to a remote-control toy car," with a detonator made from Christmas tree lights—and left it in the conference hall. It was a dud; the controller was later found in the shot-up SUV. They also reportedly failed to convert one of their assault rifles from semiautomatic to fully automatic, which, had they been successful, would have allowed them to fire more rounds in the space of four minutes. As for communications security, here, too, Farook and Malik proved to be amateurs. They tried to smash their two cell phones after the attack but ended up dumping the still forensically viable devices in garbage bins near their apartment. The FBI would later send divers into a San Bernardino lake looking for a discarded computer hard drive. Whether or not anything was recovered has not yet been publicly acknowledged.

Inside the Redlands apartment and the couple's garage, investigators would uncover an arsenal similar to what Belgian commandos found in Verviers. A largely homemade explosives inventory, including, according to San Bernardino police chief Jarrod Burguan, twelve more pipe bombs, hundreds of tools used for making IEDs, two thousand 9mm rounds, more than twenty-five hundred .223 rounds, and hundreds of .22 long rifle rounds. The pipe bombs were cookie-cutter versions of the kind laid out in *Inspire* magazine, the online journal of al-Qaeda in the Arabian Peninsula (AQAP), and formalistically the digital media forerunner to *Dabiq*. The most famous article published in *Inspire* was in its premiere issue, launched in June 2010, titled, "Make a bomb in the kitchen of your mom," a how-to guide for lone wolves without access to military-grade weaponry who still wanted to kill the kuffar. Farook and Malik followed the directions in this article closely but not well enough, it seems. (A more recent issue of *Inspire* also explained how to use a Christmas tree lamp to build an igniter for a timed hand grenade—another do-it-yourself innovation the couple made use of.)

Malik was a Pakistani national who had grown up in Saudi Arabia. In 2007 she returned to her birthplace and enrolled in Bahuddin Zakir University in the Punjab city of Multan, known as a hotbed for Islamic radicalism, particularly the ideology of subcontinental jihadist group Lashkar-e-Taiba. Malik studied pharmacology. One of her former professors described her as "a very hardworking and submissive student." In April 2013 Malik began taking courses at Al-Huda Institute, one of a chain of all-women's religious school in the same city, to study the Quran. Although it has not been linked to any known jihadist groups, Al-Huda has a reputation for inculcating a conservative strain of Islam in its pupils. Women, for instance, are encouraged to cover their faces with the niqab. Her enrollment was to last for eighteen months, but she left early, in May 2014, to marry Farook. The Al-Huda coordinator in Multan told the *New York Times*: "Had she completed our course, I'm sure nothing like this would have happened."

Malik connected with Farook via an online dating service and possibly first met in person on a trip back to Saudi Arabia in the fall of 2013. In the summer of 2014, she emigrated to the United States on a K1 "fiancé" visa and was granted permanent residency the following year, having cleared all the relevant background checks and bureaucratic hurdles. Saudi intelligence sources would later claim that they had absolutely nothing on her; her life had passed in the Wahhabist kingdom without incident.

On December 5, 2015, ISIS issued a broadcast on its al-Bayan Radio claiming credit for the San Bernardino attacks and referring to Farook and Malik as "martyrs." All the organization had to go on was Malik's mid-massacre pledge of allegiance to al-Baghdadi on Facebook. To date, there was no evidence that Malik or Farook had any real contact with ISIS operatives in the United States or abroad. If anything, they became two of al-Adnani's invisible soldiers the moment Malik pushed "post" on her cell phone and her pledge of allegiance was uploaded to the Internet. The indictment on December 17 of a third man, Enrique Marquez Jr., charged with providing two of the rifles Farook and Malik used in the attack, would complicate the search for the killers' motives and affiliation.

Marquez had been Farook's neighbor going back a decade; he converted to Islam in 2007, largely at Farook's prompting. A great admirer of Anwar al-Awlaki, the American-born al-Qaeda cleric who would be killed in a US drone strike in Yemen in 2011, Farook would provide Marquez with the core curriculum for self-radicalization, including Abdullah Azzam's tract "Defense of Muslim Lands," al-Awlaki's lectures, copies of *Inspire*, and videos put out by al-Shabaab, the Somali al-Qaeda affiliate. Farook wanted to join AQAP, according to the criminal complaint against Marquez, and for years the two jointly planned to carry out acts of terrorism in Southern California, including against their mutual alma mater, Riverside Community College (the library or cafeteria, to maximize casualties), and major State Route 91 at rush hour. They attended gun ranges together in 2012. Then Marquez says he distanced himself from Farook, although the latter's brother was a witness at Marquez's wedding to a woman known only as "M.C.," a Russian citizen who Marquez says paid him two hundred dollars per month to enter into a false marriage for immigration purposes. He came to law enforcement's attention a day after the attack when he called 911 and said he was suicidal. Why? Because the San Bernardino shooter was his neighbor Farook and two of the rifles used were Marquez's; he'd given them to Farook, he said, "for safe storage."

The days following San Bernardino, the worst terrorist attack on US soil since 9/11, the media and US officials would hunt for an intelligible cause. Was it "ISIS-plotted" or "ISIS-inspired," or perhaps driven by another jihadist brand, such as al-Qaeda? "As the investigation has progressed," David Bowdich, the FBI's assistant director in charge of the Los Angeles field office, told reporters on December 7, "we have learned and believe that both subjects were radicalized and have been for quite some time." But radicalized by what and by whom?

The prevalence of content by al-Awlaki and al-Shabaab in the Farooks' possession, and in Marquez's recollection to the FBI, would lead some to suggest that this had nothing to do with ISIS at all, no matter Malik's Facebooked bayat to al-Baghdadi made while her gun barrel was still smoking. An earlier hypothesis, that Malik may have brainwashed Farook into becoming a jihadist, was ruled out given the latter's long-standing fixation with committing an act on US soil, as attested by Marquez. But by the time this third man was under indictment, and the criminal complaint against him published, another clue was furnished. According to Joel T. Anderson, the FBI agent who investigated Marquez's role in buying weapons for Farook, early in the morning on December 2, between 8:43 and 8:47 a.m., or twenty minutes or so before Farook sat down next to Patrick Baccari at the Inland Regional Center, Malik had made a trawl on social media, looking for materials related to ISIS. Did this mean that perhaps the couple had no real inspiration or favored "brand" of jihad, until the very last hours of their lives?

"The most interesting thing about the Farook and Malik case," Robin Simcox told us, "is that it was not as if they had just stumbled upon jihadism." Farook had all the hallmarks of being an evolving al-Qaeda jihadist: he admired Azzam, he followed the activities of al-Shabaab, and he immersed himself in the lectures of al-Awlaki and the articles of *Inspire*. "Shabaab, AQAP, and Awlaki have been calling for attacks in the West for *years*. Yet it took the rise of ISIS to compel Farook to take up the call. That means there is something unique about the ISIS brand that resonates with men like Farook in a way that al-Qaeda's did not. That may have something to do with ISIS's success on the ground. Pledge allegiance to ISIS and you are joining the winning team."

CLOSER TO ROME

In November 2015, the United Nations' sanctions monitoring team warned that Libya was emerging as a key stronghold for the Islamic State and a possible "fallback" base if it is defeated in Iraq and Syria. The consolidation of an ISIS base on the shoreline of Europe was hardly in doubt. Patrick Prior, the Defense Intelligence Agency's top counterterrorism analyst, said ISIS's presence in Libya was "the hub from which they project across all of North Africa."

Reading ISIS's entrenchment in Libya as preparation for a retreat from the Fertile Crescent was perplexing once the details of the UN's own report were examined. As ISIS faced increased pressure in Iraq and Syria, many of its Libyan fighters were said to be returning home to shore up its franchises there. The group had announced three wilayats in 2014: Wilayat Tripolitania (including Tripoli and Sirte), Wilayat Barqa (the Cyrenaica Province), which includes Derna and Benghazi, and Wilayat Fezzan in the south. The report stated that around 3,500 Libyan nationals had joined jihadi groups in Syria and Iraq, and 800 had returned to Libya to join the local ISIS affiliate, the total size of which, according to one UN estimate, was between 2,000 and 3,000. What was notable was the composition of this ISIS contingent that had moved back to Libya.

Most of the Libyan ISIS members who returned home in early 2014, the UN report noted, were from al-Battar Brigade, many of them from Derna, a hotbed of Islamist militancy that had been the largest per capita contributor of foreign fighters to ISIS's predecessor during the years of the American occupation of Iraq. Named after one of the armed groups that fought against Muammar Gaddafi, al-Battar had fought in Syria early on in the conflict, around a year before al-Baghdadi unilaterally announced a merger with Jabhat al-Nusra to form ISIS.

In Syria and Iraq, Libyan jihadis are widely credited with some of ISIS's key operations, including suppressing a tribal rebellion in Deir Ezzor and taking areas in Kirkuk during ISIS's blitzkrieg across central Iraq in the summer of 2014. Al-Battar was notorious for incessant suicide attacks and merciless killing rampages after the takeover of areas. Although most of its rank and file comes from Libya, the faction includes foreign fighters from Europe, mostly from Belgium and France, and from Tunisia. Along with Chechen and Uzbek fighters in other factions, the al-Battar Brigade, numbered in the hundreds, has acted as "special forces" or "commandos" for the group. ISIS has only a few other organized groups that match its strength, including Jaysh al-Khilafa, or the Caliphate Army, and Jaysh al-Badiya, or the Desert Army. It was hardly a sign of weakness that ISIS was able to spare such forces.

The war with al-Qaeda was waged in Libya, too. When al-Battar began filtering back to Libya, they joined the newly proclaimed ISIS branch that had evolved out of the Islamic Youth Shura Council. ISIS had orchestrated the creation of its Libyan branch by sending its former governor of Salah-ad-Din Wissam al-Zubaydi, known variously as Abu Nabil al-Anbari and Abu Mughira al-Qahtani, who had been credited for the takeover of Baiji and Tikrit. Al-Zubaydi, a former policeman in Saddam Hussein's regime, was allegedly accompanied by a cell of half a dozen men, all of whom were former members of Saddam's military-intelligence apparatus. In late 2014 and early

2015, al-Zubaydi constructed ISIS's infrastructure by annexing profit-making criminal networks, helping to make ISIS self-sufficient, and by poaching recruits from among local jihadi groups, specifically al-Qaeda. ISIS had also sent its most senior cleric, Turki al-Binali, to Libya.

With the failure of NATO even to really try post-Gaddafi stabilization, Libya emerged as a playground for jihadists in Africa, from Somalia, Mali, Nigeria, Algeria, and Egypt. Al-Qaeda has certainly seen the advantages of Libya. Among those who saw the advantage of Libya was the one-eyed cigarette-smuggler-turned-holy warrior Mokhtar Belmokhtar, who has spent time in Libya. Belmokhtar, a former commander of al-Qaeda in the Islamic Maghreb who now leads his own splinter faction, which is pledged to al-Qaeda, was made famous by the attack on the Amenas gas plant in Algeria in January 2013.

The importance of Libya for ISIS was emphasized by al-Zubaydi. "Libya has a great importance because it is in Africa and south of Europe," he said in an interview with *Dabiq* magazine. "It also contains a well of resources that cannot dry. . . . It is also a gate to the African desert stretching to a number of African countries."

For all its relative success in Libya, however, ISIS has struggled in absolute terms. Conditions would appear to be favorable. Al-Qaeda operatives or former members played a major role in the fight against the al-Gaddafi regime. The lawlessness of postrevolutionary Libya presented a perfect environment for ISIS: hundreds if not thousands of Libyan and Tunisian jihadists in Syria either trained or crossed through the country; the country is also predominantly tribal, and the porous borders and hinterlands in southern Libya are potential breeding grounds for the group. But it seems that where al-Qaeda has established presence, such as in Africa and Yemen, ISIS does not do well. Also, the coherence of Libya's tribes in Libya has blunted its ability to exploit social and religious divides in the way it did elsewhere.

The campaign there is one of "vexation and exhaustion," in accordance with Abu Bakr Najji's *The Management of Savagery*. Attacks on Libya's security checkpoints, tourism market (or what's left of it), and oil infrastructure characterize its play for dominance in a prominent outpost in the Maghreb. A presence here places ISIS fewer than five hundred miles from coast of Sicily. After Paris and San Bernardino, al-Baghdadi needn't conquer Rome to terrify the West. His observable battalions are close enough to Europe's shores already. And his invisible armies are even closer.

THE GULF AND ISIS

The operational relevance of Libya for ISIS is paralleled by the strategic importance of the Gulf states, and specifically Saudi Arabia. These countries—allies of the West and the hubs for the region's most inflammable products, namely oil, gas, religion, and sectarianism—present an ideal target for the group. In all of his speeches since the establishment of a caliphate, Abu Bakr al-Baghdadi has mentioned the Gulf monarchies, often focusing on Saudi Arabia. During his first appearance at the pulpit of Mosul's Great Mosque, he told his followers that he might not afford them the life provided by the Gulf monarchies but he would bring them dignity and honor under the canopy of the long-promised caliphate. On May 14, 2015, he castigated the Saudi-led Operation Decisive Storm in Yemen, aimed at supporters of the old regime and the Iranian-backed Houthi rebels, as a "storm of illusion" and a "desperate move to turn people away from the Islamic State." His audio message on December 26, 2015, also attacked the "Islamic Coalition," an alliance of around thirty-four countries formed in Riyadh with a stated objective of fighting terrorist organizations.

Saudi Arabia and other Gulf states joined the United States's air campaign against ISIS in the summer of 2014, mostly operating in the skies of Raqqa and Deir Ezzor, as well as in Kobane. But they have substantially scaled back their involvement in the fight since the Yemen campaign began. It was therefore curious that ISIS, with its sectarian bent, would attack the anti-Houthi campaign, when other Islamists in Syria offered to lend hands in the fight against the Houthis, who originate from the Zaidi branch of Shiism, though the group is heavily influenced by the doctrine of *wilayat al-faqih* (the Guardianship of the Cleric, the Islamic Republic of Iran's official ideology).

Although the Gulf states are frequently criticized for failing to adequately fight ISIS, there is a constant tug-of-war between the two sides. The Gulf states' out-of-character military intervention in Yemen undermined ISIS and its rhetoric as the custodian of Sunnis in the region. Many of those who had at least secretly wished ISIS would continue its march, for reasons ranging from opposition to Iran to the Gulf states' support for the anti-Brotherhood coup in Egypt in the summer of 2013, started to look away.

The Gulf states' willingness to use their fancy, Western-supplied weaponry stole ISIS's thunder and, along with the Syrian rebels' impressive gains in northern Syria in early 2015, which coincided with the Yemen offensive, caused probably more damage to the group's momentum and popularity than months of air strikes by Western countries.

Jamal Khashoggi, a prominent Saudi writer, explained the situation at the time for the London-based *Al-Hayat* newspaper: "Victory generates followers and power attracts vulnerable individuals hostile to the regime. These [individuals] have found in ISIS, especially during the Syrian downfall period, a way to seek revenge against an unjust system which oppressed their people and loved ones. Therefore, the emergence of an alternative, combining strength, power and moderation is enough to pull the rug out from under ISIS."

Aside from the recruitment of Gulf nationals as fighters in its heartlands in Iraq and Syria or as suicide attackers in their own countries, as happened in the bombing of mosques in Saudi Arabia and Kuwait in 2015, ISIS's inability to establish itself as a powerful mobilizer in the Gulf region is a spectacular failure—highlighting again that ISIS's worst enemies are fellow Sunni Muslims capable of undermining its monopoly and claims for legitimacy. The number of Gulf citizens who have joined ISIS remains lower than those coming from other countries: according to the Soufan Group, 2,275 Saudi citizens are fighting with ISIS, compared to nearly 5,000 from Tunisia.

These figures show a dismal performance for ISIS when it comes to infiltrating such a strategic region, particularly if seen against the potential opportunities it has within these nations: the flow of funds to support Islamists in Syria since 2011, the polarized sectarian landscape, and the widespread culture of martyrdom relative to other areas.

But ISIS's infiltration of the Gulf is still a work in progress. ISIS's foray in the Gulf began in Saudi Arabia in November 2014, when a gunman shot at a Shia gathering at a shrine in the city of Ahsa. Six months later, the group carried out two attacks in Shia mosques on two consecutive Fridays in Qatif and Dammam in the Shia-dominated Eastern Province. In June 2015, it carried out a similar attack in Kuwait.

ISIS's attacks put clerics in the Saudi kingdom and outside in a bind, whereby they would either have to condemn the attacks and thus side with the Shia against Sunnis, anathema to the most conservative sections of the population and the official clergy, or not condemn the attacks and increase the accusations from abroad that the Saudis were in league with ISIS. In the event, the attacks on the mosques led to a rare admonition of the kingdom's top clerics by the late King Abdullah to stop "laziness" and do more to combat the ideology of ISIS.

Besides exploiting religious and sectarian fault lines in this region, ISIS also seeks to appeal to current and former jihadists and sympathizers, many of whom have been incarcerated or dispersed as a result of the wars in Afghanistan and Iraq and the almost simultaneous Saudi crackdown on an al-Qaeda insurrection at home from 2003 to 2005. ISIS seeks to ride a new wave of jihadism in the Gulf region. Many of those who fought with or rhetorically supported jihadists against the Saudi government remain in prison, their financial and social networks disrupted over the decade preceding the Arab uprisings, and ISIS hopes to pick up where al-Qaeda left off.

This attempt to supplant al-Qaeda is part of a broader strategy. By appealing to established jihadists in the Gulf and elsewhere, especially in Africa, ISIS aims to re-assemble the scattered jihadi networks dispersed after 9/11. Its attempts to infiltrate the Gulf, the acceptance of allegiance of Boko Haram in Nigeria and attempts to attract the Tuareg people in northern Mali and across the Sahel as well as Somalia's al-Shabab are driven by the same ambition. Appeal to such demographics provides ISIS not only with greater legitimacy but also with decades of cumulative experience, battle-hardened and committed fighters and indispensable networks to further develop its global "brand."

Winning over such individuals is not just an issue of manpower. Many of those whom ISIS seeks to recruit were part of the so-called Islamic Awakening that existed in Saudi Arabia and, to a lesser degree, in the wider neighborhood from the 1960 to 1990s, an era that helped formulate much of the thinking and discourse of modern jihadism in the region. After all, many of the leaders and ideologues of modern jihad, such as Osama bin Laden, Abdullah Azzam, and Abu Muhammed al-Maqdisi, either influenced or were influenced by this movement.

The religious weight of Saudi Arabia, as the site of Islam's holy sites in Mecca and Medina, is also key for the legitimacy of ISIS as a self-styled caliphate, particularly if combined with the seats of former Islamic Umayyad and Abbasid dynasties. ISIS's failure to effectively project power and strength in the Gulf region is a major flaw in its narrative, but one that it hopes to overcome, especially as sectarian tensions in the region appear to be spiraling out of control.

For the West, any progress for the group in the Gulf region could have wide implications not only because these countries are sworn Western allies but also because the slow revival of old financial networks that had been significantly undercut since the 9/11 attacks could bolster ISIS internationally.

The reactivation of such networks began in earnest after the militarization of the Syrian uprising in late 2011, when private donors across the region organized aid and funding first to address the deteriorating humanitarian situation in the country and later to sponsor armed groups fighting the regime of Bashar al-Assad.

These networks are often murky. Islamist groups that cooperate on the battlefield with jihadist organizations, as in Syria, Libya, and Yemen, end up creating a loose network of financing that is hard to monitor or control. While most of the Gulf countries banned ad hoc private donations and restricted relief work to state-owned or nongovernmental entities, countries like Kuwait had relatively relaxed financial laws and thus became financial hubs for sending money to Syria and other restive countries. While ISIS's economic model depends primarily on extortion, confiscation, taxes, and trade in areas under its control, the revival of old financial networks could supplement the group's nascent international network and bolster its ability to strike abroad.

19

CONFESSIONS OF
AN ISIS SPY
A MEETING IN ISTANBUL

It took some convincing, but the man called Abu Khaled finally told his story. Since the early, more hopeful days of the Syrian revolution, he joined the ranks of the Islamic State and served with its "state security" branch, the Amn al-Dawla, training jihadist infantry and foreign operatives. Now, he said, he had left ISIS as a defector—making him a marked man.

Abu Khaled saw firsthand, he said, what amounted to the colonial arrogance of Iraqi and other foreign elites in the ISIS leadership occupying large swaths of his Syrian homeland. If he were telling the truth, he had extraordinary, granular information about the way ISIS operates: who is really in charge, how they come and go, what divisions there are in the ranks of the fighters and the population. He was in a position to explain the banality of the bureaucracy in a would-be state, and the extraordinary savagery of the multiple security services ISIS has created to watch the people—and to watch each other. He could also tell me why so many remain beholden to a totalitarian cult, which, far from shrinking from its atrocities and acts of ultra-violence, glories in them.

Abu Khaled had worked with hundreds of foreign recruits to the ISIS banner, some of whom had already traveled back to their home countries as part of the group's effort to sow clandestine agents among its enemies.

But Abu Khaled didn't want to leave his wife and an apartment he'd just acquired in the suburbs of embattled Aleppo. He didn't want to risk the long journey to Istanbul. Since he'd bailed out of ISIS, he said, he'd been busy building his own seventy-eight-man *katiba*, or battalion, to fight his former jihadist comrades.

The worst terrorist bombing in modern Turkish history had just been carried out by ISIS operatives in the streets of Ankara, killing more than one hundred people in a NATO country, reinforcing yet again one of the core ideological conceits of the putative caliphate: borders are obsolete, and ISIS can get to you anywhere, as it wants everyone to know. There was at least a possibility Abu Khaled was *still* a spy for ISIS, and that he was part of an operation to collect new hostages.

For Abu Khaled, assuming he was telling the truth, the risks were much greater. ISIS might track him all the way into the "Land of Unbelief" and deal with him there. Indeed, it did just that with two Syrian activists from Raqqa, who were beheaded in Sanliurfa. And there were agents Abu Khaled had trained himself who had left Syria and Iraq for work "behind enemy lines."

"When you're in the secret service, everything is controlled," he said. "You can't just leave Islamic State territory." It would be especially hard for him because the entire border was controlled by the state security apparatus he had served. "I trained these guys! Most of them knew me."

"I can't go," he said more than once. "I'm *kafir* now," an infidel, a nonbeliever in the view of the caliphate. "I was Muslim and now I'm *kafir*. You can't go back, from Muslim to *kafir*, back to Muslim again." The price you pay is death.

Given the circumstances, it seemed possible, even preferable, that he leave Syria for good, and bring his wife to Istanbul, so they could make their way eventually to Europe. But he refused even to consider such a thing. Abu Khaled said he was prepared to die in Syria. "You have to die somewhere," he said. "People die in bed more than people who die in wars. What if something like this happened to your country? Are you willing to die for your country, the next generation, or do you run away?"

Abu Khaled eventually relented and agreed to an in-person interview at the end of October 2015. He borrowed about one thousand dollars to make the long, 750-mile journey by car and bus from Aleppo to Istanbul, and then back again. And so for three long days, in the cafés, restaurants, and boulevards of a cosmopolis, on the fault line between Europe and the Middle East, through the haze of smoke, he lit one cigarette after another and sipped his bitter Turkish coffee. And Abu Khaled sang.

"All my life, okay, I'm Muslim, but I'm not into Sharia or very religious," he said early on. "One day, I looked in the mirror at my face. I had a long beard. I didn't recognize myself. It was like Pink Floyd. 'There's somebody in my head but it's not me.'"

Not many recovering jihadists have a word-perfect recall for "Brain Damage." But Abu Khaled is not a fresh young fanatic anxious for martyrdom; he is a well-educated multilingual Syrian national of middle age whose talents, including his past military training, the ISIS leadership had found useful.

Like many of his compatriots, Abu Khaled had spent a large part of a war that has gone on for half a decade based in southern Turkey. He joined ISIS on October 19, 2014, he said, about a month after Operation Inherent Resolve expanded its aerial bombardment campaign to Raqqa, the eastern province where ISIS keeps its "capital."

Abu Khaled felt compelled to sign up because he believed America was an accomplice to global conspiracy, led by Iran and Russia, to keep the tyrant Bashar al-Assad in power. How else could it be explained that the United States was waging war only against Sunnis, and leaving an Alawite-run regime guilty of mass murder by almost every means and its Iranian Shia armies untouched?

Abu Khaled was curious, too. "I went there practically as an adventure," he said. "I wanted to see what kind of people were there. Honestly, I don't regret it. I wanted to know them. Now they are my enemy—and I know them very well."

The procedure that took him into ISIS ranks was thoroughly organized. He approached a checkpoint at the Turkish-Syrian border town of Tal Abyad when it was in ISIS's hands. "They asked me, 'Where are you going?' I said: 'Raqqa.' They asked me why. I told them I wanted to join ISIS. They checked my luggage."

Once in Raqqa he had to go to the "Homs embassy," the name for the ISIS administrative building where all Syrians had to apply. He spent two days there, after which he was transferred to what was called the "Border Administration Department." All this in his own country, which ISIS informed him no longer existed.

"They considered me an immigrant because I had been living outside the caliphate." So Abu Khaled had to be "naturalized" first, and had to pass a citizenship interview conducted by an Iraqi named Abu Jaber.

"Why do you want to become a holy warrior?" he was asked. He said something perfunctory about fighting the Crusader-infidels, he recalls. Apparently it passed Abu Jaber's smell test.

The next stage was indoctrination: "I went to Sharia court for two weeks. You have to go take classes. They teach you how to hate people." Abu Khaled laughed. He was taught the ISIS version of Islam—that non-Muslims have to be killed because they are the enemy of the Islamic community. "It's brainwashing," he said.

The clerics responsible for this indoctrination were know-nothing striplings from foreign countries. "There was one guy I remember from Libya, maybe he was in his mid-twenties." What kind of Islamic authority could someone so young have, Abu Khaled wondered. And where were all the Syrians?

In his first weeks with ISIS, Abu Khaled met Germans, Dutchmen, Frenchmen, Venezuelans, Trinidadians, Americans, and Russians—all freshly arrived to "remain and expand," as the ISIS mantra goes, and to be custodians of the one true faith.

As might be expected, new additions to this jihadist internationale don't have even conversational Arabic, so a polyglot volunteer, such as Abu Khaled, is particularly valued. He has fluent Arabic, English, and French, and was therefore seized upon right away as an interpreter. "I had two groups," he said. "On the left I had the French and was translating from Arabic to French; on the right I had the Americans, translating from Arabic into English."

As part of its agitprop, ISIS often shows its *muhajireen*, or foreign fighters, setting their passports ablaze in a ritual designed to demonstrate that there's no going back. Whether from Bruges or Baton Rouge, they have all repudiated their nationality in Dar al-Harb, the land of war and depravity and godlessness, in order to become inhabitants of Dar al-Islam, the land of faith and peace (once it finishes fighting wars). But this is mostly for show. Previously, most new arrivals either kept their passports or "handed them over." To whom? "Human Resources," said Abu Khaled.

But that relatively relaxed personnel policy has changed in recent days. ISIS is increasingly restrictive and controlling as it has begun to lose battles, some of them at tremendous cost.

Before the fight for the Kurdish town of Kobane in 2014, the caliphate had an aura of invincibility, and people from around the world were rushing to envelop themselves in the black flag of messianic victory. But in that battle, which lasted for months, Kurdish paramilitaries backed by US airpower fought well, while ISIS—at least as far as Abu Khaled characterizes it— needlessly sent thousands to their slaughter, without any tactical, much less strategic, forethought. The jihadist army had lost between 4,000 and 5,000 fighters, most of them non-Syrians.

"Double this number are wounded and can't fight anymore," Abu Khaled said. "They lost a leg or a hand." Immigrants, then, are requisitioned as cannon fodder? He nodded. In September 2014, at the apogee of ISIS's foreign recruitment surge, he says the influx of foreigners amazed even those welcoming them in. "We had like three thousand foreign fighters who arrived every day to join ISIS. I mean, every day. And now we don't have even like fifty or sixty."

This sudden shortfall has led to a careful rethinking by ISIS high command of how inhabitants outside of Syria and Iraq can best serve the cause. "The most important thing," Abu Khaled said, "is that they are trying to make sleeper cells all over the world." The ISIS leadership has "asked people to stay in their countries and fight there, kill citizens, blow up buildings, whatever they can do. You don't have to come."

Some of the jihadists under Abu Khaled's tutelage have already left al-Dawla, the state, as he puts it, and gone back to their nations of origin. He mentioned two Frenchmen in their early thirties. What were their names? Abu Khaled claimed not to know. "We don't ask these kinds of questions. We are all 'Abu Something.' Once you start asking about personal histories, this is the ultimate red flag."

Following the Paris terrorist attacks on November 13, 2015, which occurred almost a month after their initial meeting in Turkey, one of the authors contacted Abu Khaled. Now back in Aleppo, he said that he was fairly certain that one or both of these French nationals were involved in some way in the coordinated assault, the worst atrocity to befall France since World War II, which killed at least 132 and left almost as many critically wounded. He said he was waiting to see their photographs published in the international press.

The first, he said, was a North African, possibly from Algeria or Morocco, bald, of average height and weight. The other was a short, blond-haired, blue-eyed Frenchman, very likely a convert to Islam, who had a wife and a seven-year-old son.

It seemed like the kind of information that those looking to counter ISIS would find useful. Did you warn anyone about these two? "Yes," he responded, and left it at that.

"Suicide bomber is a choice," said Abu Khaled, stubbing out a Marlboro Red and lighting a new one. "When you join ISIS, during the clerical classes, they ask: 'Who will be a martyr?' People raise their hands, and they go off to a separate group."

The number of recruits is declining but, at least in those indoctrination classes, there's no want of young men looking for a quick trip to Paradise. "They keep volunteering," said Abu Khaled.

In the wide world outside al-Dawla al-Islamiya, the Islamic State, we have caught occasional glimpses of these incendiary young zealots. There was, for instance, Jake Bilardi, a disaffected Australian eighteen-year-old, who, judging by the blog he left while still in Melbourne, made a rather seamless transition from Chomskyism to *takfirism*, before detonating himself at a checkpoint in Iraq.

Abu Abdullah al-Australi, as he went to his death in Ramadi, was convinced that he was carrying out a noble act of self-sacrifice, turning kamikaze for the caliphate. For him, jihad began at home. "The turning point in my ideological development," he'd written, coincided with the "beginning of my complete hatred and opposition to the entire system Australia and the majority of the world was based upon. It was also the moment I realized that violent global revolution was necessary to eliminate this system of governance and that I would likely be killed in this struggle." He was right about that last part, if not quite about how his fellow revolutionaries determined his use value.

For pragmatic reasons, ISIS has encouraged homogeneity within the ranks of its *katibas*, much as the republicans did with their international brigades during the Spanish Civil War. One of the best-trained and best-equipped *katibas*, or battalions, is named for Anwar al-Awlaki, the American-born al-Qaeda cleric who was killed by a US drone strike in Yemen in 2011. "Everything is in English for this *katiba*," Abu Khaled said. "And we have another one with a lot of Americans called Abu Mohammed al-Amiriki. It's named for a guy from New Jersey. He got killed in Kobane. This *katiba* also has a lot of foreigners."

Lately, however, ethnically or linguistically delimited *katibas* are being dissolved and reconstituted into mixed ones, owing to the unintended consequence of having too many people from one place, or with one language, assembled together. Al-Battar, one of the strongest battalions in the ISIS army, was made up of 750 Libyans. Its men, ISIS found, were more loyal to their emir than they were to the organization. So al-Battar was disbanded.

Not long after joining ISIS, Abu Khaled had intended to found a Franco-phone *katiba* of around seventy to eighty fighters who didn't speak any Arabic. The men drew up a petition and signed it, and Abu Khaled took it to ISIS headquarters in Raqqa. The petition was denied. Why? "They told me, 'We had a problem before with the Libyans. We don't want the French in one katiba.'"

Russian speakers, too, are considered rogue troublemakers in al-Dawla. All fighters from the Caucasus or former Soviet republics tend to be referred to by the catch-all word "Chechens." And while Abu Umar al-Shishani is one of the most recognized (and overhyped) battlefield commanders in ISIS, "Chechens" are running their own outfits with very little supervision or command-and-control from Raqqa. This has caused heightened vigilance among the Arab or regional jihadists. "I was in Raqqa once, and there was five or six Chechens. They were mad about something. So they came to see the emir of Raqqa. He was so afraid, he ordered ISIS to deploy snipers to the roofs of buildings. He thought the Chechens would attack. The snipers stayed there for two hours."

ISIS's heralded end of the artificial borders imposed by European imperial powers has led to the unintended consequence of jihadist imperialism. The ISIS leadership, after all, is mainly Iraqi, and if there is a political, as opposed to religious, objective underlying all its activity, it is the restoration of Sunni power in Baghdad. Indeed, the franchise in Mesopotamia can be considered more "nationalist" in orientation than the one in the Levant, where *muhajireen* drunk on the "end of Sykes-Picot" seem not to realize they're being exploited by the former henchmen of Saddam Hussein.

Structured rather like the regional *Mukhabarat*, or intelligence agencies, of the traditional Arab tyrants ISIS supposedly wants to extirpate, ISIS's *amniyat* consists of four separate agencies or branches, each with its own role.

There is Amn al-Dakhili, which is tantamount to ISIS's interior ministry. It's charged with maintaining security for each city.

Then there is Amn al-Askari, or ISIS military intelligence, its reconnaissance men and anatomists of enemy positions and fighting capabilities.

Amn al-Kharji is ISIS foreign intelligence, whose operatives are sent behind "enemy lines" to conduct espionage or plot and perpetrate terrorist operations. But "enemy lines" doesn't just refer to countries and cities of the West; any areas in Syria controlled by the Free Syrian Army or the Assad regime, and thus not technically within the boundaries of the caliphate, require foreign assets to penetrate.

This is crucial for how the organization "expands" in Syria and Iraq—by dispatching sleepers to recruit agents and informants, or gather information about rival groups, be they other militias or state armies. Abu Khaled emphasized repeatedly that tradecraft rather than martial puissance is what makes ISIS so formidable at seizing and keeping terrain.

Others agree. In April 2015, *Der Spiegel*'s Christoph Reuter published an exposé based on captured internal ISIS documents showing the careful compartmentalization of the *amniyat*.

"The agents were supposed to function as seismic signal waves," Reuter wrote, "sent out to track down the tiniest cracks, as well as age-old faults within the deep layers of society—in short, any information that could be used to divide and subjugate the local population." Who were the elite families? How did they make their money? Were any of their sons secretly gay? What could be used to blackmail them into submission or compliance?

The entire apparatus was honeycombed with semiautonomous fiefs, often tasked with keeping track of what the others were up to. "A general intelligence department reported to the 'security emir' for a region who was in charge of deputy emirs for individual districts. A head of secret spy cells and an 'intelligence service and information manager' for the district reported to each of these deputy emirs. The spy cells at the local level reported to the district emir's deputy. The goal was to have everyone keeping an eye on everyone else."

This naturally puts one in mind of the KGB or Stasi—hardly a coincidence given that many of the top-ranking ISIS officials are former members of Saddam Hussein's *mukhabarat* and therefore past pupils of Warsaw Pact security organs. In fact, the man who constructed the ISIS franchise in Syria, the now-deceased Haji Bakr, had once been a colonel in Saddam's air defense intelligence service.

Abu Khaled said that the ministry of fear Haji Bakr built has only thrived since.

"A week before I defected, I was sitting with the chief of Amn al-Kharji,

Abu Abd Rahman al-Tunisi. They know the weak point of the FSA. Al-Tunisi told me: 'We are going to train guys we know, recruiters, Syrians. . . . Take them, train them, and send them back to where they came from. We'll give them $200,000 to $300,000. And because they have money, the FSA will put them in top positions.'"

"This is how ISIS took over Syria," said Abu Khaled. "It has plants in the villages and areas run by the FSA, and its people are in the FSA."

In other words: Not all of America's supposed allies in Syria are what they seem. Some of them, according to Abu Khaled, are being manipulated by people secretly working for ISIS instead.

Abu Khaled was made a member of Amn al-Dawla. This is its Shin Bet or FBI, responsible for running counterintelligence operations (weeding out foreign spies from the FSA, the Assad regime, or Western or regional services), intercepting communications internally (such as phone calls or unauthorized Internet connections), and maintaining the organization's detention program. The British-born Mohammed Emwazi, whom the media nicknamed "Jihadi John" after his recorded decapitations of Western hostages and who was very likely killed by a US drone strike on November 13, 2015—although in January 2016, *Dabiq* confirmed his death, saying he was shot in the back in a battle in Syria—was also a member of Amn al-Dawla.

"When anyone from any of these four branches is at work," Abu Khaled explained, "they are masked." But sometimes ISIS's fondness for media attention gets the better of it. Emwazi's identity, Abu Khaled said, was only confirmed because an informant for a regional government obtained unedited footage of the Briton running around Raqqa without his mask and delivered it to London.

While the agents for each branch are typically Syrian, their chiefs are not. For some reason Abu Khaled can't explain, the chiefs of the *amniyeen* tend to be Palestinians from Gaza.

Like any state bureaucracies, territoriality gives rise to factionalism and infighting. "We have the military and the *amniyeen*," Abu Khaled said. "They don't like each other. When I used to train the *amniyeen*, my friends from the military used to tell me, 'So now you are working for the *kufar*?'" He smiled. The infidels.

Abu Khaled's main role was in training the frontline local security for al-Bab. This took place in a camp about five kilometers north of the city and the daily protocol was intense. Reveille was at five thirty in the morning. The jihadists would all gather for a one-hour workout. Abu Khaled got on site at seven and gave lessons until noon. He taught battlefield tactics and operational awareness: how to secure a perimeter or launch a sortie.

The fighters were then allowed to rest for two hours before training commenced again. At five thirty in the evening, they were relieved, but not to a camp barracks. "The guys would go back to the places where they slept because it wasn't safe to stay over in the camp," he said.

They stayed at the residence of Aleppo-born Abu Mohammed al-Adnani, the spokesman and second-most powerful man in this terror army. Adnani, a senior member of ISIS's Shura Council—its main decision-making body—is responsible for appointing the *wali*, or governor, for each of four *wilayat*, or provinces. Adnani also names the chiefs of all four branches of the security services, as well as the chief of staff for the ISIS military administration. He is very mercurial. "I don't even think he consults with the *khalifa* [the caliph] for replacing people or firing people," Abu Khaled said. (This seemed exaggerated: the Shura Council, headed by Abu Bakr al-Baghdadi, likely does authorize— or at least rubber-stamps—the selection and deselection of *walis*.) "Every visit, he puts people in jail, he fires people. Before I came to al-Bab, Adnani appointed a new *wali* from Iraq, a new chief of security from Iraq. Now in Syria we don't have any Syrians as *walis*. Foreigners from Saudi Arabia, Tunisia, Iraq—but not Syrians. Tunisia should really open its embassy in Raqqa, not Damascus. That's where its people are."

Adnani divides his time between Raqqa and al-Bab, where Abu Khaled claims to know all of his residences, including the one used by the soldiers that Abu Khaled trained. Adnani is largely inconspicuous, always traveling in "an old car" and with a security detail that tends not to advertise its presence.

The ISIS leaders, according to Abu Khaled, conduct regular tours of their caliphate virtually incognito as they check on whether the "state" is functioning as it should. And if it's not, then heads will roll in both the literal and figurative sense.

Abu Khaled said he once shared a frontline position with Baghdadi himself. "One time, we were around Kweris airport," he said, an isolated and— until recently—besieged regime outpost in ISIS country near Aleppo. "And al-Baghdadi came there. We didn't know at the time, only after he left. Some people saw him but didn't realize it was him. When Islamic State leaders travel, they don't come with high-profile bodyguards. You don't even know they're there."

Perhaps the foregoing story is true, or perhaps it's part of a carefully tended personality cult, without which no absolutism can survive and self-perpetuate.

The tales about these secret visits are reminiscent of those told about Harun al-Rashid, the fifth Abbasid caliph of Baghdad when it was at its height in the eighth century. Although al-Rashid was real, his rendering by posterity was more informed by his recurring, fictionalized role in *The Thousand and One Nights*.

At times, Abu Khaled seemed an unwitting Scheherazade, trafficking more in third-hand rumors and gossip—caliphate cock-and-bull—than in what he'd witnessed himself. Yet even these stories were illuminating insofar as they demonstrate the care with which ISIS sells its own legend internally.

Another anecdote about Baghdadi, for instance, is almost surely a fabrication by clever political technologists for intentional dissemination through the jihadist grapevine.

Once, it is said, Baghdadi traveled to Minbij, the other main city ISIS controls in Aleppo, whereupon he got into a car accident. The man whose car he dinged was incensed and started shouting at the caliph, whose identity he didn't know, right there on the street, in front of passersby.

"I'm going to take you to the court!" the man screamed at Baghdadi. "Let's go," Baghdadi answered him. And off the two went, to the Sharia court in Minbij. In front of a clerical magistrate who knew the defendant's identity even if the plaintiff did not, Baghdadi admitted that the smash-up was indeed his fault. The judge ordered the caliph to pay a fine.

"They hold themselves to account, like everybody else," Abu Khaled said. "This kind of thing, believe me, they are very good at."

Abu Khaled credits this notion of "equality before the law" as one of the main pillars of ISIS's populist political program. And he said he experienced it firsthand.

His personal computer, he said, was at one point confiscated by Amn al-Dawla so that it could be checked for any sign of disloyalty or treason. The machine was lost, a casualty of the jihadist bureaucracy. "So I had to take them to court. I swear to God, the judge, he picked up the phone: 'Okay, guys, you have twenty-four hours. I need his computer. Or you have to compensate him for the computer. Otherwise, I'm going to put you in the square and thrash you in front of everybody.' You can be a nobody and still seek justice. This is one reason people who hate ISIS still respect them."

But, of course, ISIS doesn't just enforce its will through respect, he noted. When that appeal falls short, ISIS turns to a complementary method of controlling its population: fear. Then Abu Khaled mentioned the cage.

"They have a cage in this square," he said, describing the place where ISIS justice is meted out in al-Bab. This is the same place where beheadings take place from time to time. But the cage is always there, and there's almost always someone inside.

"They put people in it for three days. And they say why he is there," Abu Khaled told us. "One time, a man went to the court as a witness and he lied. They put him in the cage for three days. One guy was hanging out with girls; they weren't his relatives and not married. He spent three days. For cigarettes, you spend like one day, two days, three days. It depends."

Abu Khaled was describing a place one of the authors had been while visiting al-Bab during Ramadan 2012, in the relatively early days of the revolt against the Assad regime, when the town was still controlled by local rebel forces, and the fighter jet-chasing Barry Abdul Lattif had offered visiting journalists a tour. This was the same town that came alive at night when activists, rebels, or local civilians transformed themselves into ad hoc cleanup crews—the Free Syrian Street Sweepers—picking up detritus and rubble left over from regime shelling, or manning field hospitals in the basement of the local mosque, because the real hospital in al-Bab had been targeted and badly damaged by the Syrian military.

There was even an all-night café in those days where you could watch international news, drink smoothies, smoke *shisha*, and talk endlessly about everything and anything, without the fear that Assad's *mukhabarat* would be listening in. All that is gone now, Abu Khaled assured the author. The café is closed. No one comes out at night anymore because there's an ISIS-enforced curfew. And the locals have to worry about everything they say, and to whom.

As with Bashar al-Assad and Saddam Hussein, so with Abu Bakr al-Baghdadi. ISIS is absolutely paranoid about infiltration, and its wild dragnets for capturing fifth columnists and foreign agents seem premised on preemption rather than exposure. Fear must be maintained to keep people from so much as thinking of resistance. And in the frenzy, inevitably, ISIS devours some of its own. "One time they beheaded a Kuwaiti guy they said was working for MI6. They wrote on his body that he was a British spy—and he was the chief of the *amniyat* in al-Bab."

Abu Khaled, deadpan, took a long drag on his Marlboro and sipped some of his tea.

He argued that the paranoia is well founded. ISIS, he believes, is absolutely run through with spies and informants of all persuasions. A Russian in Raqqa, he says, was found to be working for Vladimir Putin's services. "They had video, he admitted to it. I don't know if it was under pressure, but he confessed." Another man, a Palestinian, was accused of working for Mossad. Both were executed.

Abu Khaled listed the crimes of high treason: "Working with the FSA that's capital punishment. Working with the *mukhabarat*, CIA, or foreigners—capital punishment."

There was one example that was especially vivid in his mind. "One time, they executed a guy, he was throwing SIM cards around places ISIS keeps its government services." Abu Khaled kept calling them that, but it soon became apparent that he was referring to tracking devices—possibly GPS-based, possibly a variation of RFID, or radio frequency identification chips, with signals that can be picked up by coalition drones and jets. "These were for the coalition airplanes to spot targets," said Abu Khaled. "They arrested the guy. They cut off his head and left his body and head to rot in the square for three days. His head was on a stick."

Don't like the pita at your local restaurant? Call the Hisbah, the ISIS morality police. Think the joint is unsanitary or infested with vermin? Call the Hisbah. "They are severe. If your restaurant is found to be unclean, they'll shut you down for fifteen days until you comply."

What you consume in the caliphate is of course heavily regulated. Alcohol is haram, and if you're found to be drinking, you're likely to receive eighty lashes there in al-Bab's central square as punishment.

The Hisbah "drive around inspecting what everybody is doing," Abu Khaled said. "In al-Bab, there [are] maybe fifteen to twenty of them. Not a lot, but you see them all over. They have a van with a speaker and they shout: 'It's prayer time! Go to mosque! Hurry up! Shut your business. You, woman, cover your face!'"

"Women are living in fear in al-Bab," said Abu Khaled. "You see a woman walking in the street, sometimes she can't see at nighttime because of the niqab," the veil covering her face entirely. "It's very hard to see out of the niqab during the day, much less in the dark. Then you hear, 'Cover your head! Go home!'"

But ISIS cannot rely entirely on fear to rule, and it has to bring in new recruits all the time, so indoctrination is a major part of its program. It accepts volunteers from the hated Free Syrian Army, from various Islamist militias, or Jabhat al-Nusra. But it makes the barrier for entry very high and limits their choices of assignment. Someone joining after having served in a rival group has to attend a Maoist-like reeducation camp for three months and "repent." And there are lifelong limitations on what you can do from then on, and where you can go.

"You can't stay or go back to your home city. Let's say I'm from al-Bab and was with the FSA. Now I want to join ISIS. Okay, I have to go to the camp for three months, and then after three months they will send me somewhere for one year, and I have no right to go back to al-Bab."

And because the caliphate wants to create future generations of willing executioners, it is very careful about educating the young, as well. Former teachers in Syria have been invited back to teach students in ISIS-held cities, but they have to take classes for three months and repent for having worked with the regime. Homeschooling is haram because the curriculum can't be controlled. Abu Khaled knew an English teacher who was arrested for teaching students out of his house.

There are also distinct perks and dispensations for those having a bit of power in al-Dawla. Abu Khaled, like other ISIS members, was paid a hundred dollars per month, in US greenbacks, not Syrian lira, despite the latter being the coin of the realm in al-Bab. Currency exchange houses exist in the city where ISIS employees can take their salaries for conversion, although they scarcely need to, given the freebies that come with ISIS employment.

"I rented a house, which was paid for by ISIS," Abu Khaled said. "It cost $50 per month. They paid for the house, the electricity. Plus, I was married, so I got an additional $50 per month for my wife. If you have kids, you get $35 for each. If you have parents, they pay $50 for each parent. This is a welfare state.

"This is why a lot of people are joining," said Abu Khaled. "I knew a mason who worked construction. He used to get 1,000 lira per day. That's nothing. Now he's joined ISIS and gets 35,000 lira—$100 for himself, $50 for his wife, $35 for his kids. He makes $600 to $700 per month. He gave up masonry. He's just a fighter now, but he joined for the income."

ISIS likes a tidy state and maintains one courtesy of the Diwan al-Khadamat, or Office of Services, which Abu Khaled likened to city hall. Here, too, the bureaucracy is impressive. Diwan al-Khadamat includes a sanitation department, a parks department, a building licensing department, and an electric utility. It also runs an agriculture department to cultivate the farmland ISIS has either purchased or, as is more often the case, confiscated from enemies of the state.

Anyone wanted by ISIS who runs away will have all his property and assets seized. "Land, houses, stores, everything. The building I used to live in in al-Bab belonged to a guy they accused of working for the regime," Abu Khaled said. "So they seized the whole building. They came with a notice of eviction for everybody living there. 'You have twenty-four hours to leave the building,' it said."

All businesses have to pay taxes—there's a collection every month, orchestrated by Jibaya, the ISIS IRS, whom you'd be foolish to evade or try to cheat. The Hisbah, too, perform patrols like mob enforcers to inspect all local businesses and make sure they're charging the proper prices for goods and services, and keeping accurate ledgers. "You have to pay a percentage, like 2.5 percent you have to pay from your gross sales to ISIS." Do the Hisbah skim off the top? "Yes," Abu Khaled said. ISIS charges whatever rates it chooses for the scarce electricity. "And you have to pay for the water. You have to pay for the city. For the cleaning, the garbage. Plus, when you bring any stuff from outside the Islamic State, you have to pay taxes. Vegetables or fruit—anything from Turkey or FSA areas, you have to pay taxes."

ISIS also levies fines for all manner of civil infractions, especially cigarette smoking or smuggling. This is a sore subject for Abu Khaled, a hopeless chain smoker, but he recognizes it's a huge source of revenue for the caliphate. Cigarettes are forbidden because they're harmful for the body, like alcohol. Yet because virtually every Syrian wants to smoke, ISIS realizes that it can make a windfall from the inevitable contraband. "A Saudi came to see my neighbor," Abu Khaled said. "He knocked on my neighbor's door and then on my door. I had an air freshener for the cigarettes. He asked, 'Where is my neighbor?'

I said, 'I don't know.' Then he said: 'You have something nice-smelling in your house. Man, I know you have cigarettes—please, can I come in and have a smoke?'"

Quranic obscurantism meets economic pragmatism throughout the ISIS administration. In dealing with antiquities, for instance, many of which in Syria and Iraq date back to the days of the biblical prophets, ISIS declares that any pre-Islamic art that once was "worshipped" is supposed to be marked for destruction, whereas anything else—such as Babylonian or Roman coins—is eligible for sale on the international black market, which doesn't lack for eager buyers. No doubt it helps ISIS's archaeological logic that smaller artifacts tend not to be idolatrous, and in practice it's the enormous monuments or statues that can't be quietly ferreted out to Turkey or Iraqi Kurdistan that are targeted for destruction.

Many compromises and corner-cuttings have to take place to keep al-Dawla, the State, in clover. Abu Khaled offered two important examples of ISIS bartering with, and extorting, its avowed enemies.

Oil, naturally, is a big source of revenue. ISIS controls of all of Syria's eastern oil fields, making it the premier energy supplier for the country and a racketeer for fuel. The Bab al-Salameh crossing, which is now ISIS's only means of entry into northern Syria, is responsible for feeding the entire caliphate, from Aleppo to Fallujah. "So imagine how many trucks are crossing every day," Abu Khaled said. Yet Bab al-Salameh is controlled on the Syrian side by the non-ISIS rebels, and of course on the Turkish side by the government in Ankara. Why can't either the Syrians or the Turks simply shut down the crossing and deprive ISIS of its revenue stream?

"Because there is no choice. ISIS has the diesel, the oil. Last time, a little bit before Ramadan, the rebels closed ISIS's crossing." ISIS responded by turning off the tap. "The price of oil in Syria went up. The bakeries stopped because there was no diesel. The cars, the hospitals, everything shut down."

There's a knock-on effect to the ISIS energy racket. Abu Khaled says that everything in Syria works on generators now. "I have a huge generator, I can fuel a small area, and people pay me for the power." And because he could purchase his diesel fuel at cut-rate prices owing to his ISIS membership—one-sixth the cost to civilians—he became a minor energy baron in his own right.

ISIS also, famously, sells Assad's oil back to him. "In Aleppo, people have electricity for maybe three or four hours per day. The electricity station is in

Asfireh, ISIS-controlled territory, near Kweris airport. So the regime pays for the fuel to run the station. It pays the salaries for the workers because they're specialized and can't be replaced. And ISIS takes fifty-two percent of the electricity and the regime takes forty-eight percent. That's the deal they have with Assad."

For all its means of self-enrichment, ISIS hasn't forgotten about the little guy. It has constructed a social safety net for those it rules in its Islamic welfare state, a linchpin of which is al-Baghdadi's own Affordable Care Act.

ISIS members are entitled to free medical treatment and pharmaceuticals, and *anyone* living in the caliphate can apply for free health care, provided need can be established. "You can go to the doctor or hospital for no money," Abu Khaled said. "If you can't go to the doctor or hospital in Islamic State territory, if you have to go abroad, they pay you. No matter what the amount. If you have cancer and you need chemotherapy in Turkey, they will pay for everything, including your hotel. Even if it's tens of thousands of dollars."

And doctors in al-Bab hardly complain about losses because medicine is one of the most profitable careers one can have in al-Dawla. Physicians are paid between $4,000 and $5,000 a month to keep them from running off to Turkey.

For these reasons, Abu Khaled said, Syria is the "five-star jihad," at least compared to Iraq. "Over there is nothing, but you come to al-Bab, there are coffee shops, there are nice things. You can have a decent life."

So why would he, or anyone, for that matter, want to leave? "Because of what I saw at the farm," he answered.

"I know one guy, he has a farm. Every day, every weekend when he went to the farm, he found bodies underground. These were people who'd been killed and ISIS threw their corpses into his farm." The more the farmer tilled the earth, as in an Aleppine Verdun, the more he kept bringing up the bodies. "The farmer would dig and he'd uncover a hand or foot."

Abu Khaled, at the request of the farmer, went to see the emir of al-Bab to complain of the human disposal problem. The emir told him that he'd investigate and get back to Abu Khaled in due course. "A few days later, I saw the emir in the street. I asked, 'What happened?' He said, 'That's not us. We don't know who's dumping these bodies.'" Did Abu Khaled believe the emir? Of course not. "But you can't call the emir a liar."

A few days later, the farmer told Abu Khaled he had something to show him. He said that whereas before ISIS had at least dug shallow graves for its prey, now it was just dumping the corpses on the topsoil. "All over the farm, the olive trees—there were bodies everywhere."

So Abu Khaled went back to see the emir and told him that he must come and see for himself. The emir agreed. He told Abu Khaled to get in his car—his BMW X5, to be exact—and he drove them both to the agrarian mausoleum.

Abu Khaled said, "I told him, 'Man, you have a nice car.'" He answered me: 'Alhamdulillah, the Islamic State is very rich!'"

Abu Khaled found the bodies at once. But the emir was adamant: ISIS, he said, wasn't responsible for these deaths. By now, however, Abu Khaled had proof that this was a falsehood. The same man who had been caught and beheaded for depositing "SIM cards" around strategic sites in al-Bab, presumably for coalition spotters, was one of the corpses. "I knew it was him," Abu Khaled said, "because he was wearing a black-and-white Adidas tracksuit. I told the emir, I said, 'Come on, man. That's yours.'"

Twenty-four hours later, the emir called Abu Khaled and told him, "We're going to buy the farm. Ask the farmer how much he wants for it."

Even though ISIS terror had struck inside Turkey the week prior to the author's meeting with Abu Khaled, the Islamic State felt very far away. Truly, Abu Khaled said, the people who run it want their subjects to live as if in a world of their own, captive minds in a closed society. But the real world is a small place, and this defector from the ISIS intelligence services said he was not the only one who had grown restive.

"People started feeling bad about all the lying," he said. "If you read the news . . . There's no TV, just an ISIS newspaper, *Akhbar Dawli Islamiya*. It says we're still in Kobane," a Kurdish city retaken from ISIS with the help of US-led bombing raids last year.

The pervasive mendacity in the caliphate competes with a climate of ceaseless recrimination and denunciation: Two Minutes of Hate directed every day, at everyone. And typically the accusers are not Syrians but the *muhajireen*, the foreign fighters, who haven't spent 1 percent of the time most residents of al-Bab have spent in Syria. They are an arrogant and unruly gang, increasingly seen, according to Abu Khaled, as colonial occupiers.

They see themselves as superior—holier than thou in the proper definition. "First of all, to most ISIS fighters—especially the foreigners—everybody in al-Bab, everybody in Syria, is *kafir*. Period. They treat people in this way, which is wrong. Even by ISIS's standards, that's clearly wrong. They are Muslims, they have to be treated as Muslims.

"Foreigners are telling Syrians how to dress, how to live, how to eat, how to work, how to cut their hair. Maybe the only place in the world where there is no barbershop is al-Bab. They're all closed. Because you can't cut your hair. You have either long hair, or you must wear it the same exact length everywhere. You can't cut your beard, you can't trim it. You have to let it grow." Abu Khaled said that the penalty for men with too-short beards was thirty days in prison.

And just like under Syrian dictator Bashar al-Assad, ISIS has presided over an atmosphere of mutual suspicion, where the errant joke or critical observation can land you in the cage, or worse. Abu Khaled has a big mouth and is amazed he wasn't killed before he managed to flee. "One time, a guy was telling me: 'You see this victory against the FSA? . . . It's because God is fighting with us!' So I told him: 'So why didn't God and the angels fight with us when we fought the Kurds in Kobane?'"

Abu Khaled was told that if he kept talking like that, he'd lose his head.

Nor was his sense of irony directed merely at the braggadocio of the *muhajireen*. He had been present at the battle for Kobane. Abu Khaled had witnessed firsthand just how poorly ISIS's soldiers fought: more like F Troop than Delta Force.

"The first time I realized that ISIS fighters are not well trained was the last day of Ramadan, this year [2015]." Abu Khaled was leading a charge against Kobane, and he and his men bivouacked in Sarrin, one of the nearby towns ISIS controls in the Aleppo countryside. He decided to attack a series of villages held by Kurdish forces.

Abu Khaled was commanding three ISIS units. One of them was dispatched to Khalat Hadid; another to the village of Nour al-Ali; a third to the small village of Ras al-Ayn. The assault began at one o'clock in the morning and involved missiles, mortars, and tanks.

"We took Khalat Hadid within forty-five minutes," Abu Khaled said. "Then my guys ran away." They ran away? That's right. " 'It's free,' they told me," that is, liberated. Apparently they mistook the fall of a village for the permanent seizure of one. Meanwhile, the other two units refused to enter their designated villages. "They said, 'Ah, it's too late, blah, blah,'" Abu Khaled recalled, in disgust. So they returned to Sarrin not so much in defeat as in indifference. Then the coalition started hitting the ISIS locations at 4 a.m. Warplanes killed twenty-three of Abu Khaled's men within a few minutes.

Abu Khaled interrogated his soldiers to find out why they had not fought that night. "Why didn't you go?" he asked some of those who'd gone AWOL. "I mean, we were three groups. One of you attacked, the others didn't."

Their response: They were tired of being sent to certain death.

"We had pickup trucks, machine guns. And the Americans were flying all over us. When we left the town, we got bombed. But when we went back to the town, we were fine. The town had never been hit. Then the Kurds besieged it. So we fled, and destroyed all our cars, vehicles, weapons. I destroyed my own car."

Abu Khaled estimates that ISIS lost up to five thousand men in the vain attempt to capture Kobane. They went like lemmings over a cliff, without any strategic forethought as to how best to fight both the world's most powerful air force and one of Syria's most accomplished militias.

"Everybody I know at that time is dead," Abu Khaled said. "I trained a Turkish battalion, like a hundred and ten people. We had to stop the training after two weeks because they had to go to Kobane. All of them got killed except three. And those three aren't fighting anymore. I saw one a few days before I defected. He said, 'I'm not going back.'"

Abu Khaled illustrated just how incompetent he found the ISIS infantry. He used silverware. "Here's Kobane," he said. "Here's open land, five kilometers of it until the first ISIS position. When we sent the fighters to Kobane, we sent them one by one. Walking. The logistics for them—weapons, food—came on a bike. Most of the time, the bike couldn't make it. It'd get hit by an air strike. So the ones who made it, they entered houses."

They were instructed to stay inside the house and not do anything. They remained for a day or two. Then, inevitably, one of them stuck his head out a window. "And then the house would get bombed and they'd all get killed!" Abu Khaled let out a mirthless laugh. "People started to think there was an ISIS conspiracy to kill everybody."

He also found it remarkable that, for all the many months of the siege of Kobane, ISIS fighters came and went as they pleased across the Syrian-Turkish border. The second-largest army in NATO stationed soldiers, tanks, and armored personnel carriers within spitting distance of one of the most intense war zones of the Syria conflict and did virtually nothing, apart from sometimes firing water cannons at Kurds trying to flee into Turkey.

"I don't know the relationship between ISIS and Turkey," Abu Khaled said. "During the Kobane war, shipments of weapons arrived to ISIS from Turkey. Until now, the gravely wounded go to Turkey, shave their beards, cut their hair, and go to the hospital. Somebody showed me pictures in Kobane. You see ISIS guys eating McDonald's french fries and hamburgers. Where did they get it? In Turkey."

Abu Khaled has spent plenty of time in southern Turkey and says ISIS sympathizers don't even try to hide their proselytizing efforts there. In Kilis, a border town, there are two important mosques, he said. "This one [is] for the Islamic State. You go there, everybody says, 'You want to go to Syria?' They arrange your travel back and forth. And the other mosque is for Jabhat al-Nusra."

During the June 2014 invasion of Mosul, ISIS took forty-nine hostages, including diplomats, soldiers, and children, by raiding the Turkish consulate there. Their release, three months later, went largely unexplained by either party, fueling suspicion that Ankara had either paid a ransom or brokered a prisoner swap with ISIS. Abu Khaled said he knows for certain that the exchange took place because he met two of the jihadists who were swapped for the forty-nine captives.

"They were prisoners of the FSA," he said, "held for seven or eight months. Right after ISIS captured the Turks, within twenty-four hours, these guys told me . . . 'We were transferred to the custody of Turkish intelligence, which took us on a plane to Istanbul.'" The ISIS detainees weren't kept in a prison, Abu Khaled says his informants told him, but in "a nice building" with a round-the-clock guard. "They were well taken care of. Then they were exchanged."

Eventually, the brutality and the incompetence and the lies became too much for Abu Khaled to take. But he was serving as an agent of Amn al-Dawla, the caliphate's state security. So he couldn't simply run away from ISIS; he had to plan and prepare his escape and hope that he wasn't caught and undone in the planning and preparation. "When you're in the secret service," Abu Khaled said, "everything is controlled. You can't just leave Islamic State territory. It was especially hard for me because all the border is controlled by the state intelligence. And I trained these guys! Most of them knew me. I was very well known in al-Bab. So this was also how I got out."

Abu Khaled's defection was a very near thing. It started with a friend he had in al-Bab who ran an illegal business printing fake IDs, the kind still issued by the Assad regime. The way ISIS border control works is that if you're a mere civilian, you can more or less come and go as you please, provided you have identification. Abu Khaled's passport was still with "Human Resources" in Raqqa. So he needed papers and they had to be a ringer for authentic ones. He had an ID made for twenty dollars with a photograph of him clean-shaven, which he said was taken before his enlistment in ISIS. He stressed that this bore not even a ghost of a resemblance to the appearance he'd adopted for almost a year as a jihadist.

He decided to make his move in early September. And he went solo, at least at first. "When I left, I didn't tell my wife. I told her only that I wanted to go to Raqqa. 'I have something to do in Raqqa.' I left my gun at home— my AK. I had a handgun with me. If you belong to ISIS, you have to have a weapon on you when you are on the street. I had my uniform. I left home at seven in the morning. I went to my friend's house, the same one who made the ID. I changed my clothes, I left my weapon at his place. He gave me the new ID. I cut my beard, not completely off, because I didn't want to get arrested for having no beard. But I looked closer to the ID photo."

Abu Khaled hopped a motorcycle from al-Bab and drove to Minbij. From there he hired a minibus, which took him to Aleppo. He says he could have actually hired a bus in al-Bab but for the fact that in every terminal, ISIS had *amniyeen*, members of the security forces, standing guard to survey the passengers. He was sure he'd be recognized in al-Bab. But the agents in Minbij had no idea who he was. "I gave them the fake ID." They let him board the bus.

When Abu Khaled arrived in Aleppo—territory held by rebels, not ISIS—he immediately called his wife. "I told her, 'In one hour, you have to leave.' I told her to gather her stuff, some clothes to wear, in a small bag, and take a cab. Within forty-five minutes, she was on her way, with her mother, brother, and sister. Two, three hours later, they were all there."

Since leaving the Islamic State, Abu Khaled has built himself a new fighting force—this one to battle ISIS, and the Assad regime as well. The Islamist super-brigade Ahrar al-Sham has evidently helped him finance his start-up army, although he says his *katiba* remains independent. "They gave us ten thousand lira. So it's like twenty dollars per soldier." This is the minimum monthly salary to keep a small militia in Syria.

"There are two ISIS brigades in northern Aleppo fighting us," he said, "and I know the emirs for both of them. One is from Morocco, the other is from Libya. I know how they think and how they fight."

When asked if he wanted a bit of respite, after everything he's been through, Abu Khaled shook his head no, and said, "I'm not scared of dying."

Abu Khaled walked from Laleli to the Sultanahmet district of Istanbul, meandering toward the Blue Mosque, the celebrated Ottoman complex. It might be the last time he ever got to see it. Female visitors, as signs everywhere instruct, are supposed to wear headscarves out of respect. But as he passed through the courtyard of Sultan Ahmet Camii, he spotted a woman in her twenties. She walked up the steps uncovered. But no one stopped her. Abu Khaled looked at her, as if he'd had an important revelation. "Syria will be like this again one day," he said.

He wandered around the courtyard of the Blue Mosque briefly before exiting out onto the Hippodrome. Then Abu Khaled stopped for a second and looked up. Not a week earlier, he said, a Russian warplane had bombed not far from his new home in Aleppo. The walls of his house shook. "Bashar has taught every Syrian to stare at the sky," he said. "There are no planes here."

EPILOGUE

How has ISIS fared in its briar patches in the Levant and Mesopotamia? Judging by a shrinking geographical landscape, and a renewed emphasis on "foreign operations," it has taken a conspicuous beating. The army of terror gave up 14 percent of its terrain across Syria and Iraq in 2015, according to the British defense firm IHS. That said, most of its losses have been tactical rather than strategic. ISIS is still entrenched in the areas, and among the constituencies, of the Euphrates River Valley and the Sunni Arab tribal heartlands of eastern Syria and western Iraq. Ramadi was a late addition to the caliphate's collection of provincial capitals, one whose sacking cost the Iraqi government more than its eventual recapture cost ISIS. The retaking of the city also made the prospect of capturing the larger and more important city of Mosul more remote.

Based on the testimony of past and present ISIS members, the American-led direct war from above and the proxy war from below have both badly hindered and accidentally behooved the jihadists.

Abu Barzan, the leader of Usud al-Sharqiyyah, one of the groups driven out of Deir Ezzor when ISIS overran the province, said that the depletion of al-Baghdadi's elite ground forces since Operation Inherent Resolve began has led to a shortfall in resolute and professional holy warriors, bringing ISIS to rough parity with the lackluster rebel groups it had once easily vanquished. "Their fighters are now like our fighters," Abu Barzan told one of the authors in early 2016. "The foreigners were their best forces and many of them have been killed in battles and air strikes. The new ones do not have the same experience."

Another problem is one of recruitment and societal outreach. Few want to cast their lot with an insurgency that has got an enormous bull's-eye painted on its back. Defections of rival or independent rebel groups to ISIS in 2014, combined with the addition of foreign fighters, helped the organization spearhead many of the battles that enabled it to conquer a third of Syria. But these defections have dwindled. Small provincial factions continue to join publicly or in secret, primarily in Deraa and the hinterlands near Palmyra, but elsewhere the enlistment has stopped.

Worse still for al-Baghdadi, the trend of defections has been mainly in the opposite direction. ISIS has been hemorrhaging loyalists, often depriving it of some of its best-trained and most-disciplined cadres. Al-Baghdadi indicated as much during his defiant audio message in December: "the greater the adversity, the more pretending hypocrites it rejects and the purer and more robust and steadfast it becomes." Many of the local Syrian and Iraqi recruits in particular had an irreplaceable nous for policing their hometowns; with their departure comes the added need to bring foreigners in at the risk of perpetuating an already pervasive perception of ISIS as just another species of colonial occupier. Former FSA and Islamist fighters have migrated out of the caliphate or simply asked to quit the battlefield for whatever reason. Contrary to media reports, ISIS members can ask to be dismissed from military service if they have valid excuses, such as having to look after their families.

ISIS has, as we've seen, implemented a stopgap measure to keep its militants at home and on the front line, banning travel outside the caliphate except under extenuating circumstances (such as urgent medical requirements). Even residents who move from one wilayah to another have to provide a convincing reason for doing so. So they've taken to lying.

Karim, a former ISIS sympathizer from Deir Ezzor, said he tried to trick the amniyat into allowing him to escort his ailing mother to a hospital in Turkey. A local ISIS doctor countered that Karim's mother didn't need to leave the caliphate at all and that her condition could be adequately treated at a hospital in Mayadeen, Deir Ezzor. So Karim fled. He left his area with two friends in the early hours of the morning, only to be stopped by an ISIS patrol that confiscated the party's IDs for further investigation. Fearing that he'd be arrested, Karim finally smuggled himself out of Syria via desert roads through Palmyra, where ISIS's checkpoint was somewhat more relaxed.

For all the erosion in fellow travelers and gun-toting mujahidin, ISIS still does not yet anticipate a rebellion from within, or another sahwa, largely because it's spent most of its rulership preparing for just such a contingency.

Andropov-style counterintelligence remains the group's stock-in-trade and despite the sustained coalition counterpropaganda campaign to depict ISIS as crumbling from within, security officials and local administrative personnel actually demonstrate few signs of paranoia. Internal opposition remains, at this stage, more nuisance than mortal danger, at least so long as ISIS operatives can successfully assassinate dissidents "abroad," restrict internal Internet access, and ban satellite television.

The war has also yet to noticeably change the way ISIS governs. Here the unintended consequences of coalition sorties have actually benefited the organization's recruitment efforts from Fallujah to al-Bab. The bombardment of infrastructure and industry, particularly in eastern Syria, has led to ruined livelihoods. Boys of workable age have thus been forced into joining ISIS just to make money. Similarly, poorer families that cannot afford the risky and expensive voyage to Europe by way of Turkey, Jordan, or Lebanon have seen their children transformed into "cubs of the caliphate" for lack of any viable economic alternative, with families that are already internally displaced within Syria being the most susceptible.

The Syria and Russian air forces' contribution to the conflict has exacerbated the phenomenon of child soldiering. One family of eight, for example, left Deir Ezzor city because of the constant shelling and bombardment and relocated to an ISIS-controlled town in the countryside. The family's breadwinner could not find a job to sustain his four daughters and two sons, one of whom is disabled. So the father sent his able-bodied boy to join ISIS, just for the four-hundred-dollar monthly salary and requisite family subsidy. The son was since dispatched to fight in Hasaka province.

A high-level military official in the coalition told one of the authors in September 2015 that he recognized the deleterious financial effect Operation Inherent Resolve was having on those living under ISIS rule, but suggested that the worsening economics could lead people to rise up against the group or cooperate with foreign countries fighting it. This is more wishful thinking than a sound policy because it ignores the fact that the air strikes have disrupted a more or less functioning wartime economy, which *predated* ISIS's arrival.

After the collapse of the Assad regime in much of Syria in 2012 and 2013, citizens had to rely on local resources and ad hoc means of subsistence to stay alive. In the east, cheap oil allowed farmers to operate engines to pump water from the Euphrates River to better irrigate their farmland. Poorly refined oil was also used to operate heavy machinery and vehicles for transport and agricultural. Whole families and armed militias could find work in primitive refineries or as the security detail protecting oil tankers. This bottom-up hydrocarbon industry actually revitalized local markets hit hard by the war and ensured the steady flow of electricity and water. When ISIS took over the Jazira, it managed the resources and profited from them but smartly didn't completely monopolize this war economy. The same families continued to work in the oil industry, just under new management. ISIS installed price caps and a form of regulation, but never so asphyxiating as to alienate those under its control. Air strikes are doing permanent damage to a system of self-enrichment that never depended on ISIS in the first place. As such, popular rebellion has mostly been against the United States, not the takfiris.

ISIS propaganda has also adroitly performed its moral jujitsu on who the true author of this new form of Syrian suffering must be: the Crusaders. Air strikes have taken out bridges that connect urban centers to adjacent villages, making life for the average citizen of the caliphate much harder. Tradesmen in Deir Ezzor now have to use boats to get from one place to another; a trip that formerly took thirty minutes can now take, at minimum, two hours. In some border regions, damaged or destroyed infrastructure has actually led Syrians to travel first into Iraq to get to a nearby destination in Syria, making them even more reliant on ISIS administration, which has "abolished" the border between the two countries and is thus seen as an expedient rather than hindrance to mobility.

The US administration, according to the same senior military official cited above, asked the Iraqi government to stop paying the salaries of government employees living under ISIS dominion, which Baghdad apparently did in July 2015, the better to foment popular unrest. The plan backfired. In October, Iraqi officials told Reuters that cutting public salaries "plunged people into hardship and could help the insurgents tighten their grip." Younes Khalaf, a retired border policeman from Mosul, who was supporting seven on his pension, told the news agency, "The government has severed its last tie to us. The situation has never been as miserable as it is now."

A Baathist style of population control has come in handy in other parts of Iraq, where a culture of baksheesh has often meant owing multiple gangs costly sums of payoff money. A former businessman in Mosul currently living in London told one of the authors that before ISIS's takeover of the Ninewah capital, he'd paid fifty dollars a month in extortion to al-Baghdadi's bagmen and roughly the same amount in bribes for crooked Iraqi government employees for having bribed the takfiris. "After ISIS took over, at least I only had to pay once," he joked.

"After four decades of poor governance at the hands of Saddam Hussein's Baath Party regime and Nouri al-Maliki's Dawa Party regime, Iraq is a failed state," said Ali Khedery, the former US diplomat who served consecutive ambassadors in the Green Zone. "Baghdad's endemic corruption; systemic use of rape, torture, and murder; foreign and domestic military adventures; ethnic cleansing, and at times genocide, have all conspired to erode the fragile Iraqi national identity and harden the sense of self that existed for centuries prior to the formation of the modern Iraqi state in 1920: the tribal, the ethnic, the sectarian."

The deadly dialectic between Sunni and Shia extremism conceived by Abu Musab al-Zarqawi is tearing the country apart. Nowhere is this fact more on display than in Diyala province, home to over a million people, half Sunni, a quarter Shia, and a quarter Kurdish. In January 2015, ten Humvees arrived in a village in Muqdadiyya, a town that lies eighty miles north of Baghdad. The vehicles offloaded a dozen or so men, a combination of Shia militiamen and Iraqi Security Forces personnel who proceeded to round up seventy-two unarmed residents and take them into a nearby field. "For about two hours, they were forced to kneel and stare at the ground as the fighters selected their targets and led them to a spot behind a mud wall," one eyewitness recounted. The bodies were later discovered, with gunshot wounds. The victims were of all ages, up to seventy years old.

Rafid Jaboori, Iraqi prime minister Haider al-Abadi's now-resigned spokesperson, said at the time, in what has become Baghdad boilerplate following allegations of government war crimes, the "prime minister has ordered an urgent investigation and we are awaiting the results." Al-Abadi denounced the atrocities and those who "commit killings and aggression on sanctities, set fire to people's homes and assault their souls and properties in areas liberated from Daesh," he said. "Those [acts] are no less dangerous than terrorism."

Except the killings and aggression have only risen in the intervening period. A year later, Diyala has once more gone up in flames. On January 11, 2016, ISIS set off two consecutive bombs at a shopping complex in Muqdadiyya, massacring fifty-one people. Although it claims to have selected this target as gathering point for the Popular Mobilization Units, the victims were mostly Sunni civilians. The next day, January 12, agents of the Badr Corps and

League of the Righteous responded by burning Sunni homes and mosques and killing a dozen or so civilians.

This time, Sunni MPs boycotted Iraqi parliament in protest to the militia rampages, urging that the Popular Mobilization Units in the area be disarmed. Two legislators, Nahida al-Daini and Raad al-Dahlaki, the head of the parliamentary Committee on Immigration and Displacement, calculated that forty-three people had been killed and nine mosques set on fire within the space of a week. Hadi al-Amiri called the accusations against his Badr Corps a "great conspiracy" to stoke Sunni-Shia tensions. He also blamed Iraqi journalists trying to cover the violence and Sunni MPs for spreading malicious gossip. Diyala's police chief, a close ally of al-Amiri and the Badr Corps, also gave orders to arrest anyone spreading "rumors," which is to say telling the truth.

It would be bad enough if Iraqi Sunnis were the only quarry of Suleimani's proxies. The same month as Diyala's tit-for-tat carnage, three American contractors with General Dynamics were kidnapped by a Shia militia in the Dora district of Baghdad. Two of them had been helping to train soldiers from Iraq's Counter Terrorism Service, one of the few professional military units in the Iraqi army. According to CBS News, the US embassy in Iraq received advance warning that Iranian-backed proxies were looking to capture Americans again. As of this writing, all three are still being held, reportedly in Sadr City, once a cynosure for Iranian proxy violence against US soldiers. But their abduction conforms to an underreported trend of similar kidnappings— eighteen Turkish construction workers in September 2015; twenty-six Qatari falconers in December—all by Shia militias.

One Western intelligence officer working to recover the General Dynamics employees relayed to one of the authors in late January 2016 that the principal suspect is the League of the Righteous, the very same militia that carried out the 2007 raid in Karbala that killed five US soldiers in an operation planned and orchestrated by the Quds Force. US hostages in Iraq are of course an insurance policy to allow Suleimani to continue his creeping takeover of Iraq's security apparatus with absolute impunity. "Any such American force will become a primary target for our group," said Jafar Hussaini, a spokesman for the Hezbollah Brigades, the one militia actually designated a terrorist entity by the United States. "We fought them before and we are ready to resume fighting."

There are currently 4,450 US servicemen stationed in Iraq, plus an additional 7,000 American contractors. So that a noted Special Group has already resorted to the old habit of targeting Americans ought to greatly worry the Obama administration, particularly as it has cited this exact contingency as its excuse for not countering Iranian influence in Syria. Both the League of the Righteous and the Hezbollah Brigades have deployed to Aleppo, where they are helping the al-Assad regime and Russia's charge to retake that province's capital city from the opposition. In other words, the very militias that a year ago received direct US air support to recapture Amerli from ISIS are today taking advantage of the US having quarantined ISIS in Iraq to redeploy manpower next door to try to eradicate US-armed anti-ISIS rebels—and are being met with US indifference. Inhabitants of the region can be forgiven for thinking that Washington's foreign policy seems cooked up by the Mad Hatter.

All of the foregoing ironies and contradictions can at least be parsed from open-source material. More scandalous is how US intelligence has once again been manipulated and spun to suit the public relations needs, and political caprices, of another White House. The *Daily Beast* reported in late August and early September 2015 that more than fifty analysts at US Central Command in Tampa, Florida, formally protested that their assessments of ISIS and al-Nusra were being systematically altered to suggest greater progress was being made than the evidence warranted. A written complaint submitted to the Pentagon's inspector general contained the word *Stalinist* to describe the culture of coercion and intimidation within the US Defense Department to offer a rosy appraisal of Operation Inherent Resolve. "Senior CENTCOM intelligence officials who reviewed the critical reports sent them back to the analysts and ordered them to write new versions that included more footnotes and details to support their assessments," the magazine's Nancy Youssef and Shane Harris wrote, citing two officials versed in the text of the complaint. Specifically, the assassination of midlevel ISIS officials was rendered as more significant culls of the senior leadership, and strikes on the organization's oil refineries and equipment were deemed to have taken bigger chunks out of its billion-dollar black-market economy than the evidence warranted. As Derek Harvey told one of the authors at the time, such a rewriting of a terrorist network's capability was in keeping with long-standing practice. "Whether al-Qaeda was destroyed or no longer a factor—we were told to cease and desist that kind of analysis," Harvey said. "Al-Qaeda core was declared all but dead by the Obama administration," a determination seriously undermined by intelligence recovered by Navy

SEALs from the raid that killed Osama bin Laden at his compound in Abbottabad, Pakistan, in 2011.

If the coalition's air war is accidentally strengthening ISIS's appeal in Syria, or leading to widening a sectarian chasm in Iraq, then Russia's intervention in the region is actually calculated to do so. Thanks to Vladimir Putin, al-Assad has won back a mere 1.3 percent of lost territory—and won it back primarily from non-ISIS rebels. The Kremlin's objective of securing its client regime in the Levant has "largely been achieved," IHS has concluded.

So it has, but at what price? In Aleppo, one hundred thousand civilians made a mad dash for the Turkish border in early February 2016 because the Russian bombing raids were so frequent and so severe that they simply had no place left in Syria to hide. "Sometimes there are so many airstrikes," Abdulrahman Alhassan, a volunteer with the Syrian White Helmets search-and-rescue team, told the *Observer*, "we are just waiting and waiting at our headquarters, and the jets don't leave the skies." The situation was much the same in southern Syria, where in the first weeks of 2016, Russian warplanes aided a pro-regime advance into the opposition-held town of Sheikh al-Maskin in central Deraa, waging more than one thousand air strikes against the armed factions of the Southern Front. The result was the empowerment of the pro-ISIS Shuhada al-Yarmouk and the hardline jihadist Muthanna Movement, which together consist of around 3,500 militants in a province that has traditionally been hostile to the Zarqawists. One Israel Defense Forces commander baldly told the *Financial Times* that Russia's intervention is making ISIS "stronger and stronger" on Israel's doorstep.

Putin's war is also precipitating a massive internal displacement crisis, with 150,000 rendered homeless in Deraa, according to a rebel-linked news monitor. "Since most of the displaced people are from the big towns and their numbers are huge it is difficult for small settlements in the province to absorb them," activist Mohammed al-Hariri told the website All4Syria. At roughly the same time, the regime struck an accord with ISIS fighters in the Damascus suburbs to relocate them from the area. They have but one direction to head, southward, in a migration of extremism that will further imperil the Southern Front's hold on territory and threaten its supply lines and, eventually, overwhelm what Jordan has seen as a workable buffer zone between itself and jihadist takeover to its north.

Russia has also gone after prominent anti-ISIS rebels in Damascus. On Christmas Day 2015, it assassinated Zahran Alloush, the commander of Jaysh al-Islam, or the Army of Islam, in an air strike in the Ghouta district of the Syrian capital, where al-Assad's military unleashed sarin gas in 2013. Alloush's political reputation was complicated, to say the least. Many Syrians committed to the same cause of the regime's overthrow saw him as a Salafist "fascist" whose anti-Alawite bigotry was the mirror image of the regime's anti-Sunni variety. Many also blamed him for the abduction of human rights campaigner Razan Zeitouneh in 2013, although Alloush serially denied responsibility. His record as a battlefield commander was less complicated, however. He was one of the earliest, if not the earliest, rebel leader to unequivocally and consistently battle ISIS.

Unlike other factions that reluctantly or halfheartedly fought the organization, the Army of Islam single-handedly kept ISIS from establishing a permanent foothold in the Damascus region, for which one might have thought both al-Assad and his foreign sponsors would have been grateful. They weren't. Russia made sure to target and kill him weeks before Alloush's emissaries were to attend dead-on-arrival peace negotiations in Switzerland, orchestrated by the US State Department. His death rallied Syrians wary of him around the Army of Islam and left few in doubt as to Putin's real, as opposed to stated, war aims.

When Russian warplanes are not busy bombing bakeries or Doctors Without Borders hospitals along ISIS-free longitudes, they're hitting civilians exclusively in areas where ISIS *does* maintain garrisons. Deir Ezzor has suffered some of the worst aerial massacres to date. Omar Abu Layla runs Deir Ezzor 24, a pro-opposition online news portal for the province. He sent the authors a month-by-month breakdown of Russian air strikes in the eastern region, along with the confirmed and named civilian fatalities—a total of 115, including 6 women and 14 children. November 2015 was the cruelest month, with 55 air raids on Deir Ezzor, one of them killing 71 civilians in the border city and jihadist ratline corridor of Albu Kamal. Perversely, ISIS has gained ground in Deir Ezzor since the Russian air campaign commenced.

The geopolitical paradox of seconding terrorists into a notionally counterterrorist intervention has also taken on new dimension since then. Russia Spetsnaz commandos "equipped with Howitzer artillery, supported by warplanes and backed by elite units from Lebanon's Hezbollah ... have been entering the fierce battles in the heights and towns of Latakia," as sources in a joint operations room run out of Damascus told Kuwaiti newspaper *Al-Rai*. The constituent parties of this command center are the militaries or paramilitaries of Moscow, Baghdad, Tehran, and Damascus, plus the Party of God, a collective alliance churlishly nicknamed the "4+1"—a play on P5+1, the acronym used to refer to the five permanent members of the UN Security Council plus Germany, all of which negotiated an arms control agreement with Iran over the latter's nuclear program.

According to Lebanese Hezbollah, Russia is directly arming its militants in Syria, a claim seemingly bolstered by Mikhail Bogdanov, Russia's deputy minister of foreign affairs, who has refused to classify the group that pioneered the car bomb and killed 241 US servicemen and 58 French paratroopers in the 1983 Marine barracks bombing in Beirut as any kind of rogue actor. Moscow, Bogdanov said, "maintains contacts and relations with [Hezbollah] because we do not consider them a terrorist organization."

The primus inter pares of the 4+1 alliance is of course Suleimani's Quds Force, if for no other reason than it now controls, directly or indirectly, most of the al-Assad regime's security establishment and attendant war machine. The expeditionary arm of the Revolutionary Guards Corps has sent upwards of two thousand "advisers" to Syria. Hundreds of them have since returned in boxes to Tehran, where they have been buried under state obsequies for their "martyrdom" in a foreign land, as Iranian state media now openly reports. Suleimani's agents have also conscripted or cajoled thousands of undocumented Afghan refugees in Iran, some apparently as young as twelve years old, into joining a Shia holy war against "terrorists" for the promise of a thousand dollars a month. Here foreign fighters have been requisitioned on behalf of the ayatollah much the same way they have been on behalf of the caliph—as cannon fodder.

Afghan fighters who join the so-called Fatemiyoun Brigade are sent by the Quds Force to "conduct dangerous military operations such as advancing against well-entrenched ISIS military positions with only light automatic weapons and without artillery support," in the words of Human Rights Watch. Seventeen-year-old "Masheed Ahmadzai" (not his real name) explained to the NGO that after twenty-one days of military training in Tehran, he and other Afghan refugees were sent first to Damascus, then on to Palmyra. "Daesh was advancing, and the Arabs were retreating," Ahmadzai said. "The Syrians were too afraid to fight. So they ordered us to the front to fight against Daesh. There were almost no Syrians with us. They said that if we refused to advance, they would shoot all of us, saying we could not retreat. If people still refused, the commander would shoot them in the leg. He shot two people in my ground that way. The commander was Iranian, Hodji Heydar, also called Abu Hamed, from the Iranian Revolutionary Guard."

While the al-Assad's regime's atrocities have been well documented in the five years since the Syrian revolution began, it remains the case that because the West is now at war with ISIS, the Western popular imagination has been primed to look on the black-clad head-loppers and crucifiers as a preternaturally malevolent force in the Middle East. The cynical relationship between the "secular" dictatorship in Damascus and the theocratic one in Raqqa has thus been elided, much to the delight of the former, now the prime beneficiary of the world's fixation on the latter. Al-Assad has been further immunized to carry on killing and dispossessing Sunni rebels he pleases, as US secretary of state John Kerry blames the victims for not negotiating in Geneva while they are being pulverized by barrel and carpet bombs dropped by Russian and Syrian aircraft in Aleppo.

Tyrants have long understood the inverse proportion between empathy and corpses. One death, said Stalin, with some measure of experience, is a tragedy; one million is a statistic.

Still, statistics can give some perspective. The Syrian Network for Human Rights found that between January and July 2015, the regime killed 7,894 civilians. ISIS killed 1,131. As we've seen, the methods of murder did not vary wildly and in some cases, such as the immolation of the living, were identical. As this book goes to print, the United Nations Human Rights Council has published the findings of a comprehensive, five-year investigation into systematic detention, torture, and killing of prisoners held by al-Assad's security forces, al-Nusra, and ISIS. Drawing on documentary evidence and more than six hundred interviews (the majority of them with ex-prisoners), the report makes not only for chilling but edifying reading.

What calculus do we employ for determining evil, or judging its singular enormity versus its notorious "banality"? Is an executioner in a long beard and a dishdasha somehow worse than one with a trimmed mustache and military fatigues? In early 2014, a detainee held by the Syrian regime at Sednaya, the prison from which al-Assad released untold jihadists at the start of the uprising, "was killed after guards entered the cell and subjected him to severe beating, including kicking to the head and vital organs. Other prisoners present were ordered to face the wall while the man was heard screaming. The victim was left vomiting blood. A former cellmate explained how the man asked him to tell his wife and family what happened to him. 'He died. We closed his eyes, wrapped him in a military blanket and read the Quran in our hearts.'"

At around the same time, at an ISIS-run prison in Jarablus, Aleppo, another detainee "witnessed a 27-year-old man being taken out of his cell, and screaming while he was beaten with a metal bar. When he was brought into the cell, the man was foaming from the mouth. When his cellmates called for medical attention, the guards said 'let him suffocate.'" That man died, too.

"The raping and butchering in Chinese cities," Orwell wrote in an essay reflecting on the Spanish Civil War, and specifically how that curtain-raiser conflict war had been misremembered in real time, "the tortures in the cellars of the Gestapo, the elderly Jewish professors flung into cesspools, the machine-gunning of refugees along the Spanish roads—they all happened, and they did not happen any the less because the *Daily Telegraph* has suddenly found out about them when it is five years too late." Nor, one would add, can the crimes of Syria's original culprit be confined to historical footnotes because it is five years later and cable news channels prefer to talk only of jihad.

When Operation Inherent Resolve got under way, ISIS appeared unstoppable. Their slogan, "remaining and expanding," seemed mind-bogglingly plausible because of the swath of territory it had already gobbled up and the parlous state of its state or nonstate opponents: vanished Iraqi army battalions; beheaded Syrian (Sunni) army conscripts; fleeing Kurdish peshmerga. Eighteen months of air strikes, plus the firsthand accounts of growing ISIS defectors, have demystified the organization's martial prowess. Lost cities, towns, and villages have also done their part to force an already-overstretched jihadist insurgency into beating its own ignominious retreats. Nevertheless, ISIS is resilient and adaptive and has demonstrated a cunning capacity to fashion its weaknesses into newfound strengths.

Better than its international enemies, it has grasped the opportunity in the many vulnerable short-term alliances or condominiums that have arisen in opposition to its caliphate—between the Free Syrian Army and the People's Defense Units; the Pentagon and the Quds Force; the Kremlin and the Party of God—and how best to exploit them to its own advantage through propaganda or terrorism. It has often become difficult to discern, for instance, where ISIS conspiracy theory ends and US foreign policy begins, particularly with respect to American acquiescence to Russian and Iranian intervention. Counterterrorism absent geopolitical forethought has aided the takfiris in the battle of ideas. They have relied, after all, not just on stolen tanks and oil wells to keep themselves in business, but on the belief shared by millions they rule—

and millions they don't—that there indeed exists a worldwide plot to keep the Sunnis down.

The post-ISIS landscape, whenever it arrives, portends many foreseeable sideshow conflicts as the contemporary Middle East is being altered forever, courtesy of US and Russian bombers and manifold militias. In this sense, ISIS has achieved one stated objective: the abolition of "Sykes-Picot" borders. Iran has assumed command of whole segments of Syria and Iraq's security establishments, creating a virtual occupation army in the first country and an ineradicable deep state in the second. Syrian Kurds, backed by one NATO member, are erecting a semiautonomous statelet, to the enervation of another NATO member. More than 4.5 million Syrians are now external refugees, living in tent cities in Lebanon, Turkey, Jordan, and Iraq, or trying to reach Europe by desperate—in some cases suicidal—means. Their numbers are growing by the day and the wave of immigration has driven knock-on social crises from Hungary to Slovakia to Germany to France, boosting the fortunes of far-right and isolationist political elements, which confirm ISIS's appraisal of the West as inimical to Muslims. ISIS has also exploited the humanitarian exodus by masquerading as refugees, the better to smuggle into Europe and conduct terrorist operations. Meanwhile, its heartland region in eastern Syria and western Iraq remains largely uncontested and it is building legionary outpost from Palestine to Afghanistan, capitalizing on the chaos of other failed or defunct authorities there. We concluded more than a year ago that "the army of terror will be with us indefinitely." Unfortunately, we have little cause to adjust this assessment.

ACKNOWLEDGMENTS

The authors are profoundly grateful to those whose knowledge and experience helped to bring an awful story to life.

Our discussion of the early years of the Iraq insurgency and then the Sahwa owes enormously to our very own "Council of Colonels." Derek Harvey, Rick Welch, Jim Hickey, and Joel Rayburn, whose friendship is already a nice return on this investment—all gave hours of themselves to be interviewed and in some cases re-interviewed via frantic emails dispatched at three in the morning.

Major General Doug Stone ran the Sing Sing for al-Qaeda in Iraq for a little more than a year, which was long enough for him to surmise that there were jihadists trying to *break into* Camp Bucca. Ali Khedery and Emma Sky explained how decisions taken in Washington, particularly toward the end of the Iraq War, affected fortunes in Baghdad (and Ninewah and Anbar and Salah ad-Din). Laith Alkhouri, whose job it is to listen daily to what terrorists are saying to one another, proved an excellent and humorous dragoman in what is no doubt a still-terrified Starbucks in midtown Manhattan. Shiraz Maher took time out of finishing his dissertation on jihadism to explain the various categories of foreign fighters flocking to join ISIS. Martin Chulov and Christoph Reuter, two of the finest Middle East correspondents in print, generously shared their own fieldwork with us to help us ferret out some of the more obscure details from the Syria conflict. Tony Badran, who has made a life's work of studying the House of Assad, illuminated Syria's collusion with the very terrorism it now claims to be fighting.

NOW Lebanon's Hanin Ghaddar, apart from being the bravest and most principled editor we know, allowed work originally written for her magazine to be reproduced in this book. As did *Foreign Policy*'s Benjamin Paulker. Nearly all of the reporting featured in the six additional chapters of this revised and expanded edition is a result of the encouragement and guidance of three mentors at the *Daily Beast*: John Avlon, Christopher Dickey, and Noah Shachtman, all of whom generously allowed one of the authors to take a leave of absence to delve back into this grim subject matter after sending him on a Smiley-esque journey to Istanbul to interview a former ISIS spy.

The *Guardian*'s Paul Webster, *Foreign Affairs*'s David Mikhail and Kathryn Allawala, and *Foreign Policy*'s David Kenner commissioned essays from the authors that led to research about ISIS before there was a book.

Lidiya Dukhovich, Olga Khvostunova, Boris Bruk, Grace Lee, Dmitry Pospelov at the Institute of Modern Russia, and James Miller, Catherine Fitzpatrick, and Pierre Vaux at the *Interpreter* were already accustomed to fielding menacing or bewildering phone calls from another part of the world before being treated to a few award-winning examples of these from the Middle East.

Alex Rowell read our drafts in their early stages and, as ever, offered insights, which ended up in the original manuscript. Stefan Beck, Aymenn Jawad al-Tamimi, and Robin Simcox did the same for the second edition.

Colleagues, friends, and family who were similarly indulgent, patient, or helpful in seeing this project to completion include Linda Weiss, Leslie Wilson, Ric Peterson, Stephanie Weiss, Stephen Weiss, Eliot Weiss, Jessica Weiss, Jean Weiss, Augie Weiss, Michael Pregent, Chris Harmer, Jessica Lewis McFate, Aaron Stein, Ilhan Tanir, Wladimir van Wilgenburg, Yusuf Sayman, Ceren Kenar, Omar Abu Layla, Nancy Youssef, Shane Harris, Paul Cruickshank, Anne Giudicelli, Farha Barazi, Mariam Hamou, Bayan Khatib, Nada Kiwan, Qusai Zakarya, Ammar Abdulhamid, Lina Sergie, Phillip Smyth, Mubin Shaikh, Mike Giglio, Hamdi Rifai, Sean Penn, Mishaal al-Gergawi, Mahmoud Habboush, Craig Larkin, Abdulsalam Haykal, Ahmed Hassan and Abdulhamid Hassan, Kareem Shaheen, Sultan Al Qassemi, Iyad al-Baghdadi, Abdullah al-Ghadawi, Elizabeth Dickinson, Faisal al-Yafai, Nick March, Hussain Abdullatif, Ghazi Jeiroudi, Abdulnaser Ayd, Abdulrahman Aljamous, Mousab al-Hammadi, and everyone at the *National* and Delma Institute.

And the team at Regan Arts who put this book together in record time: Judith Regan, Lucas Wittmann, Emily Greenwald, and Lynne Ciccaglione.

Mustafa L. and John Bundock started out as fact-checkers on the book's first edition and gradually became research assistants. Kyle Orton, for whom we will all be working one day, performed the same dual function for this revision. Any errors of fact or interpretation remain our own.

Finally, much of what we know from ISIS-occupied territory is thanks to the work of two courageous media organizations: Deir Ezzor 24 and Raqqa Is Being Slaughtered Silently. The Syrians who risk their lives to expose the army of terror are reason enough not to lose hope.

NOTES

INTRODUCTION

x Islamic State of Iraq and al-Sham: Technically "ISIS" no longer exists. The official name for the organization is now the Islamic State. We have stuck with "ISIS" purely for the sake of convenience, realizing that there's an intense debate on nomenclature. *Daesh*, which many of our interviewees use, is the Arabic acronym for "Dawla al-Islamiya fil Eraq wa Sham," or the Islamic State in Iraq and al-Sham. Although the acronym doesn't have a specific meaning, it is considered pejorative because of the hard sound of its pronunciation. The combination of letters in Arabic connotes thuggishness, harshness, and obtuseness.

CHAPTER 1

2 Zarqa was the biblical staging ground: Loretta Napoleoni, *Insurgent Iraq: Al-Zarqawi and the New Generation* (New York: Seven Stories Press, 2005) 29–30.

2 Zarqawi was an unpromising student: Napoleoni, *Insurgent Iraq*, 260.

2 He drank and bootlegged alcohol: Mary Anne Weaver, "The Short, Violent Life of Abu Musab al-Zarqawi," *The Atlantic*, July 1, 2006, www.theatlantic.com /magazine /archive/2006/07/the-short-violent-life-of-abu-musab-al-zarqawi /4983.

2 His first stint in prison: Loretta Napoleoni, "Profile of a Killer," *Foreign Policy*, October 20, 2009, foreignpolicy.com/2009/10/20/profile-of-a-killer.

3 Worried that her son was descending: Weaver, 2006.

4 It was a city of perpetual waiting: Jean-Charles Brisard, *Zarqawi: The New Face of Al-Qaeda* (New York: Other Press, 2005) 16.

5 If Azzam was the Marx: Fawaz A. Gerges, *The Far Enemy: Why Jihad Went Global* (New York: Cambridge University Press, 2005) 135.

5 Untold millions of dollars passed through: Lawrence Wright, *The Looming Tower* (New York: Vintage, 2007); Gerges, *The Far Enemy*, 134.

5 Some of the world's most notorious: Gerges, *The Far Enemy*, 76.

6 By the end of the decade: Peter L. Bergen, *The Osama bin Laden I Know: An Oral History of al Qaeda's Leader* (New York: Free Press, 2006), 64–65.

6 He had been the emir: Bergen, *The Osama bin Laden I Know*, 63, 66–67.

6 In late November 1989: Napoleoni, *Insurgent Iraq*, 52–53.

6 Theories as to the likely culprits: Bergen, *The Osama bin Laden I Know*, 93.

6 One of the arrivals: Weaver, 2006.

7 Rather than return to Amman: Brisard, *Zarqawi*, 17.

7 Among those he encountered were the brother of Khalid Sheikh Mohammed: Brisard, *Zarqawi*, 21.

7 Despite his remedial Arabic: Ibid.

7 He also met his future brother-in-law: Brisard, *Zarqawi*, 21; Bergen, *The Osama bin Laden I Know*, 32.

7 Al-Hami had lost a leg to a land mine: Weaver, 2006.

7 She traveled to Peshawar for the wedding: "هذا بياذ للناس ـ أبو مصعب لازرقاوي," YouTube video, 34:05, posted by قا ansaralshari3a, March 25, 2012, www.youtube.com/watch?v=EUrLMFautCI.

7 According to al-Hami: Brisard, Zarqawi, 22.

7 Al-Hami returned to Jordan: Brisard, *Zarqawi*, 23–24.

7 Al-Zarqawi cast his lot with the Pashtun warlord: Brisard, *Zarqawi*, 24.

8 graduating the masterminds: "KSM trains at Sada camp," GlobalSecurity.org, last modified January 11, 2006, www.globalsecurity.org/security/profiles/ksm_trains_at_sada_camp.htm; "Hambali trains at Sada camp," GlobalSecurity.org, last modified January 11, 2006, www.globalsecurity.org/security/profiles/hambali_trains_at_sada_camp.htm.

8 As recounted by Loretta Napoleoni: Napoleoni, *Insurgent Iraq*, 55.

8 The first was "the days of experimentation": Ibid.

8 The second was the "military preparation period": Ibid.

8 Clausewitz for terrorists: Ibid.

8 Al-Zarqawi returned to Jordan in late 1993: Brisard, *Zarqawi*, 28.

8 The Mukhabarat fears were borne out: Brisard, *Zarqawi*, 29.

9 Together, in a Levantine shadow play: Brisard, *Zarqawi*, 36.

9 Al-Maqdisi was a pedantic scholar: Brisard, *Zarqawi*, 37.

9 "He never struck me as intelligent": Jeffrey Gettleman, "Zarqawi's Journey: From Droupout to Prisoner to Insurgent Leader," *New York Times*, July 13, 2004, www.nytimes.com/2004/07/13/international/middleeast/13zarq.html.

9 Al-Maqdisi gave al-Zarqawi: Brisard, *Zarqawi*, 226–27.

9 Aware that the Mukhabarat was tracking: Brisard, *Zarqawi*, 39.

9 Al-Zarqawi was charged and convicted: Weaver, 2006.

10 Amin was further instructed: Napoleoni, *Insurgent Iraq*, 64–65.

10 Both men were sentenced in 1994: Brisard, *Zarqawi*, 43.

10 It made him more focused: Weaver, 2006.

10 He got his underlings: Brisard, *Zarqawi*, 48.

10 "He could order his followers": Gettleman, 2004.

10 By means of coercion or persuasion: Brisard, *Zarqawi*, 48.

10 He beat up those he didn't like: Ibid.

11 "The note was full of bad Arabic, like a child wrote it": Gettleman, 2004.

11 Unable to develop arguments: Ibid.

11 At one point, he was thrown into: Napoleoni, *Insurgent Iraq*, 70.

11 Al-Zarqawi assumed the title of emir: Napoleoni, *Insurgent Iraq*, 75–76.

11 The mentor-scholar helped: Weaver, 2006.

11 A few of these even caught the attention of bin Laden: Bruce Riedel, *The Search for Al Qaeda: Its Leadership, Ideology, and Future* (Washington, D.C.: Brookings Institution Press, 2010), 93–94.

11 According to "Richard," a former top-ranking counterterrorism official: Interview with former top-ranking counterterrorism official, December 2014.

12 Many Islamists who hadn't actually (or successfully) committed terrorism: Brisard, *Zarqawi*, 57.

12 able to depart in the summer of 1999: Brisard, *Zarqawi*, 59.

12 He was arrested briefly in Peshawar: Napoleoni, *Insurgent Iraq*, 97.

12 Told that he would only get his passport back: Brisard, *Zarqawi*, 67.

13 Al-Zawahiri . . . was present at the meeting: Bryan Price, Dan Milton, Muhammad al-Ubaydi, and Nelly Lahoud, "The Group That Calls Itself a State: Understanding the Evolution and Challenges of the Islamic State," Combating Terrorism Center at West Point, December 16, 2014, www.ctc.usma.edu/posts /the-group-that-calls-itself-a-state-understanding-the-evolution-and-challenges -of-the-islamic-state.

13 In the early 1990s al-Qaeda had targeted: Bergen, *The Osama bin Laden I Know*, 197.

14 One of these contacts was Abu Muhammad al-Adnani: Price et al., 2014.

14 The camp was built with al-Qaeda money: Brisard, *Zarqawi*, 71–72.

14 according to former CIA analyst Nada Bakos: "Tracking Al Qaeda in Iraq's Zarqawi Interview With Ex-CIA Analyst Nada Bakos," Musings on Iraq blog, June 30, 2014, musingsoniraq.blogspot.com/2014/06/tracking-al-qaeda-in-iraqs-zarqawi.html.

15 Al-Zarqawi fielded mainly Palestinian and Jordanian recruits: Brisard, *Zarqawi*, 72.

15 the Soldiers of the Levant were: Weaver, 2006.

15 Some of the camp's graduates: Napoleoni, *Insurgent Iraq*, 125–26; Brisard, *Zarqawi*, 88.

15 The Jordanians claimed: Napoleoni, *Insurgent Iraq*, 125–26; Weaver, 2006.

16 Soldiers of the Levant grew exponentially: Weaver, 2006.

16 Between 2000 and 2001: Ibid.

16 Al-Zarqawi repeatedly refused: Napoleoni, *Insurgent Iraq*, 98–99; Weaver, 2006.

16 "I never heard him praise anyone apart from the Prophet": Napoleoni, *Insurgent Iraq*, 98–99.

16 Whether owing to hubris: Weaver, 2006.

17 One of al-Zarqawi's lieutenants in Herat: Brisard, *Zarqawi*, 77.

17 After the September 11 attacks: Brisard, *Zarqawi*, 115.

17 The targets of this superconglomerate were two: Napoleoni, *Insurgent Iraq*, 106–07; Brisard, *Zarqawi*, 115–16, 122.

17 On February 3, 2003: Napoleoni, *Insurgent Iraq*, 116–17.

17 "We first knew of Zarqawi . . .": Interview with one of the authors, December 2014.

19 "Jihadists gain more from friendships . . .": Ibid.

19 Al-Zarqawi and his convoy: Napoleoni, *Insurgent Iraq*, 109.

19 He visited a Palestinian refugee camp: Brisard, *Zarqawi*, 96, 99–100.

19 Shadi Abdalla, bin Laden's former bodyguard: Brisard, *Zarqawi*, 95.

20 Al-Zarqawi also went to Syria: Brisard, *Zarqawi*, 96.

20 A high-level source in Jordanian intelligence told: Weaver, 2006.

21 As early as October 2002: Riedel, *The Search for Al Qaeda*, 87–88; Gerges, *The Far Enemy*, 252.

21 Six months later, bin Laden addressed the people: Riedel, *The Search for Al Qaeda*, 88.

22 In opposition to this, bin Laden advocated: Ibid.

22 he put out a global casting call: Riedel, *The Search for Al Qaeda*, 10–11, 87–89, 132.

22 To hurt the "far enemy,": Riedel, *The Search for Al Qaeda*, 88.

CHAPTER 2

23 Bin Laden's injunction was fully realized: Kevin Woods, James Lacy, and Williamson Murray, "Saddam's Delusions," *Foreign Affairs*, May/June 2006, www.foreignaffairs.

com/articles/61701/kevin-woods-james-lacey-and-williamson-murray/saddams
-delusions.

23 But he had very much prepared: Michael R. Gordon and Bernard E. Trainor, *The Endgame: The Inside Story of the Struggle for Iraq, from George W. Bush to Barack Obama* (New York: Vintage Books, 2013), 20–21.

23 He beefed up one of his praetorian divisions: Ibid.

23 In their magisterial history of the Iraq War: Ibid.

23 The man who anatomized this strategy: Gordon & Trainor, *The Endgame*, 18–20.

24 Added to their ranks were more disaffected Iraqis: Gordon & Trainor, *The Endgame*, 14; "Coalition Provisional Authority Order Number 1: De-Ba'athification of Iraqi Society," The Coalition Provisional Authority, May 16, 2003, www.iraqcoalition.org /regulations/20030516_CPAORD_1_De-Ba_athification_of_Iraqi_Society_.pdf; Sharon Otterman, "IRAQ: Debaathification," Council on Foreign Relations, April 7, 2005, www.cfr.org/iraq/iraq-debaathification/p7853#p9.

25 To distinguish the latter from disfigured veterans: Brian Owsley, "Iraq's Brutal Decrees Amputation, Branding and the Death Penalty," Human Rights Watch /Middle East, June 1995, www.hrw.org/reports/1995/IRAQ955.htm.

25 The regime thus introduced a proscription: Napoleoni, *Insurgent Iraq*, 146.

25 Some of Iraq's new-minted faithful: Joel Rayburn, *Iraq After America: Strongmen, Sectarians, Resistance* (Stanford, California: Hoover Institution Press, 2014), 101.

25 "Saddam believed . . .": Rayburn, *Iraq After America*, 102.

25 Many graduates of the program, Rayburn notes: Ibid.

25 One such person was Khalaf al-Olayan: Rayburn, *Iraq After America*, 113.

26 Mahmoud al-Mashhadani showed the folly: Rayburn, *Iraq After America*, 114.

27 It was for this reason that George H. W. Bush: Gordon & Trainor, *The Endgame*, 5.

27 The elder Bush had hoped: Ibid.

28 "At first no one fought . . .": Rayburn, *Iraq After America*, 105.

28 That question was carried out by a twenty-six-year-old Moroccan man: Carolina Larriera, "Remembering Sergio Vieria de Mello Ten Years After the Attack on the UN in Baghdad," *The Huffington Post*, October 19, 2013, www.huffingtonpost.com /carolina-larriera/remembering-sergio-vieira_b_3779106.html.

28 This "embellishment" evidently included the Brazilian diplomat's role: Christopher Hitchens, "Why Ask Why?: Terrorists Attacks Aren't Caused by Any Policy Except That of the Bombers Themselves," *Slate*, October 3, 2005, www.slate.com/articles /news_and_politics/fighting_words/2005/10/why_ask_why.html.

28 "According to Harvey, it gave Zarqawi's men the cars . . .": Gordon & Trainor, *The Endgame*, 22; "Iraq's Security Services: Regime Strategic Intent—Annex C," Central Intelligence Agency, April 23, 2007, www.cia.gov/library/reports/general-reports-1 /iraq_wmd_2004/chap1_annxC.html; "Special Security Organisation—SSO: Al Amn al-Khas," GlobalSecurity.org, last modified July 28, 2011, www.globalsecurity .org/intell/world/iraq/khas.htm.

29 "The idea was, if you understood who the terrorists were": Derek Harvey interview with one of the authors, October 2014.

29 According to a study conducted by the Jamestown Foundation: Murad Batal al-Shishani, "Al-Zarqawi's Rise to Power: Analyzing Tactics and Targets," *Terrorism Monitor*, Vol. 3, No. 22, The Jamestown Foundation, November 18, 2005, www.jamestown.org/single/?tx_ttnews%5Btt_news%5D=610&no_cache=1# .VIk1cDHF8ei.

30 The same month Monotheism and Jihad bombed the Jordanian embassy: Riedel, *The Search for Al Qaeda*, 100, 105; Lawrence Joffe, "Ayatollah Mohammad Baqir

al-Hakim," obituary, *The Guardian*, August 29, 2003, www.theguardian.com/news
/2003/aug/30/guardianobituaries.iraq.

28 In fact, it was al-Zarqawi's father-in-law, Yassin Jarrad: Napoleoni, *Insurgent
Iraq*, 108, 160–161; "Imam Ali Mosque," GlobalSecurity.org, last modified
July 9, 2011, www.globalsecurity.org/military/world/iraq/an-najaf-imam-ali.htm;
Bassem Mroue, "Alleged Al Qaeda Militant Is Hanged," *The New York Sun* via The
Associated Press, July 6, 2007, www.nysun.com/foreign/alleged-al-qaeda-militant
-is-hanged/57989; Ben Wedemean, "FBI to Join Mosque Bombing Probe," CNN
.com, September 1, 2003, www.cnn.com/2003/WORLD/meast/08/31/sprj.irq
.main.

30 A letter said to have been written: Musab Al-Zarqawi, "Letter from Abu Musab
al-Zarqawi to Osama bin Laden," Council on Foreign Relations, February 1, 2004,
www.cfr.org/iraq/letter-abu-musab-al-zarqawi-osama-bin-laden/p9863.

31 nemeses ... was the Badr Corps: For the sake of consistency, we have chosen to use
Badr Corps throughout, however, it was eventually renamed the Badr Organization.

31 "They have placed cadres ...": Ibid.

31 "If we succeed in dragging them into the arena of sectarian war": Ibid.

32 That figure may have been exaggerated: "Iraq: Islamic State Executions in Tikrit,"
Human Rights Watch, September 2, 2014, www.hrw.org/news/2014/09/02/iraq
-islamic-state-executions-tikrit.

32 Members of the first two categories were taken elsewhere: "Iraq: ISIS Executed
Hundreds of Prison Inmates," Human Rights Watch, October 30, 2014, www.hrw
.org/news/2014/10/30/iraq-isis-executed-hundreds-prison-inmates.

32 Al-Zarqawi proved a pioneer: Brisard, *Zarqawi*, 142–43.

32 An imprecation was then recited by his captor: Brisard, *Zarqawi*, 131.

33 Though al-Zarqawi retained an audiovisual squad: Brisard, *Zarqawi*, 143.

33 Writing to his former protégé: Riedel, *The Search for Al Qaeda*, 103.

33 As former CIA analyst Bruce Riedel has observed: Riedel, *The Search for Al Qaeda*,
102–03.

33 As scholar Michael W. S. Ryan has noted: Michael W. S. Ryan, "Dabiq: What
Islamic State's New Magazine Tells Us about Their Strategic Direction, Recruitment
Patterns, and Guerilla Doctrine, the Jamestown Foundation, August 1, 2014,
jamestown.org, August 1, 2014, www.jamestown.org/programs/tm/single/?tx
_ttnews%5B[tt_news]%5D=42702.VscOBPlrLjY.

34 Before Blackwater USAattained international notoriety: "Four Blackwater Agents
Hung in Fallujah Iraq March 31, 2004," YouTube video of ABC broadcast, 2:41,
posted by WARLORDSMEDIUM, December 11, 2011, www.youtube.com
/watch?v=bln0q8E5onE.

34 The failure of foresight seems staggering: Gordon & Trainor, *The Endgame*, 23,
56–57.

34 According to Wael Essam, a Palestinian journalist: Interview with the authors,
November 2014.

34 The beheading of Nicholas Berg: Gordon & Trainor, *The Endgame*, 113.

36 the main American weapon being deployed against the Zarqawists: Gordon &
Trainor, *The Endgame*, 114.

36 McChrystal assessed that the threat posed: Ibid.

36 By then adept at the uses of psychological warfare: Bergen, *The Osama bin Laden I
Know*, 364.

37 It was also accompanied by F/A-18 Hornet jets: Gordon & Trainor, *The Endgame*,
117–18.

37 In total, three "torture houses" were uncovered in the city: Gordon & Trainor, *The Endgame*, 119.

38 Roughly a quarter of all insurgents killed: Lt. Colonel Kenneth Estes, *US Marine Corps Operations in Iraq, 203-2006* (Marine Corps History Division), 66; *CQ Researcher, Global Issues: Selections from CQ Researcher* (CQ Press, 2014), ebook.

38 America was waging a "total war against Islam,": Napoleoni, *Insurgent Iraq*, 183.

38 In December 2004 bin Laden answered al-Zarqawi's bayat: Ibid.

38 The title was somewhat misleading: Riedel, *The Search for Al Qaeda*, 105.

39 As the former CIA analyst Bruce Riedel recounts, some al-Qaeda ideologues: Riedel, *The Search for Al Qaeda*, 12–13.

39 The ideologue invoked: Riedel, *The Search for Al Qaeda*, 100.

39 As Riedel observes: Riedel, *The Search for Al Qaeda*, 106.

39 He had intertwined: Riedel, *The Search for Al Qaeda*, 106; "Mapping the Global Muslim Population," PewResearch, October 7, 2009, www.pewforum.org/2009 /10/07/mapping-the-global-muslim-population.

39 He had, according to his Saudi admirer: Riedel, *The Search for Al Qaeda*, 105.

CHAPTER 3

42 One insurgent stronghold was Haifa Street: Gordon & Trainor, *The Endgame*, 123; "Haifa St, Baghdad, Iraq," Google Maps, accessed January 17, 2015, www.google .com/maps/place/Haifa+St.,+Baghdad,+Iraq/.

42 Haifa Street had by now become a totem: Gordon & Trainor, *The Endgame*, 123.

43 Local loyalties in Dora, yet another district of Baghdad infiltrated by insurgents: Ibid.

43 The ease with which the provincial capital collapsed: Gordon & Trainor, *The Endgame*, 124.

44 They were especially brutal to any Iraqi soldier: Gordon & Trainor, *The Endgame*, 126.

44 Al-Zarqawi's sinister strategy: Translation of *The Management of Savagery* by William McCants. Abu Bakr Najri, *The Management of Savagery: The Most Critical Stage Through Which the Umma Will Pass*, May 23, 2006, azelin.files.wordpress .com/2010/08/abu-bakr-naji-the-management-of-savagery-the-most-critical -stage-through-which-the-umma-will-pass.pdf.

47 fewer than 1 percent of all Sunnis cast ballots: Rayburn, *Iraq After America*, 110.

47 On February 28, 2005, a suicide bomb killed: Warzer Jaff and Robert E. Worth, "Deadliest Single Attack Since Fall of Hussein Kills More Than 120," *New York Times*, February 28, 2005, www.nytimes.com/2005/02/28/international/middle east/28cnd-iraq.html.

47 In one horrifying instance: "Interview Col. H.R. McMaster," Frontline End Game, June 19, 2007, www.pbs.org/wgbh/pages/frontline/endgame/interviews/mcmaster .html.

48 "If they perceive failure, they may take other actions . . .": Gordon & Trainor, *The Endgame*, 36.

48 "Al-Zarqawi, or the Iraqis he had working for him . . .": Interview with one of the authors, December 2014.

49 It also contains the largest phosphate mines in the Middle East: Napoleoni, *Insurgent Iraq*, 190.

49 Building on Such's experience in Hit: "Anbar Before and After The Awakening Pt. IX: Sheik Sabah Aziz of the Albu Mahal," Musings on Iraq blog, January 23, 2014, musingsoniraq.blogspot.com/2014/01/anbar-before-and-after-awakening-pt-ix.html.

49 In the Albu Mahal's Hamza Battalion. Hannah Allam and Mohammed al Dulaimy, "Marine-led Campaign Kill Friends and Foes, Iraqi Leaders Say," McClatchy DC via Knight Ridder Newspapers, May 16, 2005, www.mcclatchydc.com/2005/05/16 /11656_marine-led-campaign-killed-friends.html.

49 The graduates of the Qa'im program: Gordon & Trainor, *The Endgame*, 172; Rayburn, *Iraq After America*, 110–11.

49 A third of the Desert Protectors' members quit: Ibid.

50 Appalled by how the Sunni boycott: Col. Gary W. Montgomery and Timothy S. McWilliams, eds., *Al-Anbar Awakening: From Insurgency to Counterinsurgency in Iraq, 2004–2009*, Vol. 2, Marine Corps University Press, 2009, www.marines .mil/Portals/59/Publications/Al-Anbar%20Awakening%20Vol%20II_Iraqi%20 Perspectives%20%20PCN%2010600001200_1.pdf.

50 Its first initiative was to encourage Sunnis: Monte Morin, "Officer Killed by Suicide Bomb Had High Hopes for Ramadi," *Stars and Stripes*, January 9, 2006, www.stripes.com/news/officer-killed-by-suicide-bomb-had-high-hopes-for -ramadi-1.43384.

50 On the fourth day of the glass factory drive: Monte Morin, "Suicide Bomb Kills Dozens of Iraqi Police Recruits, Two Americans," *Stars and Stripes*, January 6, 2006, www.stripes.com/news/suicide-bomb-kills-dozens-of-iraqi-police-recruits-two -americans-1.43269.

50 Still too vulnerable to al-Zarqawi's strong-arm tactics: Stephen Biddle, Jeffrey A. Friedman, and Jacob N. Shapiro, "Testing the Surge: Why Did Violence Decline in Iraq in 2007?" *International Security*, Vol. 37, No. 1, Summer 2012, 20.

CHAPTER 4

52 Sunni voter turnout was around 80 percent: Rayburn, *Iraq After America*, 119.

52 Additionally, less moderate non-al-Qaeda insurgents: Gordon & Trainor, *The Endgame*, 191–92.

53 Kanan Makiya, a well-learned scholar of Saddam's Iraq: Kanan Makiya, *Cruelty and Silence: War, Tyranny, Uprising, and the Arab World* (New York: Jonathan Cape, 1993).

53 He founded his own paramilitary organization: Nada Bakri, "In Lebanon, New Cabinet Is Influenced by Hezbollah," *New York Times*, June 13, 2011, www.nytimes .com/2011/06/14/world/middleeast/14lebanon.html.

54 The Battle of Najaf in August 2004: Gordon & Trainor, *The Endgame*, 101.

54 He was an operative for the Quds Force's Department 1000: Ibid.

54 The Supreme Council for Islamic Revolution in Iraq (SCIRI): Rayburn, *Iraq After America*, 15–17.

54 SCIRI's armed wing: "Iraqi Miniser's Son Misses Flight, Forces Plane Back: Airline," Reuters, March 6, 2014, www.reuters.com/article/2014/03/06/us-lebanon -iraq-plane-idUSBREA2519B20140306; Rayburn, *Iraq After America*, 73–75.

54 "The mullahs ran a very subversive campaign": Interview with one of the authors, June 2014.

54 A former CIA officer not long ago described Suleimani: Dexter Filkins, "The Shadow Commander," *The New Yorker*, September 30, 2013, www.newyorker.com /magazine/2013/09/30/the-shadow-commander.

55 For Petraeus, Iran had: Gordon & Trainor, *The Endgame*, 423.

55 Not only had the Quds Force officer: Gordon & Trainor, *The Endgame*, 313, 351–52.

55 Al-Muhandis was selected to oversee: Gordon & Trainor, *The Endgame*, 151, 159; Filkins, 2013.

55 When detonated, the heat from the EFP: David Axe, "Real E.F.P.: Pocket-Sized Tank Killer," Defense Tech, February 14, 2007, defensetech.org/2007/02/14/real-e-f-p-pocket-sized-tank-killer.

56 Another JSOC raid in Erbil: Gordon & Trainor, *The Endgame*, 324–25.

56 "By exposing Iran's secret deal": "Treasury Targets Key Al-Qa'ida Funding and Support Network Using Iran as a Critical Transit Point," US Department of the Treasury, July 28, 2011, www.treasury.gov/press-center/press-releases/Pages/tg1261.aspx.

57 "They were there, under Iranian protection, planning operations": Filkins, 2013.

57 After December 2005 SCIRI was placed: Gordon & Trainor, *The Endgame*, 140.

57 "We either stop them or give Iraq to Iran": Gordon & Trainor, *The Endgame*, 141.

57 But, by way of trying to limit the damage: Ibid.

57 The counterpart brigade in charge of West Baghdad: Gordon & Trainor, *The Endgame*, 146.

58 According to a State Department cable: "Islamic Human Rights Organization Alleges Iraqi Forces Detainee Abuse in Ninewa," WikiLeaks, June 16, 2005, wikileaks.org/plusd/cables/05BAGHDAD2547_a.html.

58 Other Iraqi government institutions: Gordon & Trainor, *The Endgame*, 222.

58 Hospitals, meanwhile, were refashioned: Gordon & Trainor, *The Endgame*, 221–222.

58 It also had ready access: Ibid.

58 When US soldiers finally opened the door: Gordon & Trainor, *The Endgame*, 185–86.

59 Only the "most criminal terrorists" were detained: Ibid.

59 Testifying to the grim cooperation: Edward Wong and John F. Burns, "Iraqi Rift Grows After Discovery of Prison," *New York Times*, November 17, 2005, www.nytimes.com/2005/11/17international/middleeast/17iraq.html.

60 In 2006, the US government found: "Testimony of Dr. Matthew Levitt, Fromer-Wexler fellow and director of the Stein Program on Counterterrorism and Intelligence at The Washington Institute for Near East Policy," US House Financial Services Committee, November 13, 2014, financialservices.house.gov/uploadedfiles/hhrg-113-ba00-wstate-mlevitt-20141113.pdf.

60 According to Laith Alkhouri: Interview with one of the authors, November 2014.

60 From 2005 to 2010 subsidies from Gulf Arab donors: US House Financial Services Committee, 2014.

60 Oil smuggling from the Bayji Oil Refinery: Gordon & Trainor, *The Endgame*, 231; Benjamin Bahney, Howard J. Shatz, Carroll Ganier, Renny McPherson, and Barbara Sude, *An Economic Analysis of the Financial Records of al-Qa'ida in Iraq* (National Defense Research Institute, 2010), e-book.

60 A Defense Intelligence Agency assessment: Gordon & Trainor, *The Endgame*, 231.

60 Iraq's resources had by then eclipsed: US House Financial Services Committee, 2014.

60 In July 2005 al-Zawahiri sent al-Zarqawi a letter: "Zawahiri's Letter to Zarqawi (English Translation)," Combating Terrorism Center at West Point, October 2013, www.ctc.usma.edu/posts/zawahiris-letter-to-zarqawi-english-translation-2.

61 Al-Zawahiri counseled al-Zarqawi to avoid the "mistake of the Taliban": Riedel, *The Search for Al Qaeda*, 104.

61 There was one enemy: Combating Terrorism Center at West Point, 2013.

61 Fearing that the Islamic Republic's response: Riedel, *The Search for Al Qaeda*, 104.

64 The CIA leaked the critical missive: Riedel, *The Search for Al Qaeda*, 103.

64 The day of the bombing: Ellen Knickmeyer and K.I. Ibrahim, "Bombing Shatters Mosque in Iraq," *Washington Post*, February 23, 2006, www.washingtonpost.com/wp -dyn/content/article/2006/02/22/AR2006022200454.html.

64 Grand Ayatollah Ali al-Sistani called for peaceful protests: Ibid.

64 One of Iraq's NGOs found: Gordon & Trainor, *The Endgame*, 194.

64 The al-Askari Mosque bombing accomplished: Ellen Knickmeyer and Muhanned Saif Aldin, "Tense Calm Prevails as Iraqi Forces Seal Off River Town," *Washington Post*, October 18, 2006, www.washingtonpost.com/wp-dyn/content/article/2006 /10/17/AR2006101700254.html; Rayburn, *Iraq After America*, 120.

64 Bodies were dumped in the Tigris River: Joshua Partlow and Saad al-Izzi, "Scores of Sunnis Killed in Baghdad," *Washington Post*, July 10, 2006, www.washingtonpost .com/wp-dyn/content/article/2006/07/09/AR2006070900139.html; Gordon & Trainor, *The Endgame*, 214.

64 The Mahdi Army also set up checkpoints: Jon Lee Anderson, "Inside the Surge," *The New Yorker*, November 19, 2007, www.newyorker.com/magazine/2007/11/19 /inside-the-surge; "Ghazaliya, Baghdad, Iraq," Google Maps, accessed January 17, 2015, www.google.com/maps/place/Ghazaliyah,+Baghdad,+Iraq/@34.0092759, 43.8541015,9z/data=!4m2!3m1!1s0x15577d6b25af61b3:0x1c37973c4265e31e; Gordon & Trainor, *The Endgame*, 213–14.

64 Uniformed Iraqi policemen were enlisted: Gordon & Trainor, *The Endgame*, 213–14.

64 Sunni insurgents paid the Shia back: Rayburn, *Iraq After America*, 87–88.

64 Al-Qaeda in Iraq and other Islamist insurgent groups: Gordon & Trainor, *The Endgame*, 213–14.

64 This was the issue put forth in a classified memo: "Text of U.S. Security Adviser's Iraq Memo," *New York Times*, November 29, 2006, www.nytimes.com/2006/11/29 /world/middleeast/29mtext.html.

64 "Reports of nondelivery of services to Sunni areas": Ibid.

65 He may once even have escaped: Riedel, *The Search for Al Qaeda*, 106.

65 To find al-Zarqawi through his underlings: Gordon & Trainor, *The Endgame*, 206.

65 US forces discovered that their target: Ibid.

65 Iraqi soldiers found al-Zarqawi first: Gordon & Trainor, *The Endgame*, 207.

65 Jordanian intelligence, which had claimed: Dexter Filkins, Mark Mazzetti and Richard A. Oppel Jr., "How Surveillance and Betrayal Led to a Hunt's End," *New York Times*, June 9, 2006, www.nytimes.com/2006/06/09/world/middleeast/09raid .html.

65 All forgoing words of caution to the contrary: Riedel, *The Search for Al Qaeda*, 106.

66 The Mujahidin Advisory Council he installed: Eben Kaplan, "Abu Hamza al-Muhajir, Zarqawi's Mysterious Successor (aka Abu Ayub al-Masri)," Council on Foreign Relations, June 13, 2006, www.cfr.org/iraq/abu-hamza-al-muhajir-zarqawis -mysterious-successor-aka-abu-ayub-al-masri/p10894.

66 Al-Masri had belonged to: Gordon & Trainor, *The Endgame*, 230.

66 For one thing, he took the Iraqization program further: Rayburn, *Iraq After America*, 121; Ahmed S. Hashim, "The Islamic State: From al-Qaeda Affiliate to Caliphate," *Middle East Policy Council*, Vol. 21, No. 4, Winter 2014, www.mepc.org/journal /middle-east-policy-archives/islamic-state-al-qaeda-affiliate-caliphate.

66 Its demesne was Ninewah, Anbar, and Salah ad Din provinces: Rayburn, *Iraq After America*, 121, 136.

66 Iraq's first emir appointed leader, Abu Omar al-Baghdadi: Gordon & Trainor, *The Endgame*, 230; Rayburn, *Iraq After America*, 128.

66 After his succession became public, US forces captured: Gordon & Trainor, *The Endgame*, 230.

67 Al-Zarqawi, he said, saw himself in messianic terms: Ibid.

67 "He came from outside . . .": Interview with one of the authors, October 2014.

67 Both men wanted to establish: Gordon & Trainor, *The Endgame*, 230; Hashim, 2014.

67 Most of the Sunni groups that joined ISI protested: Hashim, 2014.

67 ". . . Ultimately, they resorted to killing jihadists . . .: Interview with one of the authors, November 2014.

68 In May 2014 he issued a statement: Price et al., 2014.

68 Digital intelligence on ISI: Bill Roggio, "Iraqi Troops Kill Senior al Qaeda in Iraq Leader," The Long War Journal, November 7, 2008, www.longwarjournal.org /archives/2008/11/iraqi_troops_kill_se.php.

69 The *Wall Street Journal* reported: Greg Jaffe, "At Lonely Iraq Outpost, GIs Stay as Hope Fades," *Wall Street Journal*, May 3, 2007, www.wsj.com/articles/SB1178133 40417889827.

69 Abu Ghazwan's overview: Gordon & Trainor, *The Endgame*, 233.

69 He had once been a detainee of the coalition: Gordon & Trainor, *The Endgame*, 233; "Fire Marshal Ronald P. Bucca," Officer Down Memorial Page, accessed January 17, 2015, www.odmp.org/officer/16195-fire-marshal-ronald-p-bucca.

69 In Bucca, al-Rahman did not just learn: Gordon & Trainor, *The Endgame*, 32–33, 233–34.

70 As Michael Gordon and Bernard Trainor recount: Gordon & Trainor, *The Endgame*, 234.

CHAPTER 5

71 "The history of the Anbar Awakening is very bitter . . .": a former high-ranking official: Interview with the authors, August 2014.

72 Barrels of purloined crude were imported: Gordon & Trainor, *The Endgame*, 244.

72 Two sheikhs from the Albu Aetha and Albu Dhiyab tribes: Myriam Benraad, "Iraq's Tribal 'Sahwa': Its Rise and Fall," Middle East Policy Council, Vol. 18, No. 1, Spring 2011, www.mepc.org/journal/middle-east-policy-archives/iraqs-tribal-sahwa-its -rise-and-fall.

72 Nighttime vigilantism gained: Gordon & Trainor, *The Endgame*, 244.

72 What made Ramadi different: Kirk Semple, "Uneasy Alliance Is Taming One Insurgent Bastion," *New York Times*, April 29, 2007, www.nytimes.com/2007/04/29 /world/middleeast/29ramadi.html.

72 al-Rishawi was ready to cut a new deal: Gordon & Trainor, *The Endgame*, 250.

72 "People with ties to the insurgents . . ."a US lieutenant had told the journalist George Packer: George Packer, "The Lesson of Tal Afar," *The New Yorker*, April 10, 2006, www.newyorker.com/magazine/2006/04/10/the-lesson-of-tal-afar.

73 The council quickly expanded: Gordon & Trainor, *The Endgame*, 252.

73 Just before New Year 2007: Gordon & Trainor, *The Endgame*, 253.

73 Al-Rishawi's general success: Ibid.

73 "I swear to God . . ." the sheikh told the *New York Times*: Edward Wong, "An Iraqi Tribal Chief Opposes the Jihadists, and Prays," *New York Times*, March 3, 2007, www.nytimes.com/2007/03/03/world/middleeast/03sheik.html.

73 He was assassinated by the jihadists: Alissa J. Rubin and Graham Bowley, "Bomb Kills Sunni Sheik Working With US in Iraq," *New York Times*, September 13, 2007, www.nytimes.com/2007/09/13/world/middleeast/13cnd-iraq.html.

74 The emir told him that while foreign occupiers: Gordon & Trainor, *The Endgame*, 263.

74 The new strategy demanded confronting: Jason Burke, *The 9/11 Wars* (New York: Penguin, 2012), 267.

74 Petraeus and Marine Lieutenant General James Mattis: Burke, *The 9/11 Wars*, 265.

74 A mixture of soldiering and policing: Joint Chiefs of Staff Joint Publication 3-24, *The Petraeus Doctrine: The Field Manual on Counterinsurgency Operations*, US Army, 2009.

75 In 2007, the US Government Accountability Office: Glenn Kessler, "Weapons Given to Iraq Are Missing," *Washington Post*, August 6, 2007, www.washingtonpost .com/wp-dyn/content/article/2007/08/05/AR2007080501299.html.

75 The US military's solution was a partition: Burke, *The 9/11 Wars*, 271.

75 A military intelligence analysis: Gordon & Trainor, *The Endgame*, 209.

76 Furthermore, the overwhelming cluster of attacks: Ibid.

76 If a detonated IED turned out to be a dud: Gordon & Trainor, *The Endgame*, 210.

76 As they had done the prior year in Ramadi: Gordon & Trainor, *The Endgame*, 370.

76 The group's fallback base was in nearby Buhriz: Ibid.

77 Sergeant 1st Class Benjamin Hanner told the *Washington Post*: Joshua Partlow, "Troops in Diyala Face A Skilled, Flexible Foe," *Washington Post*, April 22, 2007, www.washingtonpost.com/wp-dyn/content/article/2007/04/21/AR2007042101467 _pf.html.

77 Shawn McGuire, a staff sergeant, recalled to Michael Gordon and Bernard Trainor: Gordon & Trainor, *The Endgame*, 375.

77 In an interview with the *Washington Post*: Jackie Spinner, "Marines Widen Their Net South of Baghdad," *Washington Post*, November 28, 2004, www.washingtonpost.com /wp-dyn/articles/A16794-2004Nov27.html.

78 After being handed a list of the top-ten al-Qaeda in Iraq operatives: Gordon & Trainor, *The Endgame*, 381.

78 In Ameriya, a neighborhood: Gordon & Trainor, *The Endgame*, 384.

78 No doubt leery of seeing a replay: Ibid.

79 In a June 2010 Pentagon news briefing: Gen. Raymond Odierno, "DOD News Briefing with Gen. Odierno from the Pentagon," US Department of Defense, June 4, 2010, www.defense.gov/transcripts/transcript.aspx?transcriptid=4632.

80 In *Iraq After America*, Joel Rayburn recounts: Rayburn, *Iraq After America*, 124.

80 Several months before his death, he had conducted a Skype call: Interview with one of Jibouri's interlocutors, November 2014.

81 Dr. Jaber al-Jabberi . . . told: Interview with one of the authors, August 2014.

CHAPTER 6

83 The internationally publicized and condemned torture: Alissa J. Rubin, "US Military Reforms Its Prisons in Iraq," *New York Times*, June 1, 2008, www.nytimes .com/2008/06/01/world/africa/01iht-detain.4.13375130.html.

83 According to one US military estimate: Interview with Joel Rayburn, October 2014.

83 Owing to the spike in military operations: Craig Whiteside, "Catch And Release in the Land of Two Rivers," War on the Rocks, December 18, 2014, warontherocks .com/2014/12/catch-and-release-in-the-land-of-two-rivers.

83 In a PowerPoint presentation he prepared for Central Command: Major General D.M Stone, "Detainee Operations," United States Marine Corps, PowerPoint presentation, November 2014.

85 A former ISIS member interviewed by the *Guardian*: Martin Chulov, "Isis: The Inside Story," *The Guardian*, December 11, 2014, www.theguardian.com/world/2014 /dec/11/-sp-isis-the-inside-story.

85 Abu Ahmed recounted: Ibid.

86 Craig Whiteside, a professor at the Naval War College: Whiteside, 2014.

87 Anthony Shadid, then a foreign correspondent for the *Washington Post*: Anthony Shadid, "In Iraq, Chaos Feared as US Closes Prison," *Washington Post*, March 22, 2009, www.washingtonpost.com/wp-dyn/content/article/2009/03/21/AR20090 32102255_pf.html.

87 "It was easy to capture al-Qaeda people," Rayburn told us: Interview with one of the authors, October 2014.

88 No longer useful to al-Maliki: Burke, *The 9/11 Wars*, 430.

88 Conditions were especially grim in Diyala: Gordon & Trainor, *The Endgame*, 591.

88 Such prejudicial justice didn't apply to Shia prisoners: Gordon & Trainor, *The Endgame*, 592.

89 Shadid interviewed Colonel Saad Abbas Mahmoud: Shadid, 2009.

89 The original plan for the Awakening: Gordon & Trainor, *The Endgame*, 591.

89 The Iraqi agency tasked: Gordon & Trainor, *The Endgame*, 593.

89 Al-Maliki showed little interest: Ibid.

89 Mullah Nadim Jibouri . . . claimed: Interview with one of the authors, November 2014.

90 The US assessment of Maliki's dictatorial tendencies: Gordon & Trainor, *The Endgame*, 614.

90 Odierno, with good reason, saw: Gordon & Trainor, *The Endgame*, 609.

91 He would need to form a government: Gordon & Trainor, *The Endgame*, 617.

92 The following day, Iraq's president: Rayburn, *Iraq After America*, 213–14.

92 Al-Maliki formed a government eventually: Gordon & Trainor, *The Endgame*, 620.

92 Odierno saw how flagrant manipulation: Gordon & Trainor, *The Endgame*, 619.

92 Vice President Joseph Biden . . . is recorded: Gordon & Trainor, *The Endgame*, 615.

92 "I know one guy . . ." Khedery told us: Interview with one of the authors, November 2014; Ali Khedery, "Why We Stuck With Maliki—and Lost Iraq," *Washington Post*, July 3, 2004, www.washingtonpost.com/opinions/why-we-stuck -with-maliki—and-lost-iraq/2014/07/03/0dd6a8a4-f7ec-11e3-a606-946fd632f9f1 _story.html.

93 As much as the consequences of the surge: "Blowback Against Glenn Greenwald #1," Anonymous Mugwump blog, May 25, 2013, anonymousmugwump.blogspot .co.uk/2013/05/blowback-against-glenn-greenwald-1.html

93 There was actually very little debate: "Five Myths About ISIS," Anonymous Mugwump blog, October 5, 2014, anonymousmugwump.blogspot.co.uk/2014/10 /five-myths-about-isis.html.

93 But al-Maliki did not: Gordon & Trainor, *The Endgame*, 673–674.

94 Al-Hashimi was allowed to fly off: Adrian Blomfield and Damien McElroy, "Iraq in Fresh Turmoil as Prime Minister Nuri al-Maliki Orders Arrest of Vice President," *The Telegraph*, December 19, 2011, www.telegraph.co.uk/news/worldnews/ middleeast/iraq/8966587/Iraq-in-fresh-turmoil-as-Prime-Minister-Nuri-al-Maliki -orders-arrest-of-vice-president.html.

95 He remained in exile: Associated Press in Baghdad, "Iraq Vice President Sentenced to Death Amid Deadly Wave of Insurgent Attacks," *The Guardian*, September 9, 2012, www.theguardian.com/world/2012/sep/09/iraq-vice-president-hashemi -death-sentence.

95 They claimed to be searching the site for the killer: Joel Rayburn, "Iraq Is Back on the Brink of Civil War," *New Republic*, May 8, 2013, www.newrepublic.com /article/113148/iraqs-civil-war-breaking-out-again.

96 According to the Obama administration: Jessica D. Lewis, "Al-Qaeda in Iraq Resurgent," *Middle East Security Report 14*, Institute for the Study of War, September 2013, www.understandingwar.org/sites/default/files/AQI-Resurgent-10Sept_0.pdf.

96 ISIS takeover of Fallujah: Sinan Adnan and Aaron Reese, "Beyond the Islamic State: Iraq's Sunni Insurgency," *Middle East Security Report 24*, Institute for the Study of War, October 2014, www.understandingwar.org/sites/default/files/Sunni%20 Insurgency%20in%20Iraq.pdf

CHAPTER 7

97 Abd al Sattar al-Rishawi, the Anbar Awakening leader: Edward Wong, "An Iraqi Tribal Chief Opposes the Jihadists, and Prays," *New York Times*, March 3, 2007, www.nytimes.com/2007/03/03/world/middleeast/03sheik.html.

98 As scholar Eyal Zisser has noted: Eyal Zisser, "Hafiz al-Asad Discovers Islam," *Middle East Quarterly*, March 1999, www.meforum.org/465/hafiz-al-asad-discovers -islam.

98 Up until recently, for example, despite a national Syrian law: Fares Akram, "Hamas Leader Abandons Longtime Base in Damascus," *New York Times*, January 27, 2012. www.nytimes.com/2012/01/28/world/middleeast/khaled-meshal-the-leader-of -hamas-vacates-damascus.html.

98 Today the regime relies overwhelmingly on the paramilitary assets: David Axe, "Iran Transformed Syria's Army into a Militia that Will Help Assad Survive Another Year," Reuters, December 17, 2014, blogs.reuters.com/great debate/2014/12/16/iran -transformed-syrias-army-into-a-militia-that-will-help-assad-survive-another-year; Amos Harel, "Iran, Hezbollah Significantly Increases Aid to Syria's Assad," *Haaretz*, April 6, 2012, www.haaretz.com/news/middle-east/iran-hezbollah-significantly -increase-aid-to-syria-s-assad-1.422954.

98 In 2007, US Central Command announced: "Three Major Terror Busts in Iraq— Iran, Syria Connections Exposed, Say US Officials," ABC News, March 22, 2007, abcnews.go.com/blogs/headlines/2007/03/three_major_ter; Burke, *The 9/11 Wars*, 171.

98 According to Major General Kevin Bergner: Bill Roggio, "Al Qaeda in Iraq Operative Killed Near Syrian Border Sheds Light on Foreign Influence," The Long War Journal, October 3, 2007, www.longwarjournal.org/archives/2007/10/al_qaeda _in_iraq_ope.php.

98 A study published in 2008: Peter Bergen, Joseph Felter, Vahid Brown, and Jacob Shapiro, *Bombers, Bank Accounts, & Bleedout: Al-Qa'ida's Road In and out of Iraq*, Combating Terrorism Center at West Point, July 2008, https://www.ctc.usma.edu /wp-content/uploads/2011/12/Sinjar_2_FINAL.pdf.

99 "In border villages and cities," the CTC study stated: Ibid.

99 Al-Assad, of course, has always denied: Ibid.

100 as Jason Burke's *The 9/11 Wars* demonstrates: Burke, *The 9/11 Wars*, 171.

100 Bassam Barabandi, a former diplomat: Interview with one of the authors, December 2014.

100 The former diplomat described for us: Interview with one of the authors, December 2014.

100 Tony Badran, an expert on Syria: Interview with one of the authors, December 2014.

101 Badran mentioned . . . the curious case: "Death of a Cleric," *NOW Lebanon*, October 5, 2007, now.mmedia.me/lb/en/commentaryanalysis/death_of_a_cleric.

101 As recounted by journalist Nicholas Blanford: Ibid.

101 Blanford argued that al-Qaqa: Ibid.

101 Habash said that he first met al-Qaqa in 2006: Interview with one of the authors, December 2014.

102 "According to reports in the Arabic press": Interview with one of the authors, December 2014.

103 Fatah al-Islam later posted: Graham Bowley and Souad Makhennet, "Fugitive Sunni Leader Thought to Have Been Captured or Killed in Syria," *New York Times*, November 10, 2008, www.nytimes.com/2008/12/10/world/africa/10iht-syria.4 .18569673.html.

104 most of the insurgents Syria had funneled: Gordon & Trainor, *The Endgame*, 231.

104 "crisis management cell": Ian Black and Martin Chulov, "Leading Syrian Regime Figures Killed in Damascus Bomb Attack," *The Guardian*, July 18, 2012, www .theguardian.com/world/2012/jul/18/syrian-regime-figures-bomb-attack; Michael Weiss, "What the Assault on the Assad Regime Means," *The Telegraph*, July 20, 2012, blogs.telegraph.co.uk/news/michaelweiss/100171767/what-the-assault-on-the -assad-regime-means.

104 Abu Ghadiyah, the Treasury Department alleged: Bill Roggio, "US Strike in Syria 'Decapitated' al Qaeda's Facilitation Network," The Long War Journal, October 27, 2008, www.longwarjournal.org/archives/2008/10/us_strike_in_syria_d.php.

104 According to a State Department cable: "Gen. Petraeus's Meeting with P.M. Maliki," WikiLeaks, January 7, 2009, www.wikileaks.org/plusd/cables/09BAGHDAD31 _a.html.

105 He was an al-Qaeda financier: "Treasury Designates Members of Abu Ghadiyah's Network Facilitates Flow of Terrorists, Weapons, and Money from Syria to al Qaida in Iraq," US Department of the Treasury, February 28, 2008, www.treasury.gov /press-center/press-releases/Pages/hp845.aspx.

105 Abu Ghadiyah's predecessor: James Joyner, "Zarqawi Financial Network Independent," Outside the Beltway, January 25, 2005, www.outsidethebeltway.com /zarqawi_financial_network_independent.

105 Petraeus had even sought permission: Gordon & Trainor, *The Endgame*, 461.

105 Stanley's McChrystal's JSOC: Roggio, October 2008.

106 He asked al-Assad to end: Gordon & Trainor, *The Endgame*, 577.

106 Maura Connelly, the chargé d'affaires: "UK Foreign Secretary Miliband's Nov. 17–18 Trip to Damascus," WikiLeaks, November 19, 2008, www.wikileaks.org/plusd /cables/08DAMASCUS821_a.html.

106 Perhaps it was with the forgoing episode: "Cable 09DAMASCUS384, Re-engaging Syria: Dealing with Sarg Diplomacy," WikiLeaks, June3, 2009, wikileaks.org/cable /2009/06/09DAMASCUS384.html.

107 In December 2014, Martin Chulov: Chulov, December 2014.

107 More than one hundred people: Ibid.

107 In November 2009, his government aired: Steven Lee Myers, "Iraq Military Broadcasts Confession on Bombing," *New York Times*, August 23, 2009, www .nytimes.com/2009/08/24/world/middleeast/24iraq.html.

107 But it recalled its ambassador from Damascus: "Iraq and Syria Recall Envoys," Al Jazeera, August 25, 2009, www.aljazeera.com/news/middleeast/2009/08 /20098251602328210.html.

108 One of the men he refused to turn over: Khaled Yacoub Oweis, "US Security Team to Visit Syria, Focus on Iraq," Reuters, August 11, 2009, www.reuters.com /article/2009/08/11/us-syria-usa-sb-idUSTRE57A5Y120090811.

108 For a short time, al-Assad had tried: Gordon & Trainor, *The Endgame*, 610; Hugh Naylor, "Syria is Said to Be Strengthening Ties to Opponents," *New York Times*, October 7, 2007. www.nytimes.com/2007/10/07/world/middleeast/07syria .html.

108 Iraqi Foreign Minister Hoshyar Zebari told: Tony Badran, "The 'Lebonization' of Iraq," *NOW Lebanon*, December 22, 2009, now.mmedia.me/lb/en/commentary analysis/the_lebanonization_of_iraq.

108 The Iraqi general struggled: Chulov, December 2014.

109 As relayed in a State Department cable: "Syrian Intelligence Chief Attends CT Dialogue With S/CT Benjamin," WikiLeaks, February 24, 2010, wikileaks.org /plusd/cables/10DAMASCUS159_a.html.

109 He explained that his own peculiar method: Ibid.

109 The answer to that question lay in Mamlouk's follow-up: Ibid.

CHAPTER 8

110 ISIS's history, according to its magazine *Dabiq*'s reconstruction: "The Return of Khilafah," *Dabiq*, Issue 1, July, 2014, media.clarionproject.org/files/09-2014/isis-isil -islamic-state-magazine-Issue-1-the-return-of-khilafah.pdf.

111 The first victory was the killing of Sa'ad Uwayyid: Bill Roggio, "US Kills Senior Syrian-based al Qaeda Facilitator in Mosul," The Long War Journal, January 28, 2010, www.longwarjournal.org/archives/2010/01/us_kills_senior_syri.php.

111 A US official later said: Ibid.

111 Al-Rawi named two couriers: Gordon & Trainor, *The Endgame*, 623.

111 Laith Alkhouri, the counterterrorism expert, said: Interview with one of the authors, November 2014.

112 "The adoption of that title . . .": Ibid.

112 He is said to have lived in modest quarters: Ruth Sherlock, "How a Talented Footballer Became World's Most Wanted Man, Abu Bakr al-Baghdadi," *The Telegraph*, November 11, 2014, www.telegraph.co.uk/news/worldnews/middleeast /iraq/10948846/How-a-talented-footballer-became-worlds-most-wanted-man -Abu-Bakr-al-Baghdadi.html.

112 He wore glasses: Ibid.

112 Dr. Hisham al-Hashimi, an expert on ISIS: Interview with one of the authors, December 2014.

112 According to one of his neighbors: Sherlock, November 2014.

113 by late 2003 al-Baghdadi had founded his own Islamist insurgency: Hashim, 2014.

113 A year later, he was arrested: Chulov, December 2014.

114 Abu Ahmed, the former high-ranking ISIS member: Ibid.

114 according to Abu Ahmed: Ibid.

114 He was released: Ibid.

115 The year 2007 proved to be: Hashim, 2014.

119 "The brutality, the tradecraft . . .": Interview with one of the authors, October 2014.

119 Harvey's insight is all the more compelling: Ben Hubbard and Eric Schmitt, "Military Skill and Terrorist Technique Fuel Success of ISIS," *New York Times*, August 27, 2014, mobile.nytimes.com/2014/08/28/world/middleeast/army-know -how-seen-as-factor-in-isis-successes.html.

120 The first is Abu Abdul Rahman al-Bilawi: Ruth Sherlock, "Inside the Leadership of Islamic State: How the New 'Caliphate' Is Run," *The Telegraph*, July 9, 2014, www

.telegraph.co.uk/news/worldnews/middleeast/iraq/10956280/Inside-the-leadership
-of-Islamic-State-how-the-new-caliphate-is-run.html.

120 He was born in al-Khalidiya, in Anbar: Hisham al-Hashimi, "Revealed: The Islamic
State 'Cabinet,' From Finance Minister to Suicide Bomb Deployer," *The Telegraph*,
July 9, 2014, www.telegraph.co.uk/news/worldnews/middleeast/iraq/10956193
/Revealed-the-Islamic-State-cabinet-from-finance-minister-to-suicide-bomb
-deployer.html.

120 Somewhere in between, according to the *Wall Street Journal*: Siobhan Gorman, Nour
Malas, and Matt Bradley, "Brutal Efficiency: The Secret to Islamic State's Success,"
Wall Street Journal, September 3, 2014, www.wsj.com/articles/the-secret-to-the
-success-of-islamic-state-1409709762.

120 Iraqi and Syrian militants believe that al-Anbari: Siobahn Gorman, Nour Malas,
and Matt Bradley, "Disciplined Cadre Runs Islamic State," *Wall Street Journal*,
September 3, 2014, www.wsj.com/articles/SB20001424052970204545604580127823
357609374.

121 according to a cache of internal documents: "Exclusive: Top ISIS Leaders Revealed,"
Al Arabiya News, February 13, 2014, english.alarabiya.net/en/News/2014/02/13
/Exclusive-Top-ISIS-leaders-revealed.html.

121 Another former US detainee: Hubbard & Schmitt, 2014.

122 One final graduate of both Bucca: "3 Senior ISIS Leaders Killed in US Airstrikes,"
CBS News, December 18, 2014, www.cbsnews.com/news/3-senior-isis-leaders
-killed-in-u-s-airstrikes.

122 A former lieutenant colonel: Sherlock, July 2014.

122 Michael Pregent, another former US military: Interview with one of the authors,
October 2014.

123 Known internationally as the "red-bearded jihadist": "Red-Bearded Chechen Fighter
Is Face of ISIS," Sky News, July 3, 2014, news.sky.com/story/1293797/red-bearded
-chechen-fighter-is-face-of-isis.

123 Abu Omar al-Shishani, or Tarkhan Batirashvili: Gorman et al. "Disciplined Cadre,"
2014.

123 He fought in the 2008 Russo-Georgian war: Nina Akhmeteli, "The Georgian Roots
of Isis Commander Omar al-Shishani," BBC News, July 8, 2014, www.bbc.com
/news/world-europe-28217590.

123 Al-Shishani even hung up the phone: Ibid.

123 Released in 2010: Bassem Mroue, "Chechen in Syria a Rising Star in Extremist
Group," Associated Press, July 2, 2014, bigstory.ap.org/article/chechen-syria-rising
-star-extremist-group.

123 Teimuraz told the BBC: Akhmeteli, 2014.

124 Some of them even made impressive incursions: Mroue, 2014.

124 Menagh finally fell: Nour Malas and Rima Abushakra, "Islamists Seize Airbase Near
Aleppo," *Wall Street Journal*, August 6, 2013, www.wsj.com/articles/SB10001424127
887323420604578652250872942058.

124 Largely a morale boost: Anne Barnard and Hwaida Saad, "Rebels Gain Control of
Government Air Base in Syria," *New York Times*, August 5, 2013, www.nytimes
.com/2013/08/06/world/middleeast/rebels-gain-control-of-government-air-base-in
-syria.html; Michael Weiss, "Col. Oqaidi on al-Qaeda, UN Inspectors, and Kurdish
Militias," *NOW Lebanon*, August 18, 2013, now.mmedia.me/lb/en/interviews/col
-oqaidi-on-al-qaeda-un-inspectors-and-kurdish-militias.

124 Khalid wrote in a statement: Joanna Paraszczuk, "Military Prowess of IS
Commander Umar Shishani Called Into Question," Radio Free Europe Radio

Liberty, November 6, 2014, www.rferl.org/content/umar-shishani-military-prowess
-islamic-state/26677545.html.

125 In November 2014, Kadyrov announced: Joanna Paraszczuk, "The Chechen Leader
With a Grudge and the IS Commander with Nine Lives," Radio Free Europe Radio
Liberty, November 14, 2014, www.rferl.org/content/islamic-state-why-kadyrov
-claims-shishani-killed/26692100.html.

CHAPTER 9

126 Bashar al-Assad gave an interview: "Interview With Syrian President Bashar al-
Assad," *Wall Street Journal*, January 31, 2011, www.wsj.com/articles/SB10001424052
74870383320457611471244112894.

126 Just three days before his interview: "Syria: Gang Attacks Peaceful Demonstrators;
Police Look On," Human Rights Watch, February 3, 2011, www.hrw.org/news
/2011/02/03/syria-gang-attacks-peaceful-demonstrators-police-look; Lauren
Williams, "Syria Clamps Down on Dissent with Beatings and Arrests," *The
Guardian*, February 24, 2011, www.theguardian.com/world/2011/feb/24/syria
-crackdown-protest-arrests-beatings.

126 on February 17, a spontaneous protest erupted: Molly Hennessy-Fiske, "Syria:
Activists Protest Police Beating, Call for Investigation," *Los Angeles Times*, February
17, 2014, latimesblogs.latimes.com/babylonbeyond/2011/02/syria-activists-protest
-police-beating-call-for-investigation.html.

126 Although the protest was carefully directed: Ibid.

126 That demonstration came to an end: Rania Abouzeid, "The Syrian Style of
Repression: Thugs and Lectures," *TIME*, February 27, 2011, content.time.com
/time/world/article/0,8599,2055713,00.html.

127 Similar protests soon broke out in Damascus: Dane Vallejo and Michael Weiss,
"Syria Media Briefing: A Chronology of Protest and Repression," The Henry
Jackston Society, May 2011, henryjacksonsociety.org/cms/harriercollectionitems
/Syria+Media+Briefing.pdf.

127 One woman held at the Palestine Branch: Fergal Keane, "Syria Ex-Detainees Allege
Ordeals of Rape and Sex Abuse," BBC News, September 25, 2012, www.bbc.com
/news/world-middle-east-19718075.

128 "It was clear they had died very recently": Garance le Caisne, " 'They were torturing
to kill': inside Syria's death machine," *The Guardian*, October 1, 2015, http://www
.theguardian.com/world/2015/oct/01/they-were-torturing-to-kill-inside-syrias
-death-machine-caesar.

128 Stephen Rapp, the State Department's ambassador at large: Josh Rogin, "US: Assad's
'Machinery of Death' Worst Since the Nazis," *The Daily Beast*, July 7, 2014, www
.thedailybeast.com/articles/2014/07/07/u-s-assad-s-machinery-of-death-worst
-since-the-nazis.html.

128 one of the favored slogans: "The Syrian regime says, 'Al Assad or we'll burn the
country down,'" YouTube video, 7:24, posted by Tehelka TV, October 30, 2013,
www.youtube.com/watch?v=wNBGHaTkgW8.

129 What Zakarya meant: James Reynolds, "Syria Torture Accounts Reinforce Human
Rights Concerns," BBC News, July 3, 2012, www.bbc.com/news/world-middle
-east-18687422.

129 said Shiraz Maher, an expert on radicalization: Interview with one of the authors,
November 2014.

129 In 2010 Nibras Kazimi published: Nibras Kazimi, *Syria Through Jihadist Eyes: A
Perfect Enemy* (Stanford, CA: Hoover Press, 2010), 63.

130 "The sectarianism was carefully manufactured . . .": Interview with one of the authors, November 2014.

130 According to one who was detained: Ruth Sherlock, "Confessions of an Assad 'Shabiha' Loyalist: How I Raped and Killed for £300 a Month," *The Telegraph*, July 14, 2012, www.telegraph.co.uk/news/worldnews/middleeast/syria/9400570/Confessions-of-an-Assad-Shabiha-loyalist-how-I-raped-and-killed-for-300-a-month.html.

130 Most of them were women and children: Stephanie Nebehay, "Most Houla Victims Killed in Summary Executions: UN," Reuters, May 29, 2012, www.reuters.com/article/2012/05/29/us-syria-un-idUSBRE84S10020120529.

130 The shabiha were readily identifiable: Harriet Alexander and Ruth Sherlock, "The Shabiha: Inside Assad's Death Squads," *The Telegraph*, June 2, 2012, www.telegraph.co.uk/news/worldnews/middleeast/syria/9307411/The-Shabiha-Inside-Assads-death-squads.html.

130 an investigation by the United Nations: "Report of the Independent International Commission of Inquiry on the Syrian Arab Republic," Human Rights Council, 21st Session, August 15, 2012, www.ohchr.org/Documents/HRBodies/HRCouncil/RegularSession/Session21/A-HRC-21-50.doc.

131 Victoria Nuland accused Iran: Chris McGreal, "Houla Massacre: US Accuses Iran of 'Bragging' about Its Military Aid to Syria," *The Guardian*, May 29, 2012, www.theguardian.com/world/2012/may/29/houla-massacre-us-accuses-iran.

131 With as many as one hundred thousand recruits: Sam Dagher, "Syria's Alawite Force Turned Tide for Assad," *Wall Street Journal*, August 26, 2013, www.wsj.com/articles/SB10001424127887323997004578639903412487708.

131 Revolutionary Guards Corps operative Sayyed Hassan Entezari said: Axe, 2014.

131 Each brigade of the National Defense Force: Ibid.

131 Reuters conducted interviews: "Insight: Syrian Government Guerrilla Fighters Being Sent to Iran for Training," Reuters, April 4, 2013, www.reuters.com/article/2013/04/04/us-syria-iran-training-insight-idUSBRE9330DW20130404.

132 The camp at which Samer: Farnaz Fassihi, Jay Solomon, and Sam Dagher, "Iranians Dial Up Presence in Syria," *Wall Street Journal*, September 16, 2013, www.wsj.com/articles/SB10001424127887323864604579067382861808984.

132 According to an Iranian military officer: Ibid.

132 the National Defense Force has already: Michael Weiss, "Rise of the Militias," *NOW Lebanon*, May 21, 2013, now.mmedia.me/lb/en/commentaryanalysis/rise-of-the-militias.

132 Christian witnesses who spoke to the NGO: "No One's Left," Human Rights Watch, September 13, 2013, www.hrw.org/reports/2013/09/13/no-one-s-left-0.

132 between March 2011 and February 2015: "Executions by Burning: A Practice by Syrian Government Forces," Euro-Mid Observer for Human Rights, February 2015, http://euromid.org/uploads/reports/Executions_by_burning_EN.pdf.

133 This has resulted in high-profile Iranian fatalities: Filkins, 2013.

133 Tehran has relied not only on operatives: Farnaz Fassihi and Jay Solomon, "Top Iranian Official Acknowledges Syria Role," *Wall Street Journal*, September 16, 2012, online.wsj.com/news/articles/SB10000872396390443720204578000482831419570.

133 Several members of the Ground Forces: Will Fulton, Joseph Holliday, and Sam Wyer, *Iranian Strategy in Syria*, AEI's Critical Threats Project & Institute for the Study of War, May 2013, www.understandingwar.org/sites/default/files/IranianStrategyinSyria-1MAY.pdf.

133 A report published by the Institute for the Study of War: Ibid.

133 former Syrian prime minister Riyad Hijab declared: Karim Sadjadpour, "Iran: Syria's Lone Regional Ally," Carnegie Endowment for International Peace, June 9, 2014, carnegieendowment.org/2014/06/09/syria-s-lone-regional-ally -iran.

133 As early as May 2011: "Administration Takes Additional Steps to Hold the Government of Syria Accountable for Violent Repression Against the Syrian People," US Department of the Treasury, May 18, 2011, www.treasury.gov/press -center/press-releases/Pages/tg1181.aspx.

133 Such support, as later came to light, included: Michael R. Gordon, "US Presses Iraq on Iranian Planes Thought to Carry Arms to Syria," *New York Times*, September 5, 2012, www.nytimes.com/2012/09/06/world/middleeast/us-presses-iraq-on-iranian -planes-thought-to-carry-arms-to-syria.html.

134 In 2012, when the Iraqis stopped denying: Ibid.

134 According to US intelligence: Arash Karami, "Iran News Site Profiles Head of Iraq's Badr Organization," *Al-Monitor*, November 13, 2014, www.al-monitor.com/pulse /originals/2014/11/iran-news-site-profiles-badr-org.html.

134 In January 2014 the Meir Amit Intelligence: William Booth, "Israeli Study of Foreign Fighters in Syria Suggests Shiites May Outnumber Sunnis," *Washington Post*, January 2, 2014, www.washingtonpost.com/blogs/worldviews/wp/2014/01 /02/israeli-study-of-foreign-fighters-in-syria-suggests-shiites-may-outnumber -sunnis.

134 Hezbollah brigades have also lost: Phillip Smyth, "From Karbala to Sayyida Zaynab: Iraqi Fighters in Syria's Shi'a Militias," Combating Terrorism Center at West Point, August 27, 2013, www.ctc.usma.edu/posts/from-karbala-to-sayyida-zaynab-iraqi -fighters-in-syrias-shia-militias.

134 So has Muqtada al-Sadr's Mahdi Army: Suadad al-Salhy, "Iraqi Shi'ite Militants Fight for Syria's Assad," Reuters, October 16, 2012, www.reuters.com/article /2012/10/16/us-syria-crisis-iraq-militias-idUSBRE89F0PX20121016.

134 Phillip Smyth, an expert on the Special Groups: Phillip Smyth, "Breaking Badr, The New Season: Confirmation of the Badr Organization's Involvement in Syria," Jihadology blog, August 12, 2013, jihadology.net/2013/08/12/hizballah -cavalcade-breaking-badr-the-new-season-confirmation-of-the-badr-organizations -involvement-in-syria.

134 Iran has even sent "thousands": Farnaz Fassihi, "Iran Pays Afghans to Fight for Assad," *Wall Street Journal*, May 22, 2014, www.wsj.com/articles/SB1000142405270 2304908304579564161508613846.

134 Others are allegedly ex-Taliban fighters: Nick Paton Walsh, " 'Afghan' in Syria: Iranians Pay Us to Fight for Assad," CNN, October 31, 2014, www.cnn.com/2014 /10/31/world/meast/syria-afghan-fighter.

135 No Iranian-run subsidiary has been: Martin Chulov, "Syrian Town of Qusair Falls to Hezbollah in Breakthrough for Assad," *The Guardian*, June 5, 2013, www .theguardian.com/world/2013/jun/05/syria-army-seizes-qusair.

135 one Party of God paramilitary confessed: Mona Alami, "Hezbollah Fighter Details Ops in Qusayr," *NOW Lebanon*, June 4, 2013, now.mmedia.me/lb/en/interviews /hezbollah-fighter-details-ops-in-qusayr.

135 Abu Rami told the *Guardian* in July 2013: Martin Chulov and Mona Mahmood, "Syrian Sunnis Fear Assad Regime Wants to 'Ethnically Cleanse' Alawite Heartland," *The Guardian*, July 22, 2013, www.theguardian.com/world/2013/jul/22 /syria-sunnis-fear-alawite-ethnic-cleansing.

135 al-Assad's first post-uprising interview: Andrew Gilligan, "Assad: Challenge Syria at Your Peril," *The Telegraph*, October 29, 2011, www.telegraph.co.uk/news/worldnews /middleeast/syria/8857898/Assad-challenge-Syria-at-your-peril.html.

136 But in February 2012: Wyatt Andrews, "Clinton: Arming Syrian Rebels Could Help al Qaeda," CBS News, February 27, 2012, www.cbsnews.com/news/clinton-arming -syrian-rebels-could-help-al-qaeda.

136 The Violations Documentation Center: Glenn Kessler, "Are Syrian Opposition Fighters, 'Former Farmers or Teachers or Pharmacists'?" *Washington Post*, June 26, 2014, www.washingtonpost.com/blogs/fact-checker/wp/2014/06/26/are-syrian -opposition-fighters-former-farmers-or-teachers-or-pharmacists.

136 As Ambassador Frederic Hof: Frederic Hof, "Saving Syria is No 'Fantasy,' " *Politico*, August 11, 2014, www.politico.com/magazine/story/2014/08/mr-president-saving -syria-is-no-fantasy-109923.html.

137 he issued a general amnesty: "Assad Orders New Syrian Amnesty," Al Jazeera, June 21, 2011, www.aljazeera.com/news/middleeast/2011/06/2011621944198405.html.

137 the infamous Sedanya prison that houses the violent Islamists: Leila Fadel, "Syria's Assad moves to allay fury after security forces fire on protesters," *Washington Post*, March 26, 2011, https://www.washingtonpost.com/world/syrias-assad-moves-to -allay-fury-after-security-forces-fire-on-protesters/2011/03/26/AFFoZDdB_story .html.

137 Muhammad Habash, the former Syrian: Mohammed Habash, "Radicals Are Assad's Best Friends," *The National*, January 1, 2014, www.thenational.ae/the nationalconversation/comment/radicals-are-assads-best-friends.

137 There is a famous photograph: Joshua Landis, "Syria's Top Five Insurgent Leaders," Syria Comment blog, October 1, 2013, www.joshualandis.com/blog/biggest -powerful-militia-leaders-syria.

137 Future ISIS members were also granted amnesty: Ahmad al-Bahri, "ISIS Restructures Raqqa Under its New Ruling System," Syria Deeply, November 17, 2014, www.syriadeeply.org/articles/2014/11/6388/isis-restructures-raqqa-ruling -system.

137 according to the US State Department: "Designations of Foreign Terrorist Fighters," US Department of State, September 24, 2014, www.state.gov/r/pa/prs /ps/2014/09/232067.htm.

138 a twelve-year veteran of Syria's own Military: Ibid.

139 in January 2014, Major General Fayez Dwairi: Phil Sands, Justin Vela, and Suha Maayeh, "Assad Regime Set Free Extremists from Prison to Fire Up Trouble during Peaceful Uprising," *The National*, January 21, 2014, www.thenational.ae/world/syria /assad-regime-set-free-extremists-from-prison-to-fire-up-trouble-during-peaceful -uprising.

140 More intriguingly, Fares claimed: Ruth Sherlock, "Exclusive Interview: Why I Defected from Bashar al-Assad's Regime, by Former Diplomat Nawaf Fares," *The Telegraph*, July 14, 2012, www.telegraph.co.uk/news/worldnews/middleeast /syria/9400537/Exclusive-interview-why-I-defected-from-Bashar-al-Assads -regime-by-former-diplomat-Nawaf-Fares.html.

140 According to journalist Rania Abouzeid: Rania Abouzeid, "The Jihad Next Door," *Politico*, June 23, 2014. www.politico.com/magazine/story/2014/06/al-qaeda-iraq -syria-108214.html.

140 Among those making the journey: Ibid.

140 Major General Dwairi told the *National*: Sands et al., 2014.

140 Al-Jolani's first point of contact in Hasaka: Abouzeid, 2014.

140 What has been established: Ibid.

141 Al-Jolani's cell allegedly waged: "Extremism Hits Home Stopping the Spread of Terrorism," *Per Concordian*, Vol. 5, No. 3, 2014, www.marshallcenter.org /mcpublicweb/MCDocs/files/College/F_Publications/perConcordiam/pC_V5N3 _en.pdf.

141 Laith Alkhouri said.: Interview with one of the authors, November 2014.

142 Al-Jolani later explained to Al Jazeera: "Full Interview with Abu Mohammad al -Jolani," Internet Archive, posted by Abe Khabbaab (ابو خباب لامهاجر), archive.org /details/golan2.

142 Al-Zawahiri issued two communiqués: Sheikh Ayman Al-Zawahiri, "Move Forward, O Lions of Sham," The Global Islamic Media Front, 2012, azelin.files .wordpress.com/2012/02/dr-ayman-al-e1ba93awc481hirc4ab-22onward-oh-lions -of-syria22-en.pdf.

142 Al-Zawahiri excoriated the al-Assad regime: Sheikh Ayman Al-Zawahiri, "Move Forward, O Lions of Sham," The Global Islamic Media Front, April 26, 2012, worldanalysis.net/modules/news/article.php?storyid=2125.

CHAPTER 10

144 as the Associated Press reported: Bradley Klapper and Kimberly Dozier, "Al-Qaeda Building Well-Organized Network in Syria: US Intelligence Officials," *National Post*, August 10, 2015, news.nationalpost.com/2012/08/10/al-qaeda-building-well -organized-network-in-syria.

144 And al-Zawahiri's exhortation had paid off: Bradley Klapper and Kimberly Dozier, "US Officials: al-Qaeda Gaining Foothold in Syria," Yahoo! News, August 10, 2012, news.yahoo.com/us-officials-al-qaida-gaining-foothold-syria-201207990.html.

144 The rebels were also growing: Julian Borger, "Syria Crisis: West Loses Faith in SNC to Unite Opposition Groups," *The Guardian*, August 14, 2012, www.theguardian .com/world/2012/aug/13/syria-opposition-groups-national-council.

144 In a survey of the opposition: "Syrian Opposition Survey: June 1– July 2, 2012," The International Republican Institute and Pechter Polls, iri.org/sites/default /files/2012%20August%2017%20Survey%20of%20Syrian%20Opposition,%20 June%201-July%202,%202012.pdf.

145 On December 11, 2012, the US Treasury Department: "Treasury Sanctions Al- Nusrah Front Leadership in Syria and Militias Supporting the Asad Regime," US Department of the Treasury, December 11, 2012, www.treasury.gov/press-center /press-releases/Pages/tg1797.aspx.

145 In December 2012, Syrians held: Ruth Sherlock, "Syrian Rebels Defy US and Pledge Allegiance to Jihadi Group," *The Telegraph*, December 10, 2012, www .telegraph.co.uk/news/worldnews/middleeast/syria/9735988/Syrian-rebels-defy -US-and-pledge-allegiance-to-jihadi-group.html.

145 the first al-Qaeda agent to confirm: Rania Abouzedi, "How Islamist Rebels in Syria Are Ruling a Fallen Provincial Capital," *TIME*, March 23, 2013, world .time.com/2013/03/23/how-islamist-rebels-in-syria-are-ruling-a-fallen-provincial -capital.

146 US Marines had famously helped: Paul Wood, "The Day Saddam's Statue Fell," BBC News, April 9, 2004, news.bbc.co.uk/2/hi/middle_east/3611869.stm.

146 Suddenly Islamists had just toppled: Rania Abouzeid, "A Black Flag in Raqqa," *New Yorker*, April 2, 2013, www.newyorker.com/news/news-desk/a-black-flag-in-raqqa.

146 Pamphlets were distributed: Abouzeid, March 2013.

146 In the *New Yorker*, Rania Abouzeid reconstructed: Abouzeid, April 2013.

147 Al-Baghdadi did not confine his message: Rita Katz and Adam Raisman, "Special Report on the Power Struggle Between al-Qaeda Branches and Leadership," INSITE on Terrorism blog, June 25, 2013, news.siteintelgroup.com/blog/index.php /about-us/21-jihad/3195-special-report-on-the-power-struggle-between-al-qaeda -branches-and-leadership-al-qaeda-in-iraq-vs-al-nusra-front-and-zawahiri.

147 Al-Jolani left absolutely no doubt: Ibid.

147 What followed was a brief media intermission: Ibid.

147 Al-Zawahiri thereby "dissolved" ISIS: "Translation of al-Qaeda Chief Ayman al-Zawahiri's Letter to the Leaders of the Two Jihadi Groups," accessed January 18, 2015, s3.documentcloud.org/documents/710588/translation-of-ayman-al-zawahiris -letter.pdf.

148 Al-Suri, who was killed: Thomas Joscelyn, "Al Qaeda's Chief Representative in Syria Killed in Suicide Attack," The Long War Journal, February 23, 2014, www .longwarjournal.org/archives/2014/02/zawahiris_chief_repr.php.

148 was a veteran al-Qaeda agent: "Sources in Aleppo, Syrian Net: Syrian Regime Released from Abu Musab al-Suri and his Assistant Abu Khaled, Observers See a Threat to Washington," Aleppo Syrian Net, December 23, 2011, accessed January 3, 2015, www.sooryoon.net/archives/41907.

148 He had helped found: Caleb Weiss, "Caucasus Emirate Eulogizes Slain Ahrar al Sham Leaders," The Long War Journal, September 15, 2014, www.longwarjournal .org/archives/2014/09/caucasus_emirate_eul.php.

148 The brainchild of Sir Mark Sykes: James Barr, *A Line in the Sand: Britain, France and the Struggle That Shaped the Middle East* (New York: Simon & Schuster, 2012), p. 12.

148 The agreement was, and still is, a byword: Ian Black, "Isis Breach of Iraq-Syria Border Merges Two Wars into One 'Nightmarish Reality,'" *The Guardian*, June 18, 2014, www.theguardian.com/world/2014/jun/18/isis-iraq-syria-two-wars-one -nightmare.

149 Al-Baghdadi had earnestly taken up: Constanze Letsch, "Foreign Jihadis Change Face of Syrian Civil War," *The Guardian*, December 25, 2014, www.theguardian.com /world/2014/dec/25/foreign-jihadis-syrian-civil-war-assad.

152 On July 11 2013, Kamal Hamami: Paul Wood, "Key Free Syria Army Rebel 'Killed by Islamist Group,'" BBC News, July 12, 2013, www.bbc.co.uk/news/world-middle -east-23283079.

152 "We are going to wipe the floor with them": "New Front Opens in Syria as Rebels Say al Qaeda Attack Means War," Reuters UK, July 13, 2013, uk.reuters.com /article/2013/07/13/uk-syria-crisis-idUKBRE96B08C20130713.

152 Similarly, when ISIS "accidentally" beheaded: Richard Spencer, "Al-Qaeda–Linked Rebels Apologise After Cutting Off Head of Wrong Person," *The Telegraph*, November 14, 2013, www.telegraph.co.uk/news/worldnews/middleeast/syria /10449815/Al-Qaeda-linked-rebels-apologise-after-cutting-off-head-of-wrong -person.html.

152 It kidnapped revered opposition activists: "Rule of Terror: Living Under ISIS in Syria," Report of the Independent International Commission of Inquiry on the Syrian Arab Republic, United Nations, November 14, 2014, www.ohchr.org /Documents/HRBodies/HRCouncil/CoISyria/HRC_CRP_ISIS_14Nov2014 .pdf.

152 It established monopolistic checkpoints: Tareq al-Abed, "The Impending Battle Between FSA, Islamic State of Iraq and Syria," Al-Monitor, July 31, 2013, www .al-monitor.com/pulse/security/2013/07/syria-possible-battle-fsa-islamic-state-iraq -syria.html.

152 ISIS sent a car bomb to the base: Lauren Williams, "Islamist Militants Drive Free
Syrian Army Out of Raqqa," *Daily Star Lebanon*, August 15, 2013 www.dailystar
.com.lb/News/Middle-East/2013/Aug-15/227444-islamist-militants-drive-free
-syrian-army-out-of-raqqa.ashx.

152 ISIS then expelled the brigade: Ibid.

152 In late December 2013: Michael Weiss, "Has Sahwa Hit the Fan in Syria?" *NOW
Lebanon*, January 8, 2014, now.mmedia.me/lb/en/commentaryanalysis/529244-has
-sahwa-hit-the-fan-in-syria.

153 Among the buildings targeted: Ibid.

153 Fares had taken to comparing: Ibid.

153 "The reason Kafranbel became . . .": Ibid.

153 On New Year's Day 2014: Ibid.

154 the brigade accused it, however, of exceeding: Ibid.

154 the Islamic Front stated in a press release: Ibid.

154 This new mainstream front, Saoud told us: Interview with one of the authors,
January 2015.

154 The last group to join this budding Sahwa: Ibid.

155 If these demands were not met: Ibid.

155 On January 5 the Islamic Front announced: Ibid.

156 A shaky truce brokered: Ibid.

156 Al-Jolani blamed ISIS for the week: Ibid.

156 ISIS had raised a defiant slogan: Richard Barrett, "The Islamic State," The Soufan
Group, November 2014, soufangroup.com/wp-content/uploads/2014/10/TSG-The
-Islamic-State-Nov14.pdf.

156 Abu Omar al-Shishani . . . signed: Yossef Bodansky, "The Sochi Olympics Terror
Threat has Links to Camps in Syria that are Supported by the US," *World Tribune*,
January 24, 2014, www.worldtribune.com/2014/01/24/the-sochi-olympics-terror
-threat-has-links-to-camps-in-syria-that-are-supported-by-the-u-s.

156 On February 2, 2014, global al-Qaeda: Liz Sly, "Al-Qaeda Disavows Any Ties with
Radical Islamist ISIS Group in Syria, Iraq," *Washington Post*, February 3, 2014, www
.washingtonpost.com/world/middle_east/al-qaeda-disavows-any-ties-with-radical
-islamist-isis-group-in-syria-iraq/2014/02/03/2c9afc3a-8cef-11e3-98ab-fe5228
217bd1_story.html.

157 His real name is Maysara al-Juburi: Abu Bakr al Haj Ali, "Abu Maria: The Nusra
Leader Behind the Split with IS in Syria?," Middle East Eye, November 14, 2014,
www.middleeasteye.net/in-depth/features/changes-jabhat-al-nusra-indicate
-changes-entire-battlefield-1875666927.

157 ISIS further claims: Nibras Kazimi, "The Caliphate Attempted," Hudson Institute,
July 1, 2008, www.hudson.org/research/9854-the-caliphate-attempted-zarqawi-s
-ideological-heirs-their-choice-for-a-caliph-and-the-collapse-of-their-self-styled
-islamic-state-of-iraq.

158 A recent study conducted by the Carter Center: "Syria: Countrywide Conflict
Report #4," The Carter Center, September 11, 2014, www.cartercenter.org/resources
/pdfs/peace/conflict_resolution/syria-conflict/NationwideUpdate-Sept-18-2014
.pdf.

158 By Damascus's own admission: Kyle Orton, "The Assad Regime's Collusion
with ISIS and al-Qaeda: Assessing the Evidence," The Syrian Intifada blog,
March 24, 2014, kyleorton1991.wordpress.com/2014/03/24/assessing-the
-evidence-of-collusion-between-the-assad-regime-and-the-wahhabi-jihadists
-part-1.

158 One advisor to the regime told the *New York Times*: Michael Weiss, "Trust Iran Only as Far as You Can Throw It," *Foreign Policy*, June 23, 2014, foreignpolicy.com/2014 /06/23/trust-iran-only-as-far-as-you-can-throw-it.

158 Some of this may owe to ISIS's financial: Ibid.

158 As a Western intelligence source told the *Daily Telegraph*: Ruth Sherlock, "Syria's Assad Accused of Boosting al-Qaeda with Secret Oil Deals," *The Telegraph*, January 20, 2014, www.telegraph.co.uk/news/worldnews/middleeast/syria/10585391 /Syrias-Assad-accused-of-boosting-al-Qaeda-with-secret-oil-deals.html.

158 Frederic Hof . . . wrote: Frederic C. Hof, "Syria: Should the West Work with Assad?" Atlantic Council, July 10, 2014, www.atlanticcouncil.org/blogs/menasource/syria -should-the-west-work-with-assad.

160 Stories about pretty, middle-class teenage: Allan Hall, "One of the Teenage Austrian 'Poster Girls' Who Ran Away to Join ISIS Has Been Killed in the Conflict, UN Says," *Daily Mail*, December 18, 2014, www.dailymail.co.uk/news/article-2879272 /One-teenage-Austrian-poster-girls-ran-away-join-ISIS-killed-conflict-says.html.

160 copycats who are stopped: "Austria Detains Teenage Girls Who Wanted to Marry ISIS Fighters," NBC News, January 11, 2015, www.nbcnews.com/storyline/isis -terror/austria-detains-teenage-girls-who-wanted-marry-isis-fighters-n284096.

161 a 1940 essay by George Orwell: "George Orwell Reviews *Mein Kampf* (1940)," Open Culture, August 19, 2014, www.openculture.com/2014/08/george-orwell -reviews-mein-kampf-1940.html.

CHAPTER 11

164 ISIS's spokesman, Abu Muhammad al-Adnani: "Abu Speech: Jihadist Kurds of Halabja Attack Lead 'Islamic State' Kobani," (كرد) جهادي «خطاب» أبو «لادولة» هجوم يقود الاسلامية«رعلد كوباني ي مذ حلبجة) Al-Quds Al-Arabi, October 10, 2014, www.alquds .co.uk/?p=233274.

165 Charities that were started: "Kuwaiti Charity Designated for Bankrolling al Qaida Network," US Department of the Treasury, June 13, 2008, www.treasury.gov/press -center/press-releases/Pages/hp1023.aspx.

165 after decades of proselytization: Salem al-Haj, "Issue: Islamic Tide in Iraq's Kurdistan File Historical Reading," (ملف الاعدد: لامد اسلامي لا فـي كردستان عراق لا قراءة تاريخية) Al Hiwar. February 7, 2014, alhiwarmagazine.blogspot.ae/2014/02/blog -post_5030.html.

165 In Syria the Kurdish turn to ISIS: Jordi Tejel, *Syria's Kurds: History, Politics, and Society* (New York: Routledge, 2009), 90, 102.

165 Al-Baghdadi's deputy: "Abu Muslim al-Turkmani: From Iraqi Officer to Slain ISIS Deputy," Al Arabiya News, December 19, 2014, english.alarabiya.net/en/perspective /profiles/2014/12/19/Abu-Muslim-al-Turkmani-From-Iraqi-officer-to-slain-ISIS -deputy.html.

165 Abu al-Athir al-Absi: Radwan Mortada, "Al-Qaeda Leaks II: Baghdadi Loses His Shadow," *Al-Akhbar*, January 14, 2014, english.al-akhbar.com/node/18219.

165 Al-Absi formed a group: Suhaib Anjarini, "The War in Syria: ISIS's most Succesful Investment Yet," *Al-Akhbar*, June 11, 2014, english.al-akhbar.com/node/20133.

165 Al-Absi took a hard line: Mortada, 2014.

166 According to journalist Wael Essam: Interview with one of the authors, November 2014.

166 al-Absi was one of al-Baghdadi's staunchest defenders: Anjarini, 2014.

167 others fell out with their original insurgencies: Mitchell Prother, "ISIS's Victories May Win It Recruits from Rival Syrian Rebel Groups," McClatchy DC, June 23,

2014, www.mcclatchydc.com/2014/06/23/231236_isiss-victories-may-win-it
-recruits.html.

167 issued a joint statement disavowing: "Syria Rebel Factions, Including al Qaeda-
linked Nusra Front, Reject Authority of US-Backed Opposition SNC," CBS News,
Septembe 25, 2013,www.cbsnews.com/news/syria-rebel-factions-including-al
-qaeda-linked-nusra-front-reject-authority-of-us-backed-opposition-snc.

167 In October, seven Islamist groups: "Charter of the Syrian Islamic Front," Carnegie
Endowment for International Peace, January 21, 2013, carnegieendowment.org
/syriaincrisis/?fa=50831.

167 members of the Islamic Front: Joanna Paraszczuk, "Syria: Truce Between ISIS's Abu
Umar al-Shishani & Ahrar ash-Sham on Eastern Front in Aleppo Province, EA
Worldview, January 8, 2014, eaworldview.com/2014/01/syria-claimed-truce-abu
-umar-al-shishani-ahrar-ash-sham-eastern-front.

167 Liwa Dawud, once the most powerful: "1,000-strong Syrian Rebel Brigade Defects
to Islamic State," RT, July 11, 2014, rt.com/news/171952-thousand-strong-defect
-islamic-state.

167 fighters from the Islamic Front: Yusra Ahmed, "Nusra Front Suffers Defections to
Join Rival ISIS," Zaman Al Wasl, October 24, 2014, www.zamanalwsl.net/en
/news/7205.html.

167 ISIS benefits from the absence: Ahmed Abazid, "The Muslim Brotherhood and the
Confused Position," Zaman Al Wasl, March 28, 2014, www.zamanalwsl.net
/news/48054.html.

169 In areas fully controlled by ISIS: Liz Sly, "The Islamic State is Failing at Being a
State," *Washington Post*, December 25, 2014, www.washingtonpost.com/world
/middle_east/the-islamic-state-is-failing-at-being-a-state/2014/12/24/bfbf8962
-8092-11e4-b936-f3afab0155a7_story.html.

170 had a reputation as a drug dealer: Ruth Sherlock, "Bodyguard of Syrian Rebel
Who Defected to Isil Reveals Secrets of the Jihadist Leadership," *The Telegraph*,
November 10, 2014, www.telegraph.co.uk/news/worldnews/islamic-state/11221995
/Bodyguard-of-Syrian-rebel-who-defected-to-Isil-reveals-secrets-of-the-jihadist
-leadership.html.

170 Aamer al-Rafdan joined ISIS: Anjarini, 2014.

171 In an article for the *New Statesman*: Shiraz Maher, "From Portsmouth to Kobane:
The British Jihadis Fighting for Isis," *New Statesman*, November 6, 2014, www
.newstatesman.com/2014/10/portsmouth-kobane.

171 by September 2014 the CIA calculated: "CIA Says IS Numbers Underestimated,"
Al Jazeera, September 12, 2014, www.aljazeera.com/news/middleeast/2014/09/cia
-triples-number-islamic-state-fighters-201491232912623733.html.

171 These figures had doubled by September 2015: Eric Schmitt and Somini Sengupta,
"Thousands Enter Syria to Join ISIS Despite Global Efforts," *New York Times*,
September 26, 2015, http://www.nytimes.com/2015/09/27/world/middleeast
/thousands-enter-syria-to-join-isis-despite-global-efforts.html

171 Missionary jihadists who were driven: Interview with one of the authors, November
2014.

172 ISIS benefited from the Assadist massacres: Interviews with Syrian activists and
rebels, 2013–2014.

172 Armed with knives and light weapons: Kyle Orton, "What to do About Syria:
Sectarianism and the Minorities," The Syrian Intifada blog, December 24, 2014,
kyleorton1991.wordpress.com/2014/12/24/what-to-do-about-syria-sectarianism
-and-the-minorities.

172 Videos of torture also showed: Rafida and Nusayris are derogatory terms for Shia and Alawites respectively.

172 Saudi nationals often point to: "Kawalis al-Thawra Program, 7th episode with Mousa al-Ghannami," (داعش وجهل الاشرع حكمة بين الاحدود تطبيق-لاسا بعة الاحلقة -لا ثورة كولايس) YouTube video, 36:13, posted by لاغنامي موسد, December 20, 2014, www.youtube.com /watch?v=sYtJ0XNMoKI.

CHAPTER 12

174 Slightly overstating the power of social media: "Head to Head—Will ISIL Put an End to Iraq?" YouTube video, 47:27, posted by Al Jazeera English, November 21, 2014, http://youtu.be/XkJl9UbG2lo.

174 Two weeks before the fall of the city: Nico Prucha, "Is This the Most Successful Release of a Jihadist Video Ever?" Jihadica blog, May 19, 2014, www.jihadica .com/is-this-the-most-successful-release-of-a-jihadist-video-ever. Video can be found at ihadology.net/2014/05/17/al-furqan-media-presents-a-new-video -message-from-the-islamic-state-of-iraq-and-al-sham-clanging-of-the-swords -part-4.

176 This not only maximized its viewership: J. M. Berger, "How ISIS Games Twitter," *The Atlantic*, June 16, 2014, www.theatlantic.com/international/archive/2014/06/isis -iraq-twitter-social-media-strategy/372856.

177 In the videos, this hadith is recited: "The Failed Crusade," *Dabiq*, Issue 4, October 2014, media.clarionproject.org/files/islamic-state/islamic-state-isis-magazine-Issue -4-the-failed-crusade.pdf.

178 Al-Baghdadi claimed to be a descendent: Hashim, 2014.

184 One of ISIS's governors, Hussam Naji Allami: "Mufti 'Daash' Legitimate: Hedma Shrines of Mosul, on the Basis of the 'Modern Prophetic,'" Al-Ghad, November 17, 2014, www.alghad.com/articles/836900.

184 the US State Department created a Twitter: Think Again Turn Away, Twitter post, January 15, 2015, 11:04 a.m., twitter.com/ThinkAgain_DOS/status /555802610083852289.

184 Three days earlier, as the world was recovering: Dan Lamothe, "US Military Social Media Accounts Apparently Hacked by Islamic State Sympathizers," *Washington Post*, January 12, 2015, www.washingtonpost.com/news/checkpoint /wp/2015/01/12/centcom-twitter-account-apparently-hacked-by-islamic-state -sympathizer.

184 Though the White House downplayed: Eli Lake and Josh Rogin, "Islamic State's Psychological War on US Troops," *Bloomberg View*, January 15, 2015, www .bloombergview.com/articles/2015-01-15/islamic-states-psychological-war-on -us-troops; "ISIS Supporters Just Hacked the US Military's CENTCOM Twitter Account." Vox, posted by Zack Beauchamp, January 12, 2015, www.vox.com/2015 /1/12/7532363/centcom-hack-isis.

CHAPTER 13

186 It was this established patronage system: William D. Wunderle, *A Manual for American Servicemen in the Arab Middle East: Using Cultural Understanding to Defeat Adversaries and Win the Peace* (New York: Skyhorse Publishing, 2013).

187 the Baath Party saw: Carole A. O'Leary and Nicholas A. Heras, "Syrian Tribal Networks and their Implications for the Syrian Uprising," The Jamestown Foundation, June 1, 2012, www.jamestown.org/single/?no_cache=1&tx_ttnews %5Btt_news%5D=39452.

387 Protestors called for *fazaat houran*: "شام - عزفة روحان - ادهاء الثور ةمن بنديا با سورويا سلابم اروق" YouTube video, 7:28, posted by Shaam Network S.N.N., April 1, 2011, www .youtube.com/watch?v=Y4ww1xUrHMs.

188 Overall, tribes account for 30 percent: Nasser Al-Ayed, "Jihadists and Syrian Tribes," *Global Arab Network*, November 6, 2014, www.globalarabnetwork.com/studies /13181-2014-11-06-11-53-28.

188 Because Deir Ezzor connects Syria: Peter Neumann, "Suspects into Collaborators," *London Review of Books*, Vol. 36, No. 7, April 3, 2014, www.lrb.co.uk/v36/n07/peter -neumann/suspects-into-collaborators.

188 By the summer of 2012: Karen Leigh, "In Deir Ezzor, ISIS Divides and Conquers Rebel Groups," *Syria Deeply*, August 11, 2014, www.syriadeeply.org/articles /2014/08/5930/deir-ezzor-isis-divides-conquers-rebel-groups.

193 preferring to answer to fellow Muslims: William McCants, *The ISIS Apocalypse: The History, Strategey, and Doomsday Vision of the Islamic State* (New York: St. Martin's Press, 2015), Kindle Location 1352.

193 ISIS assassinated more than thirteen hundred Awakening militiamen: Craig Whiteside, "War, Interrupted, Part I: The Roots of the Jihadist Resurgence in Iraq," *War on the Rocks*, November 5, 2014, warontherocks.com/2014/11/war-interrupted -part-i-the-roots-of-the-jihadist-resurgence-in-iraq/.

CHAPTER 14

201 "They did not bomb the [ISIS] headquarters until June": Martin Chulov, "Isis Fighters Surround Syrian Airbase in Rapid Drive to Recapture Lost Territory," *The Guardian*, August 22, 2014, www.theguardian.com/world/2014/aug/22/isis-syria -airbase-tabqa.

202 "There is a clear shift in the ISIS strategy . . .": "ISIS Take over Syria Army Base, Behead Soldiers: Activists," *Daily Star Lebanon*, July 26, 2014, www.dailystar.com .lb/News/Middle-East/2014/Jul-26/265226-85-syria-troops-killed-in-jihadist advance-activists.ashx.

202 Assad's own cousin, Douraid al-Assad, is quoted as saying: YouTube video, 7:29, posted by Syria.truth, September 15, 2014, www.youtube.com/watch?v=zsA7FQ ywurU#t=11.

202 When the Syrian Air Force finally escalated: Anne Barnard, "Blamed for Rise of ISIS, Syrian Leader is Pushed to Escalate Fight," *International New York Times*, August 22, 2014, www.nytimes.com/2014/08/23/world/middleeast/assad -supporters-weigh-benefits-of-us-strikes-in-syria.html.

203 "[I]t's imperative that, in addition to force, there be an appeasement . . .": Price et al., 2014.

205 "What they do is attack the weaker units . . .": Ghaith Abdul-Ahad, " 'Syria is Not a Revolution Any more—This is Civil War,' " *The Guardian*, November 18, 2013, www.theguardian.com/world/2013/nov/18/syria-revolution-civil-war -conflict-rivalry.

205 In one obituary for Jazra, journalist Orwa Moqdad wrote: Orwa Moqdad, "A Rebel Killed by Rebels," *NOW Lebanon*, December 19, 2013, now.mmedia.me/lb/en /reportsfeatures/526509-the-enemy-of-the-enemy.

209 One military commander: Hassan Abu Haniya, "Structural Construction of the 'Islamic State,' " Al Jazeera Center for Studies, November 23, 2014, studies.aljazeera .net/files/isil/2014/11/20141123638165113973.htm

212 to keep the caliphate in black gold: Erika Solomon, Guy Chazen, and Sam Jones, "Isis Inc: how oil fuels the jihadi terrorists," *The Financial Times*, October 14, 2015,

http://www.ft.com/intl/cms/s/2/b8234932-719b-11e5-ad6d-f4ed76f0900a
.html#axzz3xj4hwZtV.

212 the Kremlin's avowed commitment to destroying ISIS: Tony Badran, "Minority Report: Is the link between Assad and the Islamic State a Christian One?" *Now*, May 9, 2014, https://now.mmedia.me/lb/en/commentaryanalysis/562681-minority -report.

213 "The gas goes west to Assad": Matthew M. Reed, "Revealed: Assad Buys Oil from ISIS," *The Daily Beast*, December 10, 2015, http://www.thedailybeast.com /articles/2015/12/10/isis-is-the-con-ed-of-syria.html.

214 Germany's foreign intelligence agency: "German Spies Say Isis Oil Isn't Money Gusher," *The Local*, November 7, 2014, www.thelocal.de/20141107/spies-say-isis -oil-isnt-money-gusher.

214 Zakat is extracted from annual savings: "Zakat FAQs," Islamic Relief UK, accessed January 18, 2015, www.islamic-relief.org.uk/about-us/what-we-do/zakat/zakat -faqs/#trade.

214 ISIS also imposes taxes on non-Muslims: The Islamic State blog, the-islamic-state .blogspot.ae/2014/02/blog-post_26.html.

214 ISIS seized hundreds of millions of dollars': Bronstein & Griffin, 2014.

214 it has also seized large stockpiles: "Dispatch from the Field: Islamic State Weapons in Iraq and Syria," Conflict Armament Research Ltd, September 2014, conflictarm .com/wp-content/uploads/2014/09/Dispatch_IS_Iraq_Syria_Weapons.pdf.

215 killed by American special forces in May 2015: Andrew Keller, "Documenting ISIL's Antiquities Trafficking," September 29, 2015, https://eca.state.gov/files/bureau /final_presentation_to_met_on_isil_antiquities_trafficking_for_das_keller_9.29 .2015_.pdf.

215 "that's when we saw a peak of looting activity,": Rachel Shabi, "Looted in Syria— and sold in London: the British antiquities shops dealing in artefacts smuggled by Isis," *The Guardian*, July 3, 2015, http://www.theguardian.com/world/2015/jul/03 /antiquities-looted-by-isis-end-up-in-london-shops.

CHAPTER 15

217 "its operational flexibility and discretion, is its brand and idea": Mina Al-Oraibi, "Exclusive: General Allen discusses coalition plans for defeating ISIS as regional tour starts," *Asharq al-Awsat*, October 25, 2014, http://english.aawsat.com/2014/10 /article55337867/us-gen-john-allen-at-least-one-year-until-isis-is-out-of-iraq.

217 spoke of a "culture of takfir" pervasive within rebel groups' rank and file undermining the hearts-and-minds quotient in the war against ISIS: Interview with Hassan Hassan, December 2015.

218 to be sent back to receive more training to "strengthen" their faith: Interviews by Hassan Hassan, January 2015.

218 There are, after all, approximately twenty mosques in each town that falls under ISIS control, and all have to be fully staffed to cater to their flocks: Hassan Hassan, "The secret world of Isis training camps—ruled by sacred texts and the sword," *The Guardian*, January 24, 2015, http://www.theguardian.com/world/2015/jan/25 /inside-isis-training-camps.

219 established members or commanders can study manuals such as Abu Bakr Naji's *The Management of Savagery*: Interviews with Hassan Hassan, November 2014.

219 ISIS members now routinely throw gay men off the highest buildings they can find: John Hall, "Hurled to his death in front of a baying mob: ISIS barbarians throw 'gay' man off building in another sickening day in Jihadi capital of Raqqa,"

The Daily Mail, March 4, 2015, http://www.dailymail.co.uk/news/article
-2978890/ISIS-barbarians-throw-gay-man-building-bloodthirsty-crowds
-Syria.html.

220 make a "river of blood" from the Persian army in the event: Ibn Kathir, *Khalid Bin
Al-Waleed* (Lulu.com, December 2015), page 165.

220 is glibly used by pundits to account for the entirety of the organization's ideological
underpinnings: Alastair Crooke, "You Can't Understand ISIS if You Don't Know the
History of Wahhabism in Saudi Arabia," *The World Post*, October 27, 2014, http://
www.huffingtonpost.com/alastair-crooke/isis-wahhabism-saudi-arabia_b_5717157
.html.

221 export more jihadists into ISIS ranks per capita than Saudi Arabia: Mohanad
Hashim, "Iraq and Syria: Who are the foreign fighters?" *BBC*, September 3, 2014,
http://www.bbc.com/news/world-middle-east-29043331.

221 a period that saw the influx of multinational Arabs into the Gulf states, especially
Saudi Arabia and Kuwait: Toby C. Jones, "Awakening Islam: The Politics of
Religious Dissent in Contemporary Saudi Arabia," *Middle East Journal* 66, no. 1
(Winter 2012): 187–88. Project Muse, http://muse.jhu.edu/journals/mej/summary
/v066/66.1.jones.html.

221 Bin Laden was part of the Muslim Brotherhood in Saudi Arabia: http://www
.alarabiya.net/servlet/aa/pdf/c789e942-8cf0-4fe9-9e9e-9ad365638d88.

221 The result was that Brotherhood-style politics was made still more conservative,
while Salafism was made more political: Stéphane Lacroix, *Awakening Islam:
The Politics of Religious Dissent in Contemporary Saudi Arabia* (Harvard UP:
Cambridge, MA, 2011), http://www.hup.harvard.edu/catalog.php?isbn
=9780674049642.

221 Qutb espoused *ustadhiyyat al-alam*, or supremacy over the world: Sayed Khatab,
"hakimiyyah" and "jahiliyyah" in the Thought of Sayyid Qutb." *Middle Eastern
Studies* 38 (3). Taylor & Francis, Ltd.: 145–70. http://www.jstor.org/stable
/4284246.

223 Al-Fahad has also reportedly pledged allegiance to ISIS: Robert Spencer,
"Muslim cleric who issued fatwa permitting WMD pledges allegiance to Islamic
State," *Jihad Watch*, August 25, 2015, http://www.jihadwatch.org/2015/08
/muslim-cleric-who-issued-fatwa-permitting-wmd-pledges-allegiance-to-islamic
-state.

223 His books are also in heavy circulation in ISIS-controlled areas, according to many
jihadists in Syria: Interviews by Hassan Hassan with residents and members of ISIS,
as well as claims by Syrian Islamists critical of ISIS and Maqdisi.

224 In 2009, al-Maqdisi authorized al-Binali to teach and issue fatwas, which he did
on prominent jihadi forums for years under the nom de guerre Abu Hummam al-
Athari: Shiv Malik, Ali Younes, Spencer Ackerman, and Mustafa Khalili: "The race
to save Peter Kassig," *The Guardian*, December 18, 2014, http://www.theguardian
.com/news/2014/dec/18/-sp-the-race-to-save-peter-kassig.

225 in the Rabat Mosque on the favorite subject: Aymenn Jawad Al-Tamimi,
"Islamic State Training Camp Textbook: 'Course in Monotheism'—Complete
Text, Translation and Analysis," *aymennjawad.org*, July 26, 2015, http://www
.aymennjawad.org/17633/islamic-state-training-camp-textbook-course-in.

CHAPTER 16

228 Where Noah's Ark eventually washed up: Martin Chulov, "40,000 Iraqis stranded
on mountain as Isis jihadists threaten death," *The Guardian*, August 7, 2014, www

.theguardian.com/world/2014/aug/07/40000-iraqis-stranded-mountain-isis-death
-threat.

228 "It's a disaster, a total disaster.": Loveday Morris, "Iraqi Yazidis stranded on isolated
mountaintop begin to die of thirst," *Washington Post*, August 5, 2014, https://www
.washingtonpost.com/world/iraqi-yazidis-stranded-on-isolated-mountaintop
-begin-to-die-of-thirst/2014/08/05/57cca985-3396-41bd-8163-7a52e5e72064
_story.html.

231 steadily absorbing Kurdish refugees from Syria: Sarah El-Rashadi, "Iraq's 2 million
IDPs struggling," al-monitor.com, December 30, 2014, http://www.al-monitor
.com/pulse/en/originals/2014/12/fighting-iraq-creates-2-million-refugees
.html#.

234 "because she was an American.": "US hostage Kayla Mueller 'killed by IS', say ex-
slaves," *BBC.com*, September 10, 2015, http://www.bbc.com/news/world-middle
-east-34205911.

235 rescuing journalists James Foley and Steven Sotloff: Nicholas Schmidle, "Inside the
Failed Raid to Save Foley and Sotloff," *New Yorker*, September 5, 2014, www
.newyorker.com/news/news-desk/inside-failed-raid-free-foley-sotloff.

235 authenticated by US intelligence: "American ISIS hostage is dead, family confirms,"
CBS News and The Associated Press, February 10, 2015, www.cbsnews.com/news
/kayla-jean-mueller-american-isis-hostage-is-dead-family-confirms/.

237 in the cases of both Foley: Brian Ross James Gordon Meek, and Rhonda Schwartz,
" 'So Little Compassion': James Foley's Parents Say Officials Threatened Family
Over Ransom," ABC News, September 12, 2014, abcnews.go.com/International
/government-threatened-foley-family-ransom-payments-mother-slain/story?id
=25453963.

237 and Sotloff: Lawrence Wright, "Five Hostages," *New Yorker*, July 6, 2015, www
.newyorker.com/magazine/2015/07/06/five-hostages.

237 with a password calling him a "pimp.": Shiv Malik, Ali Younes, Spencer Ackerman,
and Mustafa Khalili, "How Isis crippled al-Qaida," *The Guardian*, June 10, 2015,
www.theguardian.com/world/2015/jun/10/how-isis-crippled-al-qaida.

238 collateral damage was an "old and sick trick.": Brian Ross, Lee Ferran, and
Rym Momtaz, "Parents of American ISIS Hostage Kayla Mueller Plead for
Response From Terror Group," February 7, 2015, http://abcnews.go.com
/International/isis-claims-female-american-hostage-killed-airstrike/story?id
=28776563.

238 now flying bombing missions in al-Raqqa: Gianlucca Mezzofiore, "No, Jordan's King
Abdullah II is not personally flying planes against Isis," *International Business Times*,
February 5, 20105, http://www.ibtimes.co.uk/no-jordans-king-abdullah-ii-not
-personally-flying-planes-against-isis-1486742.

238 stopped bombing ISIS altogether: Richard Allen Greene and Schams Elwazer,
"Bombing ISIS: Arabs lag far behind West," CNN, December 10, 2015, http://
www.cnn.com/2015/12/10/middleeast/arab-countries-bombing-isis/.

238 in one of his first press conferences: Jay Solomon, "Prime Minister Haider al-Abadi
Pledges to Unify Iraq in Fight Against Islamic State," *Wall Street Journal*, September
25, 2014, www.wsj.com/articles/prime-minister-haider-al-abadi-pledges-to-unify
-iraq-in-fight-against-islamic-state-1411688702.

239 a popular reaction against ISIS: Phillip Smyth, "The Shiite Jihad in Syria and its
Regional Effects," The Washington Institute for Near East Policy, February 2015,
pages 31, 50, http://www.washingtoninstitute.org/uploads/Documents/pubs
/PolicyFocus138_Smyth-2.pdf.

239 "join the security forces to achieve this sacred goal.": Raheem Salman and Isra al -Rubei'i, "Iraq's top Shi'ite cleric issues call to fight jihadist rebels," Reuters, June 14, 2014, www.reuters.com/article/us-iraq-security-idUSKBN0EN0RV20140614.

239 before the end of the day: Loveday Morris, "Shiite cleric Sistani backs Iraqi government's call for volunteers to fight advancing militants," *Washington Post*, June 13, 2014, https://www.washingtonpost.com/world/middle_east/volunteers-flock-to -defend-baghdad-as-insurgents-seize-more-iraqi-territory/2014/06/13/10d46f9c -f2c8-11e3-914c-1fbd0614e2d4_story.html.

239 the invading British forces in Mesopotamia: Ian Rutledge, *Enemy on the Euphrates: The Battle for Iraq, 1914–1921* (London: Saqi Books, 2014), Chapter Four.

241 "good" for the Middle East and "good for the United States.": "Transcript: President Obama's Full NPR Interview," NPR, December 29, 2014, www.npr .org/2014/12/29/372485968/transcript-president-obamas-full-npr-interview.

242 boys younger than eighteen: "Iraq: Campaign of Mass Murders of Sunni Prisoners," Human Rights Watch, July 11, 2014, https://www.hrw.org/news/2014/07/11/iraq -campaign-mass-murders-sunni-prisoners.

242 According to Human Rights Watch: "Iraq Forces Executed 255 Prisoners in Revenge for Islamic State Killings—HRW," Reuters, July 12, 2014, news.yahoo .com/iraq-forces-executed-255-prisoners-revenge-islamic-state-133400715.html.

242 On August 22, 2014: "Iraq: Survivors Describe Mosque Massacre," Human Rights Watch, November 2, 2014, www.hrw.org/news/2014/11/01/iraq-survivors-describe -mosque-massacre.

243 the Badr Corps has lately been accused of: Susannah George, "Breaking Badr," *Foreign Policy*, November 6, 2014, foreignpolicy.com/2014/11/06/breaking-badr.

243 "is basically paving the way . . .": Ibid.

244 supported by US warplanes: "US Military Conducts Air Strikes Against ISIL, Airdrops Humanitarian Aid Near Amirli," United States Central Command, August 30, 2014, www.centcom.mil/en/news/articles/us-military-conducts -airstrikes-against-isil-airdrops-humanitarian-aid-iraq.

244 and led by the Badr Corps: "Ashura 'process in the rock cliff unite in support of the' resistance factions led forces Ghabban," almasalah.com, October 24, 2014, http://almasalah.com/ar/news/40335/%D8%B9%D9%85%D9%84%D9%8A% D8%A9-%D8%B9%D8%A7%D8%B4%D9%88%D8%B1%D8%A7%D8%A1 -%D9%81%D9%8A-%D8%AC%D8%B1%D9%81-%D8%A7%D9%84%D8%B5 %D8%AE%D8%B1-%D8%AA%D9%88%D8%AD%D8%AF-%D9%81% D8%B5%D8%A7.

248 Parker, a veteran journalist, left Iraq not long afterward: "Reuters Iraq bureau chief threatened, denounced over story," Reuters, April 11, 2015, www.reuters.com/article /us-mideast-iraq-reuters-idUSKBN0N20FY20150411.

249 ideological affinity with Iranian Khomeinists is hardly Iraq's best-kept secret: Matt Bradley and Julian Barnes, "New Iraq Militias Take a Lead in Tikrit Fight," WSJ .com, April 1, 2015, http://www.wsj.com/articles/new-iraq-militias-take-a-lead-in -tikrit-fight-1427936422.

249 referring to a town just outside the city: "Ruinous Aftermath: Militia Abuses Following Iraq's Recapture of Tikrit," Human Rights Watch, September 20, 2015,https://www.hrw.org/node/281164.

250 his first job for ISIS: Joby Warrick, *Black Flags: The Rise of ISIS*, (New York: Doubleday, 2015), chapter 19.

255 hasn't yet materialized as law: Moustafa Saadoun, ""It's official: Sunnis joining Iraq's Popular Mobilization Units," al-monitor.com, January 14, 2016, http://www.al

-monitor.com/pulse/originals/2016/01/iraq-sunnis-join-shiite-popular-mobilization
-forces.html#.

256 The number of mortars the Americans fired: Fazel Hawramy, Shalaw Mohammad, and David Smith, "Kurdish fighters say US special forces have been fighting Isis for months," *The Guardian*, November 30, 2015, http://www.theguardian.com/us -news/2015/nov/30/kurdish-fighters-us-special-forces-isis-combat.

CHAPTER 17

270 depriving [those inside] of foodstuffs and all essential supplies: https://www .facebook.com/Raqqa.Sl/posts/1119578281386755

270 overwhelming the Raqqa Revolutionaries Brigade entirely: "9 YPG fighters killed in attack on Ain Issa at the northwestern countryside of Al-Raqqah," January 2, 2016, http://www.syriahr.com/en/?p=41949

270 Tribes' Army was disbanded completely: "Tribes' Army disbands in north amidst accusations of YPG blockade," syriadirect.org, January 6, 2016, http://syriadirect.org /news/tribes'-army-disbands-in-north-amidst-accusations-of-ypg-blockade/.

280 "Countering Violent Extremism.": "Russia Update: Ukrainian Security Chief Accuses 'Grey Cardinal' of Directing Snipers on Maidan," *The Interpreter*, February 20, 2015, http://www.interpretermag.com/russia-update-february-20-2015/#6970.

283 But to connect their actions with ISIS is entirely incorrect: Mohammed Tuaev, "Experts: the purpose of the shelling in Derbent was military," Kavkaz-uzel.ru, December 30, 2015, http://www.kavkaz-uzel.ru/articles/275278/.

284 The Popular Mobilization Units have threatened: Michael Crowley, "Iran might attack American troops in Iraq, U.S. officials fear," Politico, March 25, 2015, www .politico.com/story/2015/03/could-iran-attack-us-troops-in-iraq-116365.

285 Terrorist attacks, claimed that: "Experts have linked the statement to a weakening Shebzuhova "Caucasus Emirate," kavkaz-uzel.ru, January 6, 2016, http://www .kavkaz-uzel.ru/articles/275548/.

285 showing militants from four regional divisions: "IG has announced the inauguration of the North Caucusus militants al-Baghdadi," kavkaz-uzel.ru, June 23, 2015, http:// www.kavkaz-uzel.ru/articles/264409/.

285 Caucasian Knot questioned: *Ibid.*

288 airborne troops who had seized Crimea in 2014: Avi Ascher-Shapiro, "Russia Now Has 4,000 People in Syria—And They're Not in a Rush to Fight the Islamic State," *VICE*, November 5, 2015, https://news.vice.com/article/russia-now-has -4000-people-in-syria-and-theyre-not-in-a-rush-to-fight-the-islamic-state.

289 to go to war on behalf of al-Assad: Jim Sciutto, "Iran's Quds Force leader traveled to Moscow in violation of U.N. sanctions, official says," *CNN*, August 7, 2015, http:// www.cnn.com/2015/08/07/politics/qasem-soleimani-iran-quds-force/.

289 proportions having changed only "marginally": Hugo Spalding, "5 Myths: Russia's False ISIS Narrative in Syria," *The Interpreter*, December 2, 2015, http://www .interpretermag.com/5-myths-russias-false-isis-narrative-in-syria/.

289 to justify its merciless campaign against the rebels: *Ibid.*

289 by targeting the Sahwah allies of Americans in Sham: Pierre Vaux and James Miller, "Putin in Syria: Even ISIS Says Russia Is Not Bombing ISIS," *The Interpreter*, November 19, 2015, http://www.interpretermag.com/putin-in-syria-even-isis-says -russia-is-not-bombing-isis/.

292 had directly displaced 35,000 people: "Tens of thousands flee Aleppo following latest wave of airstrikes in Syria," *The Guardian*, October 20, 2015, http://www.theguardian .com/world/2015/oct/20/russia-us-sign-memorandum-syria-bombings-airstrikes.

292 regime offensives in other provinces: Sarah El Deeb, "UN: At least 120,000 displaced in Syria in last month," *The Big Story*, October 26, 2015, http://bigstory .ap.org/article/049569661f954cfeb08ac3a6c0f6259c/aid-group-100000-newly -displaced-3-weeks-syria.

CHAPTER 18

293 was dead by her own hand: "Turkey bombing: Female suicide attacker hits Istanbul police station," *BBC*, January 6, 2015, www.bbc.co.uk/news/world-europe-30701483.

294 planted a car bomb, which failed to explode, in the Parisian suburb of Villejuif: "Explosion in Villejuif: the owner of the car bomb tells," *MetroNews.fr*, January 12, 2015, http://www.metronews.fr/paris/explosion-d-une-voiture-piegee-a-villejuif -nous-sommes-surs-que-c-est-coulibaly/moal!9EppJaqobIwWQ/.

297 who then turned water cannons on the stone-throwers: The Associated Press, "Two explosions hit Kurdish political rally in Turkey," *The Guardian*, June 5, 2015, www .theguardian.com/world/2015/jun/05/two-explosions-kurdish-peoples-democratic -party-rally-turkey.

297 packed with marbles and hidden in trash cans: "Turkey rally explosions 'caused by homemade bombs,'" *BBC*, June 6, 2015, www.bbc.co.uk/news/world-europe -33035450.

297 massacring thirty-two people: "Suruc massacre: 'Turkish student' was suicide bomber," *BBC*, July 22, 2015, www.bbc.co.uk/news/world-europe-33619043.

297 His older brother followed him soon afterward: Louisa Loveluck and Josie Ensor, "Suruc bomber was 'Turk with links to Isil,'" *The Telegraph*, July 22, 2015, www .telegraph.co.uk/news/worldnews/europe/turkey/11755200/Suruc-bomber-was -Turk-with-links-to-Isil.html.

298 and injured another: Gianluca Mezzofiore, "Turkey: PKK kill third policeman in Suruc suicide bombing revenge ambush in Diyarbakir," The International Business Times, July 23, 2015, www.ibtimes.co.uk/turkey-pkk-kill-third-policeman-suruc -suicide-bombing-revenge-ambush-diyarbakir-1512253.

298 "completely destroy[ing]" three ISIS positions, according to Davutoglu: "Turkey bombs Islamic State targets in Syria," *BBC*, July 24, 2015, www.bbc.co.uk/news /world-europe-33646314.

299 the Kurdistan Regional Government, in Erbil: Richard Spencer, Raziye Akkoc, and Louisa Loveluck, "Turkey launches air strikes on PKK targets in Iraq," *The Telegraph*, July 25, 2015, www.telegraph.co.uk/news/worldnews/europe/turkey/11762483 /Turkey-launches-air-strikes-on-PKK-targets-in-Iraq.html.

299 temporarily blocked Twitter in the wake of the attack: Sneha Shankar, "Turkey Suruc Attack: Court Bans Publication Of Photos And Videos Of Deadly Bombing, Blocks Twitter Access," *The International Business Times*, July 22, 2015, www.ibtimes.com/turkey -suruc-attack-court-bans-publication-photos-videos-deadly-bombing-blocks-2019362.

300 actions of ISIS and those of his own government: Louisa Loveluck, Richard Spencer, and Murat Dal, "Turkey bomb massacre kills 97 and injures over 246 at pro-Kurdish peace rally," *The Telegraph*, October 10, 2015, www.telegraph.co.uk /news/worldnews/europe/turkey/11923935/Turkey-Ankara-bomb-kills-30-at-pro -Kurdish-rally.html.

300 the Alagoz brothers returned to Syria: Zia Weise, "Ankara bombing: Perpetrators used tea house in Adiyaman to recruit for Isis—in plain sight of authorities," *The Independent*, October 15, 2015, www.independent.co.uk/news/world/middle-east /ankara-bombing-perpetrators-used-tea-house-in-adiyaman-to-recruit-for-isis-in -plain-sight-of-a6695881.html.

300 arrested four people related to the Ankara bombings: "4 arrested as part of Ankara bombing investigation," *Today's Zaman*, October 19, 2015, www.todayszaman.com /g20_4-arrested-as-part-of-ankara-bombing-investigation_401902.html.

300 sixty-seven suspects were blacklisted: "Biggest probe into ISIL in Turkey completed," *Dogan News Agency*, December 18, 2015, www.hurriyetdailynews.com/Default .aspx?pageID=238&nID=92735&NewsCatID=509.

318 if it is defeated in Iraq and Syria: Rob Crilly, "Islamic State is building a 'retreat zone' in Libya with 3000 fighters, say UN experts," *The Telegraph*, December 2, 2015, www.telegraph.co.uk/news/worldnews/islamic-state/12028246/Islamic-State-is -building-a-retreat-zone-in-Libya-with-3000-fighters-say-UN-experts.html.

318 "the hub from which they project across all of North Africa,": David D. Kirkpatrick, Ben Hubbard and Eric Schmitt, "ISIS' Grip on Libyan City Gives It a Fallback Option," *The New York Times*, November 28, 2015, www.nytimes.com/2015/11/29 /world/middleeast/isis-grip-on-libyan-city-gives-it-a-fallback-option.html.

319 between 2,000 and 3,000: "Libya a massive safe haven for ISIS now, U.N. warns," *CBS News* and *The Associated Press*, December 1, 2015, www.cbsnews.com/news /libya-safe-haven-isis-3000-fighters-un-warns/.

319 during the years of the American occupation of Iraq: Brian Fishman and Joseph Felter," Al-Qa'ida's Foreign Fighters in Iraq," Combating Terrorism Centre at West Point, January 2, 2008, https://www.ctc.usma.edu/posts/al-qaidas-foreign-fighters -in-iraq-a-first-look-at-the-sinjar-records.

319 former members of Saddam's military-intelligence apparatus: "The Arrival of Iraqi soldiers to lead to Sirte Daash Libya," *Afrigatenews.net*, July 25, 2015, 2015,http://www .afrigatenews.net/content/%D9%88%D8%B5%D9%88%D9%84-%D8%B6%D8%A8 %D8%A7%D8%B7-%D8%B9%D8%B1%D8%A7%D9%82%D9%8A%D9%8A%D9 %86-%D8%A5%D9%84%D9%89-%D8%B3%D8%B1%D8%AA-%D9%84%D9%82 %D9%8A%D8%A7%D8%AF%D8%A9-%D8%AF%D8%A7%D8%B9%D8%B4 -%D9%84%D9%8A%D8%A8%D9%8A%D8%A7-0.

320 among local jihadi groups, specifically al-Qaeda: Benoit Faucon and Matt Bradley, "Islamic State Gained Strength in Libya by Co-Opting Local Jihadists," *The Wall Street Journal*, February 17, 2015, www.wsj.com/articles/islamic-state-gained -strength-in-libya-by-co-opting-local-jihadists-1424217492.

320 its most senior cleric: Cole Bunzel, "From Paper State to Caliphate," Brookings Analysis Paper, March 2015, page 11, www.brookings.edu/~/media/research/files/ papers/2015/03/ideology-of-islamic-state-bunzel/the-ideology-of-the-islamic-state .pdf.

CHAPTER 19

332 Showed the careful compartmentalization of the *amniyat*: Christoph Reuter, "The Terror Strategist: Secret Files Reveal the Structure of Islamic State," *Der Spiegel*, April 18, 2015, http://www.spiegel.de/international/world/islamic-state-files-show -structure-of-islamist-terror-group-a-1029274.html.

EPILOGUE

349 According to the British defense firm IHS: "Islamic State's Caliphate Shrinks by 14 Percent in 2015," IHS Jane's, December 21, 2015, press.ihs.com/press-release /aerospace-defense-security/islamic-states-caliphate-shrinks-14-percent-2015.

351 Particularly in eastern Syria, has led to ruined livelihoods: Hassan Hassan, "In Syria, many families face a terrible dilemma," *National*, September 20, 2015, www .thenational.ae/opinion/comment/in-syria-many-families-face-a-terrible-dilemma.

352 "The situation has never been as miserable as it is now": Isabel Coles, "Despair, hardship as Iraq cuts off wages in Islamic State cities," Reuters, October 2, 2015, www.reuters.com/article/us-mideast-crisis-iraq-salaries-idUSKCN0RW0V620151002.

353 The victims were of all ages, up to seventy years old: Ahmed Rasheed, Ned Parker, and Stephen Kalin, "Survivors say Iraqi forces watched as Shi'ite militias executed 72 Sunnis," Reuters, January 28, 2015, www.reuters.com/article/us-mideast-crisis-iraq-killings.

353 "Those (acts) are no less dangerous than terrorism,": "Iraq's PM pledges hard line against alleged militia abuses," Reuters, January 31, 2015, www.reuters.com/article/us-mideast-crisis-iraq-killings-idUSKBN0L4OSO20150131.

353 massacring fifty-one people: "At least 51 killed in attacks in Iraqi capital, eastern town," Reuters, January 11, 2016, www.reuters.com/article/us-mideast-crisis-iraq-violence-idUSKCN0UP1R420160111.

354 killing a dozen or so civilians: Ahmed Rasheed, "Sunni mosques in east Iraq attacked after ISIS-claimed blasts," Reuters, January 12, 2016, www.reuters.com/article/us-mideast-crisis-iraq-violence-idUKKCN0UP1R420160112.

354 set on fire within the space of a week: Ahmed Rasheed and Saif Hameed, "Sunni MPs boycott Iraq parliament and govt in protest at violence," Reuters, January 19, 2016, www.reuters.com/article/uk-mideast-crisis-iraq-violence-idUKKCN0UX19.

354 Professional military units in the Iraqi army: Abigail Fielding-Smith and Crofton Black, "Baghdad kidnappings: Were American civilians working for US defence giant on 'critical' Iraq special forces programme?," Bureau of Investigative Journalism, January 19, 2016, www.thebureauinvestigates.com/2016/01/19/baghdad-kidnappings-us-civilians-worked-for-general-dynamics-defence-giant-on-critical-iraq-special-forces-deal.

354 Iranian-backed proxies were looking to capture Americans again: "Official: Americans kidnapped from Iraq interpreter's home," CBS News, January 18, 2016, www.cbsnews.com/news/americans-kidnapped-from-iraq-interpreters-home-in-dora-baghdad.

354 eighteen Turkish construction workers in September 2015: "Kidnapped Turkish construction workers freed in Iraq," BBC, September 30, 2015, www.bbc.co.uk/news/world-middle-east-34398902.

354 twenty-six Qatari falconers in December: "Qatar hunters abducted in Iraq desert by gunmen," BBC, December 16, 2015, www.bbc.co.uk/news/world-middle-east-35112774.

354 "We fought before and we are ready to resume fighting": "Kidnapping of Americans in Iraq raises fear about security," CBS News, January 18, 2016, www.cbsnews.com/news/kidnapping-of-americans-in-iraq-raises-fears-about-security.

355 The *Daily Beast* reported in late August: Shane Harris and Nancy Youssef, "Spies: Obama's Brass Pressured Us to Downplay ISIS Threat," *Daily Beast*, August 27, 2015, www.thedailybeast.com/articles/2015/08/26/spies-obama-s-brass-pressured-us-to-downplay-isis-threat.html.

355 and early September 2015: Shane Harris and Nancy Youssef, "Exclusive: 50 Spies Say ISIS Intelligence Was Cooked," *Daily Beast*, September 10, 2015, www.thedailybeast.com/articles/2015/09/09/exclusive-50-spies-say-isis-intelligence-was-cooked.html.

356 "largely been achieved," IHS has concluded: Columb Strack, "Syrian government territory grows by 1.3% with Russian military support," IHS Jane's, January 21, 2016, www.janes.com/article/57402/syrian-government-territory-grows-by-1-3-with-russian-military-support.

356 "The jets don't leave the skies": Marga Zambrana, Muhammed Almahmoud, and Emma Graham-Harrison, "Bombarded Aleppo lives in fear of siege and starvation,"

Observer, February 6, 2016, www.theguardian.com/world/2016/feb/06/aleppo
-under-bombardment-fears-siege-and-starvation.

356 "Stronger and stronger" on Israel's doorstep: Sam Jones and Erika Solomon, "Isis
empowered by shifting forces in southern Syria," *Financial Times*, January 26, 2016,
www.ft.com/cms/s/0/1784ef9c-c41d-11e5-808f-8231cd71622e.html#axzz3zrGlys6Y.

356 Mohammed al-Hariri told the website All4Syria: "Russia strikes displace over 150,000
in Daraa: rebel media," *NOW Lebanon*, February 2, 2016, https://now.mmedia.me/lb
/en/NewsReports/566560-russia-strikes-displace-over-150000-in-daraa-rebel-media.

356 to relocate them from the area: Kate Ng, "Syria and Isis reach deal to end Yarmouk
camp siege, as wounded militants begin safe passage back to strongholds,"
Independent, December 25, 2015, www.independent.co.uk/news/world/middle-east
/syria-and-isis-reach-deal-to-end-yarmouk-camp-siege-as-wounded-militants
-begin-safe-passage-back-to-a6786031.html.

357 Although Alloush serially denied responsibility: Anne Barnard, "Powerful Syrian Rebel
Leader Reported Killed in Airstrike," *New York Times*, December 25, 2015, www.nytimes
.com/2015/12/26/world/middleeast/zahran-alloush-syria-rebel-leader-reported-killed.html.

357 rebel leader to unequivocally and consistently battle ISIS: Hassan Hassan, "Syria
rebel group will survive leader's death," *National*, December 27, 2015, www
.thenational.ae/opinion/syria-rebel-group-will-survive-leaders-death.

357 told Kuwaiti newspaper *Al-Rai*: "Russia special forces aiding Hezbollah in
Latakia: report," *NOW Lebanon*, January 27, 2016, https://now.mmedia.me/lb/en
/NewsReports/566538-russia-special-forces-aiding-hezbollah-in-latakia-report.

358 Russia is directly arming its militants in Syria: Jesse Rosenfeld, "Russia Is Arming
Hezbollah, Say Two of the Group's Field Commanders," *Daily Beast*, January 11,
2016, www.thedailybeast.com/articles/2016/01/11/russia-is-arming-hezbollah-say
-two-of-the-group-s-field-commanders.html.

358 "We do not consider them a terrorist organization": "Russia says Hezbollah not
a terrorist group: Ifax," Reuters, November 15, 2015, www.reuters.com/article/us
-mideast-crisis-syria-russia-terrorgro-idUSKCN0T412520151115.

358 For the promise of a thousand dollars a month: Patrick Goodenough, "Iran
Accused of Coercing Vulnerable Afghans to Fight For Assad in Syria," CNS
News, February 4, 2016, www.cnsnews.com/news/article/patrick-goodenough
/iran-accused-coercing-vulnerable-afghans-fight-assad-syria.

358 "Without artillery support," in the words of Human Rights Watch: "Iran Sending
Thousands of Afghans to Fight in Syria," Human Rights Watch, January 29, 2016,
www.hrw.org/tet/node/285569.

359 ISIS killed 1,131: Hugh Naylor, "Islamic State has killed many Syrians, but Assad's
forces have killed more," *Washington Post*, September 5, 2015, www.washingtonpost
.com/world/islamic-state-has-killed-many-syrians-but-assads-forces-have-killed
-even-more/2015/09/05/b8150d0c-4d85-11e5-80c2-106ea7fb80d4_story.html.

359 killing of prisoners held by al-Assad's security forces, al-Nusra, and ISIS: "Out of Sight, Out
of Mind: Death in Detention in the Syrian Arab Republic," Office of the United Nations
High Commissioner for Human Rights, released to the public February 8, 2016, www
.ohchr.org/Documents/HRBodies/HRCouncil/CoISyria/A-HRC-31-CRP1_en.pdf.

360 "found out about them when it is five years too late": George Orwell, "Looking
back on the Spanish War," *New Road*, 1943, orwell.ru/library/essays/Spanish_War
/english/esw_1.

361 trying to reach Europe by desperate—in some cases suicidal—means: "Syria's refugee
crisis in numbers," Amnesty International, February 3, 2016, www.amnesty.org/en
/latest/news/2016/02/syrias-refugee-crisis-in-numbers.

INDEX